PASTORAL LETTERS
of the United States Catholic Bishops

Hugh J. Nolan, Editor

VOLUME IV
1975-1983

National Conference of Catholic Bishops
United States Catholic Conference

The bishops of the United States have provided religious and moral guidance and leadership to American Catholics since the establishment of the Church in the United States. *Pastoral Letters of the U.S. Catholic Bishops, 1792-1983*, published in a four-volume set, is a collection of statements issued by the Catholic hierarchy of the United States over the past two centuries. This publication was initiated by the Office of Publishing Services and is authorized for publication by the undersigned.

Monsignor Daniel F. Hoye

October 25, 1983   General Secretary, NCCB/USCC

I am the good shepherd.
I know my sheep
and my sheep know me
in the same way that the Father knows me
and I know the Father;
for these sheep I will give my life.
I have other sheep
that do not belong to the fold.
I must lead them, too,
and they shall hear my voice.

John 10:14-16

Acknowledgements
The Office of Publishing Services, United States Catholic Conference, is deeply grateful to all those who assisted in the compilation and production of this volume of *Pastoral Letters of the United States Catholic Bishops*. Special thanks must be given to Rev. Hugh J. Nolan for his unstinting cooperation and editorial expertise and to Russell B. Shaw, Secretary of Public Affairs of the NCCB/USCC, who suggested this undertaking.

Contents

Foreword / 1

Preface / 3

I. Social Justice for All 1975-1978

    Introduction / **9**

1975 Panama-U.S. Relations / **44**

    Statement on Feeding the Hungry: Toward a
U.S. Domestic Food Policy / **47**

    Statement on the Introduction of the
Family Viewing Period during Prime Time by
the Television Networks / **54**

    Handgun Violence: A Threat to Life / **66**

    Food Policy and the Church: Specific Proposals / **69**

    Statement on the United Nations and the Republic
of South Africa / **74**

    The Eucharist and the Hungers of the
Human Family / **77**

    Pastoral Plan for Pro-life Activities / **81**

    The Economy: Human Dimensions / **92**

    The Right to a Decent Home: A Pastoral Response
to the Crisis in Housing / **99**

    Statement on Catholic-Jewish Relations / **120**

    Resolution on Farm Labor / **126**

    Resolution on Human Life Foundation / **127**

    Resolution on New York City / **128**

1976 Political Responsibility: Reflections on an
Election Year / **129**

    Society and the Aged: Toward Reconciliation / **138**

    Political Responsibility: A Resolution of the
Catholic Bishops of the United States / **146**

    Teach Them / **148**

    Resolution of the Administrative Committee / **157**

    Let the Little Children Come to Me / **159**

    U.S.-Panama Relations / **164**

Resolution on the Pastoral Concern of the Church
for People on the Move / 167

To Live in Christ Jesus: A Pastoral Reflection
on the Moral Life / 170

Resolution in Honor of Cardinal Krol / 196

1977 Resolution on Haitian Refugees / 198

Statement on Recombinant DNA Research / 200

Statement of the United States Catholic Bishops
on American Indians / 205

Religious Liberty in Eastern Europe: A Test Case
for Human Rights / 211

The Bicentennial Consultation: A Response to the Call
to Action / 215

Resolution on *Jesus of Nazareth* / 227

Statement concerning *Human Sexuality* / 228

Principles and Guidelines for Fund Raising in the
United States by Arch/Dioceses, Arch/Diocesan
Agencies, and Religious Institutes / 232

1978 The Gospel of Peace and the Danger of War / 238

Statement on Small-Boat Refugees in
Southeast Asia / 241

To Do the Work of Justice / 243

The Plan of Pastoral Action for Family Ministry
A Vision and a Strategy / 255

Pastoral Statement of the United States
Catholic Bishops on Handicapped People / 267

Statement on the Middle East: The Pursuit of Peace
with Justice / 276

II. The Dawn of a New Era 1979-1983

Introduction / 283

1979 Political Responsibility: Choices for the 1980s / 317

Committee on Conciliation and Arbitration: Procedures
Adopted by the General Membership / 330

Brothers and Sisters to Us / 342

Resolution on Cambodia / 356

Resolution on Iran / 357

Resolution on the Papal Visit / 358

1980 Statement on Registration and Conscription for
Military Service / 360

Cultural Pluralism in the United States / 364

Resolution on the Iranian Crisis / 377

Resolution on Cuban and Haitian Refugees / 378

Statement on Tubal Ligation / 379

Pastoral Letter on Marxist Communism / 380

Catholic Higher Education and the Pastoral Mission of
the Church / 401

Called and Gifted: The American Catholic Laity / 417

Statement on Promoting Christian Unity / 424

Statement on Capital Punishment / 427

Resolution on the Hostages in Iran / 435

Resolution on El Salvador / 436

1981   Reflections on the Energy Crisis / 438

Statement on Central America / 464

Health and Health Care / 469

NCCB/USCC Mission Statement / 486

1983   Statement on Social Security / 487

Statement on Namibia / 491

The Challenge of Peace: God's Promise and Our
Response / 493

Statement on U.S. Policy in Central America / 582

Appendix

1975–1983   Chronological Table of Important Events in
the History of the Church in the
United States / 587

1975–1982   Growth of the Church in the United States / 590

Organization and Purpose of the NCCB/USCC / 591

Index / 595

Foreword

This is the fourth and latest volume of the *Pastoral Letters of the United States Catholic Bishops* published by the United States Catholic Conference. It contains the statements made collectively by the bishops from 1975 to 1983 inclusive. Marred by a national economic recession and ever increasing international tensions and wars, these eight years are truly among the more significant in our nation's history, ecclesiastical as well as secular. And all the while, the bishops have been carrying the further responsibility of a yet greater implementation of the directives of Vatican II.

There is scarcely a serious domestic problem or international one involving the United States that the bishops have not touched with a thoughtful, studied statement for these years. If any area is touched more than any other, it is social justice, in which there is a marked growth of episcopal concern. It is not that this was neglected in the past, as witness the 1919 *Program of Social Reconstruction*, but the bishops are speaking more immediately, more frequently, and more persistently on social justice issues. Mindful of Pope Paul VI's steady teaching "Peace is Justice," the bishops during these eight years have addressed much more fully and deeply international problems involving justice.

On the international level their concerns ranged from *Religious Liberty in Eastern Europe* to *The Middle East: The Pursuit of Peace with Justice* to *U.S.-Panama Relations* to *The United Nations and the Republic of South Africa* to a *Statement on Central America*. Three times the bishops expressed their heartache over how heartlessly various refugees have been mistreated. Then in 1980 the bishops published their masterful *Pastoral Letter on Marxist Communism*.

Closer to home, on the domestic scene, the prelates continued their crusade against abortion, still convinced, as they stated collectively in 1970, "Abortion is the unjust destruction of a human life and morally that is murder." They pleaded with all Americans to use their vote and vote according to their enlightened conscience. They reached out to their fellow non-Catholic Americans in the *Statement on Promoting Christian Unity* and *Statement on Catholic-Jewish Relations*.

Always giving a priority to the poor, the bishops issued a *Statement on Feeding the Hungry* and *Right to a Decent Home*. Urging a commitment to *Social Security* and proper *Health Care*, they expressed their special concern for the *Aged* and *Handicapped People*. In the depths of the recession they suggested remedies in *The Economy: Human Dimensions*.

Once again, in *Brothers and Sisters to Us*, the bishops insisted on total racial equality for all members of the human race, and to another

1

minority they addressed a *Statement on American Indians*. To help all men, they gave the marvelous directive *To Live in Christ Jesus*, developed the teaching of Christ in *Let the Little Children Come to Me*, and again followed the mandate of Christ in *Teach Them*.

In several ways these eight years are remarkable. For the first time in half a century, our nation was honored to conduct an international Eucharistic Congress. Most befittingly, the bishops issued *The Eucharist and the Hungers of the Human Family*. Another history-making event during this octave of years was a visit by Pope John Paul II, for which the bishops expressed their gratitude in a *Resolution on the Papal Visit*.

To clarify a newly developing problem in the United States, the bishops issued a *Statement on Registration and Conscription for Military Service* in 1980. This was but a prelude for the monumental history-making document: *The Challenge of Peace: God's Promise and Our Response*. It is perhaps the most important and timely Pastoral Letter ever to come from the American hierarchy in its nearly two centuries of existence. No statement of the United States bishops has ever received so much national and international notice. This Letter and the statements preceding it in this volume surely mark "The Dawn of a New Era."

The statements are edited here in such a way as to make them most meaningful. The comments by a professionally trained historian succinctly place them in their historical setting and also trace, where necessary, the statements' development from the actual dialogue on the floor. Father Nolan uses the most primary of sources, the minutes of the general meetings, all of which he attended.

Not to know and study these documents would be to miss the soul of the history of American Catholicism for these years and a significant segment of the secular history of our nation.

I bespeak a wide reading and a careful study of these statements, not only for our college and university students, but also for all literate peoples.

Joseph Cardinal Bernardin
Archbishop of Chicago
November 1, 1983

Preface

This is the fourth and the latest volume in the *Pastoral Letters of the United States Catholic Bishops*. The term *Pastoral Letters* is used in a broad sense. It is not always possible to draw a clear-cut line between the Pastorals and Statements made collectively by the American bishops, so the Statements are also included, as are the significant accompanying Resolutions for the sake of completeness. To facilitate the use of these documents, paragraphs have been numbered. These documents have been arranged chronologically. For the most part, they have emerged from the general meetings of the entire body of bishops. On occasion (usually an emergency that would not wait for a general meeting), Statements have been issued either by the President of the NCCB/USCC or the Administrative Board or Committee with proper approval. These Statements, too, have been included.

The commentaries trace rapidly the historical origin of each document, its development from the meeting floor discussions (all of which the editor attended), and give a quick glance at the effectiveness of the Statement. Because of its greater importance, the commentary on *The Challenge of Peace: God's Promise and Our Response* is much lengthier than the usually briefer comments on other Statements.

The Statements should be read in the context of the Holy Father's May 29, 1980, admonition to the Italian bishops' conference that those prelates should take up their "own responsibilities" and "revive fully the collegial tradition in force in the Church ever since the most ancient times." Addressing "the problem of a correct and well understood autonomy of the bishops' conference for defining and carrying out its own pastoral duties," His Holiness proclaimed: "You are the ones in charge of the Church in Italy, and you must be so in an ever more aware and incisive manner."

More and more the United States hierarchy, as one of the first established and most significant national episcopal conferences in the universal Church, has accepted this challenge in a nation recognized as one of the two superpowers of the world. From 1975 to 1983 there was, on the whole, a remarkable advance in the thought and the actions of the NCCB, especially in the field of human rights. The prelates have also made greater and greater efforts to publicize their Statements throughout the nation from the pulpit and in all forms of the media.

The allegation that the bishops sometimes operate in areas of limited competence—even going beyond that competence—is answered more clearly in recent Statements, which have benefited from an ever-expanding consultation process. *The Challenge of Peace*, with its incred-

3

ibly wide consultation of worldwide ecclesiastical authorities, highest government officials, and the most knowledgeable scientists and scholars in various fields, is a prime example of this increased scope.

Each individual has a significant role in the fulfillment of these Statements; he must live and act justly to make this a just society—so the prelates explained and proclaimed. They pointed out how primary and indispensable such personal responsibility is early in this set of documents with their 1976 theological directive for all areas of life, public as well as private, *To Live In Christ Jesus.*

Furthermore, in this series of documents, dealing mostly with social justice issues, a growing evangelization is noticeable, although evangelization was present in earlier Statements, e.g., 1948's *The Christian in Action,* which treats religion in education, economic life and citizenship. Readers of all the Statements should remain aware that this evangelistic note must be rather carefully worded lest it offend those not of the Catholic faith. These social justice Statements, in particular, are written to encourage and assist not only Catholic Americans in assuming their proper roles on the political, social and economic levels, but all other readers of the document, regardless of their religious beliefs. The Statements asking Americans to vote are addressed to all Americans. There is no intention, directly or indirectly, of playing down religious doctrine or prayer as witness; in the concluding section of *The Challenge of Peace,* the bishops plead for prayer and sacrifice. Even in different areas of evangelization, emphasis has to be placed on varying facets of the teaching presentation.

Climaxing this period (1975–1983) is the May 3, 1983 Pastoral Letter, *The Challenge of Peace: God's Promise and Our Response,* which faces the greatest problem since Genesis. In this letter, permitting the temporary possession of deterrent nuclear weapons during and for the sake of negotiations, the bishops speak out in true faith and call for not a mere curbing but a total elimination of the arms race through mutual verifiable disarmament. This letter does not claim to have all the answers to the arms question, but it does hope to promote and improve public debate on this most serious and pressing problem.

Cardinal Bernardin, in a presentation of the final draft, noted: "We speak not as technicians or politicians but as teachers of moral and religious principles. . . . As Catholic bishops in the United States, we face the momentous pastoral responsibility of relating moral and religious teaching to the issues facing one of the two major nuclear powers." He explained that the Pastoral Letter was designed to address both public policy and personal moral questions on war and peace. "We need," His Eminence reminded us, "to recall that as Americans and as people of faith we are expected to have our own principles and to be prepared to live by them." It is safe to write that no Statement of any other religious body in the United States has received so much notice and discussion throughout the world.

Also it is safe to write that the same pastoral type of teaching prompted all the Statements made collectively by the bishops of the United States.

The editor of this volume wishes to thank His Eminence Joseph Cardinal Bernardin for his Foreword; and to express his gratitude to the Office of Publishing Services of the United States Catholic Conference, especially Lydia Finkelstein for her constant encouragement.

Hugh J. Nolan

I. Social Justice for All
1975 – 1978

Introduction

At the closing of the November 1974 meeting, Archbishop Joseph Bernardin, former General Secretary of the NCCB and the USCC, was elected to succeed Cardinal John Krol. The archbishop, the first non-cardinal and youngest prelate (forty-six years old) to head the NCCB-USCC, received one hundred forty-three votes of the two hundred forty-eight cast on the second ballot.

Cardinal John Carberry was elected vice-president on the third ballot.

Archbishop Bernardin, in addressing the hierarchy and citing the "enormity and complexity" of the challenge, said he was "personally honored" by the trust placed in him by his fellow bishops.

Calling his new task one of service and referring to his tenure as general secretary of the NCCB-USCC for five years, the soft-spoken prelate said he would be reluctant to accept the presidency of the bishops' body if he had only his own resources to rely on.

"But," he added, "with God's help, and the knowledge that you [the bishops] will stand beside me . . . I will attempt to do the will of Christ. . . ."

One of the tasks the archbishop felt lay before him as he assumed this position of leadership in the Church, would be to help people "see the riches of the Catholic faith" and how it "speaks to people's needs and aspirations."

Stating that the NCCB is "expected to lead the Church at the national level," Archbishop Bernardin said he hoped he "would be an effective catalyst" as the NCCB-USCC sought to provide a forum for ideas transcending diocesan issues.

He expressed gratitude to the outgoing NCCB-USCC president, Cardinal Krol, and said he was delighted with the election of Cardinal Carberry as vice-president.

At a press conference and in an interview with the NC News Service following his election, the affable and capable archbishop discussed some of his views and what he hoped to see develop over the next three years.

On the priority of fostering a renewal of the faith, he told NC News: "The basic question is that of relating in positive and fruitful ways the Catholic tradition with the new situations in which people find themselves. This is a complex challenge, and it touches in a direct way on the Church's teaching mission."

One of the chief programs under way for this, he said, is the development of the *National Catechetical Directory* to provide a "tone and orientation" to the Church's teaching.

He said that the second priority, restoring a sense of moral values in today's society, is necessary because "for many people today moral values are not the determining factor in how they lead their lives."

Among the ways the bishop as a group would be involved in this area, he said, would be through a proposed pastoral statement on human values and the attempt to implement that statement through schools, both Catholic and public.

On the role of the Church in promoting social justice, he stressed the value of the bishops' conference on liberty and justice in 1976 to observe the nation's two hundredth birthday.

He also pointed to the bishops' work during the meeting to formulate a statement and develop a plan of pastoral action to meet the world food crisis.[1]

At the spring 1975 regional meetings[2] the bishops and periti discussed principally the *National Catechetical Directory*. Many of the participants of Region III (Pennsylvania and New Jersey) expressed the view that a clear and cohesive theme had not been developed throughout the draft of the *NCD*. The bishops strongly recommended that the chapter on Revelation and the chapter on Church and Community be thoroughly restudied and revised. The prelates also recommended that the entire document be reorganized to achieve a more logical presentation and to provide a clearer expression of the unifying theme.

With regard to the editorial aspects of the *NCD* draft, most participants considered it too wordy, unnecessarily repetitive, far too lengthy, and consequently too difficult to read. While recognizing the need for certain technical terms, the group urged the drafters of the document to seek clear and concise language.

Specific concerns expressed at the consultation here included:

(1) The importance of a clearer statement of faith;

(2) A more profound and extensive exploration of the importance of prayer;

(3) A more careful definition of liturgy and its place in religious education;

(4) A greater effort to resolve the theological confusion experienced by so many Catholics;

(5) Special consideration of religious education programs for the deaf, the blind, and the mentally retarded;

(6) Revision of the section on senior citizens;

---

[1]*Minutes of the Sixteenth General Meeting* of NCCB (Washington, D.C., 1974) p. 46, *The Catholic Standard and Times*, November 23, 1974 and editor's notes on the archbishop's press interview.
[2]Observers are not permitted to attend regional meetings. This account is based on *The Catholic Standard and Times*, April 24, 1975.

(7) A thorough reconsideration of the treatment of human sexuality.

Thanking all the participants, Bishop William G. Connare of Greensburg, Pennsylvania, chairman of Region III, said: "While the recommendations were extensive and in many instances radical, I see these are clear expressions of your already stated enthusiasm about the consultative process as well as a voicing of the high hopes we all share for a document which will profoundly influence the future of the Catholic Church in America."

After consultation with the Executive Committee of the U.S. Catholic Conference, Archbishop Bernardin, president of NCCB, issued a statement, *The Middle East Problem*, on the then worsening Middle East situation, April 1975.[3]

Noting that the U.S.-U.N. relations were at the moment troubled, the archbishop advised that it was of vital importance to prevent further deterioration of these relations and that key issues should be clarified in public debate. One such issue was the status of Israel in the United Nations. His Excellency warned that the suspension or the expulsion of Israel from the United Nations would threaten the viability of the United Nations as a functioning international agency. "Hence I wish to state my clear and firm opposition to any actions supporting this posture."

The president of the NCCB explained that in 1973 the U.S. Catholic Conference maintained: 1) the right of Israel to exist as a sovereign state and 2) the right of the Palestinian Arabs to a sovereign state, to compensation for past losses, and to inclusion in any negotiations. His Excellency cited that in 1973 the bishops supported *U.S. Resolution 242* as the basis for a negotiated settlement. In his conclusion the Archbishop reiterated his plea that Israel should not be deprived of the right to present its case to the U.N. "Debate and discussion involving all interested parties is a minimum requirement for a global community."

The Statement has significance since it placed on record the bishops' protest against the expulsion or suspension of Israel from the U.N. at a time when some American Jews thought the Holy See was unduly silent on the Middle East problem. It also pleaded for justice to the Palestinian Arabs so long unrecompensed.

The administrative board of the USCC opened its February 24, 1975 Statement, *Panama-U.S. Relations*: "The United States and the Republic of Panama are currently engaged in active negotiations regarding a treaty involving the Panama Canal." The board then

---

[3]The executive committee carries on the business of the NCCB between general sessions and meetings of the USCC administrative board. The executive committee is composed of the president, vice president, secretary, and treasurer of the NCCB and an elected member of the administrative board.

cautioned: "It is a moral imperative—a matter of elemental social justice—that a new and more just treaty be negotiated."

They continued that the 1903 treaty is "of dubious moral validity" and has remained unchanged "at the insistence of the more powerful of the two parties." The bishops then remarked that every nation has the right to utilize its natural resources and that the principal natural resource of Panama is and always has been its geographic location. The prelates pointed out: "If we accept the rights of Panama over her territory then instead of Panama's negotiating with the United States to obtain for herself some compensation . . . it might be reasoned that negotiations should be the other way around." The Statement shows the main benefits from the Canal should accrue to Panama, which was not the case.

Sixty-eight percent of this most valuable economic area is designated for military use, seventy percent of the goods that transit the Canal at the frozen 1914 fees are American so that "Panama, a poor nation, is subsidizing the richest nation of the world." Moreover, in sixty years, the use of the Canal has saved the U.S. armed forces in excess of $11 billion. Since property and income in the Canal Zone are exempted from Panamanian taxes, "the government of Panama is denied a major source of revenue."

These observations place the question within the context of social justice. For peace in the world, it is essential that the United States approach the Canal issue with moral sensitivity of which the new treaty will be a significant test. "The fundamental rights of the people of Panama, as well as the high ideals and long-range interest of the United States, require a new and just treaty." In their final paragraph the anxious board warned that "the whole world will be watching."

Archbishop Marcos McGrath of Panama was the most powerful force behind the thought and adoption of this Statement.

The widespread coverage of the action taken by the U.S. bishops brought a response from Brigadier General Omar Torrijos, the Panamanian head of government, who termed the Statement an "anti-colonialist gospel," and invited Archbishop McGrath to join a team of Panamanian leaders on an informational and educational tour of the United States.[4]

The USCC Department of Social Development and World Peace anticipated the occasion of "Food Day," April 17, 1975, by issuing the day before a *Statement On Feeding the Hungry: Toward a U.S. Domestic Food Policy.* "The Church," this Statement teaches, "has a particular responsibility with regard to the food crisis since Jesus identified himself with the poor and hungry . . . 'the right to eat' is a fundamental right which flows from the basic and inalienable right to life itself."

---

[4]*Christian Century*, April 16, 1976.

Happily, the department reported that the response to the bishops' November 1974 plan of action on the world food crisis "has been widespread and significant." Working with the National Catholic Rural Life Conference of Catholic Charities, the USCC continues its efforts on the food and agricultural policy and Food for Peace Program with Congress and its members.

"The United States has a responsibility in both domestic and international areas which are two different aspects of the same problem."

The Statement maintains the development of a comprehensive food policy is an urgent priority for the nation—a food policy that should work toward "full production, equitable distribution and price stability. At a time when world food shortages mean starvation for millions, a U.S. agricultural policy of full production is absolutely essential."

This Statement then addresses three areas of immediate concern: U.S. food needs, ownership and control of the resources, and full production with target prices. Of the over 37 million poor people in the United States, many "lack adequate nutrition because they lack employment and income that would enable them to buy sufficient food." Caught in the web of inflation and recession, middle and working class families "have lost ground in their battle to provide their families an adequate diet." Because of this situation: "The USCC opposes reductions in domestic food aid; in fact they must be improved and expanded as also the Food Stamp Program and the National School Lunch Program." Additional funding and permanent status for the School Breakfast Program are required, "and continued support for the school special milk program. We urge all qualified Catholic schools to provide these services for their students."

After encouraging nutritional aid to mothers, young children, and the elderly, the Statement boldly declared: "Our food policy must not be governed by profit considerations alone, but by the needs of hungry people. . . . In light of present food needs, farmers must be encouraged to produce to full capacity"—a recommendation that has not been followed to the present day despite the suffering of millions of starving people throughout the world.

Going to the heart of the food problem, the USCC repeated its plea for a guaranteed adequate income for all Americans.

"The hungry of the world have voiced their cries of anguish. We must respond to them not only with words of hope, but also with actions that will mobilize the energies, talents, and resources of the Catholic community to assist people not only around the world but in this nation as well."

Because the recommendation to produce to full capacity has not been followed on the national level, despite the millions of starving people throughout the world, on September 11, 1975, the administrative board of the USCC released the Statement *Food Policy and the Church: Specific Proposals*. The board asserted "It is evident that the 'right to eat' is still denied to many in our own country and to many more throughout the world . . . hunger and malnutrition continue to stalk many lives in several regions of the globe; at home many of the unemployed, the elderly, and the poor are forced to subsist on inadequate diets."

After praising the many helpful steps taken in the past year to alleviate hunger, the board declared that personal, voluntary efforts are essential, but they will prove inadequate to the scope of the hunger question "if they are not encompassed in a broader public policy . . . we seek to address the national policy issues which are needed to make a more just food policy a reality in our country."

Noting that the unique position of the United States as the largest food exporting nation in the world has supreme importance for the hungry of the world, the bishops offered several specific proposals on general food aid policy and then on domestic food policy in which they cited some shocking statistics, e.g., "the average cash income of a family of four on food stamps is $3,456 a year." Again the bishops supported efforts to improve and extend all the Child Nutrition Programs.

They ended their Statement on a spiritual note of great hope. Reminding a world discouraged by the hunger problem that there remains an extra measure beyond human power, "God's active presence in the world," they emphasized the importance of prayer. "He [Christ] instructed us to pray for our daily bread with confidence in the knowledge that when we ask our heavenly Father, he will give us neither a stone for bread nor a serpent for fish."

On September 10, 1975, the administrative board of the USCC issued their *Statement on the Family Viewing Policy of the Television Networks*. This Statement was occasioned by the three television networks introducing for the 1975 fall season their new policy of a "family viewing" period during prime time programming hours.

Before evaluating the policy, the board outlined certain presuppositions it felt important to the question at hand. Substantially these are:

(1) In our society today, television is the single most formative influence in shaping people's attitudes and values.

(2) Unquestionably, therefore, the experience of television is an ordinary and integral part of American home life today.

(3) The Church respects the enormous potential television has for education.

(4) American broadcasters have a global responsibility.

The Statement then mentioned that the United States Catholic Conference has been, is, and will continue to be firmly committed to the principle of voluntary self-regulation for all the communications media.

"Self-regulation is not a unilateral activity performed behind closed doors by a few powerful individuals at the top. Self-regulation, to deserve the name, is an open, accountable, and cooperative process, involving both broadcasters and the public they serve."

The board reminded all: "Self-regulation also involves cooperation on the part of the viewing public."

In their conclusion, the bishops declared that for all the reasons set forth in this Statement, the United States Catholic Conference finds the proposals contained in the FCC's report unacceptable, particularly because those proposals stand or fall upon effective self-regulation by the broadcast industry.

"Effective self-regulation has to be an open, accountable, and cooperative process. Our judgment is that to date the networks have not demonstrated a commitment to such a process" . . . "A basic weakness of commercial broadcasting is that management is incapable of exercising responsible freedom in the program decision-making process because they are trapped in a rating thralldom."

The bishops recommended that Congress investigate the program rating services which appear to exercise an inordinate influence upon television programming and which have thus far successfully resisted public scrutiny.

"As for the broadcast industry, we strongly urge all broadcast licensees, whether network affiliates or independents, whether members of the NAB or not, to reflect anew upon their responsibilities to the public they are licensed to serve and to examine how well they are meeting those responsibilities."

The prelates teach that the viewing public must respond and demonstrate to local station management that it cares and is ready to work with management for the achievement of a program schedule that serves the community's needs. "In particular, we encourage our Catholic people, under the leadership of their bishops and pastors, to take an active and affirmative role in working with their fellow citizens, especially on an interfaith basis, in pursuit of the same objectives . . . The Federal Communications Commission must demonstrate that it is more concerned about how well the public interest is served by commercial broadcasters than how well it serves the interests of commercial broadcasters."

Finally, the Statement advises: "The business community has a special responsibility for the quality of commercial broadcasting. It is their advertising dollars that either enhance or debase the medium. If all advertisers had been as sensitive to the broadcast needs of the American public, especially of the family, as some have been, this Statement might not be necessary."

The Statement had some impact in many dioceses, but its goals are still far from being fully attained.

On September 11, 1975, the Committee on Social Development and World Peace issued *Handgun Violence: A Threat to Life; Statement on Handgun Control*. The growing reality and extent of violent crime prompted this Statement. After noting that there are currently 40 million handguns in the United States, the committee remarked that in 1973, the last year for which complete figures are available, there were 28,000 firearm deaths. In 1975, it is estimated that nearly 30,000 will die from gunshot wounds. Accordingly, the bishops made five specific proposals, among which are these:

(1) A several day cooling-off period. This delay between the time of the sale and possession of the handgun by the purchaser should result in fewer crimes of passion.

(2) A ban on "Saturday night specials." These weapons are often used in street crime.

(3) Registration of handguns.

The bishops admitted that "this is a controversial issue and that some people of good faith will find themselves opposed to these measures."

Supporting the legitimate and proper use of rifles and shotguns for hunting and recreational purposes, the prelates noted the traditional principle "that individual rights to private property are limited by the universal demands of social order and human safety as well as the common good."

To date, this Statement has not been very successful in correcting this national evil.

A month later, in the *Statement on the United Nations and the Republic of South Africa*, issued by Bishop James S. Rausch, General Secretary of the United States Catholic Conference, on October 9, 1975, the Conference noted that for more than a decade, the conduct of the government of the Republic of South Africa (RSA) has been the subject of controversy among nations, and especially in the United Nations Organization. The Conference noted that in view of the RSA's flagrant violations of both the spirit and the mandate of the U.N. Charter, the U.N. General Assembly repeatedly has condemned RSA's apartheid as a "crime against humanity," and has described it as "abhorrent to the conscience of mankind."

In opposition to the thought of many nations, the bishops felt that expulsion from the U.N. of RSA would merely isolate it from the potential ameliorative influence of the full assembly of member nations, and the words of its critics would be heard only vaguely. Furthermore, the possibility of negotiating a settlement of the Namibia dispute might be postponed until, perhaps, after a bloody guerrilla war.

The prelates concluded their Statement by noting that the task of this age is to move from material interdependence to moral interdependence. It is time for all nations, especially the more powerful ones, to realize that their participation in oppression and the denial of human freedom to citizens of other lands is ultimately destructive of peace. "It is time for all nations, especially our own, to give to human dignity priority over political, military, and economic interests."

By a voice vote at their annual meeting in November 1973, the U.S. bishops agreed to help Cardinal John Krol of Philadelphia provide staff and funds for a 1976 International Eucharistic Congress in Philadelphia.

The bishops agreed to support a congress in Philadelphia after Cardinal Lawrence Shehan of Baltimore, past president of the Vatican's International Eucharistic Congress Central Committee, reported that the committee had extended an invitation to the United States to hold the forty-first congress somewhere in this country.

The central committee was again extending the invitation to the United States, he said, and Cardinal Krol had agreed to host the congress in the Philadelphia archdiocese if the bishops of the country would help him with the extensive preparatory work that goes into such a congress and assist in the funding.

The final decision as to where to hold the congress rests with the pope, who approved the recommendation of the central committee that it be held in Philadelphia.

So in 1976, for the second time in its history, the United States was chosen to host an International Congress. (The first location was Chicago in 1926.) For the bicentennial of the nation, Philadelphia, the Cradle of Liberty, was to be the scene of the International Eucharistic Congress. The motif of this congress, *The Eucharist and the Hungers of the Human Family*, was suggested by His Excellency, Archbishop Fulton J. Sheen, D.D., and was used as the title for the bishops' Pastoral. Stressing that the preparation should be primarily spiritual, centering around the "sacrament of love, a sign of unity, a bond of charity," the prelates noted that this congress, coming as it did during the bicentennial anniversary of the nation, offered an opportunity to invite others, especially visitors, to join them in affirming the religious and spiritual heritage of America.

"Let us pray," concluded the bishops, "that the Eucharistic Congress will help all of us to renew our faith, our hope, our love, and our gratitude for the greatest gift of Our Lord and Savior Jesus Christ in the Sacrament of the Eucharist; and to recommit ourselves, in union with Him, to the task of responding generously to the hungers of the human family."

In the all-out effort of the American hierarchy to make the congress a success, this Pastoral was far more widely publicized than most pastorals of the 70s. The bishops were gratified to witness the evolution of the inspiring congress programmed according to the eight major hungers of the human family listed in their Pastoral. Although Pope Paul VI was unable to come to Philadelphia, he shared with the American hierarchy the hope that the Pastoral and the congress would bear lasting fruit.

The following evaluation is taken from *Emmanuel*, a monthly published by the Priests' Eucharistic League and the Congregation of the Blessed Sacrament.

"Two things caught the planners of the congress somewhat by surprise. The first was the great numbers that attended the various conferences. Each day there were major addresses on the basic themes of the congress and numerous subsidiary presentations, all of which drew far larger crowds than hoped for. It was obvious that this was not simply a group of enthusiasts, but people who were serious about their responsibility to feed the hungers of the human family."

Each day focused on various aspects of the world's basic needs and hungers; speaker after speaker insisted that our being fed by Christ implied the obligation of genuine concern for the poor and needy. The lived dimension of a eucharistic community was stressed, and the people came to listen, to be inspired, to be fed.

The second surprise, another welcome one, was the drawing power of a small chapel situated between convention hall and the civic center. Despite the doubts of some scoffers, many thousands of people came for silent prayer before the Eucharist exposed. Here they had time to digest the matter of the various talks, and allow Christ himself to speak to them in prayer.

"In a sense, the congress was larger than life. It is impossible to describe the effect of being part of a sea of people on opening night. Prelates and some 50,000 people from all over the world dressed in native costumes, marched from center city in a procession that took over two hours to reach its destination. They believed Cardinal Krol's message proclaiming that, 'The Eucharist is and must be at the center of your lives as followers of Christ.'"[5]

At the November 1975 meeting, Cardinal Cooke, chairman of the Ad Hoc Committee for Pro-life Activities, presented a revised draft of *A Pastoral Plan for Pro-life Activities*. He emphasized that the document has a three-fold major thrust: 1. Public Information/Educational Program, 2. Pastoral Care, 3. Legislative/Public Policy Effort. Special emphasis is to be given to the first and second topics. His Eminence stressed that the pro-life effort in congressional districts is nonsectarian and nonpartisan. "Therefore, it is not controlled or financed by the Church." Encouragement should be given to people and pro-life groups to take part in the democratic process. The political activities of such groups and individuals are not the direct pastoral responsibility of NCCB, the ordinary of the diocese, or the parish.

Bishop Mark Hurley said that since this committee is a pro-life committee, the introduction should deal with broader issues than abortion alone. Other concerns such as euthanasia, death with dig-

---

[5]*"Evaluating the Congress,"* October 1976, pp. 450-51.

nity, and human experimentation should also be referred to. Cardinal Cooke asked if Bishop Hurley might make his recommendation in writing. Archbishop Borders of Baltimore, Maryland, supported Bishop Hurley's suggestion and also requested that whatever might be said should be incorporated in the *Pastoral Plan*. "We should show people that we are taking action and not just issuing another Statement." Archbishop Joseph Bernardin, summing up, observed that the consensus of the House seemed to be that strengthening and enlarging the introduction would be most acceptable. Referring to the publicity impact had by the *Food Crisis Pastoral Plan*, he expressed the hope that this plan might likewise have media impact.

Archbishop Philip Hannan asked whether efforts should be made to keep the national offices informed of the efforts conducted at the state level. Cardinal Cooke indicated that this would be most helpful.

Several other amendments, principally clarifying, were accepted by the body of the bishops and the *Pastoral Plan for Pro-life Activities* as amended was adopted by the bishops in a unanimous vote.

In 1975, the NCCB approved the publication of an updated *Ethical and Religious Directives for Catholic Health Facilities*. They mentioned that at their annual meeting in November 1971, the Directives were approved as the national code, subject to the approval of the bishops, for use in the diocese. Explaining that basic moral absolutes which underlie these Directives are not subject to change, the bishops teach that particular applications might be modified as scientific investigations and theological developments reveal new problems or cast new light on old ones.

The greatest updating is found in both "Procedures Involving Reproductive Organs and Functions"; and "Other Procedures," which includes the transplantation of organs. Allowing for further updating, the Directives declared: "The moral evaluation of new scientific developments and legitimately debated questions must be finally submitted to the teaching authority of the Church, in the person of the local bishop."

This document closes with a very complete section on "The Religious Care of the Patients."

On November 18, 1975, in his preliminary presentation on the Statement, *Right to a Decent Home: A Pastoral Response to the Crisis in Housing*, Bishop Joseph McNicholas, Chairman of the Committee on Social Development and World Peace, began by noting that the bishops in 1974 had asked that such a Statement be prepared. He reported that the housing subcommittee, under the leadership of Bishop Gallagher, has been responsible for the development of the document. The committee had sought ideas and expertise from a wide variety of persons who were knowledgeable on the issue of housing in order to prepare a document worthy of the consideration of the bishops. The Statement had received the unanimous approval of the committee and of the USCC administrative board. Pope Paul VI, in a recent statement, had said that the right to a dwelling is one of man's fundamental rights. He mentioned the committee hoped that the document would call the people of our nation to address the moral dimensions of the problem.

When Archbishop Bernardin presented the pastoral response on housing for the action of the general body, he noted that one page of the *modi* had been incorporated into the document.

After a voice vote, Archbishop Bernardin said that the *Pastoral Response to the Crisis in Housing* was declared unanimously adopted as a Statement of the USCC.

In his preliminary presentation of the Resolution, *The Economy: Human Dimensions*, addressing urgent economic problems, Bishop Joseph McNicholas said that the central domestic social justice issue before the nation was the economy. The six-page resolution was not a technical document, but rather it sought to point out the basic elements of economic distress and their moral aspects. He said that the Statement focused on the crisis of unemployment and urged policymakers to use measures to combat inflation, which do not rely upon high rates of joblessness. He concluded his introduction by adding that the document reemphasized the strong Catholic tradition of social teaching that was so relevant to the current economic distress.

When the matter was before the body for action, Archbishop Bernardin announced that the six-page resolution on economic problems had been supplemented by two pages of *modi* which had been distributed to the bishops.

Bishop McNicholas explained that in the *modi* was mention of the worldwide dimensions of economic justice, removal of any implication that the document was political, insertion of a scriptural passage, and mention of the concerns of the National Catholic Rural Life Conference.

Bishop Donohoe proposed that an addendum be attached to the document noting the success of the Statement of the bishops in 1919 on economic matters. He said that of the eleven points made in the Statement of 1919, all but one had been accepted in our society. Such an addendum would call to the mind of Catholics that statements of this kind can be very successful. Bishop McNicholas thanked Bishop Donohoe for the suggestion and noted that the addendum would be made.

After a voice vote, Archbishop Bernardin declared the document adopted by unanimous consent.

In pledging their best efforts to support the goals they mentioned, the bishops called on local parishes, dioceses, and Catholic organizations to undertake education and action programs on issues of economic justice. "We renew our commitment to assist the needy and victims of economic turmoil through programs of financial assistance and active participation in the dialogue over the formulation and implementation of just economic policies." They then called on all people to pray for our country in this time of need and "to participate in difficult decisions which can still fulfill the promise of our land."

On June 5, 1975, the California Agricultural Labor Relations Act (the first law ever enacted in any jurisdiction, federal or state, guaranteeing farm workers the right to determine, by secret ballot elections, which union, if any, they want to represent them) was signed into law by Governor Edmund G. Brown, Jr. The NCCB sincerely congratulated in their *Resolution on Farm Labor* all who participated in this process.

"We call upon all concerned—state officials, growers, and union representatives—to cooperate with one another in implementing the spirit as well as the letter of the law."

The National Conference of Catholic Bishops assured all concerned of their readiness to cooperate with the parties to the fullest possible extent in their common effort to bring about a new era of peace and justice in the agricultural industry, not only in California but also throughout the nation.

The bishops opened their *Resolution on Human Life Foundation* by commenting that just over six years ago, the Human Life Foundation, the first in the entire world, was established to encourage scientific research in natural family planning, and to promote educational efforts that would enable married couples to use responsibly those natural methods of family planning "whose safeness has been proven and whose harmony with the moral order has been ascertained" (Constitution on the *Church in the Modern World*, #87).

"In recognition and appreciation of the work of the Foundation, we pledge our continued support, encouragement, and collaboration to insure that the work so effectively begun will continue and lead to more successful achievements in the years ahead."

Since there was no objection to the resolution from the floor, the Chair declared it to be unanimously adopted.

On November 18, 1975, Archbishop William Baum, Chairman of the Committee for Ecumenical and Interreligious Affairs, explained the *Statement on Catholic-Jewish Relations* issued on the tenth anniversary of Vatican II's statement on the Jewish people, *Nostra Aetate* no. 4, was intended to address relations with the Jews from a religious rather than a political perspective. Bishop Francis Mugavero, head of the Secretariat for Jewish-Catholic Relations, presented the text for questions and clarification. He explained that the document had been approved by the administrative committee for presentation to the body of bishops and, if approved by the body of bishops, it would be released at a ceremonial celebration of the anniversary, attended by Roman Catholic and Jewish leaders. Cardinal Krol expressed his concern that the document failed to call attention to a disturbing element in Jewish-Catholic religious relations, namely, the attacks of certain Jewish organizations on the rights of Catholic parents to receive public support for secular subjects in the Church's school system. Bishop Francis Green felt that the Statement would emphasize the need to dialogue with Jews about Christ. Archbishop Joseph Ryan expressed his concern that the draft seemed to overemphasize the link of the Jews to the land of Israel.

Archbishop Baum presented, November 20, 1975, a new draft revised in light of the comments received from the bishops during the preceding session and in meetings with the committee. He particularly thanked Cardinal Krol and Archbishop Ryan for their assistance.

Melkite Archbishop Tawil asked to make an addition to the sentence: "Appreciation of this link is not to give assent to any particular religious interpretation of this bond." He moved to add the words, "nor to deny the legitimate rights of other concerned parties in the region." The motion was seconded. Archbishop Tawil urged the acceptance of the amendment to give evidence of the bishops' sensitivity to the serious situation in the Mid-East and to the efforts of the Holy Father and of the bishops in the Holy Land. Bishop Bernard Law spoke against the addition, suggesting that it was adequately covered in a subsequent sentence in the document and in the bishops' 1973 Statement on the Mid-East. Archbishop Philip Hannan supported the amendment, and expressed the view that the words "legitimate rights" contained a very helpful addition. The amendment was then brought to the floor for a vote, and the motion carried.

A two-thirds vote was required for the approval of the Statement. On a written ballot, the Statement carried: one hundred ninety affirmative, six negative.

On February 12, 1976, the administrative board of the United States Catholic Conference issued a Statement: *Political Responsibility: Reflections on an Election Year*. Noting that 1976 marked the two hundredth anniversary of the founding of the nation, the bishops remarked that it is also a year that will test the workings of this democracy. They were mindful of Watergate and other scandals in high political places. They addressed their Statement to all Americans in hopes that the upcoming elections would provide an opportunity for thoughtful debate on the issues and challenges that face the United States as well as decisions on the candidates who would lead us.

Regretting the alienation and indifference manifested in recent elections, the prelates prayed that the government would deal effectively with critical issues that affected the daily lives of our citizens. They lamented the discouragement and feelings of powerlessness affecting the young and the elderly. Accordingly, they urged all citizens to register to vote, become informed on the relevant issues, and vote freely according to their conscience. They pointed out that the Church's responsibility includes the affirmation and promotion of human rights and the obligation to call attention to the moral and religious dimensions of secular issues. They sought to make clear that the Church's participation in public affairs is not a threat to the political process or to genuine pluralism, but an affirmation of the importance of each. "We specifically do not seek the formation of a religious voting bloc; nor do we wish to instruct persons on how they should vote by endorsing candidates. We urge citizens to avoid choosing candidates simply on the personal basis of self-interest."

They singled out eight issues in all: the economy, education, food policy, housing, human rights, U.S. foreign policy, mass media, and military expenditures, although they did mention that this was not an exclusive list of issues of concern to them.

Despite the listing of so many issues and the general mention of civil and political rights, the bishops were accused of being interested in abortion alone and also of interfering in the political realm notwithstanding their clear explanation under the heading: "The Church and the Political Order."

In an effort to clarify their position and their interest, on May 6, 1976, at their spring meeting to which they decided to return, the bishops passed a resolution entitled *Political Responsibility*, in which they stated: "the Church's ministry and mission requires it to relate positively to the political order, since social injustice and the denial of human rights can often be remedied only through governmental action."

The bishops concluded that all should join together in common witness and effective action to bring about a society based on truth, justice, charity, and freedom. Notwithstanding this second clarification and the efforts of the President, Archbishop Bernardin, the bishops, up to the very hour of the election, were thought by some to be interfering, primarily because of their interest in procuring a constitutional amendment prohibiting abortion on demand.

On May 5, 1976, in the discussion of *Society and the Aged: Toward Reconciliation*, Cardinal Krol recommended four editorial changes to the draft of the Statement for greater clarity which, by the suggestion of Archbishop Peter Gerety of Newark, New Jersey, and the concurrence of Archbishop Bernardin, were referred to the appropriate committee for incorporation into the final document. Archbishop Bernardin observed that although the policy of the conference is to avoid discussion of such editorial changes, experience proves that such discussion does occur.

Archbishop Philip Hannan of New Orleans, Louisiana, then moved to amend section f, number 30 of the agenda document by inserting: "We strongly endorse continued congressional expansion and administration backing of the very successful section 202 programs. We further urge that the interest rate for section 202 loans be set at 6½%." Bishop Raymond Gallagher of Lafayette, Indiana, seconded the motion.

Archbishop Hannan said that the president of the United States does not favor expansion of programs already involving a commitment of $375 million for 14,000 units; Mr. Carter threatens to veto congressional increases in the program, noting that the interest rate of 8⅝ percent to nine percent, together with present building codes, makes such loans too expensive for middle-income people and that such loans cost the government only 6.5 percent. Archbishop Thomas Donnellan of Atlanta, Georgia, said he had some trouble in voting on a document which sets an interest rate which could very easily date the document. Bishop George Guilfoyle of Camden, New Jersey, remarked that his diocese had been turned down for a $30 million loan at the lowest possible rate rather than a specific figure.

Cardinal Dearden of Detroit, Michigan, asked why the committee had not adopted Archbishop Hannan's amendment. Bishop Maurice Dingman of Des Moines, Iowa, replied that the committee wondered about the advisability of mentioning a specific piece of legislation and an interest rate. Although the committee appreciated suggestions, it recommended they be pursued by the appropriate agency but not incorporated into the document. Bishop Joseph McNicholas of Springfield, Illinois, commented that if Archbishop Hannan's amendment were not approved, this did not mean the bishops opposed his suggestion. Bishop McNicholas recommended that a letter be circularized which bishops could sign to identify themselves with Archbishop Hannan's ideas, if they so wished. At this point Archbishop Bernardin asked if Archbishop Hannan wished to withdraw, amend, or go to a vote on his amendment. Archbishop Hannan said he would find it a contradiction to go on record for public housing for the elderly without mentioning the only law now on the books to help them. He agreed to an amendment of his amendment incorporating the motion of the lowest possible interest rate. Such an amendment to the amendment passed by voice vote, so the amendment now reads: "We strongly endorse continued congressional expansion and administration backing of the very successful section 202 programs. We further urge that the interest for section 202 be set at the lowest possible rate."

Archbishop Peter Gerety then asked how the committee felt about the amended version. Bishop Dingman thought it was too specific, since the law itself might be amended, thus creating a dilemma for legislators on where the Church stood on the issue. Bishop McNicholas opposed endorsing a specific proposal. Archbishop John Roach of St. Paul, Minnesota, favored the amendment which he saw as strengthening the document. Bishop Thomas Welsh of Arlington, Virginia, observed that the document itself says, "We must raise our voices clearly and effectively." The amendment proposed by Archbishop Hannan passed by voice vote and the final document was approved by a vote of two hundred eleven to eight.

A thorough document touching all the serious problems of the aged, this Statement shows concretely the growth of the Church leaders in their concern for social problems, a growth good to have on record.

Teach Them: Statement on Catholic Schools of May 4, 1976, was certainly accelerated by the *Catholic Schools in a Declining Church* report that 6.6 million Catholic children below college level were not enrolled in any formal religious education program.[6] In contrast with the 1972 Pastoral *To Teach as Jesus Did*, which declared the bishops' support for Catholic education in every phase, this 1976 Statement confined itself to the Church's educational ministry to children and young people, especially as expressed in Catholic schools; the focus is thus primarily upon the schools.

The bishops reasserted their support of Catholic schools because "generally these schools are notably successful educational institutions which offer not only high quality academic programs but also instruction and formation in the beliefs, values and traditions of Catholic Christianity . . . Catholic schools have a rich potential for strengthening the bonds which unite a community."

The prelates reminded all that "without Catholic and other church-related schools, spiritual values would find far less support in American society." Citing a recent report of the National Opinion Research Center that Catholic schools have a significant positive impact on those who attend them and that the Catholic public is highly supportive of them, the bishops declared "our commitment to the schools is clear and undiminished."

The Pastoral pointed out that the Catholic schools witness to the talent and potential black, Hispanic, and native American youth possess when given an educational opportunity. The Statement praised the new awareness that all faculty members are, at least by their example, an integral part of religious education and reflected on the importance of pastoral leadership.

Again in this Statement, the prelates praised the sacrifices of supporters of Catholic schools for their efforts to sustain and improve them. The Statement, reflecting the thought of many bishops, denounced the harsh injustice to nonpublic school supporters resulting from court decisions against the use of public funds for nonpublic education.[7] The bishops called "deplorable, tenuous, and at times

---

[6] Andrew M. Greely, William C. McCready, and Kathleen McCourt, *Catholic Schools in a Declining Church* (Kansas City: 1976).

[7] "The parents of children in church-related schools have reason to question the motives of the opponents of aid to children in nonpublic schools," Cardinal John Krol of Philadelphia told an interdenominational group in that city February 20, 1976. In what was a very strong statement, the cardinal called for a dialogue on school aid questions. He told his audience: "There is a growing resentment of the coalition which is helping to deprive American citizens of their religious and cultural heritage." *Catholic Trends*, March 6, 1976.

offensive," reasons given by the courts in overturning various forms of school aid legislation. The Statement concludes with a very practical program for the Department of Education of the USCC to follow. The implementation of some of the program, especially on research, was hindered, however, by the reluctance of the majority of the bishops to have another national collection of a dime per student in parochial school as suggested by Bishop William McManus of Fort Wayne, Indiana.

The bishops approved *Teach Them: Statement on Catholic Schools* by a vote of one hundred fifty-three to thirty.

In the opening sentence of *Let the Little Children Come to Me* (November 1976), the USCC Statement on early childhood care and education notes that American families live under many strong pressures today from contemporary social and economic conditions and the prevalence of secularistic values. In seeking to improve conditions of family life, "society and the Church must direct a major part of their concern and effort to very young children and their parents."

The prelates insist that all children are entitled to the best efforts of us all in regard to their care and education, although many children do not enjoy such help at present in the United States.

In the light of these rights of children and their needs, the bishops "endorse efforts within the Church which have among their purposes to strengthen and support Christian family life."

The Statement called for efforts in the Church to give guidance on early childhood development and religious formation to parents before the Baptism of their children. The bishops recommended beginning such instructions several months before Baptism. By a two hundred one to twenty-three vote, the Statement was approved.

Most American dioceses now require some instruction of the parents before the Baptism of their child.

In their *Statement on U.S.–Panama Relations,* November 10, 1976, the Conference of U.S. Catholic Bishops voted one hundred seventy to sixty-one to call for negotiation of a new treaty that will give Panama "greater sovereignty" in the Canal Zone.

Their Statement said it is a "moral imperative" to have a treaty that respects the territorial integrity, sovereignty, and economy of Panama.

The bishops called for dissolution of "the vestiges of a relationship which more closely resembles the colonial politics of the nineteenth century than the realities of an interdependent world of sovereign and equal states."

The vote, requiring a two-thirds majority for approval, came after heated debates on the third day of the bishops' four-day annual meeting.

Several bishops, among them Cardinal Carberry, objected that they did not know enough about the situation in Panama and said it would be wiser to issue such a Statement in the name of a committee that wrote it.

John Cardinal Krol of Philadelphia, Pennsylvania, objected that the Statement did not include condemnation of Soviet violations of sovereignty elsewhere in the world.

Bishop Joseph A. McNicholas of Springfield, Illinois, chairman of the committee, defended the Statement as covering only moral issues.

However, the Statement does criticize the United States military presence in the Canal Zone, "which extends U.S. military influence into much of Latin America through the programs of the U.S. Southern Command.

"For the Panamanian government to be so closely tied without a choice to the military policy of the United States in Latin America constitutes a continuing political problem which casts doubt upon the independence of Panama."

The Statement said, "We wish also to express our pastoral concern and public support for a negotiated treaty which will protect the welfare of the people living and working in the Canal Zone.

"We especially call attention to the need for an agreement which will provide for the economic security of Americans presently employed in the Canal Zone."

The efforts of the Panamanian Archbishop Marcos McGrath had a great influence on this Statement's being accepted by the bishops and as with the 1975 administrative board's Statement on *Panama-U.S. Relations*, the Panamanian government was delighted with the 1976 Statement.

At their November 1976 meeting, the bishops voted unanimously for a *Resolution on the Pastoral Concern of the Church for People on the Move* which supports the 400,000 people a year who immigrate into the United States. The Resolution gives strong support to undocumented immigrants and advocates 1) that quota-ceilings for natives of Mexico and Canada be increased to 35,000 persons per year; and 2) that the American citizen child, regardless of age, be in a position to facilitate his or her parents' immigration."

The ultimate goal the Resolution requested was "the achievement of that just social order where emigration of capital, export of technical assistance, the concessions of favorable terms of trade to the less developed countries, and similar arrangements will provide that no one is forced to emigrate for his freedom and his human dignity and all are free to do it in pursuit of their happiness."

The Resolution was in part prompted by a recent immigration law making it difficult for families from Mexico to be reunited in this country. It had only limited success.

Immigration legislation passed by the Senate in May 1983 and being considered in the House late July 1983 offers "too little in the way of relief for the vast underclass of undocumented (illegal) aliens,"[8] according to the Ad Hoc Committee for Hispanic Affairs of the National Conference of Catholic Bishops. The committee criticized both the Senate and House versions of immigration reform, saying the bills "propose restrictive and potentially discriminatory measures."

The Pastoral Statement, *To Live in Christ Jesus*, November 8, 1976, was prompted by the contemporary onslaught on morality which had been gaining devastating momentum for several years. Cardinal Manning of Los Angeles, California, lamented to the bishops: "Pornographic materials can be purchased at almost every corner in Los Angeles." Bishop John McDowell, the articulate auxiliary of Pittsburgh, was named chairman of the committee assigned in November 1975 to compose a pastoral on moral values. Some idea of the work that went into the composition can be gathered from the realization that more than 8,000 letters were sent to scholars, scholarly societies, seminaries, colleges, and universities throughout the world asking for input. Dialogues with those who responded and subsequent consultation followed with almost countless meetings. The committee labored through four drafts, and on the final morning of the meeting, a final effort was made to delay action on the document. Some bishops felt it did not express enough compassion for those who find it difficult to follow the Church's teaching. Bishop Francis Mugavero of Brooklyn, New York, who had recently released his own pastoral on sexual ethics, moved to recommit the document to the NCCB Ad Hoc Committee on Moral Values. He said he supported the document and the principles in it but believed its tone would prevent it from reaching the widest number of people. "If it lacks understanding and compassion, it fails in its teaching role," he said. A few of the bishops thought the Pastoral was coming too soon after the Detroit meeting, "A Call to Action," whose resolutions, which touched some of the subjects in the Statement, would not be considered by the body of the bishops until their next meeting. These few bishops feared that the issuance of the Pastoral before a study of Detroit's resolutions would show a certain insensitivity on the part of the NCCB.

After an hour's debate in which Cardinal Krol read a laudatory evaluation by a promising young moralist, Father Francis DiLorenzo, the bishops voted one hundred sixty-two to twenty-five to publish the Pastoral after consideration of the final draft which was given to the bishops. They were told to discuss their suggestions once more. Then the general body of the bishops went over the document sentence by sentence, taking more than three hours. Each change required a majority vote. The entire amended document passed by a one hundred seventy-two to twenty-five vote.

---

[8]*Our Sunday Visitor*, July 24, 1983.

The Pastoral focused its moral standards on Christ's two laws of love of God and fellow man as so completely exemplified in the life of Jesus; hence the title: *To Live in Christ Jesus: A Pastoral Reflection on the Moral Life*.

The letter rejects the notion that valid sacramental marriages can be dissolved and condemns premarital and extra-marital relations. In reply to the increasing voice of the homosexual, the document teaches homosexual actions are wrong but calls for compassionate pastoral care of homosexuals and condemns discrimination against them. It states that justice requires programs and individual efforts to overcome the effects of past discrimination against racial and ethnic minorities. Questioning whether war as it is waged today can be morally justified, the Pastoral strongly proclaims it is wrong to launch a nuclear attack on civilian populations or to threaten such an attack as part of a strategy of military deterrence.

The letter has been well received, with several colleges using it as a basic text for their moral courses, and has been more widely disseminated than most of the other NCCB Statements through adult education courses on the parish level. It has been used by several of the American hierarchy in the refutation of *Human Sexuality*.[9]

The New York Times noted: "The letter repeats the moral standards of the Vatican's *Declaration on Sexual Ethics* issued earlier this year.[10]

Cardinal Krol, chairman of the Ad Hoc Committee for the International Eucharistic Congress, furnished an extensive information report on the activities and success of the forty-first International Eucharistic Congress, held in Philadelphia, August 1-8, 1976. He then introduced a resolution: that the Conference recommended the continuation of Operation Rice Bowl, Operation SIGN, Operation Faith Sharing, and the liturgical and religious education of all Catholics for Jesus, the Bread of Life.

In response to a question from Cardinal Carberry, Cardinal Krol indicated that the Board of Catholic Relief Services had already decided to continue Operation Rice Bowl in 1977, which in Philadelphia alone brought more than $600,000 to efforts for the relief of hunger. He also indicated that the proposed resolution did not require the establishment of any permanent office, but could be implemented on a diocesan basis. He noted further that the resolution constituted a set of recommendations, not mandatory programs. Later in the meeting, the Conference overwhelmingly approved the resolution on a voice vote.

---

[9]Written by a Catholic Theological Society of America Committee on the Study of Human Sexuality, chaired by Reverend Anthony Kosnick and published by the Paulist Press in 1977 for the Committee but not for the Society.
[10]November 12, 1976.

Operation Rice Bowl is a program of education, fasting, and sacrifice to emphasize the world hunger situation; Operation SIGN is a program in which youth give volunteer service; Operation Faith Sharing is a program of home visitations to invite the unchurched to open houses and Church programs; and Bread of Life is a religious education and liturgical program.

At the request of Bishop Leo Maher of San Diego, California, Archbishop Quinn introduced a lengthy resolution which ended: "Resolved by the National Conference of Catholic Bishops, that the members of this Conference, in behalf of all the members of the Catholic Church in the United States of America, do hereby express our profound gratitude and heartiest congratulations to His Eminence, John Cardinal Krol, on the tremendous success of his tireless efforts to bring the forty-first International Eucharistic Congress to Philadelphia during the nation's bicentennial, and to continue its enduring effect as an instrument of spiritual renewal in the Church."

The Resolution was adopted by acclamation, the members standing to applaud for Cardinal Krol. His Eminence thanked the bishops and expressed special appreciation for the efforts of Bishop Lohmuller, executive vice-chairman of the Eucharistic Congress.

In their endeavor to extend further social justice to all, the two hundred forty-six bishops, assembled from May 2-5, 1977, in Palmer House, Chicago, adopted early in the meeting three statements that deal directly with social justice: *Religious Liberty in Eastern Europe: A Test Case for Human Rights; Statement on The American Indian;* and a *Resolution on Haitian Refugees.*

Bishop Joseph McNicholas of Springfield, Illinois, presented the *Statement on Eastern Europe,* which may have been accelerated by Cardinal Krol's comment at the previous meeting on the *Panama Statement* when His Eminence asked: "What about the violation of the sovereignty of Latvia, Lithuania, etc.?" After several strengthening amendments, the Statement was approved by a vote of two hundred fifty-two affirmative to two negative and one abstaining.

The Statement declared: "The denial of religious freedom in the countries spanning the region from Poland in the north to Bulgaria in the south is a tragic episode in humanity's efforts to defend and promote human rights. . . . No religion is spared: Christians, Jews, and Moslems all suffer . . . the suppression of religion is vigorous and comprehensive." The bishops continued: "New opportunities are present for the United States, which, if utilized, may contribute to the defense of human rights in Eastern Europe. . . . Specifically, we encourage the new administration to engage seriously in the preparations for the followup to the Helsinki Agreement scheduled for 1977. . . . We [the bishops] pledge ourselves to continue to make public advocacy of human rights a matter of our prime concern." In a most charitable way, the prelates concluded: "As we pray for the persecuted Church throughout the world, we also pray for its per-secutors." They then turned their attention to a historic domestic problem.

The *Statement on the American Indian* was five years in formulation. It began with a Statement on American Indians presented by the Subcommittee on Native Americans. This Statement was approved by the Committee on Social Development and World Peace and sub-mitted for approval to the administrative board, to be issued as a Statement of the Committee on Social Development and World Peace. After discussion, the paper was withdrawn for modification and then resubmitted for board action in February 1977. During that meeting, the administrative board recommended that in light of the very important subject matter of the Statement, the document be submit-ted to the full membership of the USCC for issuance by that body.

The Statement is addressed especially to American Indians and to those in ministry with them as well as to the broader Catholic community.

The subcommittee sought advice regarding the Statement from many Indians, from clergy, religious, and lay persons working with Indians, and from several theologians and historians knowledgeable in Indian affairs. In addition, the Statement was greatly influenced by the April 1975 Statement of the Bishops of Minnesota and the Labor Day 1975 Statement of the Bishops of Canada, both of which address the relationship of the Church with American Indians. The Statement takes its major direction from the *Exhortation on Evangeli-zation in the Modern World*, issued by Pope Paul VI in December 1975.

In the context of the themes articulated by Pope Paul's message, the Statement attempts to express simply the Church's concern for American Indians today both within the Church and in society. This Statement recommends an ongoing evaluation of the Church's min-istry with American Indians in all its aspects and urges that liturgical forms, educational programs, and other services be adapted to reflect the needs and unique cultural identity of the Indian peoples. It also encourages cooperation with Indians in their struggle to achieve social justice within the American society.

Twelve *modi* (possible modifications) to the document were sub-mitted to the general body of the bishops. After some sharp discus-sion, e.g., about too much self-accusation, the Statement received the necessary two-thirds vote, two hundred fifty-four to eight with three abstentions.

Some prelates were still disappointed in the document. Arch-bishop Thomas A. Connolly commended Bishop McNicholas's Com-mittee's work; yet he said he opposed the entire Statement. He described it as much ado about nothing, since Indian leaders would see this as a group of pious, inconsequential statements which did nothing to alleviate the sad condition of Indians. "We need something to give them," he said, "such as hospitalization or unemployment insurance, etc."

On May 2, 1977, the Ad Hoc Committee on Migration and Tourism presented to the NCCB a *Resolution on Haitian Refugees* which the conference of bishops accepted. The Resolution states that among the groups of immigrants who have lately sought refuge in our country, few have met such official opposition, hostility, and discrimination as have the refugees from Haiti. "Some have been deported, some are presently held in American jails, and the majority are still denied refugee status and the right to work and move freely within this society."

Specifically, the committee urged the immediate cessation of all deportation proceedings against Haitian refugees, release of all Haitian refugees now imprisoned solely for reason of immigration, and the granting of amnesty or full refugee rights to all such Haitians now in this country. The Resolution demanded that the United Nations convention and protocol relating to the status of refugees be scrupulously adhered to by our government and not be restrictively interpreted as applying only to persons fleeing from particular kinds of repressive societies.

The committee exhorted the appropriate committees of the House and Senate to hold full and extensive hearings on the status of human rights in Haiti, given the expressed dissatisfaction of many in the Haitian community both with such hearings as have been held in the recent past and the report issued on December 21, 1976, by the Department of State on human rights and U.S. policy.

Finally, the bishops expressed their gratitude to all who have reached out in fraternal solicitude to these recent arrivals and urged all those churches which have not inaugurated such programs of help to the Haitians to do so as soon as practical.

Many religious eyes of the nation were on the May 1977 assembled body of bishops to see how they would react to the one hundred eighty-two resolutions from the innovative "Call to Action" bicentennial meeting in Detroit. The resolutions touched almost every area of life—political, economic, and social as well as spiritual. Consideration of the resolutions and a response represented a monumental task. The prelates approached the problem systematically and thoroughly. Bishop Joseph McNicholas of Springfield, Illinois, headed the committee formulating the response. A copy was sent to each bishop who was then asked to submit his modifications. At the meeting the suggested modifications were given to the bishops for their study. On the afternoon of May 4, 1976, the bishops split into groups and were free to go into any of the eight categories, e.g., Personhood, Family, Justice and Peace, etc., which covered the subject matter or classification of the one hundred eighty-two resolutions. The input of these meetings was then collated and shared with the bishops.

Finally, on Thursday morning, May 6, the body of bishops, with
Bishop McNicholas responding for the committee, took each *modi* or
suggested amendment and any further modifications that might be
suggested from the floor and voted on each one separately, a procedure that took nearly four unbroken hours. Rarely has more collective work gone into a single Statement. It came forth as a balanced
Statement appreciative of the work and consultation offered by the
Detroit gathering. It easily received the necessary two-thirds vote.

In presenting the *Resolution on Jesus of Nazareth*, Bishop Joseph R.
Crowley suggested that since the Church is inclined to speak out
when it does not approve of particular movies, in a situation like this,
it should also speak favorably of a broadcasting effort that dealt with
an important issue in a sensitive fashion. Bishop Thomas Welsh of
Arlington, Virginia, asked whether the "sponsors" should be mentioned as well. Bishop Crowley accepted this as a friendly amendment. The Resolution as amended was then passed by voice vote.
Bishop John Dougherty requested that it be noted in the minutes that
the vote was *unanimous*.

In many ways a pioneering *Statement on Recombinant DNA*[11] *Research*
was written by the Bishops' Committee for Human Values and published by the National Conference of Catholic Bishops on May 2, 1977.
Endeavoring to simplify an unusually difficult project and debate, the
Statement still remains challenging reading for the average person.

While admitting it had several purposes in making the Statement,
the committee declared: "A primary objective is educational," since
the general public should be informed about such research and its
risks, some still unknown.

The bishops wanted to call attention to the moral dimensions
beyond the hazards issue and to offer some guidelines in moral reasoning concerning recombinant DNA research.

They proposed the dilemma: "investigation involving recombinant DNA promises great theoretical advances" with possible practical applications in medicine and agriculture. However, since the
research in some cases involves pathogenic substances and new organisms, it may involve "unknown and potentially grave risks."

After noting that the National Institutes of Health had issued
safeguards for its grantees doing this type of research, the bishops'
committee stated there are several basic ethical questions about
recombinant DNA research that must be addressed: e.g., "Are the
N.I.H. guidelines adequate? What is the responsibility of the United
States on an international level in dealing with recombinant DNA?
How far do we want to advance in genetic engineering?

Observing that each scientific advance does not necessarily constitute real human progress, the bishops teach that collaboration

[11]DNA stands for deoxyribonucleic acid.

between the scientific fraternity and an alerted public is necessary "if wisdom and humility are to effect enlightened public policy."

To promote an enlightened public policy conscious of the moral implications in this research was the major purpose of this Statement.

The *Statement concerning Human Sexuality*, issued November 15, 1977, explains that the Committee on Doctrine exists to assist the bishops in their apostolic mandate "to profess the truth in love" (Eph 4:15). It is in this perspective that the Statement considered the book *Human Sexuality, New Directions in American Catholic Thought* (Paulist Press, 1977), the final report of a committee established by the Catholic Theological Society of America.[12] After recognizing the importance of theological discussion, the Statement reminds both bishops and theologians that they have certain obligations: They are bound by the written Word of God along with the Sacred Tradition; and the *sensus fidei*, the documents which the faith of the Church has set forth.

The committee that drafted the Statement mentions that it does not object to a theological study of sexuality, but it does reject the idea that a tentative study such as *Human Sexuality* can offer "helpful pastoral guidelines to beleaguered pastors, priests, counsellors, and teachers," or guidance for the faithful in forming their consciences on sexual matters. In the judgment of the bishops' committee, this study "contradicts theological tradition and the Church's clear magisterial teaching refined over the centuries and recently reaffirmed in the Vatican *Declaration on Sexual Ethics*, and the American bishops' pastoral letter, *To Live in Christ Jesus*."

The Statement comments that in fidelity to God's plan, the Church has condemned such behavior as fornication, adultery, and masturbation as sinful. The unitive and procreative dimension of human sexual activity as it came from the hands of God can be properly realized only within the marriage covenant.

While recognizing the importance of empirical studies, the committee declares the inadequacy of such studies by themselves to establish moral norms or alter them. The committee warns that they do not find in the study a sufficiently critical attitude toward specific social analyses. "The authors of the report neglect this balance in their effort to explore a broader concept of human sexuality. The goals of human sexuality substituted by the report (creative integration, intrapersonal and interpersonal growth) are too vague to apply with any kind of precision or assurance. In effect, they remove the essential connection between sexual activity and procreation, sexual activity and marital love."

By abandoning norms that make specific demands, the report reaches the conclusion that sexual activity outside of marriage can be

---

[12]This volume was published not by the Catholic Theological Society but only under the auspices of the committee writing the report.

permissible, even virtuous, feared the bishops, and they warned that pastors, confessors, counsellors, and teachers cannot adopt these guidelines and remain faithful to the mission of proclaiming God's Word which has been entrusted to them.

The committee rebukes the report for giving too little attention to the supernatural aspects of marital love and declares that Christians cannot be satisfied with a minimal sexual morality if they are to reach the perfection to which God is calling them. After expressing a full appreciation of compassion towards the sinner, the Statement warns "against the temptation to respond to this need for pastoral compassion by weakening the demands of sound morality."

The bishops close their Statement by quoting Pope Paul VI on the occasion of the canonization of St. John Neumann: "Understanding? Yes! Sensitivity? Yes! But supernatural sensitivity to Christ and to His Cross and Resurrection."

To prevent the abuse of the great generosity of American Catholics and to keep a rightful order in the soliciting of financial support, the NCCB promulgated after the November 1977 meeting, *Principles and Guidelines for Fund Raising*.

The NCCB in the formation of these *Guidelines* worked in close conjunction with the Leadership Conference of Women Religious, and the Conference of Major Superiors of Men, both of whom agreed to promulgate these directives and to assist in the proper ordering of fund-raising activities. Pastors, who often thought their parishes were being milked dry by "outsiders," as well as the bishops looked on this document as a step in the right direction and approved heartily of it.

The bishops outlined carefully the techniques to be used in all fund-raising and demanded a strict accountability from all engaged in soliciting funds for religious purposes.

Archbishop Thomas Donnellan of Atlanta, Georgia, at the November 1977 meeting submitted a written report containing proposed *Guidelines and Principles for Fundraising*. He noted that the proposal had been approved by both conferences of major superiors of men and women. Archbishop Bernardin said that any changes made by the bishops would have to be resubmitted to these conferences in keeping with Vatican directives.

Bishop Norman McFarland suggested that the guidelines include references to the NCCB Manual on Accounting. In response to questions by Archbishop John Roach and Bishop Maurice Dingman, Archbishop Donnellan stated that the meaning of "public subscription" is not univocal. Bishop Hugh Donohue suggested that a termination date be attached to any permission to solicit funds. Archbishop Bernardin referred these and similar suggestions to the representatives of the three groups involved. Before the document is printed, said Archbishop Bernardin, the three groups should consider all the suggestions.

The Statement passed on a voice vote.

In the April 1972 meeting, Auxiliary Bishop William McManus reported that the *General Catechetical Directory* from the Vatican had been translated by the USCC Department of Education and is enjoying wide success on both the diocesan and parish levels. He then explained a USCC plan for a National Catechetical Directory.

Cardinal Carberry asked if a "yes" vote meant approval of the entire national catechetical plan. Bishop McManus replied that the two committees involved would use the plan as a model. The cardinal asked if the final document would be submitted to the bishops for their approval. Bishop McManus said: "Yes."

The major concern of the bishops was expressed by the Philadelphia Auxiliary Bishop John Graham, who remarked that if a National Catechetical Directory were to have widespread support, it ought to involve the bishops in its entire task of preparation. He said that sometimes middle management does not seem to carry out the policy directives of bishops, and he cited as an example that the instrument for evaluating religion texts had not quieted the concerns of many people. He noted that the *Basic Teachings for Catholic Religious Education* prepared by a committee of bishops had not been well received in some religious education centers. "Unless the bishops are in on the work of preparing a National Catechetical Directory," he cautioned, "the document will not express a wide consensus. A catechetical directory deals with the faith," he warned, "and to the bishops more than anyone else has been given the task of safeguarding that faith. I admire that plan," he said, "and I ask that bishops be in on its implementation."

Cardinal Krol added that one of the key questions in the discussion concerned the active and continued role of the bishops in the first and continued stages of the development of the National Catechetical Directory.

Bishop Joseph McNicholas moved to amend the plan by providing a ten- to twelve-member committee, four of whom would be bishops. Bishop McManus called this a perfecting amendment acceptable to his committee. The amendment passed by a voice vote. It was decided that the President, Cardinal John Krol, would appoint the committee. The motion to accept the new plan for the formulation of a National Catechetical Directory was adopted by voice vote.

After several progress reports at succeeding meetings and unusually wide consultation of experts, Archbishop John J. Whealon of Hartford, Connecticut, presented the draft of the Directory at the November 1977 meeting, chapter by chapter, and indicated to the body of bishops those amendments that the Policy and Review Committee had considered essentially stylistic or minor in nature. These amendments were voted *in globo.*

Finally, the bishops approved by a vote of two hundred sixteen to twelve the draft of a *National Catechetical Directory*, "Sharing the Light of Faith." This vote came after four days of lively debate during which more than three hundred amendments were considered, one hundred of which came from Bishop Thomas Welsh of Arlington, Virginia. It took four years to write the two hundred fifty-four page draft, which involved consultation on practically every level. It must not be mistaken for a catechism.[13] It is a book of background information, norms, and guidelines for the direction of religious educators and formation programs in the United States.

The Vatican, after making a few qualifications, approved the *Directory*.

The Statement, *The Gospel of Peace and the Danger of War*, was published by the USCC administrative board on February 15, 1978. An accelerating arms race throughout the world, especially in the superpowers of the United States and the U.S.S.R., occasioned this Statement.

Opening their reflections with a quotation from Pope Paul VI proclaiming "the absurdity of modern war and the absolute necessity of peace,"[14] the bishops echo Paul's teaching that the arms race is "a danger, an injustice, and a mistake" for the human family. For the United States, these papal words have a special significance. "No nation has a more critical role in determining the delicate balance between the dangers of war and the possibilities of peace."

Admitting that the United States does not bear this responsibility alone, the board cites two 1978 events that "will highlight the U.S. role and responsibility in the arms race": the forthcoming VIII Special Session of the United Nations on Disarmament; and the continuing debate in the United States about the SALT II agreement with the Soviet Union limiting nuclear weapons.[15]

Disclaiming any intention of going into a detailed analysis of either of these topics, the bishops insist "the primary moral imperative is that the arms race must be stopped and the reduction of armaments must be achieved." The prelates explain that contemporary Catholic teaching on war and peace supports those who choose nonviolence as a witness to the Gospel, but it also allows that some uses of force in defense of the common good are legitimate. Both of these moral positions are rooted in the Gospel.

But beyond this moral analysis, the Church must teach the meaning of peace and call governments and their peoples to pursue peace wholeheartedly, even to undertaking reasonable risks for peace.

---

[13]*Our Sunday Visitor*, December 4, 1977.
[14]"No Violence, Yes to Peace," January 1, 1978.
[15]Philadelphia Archdiocesan Archives, Krol papers.

"As the Church in this nation," the bishops concluded their Statement, "we seek to be a moral voice placing restraints on war, a prophetic voice calling for peace, and a prayerful community which has the courage to work for peace."

This Statement became a forerunner of the much lengthier and detailed statements.[16] In his September 6, 1979, testimony for the USCC before the Senate Foreign Relations Committee on the Salt II Treaty, Cardinal John Krol said: "We cannot regard the Salt II Treaty as a major achievement in arms control. It certainly is not an arms reduction treaty; it is more accurately characterized as a measure which regulates the expansion of the arms race."[17]

One of the saddest flights to safety in modern history was that of the refugees from Southeast Asia, Vietnam, Laos, and Cambodia, after the United States withdrew from the Vietnam War in 1973. Over sixty percent of the refugees fleeing oppressive actions by new Communist regimes were children. In the suicidal small boat movement from Vietnam, out of every two persons who started out, only one survived.

In view of these conditions, the administrative committee of the NCCB released on February 16, 1978, a *Statement on Refugees in Southeast Asia* which urged the President and Congress of the United States to respond in a more humane manner to the anguished cries of these people of Southeast Asia seeking freedom.

The committee observed that the generous hospitality of Thailand has already been overtaxed even to the risk of invasion by surrounding well-armed Communist nations. After the January 25, 1978, admission of an additional 7,000 boat refugees, a stop gap measure, the prelates pleaded for an established admission procedure "to avoid unimaginable disaster." The bishops begged the United States and all other nations to continue the ancient tradition of rendering aid to boats in distress on the high seas.

Quoting Pope Paul VI, "The pastoral care of migrants has always attracted the motherly attention and solicitude of the Church," the committee called on the dioceses, parishes, and individual Catholics of the United States to expand their endeavors to sponsor and resettle the refugees. On the part of the U.S. Catholic Church there was a magnificent response. Over 637,633 Southeast Asian refugees were successfully resettled in this nation as of March 31, 1983.

At the November 1977 meeting, Archbishop Bernardin completed his term as president. Under the nominating process, ten names had been selected for the presidential slate. Both the first and second

---

[16] Philadelphia Archdiocesan Archives, Krol papers.
[17] The most complete follow-up on *The Gospel of Peace* Statement is *The Challenge of Peace: God's Promise and Our Response*, a Pastoral Letter on War and Peace issued May 3, 1983, by the NCCB.

ballots for the presidency were inconclusive. The final ballot for the presidency listed the two candidates receiving the highest number of votes on the second ballot: Archbishop John R. Quinn of San Francisco and Archbishop John R. Roach of St. Paul. The results were Archbishop Quinn one hundred forty-six and Archbishop Roach one hundred twelve. Archbishop Quinn was therefore elected president of the Conference. Later Archbishop Roach was elected vice-president of the Conference.

Born in Riverside, California, in 1929, Archbishop John R. Quinn studied at the Gregorian University in Rome and became a professor of theology at Immaculate Heart Seminary, San Diego, California, later becoming rector of that institution. From 1968 to 1972, he was provost of the University of San Diego, in 1967 was named Auxiliary Bishop of San Diego, in 1971 was named Bishop of Oklahoma City and Tulsa, and in 1977 was promoted to Archbishop of San Francisco.

Upon being elected president of the NCCB, the debonair Archbishop Quinn acknowledged that to be elected president "is a very great honor and a mark of confidence . . . I share our common admiration at this particular moment for Archbishop Bernardin and for the sensitive, intelligent, and courteous way in which he has dealt with persons and issues during these past three years."

The president-elect said that he was looking forward "to my term of service to you in our collegial effort to respond to the demands and opportunities for the Church in our country. It is good to know that I will enjoy the constant help of Archbishop Roach, of Bishop Kelly, and Archbishop Maguire, as well as the valued and indispensable support of the outstanding staff of our Conference."

Cardinal Krol, in the name of the bishops, thanked Archbishop Bernardin for his leadership as president of the Conference. His Eminence said that Archbishop Bernardin, as we knew three years ago, and know better today, is a man of remarkable activity, energy, intelligence, vision, and pastoral dedication—a bishop whose deep love for the Church and its people impels him to give of himself without stint or hesitation. His style of leadership is collegial, marked by gentleness of manner and deep respect for the views and concerns of others. His genius for consensus without compromise of principle is born of remarkable patience and perseverance. His strength derives from total commitment and integrity. His word, spoken softly with admirable candor and compassionate determination, is his bond.

The outgoing president, Archbishop Joseph Bernardin, thought that the major successes of the NCCB over the past three years were "an increased political involvement in pro-life issues, a clear statement of the Church's view on sexual morality through the Pastoral, *To Live in Christ Jesus*, the successful resettlement of thousands of Vietnamese, and especially through its statements, an excellent record on all major questions of national and international social justice."[18]

He felt that the five major issues faced by the NCCB during his presidential tenure were "respect for human life; the role of women in society and the Church; moral values and contemporary society; national and international problems of social justice; and religious education and formation." He also admitted that while there were no "crushing failures by the NCCB in the last three years, the American bishops still face many serious, continuing long-term problems which are not going to be solved soon or easily." He cited that among them are a fundamental difficulty among many Catholics in accepting the teaching authority of the Church; the continued legality of "virtual abortion on demand" in the United States; and the refusal of some Catholics to accept the Vatican's continued ban on the ordination of women.

In the May 1978 meeting, Auxiliary Bishop Thomas Lyons of Washington, D.C., introduced the *Plan of Pastoral Action for Family Ministry*. Bishop Lyons noted that this present document is intended to be a Plan and not a Pastoral Letter dealing with the theology of marriage and family. In order to explain the context and implications of the Plan and to prepare the bishops for further discussion of it at the afternoon's workshops, he called upon Bishop Francis Stafford to make a presentation of the background and objectives of the Plan.

Bishop Stafford then presented an explanation of the proposed Plan. The Plan, as presented, is a response by the Bishops' Conference to the *Final Report on the USCC Ad Hoc Commission on Marriage and Family Life*, and chiefly to its main recommendation which calls for an action plan or vision for the Church's pastoral ministry for families.

In summary, Bishop Francis Stafford said that as bishops, we are asked to make a deep and conscious commitment to reshaping our sense of pastoral ministry, so that we see the Church not simply as many isolated individuals, but also as people living in the basic relationship of the family. When we think of the sacramental life, we should consider how the family can be a part of the sacramental celebration. When we think of education, we ought to think of how to develop the family with the educational endeavor. When we think of parish renewal, we also ought to have a sense that parishes are, to a great extent, made up of families who form the larger family of God, the Church. It means that in participating in ministry to families, we see them not as problems but as mysteries, i.e., truths that do lie not beyond us but as truths that comprehend us. We look for this participation primarily in the education of spiritual data such as creative fidelity, hope, and love.

---

[18] *Our Sunday Visitor*, November 20, 1977.

Bishop Stafford went on to say in substance that with your consent, this Plan will place the Church on record for putting family life and pastoral ministry for families as a top priority in the National Conference of Catholic Bishops as well as in our dioceses and parishes. In a word, this Plan crystallizes our genuine commitment, at the same time allowing for a flexible response in terms of the special needs of each region, diocese, and parish. It does not give in to the temptation to merely present one simplistic "program" for family renewal but rather commits us to the process of pastorally listening to families' needs, planning our own strategies of action, and laying the foundations for a decade of research and development of quality programs for family assistance and pastoral ministry. We can no longer rest content if we simply have a program of marriage preparation, a sufficient tribunal process, and a diocesan marriage counseling agency. In approving this Plan, we positively choose a process of developing concrete ways of embodying family life values.

"To accomplish this, I might point out that this Plan of pastoral action lays down as a goal the introduction of a quality pastoral ministry for families, often called family ministry. This includes both the pastoral and social mission of families themselves."

After Bishop Stafford's presentation, there were a number of questions and suggestions.

In particular, Bishop Joseph Francis called attention to the sections of the Plan dealing with minority families and asked that these sections be more precise. Also, he added, the Plan should speak to minorities as to equals. Bishop Stafford gave assurance that the minority family would be given careful attention in the development of the project.

Bishop Stafford then moved that the bishops approve the *Plan of Pastoral Action for Family Ministry* for implementation. Bishop Lyons seconded the motion. There were a number of amendments.

Bishop Romeo Blanchette introduced an amendment to substitute "Catholic Church in the United States" for "American Catholic Church" wherever that occurred in the text. Bishop John J. Sullivan seconded it and the amendment carried without dissent.

Following the formal amendments, Bishop Mark Hurley suggested that the tone would be improved if the document were made to reflect more explicitly the situation of the family in the United States.

The vote was taken and the *Pastoral Plan for Family Ministry* was passed as amended.

Bishop Stafford then thanked the staff and consultants for their contribution toward developing the pastoral Plan.

In the opening paragraphs of the November 1978 *Pastoral Statement of U.S. Catholic Bishops on Handicapped People*, the bishops declared themselves "to be committed to working for a deeper understanding of both the pain and the potential of our neighbors who are blind, deaf, mentally retarded, emotionally impaired, who have special learning problems, or who suffer from single or multiple physical handicaps—all those whom disability may set apart."

The purpose of the Pastoral is to move people to "reexamine their attitudes toward their handicapped brothers and sisters and to promote their well-being" with the justice and compassion our Lord so clearly desires and to integrate the handicapped and their gifts more fully into the Christian community.

Warning that "what the handicapped need first of all is acceptance," the bishops cautioned, "no acts of charity can be of lasting value unless they are informed by a sincere and understanding love." The prelates proclaimed unconditionally that we must love others from the inside out, so to speak, accepting their difference from us in the same way that we accept our difference from them.

Then, in a concise fashion, the Pastoral traces the history of the Church's response to the handicapped in the general ecclesial community, on the parish level, and the diocesan level.

The bishops ended their Pastoral on an optimistic note, hoping that the Church's example "will fuel the stronger, more broadly based efforts called for by contemporary circumstances . . . every man, woman, and child has the right to develop his or her potential to the fullest."

A few modifications and some strengthening notes were added to this Statement, but there was really no opposition or debate. It is too early to evaluate whether or not this effort will prompt greater state and federal interest in the handicapped.

Archbishop Bernardin introduced at the November 1978 meeting the *Statement on the Middle East* and explained that the decision to prepare such a statement was made by the administrative committee at its September meeting. It was felt that because of the extraordinary developments which have taken place in the Middle East in recent months, it would be appropriate for the Conference to speak again at this time, both to reaffirm the moral principles which must underlie any just settlement and to encourage the diplomatic initiatives which had been taken to establish stability in the area. In particular, the administrative committee felt that this was a good time to update the 1973 Statement, which was then generally acclaimed as a significant contribution to the dialogue on the Middle East. The basic thrust of that Statement, the bishops thought, is still valid, and relating the principles contained in it to the current situation would be a good exercise of our office as pastors who are concerned about the well-being of all peoples and, in a particular way, the peoples who inhabit a land that is sacred to Judaism, Christianity, and Islam.

Because a Statement of this kind touches various groups within the Conference, Archbishop John Quinn appointed a small ad hoc committee to supervise the preparation of the Statement: Bishop Edward Head, Chairman of the Committee on Social Development and World Peace; Bishop Bernard Flanagan, who has long been involved in the Catholic-Jewish dialogue; and Archbishop Bernardin as chairman. Consultations had been made with many persons, both inside and outside the Conference, who have an interest in the matter.

Father Bryan Hehir then summarized major developments in the Middle East since 1973 and commented on the rationale for the 1978 Statement. In view of several changes in the Middle East picture, the 1978 Statement seeks to indicate what the position of the NCCB is today. Father Hehir concluded that the 1978 Statement, in addition to restating the basic principles of 1973, also deals with the two new issues, Lebanon and Camp David. He noted that the Lebanon section summarizes what has been said in three extensive statements by Archbishop Bernardin and Quinn, and that the Camp David section acknowledges the significant value of the agreements but argues that they must be seen as part of a larger process which would deal with other questions left unresolved by Camp David.

Bishop Broderick announced that Catholic Relief Services had funneled $6.5 million in relief supplies and funds to Lebanon in the last eighteen months and intended to increase that amount in the months ahead. This important fact should be made known in the Statement, as Catholics are sometimes criticized for not doing anything in the Lebanon crisis.

Cardinal Cooke asked if the proposed Statement would be open to amendments regarding what Catholic Relief Services is doing for the plight of Christians in Lebanon. Archbishop Bernardin replied that such amendments would be welcome. Archbishop Bernardin then moved that the *Statement on the Middle East* be approved to be published as a Statement of the NCCB. Bishop Unterkoefler seconded the motion.

A number of amendments were presented to the ad hoc committee for review. Several were accepted and did much to strengthen the documents.

Bishop Mark Hurley stressed the importance of placing this Statement in the context of the Conference's speaking out against human rights violations throughout the world.

A ballot was taken and the *Statement of the Middle East* passed two hundred thirteen to eight.

Panama-U.S. Relations

A Statement of the Administrative Board of the United States Catholic Conference

February 24, 1975

1. The United States and the Republic of Panama are currently engaged in active negotiations regarding a treaty involving the Panama Canal. It is a moral imperative—a matter of elemental social justice—that a new and a more just treaty be negotiated.

2. The history of the negotiations spans a seventy-year period, beginning with the original treaty of 1903 by which the United States assumed virtually sovereign and perpetual control over the heartland of the Panamanian Isthmus. More recently, in February 1974, the two nations signed the Kissinger-Tack Agreement on Principles, which provides a significant basis for a new treaty.

3. Why is a new treaty imperative? In the first place, the 1903 treaty is, in itself, of dubious moral validity, drafted as it was when international affairs were frequently determined by precepts of power. Since that time, and despite the seventy years that have passed in this century in which other peoples have achieved their independence or have established functional control over their territory, this treaty has remained essentially unchanged at the insistence of the more powerful of the two parties.

4. In the second place, a more fundamental issue is the right of every nation to utilize its natural resources for the development of its people. In his 1963 encyclical *Pacem In Terris*, Pope John XXIII emphasized this basic principle of international justice which had been strongly affirmed in the previous year's declaration of the U.N. General Assembly (Resolution 1803, XXVII, December 14, 1962). Nations, the Holy Father stressed, "have the right to play the leading part in the process of their own development" and "no country may unjustly oppress others or unduly meddle in their affairs."

5. The principal natural resource of Panama is and always has been its geographic location and its configuration. The treaty of 1903 established a monopoly, "in perpetuity," in favor of another government over the principal natural resource of the Republic of Panama.

6. The question, therefore, lies in whether or not we accept the fact that Panama is a free and independent nation. As such, her claims over the Canal area are a simple consequence of her basic right. In other words, if we accept the rights of Panama over her territory, then instead of Panama negotiating with the United States to obtain for herself some compensation for the use of the Canal and the Canal

Zone, it might be reasoned that negotiations should be the other way around. The main benefits from the Canal should accrue to Panama, as a nation with principal control over its natural resources, and a fair compensation should accrue to the United States for its investment in Panama.

7.   Besides the political, social, and cultural consequences of the 1903 treaty that argue strongly for a fundamental revision of U.S.-Panamanian relations, economic considerations are also considerable. It is worth reviewing, in this regard, some of the main benefits that accrue to each side as recently cited by the Archbishop of Panama, Marcos McGrath, C.S.C.:

8.   (a) The Canal Zone, which measures roughly ten by fifty miles in area, is the heartland, the most valuable economic area of Panama. Present use represents a significant waste of this natural resource: only 3.6 percent of the land is occupied by Canal installations; some twenty-five percent is not utilized at all, and sixty-eight percent is designated for military use. For this entire territory, including fourteen military bases established without any negotiations with Panama as to their location, the United States pays an annual $1.9 million, as contrasted, for example, to the $20 million paid annually for three bases in Spain.

9.   (b) Since seventy percent of the goods that transit the Canal come from or go to U.S. ports, the noncommercial fees, frozen until this year at the 1914 level, have represented an annual saving to U.S. commerce of $700 million. In this way, Panama, a poor nation, is subsidizing the richest nation of the world and world commerce in general.

10.   (c) The savings to the U.S. Armed Forces in the use of the Canal in the sixty years since its inauguration are calculated in excess of $11 billion.

11.   (d) The U.S. military investment in the Canal Zone is more than double the total civil investment, an expense that goes far beyond any notion of mere defense of the Canal. In fact, the U.S. Southern Command, located in the Canal Zone, is a training center for military from all over Latin America and a nerve center of military contact throughout the continent. Surely military bases established within a nation should be the object of negotiation.

12.   (e) Nearly twenty percent of the gross national income of the Republic of Panama derives from the Canal Zone economy, mostly in indirect form, through salaries and sales. The rise and fall of this income according to fluctuations in building and other operations within the Canal Zone, factors beyond the control of the Republic, has a strongly distorting effect upon the Panamanian economy.

13.   (f) Since property and income in the Canal Zone are exempted from Panamanian taxes, the government of Panama is denied a major source of revenue. As a result, it has not been fully able to undertake

programs of economic infrastructures and socio-economic development, particularly for the impoverished rural areas.

14. While these observations do not attempt to treat all questions relating to the Panama Canal issue, they do serve to place the question within an overall context of international social justice.

15. For peace in the world, which can come only with justice in the world, it is essential that we citizens of the United States, including our elected representatives, approach the Panama Canal issue with the same moral sensitivity we would apply to issues of justice within our own society.

16. Our national response to the new treaty will be a significant test of that sensitivity. Not only the rest of the Americas, but the whole world will be watching. The fundamental rights of the people of Panama, as well as the high ideals and long-range interests of the United States, require a new and just treaty. It can become a sign of and a significant contribution toward world peace based upon justice and fraternity between peoples.

Statement on Feeding the Hungry: Toward a U.S. Domestic Food Policy

*A Statement of the Department of
Social Development and World Peace
United States Catholic Conference*

April 16, 1975

1. The Department of Social Development and World Peace of the United States Catholic Conference takes the occasion of "Food Day," April 17, 1975, to urge Catholics to deepen their understanding of the food crisis and commit themselves to continued reflection and action to feed the hungry both here and abroad. The Church has a particular responsibility with regard to the food crisis since Jesus identified himself with the poor and hungry. We recognize with the 1974 Synod of Bishops the "right to eat" as a fundamental right which flows from the basic and inalienable right to life itself. It is for this reason that we look upon feeding the hungry as a requirement of justice.

2. Last November the Catholic bishops of the United States adopted a pastoral plan of action on the world food crisis. The response to the bishops' program has been widespread and significant. Many dioceses, parishes, and other organizations instituted educational programs and raised funds for international humanitarian relief efforts.

3. The USCC has engaged in a sustained effort to influence public policy on food issues. Working with the National Catholic Rural Life Conference, Catholic Relief Services, and the National Conference of Catholic Charities, the USCC has testified before Congress on food and agricultural policy and the Food for Peace Program. The USCC has also opposed efforts to increase the price of food stamps, and has supported increased funding for food and nutrition development in our foreign assistance programs.

4. The grave international consequences of food shortages must be a continuing concern of the American people. However, we must not neglect the very serious food and nutrition needs in our country. The United States has a responsibility in both domestic and international areas. These responsibilities should not be seen in conflict with each other, but viewed as different aspects of the same problem.

5. The development of a comprehensive food policy is an urgent priority for the nation. Our government is currently considering various food issues. It will be necessary to weigh the competing interests of consumers, producers, and middlemen in the food distribution system. Farmers seek reasonable prices for their products; food processors, retailers, and distributors are concerned about adequate return on their investment; consumers worry about rising food costs. Lower income consumers have a particular concern about the future of food stamps and other federal nutrition programs. In addition, policymakers need to evaluate the interests and unique responsibilities of the United States vis-a-vis world markets and international needs.

6.   In the midst of these competing interests, our food policy should work toward full production, equitable distribution, and price stability. At a time when world food shortages mean starvation for millions, a U.S. agricultural policy of full production is absolutely essential. At the same time, U.S. food policy should not force low-and middle-income consumers and independent farmers to bear an unfair burden.

7.   In view of these considerations, we shall address three areas of immediate concern: U.S. food needs and nutrition programs, ownership and control of resources, and full production and target prices.

I. U.S. Food Needs and Nutrition Programs

8.   Many people in the United States continue to suffer from hunger and serious malnutrition. Rapid inflation in food prices, high levels of unemployment, and a deep recession have meant a significant increase in hunger in America. While the problem is less severe in the United States than in other countries, it is no less harsh for those who endure it.

9.   Hunger and malnutrition in this country are essentially the result of economic factors. Nutritional studies indicate that malnutrition rises as income declines and that the worst hunger is among the very poor. The consequences of malnutrition are very serious, especially for young children. It reduces productivity, motivation, and educational performance, lowers resistance to disease, inhibits growth and development, and can even result in a shorter life span.

10.   There are over 37 million poor people in the United States. Many people lack adequate nutrition because they lack employment and income that would enable them to buy sufficient food. Their situation has worsened as the economy has declined. Public assistance and social programs have not kept pace with inflation. Jobs have become almost impossible to find as unemployment approaches nine percent. In addition, many elderly persons living on fixed incomes are also victims of serious malnutrition. Middle and working class families are victims of similar economic pressures. Caught in the web of inflation, recession, and high taxes, many of them have lost ground in their battle to provide their families an adequate diet.

In the last decade, the federal government has expanded programs aimed at providing an adequate diet for all Americans. Expenditures on domestic food programs have risen to an estimated $5.8 billion in the present fiscal year.

11. Recently it has been proposed that existing child nutrition programs be eliminated and a block grant approach be substituted which would cut $600-700 million from nutrition assistance. The USCC opposes reductions in domestic food aid. We urge Congress to resist attempts to eliminate these nutrition programs or reduce funding for food assistance. Instead, these programs should be reformed to eliminate inequities and administrative problems that may prevent eligible persons from participating. They must be expanded to meet increasingly serious needs during this time of economic decline.

A. Families

12. The food stamp program is the basic form of federal nutrition assistance for American families. This program now serves more than 18 million people, although studies indicate that it reaches less than half of those who may be eligible.

13. The food stamp program must be maintained and improved. We strongly oppose any increase in the price of food stamps. We support the recent action of Congress to prevent the proposed food stamp price increases and commend the President for his decision to accept that action. Appropriate steps should be taken to guarantee that the benefits of the program go to those who are actually in need. In addition, modifications are required to speed up the certification process and improve the outreach effort to involve other qualified families while guaranteeing that eligibility requirements are enforced.

B. School Children

14. The federal government now provides nutritional assistance to nearly 25 million children through the National School Lunch Program. The program has both nutritional and educational value and should be extended and improved. Specifically, we support efforts to include the children of unemployed parents in the free lunch program and include orphanages and day-care centers in the subsidy program. We also support proposals to provide additional subsidies to cover increased costs in school lunch programs resulting from inflation.

15. The School Breakfast Program serves an adequate breakfast to almost two million children every school day. A nutritional breakfast has obvious educational and health benefits for low-income children who would otherwise go to school hungry. The level of the present program does not begin to meet the overall need. Additional funding and permanent status for the breakfast program are required.

16. Another undertaking that merits continued support is the special milk program. Many schools, especially those without hot lunch programs, benefit from this successful effort to provide milk to school children at reduced prices.

17. Many Catholic school students participate in these three programs. The Congress should be commended for recognizing the nutritional needs of nonpublic school children. We urge all qualified Catholic schools to provide these services for their students.

C. Mothers and Young Children

18. Infants, young children, and expectant or nursing mothers have special nutritional needs. Food assistance at these stages can have major impact on the elimination of birth defects, mental retardation, and malnutrition in newborn children. The Women, Infants, and Children Program (WIC) is designed to provide high protein diet supplements to low-income women, infants, and young children. We strongly support the continued existence and expansion of this unique and important program.

D. Older Americans

19. The nutritional problems of the elderly living alone and on fixed income are especially tragic. They often lack the financial resources or physical health necessary to provide an adequate diet. The Older Americans Act provides funds for community feeding programs for the elderly through communal dining rooms and meals-on-wheels programs along with a range of supportive services. Unfortunately, many of our senior citizens with nutritional problems are not reached by this program. In addition to its food benefits, a fully implemented program would diminish our society's reliance on institutional care for the elderly. We endorse the program and efforts to expand its availability. It is an important effort to meet the needs of our senior citizens.

E. Nutrition Education

20. An essential element of a national policy against hunger and malnourishment is nutrition education. Consumers need opportunities to improve their knowledge regarding foods and eating habits and to better understand the relationship between health and nutrition. Schools and other institutions should be encouraged to provide broader programs in practical nutrition education.

II. Ownership and Control of Resources

21. Recent food shortages have made us acutely aware that U.S. food and agricultural policies have a massive impact on the availability, quality, and prices of food not only in this country but throughout the world. Because food is a unique resource necessary to life itself, our great capacity to produce it carries with it awesome responsibilities. Our food policy must not be governed by profit considerations alone, but by the needs of hungry people.

22. A disturbing phenomenon in the United States is the increasing concentration occurring in the food production system. We have experienced a rapid decline in the number of farms in the United States over the last two decades and a substantial migration of families from rural areas to already overcrowded urban centers. The high costs of land, technology, and credit make it virtually impossible for young people to go into agricultural production on their own. Governmental policies have often fostered the promotion of capital incentive, corporate controlled agriculture. Our federal and local tax structures create incentives for wealthy nonfarm investors in agriculture, but do little for the competent full-time farmer. We support an agricultural system based upon widespread ownership of resources and the means of production. Legislation is needed now to inhibit further encroachment upon agriculture by nonfarm corporations and to insure that our land is kept in the hands of those who work it.

23. We are also concerned about the diminishing level of competition in the food processing and distribution system. In some sectors of the food industry, fewer companies are controlling more and more of the market. This trend toward increasing concentration of control can lead to excessive profit and even higher prices for consumers. We urge a comprehensive study of noncompetitive forces in the food industry and appropriate antitrust action to eliminate monopolistic practices.

24. Decisions about the use of land and resources are often made without rational planning or sufficient concern for the environmental and human costs of those decisions. Suburban sprawl, surface mining, industrial development, and other demands on the land are diverting over one million acres from agricultural use each year with potentially serious consequences for future food production. A more integrated and rational process for land use planning is necessary. With regard to agricultural land, the primary objective of land use legislation should be the conservation of such land for its unique food producing value and protection of a dispersed pattern of ownership.

III. Full Production and Target Prices

25. In light of present food needs, farmers must be encouraged to produce to full capacity. To cut back on production in the face of unmet world needs would be morally and ethically untenable. Neither is it acceptable, however, to ask farmers to assume total financial responsibility for the risks involved in full production without some protection. Widely fluctuating prices for farm products mean at least uncertainty, and perhaps disaster, for small farmers. A system of equitable target prices should be established and reviewed at regular intervals to assure farmers a fair return on their investment and labor. Price supports can be set at levels that will not result in excessively high food prices for consumers, yet provide adequate protection for producers.

26. At the same time, we support the establishment of reserves of essential commodities to maintain price stability and to safeguard against future world food shortages. These reserves must be federally regulated in a manner that does not jeopardize a just return for farmers.

Conclusions

27. The debate over American food policy must be seen in a larger context. Hunger and malnutrition flow from basic failures in our society's social and economic structures. Hunger is often the result of persistent poverty, and food programs only supplement inadequate income. They cannot substitute for economic resources, jobs, decent wages, equal opportunity, or the power to change economic and political institutions. These programs are not a solution to poverty, racial discrimination, inequitable taxation, or the isolation of the elderly. Fundamentally, our nation must provide jobs for those who are able to work and a minimal income to those who cannot. The U.S. Catholic Conference has consistently supported programs that would guarantee an adequate income for all Americans. We renew that call today.

28. At this point, however, Church institutions, parishes, and individual church members must seek out and help those in our midst who lack food. For as Pope Paul has said, it is not enough to point to injustice and human need. "Such words will lack real weight unless they are accompanied for each individual by a livelier awareness of personal responsibility and effective action."

29. At the same time, the Church must also participate in a rigorous and competent analysis of structures and systems that result in poverty and hunger. We must become advocates of change so that structures are adapted to meet the serious needs of those who now go hungry. In his Apostolic Letter, *A Call to Action*, Pope Paul says Christian organizations "have to express in their own way and rising above their particular nature, the concrete demands of Christian faith for a just, and consequently, necessary, transformation of society."

30. The hungry of the world have voiced their cries of anguish. We must respond to them not only with words of hope, but with actions that will mobilize the energies, talents, and resources of the Catholic community to assist people not only around the world but in this nation as well.

Statement on the Introduction of the Family Viewing Period during Prime Time by the Television Networks

A Statement of the Administrative Board of the United States Catholic Conference

September 10, 1975

I. Introduction

1. With the 1975 fall season, the three television networks have introduced their new policy of a "Family Viewing" period during prime time programming hours.

2. In summary, the following guidelines will be observed by the networks. The first hour of network entertainment programming in prime time and the immediately preceding hour are to be set aside as a "Family Viewing" period. Secondly, in the occasional case when an entertainment program broadcast during the "Family Viewing" period contains material which may be unsuitable for viewing by younger family members, a "viewer advisory" will be broadcast in audio and video form. Moreover, viewer advisories will also be employed during the later evening hours for any program containing material that might be disturbing to significant portions of the viewing audience. Finally, broadcasters will endeavor to inform publishers of television program listings of these programs that will contain "advisories." A responsible use of "advisories" in promotional material is also urged upon broadcasters.

3. This new network policy on family viewing is the result of conversations that the chairman of the Federal Communications Commission had with network leaders in the early part of this year. The results of those negotiations were made public by the Commission in its "Report on the Broadcast of Violent, Indecent and Obscene Material" on February 19, 1975 (FCC 75-202,30159). The report, which was in response to congressional directives on the subject, addresses the "specific positive action taken and planned by the Commission to protect children from excessive programming of violence and obscenity." The acceptance by the Commission of the "Family Viewing" concept constitutes the major element of this plan.

II. Presuppositions

4. Before evaluating this "Family Viewing" policy, we wish to outline certain presuppositions which the United States Catholic Conference views as important and relevant to the question at hand.

5. (1) In our society today, television is the single most formative influence in shaping people's attitudes and values. It is not only the power the medium itself possesses that supports this proposition. Of even greater significance is the cumulative effect upon an individual of his daily television experiences, frequently passive and uncritical, from early childhood until the evening of life. By the time they have completed high school, most children have spent more hours before a television set than they have in the classroom. The average adult also spends considerable time each day viewing television.

6. (2) Unquestionably, therefore, the *experience* of television is both an *ordinary* and *integral* part of American *home life* today. Hence it follows that any evaluation of the role that television plays in the American experience must focus on the actualities, first, of substantial daily viewing by the average American, and second, of the home environment in which the viewing is experienced. We are not dealing then with the occasional entertainment experience that a child or adult may have by going out of the home to see a movie. Much less are we dealing with the even rarer entertainment experience of a nightclub show.

7. (3) The Church respects the enormous potential that television has: for education; for providing full and accurate information so essential to enlightened public opinion; for building understanding and community among men and nations; for preserving and, indeed, creating art; for providing entertainment and relaxation that recreate the human spirit and emotions.

8. In the face of this enormous potential, broadcasters cannot view themselves as merely entertainers or technicians. Because social communications are so central to modern life, the vocation of a broadcaster is a calling of high honor—and of heavy responsibility. The broadcaster, more than others, helps to shape the very ethos of the world in which we live.

9. (4) It should be noted as well that American broadcasters' responsibilities go far beyond the frontiers reached by their signals. They have a global responsibility because they belong to an industry that has established American international leadership in the technology, the content, and the style of contemporary mass communications. One example is enlightening: during 1974, of 1,707 film entertainment programs shown on Brazilian television, 1,267 programs were of American origin; only ten were Brazilian productions. American broadcasters cannot therefore take a parochial or narrowly nationalistic view of their responsibilities. They must be increasingly sensitive to the cultural and moral imperatives of societies other than our own. The American people, sharing as they do a collective responsibility in our interdependent world, have every right and duty to protest whenever broadcasters may manifest indifference or insensitivity to the needs of their sisters and brothers across the world. In a word, the question of the broadcast of violent, indecent, and obscene material has to be viewed from an international as well as a domestic perspective.

III. USCC Evaluation of the "Family Viewing" Policy

10. At the very outset of our evaluation of the FCC acceptance of the "Family Viewing" policy, it seems important to state that if our opinion of the Commission's recommendations must be largely negative, it is not because we have failed to appreciate the most difficult task of the commissioners.

11. The FCC report (p. 3) quite rightly observes that "administrative actions regulating violent and sexual material must be reconciled with constitutional and statutory limitations on the Commission's authority to regulate program content." Not only do we support this observation but we would oppose any recommendation that would call for the direct involvement by government in the content area of programming. Section 326 of the Communications Act specifically prohibits the Commission from exercising the power of censorship. This prohibition must be maintained.

12. Opposition to *direct* governmental involvement in program content, however, does not call in question the role required of the Commission by the same Communications Act, namely, that it ensure that broadcast licensees operate in a manner consistent with the public interest. The *Red Lion* decision of the Supreme Court explicitly reminded broadcasters that they are "public trustees" with fiduciary responsibilities to their communities. We strongly support the Commission's policy that program service in the public interest is an essential part of every licensee's obligation.

13. Nor again, by opposing *direct* involvement by government, do we intend to cast any doubt on the obligation that Congress has to legislate effectively against the broadcast of violent, obscene, or indecent material. Specifically, we support the Commission's legislative proposal that Congress amend Section 1464 of Title 18, United States Code, in order to remove the present uncertainty of the Commission as to whether it has statutory authority to proceed against the video depiction of obscene or indecent material (*Report*, p. 9).

14. In the light of the constraints placed on it by the Constitution and Section 326 of the Communications Act, the Commission understandably notes that it "walks a tightrope between saying too much and saying too little" when applying the public interest standard to programming. In the present instance, the Commission decided that "regulatory action to limit violent and sexually-oriented programming which is neither obscene nor indecent is less desirable than effective self-regulation" (*Report*, p. 3). Hence, the chairman of the Commission met with broadcast industry leadership in the hope that he might "serve as a catalyst for the achievement of meaningful self-regulatory reform."

15. Although the effort of the chairman is commendable, our judgment is that the results are unacceptable. Our reasons are as follows:

16. (1) *Self-regulation must be open, accountable, and cooperative.* The United States Catholic Conference has been, is, and will continue to be firmly committed to the principle of voluntary self-regulation for all the communications media. We therefore share the Commission's conviction that broadcast self-regulation is the basic solution to the problems at hand. However, we strongly disagree with the Commission's apparent conviction that a few modifications in the status quo will enable the networks to achieve "meaningful self-regulatory reform" in the area of broadcast entertainment.

17. Self-regulation is not a unilateral activity performed behind closed doors by a few powerful individuals at the top. Self-regulation, to deserve the name, is an *open*, *accountable*, and *cooperative* process, involving both broadcasters and the public they serve.

18. We are far from convinced that broadcast management is genuinely *open* to dialogue with the public or accountable to it. The very corporate structure of the networks, for example, is such a forbidding and complicated maze that it appears designed to guarantee that, insulated from public scrutiny, top management may, without fear of challenge or other encumbrance, pursue the uniquely important goal of maximizing profits. And yet, of all the communications media, broadcasting should be the one most open to dialogue with the public, precisely because the airwaves belong to the public and broadcasters are public trustees with fiduciary responsibilities to their communities. The polished rhetoric of industry public relations releases is not dialogue but self-serving monologue. In spite of good intentions, the series of closed meetings which the chairman of the Commission held with the inner circle of network top management strikes us as having little to do with openness to public dialogue or public accountability. Even worse, it can only serve in effect to strengthen the claims currently being made by some broadcasters that the public does not really own the airwaves.

19. Neither will the quality of openness and accountability characterize industry self-regulation as long as the public is without ready access to reliable advance information about broadcast entertainment programming. This need for information is not satisfied by industry-generated publicity releases or advisories. Books, plays, records, movies, circuses, exhibits of all manner are also the object of publicity and promotion, but before buying, the interested consumer has critical evaluations of the product available to guide his or her choice. Since, apart from summer repeats, broadcast entertainment is essentially a one-time presentation, reliable advance program information would only be possible were networks and local stations to adopt and implement a policy of prescreening *all* entertainment programs for critical review. We are aware, of course, that the "rating-game" approach to television entertainment effectively precludes even the consideration of any prescreening policy that might, in effect, serve to restrict potential audiences. Without it the broadcast industry cannot justify claim to be open and accountable to the public it claims to serve. One might have expected that the chairman of the Commission would have seen this as an important question to have posed to network top management.

20. Self-regulation is also a *cooperative* activity that should involve every local broadcaster. A frequent complaint of the local broadcaster is that he is rarely consulted or otherwise actively involved by the networks in the decision-making process with regard to network entertainment programming. To the best of our knowledge, top network management did not invite the *prior* counsel of their affiliate stations on the subject of whether there ought to be a family viewing period during prime time. Neither are we aware that the Commission sought the opinion of the affiliates in the matter. If the decision has been unilaterally taken by the networks and accepted by the Commission, it may be because, were it left to local affiliate management, who alone must bear the ultimate responsibility to the public, many of them might have rejected the idea on the grounds that their prime time audience is a family audience. At the very least, they might have demanded stricter and more precise standards.

21. Self-regulation also involves *cooperation* on the part of the *viewing public*. No system will succeed unless it enjoys public confidence and support. Part of our complaint is that neither the networks nor the Commission made any effort to consult the public on whether it was indeed prepared to accept the introduction of a distinction between family-type and adult programming and, if so, under what conditions. We seriously doubt that the average parent would or should find it reasonable to insist the older children be excluded from watching television in their own home after certain time periods. By what mandate or legal title, parents might rightfully demand, can the Commission and the networks unilaterally decide that henceforth minor

children are entitled to enjoy only a limited access to evening television entertainment? A more than lurking suspicion remains that
the audience for prime time television is after all not the general
American public but older teenagers, young adults, and the affluent
who have the money to spend on the products advertised. In short,
children, the poor, and the aged are to be disenfranchised. How all
of this relates to high-sounding network appeals to creativity and
First Amendment guarantees or is to be reconciled with serving the
public interest is difficult to perceive.

22. (2) *Commercialism—Core Problem.* And so we come to what must
be acknowledged as the *core* obstacle to effective self-regulation in the
broadcast industry—its complete domination by commercial interests. What American commercial television is all about is not primarily
either information or entertainment, neither news nor culture. Its
primary objective is to create a meeting place for consumers and
advertisers. American television is essentially concerned with the sale
of consumers to advertisers.

23. As long as this equation controls programming decisions, especially during prime time when network competition is keenest, the
central concern of broadcast management has to be to air that type
of program which will deliver the greatest possible audience. And
what kind of programming is this? Look at the record. Do we find
serious dramatic works or programs that might challenge viewers to
confront disturbing social issues or documentaries that might open
American minds and hearts to understanding and compassion for the
powerless at home and abroad? What has the average American viewer
of prime time entertainment programming learned about the global
village, the interdependent world in which we are said to live—about
Africa, Latin America, Asia, Oceania? The record will reveal that
network management programming decisions have much more to do
with appealing to the alleged lowest common denominator of audience interest: smart comedy, crime, violence, and sex. Were the record
otherwise, the Commission would never have been mandated by
Congress to undertake its study.

24. (3) *Lessons Learned From Motion Picture Code and Rating Program.*
On page five of the Commission's report, it is stated that "the Chairman raised the possibility of the adoption of a rating system similar
to that used in the motion picture industry." We believe that some
sobering conclusions might have emerged for the members of the
Commission had they reflected on what has happened to American
motion pictures since October 7, 1968, when the Motion Picture Association of America (MPAA) first announced the details of its new and
expanded plan of movie industry self-regulation.

25. The MPAA plan bore the title "The Motion Picture Code and Rating Program." We wish to emphasize that it was a *code* as well as a rating program. At the top of the document appears a section entitled "Declaration of Principles of the Code of Self-Regulation of the Motion Picture Association." A few excerpts from this section are of interest:

> This Code is designed to keep in close harmony with the mores, culture, the moral sense and change in our society.
> The objectives of the Code are:
> 1. To encourage artistic expression by expanding creative freedom; and
> 2. To assure that the freedom which encourages the artist remains responsible and sensitive to the standards of the larger society.
> We believe self-restraint, self-regulation, to be in the American tradition. The results of self-discipline are always imperfect because that is the nature of all things mortal. But this Code, and its administration, will make clear that freedom of expression does not mean toleration of license.
> The test of self-restraint—the rule of reason—lies in the treatment of a subject for the screen.

26. Under the second section of the MPAA document which is entitled "Standards for Production" there are eleven standards enunciated which will determine whether a motion picture will qualify for a Code Seal of Approval. Those standards read as follows:

(a) The basic dignity and value of human life shall be respected and upheld. Restraint shall be exercised in portraying the taking of life.

(b) Evil, sin, crime, and wrong-doing shall not be justified.

(c) Special restraint shall be exercised in portraying criminal or anti-social activities in which minors participate or are involved.

(d) Detailed and protracted acts of brutality, cruelty, physical violence, torture, and abuse shall not be presented.

(e) Indecent or undue exposure of the human body shall not be presented.

(f) Illicit sex relationships shall not be justified. Intimate sex scenes violating common standards of decency shall not be portrayed.

(g) Restraint and care shall be exercised in presentations dealing with sex aberrations.

(h) Obscene speech, gestures, or movements shall not be presented.

(i) Undue profanity shall not be permitted.

(j) Religion shall not be demeaned.

(k) Words or symbols contemptuous of racial, religious, or national groups shall not be used so as to incite bigotry or hatred.

(l) Excessive cruelty to animals shall not be portrayed and animals shall not be treated inhumanely.

27. The Motion Picture Code and Rating Program envisioned two distinct questions for its administration. The first question pertained to these Standards for Production; if the submitted motion picture conformed to the standards, it would be issued a Code Seal of Approval. If it did not qualify for a Code seal, it could only be rated (X). For a Code-approved film, a second question was then to be applied, namely, which of the first three ratings (G, M, or R) were to be applied.

28. The United States Catholic Conference and the National Council of Churches endorsed in principle this MPAA program "as being consistent with the rights and obligations of free speech and artistic expression, as well as with the duty of parents and society to safeguard the young in their growth to responsible adulthood." The churches, "relying on the good faith of the industry," gave "genuine and full support to this plan" and urged "its conscientious implementation on every level of production, distribution, and exhibition."

29. The churches maintained their support of the MPAA plan for over two and a half years. Finally, on May 18, 1971, after a detailed statement of concern published a year previously, the churches, because they could no longer in good conscience be party to a charade, withdrew their support.

30. How could a plan which had been welcomed with genuine enthusiasm only two and a half years previously have failed so miserably? The best of motivation and the highest good faith could not stand up to the pressures of commercial competition. Within a few short weeks of the introduction of the Code and Rating Plan, there began to emerge an attitude on the part of some film producers that "now that the kids are protected, anything goes." And in no short order, almost everything did go—including the standards for production, which, as noted previously, were to determine whether films qualified for the Code Seal of Approval. Although the MPAA has not formally advised the public, the Code is officially dead. All that remains is the rating aspect of the original plan.

31. One result of all this is that the theatrical motion picture as such has become a lost experience for the majority of Americans. For the industry, in spite of the occasional box-office successes that keep some of the Hollywood glitter going, the loss of the general audience has resulted in serious financial reverses for many producers and exhibitors across the industry. Perhaps the worst consequence of all for American society is that too many of the creative community of producers, writers, directors, and actors have been replaced by hacks whose artistic perception is limited to "exploit-the-audience-with-sex-and-violence."

32. Our purpose in this review is not to focus on the problem of the motion picture industry but to raise the question of why a reasonable person would be expected to accord greater confidence to effective self-regulation by the television networks than to the MPAA. To the credit of the MPAA, it has involved itself in broad consultation with representatives of the public before introducing its Code and Rating Program and continued to collaborate with them in an effort to make the program work. Again, the film industry prescreens its product for public review and takes its chances at the box office. As already noted, the broadcast industry's self-regulation is a closed shop and, short of the risk of challenge at license renewal time, is not otherwise accountable to the public. In fact, the networks do not even have to face that risk—except in the narrow area of their owned and operated stations.

33. We have no confidence that once the commercial broadcast industry as presently constituted is permitted without challenge to introduce what is in effect a rating system for programming, the identical excesses that have occurred in the motion picture medium will not be visited upon the American public—but this time not at the local theater but in the American home. In making this judgment we are not limiting our concern to the pressures of commercial competition presently experienced by the networks. We are also looking down the road when the networks will have to face the added competition from pay-television, video-cassettes, video-discs, and whatever else technological genius may develop.

34. *(4) Greater Handicaps for Parents and Family Life.* We have placed great emphasis upon television's role in American family life. We do not think that it is possible to exaggerate the centrality and importance of this role, especially at a time in our history when the very structure of family life is seriously threatened. We therefore commend the Commission when it states (*Report*, pp. 7-8):

> Parents in our view, have—and should retain—the primary responsibility for their children's well-being. This traditional and revered principle . . . has been adversely affected by the corrosive processes of technological and social change in twentieth-century American life. Nevertheless, we believe that it deserves continuing affirmation.
> Television . . . also has some responsibilities in this area. . . . The Commission has sought to remind broadcasters of their responsibility to provide some measure of support to concerned parents.

35. However, we must also seriously fault the Commission for then making recommendations which, in the light of our foregoing observations, will only serve to create even greater handicaps for parents as they struggle not only to assure the well-being of their children, but also to preserve family life which is so essential to the well-being of this or any nation.

36. *(5) Specific Criticism of "Family Viewing" Plan.* Although it may seem unnecessary to comment on the specific recommendations that the FCC report has proposed for the fall 1975 television season, we will do so anyway with the understanding, however, that these criticisms are secondary to our already stated core concerns.

37. (a) Inspection of the report reveals that the 7:00-9:00 p.m. "Family Viewing" period, which appears to have been the initial FCC objective, will hold only in fact for the Eastern and Western time zones. For the Midwest it will mean a 6:00-8:00 p.m. period and for the Rocky Mountain time zone 5:00-7:00 p.m. Why? The Commission lamely acknowledges that the networks had informed it that "a standard based on a 9:00 p.m. local time would require prohibitively expensive separate program transmissions to each time zone." This concession to commercial considerations is incredible. It hardly demonstrates an honest commitment by the networks to American parents.

38. (b) The use of the so-called "advisory warnings," the second point in the FCC proposals, is an equally incredible concession. "Viewer advisories," the report states, "will be broadcast in audio and video form *in the occasional case* when an entertainment program broadcast during the *Family Viewing* period contains material which may be unsuitable for viewing by younger family members" (emphasis added). Not only does this "advisory warning" concession open the door to abuse in order to attract larger audiences; there is something far more disturbing about it. It leads to the obvious conclusion that neither the Commission nor the networks are single-minded about keeping the "Family Viewing" period inviolate.

39. (c) The combination of "viewer advisories" and the "advance notice" to be given about such advisories clearly implies that a television *rating system*, almost as developed as that of the motion picture industry, is about to be foisted upon the American public without, however, it being candidly identified as a rating system and, of course, without any previous public debate as to the merits of same.

40. (d) Granted the advisory or rating system proposal, who is going to be making the necessary judgments as to material "which may be unsuitable for viewing by younger family members" or concerning programs, "in the later evening hours," which "contain material that might be disturbing to significant portions of the viewing audience?" The Commission report makes much of the "subjectivity" of these matters. But even if artistic and moral considerations were actually as subjective as the approach of the Commission would imply, there is no reason to conclude, as the Commission does in fact conclude, that such decisions must be left to the networks. This, of course, touches on the basic issue: despite the fervent rhetoric of the FCC report, the networks continue to be answerable to no one but themselves. In some respects, the report of the Commission is an insult to the public's intelligence and inescapably lends credence to the suspicion that the main function of the FCC is, after all, to act as a buffer between the networks and public accountability.

41. (e) An integral part of the Commission's plan involves the incorporation of the "Family Viewing" period concept and the advisory warnings into the Television Code of the National Association of Broadcasters. It appears unnecessary to observe that the NAB as presently constituted has been neither organized for, nor is it capable of, taking on any serious representation role for the public interest. The NAB is a trade organization whose function is to argue for the interests of its members before the government and the public. Moreover, since no more than sixty percent of all stations belong to this voluntary organization, NAB cannot even speak for the entire industry. Nor, in fact, can it effectively discipline its members who choose not to abide by its Standards and Practices rules. Finally, the FCC has not yet secured agreement of the independent television stations to support the NAB TV Code's incorporation of "Family Viewing," despite the fact that the NAB voted to give independents a waiver on restrictions against sex and violence until September 1977, for any programs under contract since last April.

IV. Conclusions

42. For all the reasons set forth in this Statement, the United States Catholic Conference finds the proposals contained in the FCC's report to be unacceptable. Our principal reason is that those proposals stand or fail upon effective self-regulation by the broadcast industry.

43. Effective self-regulation has to be an open, accountable, and cooperative process. Our judgment is that to date the networks have not demonstrated a commitment to such a process. Moreover, we seriously question whether such a commitment is even possible for the networks as long as no industry effort is undertaken to reduce the impact of commercial pressures upon their program decision making. In this connection, the "rating game" must be addressed specifically. A basic weakness of commercial broadcasting is that management is incapable of exercising responsible freedom in the program decision-making process because they are trapped in a rating thralldom.

44. If ratings objectively identified the needs of the public, they would be a true service both to broadcasters and the public they are to serve. We doubt anyone can make a case in favor of the rating organizations that would prove them to be providing a constructive service to the medium or the public. We therefore recommend that Congress investigate the program rating services which appear to exercise an inordinate influence upon television programming and which have thus far successfully resisted public scrutiny.

45. As for the broadcast industry, we strongly urge all broadcast licensees, whether network affiliates or independents, whether members of the NAB or not, to reflect anew upon their responsibilities to the public they are licensed to serve and to examine how well they are meeting those responsibilities. We fully appreciate that service to the community by commercial broadcasters cannot be delivered without a profitable operation. Yet the profit motive can never justify programming that debases rather than builds community.

46. As for the viewing public, it must respond and demonstrate to local station management that it cares and is ready to work with management for the achievement of a program schedule that serves the community's needs. In particular, we encourage our Catholic people, under the leadership of their bishops and pastors, to take an active and affirmative role in working with their fellow citizens, especially on an interfaith basis, in pursuit of the same objectives. Neither networks nor advertisers, neither Hollywood nor government can influence station managers who have their communities strongly behind them.

47. For its part, the Federal Communications Commission must demonstrate that it is more concerned about how well the public interest is served by commercial broadcasters than how well it serves the interests of commercial broadcasters. In particular, a scrupulous enforcement of the spirit as well as the letter of the community ascertainment requirement is essential.

48. Moreover, recent efforts either to exempt certain broadcasters from the requirement to ascertain community problems or to reduce the requirements for others must be resisted by the Commission. The Commission must also fully support the right of the public to challenge license renewals. This requires that communities have access to all necessary information and be afforded adequate time to exercise the right to challenge.

49. Finally, the business community has a special responsibility for the quality of commercial broadcasting. It is their advertising dollars that either enhance or debase the medium. If all advertisers had been as sensitive to the broadcast needs of the American public, especially of the family, as some have been, this Statement might not be necessary.

Handgun Violence: A Threat to Life

A Statement of the Committee on
Social Development and World Peace
United States Catholic Conference

September 11, 1975

The Problem

1. There are currently 40 million handguns in the United States.[1] More than 2.5 million new handguns will be manufactured and sold this year. In most of our cities and rural areas, purchasing a weapon is as easy as buying a camera.

2. In 1973, the last year for which complete figures were available, there were 28,000 firearms deaths.[2] In 1975, it is estimated that nearly 30,000 will die from gunshot wounds. Added to this are over 100,000 people wounded by guns each year, the victims of 160,000 armed robberies and 100,000 assaults with guns.[3]

3. Gun accidents are now the fifth most common accidental cause of death according to the National Safety Council. In 1973, 2,700 people died in gun-related accidents.

4. Some have suggested that homeowners and citizens should arm themselves to protect their families from murder, assault, or robbery. The sad fact is that a handgun purchased for protection is often used in a moment of rage or fear against a relative or acquaintance. A recent study in the Cleveland area indicates guns purchased for protection resulted in the deaths of six times as many family members, friends, and neighbors as intruders or assailants.[4] The *1973 FBI Uniform Crime Report* indicates that of all murders almost twenty-five percent involved one family member killing another and an additional forty percent occur among people who are acquainted. Most homicides are not the result of criminal design but rather they are the

---

[1] Estimate of the Division of Alcohol, Firearms, and Tobacco, U.S. Department of the Treasury. Handgun refers to a firearm held and fired by the hand, usually a pistol or revolver. It does not include rifles, shotguns, long guns, or other shoulder arms.

[2] There were 13,070 murders involving firearms according to *Crime In The United States 1973*, the FBI Uniform Crime Report (September 1974). In addition, there were 2,700 deaths involving firearms accidents according to *Accident Facts*, National Safety Council. And, approximately 13,317 people committed suicides with firearms, according to the National Center for Health Statistics.

[3] *Crime In The United States 1973*, FBI Uniform Crime Report, September 1974.

[4] A 1968-1972 study of the Medical School of Case Western University. Of the one hundred thirty-one persons killed, one hundred fourteen were family members or acquaintances killed because a gun was present in the home and seventeen were robbers or other persons engaged in criminal activity.

outcome of quarrels and arguments among spouses, friends, and acquaintances. In these situations, it is the ready availability of handguns that often leads to tragic and deadly results.

5. Handguns play a disproportionate role in gun violence. They account for fifty-three percent of all murders, yet make up only twenty percent of all firearms. The problem is growing. The annual sales of handguns have quadrupled in the last ten years.

A National Firearms Policy

6. The growing reality and extent of violent crime is of great concern to the Committee on Social Development and World Peace and to all Americans. It threatens more and more of our citizens and communities. The cost of this violence in terms of human life and suffering is enormous. We speak out of pastoral concern as persons called to proclaim the Gospel of Jesus, who "came that they may have life and have it to the full" (Jn 10:10). We are deeply committed to upholding the value of human life and opposing those forces which threaten it.

7. One of these factors is the easy availability of handguns in our society. Because it is so easily concealed, the handgun is often the weapon of crime. Because it is so readily available, it is often the weapon of passion and suicide.

8. This is clearly a national problem. No state or locality is immune from the rising tide of violence. Individual state and local action can only provide a partial solution. We must have a coherent *national* firearms policy responsive to the overall public interest and respectful of the rights and privileges of all Americans. The unlimited freedom to possess and use handguns must give way to the rights of all people to safety and protection against those who misuse these weapons.

9. We believe that effective action must be taken to reverse this rising tide of violence. For this reason, we call for effective and courageous action to control handguns, leading to their eventual elimination from our society. Of course, reasonable exceptions ought to be made for the police, military, security guards, and pistol clubs where guns would be kept on the premises under secure conditions.

10. We recognize that this may be a long process before truly comprehensive control is realized. We therefore endorse the following steps to regulate the use and sale of handguns:

   (1) A several day cooling-off period. This delay between the time of the sale and possession of the handgun by the purchaser should result in fewer crimes of passion.

   (2) A ban on "Saturday Night Specials." These weapons are cheap, poorly made pistols often used in street crime.

   (3) Registration of handguns. This measure could provide an improved system of tracing weapons by law enforcement officials.

Registration will tell us how many guns there are and who owns them.

(4) Licensing of handgun owners. Handguns should not be available to juveniles, convicted felons, the mentally ill, and persons with a history of drug or alcohol abuse.

(5) More effective controls and better enforcement of existing laws regulating the manufacture, importation, and sale of handguns.

11. These individual steps will not completely eliminate the abuse of handguns. We believe that only prohibiting the importation, manufacture, sale, possession, and use of handguns, with the exceptions we have already cited, will provide a comprehensive response to handgun violence.

Conclusion

12. We realize this is a controversial issue and that some people of good faith will find themselves opposed to these measures. We acknowledge that controlling possession of handguns will not eliminate gun violence, but we believe it is an indispensable element for any serious or rational approach to the problem.

13. We support the legitimate and proper use of rifles and shotguns for hunting and recreational purposes. We do not wish to unduly burden hunters and sportsmen. On the contrary, we wish to involve them in a joint effort to eliminate the criminal and deadly misuse of handguns.

14. We are, of course, concerned about the rights of the individual, as these rights are grounded in the Constitution and in the universal design of our Creator. We are convinced that our position is entirely in accord with the rights guaranteed by our Constitution, and particularly with the Second Amendment to the Constitution, as these rights have been clarified by the United States Supreme Court. We affirm the traditional principle that individual rights to private property are limited by the universal demands of social order and human safety as well as the common good.

Food Policy and the Church Specific Proposals

*A Statement of the Administrative Board of the
United States Catholic Conference*

September 11, 1975

1. In October 1974, the Fourth International Synod of Bishops described "the right to eat" as fundamental to human dignity. In November 1974, the National Conference of Catholic Bishops adopted a pastoral plan of action designed to mobilize the Catholic community in the United States in an effort to realize the right to eat for millions threatened last year by starvation and malnutrition.

2. One year later it is evident that "the right to eat" is still denied to many in our own country and to many more throughout the globe. Although the threat of starvation has been reduced significantly during the past year, the presence of hunger and malnutrition continue to stalk many lives in several regions of the globe; at home many of the unemployed, the elderly, and the poor are forced to subsist on inadequate diets.

3. In the past year, however, many helpful steps were taken in the religious communities and in the wider society. Perhaps the most significant was the meeting of the World Food Conference held in Rome last November. Throughout the United States, programs were conducted in our dioceses, parishes, and schools, and policies and practices adopted by individuals, Catholic families, priests' senates, and religious communities to help alleviate the problem of global and domestic hunger. The media used their powers of persuasion and education to publicize the issue of hunger. Finally, in the Congress and in parts of the Administration, initial efforts have been made to shape a coherent, just, and generous food policy.

4. All these actions are significant, but public policy has a unique importance. Personal, voluntary efforts are essential, but they will prove inadequate to the scope of the hunger question if they are not encompassed in a broader public policy which links them to a systematic program of action. In this Statement, continuing the effort of policy debate, public education, and pastoral leadership we began last year, we seek to address the national policy issues which are needed to make a more just food policy a reality in our country.

A. Food and Foreign Policy

5. The World Food Conference produced a series of proposals for combatting hunger and malnutrition on a global basis. The unique position which the United States holds as the largest food exporting nation in the world means that our response to these proposals has supreme importance for the hungry of the world.

6. Since the Food Conference, a serious and sustained debate has been carried on in the Congress and within the Administration about our food policy. Some of the fruits of the debate are now taking the form of specific legislative proposals. We believe the following ideas contained in some of these proposals deserve serious public consideration and support.

I. Food Aid

7. The restructuring of U.S. food aid policy should include: 1) clear policy guidelines separating food aid from strategic and political considerations; 2) a specific policy commitment to give priority in food aid to the U.N.-designated "most severely affected nations"; this commitment should be specified in the language of the law; 3) the establishment of a guaranteed minimum of food aid to be provided each year; 4) the establishment of a guaranteed minimum of food aid to be provided on a donation basis through nongovernmental agencies rather than through concessional sales.

II. Grain Reserve

8. The World Food Conference proposal for an international system of national grain reserves needs the continued support and leadership of our government and should receive whatever legislative support is needed to allow the United States to participate in the system.

III. International Fund for Agricultural Development

9. Our government's pledge to contribute $200 million to the Fund is most welcome; this pledge should receive congressional support and implementation.

IV. Foreign Assistance

10. The foreign assistance program presently being debated in Congress should include several of the elements which have been proposed: 1) the separation of economic from military aid; 2) the support for multilateral aid programs; 3) the focusing of U.S. aid programs on the needs of the small farmer and the rural poor.

B. Domestic Food Policy

11. Many Americans face the reality of hunger and malnutrition intensified by high levels of unemployment, inflated food prices, and persistent poverty. Two federal programs are now under governmental review: food stamps and child nutrition programs.

I. Food Stamps

12. We support a major review of the food stamp program. Yet, we are concerned that reform efforts not lead to a diminished commitment to assist poor and working poor families. True reform seeks to make adequate assistance available where it is needed, but protects against abuses and excesses.

13. Unfortunately, the current debate over the value of the food stamp program is clouded by misunderstandings. Opponents maintain that the program is growing at uncontrollable rates and that affluent families and students are taking advantage of it. Some problems and abuses do exist; however, the evidence does not support these sweeping indictments.

14. (a) *Growth of the Program.* The growth of food stamps is the result of three factors: the introduction of food stamps to additional counties, the conversion of many counties from food commodities programs to food stamps, and the increase in unemployment. Begun as a pilot program in 1961, food stamps or food commodities were available in virtually every county in the nation by 1971. Between that year and mid-1974, the number of participants in the two programs remained at 14.9 million. In the last year, however, the serious rise in unemployment brought participants to a level of 19.5 million. Since April, the number of people receiving stamps has declined, and the USDA projects a lower level of participants and costs by 1980. These figures indicate that the program is not out of control, but is responding to the severe economic stress of the last year.

15. (b) *Income of Participants.* According to USDA, eighty-seven percent of all food stamp participants have family incomes of less than $6,000 after taxes and the average cash income of a family of four on food stamps is $3,456 a year. Congress has already acted to prohibit the eligibility of students who are dependents of affluent families, and this provision will take full effect this month. The evidence suggests that food stamps continue to offer nutritional assistance to the poor and the near-poor who are least able to afford a nutritional diet.

16. (c) *Policy Reform.* The food stamp program must be maintained and improved. We oppose drastic cuts and attempts to eliminate the working poor or unemployed from its coverage.

17. We support measures that will tighten up administration, improve responsiveness, and reduce certification errors. We do not support modifications that will penalize the working poor and result in disincentives for participants to work.

18. Any changes in the family asset limitations should not require the elderly or recently unemployed to sell their automobile, necessary household goods, and personal effects in order to become eligible for food stamps.

19. We have opposed and will continue to oppose increases in food stamp prices that will have an adverse impact on the ability of needy families to obtain adequate nutrition.

20. Although the evidence indicates there are very few non-needy families on food stamps, we would support a reasonable gross income limit that would disqualify affluent families from receiving food stamps under any circumstances. We would oppose efforts to set this limit so low that it would eliminate families actually in need.

21. Ultimately, the future of food stamps is linked to reform of the welfare system. Fundamentally, our nation must provide jobs for those who can and should work and an adequate income for those who cannot. Until such a policy is implemented, the food stamp program deserves the support of our country's public officials and citizens.

II. Child Nutrition

22. We have consistently supported efforts to improve and extend the child nutrition programs, including the School Lunch and Breakfast, the Special Supplemental Feeding Program for Women, Infants and Small Children, and the Special Milk Program. These programs provide particularly important health and education benefits for children in public and nonpublic schools. We support recent congressional efforts to strengthen these programs. We urge Congress to act swiftly and the President to sign this legislation into law.

Concluding Remarks

23. Enlightened government food policies and individual generosity are necessary to alleviate the world food problem, but they alone are not sufficient. Christians believe that despite the most inventive programs and the best of intentions, there remains an extra measure beyond human power, that is, God's active presence in the world. Christians also believe that prayer can solicit God's presence. The complexities of the food problem tax human ingenuity and invite Christians' efficacious prayers. Our Lord's belief in the power of prayer is enlightening and consoling; he instructed us to pray for our daily bread with confidence in the knowledge that when we ask our heavenly Father, he will give us neither a stone for bread nor a serpent for fish.

Statement on the United Nations and the Republic of South Africa

A Statement by Bishop James S. Rausch,
General Secretary, United States
Catholic Conference

October 9, 1975

1. For more than a decade, the conduct of the government of the Republic of South Africa (RSA) has been the subject of controversy among nations, and especially in the United Nations Organization. Furthermore, the RSA's conduct is a source of embarrassment and consternation to supporters of the principle of universality of membership in the United Nations.

2. Two principal issues place the U.N.-RSA relations in jeopardy:

(1) RSA's policy of separate development (apartheid) violates many of the basic human rights of the majority of its citizens who are black. Among these violations are infringement on the right to travel within their own country, search and seizure at will of police, imprisonment under cover of a myriad of laws restricting black people, labor contracts which separate working men from their families for extended periods of time and force them to live in inhuman barrack conditions. In addition, in its efforts to resolve its racial problem, RSA is carrying out its plan to confine its black population to Bantustans—areas amounting to thirteen percent of the land, but which would, when fully developed, contain about eighty percent of the total population of the Republic.

(2) The most specific charge against RSA is its position on Namibia (South West Africa). In October 1966, the U.N. General Assembly terminated South Africa's mandate over Namibia and placed the territory under the direct responsibility of the United Nations. In 1969, the U.N. Security Council adopted a resolution calling on South Africa to withdraw immediately from Namibia. In the interim, the RSA has resisted the jurisdiction of the United Nations (jurisdiction confirmed by the International Court of Justice four years ago) in the latter's efforts to establish an independent, majority-rule government in Namibia, which was clearly the intention of the U.N. resolutions. RSA has, on the contrary, refused to withdraw from the territory and has gone forward in planning elections under its own supervision in anticipation of installing its Bantustan system in Namibia. Such elections are not likely to give assurance to the world that the genuine desires of the majority of Namibian people will be respected.

3.   In view of these flagrant violations of both the spirit and the mandate of the U.N. Charter, the U.N. General Assembly repeatedly has condemned RSA's apartheid as a "crime against humanity," and has described it as "abhorrent to the conscience of mankind."

4.   Despite serious differences among member states about the appropriate international actions to deal with South Africa's violations, the Security Council in 1963 passed a resolution calling upon all member states to cease the sale and shipment of military arms and equipment to South Africa. This arms embargo was later extended to include equipment and materials for the manufacture and maintenance of arms and ammunition.

5.   South Africa's continued pursuit of apartheid, its constant build-up of military power, and its insistence upon ignoring the U.N. resolutions finally prompted the Security Council, in June 1975, to consider whether, under the provisions of Article VII of the U.N. Charter, RSA is a potential threat to international peace.

6.   In view of the intransigence of the RSA relative to the U.N. resolutions, the General Assembly has taken the position that the Security Council enforcement action, under Article VII, is essential to effect an appropriate change, and that "universally applied mandatory economic sanctions are the only means of achieving a peaceful solution." To date, however, the Security Council has not taken such enforcement action against RSA.

7.   Adherence to the principle of the universality of a membership in the United Nations cannot obscure certain practices of a nation whose very conduct erodes the strength and vitality of the United Nations itself. The history of RSA's relations with the United Nations presents ample evidence to question RSA's status as a member in full standing in the United Nations.

8.   Last year the General Assembly refused to seat the RSA's delegation; it may do the same this year. While expulsion from U.N. membership is the prerogative of the U.N. Security Council, such drastic action should be undertaken only after all other efforts have failed and reasons clearly exist meriting such a measure.

9.   Expulsion at this time would merely isolate RSA from the potential ameliorative influence of the full assembly of member nations, and the words of its critics would be heard only remotely. Furthermore, the possibility of negotiating a settlement of the Namibia dispute might be postponed until, perhaps, after a bloody guerilla war.

10. However, mere exhortation against the conduct of RSA and voluntary prohibition by member nations appears to be ineffective. The conduct of the Republic of South Africa has continually placed severe strains on the U.N.'s delicate apparatus. Certainly the peace and tranquility in Southern Africa has not been fostered by the Republic's apartheid policies and practices. Repeated efforts by the U.N. Assembly

to change the Republic's racist policies and its position on Namibia appear to have been minimal at best.

11. The time indeed may come when the Security Council is compelled to expel RSA from U.N. membership. The Security Council will have to weigh carefully the real effects of such an action—beyond the rhetoric—against the always-to-be-desired course of dialogue, negotiation, and peaceful settlement. Article 41 of the Charter provides a number of options, including mandatory sanctions, within the framework of the United Nations, to attempt to effect more universally acceptable conduct by a member nation.

12. In the case of RSA, its conduct warrants serious consideration for the U.N. Security Council to invoke mandatory sanctions. Of course such action, to be faithful to the intention of the Charter and to achieve a significant measure of effectiveness, requires sincere commitment and genuine efforts to enforce the mandate by all the nations.

13. In an interdependent world, the future of all nations and peoples is tied to the fate of each. The bonds of material interdependence we share range from economic ties through our ecological heritage to nuclear danger. The task of the age is to move from material interdependence to moral interdependence. It is time for all nations, especially the more powerful ones, to realize that their participation in oppression and the denial of human freedom to citizens of other lands is ultimately destructive of peace. It is time for all nations, especially our own, to give to human dignity priority over political, military, and economic interests.

14. Pope Paul stated the issue well at his meeting with the U.N. Special Committee on Apartheid in 1974:

> As long as the rights of all the peoples, among them the right to self-determination and independence, are not duly recognized and honored, there cannot be true and lasting peace, even though the abusive power of arms may for a time prevail over the reactions of those opposed. For as long as, within the individual national communities, those in power do not nobly respect the rights and legitimate freedoms of the citizens, tranquillity and order (even though they can be maintained by force) remain nothing but a deceptive and insecure sham, no longer worthy of a society of civilized beings. Therefore, from our vantage point, we earnestly call upon all men of good will to recognize this and to give heed to the just yearnings of individuals and peoples.

The Eucharist and the Hungers of the Human Family

A Pastoral Statement Issued by the National Conference of Catholic Bishops

November 20, 1975

1. At Thanksgiving, Americans join in gratitude to God for His gifts to this nation and its people. The act of giving thanks is one in which Catholics are privileged to participate in a special way in the celebration of the Eucharist. The word, eucharist, means "thanksgiving," and the Eucharist is the supreme act of thanks in which Christ offers perfect worship to the Father and gives Himself as the perfect gift of love to those who believe in Him.

2. Next August the forty-first International Eucharistic Congress will be celebrated in the United States at Philadelphia. In the intervening months we Catholics of the United States will be preparing for that great event, which will constitute a magnificent public witness to our faith in Jesus Christ, Our Lord in the Eucharist, and our love for Him. The preparation will be primarily spiritual, as we work together to renew ourselves and the Church.

3. The Eucharistic Congress gives us a special opportunity for spiritual and intellectual growth focused on the Eucharistic liturgy, which is simultaneously "a sacrament of love, a sign of unity, a bond of charity, a paschal banquet in which Christ is consumed, the mind is filled with grace, and a pledge of future glory is given to us" (Vatican Council II, *Constitution on the Sacred Liturgy*, 47). In the Congress, we are offered means to manifest publicly our faith and love for this great gift. Coming as it does during our nation's bicentennial anniversary, the Congress also affords Catholics an occasion to invite others to join them in affirming the religious and spiritual heritage of America. It renews and strengthens our commitment to the work of spreading Christ's reign of justice and charity in the world.

4. We should all seize this opportunity, not only by participating, if possible, in the Congress itself, but also by participating fully in the programs of spiritual renewal which will be offered by dioceses and parishes throughout our nation.

5. As this season is an appropriate time to begin intensive preparation, it is also a fitting time to recall that there are many persons in our nation and our world who experience profound hungers which crave to be satisfied. There is no one of us who does not hunger in some way, or in many ways: for, besides physical hunger, human beings have deep emotional, intellectual, and spiritual hungers.

6.   Pleasure, power, or possessions may temporarily quiet the pangs of some hungers. They cannot satisfy us on the deepest levels of our personhood. Only God can do that. "You have made us for Yourself, O God, and our hearts are restless until they rest in You" (St. Augustine, *Confessions*, 1,1).

7.   God the Father loves us so much that He sent His only Son to become one of us and redeem us. Jesus loves us so much that, even after His death, resurrection, and ascension, He remains with us. He is, after all, Emanuel, "God with us," but now through His living, sanctifying Spirit. We now encounter Him in new ways: in other human beings; in any place where people gather in His name (Mt. 18:20); in the inspired words of Holy Scripture; in His Church, particularly her liturgical celebrations; in the person of His minister; and especially in the sacraments, preeminently the sacrament of the Eucharist.

8.   In the Eucharist, which is Jesus really present, God satisfies our deepest hungers. The Sacrifice of the Mass is Christ's supreme act of reconciliation. "Truly partaking of the body of the Lord in the breaking of the Eucharistic bread, we are taken up into communion with Him and with one another. 'Because the bread is one, we though many, are one body, all of us who partake of the one bread' (1 Cor 10:17). In this way all of us are made members of His body (cf., 1 Cor 12:27), 'but severally members of one another' (Rom 12:15)" (Vatican Council II, *Dogmatic Constitution on the Church*, 7). The Eucharist is indeed the Sacrament of Unity, "by which the unity of the Church is both signified and brought about" (Vatican Council II, *Decree on Ecumenism*, 2).

9.   The theme of the Congress, "The Eucharist and the Hungers of the Human Family," reminds us that men and women hunger not only for food, but also for God, not only for bread in this life but for the Bread of Life itself: for Christ, really present in the Eucharist, really received in Holy Communion, leading us to the Father. The Eucharist responds to our needs and concerns—our many hungers— as human beings. The eight days of the Eucharistic Congress will be devoted to eight separate human "hungers" and the relationship of the Eucharist to them.

10.   (1) *Hunger for God*. If we lack God, it matters little what else we have. Estranged from God, we are estranged from our own destiny and fulfillment. Human life absorbed in itself is diminished and lacking in purpose. The Eucharist is a special means given to us by Jesus for overcoming our estrangement from God. It is as Christ tells us: "The man who feeds on my flesh and drinks my blood remains in me, and I in him" (Jn 6:56).

11.   (2) *Hunger for Bread*. Many persons today are physically hungry. Certainly the solution to starvation and malnutrition requires increased

production and improved distribution of food. But it also requires "a concerted act of solidarity" by the nations and peoples of the world (Synod of Bishops, 1974, *Statement on Human Rights and Reconciliation*). Our sharing in the Eucharist inspires us to such solidarity, as well as to actions which express it; for sincere celebration of the Eucharist "must lead to various works of charity and mutual help" (Vatican Council II, *Decree on the Ministry and Life of Priests*, 6).

12. (3) *Hunger for Freedom and Justice.* The quest for human freedom and justice is not optional for Catholics, nor is it a small part of the Church's mission. Participation in the struggle for freedom and justice is a duty for each one of us, as it is a central element of the Church's mission of redemption and liberation. In the Eucharist we find the source of our deepest commitment to the loving service of our brothers and sisters. It is especially timely for us to reflect on these facts at this season of the year, when we are called upon to express our solidarity with the poor and powerless of our nation through the Campaign for Human Development.

13. (4) *Hunger for the Spirit.* In considering this theme, the Eucharistic Congress will focus in a special way on religious vocations and the need for commitment by the clergy and religious of the world. It is most appropriate that this be done in the context of the Eucharist, for it is the special role of clergy and religious to give witness to the transcendent, God-centered nature of human life and striving, which the Eucharist supremely expresses. This is no "perishable food but . . . food that remains unto life eternal, food which the Son of Man will give you" (Jn 6:27).

14. (5) *Hunger for Truth.* Jesus proclaimed that He is "the Way, the Truth, and the Life" (Jn 14:6). We see, therefore, that knowledge of truth in the act of faith means more than just an intellectual understanding of abstract concepts. It also means commitment to a Person. Our most direct and profound encounter with this Person who is Truth occurs in the sacrament of the Eucharist. Here grace strengthens both our acceptance of what faith teaches and our loving commitment to the Person who stands at the center of faith.

15. (6) *Hunger for Understanding.* Our times experience the tragedy of estrangement between nations, races, classes, churches, and even generations. Members of the same family are sometimes strangers to each other. Children feel that they are not understood by their parents; parents feel the same with respect to their children. The need for reconciliation is clear. How better achieve such reconciliation than at the Table of the Lord; for "the liturgy in its turn inspires the faithful to become of one heart in love" (Vatican Council II, *Constitution on the Sacred Liturgy*, 10).

16. (7) *Hunger for Peace.* In an era of tension and violence, the limits of human instruments for peace are all too evident. Christ is our peace, and Christ Himself in the Eucharist provides us with both our model and best hope of peace. For it is He "who made the two of us one by breaking down the barrier of hostility that kept us apart" (Eph 2:4). It is here, in the Eucharist, that "all education in the spirit of community must originate" (Vatican Council II, *Decree on the Ministry and Life of Priests*, 6).

17. (8). *Hunger for Jesus—The Bread of Life.* All men and women hunger for Christ, consciously or not. It is the Lord, worthily and maturely received in Holy Communion, who brings about our loving unity with one another and with Him. Without the Eucharist, our lives in all their dimensions would be lacking in something essential; in the Eucharist we find means to conquer our weakness and tendency to sin and to live according to God's will for us. "Let me solemnly assure you if you do not eat the flesh of the Son of Man and drink his blood, you have no life in you. He who feeds on my flesh and drinks my blood has life eternal, and I will raise him up on the last day" (Jn 6:53-54).

18. The mysterious reality of the Eucharist—"My flesh is real food and my blood real drink" (Jn 6:55)—is a puzzle to some, a scandal to others. It has always been so. After Jesus promised the Eucharist, "many of his disciples remarked, 'This sort of talk is hard to endure! How can anyone take it seriously?' . . . From this time on, many of his disciples broke away and would not remain in his company any longer" (Jn 6:60-66).

19. But for those who believe in Jesus' teaching because they believe in Jesus Christ Himself, the Eucharist is, among all His gifts to us, the most cherished and the cause of our deepest gratitude. After some of his disciples had left Him, Jesus asked the Twelve: "Do you want to leave me too?" Simon Peter answered—for them and for us. "Lord, to whom shall we go? You have words of eternal life. We have come to believe; we are convinced that you are God's holy one" (Jn 6:67-69). Let us pray that the Eucharistic Congress will help all of us to renew our faith, our hope, our love, and our gratitude for the great gift of Our Lord and Savior Jesus Christ in the sacrament of the Eucharist; and to recommit ourselves, in union with Him, to the task of responding generously to the hungers of the human family.

Pastoral Plan for Pro-life Activities

A Statement Issued by the
National Conference of Catholic Bishops

November 20, 1975

> *All should be persuaded that human life and the*
> *task of transmitting it are not realities bound*
> *up with this world alone. Hence they cannot be*
> *measured or perceived only in terms of it, but*
> *always have a bearing on the eternal destiny of*
> *men . . . For God, the Lord of life, has conferred*
> *on men the surpassing ministry of safeguarding*
> *life in a manner which is worthy of man. There-*
> *fore from the moment of its conception, life must*
> *be guarded with the greatest care, while abor-*
> *tion and infanticide are unspeakable crimes.*

Constitution on the Church
in the Modern World

1. Respect for human life has been gradually declining in our society during the past decade. To some degree this reflects a secularizing trend and a rejection of moral imperatives based on belief in God and His plan for creation. It also reflects a tendency for individuals to give primary attention to what is personally rewarding and satisfying to them, to the exclusion of responsible concern for the well-being of other persons and society. These trends, along with others, have resulted in laws and judicial decisions which deny or ignore basic human rights and moral responsibilities for the protection and promotion of the common good. In this category are efforts to establish permissive abortion laws, the abortion decisions of the United States Supreme Court in 1973 denying any effective legal protection to the unborn child, and the growing attempts to legitimatize positive euthanasia through so-called "death with dignity" laws.

2. In the Declaration of Independence, our Founding Fathers point to the right to life as the first of the inalienable rights given by the Creator.

3. In fulfillment of our pastoral responsibilities, the members of the National Conference of Catholic Bishops have repeatedly affirmed that human life is a precious gift from God; that each person who receives this gift has responsibilities toward God, toward self, and toward others; and that society, through its laws and social institutions, must protect and sustain human life at every stage of its existence. Recognition of the dignity of the human person, made in the image of God, lies at the very heart of our individual and social duty to respect human life.

4.   In this Pastoral Plan we hope to focus attention on the pervasive threat to human life arising from the present situation of permissive abortion. Basic human rights are violated in many ways: by abortion and euthanasia, by injustice and the denial of equality to certain groups of persons, by some forms of human experimentation, by neglect of the underprivileged and disadvantaged who deserve the concern and support of the entire society. Indeed, the denial of the God-given right to life is one aspect of a larger problem. But it is unlikely that efforts to protect other rights will be ultimately successful if life itself is continually diminished in value.

5.   In focusing attention on the sanctity of human life, therefore, we hope to generate a greater respect for the life of each person in our society. We are confident that greater respect for human life will result from continuing the public discussion of abortion and from efforts to shape our laws so as to protect the life of all persons, including the unborn.

6.   Thus this Pastoral Plan seeks to activate the pastoral resources of the Church in three major efforts:

(1) an educational/public information effort to inform, clarify, and deepen understanding of the basic issues;

(2) a pastoral effort addressed to the specific needs of women with problems related to pregnancy and to those who have had or have taken part in an abortion;

(3) a public policy effort directed toward the legislative, judicial, and administrative areas so as to insure effective legal protection for the right to life.

7.   This Pastoral Plan is addressed to and calls upon all Church-sponsored or identifiably Catholic national, regional, diocesan, and parochial organizations and agencies to pursue the three-fold effort. This includes ongoing dialogue and cooperation between the NCCB/USCC on the one hand, and priests, religious, and lay persons, individually and collectively, on the other hand. In a special way, we invite the continued cooperation of national Catholic organizations.

8.   At the same time, we urge Catholics in various professional fields to discuss these issues with their colleagues and to carry the dialogue into their own professional organizations. In similar fashion, we urge those in research and academic life to present the Church's position on a wide range of topics that visibly express her commitment to respect for life at every stage and in every condition. Society's responsibility to insure and protect human rights demands that the right to life be recognized and protected as antecedent to and the condition of all other rights.

9.   Dialogue is most important—and has already proven highly fruitful—among churches and religious groups. Efforts should continue at ecumenical consultation and dialogue with Judaism and other Christian bodies, and also with those who have no specific ecclesial allegiance. Dialogue among scholars in the field of ethics is a most important part of this interfaith effort.

10. The most effective structures for pastoral action are in the diocese and the parish. While recognizing the roles of national, regional, and statewide groupings, this Plan places its primary emphasis on the roles of diocesan organizations and the parish community. Thus, the resources of the diocese and parish become most important in its implementation.

I. Public Information/Education Program

11. In order to deepen a respect for human life and heighten public opposition to permissive abortion, a two-fold educational effort presenting the case for the sanctity of life from conception onwards is required.

12. The first aspect, a public information effort, is directed to the general public. It creates awareness of the threats to human dignity inherent in a permissive abortion policy, and the need to correct the present situation by establishing legal safeguards for the right to life. It gives the abortion issue continued visibility, and sensitizes the many people who have only general perceptions of the issue but very little by way of firm conviction or commitment. The public information effort is important to inform the public discussion, and it proves that the Church is serious about and commited to its announced long-range pro-life effort. It is accomplished in a variety of ways, such as accurate reporting of newsworthy events, the issuance of public statements, testimony on legislative issues, letters to editors.

13. The second aspect, an intensive long-range education effort, leads people to a clearer understanding of the issues, to firm conviction, and to commitment. It is part of the Church's essential responsibility that it carry forward such an effort, directed primarily to the Catholic community. Recognizing the value of legal, medical, and sociological arguments, the primary and ultimately most compelling arguments must be theological and moral. Respect for life must be seen in the context of God's love for mankind, reflected in creation and redemption, and man's relationship to God and to other members of the human family. The Church's opposition to abortion is based on Christian teaching on the dignity of the human person, and the responsibility to proclaim and defend basic human rights, especially the right to life.

14. This intensive education effort should present the scientific information on the humanity of the unborn child and the continuity of human growth and development throughout the months of fetal existence; the responsibility and necessity for society to safeguard the life of the child at every stage of its existence; the problems that may exist for women during pregnancy; and more humane and morally acceptable solutions to these problems.

15. The more intensive educational effort should be carried on by all who participate in the Church's educational ministry, notably:

(a) Priests and religious, exercising their teaching responsibility in the pulpit, in other teaching assignments, and through parish programs.

(b) All Church-sponsored or identifiably Catholic organizations, national, regional, diocesan, and parochial, carrying on continuing education efforts that emphasize the moral prohibition of abortion and the reasons for carrying this teaching into the public policy area.

(c) Schools, CCD, and other Church-sponsored educational agencies providing moral teaching, bolstered by medical, legal, and sociological data, in the schools, etc. The USCC Department of Education might serve as a catalyst and resource for the dioceses.

(d) Church-related social service and health agencies carrying on continuing education efforts through seminars and other appropriate programs, and by publicizing programs and services offering alternatives to abortion.

16. Although the primary purpose of the intensive educational program is the development of pro-life attitudes and the determined avoidance of abortion by each person, the program must extend to other issues that involve support of human life: there must be internal consistency in the pro-life commitment.

17. The annual Respect Life Program sets the abortion problem in the context of other issues where human life is endangered or neglected, such as the problems facing the family, youth, the aging, the mentally retarded, as well as specific issues such as poverty, war, population control, and euthanasia. This program is helpful to parishes in calling attention to specific problems and providing program formats and resources.

II. Pastoral Care

18. The Church's pastoral effort is rooted in and manifests her faith commitment. Underlying every part of our program is the need for prayer and sacrifice. In building the house of respect for life, we labor in vain without God's merciful help.

19. Three facets of the Church's program of pastoral care deserve particular attention.

20. *1) Moral Guidance and Motivation.* Accurate information regarding the nature of an act and freedom from coercion are necessary in order to make responsible moral decisions. Choosing what is morally good also requires motivation. The Church has a unique responsibility to transmit the teaching of Christ and to provide moral principles consistent with that teaching. In regard to abortion, the Church should provide accurate information regarding the nature of the act, its effects and far-reaching consequences, and should show that abortion is a violation of God's laws of charity and justice. In many instances, the decision to do what is in conformity with God's law will be the ultimate determinant of the moral choice.

21. *2) Service and Care for Women and Unborn Children.* Respect for human life motivates individuals and groups to reach out to those with special needs. Programs of service and care should be available to provide women with alternate options to abortion. Specifically, these programs should include:

(a) adequate education and material sustenance for women so that they may choose motherhood responsibly and freely in accord with a basic commitment to the sanctity of life;

(b) nutritional, pre-natal, childbirth, and post-natal care for the mother, and nutritional and pediatric care for the child throughout the first year of life;

(c) intensified scientific investigation into the causes and cures of maternal disease and/or fetal abnormality;

(d) continued development of genetic counseling and gene therapy centers and neo-natal intensive care facilities;

(e) extension of adoption and foster care facilities to those who need them;

(f) pregnancy counseling centers that provide advice, encouragement, and support for every woman who faces difficulties related to pregnancy;

(g) counseling services and opportunities for continuation of education for unwed mothers;

(h) special understanding, encouragement, and support for victims of rape;

(i) continued efforts to remove the social stigma that is visited on the woman who is pregnant out of wedlock and on her child.

22. Many of these services have been and will continue to be provided by Church-sponsored health care and social service agencies, involving the dedicated efforts of professionals and volunteers. Cooperation with other private agencies and increased support in the quest for government assistance in many of these areas are further extensions of the long-range effort.

23. *3) Reconciliation.* The Church is both a means and an agent of reconciliation. As a spiritual entity, the Church reconciles men and women to God. As a human community, the Church pursues the task of reconciling men and women with one another and with the entire community. Thus all of the faithful have the duty of promoting reconciliation.

24. Sacramentally, the Church reconciles the sinner through the sacrament of Penance, thereby restoring the individual to full sacramental participation. The work of reconciliation is also continually accomplished in celebrating and participating in the Eucharist. Finally, the effects of the Church's reconciling efforts are found in the full support of the Christian community and the renewal of Christian life that results from prayer, the pursuit of virtue, and continued sacramental participation.

25. Granting that the grave sin of abortion is symptomatic of many human problems, which often remain unsolved for the individual woman, it is important that we realize that God's mercy is always available and without limit, that the Christian life can be restored and renewed through the sacraments, and that union with God can be accomplished despite the problems of human existence.

III. Legislative/Public Policy Effort

26. In recent years there has been a growing realization throughout the world that protecting and promoting the inviolable rights of persons are essential duties of civil authority, and that the maintenance and protection of human rights are primary purposes of law. As Americans, and as religious leaders, we have been committed to governance by a system of law that protects the rights of individuals and maintains the common good. As our founding fathers believed, we hold that all law is ultimately based on Divine Law, and that a just system of law cannot be in conflict with the law of God.

27. Abortion is a specific issue that highlights the relationship between morality and law. As a human mechanism, law may not be able fully to articulate the moral imperative, but neither can legal philosophy ignore the moral order. The abortion decisions of the United States Supreme Court (January 22, 1973) violate the moral order, and have disrupted the legal process which previously attempted to safeguard the rights of unborn children. A comprehensive pro-life legislative program must therefore include the following elements:

(a) Passage of a constitutional amendment providing protection for the unborn child to the maximum degree possible.

(b) Passage of federal and state laws and adoption of administrative policies that will restrict the practice of abortion as much as possible.

(c) Continual research into and refinement and precise interpretation of *Roe* and *Doe* and subsequent court decisions.

(d) Support for legislation that provides alternatives to abortion.

28. Accomplishment of this aspect of this Pastoral Plan will undoubtedly require well-planned and coordinated political action by citizens at the national, state, and local levels. This activity is not simply the responsibility of Catholics, nor should it be limited to Catholic groups or agencies. It calls for widespread cooperation and collaboration. As citizens of this democracy, we encourage the appropriate political action to achieve these legislative goals. As leaders of a religious institution in this society, we see a moral imperative for such political activity.

Means of Implementation of Program

29. The challenge to restore respect for human life in our society is a task of the Church that reaches out through all institutions, agencies, and organizations. Diverse tasks and various goals are to be achieved. The following represents a systematic organization and allocation of the Church's resources of people, institutions, and finances which can be activated at various levels to restore respect for human life and insure protection of the right to life of the unborn.

1. State Coordinating Committee

30. A. It is assumed that overall coordination in each state will be the responsibility of the State Catholic Conference or its equivalent. Where a State Catholic Conference is in process of formation or does not exist, bishops' representatives from each diocese might be appointed as the core members of the State Coordinating Committee.

31. B. The State Coordinating Committee will comprise the director of the State Catholic Conference and the diocesan pro-life coordinators. At this level, it would be valuable to have one or more persons who are knowledgeable about public traditions, mores, and attitudes and are experienced in legislative activity. This might be the public affairs specialist referred to under the Diocesan Pro-Life Committee, or, e.g., an individual with prior professional experience in legislative or governmental service. In any case, it should be someone with a practical understanding of contemporary political techniques.

32. C. The primary purposes of the State Coordinating Committee are:

(a) to monitor the political trends in the state and their implications for the abortion effort:

(b) to coordinate the efforts of the various dioceses; and to evaluate progress in the dioceses and congressional districts;

(c) to provide counsel regarding the specific political relationships within the various parties at the state level.

2. The Diocesan Pro-life Committee

33. *a) General Purpose*
The purpose of the committee is to coordinate groups and activities within the diocese (to restore respect for human life), particularly efforts to effect passage of a constitutional amendment to protect the unborn child. In its coordinating role, the committee will rely on information and direction from the Bishops' Pro-life Office and the National Committee for a Human Life Amendment. The committee will act through the Diocesan Pro-life Director, who is appointed by the bishop to direct pro-life efforts in the diocese.

34. *b) Membership*
    (1) Diocesan Pro-life Director (bishop's representative)
    (2) Respect Life Coordinator
    (3) Liaison with State Catholic Conference
    (4) Public Affairs Advisor
    (5) Representatives of Diocesan Agencies (priests, religious, lay organizations)
    (6) Legal Advisor—representative of pro-life groups
    (7) Representatives of Parish Pro-life Committees
    (8) Congressional District Representative(s)

35. *c) Objectives*
    (1) Provide direction and coordination of diocesan and parish education/information efforts and maintain working relationship with all groups involved in congressional district activity.
    (2) Promote and assist in the development of those groups, particularly voluntary groups involved in pregnancy counseling, which provide alternatives and assistance to women who have problems related to pregnancy.
    (3) Encourage the development of "grassroots" political action organizations.
    (4) Maintain communications with National Committee for a Human Life Amendment in regard to federal activity, so as to provide instantaneous information concerning local senators and representatives.
    (5) Maintain a local public information effort directed to press and media. Include vigilance in regard to public media, seek "equal time," etc.
    (6) Develop close relationships with each senator or representative.

3. The Parish Pro-life Committee

36. The Parish Pro-life Committee should include a delegate from the Parish Council, representatives of various adult and youth parish organizations, members of local Knights of Columbus Councils, Catholic Daughters of America Chapters, and other similar organizations.

Objectives

37. (a) Sponsor and conduct intensive education programs touching all groups within the parish, including schools and religious education efforts.

38. (b) Promote and sponsor pregnancy counseling units and other alternatives to abortion.

39. (c) Through ongoing public information programs, generate public awareness of the continuing effort to obtain a constitutional amendment. The NCCB, the National Committee for a Human Life Amendment, and the State and Diocesan Coordinating Committees should have access to every congressional district for information, consultation, and coordination of action. A chairperson should be designated in each district who will coordinate the efforts of parish pro-life groups, K of C groups, etc., and seek ways of cooperating with nonsectarian pro-life groups, including right-to-life organizations. In each district, the parishes will provide one basic resource, and the clergy will have an active role in the overall effort.

40. (d) Prudently convince others—Catholics and non-Catholics—of the reasons for the necessity of a constitutional amendment to provide a base for legal protection for the unborn.

4. The Pro-life Effort in the Congressional District

41. Passage of a constitutional amendment depends ultimately on persuading members of Congress to vote in favor of such a proposal. This effort at persuasion is part of the democratic process, and is carried on most effectively in the congressional district or state from which the representative is elected. Essentially, this effort demands ongoing public information activity and careful and detailed organization. Thus it is absolutely necessary to encourage the development in each congressional district of an identifiable, tightly-knit, and well-organized pro-life unit. This unit can be described as a public interest group or a citizens' lobby. No matter what it is called:

(a) its task is essentially political, that is, to *organize people* to help persuade the elected representatives; and

(b) its range of action is limited, that is, it is focused on passing a constitutional amendment.

42. As such, the congressional district pro-life group differs from the diocesan, regional, or parish pro-life coordinator or committee, whose task is pedagogic and motivational, not simply political, and whose range of action includes a variety of efforts calculated to reverse the present atmosphere of permissiveness with respect to abortion. Moreover, it is an agency of citizens, operated, controlled, and financed by these same citizens. *It is not an agency of the Church, nor is it operated, controlled, or financed by the Church.*

43. The congressional district pro-life action group should be bipartisan, nonsectarian, inclined toward political action. It is complementary to denominational efforts, to professional groups, to pregnancy counseling and assistance groups.

44. Each congressional district should have a chairperson who may serve as liaison with the Diocesan Coordinating Committee. In dioceses with many congressional districts, this may be arranged through a regional representation structure.

5. *Objectives of the Congressional District Pro-life Group*

45. (1) To conduct a continuing public information effort to persuade all elected officials and potential candidates that abortion must be legally restricted.

46. (2) To counterbalance propaganda efforts opposed to a constitutional amendment.

47. (3) To persuade all residents in the congressional district that permissive abortion is harmful to society and that some restriction is necessary.

48. (4) To persuade all residents that a constitutional amendment is necessary as a first step toward legally restricting abortion.

49. (5) To convince all elected officials and potential candidates that "the abortion issue" will not go away and that their position on it will be subject to continuing public scrutiny.

50. (6) To enlist sympathetic supporters who will collaborate in persuading others.

51. (7) To enlist those who are generally supportive so that they may be called upon when needed to communicate to the elected officials.

52. (8) To elect members of their own group or active sympathizers to specific posts in all local party organizations.

53. (9) To set up a telephone network that will enable the committee to take immediate action when necessary.

54. (10) To maintain an informational file on the pro-life position of every elected official and potential candidate.

55. (11) To work for qualified candidates who will vote for a constitutional amendment, and other pro-life issues.

56. (12) To maintain liaison with all denominational leaders (pastors) and all other pro-life groups in the district.

57. This type of activity can be generated and coordinated by a small, dedicated, and politically alert group. It will need some financial support, but its greatest need is the commitment of other groups who realize the importance of its purposes, its potential for achieving those purposes, and the absolute necessity of working with the group to attain the desired goals.

Conclusion

58. The challenges facing American society as a result of the legislative and judicial endorsement of permissive abortion are enormous. But the Church and the individual Catholics must not avoid the challenge. Although the process of restoring respect for human life at every stage of existence may be demanding and prolonged, it is an effort which both requires and merits courage, patience, and determination. In every age the Church has faced unique challenges calling forth faith and courage. In our time and society, restoring respect for human life and establishing a system of justice which protects the most basic human rights are both a challenge and an opportunity whereby the Church proclaims her commitment to Christ's teaching on human dignity and the sanctity of the human person.

The Economy: Human Dimensions

A Statement Issued by the
Catholic Bishops of the United States

November 20, 1975

This unemployment returning again to plague
us after so many repetitions during the century
past is a sign of deep failure in our country.
Unemployment is the great peacetime physical
tragedy of the nineteenth and twentieth centu-
ries, and both in its cause and in the imprint it
leaves upon those who inflict it, those who per-
mit it, and those who are its victims, it is one
of the great moral tragedies of our time.

The Bishops of the United States,
Unemployment, 1930.

1. This was the judgment of our predecessors as they responded to the economic crisis of 1930. As pastors, teachers, and leaders, we recall and emphasize their words as our country faces important economic, social, and moral decisions in the midst of the highest unemployment since the 1930s.

I. The Church's Concern

2. Despite recent hopeful signs, the economy is only slowly and painfully recovering from the recent recession, the worst since World War II. We are deeply concerned that this recovery may lack the strength or duration to alleviate the suffering of many of the victims of the recession, especially the unemployed. It is the moral, human, and social consequences of our troubled economy which concern us and their impact on families, the elderly, and children. We hope in these limited reflections to give voice to some of the concerns of the poor and working people of our land.

3. We are keenly aware of the world-wide dimensions of the problem and the complexity of these issues of economic policy. Our concern, however, is not with technical fiscal matters, particular economic theories, or political programs, but rather the moral aspects of economic policy and the impact of these policies on people. Our economic life must reflect broad values of social justice and human rights.

II. The Church's Teaching

4.   Our own rich heritage of Catholic teaching offers important direction and insight. Most importantly, we are guided by the concern for the poor and afflicted shown by Jesus, who came to "bring good news to the poor, to proclaim liberty to captives, new sight to the blind, and to set the downtrodden free" (Lk 4:18). In addition, the social encyclicals of the popes and documents of the Second Vatican Council and the Synod of Bishops defend the basic human right to useful employment, just wages, and decent working conditions as well as the right of workers to organize and bargain collectively. They condemn unemployment, maldistribution of resources, and other forms of economic injustice and call for the creation of useful work experiences and new forms of industrial organization enabling workers to share in decision making, increased production, and even ownership. Again and again they point out the interrelation of economics and ethics, urging that economic activity be guided by social morality.

5.   Catholic teaching on economic issues flows from the Church's commitment to human rights and human dignity. This living tradition articulates a number of principles which are useful in evaluating our current economic situation. Without attempting to set down an all-inclusive list, we draw the following principles from the social teachings of the Church and ask that policymakers and citizens ponder their implications.

(a) Economic activity should be governed by justice and be carried out within the limits of morality. It must serve people's needs.[1]

(b) The right to have a share of earthly goods sufficient for oneself and one's family belongs to everyone.[2]

(c) Economic prosperity is to be assessed not so much from the sum total of goods and wealth possessed as from the distribution of goods according to norms of justice.[3]

(d) Opportunities to work must be provided for those who are able and willing to work. Every person has the right to useful employment, to just wages, and to adequate assistance in case of real need.[4]

(e) Economic development must not be left to the sole judgment of a few persons or groups possessing excessive economic power, or to the political community alone. On the contrary, at every level the largest possible number of people should have an active share in directing that development.[5]

---

[1]Vatican II, *The Church In The Modern World*, 64; John XXIII, *Mater et Magistra*, 38–39.
[2]Vatican II, *The Church In The Modern World*, 69.
[3]John XXIII, *Mater et Magistra*, 73.
[4]Pius XI, *On The Reconstruction of The Social Order*, 74; John XXIII, *Pacem in Terris*, 11. 18; Vatican II, *The Church In The Modern World*, 67; Paul VI, *A Call To Action*, 6.
[5]Vatican II, *The Church In The Modern World*, 65.

(f) A just and equitable system of taxation requires assessment according to ability to pay.[6]

(g) Government must play a role in the economic activity of its citizens. Indeed, it should promote in a suitable manner the production of a sufficient supply of material goods. Moreover, it should safeguard the rights of all citizens, and help them find opportunities for employment.[7]

6.   These are not new principles. They are drawn directly from the teachings of the Church, but they have critical relevance at this time of economic distress. Under current conditions, many of these principles are being consistently violated.

III. Dimensions of the Economic Situation

7.   In these reflections we wish to examine briefly the dimensions of our economic problems in three areas: unemployment, inflation, and distribution of wealth and income.

A. Unemployment

8.   In October, government figures show eight million persons were unemployed, representing 8.6 percent of the work force.[8] Millions of other persons have given up seeking work out of discouragement or are in part-time jobs although they desire full-time work. Taking this into account, the actual level of unemployment in our country is over twelve percent. It is estimated that 20 million people will be jobless at some time this year, and that one-third of all Americans will suffer the traumatic experience of unemployment within their families.

9.   The official unemployment rate does more than underestimate the true extent of joblessness. It also masks the inequitable distribution of unemployment. The figures for October indicate that minorities, blue collar workers, young people, and women bear a disproportionate share of the burdens of joblessness.[9]

---

[6]John XXIII, *Mater et Magistra*, 132.
[7]John XXIII, *Mater et Magistra*, 20; Vatican II, *The Church In The Modern World*, 67, 70.
[8]The Employment Situation: October 1975; U.S. Department of Labor, Bureau of Labor Statistics; November 7, 1975.
[9]Department of Labor figures for October 1975 indicate:
    (a) One out of five teenagers were jobless.
    (b) Over eleven percent of all blue collar workers were out of work.
    (c) 14.2 percent of all minority persons were unemployed.
    (d) Nearly forty percent of all minority teenagers were jobless.
    (e) One hundred thirty-four of our one hundred fifty major urban areas were officially listed as areas of substantial subemployment.

10. These realities clearly indicate that the nation's commitment to genuine full employment has been seriously eroded, if not abandoned. Since World War II, unemployment has been substantial, persistent, and drifting upward. In fact, when joblessness rose dramatically during the latest recession, it took the form of an acute and visible crisis, superimposed on a long-term unemployment problem which has persisted for decades.

11. The costs of this tragic under-utilization of our country's human resources are enormous. In economic terms, these high levels of unemployment cost literally hundreds of billions of dollars in lost productivity and tens of billions of dollars in lost revenue and increased expenses for all levels of government.

12. As lamentable as these financial costs are, the social and human impact is far more deplorable. In our society, persons without a job lose a key measure of their place in society and a source of individual fulfillment; they often feel that there is no productive role for them. Many minority youth may grow up without meaningful job experiences and come to accept a life of dependency. Unemployment frequently leads to higher rates of crime, drug addiction, and alcoholism. It is reflected in higher rates of mental illness as well as rising social tensions. The idleness, fear, and financial insecurity resulting from unemployment can undermine confidence, erode family relationships, dull the spirit, and destroy dreams and hopes. One can hardly bear to contemplate the disappointment of a family which has made the slow and painful climb up the economic ladder and has been pushed down once again into poverty and dependence by the loss of a job.

13. The current levels of unemployment are unacceptable and their tremendous human costs are intolerable. Unemployment represents a vast and tragic waste of our human and material resources. We are disturbed not only by the present levels of joblessness, but also by official government projections of massive unemployment for the rest of this decade. We sincerely hope that these figures do not represent resignation to the human and economic waste implied in these rates of unemployment. As a society, we cannot accept the notion that some will have jobs and income while others will be told to wait a few years and to subsist on welfare in the interim. For work is more than a way to earn a living. It represents a deep human need, desired not only for income but also for the sense of worth which it provides the individual.

B. Inflation

14. There are those who insist that we must tolerate high levels of unemployment for some, in order to avoid ruinous inflation for all. Although we are deeply concerned about inflation, we reject such a policy as not grounded in justice. In recent years, our country has experienced very high levels of inflation. During this past year, there has been some reduction in inflation, but there are already signs of its renewal, spurred by large increases in food and fuel prices.

15. Inflation weakens the economic stability of our society and erodes the economic security of our citizens. Its impact is most severe on those who live on fixed incomes and the very poor. The double distress of inflation and recession has led to a painful decline in real income for large numbers of people in recent years. Clearly, steps must be taken to limit inflation and its impact.

16. However, low unemployment and high inflation are not inevitable partners, as history and the experience of other industrialized countries bear out. Policymakers should seek and use measures to combat inflation which do not rely upon high rates of joblessness. For many of our fellow citizens, the major protection against inflation is a decent job at decent wages.

C. *Distribution of Income and Wealth*

17. Within our country, vast disparities of income and wealth remain. The richest twenty percent of our people receive more income than the bottom sixty percent combined. In the area of ownership, the disparities are even more apparent. The top one-fifth of all families own more than three-fourths of all the privately held wealth in the United States, while over one-half of our families control less than seven percent of the wealth.

18. The distribution of income and wealth are important since they influence and even determine our society's distribution of economic power. Catholic social teaching has condemned gross inequality in the distribution of material goods. Our country cannot continue to ignore this important measure of economic justice.

IV. Policy Directions

19. Fundamentally, our nation must provide jobs for those who can and should work and a decent income for those who cannot. An effective national commitment to full employment is needed to protect the basic human right to useful employment for all Americans. It ought to guarantee, through appropriate mechanisms, that no one seeking work would be denied an opportunity to earn a livelihood. Full employment is the foundation of a just economic policy; it should not be sacrificed for other political and economic goals. We would support sound and creative programs of public service employment to relieve joblessness and to meet the vital social needs of our people (housing, transportation, education, health care, recreation, etc.).

20. The burden and hardship of these difficult times must not fall most heavily on the most vulnerable: the poor, the elderly, the unemployed, young people, and workers of modest income. We support efforts to improve our unemployment compensation system and to provide adequate assistance to the victims of the recession. Efforts to eliminate or curtail needed services and help must be strongly opposed.

21. We continue to support a decent income policy for those who are unable to work because of sickness, age, disability, or other good reason. Our present welfare system should be reformed to serve our country and those in need more effectively.

22. Renewed efforts are required to reform our economic life. We ask the private and public sectors to join together to plan and provide better for our future, to promote fairness in taxation, to halt the destructive impact of inflation, and to distribute more evenly the burdens and opportunities of our society. We also ask that consideration be given to a more efficacious use of the land, the nation's primary resource, in order to provide gainful employment for more people. We should also explore the impact of technology and endeavor to preserve the small family farm and other approaches to economic life which provide substantial and productive employment for people. It is not enough to point up the issues in our economy and to propose solutions to our national problems while accepting uncritically the presupposition of an economic system based in large part upon unlimited and unrestrained profit.

23. We pledge our best efforts in support of these goals. We call on local parishes, dioceses, Catholic institutions and organizations to undertake education and action programs on issues of economic justice. We renew our commitment to assist the needy and victims of economic turmoil through programs of financial assistance and active participation in the dialogue over the formulation and implementation of just economic policies. We call on our people to pray for our country in this time of need and to participate in the difficult decisions which can still fulfill the promise of our land.

24. Working together with renewed vision and commitment, our country has the productive capacity and human and material resources to provide adequately for the needs of our people. We take this opportunity to renew the challenge of our fellow bishops of forty-five years ago:

> Our country needs, now and permanently, such a change of heart as will, intelligently and with determination, so organize and distribute our work and wealth that no one need lack for any long time the security of being able to earn an adequate living for himself and for those dependent upon him (The Bishops of the United States, *Unemployment*, 1930).

Appendix

25. In adopting this resolution, the bishops sought to link this effort to a major statement issued in 1919 on similar matters. Entitled, "The Bishops' Program For Social Reconstruction," the statement called for: minimum wage legislation; unemployment insurance and protection against sickness and old age; minimum age limit for working children; legal enforcement of the right of labor to organize; a national employment service; public housing; and a long term program of increasing wages.

26. It also urged: prevention of excessive profits and incomes through regulation of public utilities and progressive taxes on inheritance, income, and excess profits; participation of labor in management; a wider distribution of ownership through cooperative enterprises and worker ownership in the stock of corporations; and effective control of monopolies even by the method of government competition if that should prove necessary.

27. Most of these proposals have been enacted. Partial progress has been made toward others. The 1919 statement provides a historical framework for the current resolution and evidences a longstanding concern for economic justice on the part of the Catholic community in this country.

The Right to a Decent Home: A Pastoral Response to the Crisis in Housing

A Statement Issued by the Catholic Bishops of the United States

November 20, 1975

I. Introduction

1. The United States is in the midst of a severe housing crisis. This is a broader, more pervasive, and more complicated phenomenon than the customary photographs of urban slums and rural shacks indicate. It involves more people, more neighborhoods and communities than was thought to be the case even a few years ago. It touches millions of poor families who live in inhuman conditions, but it also involves many middle-income families whose ability to provide themselves with decent housing is being painfully tested. Rising costs of shelter, maintenance, and utilities—as well as high interest rates and regressive property taxes—are forcing many families to live in inadequate housing or to do without other basic essentials. Other low- and middle-income families have been confined to neighborhoods without adequate services, minimal safety, or necessary community life.

2. The dimensions of our housing crisis are apparent in the following statistics:

(a) One of every five families in the United States suffers from serious housing deprivation. They either live in physically inadequate buildings, suffer from severe overcrowding, or spend an excessive proportion of their income for shelter.[1]

(b) Housing costs have increased to the point that millions of families cannot obtain decent housing unless they deprive themselves of other essentials of life. Only fifteen percent of American families can afford to purchase a median-priced new home.[2]

(c) 4.7 million housing units lack adequate plumbing facilities and 5 million families live in overcrowded housing.[3]

---

[1] "America's Housing Needs: 1970 to 1980," Joint Center for Urban Studies of the Massachusetts Institute of Technology and Harvard University (Cambridge, 1973), pp. 4-7.

[2] "Availability of Homes for Middle-Income Families," Congressional Research Service, Library of Congress (Washington, 1975), p. 19.

[3] "General Housing Characteristics for the United States: 1970." Bureau of the Census, U.S. Department of Commerce. March 1972, pp. 1-53.

(d) Eighty percent of those with incomes under $5,000 experience some form of housing inadequacy.[4]

(e) Two-thirds of officially substandard housing is in rural areas and small towns.[5]

(f) It is estimated that over 23.3 million new homes will be needed between 1970 and 1980, yet housing production for the first quarter of 1975 was at the lowest level since World War II.[6]

(g) Forty percent of our available housing stock is more than thirty years old and the accompanying deterioration and abandonment are threatening many neighborhoods.[7]

(h) It is authoritatively estimated that 13.1 million American families suffer serious housing deprivation.[8]

3.   Over twenty-five years ago, the United States Congress declared the housing policy of this country to be "a decent home in suitable living environment for every American family."[9] This goal has not been achieved. The harsh and frustrating reality is that it certainly will not be achieved in the near future and may never be achieved at all. This means that millions of American families are condemned to live in poor housing or in unsuitable environments unless dramatic action is taken.

II. Housing: A Pastoral Imperative for the Church

4.   In the face of this cruel and discouraging condition, we, the bishops of the United States, cannot remain silent. The reality of this housing crisis provides a challenge to our country as we approach the bicentennial. In the past two hundred years, our nation, with the abundant blessing of God, has overcome many other complex problems and has provided a standard of living previously unknown to the world.

5.   We are not so naive as to believe that there are easy solutions to the crisis. The housing crisis is overwhelming. It touches facets of our economic, political, and social life that are extremely complicated. Any attempt to solve these intricate problems can give rise to petty

---

[4]"America's Housing Needs: 1970 to 1980." *Op. cit.,* pp. 4-12.
[5]"General Housing Characteristics for The United States: 1970." *Op. cit.* Officially substandard refers to units lacking adequate plumbing and overcrowded conditions.
[6]"America's Housing Needs: 1970 to 1980." *Op. cit.,* pp. 3-13. Also, Bureau of the Census, U.S. Department of Commerce: (1) *Housing Construction Statistics, 1889 to 1964,* p. 18, table A-1; (2) *Construction Reports, Housing Starts 1959 to 1971,* C 20 supplement; and (3) *Construction Reports, Housing Starts,* series C 20.
[7]"Detailed Housing Characteristics of The United States: 1970." Bureau of the Census, U.S. Department of Commerce, June, 1972, pp. 1-287.
[8]"America's Housing Needs: 1970 to 1980." *Op. cit.,* pp. 4-7.
[9]*The Housing Act of 1949,* Section 2.

self-interest and alarming divisions. Addressing ourselves to our own people and to the whole country, we plead with all, in both the private and the public sector, to confront our housing crisis with the courage, conviction, and talent that have brought about our greatest achievements in the past.

6.   As preachers of the Gospel, we proclaim the message of Jesus Christ who identifies Himself with the needs of the least of the brethren. The second great commandment is to love our neighbor. We cannot deny the crying needs for decent housing experienced by the least of the brethren in our society. Effective love of neighbor involves concern for his or her living conditions.

7.   We begin with the recognition that decent housing is a right. Our Catholic tradition, eloquently expressed by Pope John XXIII[10] and Pope Paul VI,[11] insists that shelter is one of the basic rights of the human person. The Second Vatican Council has said with great directness: "There must be made available to all men everything necessary for leading a life truly human, such as food, clothing, and shelter. . . ."[12]

8.   As teachers, pastors, and leaders, we have the responsibility to articulate the principles and values that govern the Church's concern for housing. We believe that each individual possesses an inherent dignity and priceless worth because he or she is created in the image and likeness of God. We also believe each person should have the opportunity to grow and develop his or her potential to the fullest extent possible. Human dignity and development are threatened whenever social and economic forces imprison or degrade people. We call on Catholics and all citizens to join us in working against these debilitating forces.

9.   In particular, we take this opportunity to reflect on the consequences of poor housing. The physical and social environment play an important role in forming and influencing the lives of people. We cannot ignore the terrible impact of degrading and indecent living conditions on people's perception of themselves and their future. The protection of the human dignity of every person and the right to a decent home require both individual action and structural policies and practices.

10.   Our faith teaches us that "the earth is the Lord's" (Ps 24) and that wealth and private property are held in trust for others. We are trustees of God's creation, and as good stewards we are required to exercise that trust for the common good and benefit of our brothers and sisters.

---

[10]*Peace on Earth*, 11. Pope John XXIII. April 1963.
[11]*A Call to Action*, 11-12, Pope Paul VI, May 1971.
[12]*Pastoral Constitution on the Church in the Modern World*, 26. December 1965.

11. The role of those who own land or other wealth is one of stewardship. While the Church has traditionally recognized the right to private property, that right is always subject to certain limitations. As the Second Vatican Council pointed out:

> God intended the earth and all that it contains for the use of every human being and people. . . . Whatever the forms of ownership may be, as adapted to the legitimate institutions of people according to diverse and changeable circumstances, attention must always be paid to the universal purpose for which created goods are meant. In using them, therefore, a man should regard his lawful possessions not merely as his own but also as common property in the sense that they should accrue to the benefit of not only himself but of others.[13]

12. This teaching is central to a discussion of the ethical and moral dimensions of the housing crisis. It imposes major responsibilities on those whose land and shelter resources or skills might help society guarantee the right to a decent home.

13. This concept of stewardship must be reflected in our concern and action on housing. It must be practiced not only by individuals but also by institutions. The Church must give witness to this trusteeship in the use of its own property and resources. Just as individual property holders are bound by this principle, so it must be reflected in public policy at each level of government.

14. Our concern is not simply for houses or programs but for the people who inhabit these dwellings or are affected by these programs. These include families whose attempts to create a stable and wholesome family life are inhibited by inadequate living conditions; people and parish communities in neighborhoods without the housing services or community life which foster love and Christian service; the many elderly whose meager incomes are consumed by housing maintenance costs, utility bills, and property taxes; and countless young families who lack the resources to acquire decent housing. The statistics we cite are not simply numbers or points on a graph; they are individual human tragedies. We are shocked by the pervasiveness and depth of our housing crisis and what this means for our country and our people.

III. National Housing Goal

15. We affirm the national housing goal first articulated in 1949: "a decent home and a suitable living environment for every American family." We believe this inclusive goal is in line with the values and principles we have already articulated, and is a suitable basis for

---

[13] *Ibid.*, 69.

national policy. We take this opportunity, however, to suggest two needed qualifications of this goal. First, decent housing must be within the *means* of each family. The cost of such a home or apartment should not deprive the family of other essentials. Second, our housing goal must allow families *freedom of choice* as to where they will live and whether they will rent or own their homes. Equal housing opportunity and the possibility of home ownership for those who desire it should be integral components of our national housing policy.

16. As we have already stated, this national goal is far from being realized. Even now, social and economic forces—and current housing policy—make its realization more and more difficult. We are faced with the cruel paradox of urgent and growing housing needs and the inability of our present system of housing production, delivery, and financing to meet this challenge.

17. The achievement of this housing goal will require a reordering of priorities and a substantial increase in expenditures for housing and community development. A realistic appraisal of our housing needs indicates that the resolution of our present crisis will be expensive and difficult.

18. In many ways, the housing crisis is an institutional one, reflecting the limitations of our political, economic, and social institutions. Effective action for better housing will depend on a competent analysis and significant changes in the structures and policies that have helped create and maintain our current housing delivery system. Our present way of financing and building housing seems not to lend itself to the resolution of our problems. The traditional law of supply and demand has not proved adequate to the task of providing decent housing for all our people. The demand, as we have seen, is present and growing, yet the response is clearly inadequate, especially for low- and middle-income people.

19. The housing crisis is, of course, part of a larger pattern of neglect. It is intricately linked to other social and economic problems. In fact, poor housing is often cited as an index or symptom of general social deprivation. We do not undertake here an in-depth examination of the relationship between housing and employment, income, education, health, crime, discrimination, environment, or transportation. However, we recognize that a lasting solution to our housing problems will require a comprehensive attack on a variety of social injustices. An essential dimension of comprehensive housing strategy is action on unemployment and inadequate income, which severely limit the ability of families to acquire decent housing. A comprehensive response to our shelter needs will include more than increased housing production and elimination of blight. This broader response requires a serious analysis of economic and tax policies, the treatment accorded neighborhoods and rural areas, the use of land and resources, as well as issues of environmental preservation and civil rights.

IV. Housing Issues

20. Questions of housing and community development are extremely complex and often technical. They involve a variety of interests: private enterprise and government participation; maximum production and environmental and consumer protection needs; increased housing needs and tight budgetary restraints; public interest and private gain; as well as questions of equity and efficiency.

A. Housing and the Economy

21. The housing crisis and proposed solutions to it are often stated in economic terms. The present housing crisis itself is often attributed to the critical state of the economy in a period of inflation and recession. However, there has been a serious housing problem for at least the last twenty-five years, during which we have experienced unparalleled prosperity. Since the problem has persisted in both good and bad economic times, it is apparent that we cannot rely on economic recovery alone to meet our housing needs.

22. Nonetheless, it is obvious that current economic difficulties have greatly intensified housing problems. For example, during the recent recession, housing production has been approximately one-half of the annual need of over 2.3 million units.[14] At this level of production, almost no housing for the poor is being constructed. Recession, inflation, and monetary policies have combined to leave the housing industry in a lamentable condition. The recent steep decline in housing production was the fifth and sharpest in the last twenty years. This situation is particularly ominous for low-income families and apartment dwellers since the production of multi-family developments is even lower. Recent economic projections show some signs of hope, but even the most optimistic forecasters predict a level of housing starts well below our requirement.

23. Another serious factor in our current difficulties is the devastating impact of inflation. Rising construction costs, high interest rates, and increasing utility bills have combined to make decent housing an unrealizable goal for many families. Studies indicate that eighty-five percent of American families cannot afford to purchase the median-priced new home.[15] The price of that median home rose from $23,400 in 1970 to $39,900 in May of 1975.[16] An income of $21,170 is needed

---

[14]The National Association of House Builders estimates that housing starts for 1975 will not exceed 1.2 million starts. The Harvard-MIT study previously cited estimates a ten-year need of 23 million new units.

[15]"Availability of Homes for Middle-Income Families." *Op. cit.,* p. 19.

[16]"New One-Family Houses Sold and For Sale," Bureau of the Census, U.S. Department of Commerce. Series C-25.

to support the median-priced *existing* home.[17] Declining production, shrinking real income, and the tendency of builders to produce higher-priced homes have severely limited the number of new homes available to middle- and moderate-income families. Low-income people face even bleaker prospects. Their rents and utility costs are climbing, yet they have virtually no place to go.

24. Another important economic factor is the availability and cost of housing credit. High interest rates substantially increase the cost of housing and often lead to a downturn in housing production. For example, the increase in the cost of buying a $25,000 home at ten percent interest rather than six percent is $19,800 over the life of a twenty-five-year mortgage.[18] National monetary policy must insure an adequate supply of affordable credit for socially desirable purposes such as housing.

25. The number, intensity, and durability of these economic downturns in housing point out the necessity for fresh approaches. More efficient use of land and materials must be sought through the use of attached dwellings, planned unit developments, and other innovations.

26. The focus of the housing crisis is shifting from problems associated with the *condition* of the structure to problems associated with the *cost* of housing. It is not that the problem of substandard housing has been solved, although progress has been made. Rather, the impact of economic factors has become so great that they must now become the central focus of efforts to remedy our housing problems.

B. Neighborhoods

27. Housing conditions cannot be separated from the surrounding environment. City services, education, community cohesiveness, safety, government responsiveness, and taxation policies are critical factors in the creation and maintenance of decent housing.

28. In our view, the key element in the deteriorating urban environment is the decline of neighborhoods. In the past, the neighborhood has played a critical role in the lives of its residents. More recently, neighborhoods have lost some of their influence and importance. Centralized decision making, suburban migration, deteriorating city services, and the loss of ethnic identity have contributed to this decline and resulted in less responsibility for local concerns. A psychological and physical process of abandonment has set in, and fewer resources and people have been available to assist neighborhoods in combating blight and indifference.

---

[17]"Availability of Homes for Middle-Income Families." *Op. cit.,*
[18]Interest on a $25,000 mortgage, payable in twenty-five years, at six percent, is $23,300; at ten percent, $43,100.

29. Our cities are composites of smaller communities. Strong neighborhoods are the cornerstone of strong cities, and decent housing is a critical factor in the survival and viability of neighborhoods.

30. We applaud the renewed interest in neighborhoods by those who live in them and govern them. The neighborhood is the most logical basis for a positive housing policy. We hope that recognition of this fact will be translated into policies and provide neighborhoods with the tools and resources necessary to survive. The local parish has a critical role to play in the revitalization of neighborhoods. Effective use of revenue-sharing and community development funds can be a step in promoting neighborhood recovery.

C. Disinvestment

31. We are particularly concerned about the abundant evidence of "redlining" or disinvestment. This is the practice by which financial institutions deny or restrict mortgage and home improvement loans in particular areas. This practice often becomes a self-fulfilling prophecy leading to the rapid decline of a neighborhood or community. Where it exists, it must be condemned; discrimination based on geography is as destructive as other forms of discrimination. We must insure fair and equal access to available credit.

32. We urge banks and savings and loan associations to meet their responsibilities in central city areas. We commend financial institutions which have chosen to intensify programs of investment in these neighborhoods. We support the principle of disclosure of lending patterns. Savers and consumers are entitled to information about the lending practices and patterns of the institutions seeking their business. We also urge individual depositors and those responsible for Church funds to encourage a responsible and sensitive lending policy on the part of the financial institutions which they patronize.

D. Racial and Economic Segregation

33. There are disturbing signs of increased racial and economic segregation in urban areas. We deplore discrimination, still present in our society, against persons because of their race, economic status, sex, or religion. Such attitudes contradict the Christian belief in the equality and inherent dignity of all people and they must be opposed.

34. Central cities are increasingly becoming islands of economic hardship populated by the elderly, racial and ethnic minorities, and the working poor. The eroding tax base of cities follows the trend of suburban migration. Exclusionary zoning continues as a major factor which limits housing opportunities for low- and middle-income families and minority persons in suburban areas. In addition to these economic hurdles, many persons still find their housing choice limited by discriminatory practices in the sale or rental of housing. Suburban communities must recognize and act on their responsibilities without utilizing improper zoning, overly rigid building codes, onerous referendum requirements, or other barriers to avoid contact with the less affluent.

35. Continued vigilance is necessary in the struggle to expand equal housing opportunity. We take this occasion to renew our support, expressed in 1966, for:

> Sound programs to assure equal housing opportunities for all, without discrimination of race, creed, or color. Here is a unique chance for responsible dialogue, for learning from successes and failures, and thus constructing harmonious communities in every part of the nation.[19]

36. The uniqueness of neighborhoods and diversity of communities are healthy signs. We have a pastoral responsibility to respond creatively to questions of ethnicity and race. Positive ethnic identity, whether it be Black-American, Hispanic-American, Irish-American, Italian-American, or any other, recognizes the worth of the individual and respects his or her particular cultural heritage and lifestyle.

37. However, heightened awareness of ethnic background cannot be allowed to lead to exclusionary practices or intergroup competition. Rather, a healthy sense of cultural pluralism should lead to a greater ability to interact with neighbors of different backgrounds in a positive way.

38. The housing needs of racial minorities remain critical and the unfulfilled dream of open housing cannot be abandoned. An absence of racial discrimination is no longer enough. We must insist upon effective programs to remedy past injustice.

E. Rural Housing

39. The housing crisis is often thought of as a predominantly urban problem. This misconception has resulted in unfortunate consequences for rural people. According to 1970 Census figures, thirty percent of Americans live outside metropolitan areas; at the same time, over sixty percent of all overcrowded housing or units without plumbing are in rural areas and small towns.[20] The housing crisis is at least as severe in rural areas as in urban centers.

40. The housing delivery system is inadequate in many small towns and rural areas. Almost half of all rural counties have no public housing agency. In addition, many rural areas do not have sufficient con-

---

[19]"On Poverty and Race Relations." United States Catholic Conference. November 1966.
[20]"General Housing Characteristics for the United States: 1970." *Op. cit.*, pp. 1-53.

struction or financial institutions which make private development feasible. While some progress has been made, disparities remain.

41. Economic factors also account for widespread housing deprivation in rural areas. The gap between housing costs and income is even wider in rural communities than in cities. Only one rural family in twenty can afford the median-priced newly constructed home. In recent years, one-third of all new housing units in rural areas have been mobile homes.

42. The simple fact is that neither rural people nor rural communities have the resources to solve their housing problems without outside assistance. It is clear that too often national housing policy has neglected rural areas.

F. Special Needs

43. Several groups in our society have particularly severe housing problems. The poor suffer disproportionately in this regard. They lack the income and economic resources to acquire and maintain adequate housing. Rising rents and utility costs, as well as a decline in the availability of low-cost housing, have intensified their problems. Four out of five families with incomes below $5,000 suffer some form of housing deprivation.[21]

44. Many elderly people have special housing problems resulting in part from their small fixed incomes, growing isolation, rising property taxes, and housing maintenance costs. New approaches to housing maintenance and health care are needed to enable the elderly to remain in their own homes and communities. Present government housing programs for the elderly do not begin to meet the need. A recent survey of federal housing for the elderly revealed that, for every senior citizen in an apartment for the elderly, there is another on a waiting list for such an apartment. The average waiting time is over twenty months.[22]

45. Migrant farmworkers also suffer serious housing deficiences. Their high mobility, low income, and regular periods of unemployment seriously hamper their efforts to obtain decent shelter. The housing available in migrant farm labor camps is often deplorable, yet effective enforcement of housing standards is rare.

46. The high levels of poverty and unemployment among Native Americans in both rural and urban areas have seriously affected their ability to acquire good housing. On Indian reservations the problems are particularly severe. Two-thirds of the housing on reservations either lacks adequate plumbing or is overcrowded. Most lending institutions are reluctant to make loans to Native Americans whose res-

---

[21]"America's Housing Needs: 1970 to 1980." *Op. cit.*, pp. 4-12.
[22]Senate Subcommittee on Housing for the Elderly, July 1975.

ervation land is held in federal trust. In addition, housing assistance is often caught in the bureaucratic maze surrounding the provision of services on Indian reservations.

47. People with physical handicaps often experience difficulty in obtaining suitable housing at a cost they can afford. The planning and construction of housing often restrict it to able-bodied people. Architectural barriers are often put in the way of handicapped people in conventional housing as well as public buildings and accommodations.

48. Housing policy must be more sensitive to the needs of these particular groups, whose problems have too often been neglected or intensified by past housing practices.

G. Housing Stock

49. The existing housing stock of nearly 70 million units is perhaps the largest single component of our national wealth. According to the 1970 Census, 27.4 million of these units are more than thirty years old. We must act now to preserve and maintain this valuable resource or it will be abandoned and lost to us.

50. Too often older housing has been allowed to simply deteriorate. Conservation of existing housing must be encouraged by modifying tax and fiscal policies which penalize those who seek to maintain and rehabilitate existing housing. These approaches can help preserve part of our housing supply and prevent the destruction and large-scale displacement of people which marked earlier urban renewal efforts.

51. Rehabilitation and housing maintenance programs which are innovative, imaginative, and economically feasible should be encouraged and implemented. The preservation of existing housing is an essential and economical approach to meeting our housing goal.

H. The Resource of Land

52. There is increasing awareness of limitations of land and resources and the implications of these limitations on efforts to house our citizens. Since only a fixed amount of land is available and housing needs are growing, legitimate questions may be raised regarding the amount of land a person owns, the manner in which the land is used, and regulation of land ownership by society.

53. The principle of stewardship discussed earlier has specific application to this question. As Pope Paul said in *Populorum Progressio*:

> . . . Private property does not constitute for anyone an absolute and unconditional right. No one is justified in keeping for his exclusive use what he does not need, when others lack necessities. In a word, according to the traditional doctrine, as found in the Fathers of the

Church, and the great theologians, "the right to property must never be exercised to the detriment of the common good.[23]

54. Land speculation is a particularly vexing problem. Where basic human rights are concerned, one person simply must not take an unreasonable gain at the expense of another. Huge increases in the cost of land, resulting in part from such speculation, seriously impair efforts to provide affordable housing to people of low and moderate income.

55. The demand for land to meet a variety of competing growth needs, such as urban expansion, highway and mineral development, parks and recreation, is forcing upon us difficult decisions with respect to the use and control of our land resources. The decisions can no longer be left to the private market alone to resolve. Since land use decisions are characteristically irreversible and hold consequences for the nation as a whole, they should be opened to some degree of public participation. Legislation is urgently needed to facilitate such participation.

V. Governmental Housing Activity

56. The federal government has for decades exerted a major influence upon the production and consumption of housing. Its involvement in the housing field is intricate and tangled, including economic and taxation policies, regulation of mortgage financing, as well as provision of housing subsidies.

57. Since decent housing is a human right, its provision involves a public responsibility. The magnitude of our housing crisis requires a massive commitment of resources and energy. Government must supplement and regulate the activities of private individuals and institutions in order to achieve our housing goals. A creative partnership of private enterprise and government is necessary. Public agencies have a particular responsibility to aid those in need as well as to oversee the development of a comprehensive housing and community development policy.

58. Fiscal and monetary policy has a dominant influence on housing. The rise and fall of inflation, employment, and productivity are felt to a pronounced degree in the housing market. Monetary policy, the availability and rate of credit, are likewise critical factors in the system of housing production and consumption.

59. Beyond these broad economic policies, the federal government utilizes two basic approaches in housing: indirect subsidies to homeowners through the tax system and direct subsidies to producers and consumers of housing.

---

[23] *Populorum Progressio*, 23. Paul VI. March 1967.

A. Indirect Action

60. Indirect housing subsidies through the tax system make up the largest share of federal housing activity. In 1972, federal housing expenditures and tax subsidies rose to a level of $15 billion of which only $2.5 billion went for direct housing subsidy programs. This indirect tax subsidy consists primarily of the deduction of mortgage interest and property taxes by homeowners. It is estimated that this deduction alone will cost $11.3 billion in 1976.

61. The higher a person's income, the more likely it is that he will be entitled to this kind of subsidy, and the higher the subsidy is likely to be.[24] In 1972, less than five percent of the taxpayers with incomes below $5,000 were entitled to this kind of subsidy, as against more than eighty percent of all taxpayers with incomes above $20,000.[25] This means:

(a) Four out of five households with incomes over $20,000 received housing subsidies through the tax systems.

(b) Only one out of twenty households with incomes below $5,000 received this form of housing subsidy.

In addition, it is estimated that in 1976:[26]

(a) The one percent of the population with incomes over $50,000 will receive more than ten percent of both direct and indirect housing subsidies (an estimated $1.4 billion in 1976).

(b) The fourteen percent of the population with incomes below $3,000 will receive less than seven percent of either direct or indirect housing subsidies ($0.9 billion).

62. We do not quarrel with the objectives of these policies. The use of tax incentives to achieve desirable social goals (i.e., home ownership) can be appropriate, but it inevitably raises questions of equity which must be addressed through public policy.

B. Direct Housing Programs

63. Since the 1930s, the federal government has used seven basic approaches to provide more direct forms of assistance to builders and consumers of housing.

(1) Mortgage insurance, begun during the Great Depression, enabled millions of middle-income families to buy homes with long-term, low down payment mortgages.

---

[24] In 1973, 112,000 people with incomes below $3,000 claimed these subsidies, and the average subsidy was twenty-three dollars. At the other end of the income scale, 118,000 people with incomes of $100,000 or more claimed these subsidies and the average subsidy was more than one hundred times the subsidy for the low-income person: $2,449.

[25] *Housing in the Seventies.* Report of the Department of Housing and Urban Development (HUD). (Washington, 1973). Pp. 2-8.

[26] By the National Rural Housing Coalition. Washington, D.C., 1975.

(2) Insurance of bank deposits and purchase of mortgages from private institutions—sometimes with a subsidy—have provided a flow of credit into housing and sustained construction during periods of tight money.

(3) Low interest rates for rental and sales housing have been direct subsidy programs since 1968. Under these programs, the federal government can reduce interest costs, thus substantially lowering the monthly cost to the consumer.

(4) Public housing is the oldest direct housing subsidy program. Begun in 1937, it provides for building, buying, or renting housing by local housing authorities. Over one million public housing units are occupied primarily by families with incomes below $4,000.

(5) Block grants recently have been made available to assist local communities in their efforts to provide adequate community development.

(6) Housing assistance payments to families and individuals are currently being tested as a new approach to the housing problems of low-income people.

(7) Large-scale leasing of housing units is a relatively new and untested approach to assist low-income people in gaining decent housing.

64. The Department of Housing and Urban Development (HUD) is responsible for administering a variety of programs in metropolitan areas across the country. The Farmer's Home Administration serves rural areas with direct lending and other programs. In the past, many of these federal programs were designed to encourage the participation of nonprofit housing development corporations. A large number of these have been established by religious organizations or community groups.

65. Currently, the federal government relies almost exclusively on its leased housing program to meet national housing needs. This is not enough. The housing crisis requires a variety of tools responsive to the many dimensions of housing need. No single program will be the answer. Programs which might be improved and used as effective vehicles for the production of housing should not be abandoned. The country needs a firm commitment by the federal government to meet our housing goal. The agencies charged with this duty must move forcefully and creatively to meet their responsibilities. Adequate funds and administrative staff must be made available to them. The free market, acting alone, cannot supply a sufficient quantity of low- and moderate-income housing to meet our needs. A new commitment of will and resources is needed if we are to make progress in providing "a decent home and suitable living environment" for all Americans.

C. *Local and State Activity*

66. Local governments control housing development through zoning and building codes and the provision of such community facilities as streets or roads, water, sewers, schools, and health and recreation centers. Many communities with older housing also have housing codes which set basic standards for all existing housing.

67. Unfortunately, on some occasions these local controls have been used to exclude minorities and the less affluent from communities and to evade common responsibilities for housing and community development. On a more positive note, however, many communities have initiated housing rehabilitation and construction programs aimed at providing adequate housing at costs which low- and middle-income people can afford.

68. Recently, many state governments have set up housing finance agencies or departments of community affairs. They assist local communities with advice and resources, sometimes providing financial assistance, and often using federal subsidy programs to help local groups.

69. These local and state efforts to provide greater housing opportunities for all our people are encouraging and should be expanded. We urge state and local governments to develop sensitive and responsible policies regarding land use and zoning disputes. We also hope local governments will use their new community development funds to assist the victims of housing deprivation.

VI. The Role of the Catholic Community

70. The Catholic community has a responsibility to act effectively to help meet the needs of those who lack adequate housing. We must confess that we have not done all we could. It is not enough for us to point to the reality of poor housing and recommend that government and other institutions take appropriate action. We must also reflect on our own responsibilities and opportunities for action. We call on individual Catholics, dioceses, and parishes, as well as other Catholic organizations, to join us in a new commitment to those who suffer from poor housing.

71. The Church alone cannot provide a significant quantitative answer to the cries for better housing. This is not its specific role, nor does it have the financial and technical resources to build all the required homes. However, it is our responsibility to proclaim the Gospel of Jesus Christ and its implications for our society. We must analyze in a competent and critical manner the aspects of housing which pertain to social justice. We must point constantly to human rights—and human suffering—involved in this issue. We must apply Christian social teaching to the resolution of the problem. We must seek to have a qualitative impact on the problem of housing deprivation in our society by attempting to change the systems and the policies that result in housing deprivation. There seem to be five possible approaches for Church involvement in housing: awareness, advocacy, providing services, stewardship, and community-building.

A. Awareness

72. The first element of the Church's response is building awareness of the extent of the housing crisis and our participation in it. Christ's concern for those in need is an essential dimension of our faith. The Catholic community must remind itself and all others that indecent housing is a moral and ethical issue demanding a response.

73. We cannot be at peace with ourselves while so many of our brothers and sisters suffer from inadequate housing. We are often unconscious participants in the systems that result in poor housing. All of us, through our involvement in the community, can assist in the development of humane and just policies pertaining to a shelter. We encourage individual Catholics to join and support organizations which have demonstrated a sincere and effective concern for better housing for all people.

74. Particular persons have particular responsibilities. Those who own rental property must maintain and manage it in a way that provides decent, sanitary, and safe housing. Landlords must respect the human dignity and rights of tenants and observe the principles of justice in setting their rents. Tenants must cultivate a respect for property and their neighbors and meet their financial obligations. Those employed in the housing field should seek to encourage a sensitive response on the part of private industry, labor unions, and government agencies.

75. We urge parishes and organizations within the Catholic community to undertake programs to promote understanding of housing problems and the role each of us might play in meeting those needs.

B. Advocacy

76. As an advocate, the Church should analyze housing needs in the light of the Gospel, make judgements, and offer suggestions. On the national level, we should attempt to educate people regarding the demands of justice in the area of housing and suggest principles upon which proposals for change might be based. We should also involve ourselves in the ongoing dialogue over housing policy and underline the moral dimensions of the problem.

77. The United States Catholic Conference will continue to monitor and participate in the development of housing and community development policy. In line with the following principles we shall encourage governmental action that:

(1) Affirms and advances the realization of the national housing policy of "a decent home and suitable living environment for all American families."

(2) Provides a variety of programmatic tools and sufficient resources to meet the housing needs of low- and moderate-income families, including the continued participation of nonprofit, community-based housing corporations.

(3) Focuses programs and resources on the special needs of the following: low-income people, rural Americans, the elderly, farmworkers, Native Americans, and the handicapped.

(4) Adapts our housing delivery system to meet the economic realities of inflation, recession, and unemployment.

(5) Recognizes the central role of the neighborhood in the survival of viable urban areas by encouraging rehabilitation and reinvestment in central cities.

(6) Encourages land use policies that provide for adequate planning and effective controls on unreasonable and wasteful development and speculation.

(7) Encourages a monetary policy and credit allocation system that provides a sustained supply of affordable credit for housing production.

(8) Encourages the integral participation of housing consumers and tenants in decisions regarding housing at local, regional, and national levels.

(9) Encourages equal housing opportunity, within a framework of cultural pluralisms, through voluntary compliance and, where necessary, legal remedies.

78. We applaud the involvement of the National Conference of Catholic Charities, the National Catholic Rural Life Conference, and the Interreligious Coalition for Housing in this area. We hope to work in collaboration with them and other groups in advancing these principles.

79. The same responsibility for action exists on the local and regional levels. We encourage local and regional organizations to work with their people and political leaders to achieve these same ends.

80. The parish is the setting for perhaps the most important Catholic response to poor housing. With its roots deep in the community, the parish can play a critical advocacy role regarding the housing problems of its people. Working with individuals, community organizations, and members of the private sector, it can harness its own resources and energies to combat decay, blight, and indifference. Parish programs of rehabilitation and housing maintenance could be initiated. In addition, parishes can join with others to utilize government programs and monitor public and private efforts to alleviate poor housing.

81. Through education and involvement, the local church can help its people gain a wider measure of justice in the area of housing.

C. Providing Services

82. The Catholic Church in this country has a long tradition of providing services to those in need. Our concern must also extend to the shelter needs of people.

83. Many dioceses, Catholic charities, and parishes have already sponsored the development of housing for low-income people and the elderly, or have initiated rehabilitation programs. Using federal programs, Catholic institutions and organizations have provided a substantial amount of housing for low- and middle-income people and for the elderly. A 1974 survey of sixty dioceses conducted by the National Housing and Human Development Alliance indicated that more than 25,000 units have been built under Catholic sponsorship in the past ten years. Over twenty congregations of religious men and women are involved in housing, with 2,600 units already constructed.

84. We strongly support these efforts and are deeply impressed by what has been achieved thus far. Given the compelling need for new housing, we believe there is an important role for nonprofit developers willing to sponsor viable and creative housing where the private market is unable or unwilling to build.

85. This special "housing ministry" requires sensitivity and adequate technical expertise. Housing sponsorship inspired by Christian values should bring a qualitative difference to housing. The housing development motivated by Christian concern must reflect a lively awareness of human need and the dignity of the person in its treatment of tenants, in its relationship to the local community, in its planning, location, and employment practices.

86. There are a variety of other social and human services relating to shelter: housing management, education in tenant rights and responsibilities, financial and personal counseling, housing and appropriate services provided by Catholic organizations and individuals.

87. Providers of housing services should endeavor to involve tenants and the local community in an integral way in housing management and the provision of services. Housing sponsorship and management under Church auspices should provide models for others. This housing ministry must be encouraged, for it offers us an opportunity to act on our principles and give witness of our concern for the poorly housed.

D. Stewardship

88. In proclaiming the principle of stewardship, we must take note of the fact that the Church is also an institution possessing land, economic, and personnel resources. While speaking to other organizations about the promotion of human rights and social justice, the Church must examine its own conscience and actions to determine if its efforts and use of resources are just. In the 1971 synod document, *Justice in the World*, the bishops state:

> While the Church is bound to give witness to justice, she recognizes that anyone who ventures to speak to people about justice must first be just in their eyes. Hence we must undertake an examination of the modes of acting and of the possessions and lifestyle found within the Church itself.[27]

89. In the particular area of housing, we might take an inventory of our property and real estate, reflect upon its utilization, and examine how it might better be put at the service of those who lack adequate shelter. We might also consider how we could make better use of our economic and personnel resources to assist those who need housing. In addition, a review of our investment policies may indicate how we might better harness our economic resources to assist in resolving the housing crisis.

E. Community Building

90. The alienation and isolation in our communities are important components of the housing problem. This more subtle concern is central to the resolution of the housing crisis. The Church is called to reconcile people with God and with one another, to bring them into a community of mutual support and love. We have noted that the Church must identify with the needs and aspirations of the community it serves. The Church should encourage the development of community organizations, neighborhood institutions, and programs concerned with housing. As Pope Paul VI pointed out in *A Call To Action*:

> There is an urgent need to remake at the level of the street, of the neighborhood, the social fabric whereby man may be able to develop the needs of his personality. Centers of special interest and of culture must be created or developed at the community and parish levels with different forms of associations, recreational centers, and spiritual and community gatherings where the individual can escape from isolation and form anew fraternal relationships.[28]

---

[27] *Justice in The World*. November 1971.
[28] *A Call To Action*, 11. Pope Paul VI. May 1971.

91. It is important to recognize that historically neighborhoods often developed side by side with the growth of the local parish. If the neighborhood is the foundation stone of the city, it is obvious that the local parish plays a critical role in many neighborhoods. Often in rural areas and small towns a similar relationship exists between the local church and the community.

92. This fact imposes great responsibilities and provides important opportunities for the local church. With the encouragement of the local diocese, Catholic parishes in urban areas should seek out a creative pastoral role in the development of sound and healthy neighborhoods. In metropolitan and rural areas alike, parishes must develop a ministry of "community-building," helping to identify and resolve serious problems through education and participation in the life of the community. It should encourage its members to become informed and involved in community affairs and housing issues.

93. The parish itself should join with other community groups and churches to gain greater housing opportunities for all people. Traditionally, the Catholic parish has rendered a major service in meeting the educational needs of communities; it should now also attempt to meet other critical human needs, including the need of a decent home and a suitable living environment.

VII. Conclusion

94. The dimensions of the crisis in housing seem overwhelming in the number of people and communities affected, the complexity of the problem, and the magnitude of the effort required to meet our housing needs. There is a temptation to feel discouraged in the face of this situation.

95. However, we do not address this crisis to emphasize the difficulty, but to issue a challenge. The greatest obstacle is apathy and indifference. We ask all those in our society—individuals, private enterprise, government, social and religious organizations—to reexamine what role they might play in eliminating poor housing in our nation. Responsibility for this problem has been passed from one segment of the community to another for too long. We pray that this Statement will not further divide, but rather unite us in a common effort to meet our housing needs. For our part, we pledge to work with others in a renewed effort to promote awareness and action on the housing crisis. Shared responsibility, ecumenical coordination, and cooperation with any group sharing our concern will mark our housing activities.

96. We are hopeful. We have faith in the basic values of people. We believe that once they understand the nature and extent of housing problems and their moral responsibility, they will respond with individual and collective action to meet housing needs. They believe, as we do, that every person has a right to a decent home in a decent environment.

97. Our hope flows from the core of the Gospel: new life springs from suffering and death. We believe our cities and rural areas can be resurrected and bloom again with renewed vitality and community life. As the prophet said:

> They shall rebuild the ancient ruins,
>   the former wastes they shall raise up
> And restore the ruined cities,
>   desolate, now for generations.
>   Is 61:4.

98. Our faith tells us that men and women are called by God to continue the work of creation, to fashion a better, more just society as we wait for the coming of the Kingdom of God. Effective action for decent housing is an essential dimension of this continuing creation.

99. This is a time for renewed dedication and action. Decent housing for all our people is a moral imperative. We pledge our support to those who carry out the demand of the traditional corporal work of mercy, "to shelter the homeless."

100. We are not suggesting a project or a program for this year or the next, nor are we calling for a reassertion of a public policy already declared, but never realized. What we are proposing is a long and determined effort, with all its frustrations, toward a better life for millions of Americans. This task is more than an element of a better society or an aspect of the common good; it is indispensable to the future health of America and its people.

101. In this undertaking, we summon our fellow Catholics and all who recognize this pressing concern to a task that calls for intelligence, resiliency, and unremitting vigor. We will find allies in this work, and we must welcome them; we will find foes who think our dream utopian and unrealizeable, and we must persuade them. The one thing we cannot do is to acknowledge the immoral situation of indecent, inadequate housing and do nothing about it. We seek in this Statement to initiate a fresh response to the unanswered pleas for help that come from the oppressed, neglected, and forgotten. We pledge our continuing efforts as we set out on the long road that offers a lasting hope for decent shelter to this nation and its people.

Statement on Catholic-Jewish Relations

A Statement Issued by the
National Conference of Catholic Bishops

November 20, 1975

1. Ten years have passed since the Second Vatican Council promulgated its statement on the Jewish people (*Nostra Aetate, no. 4*). This decade has been a period unique in Catholic-Jewish relations. The vantage point of ten years later provides a timely opportunity for the Catholic Church in the United States to recall, reaffirm, and reflect on the principles and teachings of the conciliar document, and to evaluate their implementation in our country.

2. For this task, we welcome the new *Guidelines and Suggestions for Implementing Nostra Aetate, no. 4* issued in January of this year by the Commission for Religious Relations with the Jews recently established by the Holy See. And we are reminded of the still very applicable programs recommended by the *Guidelines for Catholic-Jewish Relations* which our National Conference of Catholic Bishops issued in 1967. We are gratified that the latter have been highly regarded, especially in the Jewish community, and that some of their recommendations anticipated portions of the new *Guidelines* of the Holy See and also of several diocesan documents.

3. These two documents, themselves fruits of *Nostra Aetate, no. 4* elucidate the conciliar declaration, considerably extend its perspectives, and broaden the paths it opened. Both are eloquent testimonies to the new horizons the Second Vatican Council succeeded in bringing into Catholic view.

4. These ten years make it clear that *Nostra Aetate, no. 4* initiated a new era in Catholic-Jewish affairs. Calling for "fraternal dialogue and biblical studies" with Jews, it ended a centuries-long silence between Church and Synagogue. An age of dialogue was begun. Conversations between Catholics and Jews proliferated rapidly in many forms. Productive meetings took place on every level, from the highest intellectual exchanges to the most popular types of social gatherings, often referred to as "living room dialogues." Our own Bishops' Conference was among the first to form a national commission which sought to implement the Council document. Even before the close of the Second Vatican Council in 1965, the United States bishops had decided to establish a commission in the National Conference of Catholic Bishops to promote Catholic-Jewish understanding, and in 1967 the first full-time Secretariat for Catholic-Jewish relations was in operation.

5.   Since that time, the Secretariat has maintained fruitful contact with the major groups within the Jewish community and has been in regular communication with the dioceses of the country. Many dioceses have followed the example of our Conference and have established Commissons or Secretariats for Jewish-Catholic relations. Numerous projects have been undertaken, including, for example, a careful and systematic analysis of Catholic teaching texts in order to eliminate offensive references to Jews and replace them with materials showing Judaism in a positive light. Numerous theological discussions have been undertaken and Catholic collaboration with the Jewish community has resulted in a variety of social action programs. We are pleased to observe that many of these initiatives have been emulated on the unofficial level by many individuals and groups across the country who have shown admirable sensitivity, dedication, and expertise in promoting Catholic-Jewish amity.

6.   We do not wish to convey the impression that all our problems are behind us. There still exist areas of disagreement and misunderstanding which create tensions in both communities. We hope that the difficulties can be resolved to some degree in amicable discussion. Certainly the Catholic view on aid to nonpublic schools should be the subject of serious dialogue and concern. We are pleased that this and other exchanges have already been held on important subjects of disagreement, and it is our hope that progress will be made in mutual understanding by furthering this dialogic method.

7.   Recalling past centuries, however, invites a sobering evaluation of our progress and warns against becoming overconfident about an early end to remaining problems. Those were centuries replete with alienation, misunderstanding, and hostility between Jews and Christians. While we rejoice that there are signs that anti-Semitism is declining in our country, conscience compels us to confront with candor the unhappy record of Jewish sufferings, both past and present. We make our own the statement of *Nostra Aetate*, ". . . for the sake of her common patrimony with the Jews, the Church decries hatred, persecutions, displys of anti-Semitism staged against Jews at whatever time in history and by whomsoever" and we reaffirm with the new Vatican *Guidelines* that "the spiritual bonds and historical links binding the Church to Judaism condemn (as opposed to the very spirit of Christianity) all forms of anti-Semitism . . ." We urge all in the Church who work in the area of education, whether in the seminary, the school, or the pulpit, not only to avoid any presentation that might tend to disparage Jews or Judaism but also to emphasize those aspects of our faith which bear witness to our common patrimony and our spiritual ties with Jews.

8.   Much of the alienation between Christian and Jew found its origins in a certain anti-Judaic theology which over the centuries has led not

only to social friction with Jews but often to their oppression. One of the most hopeful developments in our time, powerfully assisted by *Nostra Aetate*, has been the decline of the old anti-Judaism and the reformation of Christian theological expositions of Judaism along more constructive lines.

9.   The first major step in this direction was the repudiation of the charge that Jews were and are collectively guilty of the death of Christ. *Nostra Aetate* and the new *Guidelines* have definitely laid to rest this myth which has caused so much suffering to the Jewish people. There remains, however, the continuing task of ensuring that nothing which in any way approaches the notion of Jewish collective guilt should be found in any Catholic medium of expression or communication. Correctly viewed, the disappearance of the charge of collective guilt of Jews pertains as much to the purity of the Catholic faith as it does to the defense of Judaism.

10.   The Council's rejection of this charge against Jews has been interpreted by some commentators as an "exoneration" of the Jewish people. Such a view of the matter still persists. The truth is that the Council acknowledged that the Jewish people never were, nor are they now, guilty of the death of Christ.

11.   *Nostra Aetate* was a new beginning in Catholic-Jewish relations and, as with all beginnings, we are faced with the task of revising some traditional understandings and judgments. The brief suggestions of the Council document have been taken up by some theologians, but their implications for theological renewal have not yet been fully explored. We therefore make a few recommendations in line with two themes of the document: the Jewish origins of the Church and the thought of St. Paul.

12.   Christians have not fully appreciated their Jewish roots. Early in Christian history, a de-Judaizing process dulled our awareness of our Jewish beginnings. The Jewishness of Jesus, of his mother, his disciples, of the primitive Church, was lost from view. That Jesus was called Rabbi; that he was born, lived, and died under the Law; that He and Peter and Paul worshipped in the Temple—these facts were blurred by the controversy that alienated Christians from the Synagogue. How Jewish the Church was toward midpoint of the first century is dramatically reflected in the description of the "Council of Jerusalem" (Acts 15). The question at issue was whether Gentile converts to the Church had to be circumcised and observe the Mosaic Law. The obligation to obey the Law was held so firmly by the Jewish Christians of that time that miraculous visions accorded to Peter and Cornelius (Acts 10) were needed to vindicate the contrary contention that Gentile Christians were not so obliged. By the third century, however, a de-Judaizing process had set in which tended to undervalue the Jewish origins of the Church, a tendency that has surfaced from time to time in devious ways throughout Christian history. Some catechists, homilists, and teachers still convey little appreciation of the Jewishness of that heritage and rich spirituality which we derive from Abraham, Moses, the prophets, the psalmists, and other spiritual giants of the Hebrew Scriptures.

13. Most essential concepts in the Christian creed grew at first in Judaic soil. Uprooted from that soil, these basic concepts cannot be perfectly understood. It is for reasons such as these that *Nostra Aetate* recommends joint "theological and biblical studies" with Jews. The Vatican *Guidelines* of 1975 encourage Catholic specialists to engage in new research into the relations of Judaism and Christianity and to seek out "collaboration with Jewish scholars." The renewal of Christian faith is the issue here, for renewal always entails to some extent a return to one's origins.

14. The Council document cites St. Paul, particularly in chapters nine to eleven of his letter to the Romans. We find in these rediscovered, precious chapters, Paul's love for his kinsmen and a firm basis for Christian reverence for the Jewish people. Admittedly, Paul's theology of Judaism has its more negative aspects; they have been adequately emphasized over the centuries in Catholic teaching. It would be well today to explore and emphasize the positive elements of Paul's thought that have received inadequate attention.

15. In these chapters, Paul reveals his deep love of the Jewish people. He tells of his willingness to accept damnation itself for the sake of his kinsmen (9:3), even though he also expresses his painful disappointment and incomprehension of Israel's failure to accept Jesus as its Messiah. Crucial to an understanding of his admiration of the Jewish people and to a Christian understanding of their situation is the following text. Written at the midpoint of the first century, Paul refers to his "kinsmen according to the flesh who are Israelites, who have the adoption as sons, and the glory and the covenants and the legislation and the worship and the promises; who have the fathers, and from whom is the Christ according to the flesh" (9:3-5), thus making clear the continuing validity of Israel's call. Paul, moreover, insists that God has by no means rejected his people. "Is it possible that God has rejected his people? Of course not. I, an Israelite descended from Abraham through the tribe of Benjamin, could never agree that God has rejected his people, the people he chose specially long ago" (11:1-2). What proof does Paul offer for the enduring validity of Israel's relationship to God even after the founding of the Church? "God never takes back his gifts or revokes his choice" (11:29).

16. Paul warns fellow Christians against showing contempt for the Jewish people by reminding them that they (Christians) are wild branches grafted into the olive tree itself to share its life. ". . . Remember that you do not support the root: it is the root that supports you" (11:18). And he invites his listeners to a love of the Jews, since they are "still loved by God for the sake of their ancestors" (11:28).

17. In effect, we find in the Epistle to the Romans (9-11) long-neglected passages which help us to construct a new and positive attitude toward the Jewish people. There is here a task incumbent on theologians, as yet hardly begun, to explore the continuing relationship of the Jewish people with God and their spiritual bonds with the New Covenant and the fulfillment of God's plan for both Church and Synagogue.

18. To revere only the ancient Jewish patriarchs and prophets is not enough. The all too common view of Judaism as a legalistic and decadent form of religion that lost all significance with the coming of Christ and all vitality after the destruction of the Temple has lingered on in the Christian centuries. The 1975 *Guidelines* put us on guard against such a view and urge us to see post-biblical Judaism as rich in religious values and worthy of our sincere respect and esteem. The *Guidelines*, in fact, discourage us from attempting to define the Jews in exclusively Christian terms, explicitly stating, "Dialogue demands respect for the other as he is" (Part 1). Again, "Christians must therefore strive to acquire a better knowledge of the basic components of the religious tradition of Judaism; they must strive to learn by what essential traits the Jews define themselves in the light of their own religious experience" (Introduction).

19. In dialogue with Christians, Jews have explained that they do not consider themselves as a church, a sect, or a denomination, as is the case among Christian communities, but rather as a peoplehood that is not soley racial, ethnic, or religious, but in a sense a composite of all these. It is for such reasons that an overwhelming majority of Jews see themselves bound in one way or another to the land of Israel. Most Jews see this tie to the land as essential to their Jewishness. Whatever difficulties Christians may experience in sharing this view, they should strive to understand this link between land and people which Jews have expressed in their writings and worship throughout two millenia as a longing for the homeland, holy Zion. Appreciation of this link is not to give assent to any particular religious interpretation of this bond. Nor is this affirmation meant to deny the legitimate rights of other parties in the region, or to adopt any political stance in the controversies over the Middle East, which lie beyond the purview of this Statement.

20. On this tenth anniversary of *Nostra Aetate*, we reaffirm our wholehearted commitment to the principles of that document as well as to the directives of the *Guidelines* of 1975. Aware of the magnitude of the task before us and of the excellence of the many practical guidelines and suggestions contained in the documents, we urge that special attention be given to the following exhortations:

(1) That all dioceses, according to their needs and circumstances, create and support whatever instrument or agency is appropriate for carrying out the recommendations of *Nostra Aetate, no. 4*, the Vatican

Guidelines of 1975, and the American Bishops' *Guidelines for Catholic-Jewish Relations* of 1967.

(2) That homilists and liturgists pay special attention to the presentation and interpretation of Scripture so as to promote among the Catholic people genuine appreciation of the special place of the Jewish people as God's first-chosen in the history of salvation and in no way slight the honor and dignity that is theirs.

(3) That Catholic scholars address themselves in a special way to the theological and scriptural issues raised by those documents which deal with the relationships of the Church with Judaism.

21. We are firm in our faith that the God of Abraham, Isaac, and Jacob and He whom we consider Israel's fairest Son will sustain us in this holy endeavor.

Resolution on Farm Labor

A Statement Issued by the
National Conference of Catholic Bishops

November 20, 1975

1. June 5, 1975, marked an important turning point in the history of farm labor relations in the United States. It was on that day that the California Agricultural Labor Relations Act was signed into law by Governor Edmund G. Brown, Jr. This is the first law ever enacted in any jurisdiction, federal or state, guaranteeing farm workers the right to determine, by secret ballot elections, which union, if any, they want to represent them. It is a good law and one that might well serve as a model for parallel legislation in other key agricultural states as well as at the congressional level in Washington. While it will not automatically resolve all of the problems involved in the farm labor dispute, it does provide the parties with a set of enforceable procedures through which they can begin, at long last, to settle their differences in an orderly manner. In short, it represents an historic step in the right direction.

2. We salute the innovative leadership of Governor Brown who set into motion the process which resulted in the enactment of this long overdue statute by an overwhelming vote of the California legislature and with the almost unanimous support of the parties involved. We sincerely congratulate all who participated in this process: members of the legislature, the many and varied grower organizations, the United Farm Workers of America, the Western Conference of Teamsters, and the technical advisors and consultants who helped to draft the statute.

3. We call upon all concerned—state officials, growers, and union representatives—to cooperate with one another in implementing the spirit as well as the letter of the law. It would be a tragedy if the purpose of the law, which holds out such promise for the future of sound labor relations in the agricultural industry, were to be thwarted in practice, for whatever reason. If experience demonstrates that either the statute itself or its administration needs to be improved, we pledge our support to this end. The National Conference of Catholic Bishops stands prepared to cooperate with the parties to the fullest possible extent in their common effort to bring about a new era of peace and justice in the agricultural industry, not only in California but throughout the nation.

Resolution on Human Life Foundation

A Statement Issued by the
National Conference of Catholic Bishops

November 20, 1975

1. Just over six years ago, the Human Life Foundation was established to encourage scientific research in natural family planning, and to promote educational efforts that would enable married couples to use responsibly those natural methods of family planning "whose safeness has been proven and whose harmony with the moral order has been ascertained (*Constitution on the Church in the Modern World*, #87). The foundation was the first of its kind in the entire world, and has played a major role in generating international interest and worldwide scientific research.

2. The National Conference of Catholic Bishops takes this occasion to recognize with approval and appreciation the dedicated work of the board of directors, the advisory committees, and the staff of the Human Life Foundation. We realize that those associated with the foundation have made generous sacrifices of time, energy, and personal interest to pursue the goals of the foundation, and we recognize the significant achievements that have resulted.

3. The work of the foundation is far from complete, and the accomplishments of the past generate a new spirit of confidence and a renewal of hope for future activities.

4. In recognition and appreciation of the work of the foundation, we pledge our continued support, encouragement, and collaboration to insure that the work so effectively begun will continue and lead to more successful achievements in the years ahead. The work of the Human Life Foundation, in which we are proud to have a part, will considerably advance the welfare of marriage and the family, by leading those who are skilled in the sciences—notably the medical, biological, social, and psychological—to pool their efforts in perfecting the natural methods of family planning so as to explain more thoroughly the various conditions favoring a proper regulation of births (cf., *Constitution on the Church in the Modern World*, #52).

Resolution on New York City

*A Resolution Passed by the Administrative Board
of the United States Catholic Conference*

November 1975

1. The current crisis facing the 8 million people of New York City is more than a fiscal crisis. It is a human crisis as well; it involves people and their health and welfare. Moreover, it is not just a problem of one city or one state. It is part of a larger urban crisis confronting many American cities and threatening the common good and dignity of many millions of our fellow citizens.

2. We are convinced that default and bankruptcy are not adequate answers. Default will mean that human life in New York City will be seriously damaged. Municipal services will be paralyzed. Assistance in human services for the poor and the sick, the young and the aged, will all but cease to exist. Hospitals may well have to suspend their services, furlough their staffs, and discharge their patients. Nursing homes and senior citizen centers are also in jeopardy. Schools, day care centers, and child care facilities may not be able to survive.

3. We are not unaware of the many factors which have contributed to New York City's problems. The dire effects of recession and inflation—the loss of thousands of jobs, the erosion of tax base and the costs of municipal and human services to sustain the less fortunate—have all contributed to the problem. We are also aware of the serious charges that poor judgments, over-spending, political opportunism and, at times, inefficient management have all played their part and must be corrected. Specific steps in this direction have already been taken.

4. We call upon our national leaders and the people of the nation to share our concern for the people of New York City; as just and equitable solutions are sought, there is no room for sectionalism and partisanship.

5. Therefore, we earnestly urge that the Congress enact and the President sign appropriate loan guarantee legislation for the City of New York. This legislation should be designed to avert default by the City and the adverse economic and social consequences that would result for the people of New York. We support these guarantees in order to provide sufficient time for the City to make the necessary program and financial adjustments to restore the City to financial stability.

Political Responsibility: Reflections on an Election Year

*A Statement of the Administrative Board
of the United States Catholic Conference*

February 12, 1976

1. This year marks the two hundredth anniversary of the founding of our republic with its remarkable system of representative democracy. It is also a year that will test the workings of this democracy. A national election is a time for decisions regarding the future of our nation and the selection of our representatives and political leaders. As pastors and teachers, we address this Statement on political responsibility to all Americans in hopes that the upcoming elections will provide an opportunity for thoughtful and lively debate on the issues and challenges that face our country as well as decisions on the candidates who seek to lead us.

I. Public Responsibility and the Electoral Process

2. We call this year a test of our democratic institutions because increasing numbers of our fellow citizens regard our political institutions and electoral processes with indifference and even distrust. Two years ago, only thirty-six percent of those eligible voted in the national congressional elections; in contrast, forty-six percent voted in 1962. In 1972, only half of the eligible citizens exercised their right to vote, down from a peak of sixty-three percent in 1960. This trend—and the alienation, disenchantment, and indifference it represents—must be reversed if our government is to truly reflect the "consent of the governed."

3. Abuses of power and a lack of governmental accountability have contributed to declining public confidence, despite significant efforts to uncover and redress these problems. Equally important, government has sometimes failed to deal effectively with critical issues which affect the daily lives of its citizens. As a result, many persons caught in the web of poverty and injustice have little confidence in the responsiveness of our political institutions. This discouragement and feeling of powerlessness are not limited to the poor who feel these most intensely, but affect many social groups, most alarmingly the young and the elderly. This leads to a loss of human resources, talent, and idealism which could be harnessed in the work of social and national progress.[1]

4.   However, we believe that the abandonment of political participation is neither an effective nor a responsible approach to the solution of these problems. We need a committed, informed, and involved citizenry to revitalize our political life, to require accountability from our political leaders and governmental institutions, and to achieve the common good. We echo the words of Pope Paul VI who declared: "The Christian has the duty to take part in the organization and life of political society."[2] Accordingly, we would urge all citizens to register to vote, to become informed on the relevant issues, to become involved in the party or campaign of their choice, to vote freely according to their conscience, in a word, to participate fully in this critical arena of politics where national decisions are made.

5.   Certain methods used in political campaigns sometimes have intensified this disaffection. We call on those seeking public office to concentrate on demonstrating their personal integrity, their specific view on issues, and their experience in public service. We urge a positive presentation of their programs and leadership abilities. In this way, they can contribute to a campaign based on vital issues, personal competence, and real choices which will help to restore confidence in our electoral process.

II. The Church and the Political Order

6.   It is appropriate in this context to offer our own reflections on the role of the Church in the political order. Christians believe that Jesus' commandment to love one's neighbor should extend beyond individual relationships to infuse and transform all human relations from the family to the entire human community. Jesus came to "bring good news to the poor, to proclaim liberty to captives, new sight to the blind and to set the downtrodden free" (Lk 4:18). He called us to feed the hungry, clothe the naked, care for the sick and afflicted, and to comfort the victims of injustice (Mt 25). His example and words require individual acts of charity and concern from each of us. Yet they also require understanding and action upon the broader dimensions of poverty, hunger, and injustice which necessarily involve the institutions and structures of economy, society, and politics.

7.   The Church, the People of God, is itself an expression of this love, and is required by the Gospel and its long tradition to promote

---

[1]Joint Economic Committee Hearings, October 20, 1975; *New York Times,* February 1, 1976; *Wall Street Journal,* February 2, 1976.
[2]*A Call to Action,* Pope Paul VI, 24, 1971.

and defend human rights and human dignity.[3] The 1971 Synod of Bishops declared that action on behalf of justice is a "constitutive dimension" of the Church's ministry and that, "the Church has the right, indeed the duty, to proclaim justice on the social, national, and international level, and to denounce instances of injustice, when the fundamental rights of man and his very salvation demand it."[4] This view of the Church's ministry and mission requires it to relate positively to the political order, since social injustice and the denial of human rights can often be remedied only through governmental action. In today's world, concern for social justice and human development necessarily require persons and organizations to participate in the political process in accordance with their own responsibilities and roles.

8. The Church's responsibility in the area of human rights includes two complementary pastoral actions: the affirmation and promotion of human rights and the denunciation and condemnation of violations of these rights. In addition, it is the Church's role to call attention to the moral and religious dimensions of secular issues, to keep alive the values of the Gospel as a norm for social and political life, and to point out the demands of the Christian faith for a just transformation of society.[5] Such a ministry on the part of every Christian and the Church inevitably involves political consequences and touches upon public affairs.

9. Christian social teaching demands that citizens and public officials alike give serious consideration in all matters to the common good, to the welfare of society as a whole, which must be protected and promoted if individual rights are to be encouraged and upheld.

10. In order to be credible and faithful to the Gospel and to our tradition, the Church's concern for human rights and social justice should be comprehensive and consistent. It must be formulated with competence and an awareness of the complexity of issues. It should also be developed in dialogue with other concerned persons and respectful of the rights of all.[6]

11. The Church's role in the political order includes the following:

(a) education regarding the teachings of the Church and the responsibilities of the faithful;

(b) analysis of issues for their social and moral dimensions;

(c) measuring public policy against Gospel values;

(d) participating with other concerned parties in debate over public policy;

---

[3]*Human Rights and Reconciliation*, Synod of Bishops, 1974.
[4]*Justice In The World*, Synod of Bishops, 1971.
[5]*Justice In The World*, ibid.
[6]*A Call To Action*, op. cit., 4, 50. *The Church In The Modern World*, Second Vatican Council, 43, 1965.

(e) speaking out with courage, skill, and concern on public issues involving human rights, social justice, and the life of the Church in society.

12. Unfortunately, our efforts in this area are sometimes misunderstood. The Church's participation in public affairs is not a threat to the political process or to genuine pluralism, but an affirmation of their importance. The Church recognizes the legitimate autonomy of government and the right of all, including the Church itself, to be heard in the formulation of public policy. As Vatican II declared:

> By preaching the truth of the Gospel and shedding light on all areas of human activity through her teaching and the example of the faithful, she [the Church] shows respect for the political freedom and responsibility of citizens and fosters these values. She also has the right to pass moral judgments, even on matters touching the political order, whenever basic personal rights or the salvation of souls make such judgments necessary.[7]

13. A proper understanding of the role of the Church will not confuse its mission with that of government, but rather see its ministry as advocating the critical values of human rights and social justice.

14. It is the role of Christian communities to analyze the situation in their own country, to reflect upon the meaning of the Gospel, and to draw norms of judgment and plans of action from the teaching of the Church and their own experience.[8] In carrying out this pastoral activity in the social arena, we are confronted with complexity. As the 1971 Synod of Bishops pointed out: "It does not belong to the Church, *insofar as she is a religious and hierarchical community*, to offer concrete solutions in the social, economic, and political spheres for justice in the world"[9] (emphasis added). At the same time, it is essential to recall the words of Pope John XXIII:

> . . . it must not be forgotten that the Church has the right and duty not only to safeguard the principles of ethics and religion, but also to intervene authoritatively with her children in the temporal sphere when there is a question of judging the application of these principles of concrete cases.[10]

15. The application of Gospel values to real situations is an essential work of the Christian community. Christians believe the Gospel is the measure of human realities. However, specific political proposals do not in themselves constitute the Gospel. Christians and Christian organizations must certainly participate in public debate over alternative policies and legislative proposals, yet it is critical that the nature

---

[7]*The Church In The Modern World, op. cit.,* 76.
[8]*A Call To Action, op. cit.*
[9]*Justice In The World, op. cit.*
[10]*Pacem in Terris,* Pope John XXIII, 160, 1963.

of their participation not be misunderstood.

16. We specifically do not seek the formation of a religious voting bloc; nor do we wish to instruct persons on how they should vote by endorsing candidates. We urge citizens to avoid choosing candidates simply on the personal basis of self-interest. Rather, we hope that voters will examine the positions of candidates on the full range of issues as well as the person's integrity, philosophy, and performance. We seek to promote a greater understanding of the important link between faith and politics and to express our belief that our nation is enriched when its citizens and social groups approach public affairs from positions grounded in moral conviction and religious belief. Our view is expressed very well by Pope Paul VI when he said:

> While recognizing the autonomy of the reality of politics, Christians who are invited to take up political activity should try to make their choices consistent with the Gospel and, in the framework of a legitimate plurality, to give both personal and collective witness to the seriousness of their faith by effective and disinterested service of men.[11]

17. The Church's responsibility in this area falls on all its members. As citizens we are all called to become informed, active, and responsible participants in the political process. The hierarchy has a responsibility as teachers and pastors to educate the faithful, support efforts to gain greater peace and justice, and provide guidance and even leadership on occasion where human rights are in jeopardy. The laity has major responsibility for the renewal of the temporal order. Drawing on their own experience and exercising their distinctive roles within the Christian community, bishops, clergy, religious, and laity should join together in common witness and effective action to bring about Pope John's vision of a well ordered society based on truth, justice, charity, and freedom.[12]

18. As religious leaders and pastors, our intention is to reflect our concern that politics—the forum for the achievement of the common good—receive its rightful importance and attention. For, as Pope Paul VI said, "politics are a demanding manner—but not the only one—of living the Christian commitment to the service of others."[13]

III. Issues

19. Without reference to political candidates, parties, or platforms, we wish to offer a listing of some issues which we believe are central

---

[11] *A Call To Action, op. cit.*, 46.
[12] *Pacem In Terris*, Pope John XXIII, 35, 1963.
[13] *A Call To Action, op. cit.*

to the national debate this year. These brief summaries are not intended to indicate in any depth the details of our positions in these matters. We wish to refer the reader to fuller discussions of our point of view in the documents listed in the summary which appears below. We wish to point out that these issues are not the concerns of Catholics alone; in every case we have joined with others to advocate these concerns. They represent a broad range of topics on which the bishops of the United States have already expressed themselves and are recalled here in alphabetical order to emphasize their relevance in a period of national debate and decision.

A. Abortion

20. The right to life is a basic human right which should have the protection of law. Abortion is the deliberate destruction of an unborn human being and therefore violates this right. We reject the 1973 Supreme Court decisions on abortion which refuse appropriate legal protection to the unborn child. We support the passage of a constitutional amendment to restore the basic constitutional protection of the right to life for the unborn child (*Documentation on the Right to Life and Abortion, 1974; Pastoral Plan on Pro-life Activities, 1975*).

B. The Economy

21. Our national economic life must reflect broad values of social justice and human rights. Current levels of unemployment are unacceptable and their tremendous human costs are intolerable. We support an effective national commitment to genuine full employment. Our strong support of this human right to meaningful employment is based not only on the income it provides, but also on the sense of worth and creativity a useful job provides for the individual. We also call for a decent income policy for those who cannot work and adequate assistance to those in need. Efforts to eliminate or curtail needed services and help in these difficult economic times must be strongly opposed (*The Economy: Human Dimensions, 1975*).

C. Education

22. All persons of whatever race, condition, or age, by virtue of their dignity as human beings, have an inalienable right to education.
23. We advocate:

(1) Sufficient public and private funding to make an adequate education available for all citizens and residents of the United States of America and to provide assistance for education in our nation's program of foreign aid.

(2) Governmental and voluntary action to reduce inequalities of educational opportunity by improving the opportunities available to economically disadvantaged persons.

(3) Orderly compliance with legal requirements for racially integrated schools.

(4) Voluntary efforts to increase racial and ethnic integration in public and nonpublic schools.

(5) Equitable tax support for the education of pupils in public and nonpublic schools to implement parental freedom in the education of their children (*To Teach as Jesus Did*, Nov. 1972).

D. Food Policy

24. The "right to eat" is directly linked with the right to life. This right to eat is denied to countless numbers of people in the world. We support a national policy in which:

(a) U.S. world food aid seriously combats hunger and malnutrition on a global basis, separates food aid from other considerations, gives priority to the poorest nations, and joins in a global grain reserve.

(b) U.S. domestic food programs meet the needs of hungry and malnourished people here in America, provide strong support for food stamps to assist the needy, the unemployed, the elderly, and the working poor, and strive to improve and to extend child nutrition programs.

(c) U.S. agricultural policy promotes full production and an adequate and just return for farmers (*Food Policy and The Church: Specific Proposals*, 1975).

E. Housing

25. Decent housing is a basic human right. A greater commitment of will and resources is required to meet our national housing goal of a decent home for every American family. Housing policy must better meet the needs of low- and middle-income families, the elderly, rural areas, and minorities. It should also promote reinvestment in central cities and equal housing opportunity. Preservation of existing housing stock and a renewed concern for neighborhoods are required (*The Right to a Decent Home*, 1975).

F. Human Rights and U.S. Foreign Policy

26. Human dignity requires the defense and promotion of human rights. Many regimes, including communist countries and some U.S. allies, violate or deny their citizens' human and civil rights, as well as religious liberty. Internationally, the pervasive presence of American power creates a responsibility to use that power in the service of human rights. In the face of regimes which use torture or detain political prisoners without legal recourse, we support a policy which gives greater weight to the protection of human rights in the conduct of U.S. affairs (*Resolution on the 25th Anniversary of the U.N. Universal Declaration of Human Rights*, 1973).

G. Mass Media

27. We are concerned that the communications media be truly responsive to the public interest. We strongly oppose government control over television programming policy, but we deplore unilateral decision making by networks. We urge that broadcasters, government, private business, and representatives of the viewing public seek effective ways to ensure accountability in the formulation and implementation of broadcast policy. We recommend exploring ways to reduce the commercial orientation of the broadcasting industry to better serve the public (*Statement on the Family Viewing Policy*, 1975).

H. Military Expenditures

28. The arms race continues to threaten humanity with universal destruction. It is especially destructive because it violates the rights of the world's poor who are thereby deprived of essential needs, and it creates the illusion of protecting human life and fostering peace. We support a policy of arms limitation as a necessary step to general disarmament which is a prerequisite to international peace and justice (*U.S. Bishops on the Arms Race*, 1971 Synod).

29. This is not an exclusive listing of issues of concern to us. We are also concerned about issues involving the civil and political rights of racial and ethnic groups, women, the elderly, and working families. We support measures to provide health care for all of our citizens and the reform of our criminal justice system. We are concerned about protection of the land and the environment as well as the monumental question of peace in the world.

IV. Conclusion

30. In summary, we believe the Church has a proper role and responsibility in public affairs flowing from its Gospel mandate and its concern for the human person and his or her rights. We hope these reflections will contribute to a renewed sense of political vitality in our land, both in terms of citizen participation in the electoral process and the integrity and accountability of those who hold and seek public office.

31. We pray that Christians will follow the call of Jesus to provide the "leaven" for society (Mt 13:34; Lk 13:20), and heed the appeal of the Second Vatican Council:

> To enlighten one another through honest discussion, preserving mutual charity and caring above all for the common good . . . to be witnesses to Christ in all things in the midst of human society.[14]

---

[14] *The Church In The Modern World, op. cit.,* 43.

Society and the Aged:
Toward Reconciliation

A Statement of the
Catholic Bishops of the United States

May 5, 1976

I. The Aged

1. America today faces a great paradox: It is an aging nation which worships the culture, values, and appearance of youth. Instead of viewing old age as an achievement and a natural stage of life with its own merits, wisdom, and beauty, American society all too often ignores, rejects, and isolates the elderly.

2. In an increasingly mobile nation, where the single-generation family as well as the extended family is weakened, the elderly often find themselves cut off from their families and their communities; about fourteen percent of elderly men and forty-one percent of elderly women live alone or with nonrelatives. Even large numbers of elderly persons not lacking for material goods find themselves unwanted and out of place.

3. Society has come to take a negative view of the elderly. This can be seen in the increasing tendency of families to rely on institutions to care for their elderly members, and in repeated efforts by some government officials to cut services and benefits for the elderly in order to ease the burden of inflation on the rest of society.

4. Society's negative image of the elderly reinforces their own negative self-image. The result of this unfortunate process is a tragically wasted human resource. The elderly are denied their God-given right to develop their potential to the fullest at every stage of life; at the same time, society is denied the fruits of that development.

5. In rejecting the elderly, we do more than perpetuate injustice: When we reject any stage of human life, we are in effect rejecting a part of ourselves and our connections with the human community. Perhaps we react to the elderly as we do because they are an unwanted reminder of our own mortality.

6. The biblical commandment to "Honor your father and mother" (Dt 5:16) reminds us that, above all else, the family ought to be a place of love, respect, and caring for the aging members of society. But often this is not the case. Many elderly people are physically, culturally, psychologically, and spiritually isolated from their families and the rest of society; equally as important, society has become

isolated from this group which composes ten percent of its membership.

7. The break between generations is weakening our values as a nation
and creating a form of discrimination—against the elderly—which
parallels more widely recognized forms of discrimination against
minorities, women, the poor, or the unborn.

8. Such a wound demands healing. Such a separation calls for reconciliation. This requires a rethinking of personal attitudes in the light
of Gospel values. Our first task is to restore to the elderly the dignity
and sense of worth which they deserve.

9. As religious people and followers of Jesus, Who calls us to reconciliation and love, we must pledge ourselves, our communities,
our influence, and our prayers to bringing about this reconciliation
between society and its elderly.

II. Human Rights and the Elderly

10. The elderly do not forfeit their claim to basic human rights because
they are old. But a brief look at the plight of many elderly people
shows that they are in fact being denied those rights. The reconciliation we seek begins with recognition of our responsibilities to the
elderly to insure their dignity and worth so that they can enjoy their
God-given rights. As Pope John has said:

> Every man has the right to life, to bodily integrity, and to the means
> which are suitable for the proper development of life; these are
> primarily food, clothing, shelter, rest, medical care, and finally the
> necessary social services. Therefore, a human being also has the
> right to security in cases of sickness, inability to work, widowhood,
> old age, unemployment, or in any other case in which he is deprived
> of the means of subsistence through no fault of his own (Pope John
> XXIII, *Peace on Earth*).

A. The Right to Life

11. The right to life is the most basic human right in the sense of
being the precondition for realization of all the others. But the right
to life of the elderly is under constant attack, both direct and indirect.

12. On one level, the elderly, along with the sick and the handicapped, are the targets of a "mercy killing" mentality which would
dispose of the unwanted. Even well-meaning legislative efforts to
cope with complex questions about when and when not to use
extraordinary technological and therapeutic means to preserve life
post genuine dangers, particularly since some would place fateful
decisions solely in the hands of physicians or the state.

13. A more subtle, although no less serious, threat to the right to life of the elderly is a social system which, by ignoring their poverty, loneliness, and despair, denies them the means and sometimes the very will to live.

14. Sociologists tell us we are nearing a time when the elderly will be divided into the "Young-Old," age fifty-five to seventy-five, and the "Old-Old," over seventy-five. The "Young-Old" will be a relatively healthy group, capable of entering second careers and influencing social patterns. The "Old-Old" will feel more clearly that they are simply awaiting death. As President Kennedy once said: "It is not enough to add new years to life; our objective must be to add new life to those years."

15. The elderly have a right to "new life": not just to material survival, but to education, recreation, companionship, honest human emotions, and spiritual care and comfort.

16. Finally, in reflecting upon the right to life of the elderly, one must note that in America women live longer than men. There are one hundred forty-three women over age sixty-five for every one hundred men. To talk of the problems of the elderly, then, is to talk in particular of the problems of elderly women who in their declining years may feel more painfully than ever the burdens of society's discrimination against women.

B. The Right to a Decent Income

17. The elderly, often living on fixed incomes, are among those who suffer disproportionately from society's economic ills of recession and inflation. The costs of food, medical care, and housing (including fuel) have risen much more sharply than overall consumer price increases; moreover, these areas take up some seventy percent of the income of the elderly, as opposed to less than sixty percent of the income of the nonaged.

18. Some twenty-two percent of the elderly have incomes below the 1971 federal poverty level and half have incomes below $5,000. Social Security and Supplemental Security Income payments, in these circumstances, remain inadequate to maintain a decent standard of living. Inflation eats away at the value of savings. Many of the elderly do not have pensions, and there are serious problems in existing pension plans.

C. The Right to a Job

19. Polls reveal that eighty-five percent of the American people are opposed to mandatory retirement ages; these often force able-bodied people out of their jobs when they still have much to offer and need the satisfaction of a meaningful job. Older workers are frequently forced out of work by technological change and are handicapped in seeking new employment by discrimination on the basis of age. A recession at any time may force many older workers into premature retirement which can be spiritually and financially draining.

20. Even those elderly who are not seeking remuneration for work are under-utilized: Some two million elderly Americans willing to do volunteer work do not have such opportunities available.

D. The Right to Health Care

21. Health care is a basic right, but it is often regarded as an expensive luxury. Despite passage a decade ago of Medicare, millions of elderly people still lack adequate medical care.

22. The percentage of health care costs for the elderly paid by Medicare has dropped in recent years and will probably continue to drop. Medicare does not pay for preventive health care, which means that many elderly persons will develop health problems unnecessarily and will receive treatment only when their problems become serious.

23. In addition, Medicare does not pay for such necessities as prescription drugs, eyeglasses, hearing aids, dentures, or dental care, all of which become extraordinarily expensive when measured against the income of most elderly persons.

24. Although only five percent of the elderly live in institutions, nursing home care is a serious problem. Well-publicized scandals have arisen concerning the operations of some nursing homes, where patient care is sacrificed while operators amass huge profits. Large numbers of elderly people are institutionalized needlessly for want of simple services, such as visiting nurses or homemakers, which would help them remain in their homes.

25. Mental health care for the elderly is even more inadequate than physical health care. An estimated one-third of the elderly in mental hospitals are there because they have nowhere else to go. Physical illnesses such as diabetes, anemia, or simply over-medication may produce behavior patterns in the elderly which are mistaken for senility.

E. The Right to Eat

26. A 1971 Administration Task Force on Aging declared that the elderly are the most severely malnourished group in society. Poor nutrition is a major factor in the incidence of poor health among them.

27. The food stamp program, hot meals program, and other efforts are a help to the elderly, but they still do not reach all those in need. The elderly are also threatened by new food stamp proposals. Some would increase the amount the elderly must pay for food stamps or create unreasonable assets limitations which would force them either to forfeit food stamps or sell their valuables, possibly their homes;

other proposed regulations determining food stamp benefit levels could result in a decrease in benefits for many of the elderly.

28. Inadequate income is not the only reason why many of the elderly have poor diets. Lack of proper kitchen facilities, nutrition education, or simple lack of companionship and incentive to eat are also factors.

F. The Right to a Decent Home

29. America has a severe housing shortage which, like other economic problems, affects the elderly more than most. Forty percent of the elderly live in homes which lack such facilities as central heating, hot water, or inside toilets. (Seventy-seven percent of the elderly live in rural areas.)

30. Many elderly persons live in homes they own as the result of a lifetime of work, but are threatened with losing their homes because of waning physical strength, rising fuel and maintenance costs, and regressive property taxes.

31. Housing is particularly important to the elderly because they are often virtually trapped in their homes by lack of transportation and fear of crime.

32. Less than half of those over sixty-five are licensed to drive. Many, particularly those in rural areas, do not have access to mass transportation, which is often costly when it is available.

33. The elderly, particularly in urban areas, live in fear because of their particular vulnerability to such crimes as burglary and mugging, as well as "white-collar" crimes such as price-fixing and fraud.

G. The Right to Equal Treatment

34. Members of minority groups in America face special discrimination at all age levels. Minority elderly persons suffer discrimination on account of their race in addition to their age, their poverty, and often their sex.

35. A serious problem facing some minority elderly is a language barrier which may prevent them from obtaining medical and social services to which they are entitled. The same barrier may prevent them from participating in the social and recreational life of their communities and neighborhoods or the liturgical life of their churches.

III. The Role of the Church

36. The Church is many things—a community of faith, a community of individuals and families, and a voice in civil society. If the Church is to help reconcile society and the elderly, it must act in all these roles. The elderly look to the Church for strength and assistance.

They want the Church to be a community where they experience the comfort of the forgiving Lord, and the hope of the risen Lord. The elderly need the concern, joy, and presence of a caring Christian community.

A. As Individuals

37. No institutional effort can be successful unless we examine our own individual attitudes and actions. We must ask ourselves how we treat the elderly in our own families and communities.

38. Do we treat them with the respect and dignity which they deserve? Do we try to draw out the best in them and share ourselves with them? Do we carry our fair share of their financial support? Do we make an effort to try to understand and meet their special needs? Are we kind and patient?

B. As Families

39. The family is the basic unit of any community and is itself an expression of love. We cannot emphasize enough the critical role of the family in caring for their aging loved ones and keeping them in their midst as valuable, contributing members. The family is where the elderly feel most comfortable and accepted. We call on each family to weigh carefully its obligation to care for an elderly father or mother, uncle or aunt.

40. Should elderly family members require a form of institutionalization, the obligations of the family remain. Responsibility for their well-being cannot be left to health care professionals and social service agencies alone. Often, only relatives and friends can provide the love and personal attention that humanize the sometimes lonely experience of institutional care.

C. As a Community

41. We take pride in the fact that the Catholic community has always made special efforts to care for the elderly; but we also acknowledge with humility that there is much still to do.

42. One valuable task which can be performed at the parish level is simply to locate the "hidden" elderly in order to bring them into parish and community life and help them obtain community and government services to which they may be entitled but which they do not receive.

43. Parish structures offer many opportunities for leadership in helping the elderly: community dining rooms, "day care," home visits, and telephone reassurance services; car pools and other transportation aids; recreation; continuing education programs.

44. We must not only help continue the education of the elderly. We must guarantee effective education for all age groups about the aging process, the rights of the elderly, and their potential for more active and satisfying lives.

45. Catholic hospitals and other health care institutions have a special responsibility in meeting the needs of the elderly, as do all forms of Church social service agencies.

46. More coordination of services and outreach are needed in diocesan as well as local programs. There are special needs and opportunities in the areas of low-cost housing, supervised housing, transportation, and job training. Many dioceses have already sponsored low-income housing programs for the elderly. We support these efforts and encourage wider participation in low-income housing programs by other dioceses and religious orders.

47. The Church at all levels has a responsibility to seek out the elderly for their input into policy decisions and to provide them with opportunities for meaningful work, both as employees and volunteers.

48. The Church also must make provisions for retired priests and religious to live in a dignified manner. Special attention must be given to communities of religious women, which face particular financial hardship in caring for retired sisters. Adequate pension plans for all Church employees are essential.

D. As Public Policy Advocates

49. In this Statement, we have called on individuals, families, the Church, and community groups to assist the elderly in realizing their human rights and living decent lives. We also recognize, however, that some problems require the attention of society as a whole, through legislative and governmental action.

50. We must raise our voices clearly and effectively as advocates for the elderly on public policy matters. Elderly people cannot compete with well-financed interest groups for national resources; like other basically powerless groups, the elderly stand to lose the most in times of economic crisis.

51. Many of the needs of the elderly will only be met adequately when the needs of others are met through a national policy guaranteeing full employment, a decent income for those unable to work, equitable tax legislation, and comprehensive health care for all. But a number of significant steps can be taken in the interim:

(a) Continued opposition to euthanasia and "death with dignity" legislation which gives undue power to the state or to physicians.

(b) A thorough review of the Social Security system to insure its continued stability.

(c) Continued opposition to cutbacks or ceilings on the Social Security cost-of-living index for the elderly which reflects actual increases in their living expenses.

(d) Reform of Medicare to provide coverage for preventive care, dental care, prescription drugs, devices such as eyeglasses and hearing aids, and increased and more readily available home health care services to allow the elderly to avoid unnecessary institutionalization.

(e) Establishment of stricter standards for nursing homes and strict enforcement of those standards.

(f) Opposition to food stamp program changes which would penalize the elderly.

(g) Expanded nutrition, education, job training, and recreation programs for the elderly.

(h) Special efforts to meet the transportation needs of the elderly.

(i) More low-income housing for the elderly. We strongly endorse continued congressional expansion and administration backing of the very successful Section 202 program. We further urge that the interest for Section 202 loans be set at the lowest possible rate:

(a) Continued reform of the pension system and wider availability of pensions.

(b) A higher priority for mental health care for the elderly.

(c) An end to age discrimination in hiring and flexibility in setting retirement ages.

(d) Special attention to programs to reduce crime against the elderly.

IV. Toward Reconciliation

52. Healing the rupture between society and its elderly members requires a major effort to change attitudes as well as social structures. In undertaking this task, we are not simply meeting the demands of charity and justice. We are accepting our own humanity, our link with past and future and, thereby, our link with the Creator. To do this is to add new life to the final stages of growth because Christ said, "I have come that they may have life and have it to the full" (Jn 10:10).

Political Responsibility
A Resolution of the Catholic Bishops of the United States

A Statement Issued by the
Catholic Bishops of the United States

May 6, 1976

1. The United States stands in the midst of an important national election year, a time for debate on national issues and decisions about our political leadership. We are deeply concerned that increasing numbers of voters seem to be choosing not to participate in this process out of distrust, apathy, or indifference. Two years ago, only thirty-six percent of those eligible voted in the national congressional elections, in contrast, forty-six percent voted in 1962. In 1972, a presidential election year, only half of the eligible citizens exercised their right to vote, down from a peak of sixty-three percent in 1960. This trend—and the alienation, disenchantment, and indifference it represents—must be reversed if our government is to reflect truly the "consent of the governed."

2. We therefore wish on this occasion to urge all citizens to participate fully in the political life of our country. We encourage them to register to vote, to become informed on the relevant issues, to become involved in the party or campaign of their choice, and to vote freely according to their consciences.

3. As part of its mission, the Church, the People of God, is required by the Gospel and its long tradition to promote and defend human rights and dignity. This view of the Church's ministry and mission requires it to relate positively to the political order, since social injustice and the denial of human rights can often be remedied only through governmental action.

4. The administrative board of the American bishops at its February 1976 meeting, adopted an important statement, *Political Responsibility: Reflections On An Election Year*. In this Statement, the board discussed the responsibility of the Church toward political life, called for a "thoughtful and lively debate" on the issues that face our country, and listed a broad range of issues central to that debate. In each case, these are matters which we have already addressed in major policy positions, and we ask interested persons to examine these statements for our specific views. These issues as listed in our earlier statement include: abortion, the economy, education, food policy, housing, human rights and foreign policy, mass media, and military expenditures.

5.   As citizens we are all called to become informed, active, and responsible participants in the political process. Drawing on their own experience and exercising their distinctive roles within the Christian community, bishops, clergy, religious, and laity should join together in common witness and effective action to bring about a society based on truth, justice, charity, and freedom. It is by participation of citizens in our democratic process that we can hope to move toward such a society.

Teach Them

A Statement Issued by the
Catholic Bishops of the United States

May 6, 1976

1. Jesus commanded His disciples to "go and teach all nations." From a tiny upper room, by the Spirit, He sent them. With fire in their hearts He sent them. To every nation and age He sent them. From those early apostolic days the flame has been passed. In the two hundred years of our own nation's history we can point with pride to St. Elizabeth Seton, Blessed John Neumann, to countless families who by their sense of educational mission answered the same call. The disciples of times past did not take Jesus' command lightly, even though they went with light hearts and willing hands into His vineyard, the world. In this time and place, we believe no other answer, now or at any future moment, is acceptable for a people who bear within them that same faith. The only worthy response is a wholehearted "yes" to the Lord's command to "go and teach."

2. As faithful servants responding to His command, we seek to meet the needs of all who hear Jesus' message or may do so. Our 1972 Pastoral, *To Teach as Jesus Did*, declared our support for Catholic education in its totality: schools, parish catechetical programs, campus ministry, young adult education, family life education, adult education. That commitment stands. In this Statement we are specifically concerned with the Church's educational ministry to children and young people, especially as it is expressed in Catholic schools.

3. A total of 8.6 million Catholic youth in this country are now enrolled in formal religious education programs, 3.5 million in Catholic schools and 5.1 million in parish catechetical programs. But, as a report published earlier this year shows, 6.6 million (3.4 million at the elementary and 3.2 million at the secondary level), more than twice the number a decade ago, now are not enrolled in formal religious education programs. In our opinion this is as much a pastoral problem as an educational one. Its solution will require additional data, thorough research and analysis, responsible decisions, and an appropriate program of action.

4. In the meantime, it is obvious that all persons with a responsibility for the Church's educational ministry—to one degree or another that means all members of the Catholic community—should reach out to these 6.6 million. This suggests some immediate steps: e.g., diocesan and parish censuses; more adult, parent, and family education; vigorous recruitment for Catholic schools and parish catechetical programs; more effective use of Catholic and other communications media for evangelization and religious education; completion of the National Cathechetical Directory; sensitive dialogue with persons who are critical of some methods of religious education; zealous contact with parents who have abandoned much of the active practice of their faith. Indeed, alienation and lack of interest among some parents may well be reasons why a substantial number of the 6.6 million children and youth are not receiving formal religious education. Coping adequately with this problem will require much time and effort.

5.   Our immediate and continuing concern is to provide the best possible education for children and young people in and out of Catholic schools. With respect to parish catechetical programs, many of the innovations and improvements of recent years deserve to be recognized and put more widely into effect.

6.   As we have said, however, our focus here is primarily upon the schools. We wish to declare our belief in their future, to offer renewed encouragement to all our collaborators in the school apostolate, to call attention to signs of progress and hope, to point to new areas for investigation and action, and to do all this in a spirit of realistic hopefulness.

7.   The remarkably positive response which has greeted *To Teach as Jesus Did* is especially heartening. Actions taken in light of its vision have done much to strengthen the Church's educational ministry. In this response we have discerned the providential working of the Spirit. The Pastoral Letter continues to afford many reasons for encouragement and confidence.

8.   Four years ago we reaffirmed our commitment to Catholic schools; we now do so again. For we hold that "Catholic schools which realize the threefold purpose of Christian education, to teach doctrine, to build community, and to serve, are the most effective means available to the Church for the education of children and young people."[1]

9.   The integration of religious truth and values with the rest of life, which is possible in these schools, distinguishes them from others. Here the Catholic, for whom religious commitment is a matter of central importance, finds an appreciation of religion which parallels his or her own. The integration is expressed above all in the lives of the teachers in Catholic schools whose daily witness to the meaning of mature faith and Christian living has a profound impact upon the education and formation of their pupils. On behalf of the entire Church we affirm our debt to these dedicated ministers of education, sisters, brothers, priests, and lay people, who teach by what they are.

---

[1] *To Teach as Jesus Did* (Washington, D.C.: National Conference of Catholic Bishops, November 1972), #101.

10. Our support of Catholic schools is matched by the support of millions of others, those who teach in them, who send their children to them, and who support them morally and financially. The present task seems to be less to win support for the schools than to mobilize the support which already exists.

11. Why do we and so many others continue to support Catholic schools in the face of many obstacles and burdens, problems not substantially different from those we outlined in our Pastoral four years ago? The reasons are compelling. Generally these schools are notably successful educational institutions which offer not only high quality academic programs but also instruction and formation in the beliefs, values, and traditions of Catholic Christianity. They are significantly effective in preparing students for life in today's Church and society. They instill in children and young people indispensable discipline of mind and heart. They have a highly positive impact on adult religious behavior.[2]

12. Another benefit of Catholic schools deserves mention. They can be a focal point for dedication, energy, and generosity of many different members of the Catholic community. This concerted focus, however, must not preclude an active participation in other forms of educational and ecclesial ministry. Catholic schools, therefore, have a rich potential for strengthening the bonds which unite a community.

13. In a significant way Catholic schools bear witness to the importance of religion in our local civic communities and in our society as a whole. When a sizeable segment of the American people undertakes to build and operate a great system of schools at considerable sacrifice, serious citizens are thereby encouraged to reflect upon the importance of religion in human life. Without Catholic and other church-related schools, spiritual values would find far less support in American society.

14. It is gratifying and encouraging that *To Teach as Jesus Did* has helped strengthen the Catholic school apostolate. Evidence of this comes from many sources, including the National Catholic Educational Association and many religious communities, which have themselves played a laudable role in "giving form to the vision" of educational ministry embodied in the Pastoral. Among the beneficial results arising, at least in part, from that effort are the following.

15. The identification of Catholic schools as institutions which express the threefold purpose of Catholic education, stated in the Pastoral as to teach, build community, and serve, has become more clear. Concrete priorities of the schools consistent with this threefold purpose

[2]Andrew M. Greeley, William C. McCready, and Kathleen McCourt. *Catholic Schools in a Declining Church* (Kansas City: Sheed & Ward, Inc., 1976).

have been brought into sharper focus.[3]

16. Programs for the formation of teachers have been strengthened. There has been increased recognition that all share in the educational ministry, not just those specifically assigned to "teach religion."[4]

17. The reciprocal relationship of the Catholic school and the community it serves has been recognized and fostered. New ways have been sought and put into effect by which the school can be of even greater service to the community.

18. Increased attention has been given to the need for a total, integrated approach to Catholic education involving schools and other educational programs. Competition and duplication have been reduced; collaboration and coordination have been increased. Significant in these encouraging developments has been the role played by parish boards of education and parish councils which have enabled the Catholic community in an orderly fashion to identify and respond to the educational needs of the total community. More and more, schools are being recognized and used as resource centers for total parish programs of education.

19. Positive changes in the instructional program have been carried forward, including greater emphasis on personalized learning which meets the unique needs and capabilities of individual students. Growing attention has been given to education for justice and for authentic human liberation.

20. Educational planning and the practice of accountability have been encouraged. At the same time a new thrust has emerged in educational administration, emphasizing not only technical skills but the role of the administrator as one who fosters community within both schools and school systems.

21. Appreciation has increased for the fact that the Catholic school is not simply an institution which offers academic instruction of high quality, but, even more important, is an effective vehicle of total Christian formation. The tendency to emphasize one aspect at the expense of the other has given way to recognition that both are necessary and possible, and indeed are being accomplished in Catholic schools.

22. In short, much that has happened in the past four years testifies to the fact that the schools not only remain an important part of the Catholic Church in the United States but continue to grow in effectiveness as that is determined by both educational and religious measures. This favorable judgment is strongly reinforced by a recently published report on educational research by the National Opinion

---

[3]*To Teach as Jesus Did*: Educational Developments since the Pastoral," *Notre Dame Journal of Education* (Vol. 6, #3, Fall 1975).

[4]*Qualities and Competencies of Teaching Religion* (Washington, D.C.: National Catholic Educational Association, 1973).

Research Center showing that Catholic schools have a significant positive impact on those who attend them and that the Catholic public is highly supportive of them.[5] In view of all this, our commitment to the schools is clear and undiminished.

23. The Second Vatican Council asked the Church "to spare no sacrifice" for Catholic schools which care "for the poor, for those who are without the help and affection of family, and those who do not have the faith."[6] In many places in the United States the Church's response has been an extremely large human and economic investment in schools whose pupils are, in the main, economically disadvantaged children residing in the poverty areas of large cities. The funding of this large investment has come from the self-sacrifice of the children's parents, support of fellow parishioners, and the generosity of contributors to diocesan funds for the subsidy of schools which lack adequate parish support for all educational expenses. This action has been notably productive in the black community where the Catholic school "has been and remains the strongest point of contact for many black people with the Catholic Church . . . . The Catholic school is a constant witness to the talented and creative potential which black youth possess and which needs only opportunity and educational nurturing."[7] Substantially the same may be said of Catholic schools which serve the unique needs of Hispanic and native American children from low-income families.

24. A steadily increasing number of economically poor parents are making heroic personal sacrifices to raise funds for the continuation of their Catholic schools. These parents are convinced that Catholic school education affords their children a realistic and hopeful opportunity "to break out of the hellish cycle of poverty,"[8] and to move into the mainstream of our nation's good living. These schools are therefore serving a critical human need within the context of a complete education which includes religious instruction and guidance.

25. The challenge confronting the total Catholic community is to approximate the self-sacrifice of poverty belt parents by increasing its contributions to interparochial and diocesan funds for the ongoing and expanded support of schools in need of annual subsidy.

26. To sustain this momentum we endorse developments and trends favorable to the continuation of strong and effective Catholic schools. In this connection we turn now to the challenges and opportunities confronting specific groups involved in educational ministry.

---

[5]Greeley, McCready, and McCourt, *ibid.*
[6]*Declaration on Christian Education*, Vatican Council II, the Conciliar and Post Conciliar Documents, #9.
[7]The Crisis of Catholic Education in the Black Community," *Special Statement* (National Office for Black Catholics, January 15, 1976).
[8]Letter of Pope Paul VI to French Social Action Groups meeting in France, July 1, 1970.

Parents

27. Parental confidence in Catholic schools, a quiet but eloquent witness reinforced by great personal sacrifice, produces in others an awareness of the importance of Catholic education's ideals and values. This confidence also encourages teachers to be available and open to parents who seek to be meaningfully involved in their children's schooling.

28. Parent-teacher conferences, home and school associations, lay boards and committees, and teacher aide programs are making progress because many thoughtful parents participate faithfully in these cooperative efforts to enrich their children's education. The benefits of home and school partnership are so evident that all parents should be made aware of their duty to be full partners with the school. The school administrator who does not recognize the importance of this cooperation may be depriving pupils of one of the unique advantages of Catholic schooling. In this cooperation there is a kind of reciprocal accountability of school to parent and parent to school. Today's Catholic school is more than a means for safeguarding faith and virtue; it is a center in which parents and teachers, guided by the Holy Spirit, collaborate in giving children a complete Catholic education.

Teachers

29. The new awareness that all members of the faculty, at least by their example, are an integral part of the process of religious education has brought with it a more conscientious approach to the selecting of teachers and the professional development of staff. Teachers' life style and character are as important as their professional credentials. We commend this trend and urge the development of appropriate ceremonies by which the Church can publicly express its appreciation for their role in the Church's educational ministry.

30. Teacher-initiated instructional programs are implementing the principles contained in the Pastoral. Educational approaches emphasizing doctrine, community, and service as central concepts have helped teachers implement methodologies which are responsive to the individual needs of students. Reciprocally, the thrust toward personalized learning with emphasis on the total educational environment makes clear that the atmosphere and relationships in the school are as much the focus of the Catholic school as is the formal religious education class. In other wider applications, numerous faculties have used the Pastoral in self-studies that are having profound, positive effects on the daily experiences of the school.

Administrators

31. In the area of school administration we note with great satisfaction the growing awareness and acceptance of the twin concepts of accountability and evaluation. This represents a recognition of the school's obligation to serve and be accountable to the Catholic community in relation to the threefold ideal set forth in the Pastoral.

32. We urge administrators to exercise their gifts of educational leadership by promoting structures and cooperative procedures which will render such accountability and evaluation meaningful and useful to all in the Catholic educational community—parents, teachers, and the Catholic community generally. They should exercise their responsibility particularly with reference to the selection, motivation, and development of teaching personnel, ever keeping in mind the apostolic goals and character of the Catholic school.

Pastors and the Community

33. The leadership role of pastors and their associates is a significant factor in the Catholic school apostolate. Through their words, their presence, and their support in so many ways they supply a needed leadership to those who look to such commitment as a sign of the importance of their own sacrifices.

34. Recognition of the pastor's increased importance as a facilitator of community among the professional educational staff of the parish is a positive development. The members of such a total educational team view one another as colleagues in a common work carried on through a variety of approaches.

35. Pastoral leadership can likewise foster in the Catholic community the realization that Catholic schools in parishes and dioceses can be immense spiritual assets which benefit all and give witness to the faith of the entire community. Such schools, like all other aspects of the educational ministry, deserve the support of all members of the Catholic community because, directly or indirectly, they serve all. Not to support such schools merely because they do not enroll all the children of the community would, in our opinion, reflect an inaccurate and damaging view of the Church's educational mission.

36. Community support is manifested also by the presence of the larger community as volunteer staff for the parish educational program and by the witness to that program which these persons give in their contacts with friends and neighbors.

United States Catholic Conference

37. We ask the Committee on Education and the Department of Education to consider the following steps:

38. (1) Careful study of recent research on Catholic schools, especially as it relates to their progress toward goals set forth in *To Teach as Jesus Did*. In a special way there is a need for careful identification of the facts, both quantitative and qualitative, concerning the Catholic school's role in educating those who have suffered economic deprivation or experienced discrimination because of racial, cultural, or linguistic differences. This will help both to demonstrate the contribution now being made in this way by Catholic schools to American society generally and to foster the formulation of proposals for further steps to maintain and strengthen this commitment, including the possibility of some form of nationwide action.

39. Professional guidance and assistance are also needed for making realistic predictions of future enrollment and estimates of future costs, notably for teachers' salaries. We will be assisted by documented success reports describing how particular school systems or individual schools have solved problems relating to downward enrollment, soaring expenses, tensions in governance, and disputes about religious instruction. For it is entirely possible that a solution in one diocese or individual school within a diocese can be replicated elsewhere. We hope also for the discovery or development of promising models, instruments, and processes to facilitate educational planning at the local level.

40. (2) Development and promotion at all levels, local, diocesan, and national, of effective programs of public relations on behalf of Catholic schools.

41. (3) Encouragement for the development and organization of parents, teachers, and other citizens which can articulate the just demands of the nonpublic school community with respect to government aid.

42. (4) Pursuit and publicizing of every appropriate constitutional possibility of public assistance to Catholic and other nonpublic school pupils.

43. We urge that the entire nation realistically acknowledge the contributions which Catholic and other nonpublic schools make to the total educational enterprise in our country. Although Congress and several state legislatures, reflecting growing public appreciation of this kind, have expressed such recognition in recent years by enacting programs to assist the education of nonpublic school children, it is a deplorable fact that courts have often overturned this legislation for reasons we and others consider tenuous and at times offensive. In doing so, they have inflicted a harsh injustice on supporters of nonpublic schools, increased their burdens, and caused serious suffering to many of them. It is our hope that this situation will be corrected by more perceptive rulings which reflect the authentic American tradition, firmly rooted in our history, concerning church and state, and which recognize both the needs and rights of nonpublic school students and parents and the best interests of American education generally. We affirm, as Pope Pius XI did some forty years ago, that "Catholics will never feel, whatever may have been the sacrifices already made, that they have done enough for the support and defense of their schools and for the securing of laws that will do them justice."[9]

44. Last September 15, the day following the canonization of St. Elizabeth Seton, who is celebrated as foundress of the parochial school system in the United States, Pope Paul VI spoke to some eighty of us concerning his hopes for our country. He spoke among other things of Catholic schools.

> We know the difficulties involved in preserving the Catholic schools and the uncertainties of the future," he said, "and yet we rely on the help of God and your own zealous collaboration and untiring efforts so that Catholic schools can continue, despite grave obstacles, to fulfill [their] providential role at the service of genuine Catholic education and at the service of your country.

45. How consistent this is with the first command of Jesus to teach. We receive these words of the Holy Father in the light of the centuries-old tradition of those who have given us so much that we take for granted. Our call now is to all who see with undimmed sight this same apostolic responsibility as their own and will join in carrying out this commitment in the years ahead: the commitment of handing on the faith to the next generation, not merely preserved, but more glorious, more efficacious, more valued by those who in their turn will take up the charge to "go and teach."

---

[9]*Christian Education of Youth*, The Encyclical Letter of His Holiness Pope Pius XI, December 31, 1929 (reprinted by the United States Catholic Conference, Washington, D.C., 1968).

Resolution of the Administrative Committee

A Resolution Passed by the
NCCB Administrative Committee

September 16, 1976

1. At the invitation of the presidential candidates of the two major parties, the Executive Committee of our Bishops' Conference has recently addressed critical contemporary issues in frank and courteous dialogue with them. We unite ourselves with this effort by our Executive Committee to make known our position and clarify issues.

2. Despite some public misperceptions concerning the nature and purpose of the meetings with the candidates, we note with gratitude that the Executive Committee has clearly articulated our Conference's policy on a broad range of foreign and domestic issues without endorsing or opposing either candidate. We reject any interpretation of the meetings with the candidates as indicating a preference for either candidate or party. There are elements of agreement and disagreement on many issues between our positions and those of the major parties, their platforms and their candidates.

3. Government has a legitimate and indeed essential role in the solution of social problems and the fostering of human rights. Our concern with government and the political process is based upon this fact and has no connection with political partisanship.

4. Abortion and the need for a constitutional amendment to protect the unborn are among our concerns. So are the issues of unemployment, adequate educational opportunity for all, an equitable food policy both domestic and worldwide, the right to a decent home and health care, human rights across the globe, intelligent arms limitation and many other social justice issues. We wish to emphasize that our profound concern for the specific issue of abortion is based on the fact that life is not only a value in itself but is absolutely fundamental to the realization of all other human values and human rights.

5. The Catholic bishops of the United States have often publicly stated—and we here reaffirm—deep commitment to the sanctity, dignity and quality of human life at all stages of development as well as to legislation and public policy which protect and promote these values in all contemporary contexts. Many of the specific issues in which these values are at stake were discussed by the Administrative Board of the United States Catholic Conference in its statement on *Political Responsibility* adopted May 6, 1976. Our concern on the broad range of issues was enumerated in testimony presented to the Democratic platform committee on May 20, 1976, and to the Republican platform committee on August 9, 1976. Most recently the Executive Committee has once again spoken to many of these matters.

6. As bishops, we have a duty to make clear the moral and religious dimensions of secular issues, to point to God's word as an authentic norm for social and political life, and to make clear the practical requirements which spiritual and moral values impose upon efforts to achieve a more just social order. At the same time, we are not supporting religious bloc voting nor are we instructing people for whom to vote. Rather, we urge that citizens make this decision for themselves in an informed and conscientious manner, in light of candidates' positions on the issues as well as their personal qualifications.

7. The issues with which the Catholic bishops are concerned, both as religious and moral leaders and as citizens, and to which the Executive Committee has spoken in recent days, will remain as valid and critical after the election as they are now. We shall continue to address the issues facing our nation by all appropriate means at our disposal.

Let the Little Children Come to Me

A Statement Issued by the
United States Catholic Conference

November 10, 1976

1. American families live under many strong pressures today. These pressures arise from contemporary social and economic conditions and from the prevalence of secularistic values.

2. Family separation is commonplace and takes various forms. Young families often live far away from relatives. In a growing number of families, father and mother both work outside the home and have little time to spend with their children at the end of the working day. There is a large number of single parents who must struggle to maintain both job and family. More than six million children of preschool age have mothers who also work outside the home. Many young children spend most of their waking hours in day-care centers or under the supervision of baby sitters—or with virtually no supervision at all. Divorce has touched the life of one child in three. Other elements in the crisis of the American family include frequent relocation, unemployment, poverty, and inadequate health care which afflict the deprived and disadvantaged.

3. Many things are needed for families to cope successfully with such conditions. Here we speak of the need for sound principles and effective programs to help parents raise and educate very young children. As matters stand, many American families find it difficult at best to be settings in which sound values are formed, personal growth occurs, and care is rendered. Yet without family stability, parental guidance, and the cooperation of a variety of institutions and agencies in the community, children cannot experience wholesome development—spiritual, physical, emotional, and intellectual.

4. The foundations of attitudes about human relationships and of social and religious values are laid before a child reaches school age. It is therefore profoundly important that from conception to age seven, children have opportunities to grow in a healthy, loving family environment. This is necessary for the present well-being of children, for the sake of the families they will form in the future, and for the present and future welfare of society itself.

5. In the past it was reasonable to assume that the extended family, closely knit neighborhood communities, and the relationship between church and family would provide a satisfactory setting for early childhood care and education. This cannot be taken for granted today. In seeking to improve the conditions of family life, society and the church

must direct a major part of their concern and effort to very young children and their parents.

6. Though the environment in which people live in their early years is often a source of problems and conflicts in adulthood, society seems more interested in trying to correct adult problems than in adopting realistic measures to prevent them in early childhood. Remedies are certainly needed for the problems of adults. But assisting families with young children today would reduce the need for remedial and rehabilitative programs for adults tomorrow.

7. Such efforts should begin with programs for prospective parents. We have in mind programs to strengthen family life, inform future parents about child development, and provide means for proper child care and education. Community agencies are aware of the needs and problems, but up to now they have not been able to deliver meaningful assistance to more than a minority of families and children who need it. While continuing to support such efforts, therefore, the Church also must reaffirm its own commitment to early childhood care and learning and to education for parenthood.

8. It is a fundamental tenet of Christian faith that each individual is created by God and uniquely gifted with a multitude of capabilities which can be developed for his or her own happiness and the good of the community. A wholesome environment, including the family itself, and a variety of enriching opportunities for education and formation from conception to adulthood, is essential for individuals to develop and use their capabilities.

9. Parents and families have the primary responsibility for fostering the growth and education of young children; "for the family is . . . the principal school of social virtues which are necessary to every society" (*Declaration on Christian Education*, 7). The relationships which parents establish with their children from the very first moments of their lives onward are crucial to the quality of life of their offspring— as infants, children, and eventually as adults (*General Catechetical Directory*, 78). But parents need help in carrying out their responsibilities. Others in the family, the Church, and the community at large have vital roles in the early growth and development of children. Older brothers and sisters, relatives, family friends, teachers, child-care professionals, parish and community leaders, and all others in a position to influence the young should be aware that they share with parents the awesome duty of providing the best in care and education.

10. Thus the task essentially involves a sharing of responsibility. "As well as the rights of parents, and of those to whom parents entrust some share in their duty to educate, there are certain duties and rights vested in civil society inasmuch as it is its function to provide for the common good in temporal matters" (*Declaration on Christian Education*, 3). When resources for the proper care and education of young children are lacking in the family and cannot be provided there, or when a child has reached the point at which formal peer group experiences are desirable, there is an important role for publicly funded services provided through privately or publicly directed agencies in accord with parental needs and wishes. Such agencies should, however, acknowledge the prior rights of parents and families and give them a real voice in determining the values and attitudes they will seek to foster.

11. As the living community of the faithful, following the risen Christ, the Church is committed to integral human development. This requires it to "offer its assistance to all peoples for the promotion of a well-balanced perfection of the human personality, for the good of society in this world, and for the development of a world more worthy of humanity" (*ibid.*). As part of its contemporary witness to Christian values and moral education, the Church has a significant interest—an interest we here affirm—in early childhood care and education.

12. As a community, we are pledged to support the growth in faith of all who have been baptized into membership in the body of Christ. But living faith can only be nurtured in children through interaction with their parents and other members of the Christian community who seek to enrich the lives of the young by communicating the Gospel message through programs of religious education and through the witness of their own dedicated lives, which is of vital importance. Individuals have a responsibility to grow in the faith—and the faith community has a responsibility to help them. The Church thus joins parents and society in a mutual concern for quality care and education of the very young.

13. As their birthright in human society, all children are entitled to the best efforts of us all in regard to their care and education. Much lip service is paid to this principle, but it is far from being realized in the United States today. Families, professionals in the field, and public and private agencies have made encouraging progress, but many needs in the area of early childhood care and education have not been addressed and satisfied.

14. Far more, for example, must be done to prepare men and women for parenthood. Programs should begin well before marriage and the birth of children. Beyond that, more resources, creativity, and commitment must be expended in meeting the needs of families and children. Though all children and families have the same basic needs and rights in this regard, some require our particular attention. These include single parents and their children; children in families where both parents work outside the home; abused and neglected children and their parents; families which must relocate frequently and as a result may lack opportunity for participation in community life and continuity in educational and formational programs for their children; handicapped children and their families; educationally disadvantaged children and exceptional children; children of bilingual and bicultural families; children in hospitals and child-care institutions and their parents.

15. In light of the needs, we endorse efforts within the Church which have among their purposes:

16. To strengthen and support Christian family life as a high ideal and priority in the Church and society by recognizing the need for parents to grow in their relationship with each other, with their children, with the Church, and with the community at large;

17. To help parents lead their children to develop and appreciate Christian values and practice Christian virtues, through which they will reach the fullness of Christian maturity and to be active in their support of those agencies in the Church and society which contribute to the development of those values and virtues;

18. To help single parents, working mothers, and families where both parents work outside the home obtain for their children child care and education which reflect their own best values and ideals;

19. To make guidance concerning early childhood development and religious formation part of the preparation which parents receive before the baptism of their children, beginning, if possible, several months before the baptism is to take place and consistently thereafter;

20. To make early education for parenthood available to engaged couples and also to adolescents as part of their general education;

21. To meet the special needs for care and education which educationally disadvantaged, exceptional, handicapped, abused, orphaned, or separated children have during their crucial early years;

22. To make adequately staffed and funded religious education programs, appropriate in purpose and design to their ages and needs, available to all children in parish communities;

23. To institute nursery school, preschool, and kindergarten programs and day-care centers in Catholic parishes where community needs warrant them.

24. Beyond this, we encourage parents in their efforts "to create a family atmosphere, inspired by love and devotion to God and their neighbors, which will promote an integrated personal and social education of their children" (*Declaration on Christian Education,* 3).

25. We ask that persons responsible for Christian education make special efforts to provide expectant parents, parents of young children, and all who influence the young, with programs to enrich their spiritual growth and better equip them for the demanding vocation of nurturing a new generation.

26. We encourage collaboration among diocesan agencies in establishing programs of early childhood care and education under Church auspices, as well as their cooperation in this area with other public and private agencies.

27. We point out the need for governmental solutions for the dilemma of young mothers who feel forced to choose between personally caring for their young children at home and going to join the labor force in order to provide economic necessities for these same children.

28. We urge that federal, state, and local governments cooperate with families, with the Church, and with other concerned parties in meeting young children's need for care and education. In this regard we look to government for meaningful legislation, adequate funding, and competent and concerned administration.

29. Finally, we urge all members of the Church and society to support constructive efforts on behalf of families and family life; to contribute in whatever ways are open to them in the development of new programs and resources for quality child care and education; and to join us in prayer for the success of our collective efforts to enrich the quality of life of parents and their children.

U.S.-Panama Relations

A Statement Issued by the
United States Catholic Conference

November 10, 1976

1. The United States and the Republic of Panama are presently engaged in negotiations about the future of the Panama Canal. These negotiations have been in progress since 1964 and have been advanced significantly since the Statement of Principles formulated by the two governments in 1974.

2. The administrative board of the U.S. Catholic Conference issued a policy statement in February 1975 which affirmed that: "It is a moral imperative—a matter of elemental social justice—that a new and more just treaty be negotiated" (*Panama-U.S. Relations*, 1975). We continue to believe that the moral imperative exists to fashion a new treaty which respects the territorial integrity and sovereignty of Panama, and dissolves the vestiges of a relationship which more closely resembles the colonial politics of the nineteenth century than the realities of an interdependent world of sovereign and equal states.

3. Since 1975, there has been extensive debate in the United States about the treaty negotiations. Issues of a political, strategic, and economic nature have been raised. In addition, the status of U.S. citizens living in the Canal Zone is a matter of concern for U.S. policy. Our purpose in this Statement is to reaffirm our stance in favor of a new treaty by specifying major issues which we believe should be in the forefront of the public debate and policy decision making in the United States.

4. Speaking as bishops of the Catholic Church, our perspective on the treaty negotiations is set by a text from Pope John XXIII's *Pacem in Terris*. In his discussion of relations between states, the Pope said: "Each of them, accordingly, is vested with the right to existence, to self-development and the means fitting to its attainment, and to be the one primarily responsible for this self-development" (para. 86). It is this principle which is at stake in the treaty negotiations: the fundamental question is the need to acknowledge in principle and in fact Panamanian sovereignty over its own territory. The terms of the 1903 treaty acknowledge the principle of Panamanian sovereignty, but prevent its exercise in any form in the Canal Zone. Without rehearsing the history or the terms of the treaty, we simply would affirm that the moral, legal, and political realities of international life today render the 1903 treaty an anachronism.

5.   The terms of the treaty make it impossible for Panama to be the primary agent of its own development, because it deprives the nation of a substantial part of its territory, income, and capacity for planning the integral development of its people. Finally, by restricting sovereignty in this way, the present relationship strikes directly at the national dignity and sense of respect which any nation needs for free and independent existence. To quote Pope John again, "Nor must it be forgotten, in this connection, that peoples can be highly sensitive, and with good reason, in matters touching their dignity and honor" (para. 89).

6.   Because the issue of sovereignty is so closely tied to the freedom and self-determination of a nation, it has become an issue of dignity and honor for the Panamanians. Given our political history, the world has a right to expect that Americans will be especially sensitive to another nation's claims for freedom, dignity, and self-determination.

7.   The implications of the sovereignty issue for Panama can be illustrated with two examples: First, as we indicated in our 1975 statement, the inability of Panama to integrate the canal and the territory comprising the Canal Zone into its national planning has significant economic consequences ranging from urban congestion in Panama City to the amount of revenue which can be garnered from operating the canal. Second, through a process of unilateral actions, the United States has developed in the Canal Zone a very substantial military presence which goes far beyond the requirements for defending the canal. The existence there of the U.S. Southern Command implies a U.S. military presence throughout Latin America. It is a continuing political problem, casting reflection on the independence of Panama, for its government to be so closely tied, without choice, to the military policy of the United States in Latin America. Without a new treaty, the Panamanians have no possibility of addressing either of these issues.

8.   We support a new treaty, therefore, because we see it as a requirement of justice between our nations. As we consider this larger question of justice, however, we wish also to express our pastoral concern and public support for a negotiated treaty which will protect the welfare of the people living and working in the Canal Zone. We especially call attention to the need for an agreement which will provide for the economic security of Americans presently employed in the Canal Zone. This too is a requirement of justice which rests upon both the United States and Panamanian governments.

9.   The issues involved between our two countries are complex; they are also emotionally violatile. The need in both countries is for reasoned discussion, a sense of the other s point of view, and a commitment to a fair resolution which will lay the basis for a long-term

relationship of respect and cooperation between our governments and our peoples. It is to achieve these objectives that we commit ourselves to a continued program of public education and discussion in the United States.

Resolution on the Pastoral Concern of the Church for People on the Move

A Resolution Approved by the
National Conference of Catholic Bishops

November 11, 1976

I was a stranger and you made me welcome.
Mt 25:35

1. The movement of people seeking their daily bread and the protection of their human rights is a growing phenomenon of our times. Large scale international migration is due chiefly to demands for plentiful and cheap labor created by technological progress and patterns of investment or to political unrest. People cross international borders for seasonal work, for temporary work, and for permanent resettlement. In all too many cases, human considerations, such as family life and family values, are sacrificed to economic ones.

2. Massive migration from underdeveloped countries and regions is a special phenomenon of our age. The United States alone receives about 400,000 new immigrants each year. Our country continues to attract immigrants as workers and refugees.

3. Many of today's immigrants are doubly marginal: they are forced to migrate because of inadequate resources and unequal distribution of goods; then, in their countries of adoption, they are sometimes ignored or subjected to new injustices. Perhaps it is because of such compounded injustice that Jesus specifically promises His Kingdom to those who recognize Him in the immigrant.

4. In his Motu Proprio *On the Pastoral Care of Migrants,* Pope Paul called for a careful balance of the immigrant's rights and duties: to the right of emigration corresponds the duty to serve the common good, especially in developing countries (e.g., the problem of "brain drain"); the right to be accepted as an immigrant is limited by the common good of the country receiving the immigrant; to the right of immigration corresponds the duty of adapting to the new environment; to the duty of serving the common good in the country of origin corresponds the duty of the state to create jobs in the country of origin.

5. As a leaven in the world, the Church is called to participate in human affairs and to recognize in the poor, the afflicted, and the oppressed the presence of the Lord summoning the Christian community to action.

6.   Seen in this evangelical perspective, immigrants, refugees, migrant workers, seamen, and other people uprooted and on the move for survival and human dignity are a theological sign to the Christian community. They are among those signs of the times to which the Second Vatican Council called our attention in order to discern the working of God's will.

7.   While the pastoral care of the Church is directed to all, it is especially imperative that it be extended to newcomers "driven by political or economic forces to move abroad" (*On the Pastoral Care of Migrants,* I, 1). Their human and spiritual needs are great. Furthermore, the Church has a natural concern in this area, for at least three reasons.

8.   First, a high percentage of the new immigrants to our nation come from traditionally Catholic countries such as Mexico, Cuba, the Philippines, the Dominican Republic, Colombia, Portugal, Haiti, etc. Second, the changed character of the new immigrant population, now predominantly Latin American, Caribbean, and Asian, finds in the transnational character of the Church an appropriate catalyst for a healthy adaptation to a new life. Third, the background of many of these immigrants has accustomed them to look to the Church not only as a source of spiritual guidance, but also as a natural point of cultural and social reference.

9.   Among the concrete issues facing newcomers to our country are questions pertaining to legislation and the administration of immigration laws, employment opportunities, and health and education benefits. Many special problems affect children, women, seamen, and undocumented immigrants.

10.   We are particularly concerned with the passage in October of 1976 of Public Law 94-571. While it does equalize visa issuance for both the eastern and western hemispheres, it causes a most serious hardship in the matter of family reunification, especially for natives of Mexico and Canada.

11.   This is exemplified, first, by the fact that, whereas over the past few years immigration from Mexico, chargeable to the numerical ceiling, has averaged in excess of 40,000 visas per year, this present law now restricts it to 20,000. Secondly, restrictive conditions have been placed in this law which affect alien parents who have children born in the U.S. Both of these restrictions will hinder family reunification.

12.   Therefore, we recommend:

(1) That quota ceilings for natives of Mexico and Canada be increased to 35,000 persons per year.

(2) That the American citizen child, regardless of age, be in a position to facilitate his or her parents' immigration.

(3) That in the light of humanitarian concerns and the preservation of family unity, a generous amnesty procedure be enacted for the undocumented aliens presently residing in the U.S.

(4) That the administration and implementation of the immigration laws be reviewed and revised in order to eliminate arbitrary selective enforcement and to reflect humanitarian concerns.

(5) That a new and broader definition of the category of *refugee* be given in order that we may provide a haven for oppressed people from any part of the world, regardless of their race, religion, color, or creed.

13. All of these concerns are treated in the pastoral response which has been prepared by the Conference's Committee on Migration and Tourism.

14. The Church, the People of God, is required by the Gospel and by its long tradition to promote and defend the human rights and dignity of people on the move, to advocate social remedies to their problems, and to foster opportunities for their spiritual and religious growth. We pledge ourselves and urge our brothers and sisters in the Lord to resist injustices against immigrants, to assist them in their need, and to welcome them into our nation and our community of faith as fellow pilgrims on the journey to the Father. It is our duty and our privilege to respond in this way to the biblical injunction: "The stranger who sojourns with you shall be as the native among you and you shall love him as yourself" (Lv 19:34).

To Live in Christ Jesus: A Pastoral Reflection on the Moral Life

A Statement of the
National Conference of Catholic Bishops

November 11, 1976

I. Introduction

Dear Brothers and Sisters in Christ:

1. We wish to share our faith with you. We wish to speak of its power, of the great hope that is in us, of the Spirit that has been poured into human hearts. We wish to discuss some moral questions of our day which affect the dignity of human persons and to respond to them in accordance with what we have seen and heard concerning the word of life. "What we have seen and heard we proclaim in turn to you so that you may share life with us."[1] We also address these words in charity and respect to our fellow Christians and to others who, although they do not share our religious beliefs, may wish to know our vision of the moral life and our perception of many of the critical issues of our day.

Christ, Our Life

2. We believe the meaning and destiny of our lives are most fully revealed to us in Jesus of Nazareth, whom we acknowledge as Son of God made man, Savior and Lord of creation. In Him are revealed two great truths: who God is, and who we are. He tells us that God, whom we are to love and serve above all else,[2] loves us more than we can hope to understand and offers us His love irrevocably. As St. Paul says: "Neither death nor life, neither angels nor principalities, neither the present nor the future, nor powers, neither height nor depth nor any other creature, will be able to separate us from the Love of God that comes to us in Christ Jesus, our Lord."[3] Jesus Himself is the new covenant, the sacred and enduring bond, between God and ourselves.[4]

3. "Whatever came to be in Him, found life . . . any who did accept Him He empowered to become children of God."[5] Christ, in whom

---

[1] 1 Jn 1:3.
[2] Cf., Dt 6:5; Mt 22:37.
[3] Rom 8:38-39.
[4] Cf., Words of Institution, Eucharistic Prayers.
[5] Jn 1:4-12.

God and man are most perfectly one, manifests in the world God's hidden plan to share His life with us, to pour out His own Spirit upon all flesh,[6] so that we who were formed in His image should be called and be children of God,[7] addressing Him in truth as "our Father."

4. Christ also reveals the response which we are to make to our calling and gives us power to make it. This is the power of God's own Spirit. "All who are led by the Spirit of God are sons of God."[8] Jesus lived and was led by the Spirit as the dynamic force of His life.[9] As Son of God made man, He loves not only His Father but each human being. He teaches us that love of God and love of neighbor spring from the same Spirit and are inseparable.[10] "If anyone says, 'My love is fixed on God,' yet hates his brother, he is a liar."[11] We are to love all human beings, even our enemies, as we love ourselves;[12] even more, we are to obey Christ's new command to love all others as He has loved us.[13]

5. By this commandment Christ tells us something new about God, about love, and about ourselves. His commandment to love is new not simply because of the scope and unselfishness of the love involved, but because it calls us to love with a divine love called charity, as the Father, Son, and Spirit do. This call carries with it the inner gift of Their life and the power of Their love, for Christ does not command what is impossible.

6. Christ's life is one of total obedience to the Father in the Spirit. His obedience entailed hunger and thirst and weariness, obscurity and rejection, suffering and death. Yet in accepting the suffering which came to Him as He walked the way of loving obedience, Jesus did not deny His humanity but realized it perfectly. In giving His Son the glorious victory over death, the Father showed His pleasure with the Son's loving obedience.[14]

7. His life challenges the lives we lead. He began His ministry by calling us to change our lives completely.[15] His very first word summons us to turn away from sin, turn toward God, and receive the gift of the Spirit.

---

[6] Acts 2:17.
[7] 1 Jn 3:1; Gal 4:5-7.
[8] Rom 8:14.
[9] Cf., Lk 4:14.
[10] Cf., 1 Jn 4:12; 20-21.
[11] 1 Jn 4:20.
[12] Cf., Lv 19:18; Mt 5:44-48, 22:37-40; Lk 10:25-28.
[13] Jn 13:34; 15:12-13.
[14] Phil 2:9-11.
[15] Cf., Mk 1:14-15.

Sin and Grace

8. We must recognize the brutal reality of sin. It is different from unavoidable failure or limitation. We all fail often through no fault of our own, and we all experience human limitations, among which the ultimate limitation is death. It is a sign of maturity to be able to accept our limitations and discover meaning in our failures.

9. Sin is different. It is a spirit of selfishness rooted in our hearts and wills which wages war against God's plan for our fulfillment. It is rejection, either partial or total, of one's role as a child of God and a member of His people, a rejection of the spirit of sonship, love, and life. We sin first in our hearts, although often our sins are expressed in outward acts and their consequences.[16]

10. There is vast goodness in our world, yet sin's effects are also visible everywhere: in exploitative relationships, in loveless families, in unjust social structures and policies, in crimes by and against individuals and against God's creation. Everywhere we encounter the suffering and destruction wrought by egoism and lack of community, by oppression of the weak and manipulation of the vulnerable; we experience explosive tensions among nations, ideological, racial, and religious groups, and social classes; we witness the scandalous gulf between those who waste goods and resources and those who live and die amid deprivation and underdevelopment—and all this in an atmosphere of wars and ceaseless preparations for war. Ours is a sinful world.

11. "But despite the increase of sin, grace has far surpassed it."[17] God remained faithful to His love for us, sending His own Son "in the likeness of sinful flesh"[18] into the midst of this sinful world. Jesus, "who was tempted in every way that we are, yet never sinned,"[19] accepted in Himself the full force of our sins, of the powers of darkness at large in the world, and of all the suffering which fidelity to God entails. So that by His obedience many might be made righteous,[20] He was faithful unto death. This was His final, irrevocable act of absolute self-giving in love to God and to us.

12. Christ's offer of love and life is valid forever. Transcending space and time, He is present to all and offers to each the life that is in Him. It is freely offered, there for the taking, unless in our freedom we choose to reject His call and not to be united with Him.

13. Because of sin we are helpless if left to ourselves, unable even to do the good we know and truly wish to do.[21] But God, who loves us

---

[16]Cf., Lk 6:43-45.
[17]Rom 5:20.
[18]Rom 8:3.
[19]Heb 4:15.
[20]Rom 5:19.
[21]Cf., Rom 7:11-15.

and is faithful to His promise, saves us from sin through Jesus. Through Baptism we enter into Christ's saving death and are buried with Him; through Baptism we enter into His saving resurrection; through Baptism we are united to His body and share in His Spirit. We who have been baptized in Christ are to consider ourselves "dead to sin but alive for God in Christ Jesus."[22] "Since we live by the Spirit, let us follow the Spirit's lead."[23]

Conversion

14. Even so, our final triumph over sin is a lifelong task. Christ's call to conversion is ever timely, for we still live in a sinful world and the power of sin is strong in us. "My inner-self agrees with the law of God, but I see in my body's members another law at war with the law of my mind; this makes me the prisoner of the law of sin in my members."[24]

15. As disciples of Jesus who accept Him as our way and desire to love God and each other as we have been loved, we must acknowledge our sinfulness. We have to undergo conversion: "a profound change of the whole person by which one begins to consider, judge, and arrange his life according to the holiness and love of God."[25] In a special way we engage in a continuing process of conversion through the sacrament of Penance, in which our sins are forgiven and we are reconciled with God and with the community of faith. We are to live the paschal mystery, which we proclaim at Mass: "Dying, He destroyed our death and, rising, He restored our life."[26] This paschal mystery is central to Christ's life and mission and to ours as His disciples.

16. Living in His spirit, we must deny ourselves, take up the cross each day, and follow in His steps.[27] Christ's atoning sacrifice is, in Cardinal Newman's words, "the vital principle in which the Christian lives, and without which Christianity is not."[28] As brothers and sisters of Jesus who are also His followers and members of His body, we must accept suffering and death as He did, and in so accepting them share His life. "If we have been united with Him through likeness to His death," so also "through a like resurrection" we shall be raised from the dead by the glory of the Father.[29] By our union with Christ we have already begun to share that risen life here on earth.

---

[22] Rom 6:11.
[23] Gal 5:25.
[24] Rom 7:22-23.
[25] *Paenitemini*, February 17, 1966.
[26] Cf., Memorial Acclamation, Roman Sacramentary.
[27] Cf., Lk 9:23-24.
[28] *Parochial and Plain Sermons*, V, 7.
[29] Rom 6:4-5.

Fulfillment

17. All of us seek happiness: life, peace, joy, a wholeness and wholesomeness of being. The happiness we seek and for which we are fashioned is given to us in Jesus, God's supreme gift of love. He comes in the Father's name to bring the fulfillment promised to the Hebrew people and, through them, to all people everywhere. He is Himself our happiness and peace, our joy and beatitude.

18. Of old the divine pattern for human existence was set forth in the decalogue. And Jesus said: "He who obeys the commandments he has from Me is the man who loves Me; and he who loves Me will be loved by My Father."[30] In the Beatitudes[31] Jesus, our brother, promises us the dignity of life as sons and daughters of God, and eternal enjoyment of a destiny which we now grasp imperfectly and which has yet to appear in its glorious fullness. Through these Beatitudes, Jesus also teaches us values we must cherish and qualities we must cultivate if we are to follow Him.

19. Living these values by the grace of Christ, we possess in some measure even now the fulfillment promised to us. As God's reign takes root within us we become "gentle and humble of heart" like Jesus[32] through deeds done in holiness, and thus "a kingdom of justice, love, and peace is furthered in this world."[33]

Guidance in Christ

20. God reveals to us in Jesus who we are and how we are to live. Yet He has made us free, able, and obliged to decide how we shall respond to our calling. We must make concrete in the particular circumstances of our lives what the call to holiness and the commandment of love require. This is not easy. We know, too, that our decisions may not be arbitrary, for 'good' and 'bad,' 'right' and 'wrong' are not simply whatever we choose to make them. And so God gives us His guidance in manifold forms.

21. The human heart is alive with desire for created goods. Behind this desire is our longing for God. "Athirst is my soul for God, the living God."[34] Our desire for created goods and our longing for the uncreated good are not in contradiction, since Christ came to perfect our nature, not to destroy it. He is the goal to whom all creatures tend, for whom all creatures long, in whom all hold together.[35] Everything good and worthwhile in the adventure of a human life is such

---

[30]Jn 14:21; cf., 15:14.
[31]Mt 5:3-12; Lk 6:21-26.
[32]Mt 11:29.
[33]Preface of Christ the King.
[34]Ps 42:3.
[35]Cf., Col 1:15-20.

because it shows forth in some way the glory of God and points back to Him. Created goods and loves are His gifts, and they tell us of their giver and His will for humanity. Though all other goods draw us in part to our perfection as individuals, members of human communities, and stewards of the world, union with God is the supreme and only perfect fulfillment. Those who follow Christ will value all that is truly human and be reminded by it of His call.

22. We rejoice in friends, in being alive, in being treated as persons rather than things, in knowing the truth. In this we are rejoicing in being ourselves, images of God called to be His children. Truth and life, love and peace, justice and friendship go into what it means to be human. Morality, then, is not simply something imposed on us from without, but is ingrained in our being; it is the way we accept our humanity as restored to us in Christ.

23. In giving us these goods and the desire for them, God wills that we be open to them and eager to foster them in ourselves and others. All these goods form a starting point for reflecting upon the meaning and purpose of our lives. In the life of every human person are reflected many elements of the "divine law—eternal, objective, and universal—whereby God orders, directs, and governs the entire universe and all the ways of the human community."[36] All these goods together bear witness to the existence of what is often called the natural moral law. No disciple of Christ will neglect these goods. We are not possessed of His Spirit, therefore, if we toss them aside with contempt, spurning the loving gifts of our Father; if we grasp at them selfishly and deny them to others; or if we make them, not their giver, the ultimate end and meaning of our lives."[37]

Conscience

24. Even when we have become conscious of these fundamental goods and have cultivated an attitude of cherishing them in ourselves and others, more remains to be done. We still must decide how to realize and affirm them in the concrete circumstances of our lives. Such decisions are called judgments of conscience. In the final analysis, they take place in the "most secret core and sanctuary" of a person, where one "is alone with God."[38]

25. We live in good faith if we act in accord with conscience. Nevertheless, our moral decisions still require much effort. We must make decisions of conscience based upon prayer, study, consultation, and an understanding of the teachings of the Church. We must have a

---

[36] Vatican Council II, *Declaration on Religious Freedom*, 3; cf., St. Thomas Aquinas, Summa Theologiae, 1-2, 91, 1 and 2; 94, 1.
[37] Cf., Vatican Council II, *Pastoral Constitution on the Church in the Modern World*, 16.
[38] *Ibid.*

rightly informed conscience and follow it. But our judgments are human and can be mistaken; we may be blinded by the power of sin in our lives or misled by the strength of our desires. "Beloved, do not trust every spirit, but put the spirits to a test to see if they belong to God."[39]

Clearly, then, we must do everything in our power to see to it that our judgments of conscience are informed and in accord with the moral order of which God is creator. Common sense requires that conscientious people be open and humble, ready to learn from the experience and insight of others, willing to acknowledge prejudices and even change their judgments in light of better instruction.

Followers of Jesus will have a realistic approach to conscience. They will accept what Jesus taught and judge things as He judges them.

The Church

26. Where are we to look for the teachings of Jesus, to hear His voice and discern His will?

27. In Scripture, whose books were written under the inspiration of the Holy Spirit. In prayer, where we grow in knowledge and love of Christ and in commitment to His service. In the events of human life and history, where Christ and His Spirit are at work. In the Church, where all these things converge. This is why the Second Vatican Council said: "In the formation of their consciences, the Christian faithful ought carefully to attend to the sacred and certain doctrine of the Church."[40]

There are many instruments and agents of teaching in the Church. All have roles in drawing out the richness of Christ's message and proclaiming it, each according to his or her gift. Although we cannot discuss their role at length here, we wish in particular to acknowledge and encourage the contributions which theologians make to this effort.

28. The Holy Father and the bishops in communion with him have been anointed by the Holy Spirit to be the official and authentic teachers of Christian life. For Jesus "established His holy Church by sending forth the apostles as He Himself had been sent by the Father (cf., Jn 20:21). He willed that their successors, namely the bishops, should be shepherds in His Church even to the consummation of the world."[41] It is their office and duty to express the teaching of Christ on moral questions and matters of belief. This special teaching office within the Catholic Church is a gift of the Lord Jesus for the benefit of all His followers in their efforts to know what He teaches, value

---

[39] 1 Jn 4:1; cf., 1 Cor 12:10.
[40] *Declaration on Religious Freedom*, 14.
[41] Vatican Council II, *Dogmatic Constitution on the Church*, 18.

as He values, and live as free, responsible, loving, and holy persons. As Christ says, "He who hears you, hears Me."[42] The authoritative moral teachings of the Church enlighten personal conscience and are to be regarded as certain and binding norms of morality.

29. Following the teaching and example of Christ in the family of the Church, we become more like Him and more perfect as the Father's children and people. Christ brings us the life of the Father and fills our lives with His Spirit. So our best answer in face of the challenges we encounter in living the Christian life is this: "In Him who is the source of my strength, I have strength for everything."[43]

II. Moral Life in the Family, the Nation, and the Community of Nations

30. We turn now to three social clusters, three concentric communities, which provide the setting for human life and fulfillment in Christ: the family, the nation, and the community of nations.

In speaking of matters which bear upon these three communities today, we treat them as moral issues in light of the values given us by Jesus Christ and His Church, in whose name we proclaim them. We cannot here discuss every important issue. Moreover, we admit that in some cases the complexity of the problems does not permit ready, concrete solutions. Nevertheless, as teachers of morality we insist that even such complex problems must be resolved ultimately in terms of objective principles if the solutions are to be valid.[44]

31. Our point of focus is the human person. "The progress of the human person and the advance of society itself hinge on each other."[45] Every human being is of priceless value: made in God's image, redeemed by Christ, and called to an eternal destiny. That is why we are to recognize all human beings as our neighbors and love them with the love of Christ.

32. This love of neighbor, inseparably linked to love of God and indeed an expression and measure of it, is summoned forth first in regard to those closest to us—the members of our own families.

[42]Lk 10:16.
[43]Phil 4:13.
[44]Many of the matters treated here have been discussed in detail in papal and conciliar documents, documents of the Holy See and the Synods of Bishops, and statements of national episcopal conferences. The references which follow note a few of the sources.
[45]Vatican Council II. *The Church in the Modern World*, 25.

The Family

33. Every human being has a need and right to be loved, to have a home where he or she can put down roots and grow. The family is the first and indispensable community in which this need is met. Today, when productivity, prestige, or even physical attractiveness are regarded as the gauge of personal worth, the family has a special vocation to be a place where people are loved not for what they do or what they have but simply because they are.

34. A family begins when a man and woman publicly proclaim before the community their mutual commitment so that it is possible to speak of them as one body.[46] Christ teaches that God wills the union of man and woman in marriage to be lifelong, a sharing of life for the length of life itself.

35. The Old Testament takes the love between husband and wife as one of the most powerful symbols of God's love for His people: "I will espouse you to Me forever: I will espouse you in right and in justice, in love and in mercy: I will espouse you in fidelity, and you shall know the Lord."[47] So husband and wife espouse themselves, joined in a holy and loving convenant.

36. The New Testament continues this imagery: only now the union between husband and wife rises to the likeness of the union between Christ and His Church.[48] Jesus teaches that in marriage men and women are to pledge steadfast unconditional faithfulness which mirrors the faithfulness of the Son of God. Their marriages make His fidelity and love visible to the world. Christ raised marriage in the Lord to the level of a sacrament, whereby this union symbolizes and effects God's special love for the couple in their total domestic and social situation.

37. Jesus tells us that the Father can and will grant people the greatness of heart to keep such pledges of loving faithfulness.[49] The Church has always believed that in making and keeping noble promises of this sort people can through the grace of God grow beyond themselves—grow to the point of being able to love beyond their merely human capacity. Yet contemporary culture makes it difficult for many people to accept this view of marriage. Even some who admire it as an ideal doubt whether it is possible and consider it too risky to attempt. They believe it better to promise less at the start and so be able to escape from marital tragedy in order to promise once again.

38. But this outlook itself has increased marital tragedy. Only men and women bold enough to make promises for life, believing that

---

[46]Cf., Gn 2:24.
[47]Hos 2:21-22.
[48]Cf., Eph 5:25-32.
[49]Cf., Mt 19:10-12.

with God's help they can be true to their word as He is to His, have the love and strength to surmount the inevitable challenges of marriage. Such unselfish love, rooted in faith, is ready to forgive when need arises and to make the sacrifices demanded if something as precious and holy as marriage is to be preserved. For the family to be a place where human beings can grow with security, the love pledged by husband and wife must have as its model the selfless and enduring love of Christ for the Church. "Husbands, love your wives, as Christ loved the Church. He gave Himself up for her."[50]

39. Some say even sacramental marriages can deteriorate to such an extent that the marital union dies and the spouses are no longer obliged to keep their promise of lifelong fidelity. Some would even urge the Church to acknowledge such dissolution and allow the parties to enter new, more promising unions. We reject this view.[51] In reality it amounts to a proposal to forgo Christian marriage at the outset and substitute something entirely different. It would weaken marriage further, while paying too little heed to Jesus' call to identify ourselves with His redeeming love, which endures all things. Its fundamental difficulty is that it cannot be reconciled with the Church's mission to be faithful to the word entrusted to it. The covenant between a man and a woman joined in Christian marriage is as indissoluble and irrevocable as God's love for His people and Christ's love for His Church.

40. Since the following of Christ calls for so much dedication and sacrifice in the face of strong, contrary social pressures, Christ's Church has a serious obligation to help His followers live up to the challenge. In worship, pastoral care, education, and counseling we must assist husbands and wives who are striving to realize the ideal of Christ's love in their lives together and with their children. Young people and engaged couples must be taught the meaning of Christian marriage. Married couples must have the support and encouragement of the Christian community in their efforts to honor their commitments.

41. It remains a tragic fact that some marriages fail. We must approach those who suffer this agonizing experience with the compassion of Jesus Himself. In some cases romanticism or immaturity may have prevented them from entering into real Christian marriages.

42. But often enough "broken marriages" are sacramental, indissoluble unions. In this sensitive area the pastoral response of the Church is especially needed and especially difficult to formulate. We must seek ways by which the Church can mediate Christ's compassion to those who have suffered marital tragedy, but at the same time we may do nothing to undermine His teaching concerning the beauty and meaning of marriage and in particular His prophetic demands

---

[50]Eph 5:25.
[51]Cf., Vatican Council II, *The Church in the Modern World*, 48.

concerning the indissolubility of the unions of those who marry in the Lord. The Church must ever be faithful to the command to serve the truth in love.[52]

Children

43. The love of husband and wife finds its ideal fulfillment in their children, with whom they share their life and love. Children are really the supreme gift of marriage who in turn substantially enrich the lives of their parents.[53]

44. Openness to children is vitally linked to growth in marital and family love. Couples have a right to determine responsibly, in accord with God's law, how many children they should have, and they may also have valid reasons for not seeking children immediately. But in marrying with the intention of postponing children indefinitely, some appear simply to wish to enjoy one another's company without distraction or to achieve an arbitrary level of material comfort. This can mark a selfish entry into what should be an experience of generous giving. Even worse, children may come to be regarded as an intrusion and a burden instead of a gift. This may lead to a rejection of the children, particularly those who are disadvantaged, either before or after birth.

45. In order to reflect seriously upon the value they assign children, couples should begin by reflecting upon their understanding of marriage itself. Do they believe God is with them in this adventure to which they have committed themselves? If so, their love will reach confidently toward the future and provide a setting in which new life can be generously accepted, take root and grow. Openness to new life, founded on faith, in turn will strengthen their love. They will come to see how the love-giving and life-giving meanings of their love are joined in loving acts of marital intercourse, linked by a necessary relationship which exists not only on the biological level but on all levels of personality.

46. One need not always act to realize both of these values, but one may never deliberately suppress either of them. The love-giving and life-giving meanings of marital intercourse are real human values and aspects of human personhood. Because they are, it is wrong to act deliberately against either. In contraceptive intercourse the procreative or life-giving meaning of intercourse is deliberately separated from its love-giving meaning and rejected; the wrongness of such an act lies in the rejection of this value.[54]

---

[52]Eph 4:15.
[53]Vatican Council II. *The Church in the Modern World,* 50.
[54]Cf., Humanae Vitae, 12, 13.

47. Some distinguish between a so-called contraceptive mentality—a deep-seated attitude of selfish refusal to communicate life and love to a future generation—and particular contraceptive acts during a marriage otherwise generally open to the transmission of life. Though there is a difference, even in the latter case an act of contraceptive intercourse is wrong because it severs the link between the meanings of marital intercourse and rejects one of them.

48. We ask Catholics to reflect on the value at stake here. The Church is not engaged in a mere quibble over means of birth regulation; it is proclaiming the value of the life-giving meaning of marital intercourse, a value attacked, though in different ways, by both the ideology of contraception and by contraceptive acts.

49. Pastoral sensitivity requires that we be understanding toward those who find it hard to accept this teaching, but it does not permit us to change or suppress it. We recognize that couples face increasing pressure in family planning. Contraceptive birth control results not only from selfishness and improperly formed conscience but also from conflicts and pressures which can mitigate moral culpability. Therefore, we ask our people not to lose heart or turn away from the community of faith when they find themselves caught in these conflicts. We urge them to seek appropriate and understanding pastoral counsel, to make use of God's help in constant prayer and recourse to the sacraments, and to investigate honestly such legitimate methods of birth limitation as natural family planning.[55] At the same time we urge those who dissent from this teaching of the Church to a prayerful and studied reconsideration of their position.

50. Our Christian tradition holds the sexual union between husband and wife in high honor, regarding it as a special expression of their covenanted love which mirrors God's love for His people and Christ's love for the Church. But like many things human, sex is ambivalent. It can be either creative or destructive. Sexual intercourse is a moral and human good only within marriage; outside marriage it is wrong.[56]

51. Our society gives considerable encouragement to premarital and extramarital sexual relations as long as, it is said "no one gets hurt." Such relations are not worthy of beings created in God's image and made God's adopted children nor are they according to God's will.[57] The unconditional love of Christian marriage is absent, for such relations are hedged around with many conditions. Though tenderness and concern may sometimes be present, there is an underlying tendency toward exploitation and self-deception. Such relations trivialize

---

[55]Cf., Vatican Council II, *The Church in the Modern World*, 52; Humanae Vitae, 24.
[56]Cf., Sacred Congregation for the Doctrine of the Faith, *Declaration on Certain Questions Concerning Sexual Ethics*, December 29, 1975.
[57]Cf., 1 Cor 6:9-10, 18.

sexuality and can erode the possibility of making deep, lifelong commitments.

52. Some persons find themselves through no fault of their own to have a homosexual orientation. Homosexuals, like everyone else, should not suffer from prejudice against their basic human rights. They have a right to respect, friendship, and justice. They should have an active role in the Christian community. Homosexual activity, however, as distinguished from homosexual orientation, is morally wrong. Like heterosexual persons, homosexuals are called to give witness to chastity, avoiding, with God's grace, behavior which is wrong for them, just as nonmarital sexual relations are wrong for heterosexuals. Nonetheless, because heterosexuals can usually look forward to marriage, and homosexuals, while their orientation continues, might not, the Christian community should provide them a special degree of pastoral understanding and care.

53. Though most people have two families, the one in which they are born and the one they help bring into being, the single and celibate have only the first. But from this experience they, too, know family values. Love and sacrifice, generosity and service have a real place in their lives. They are as much tempted as the married—sometimes more—to selfishness. They have as great a need for understanding and consolation. Family values may be expressed in different terms in their lives, but they are expressed.

The Aged

54. The adventure of marriage and family is a continuing one in which elderly people have important lessons to teach and learn. Contemporary American society tends to separate the aging from their families, isolating kin in ways that are more than physical, with the result that the wisdom of experience is often neither sought, imparted, nor further developed.[58]

55. Families should see the story of loving reciprocity through life's closing chapters. Where possible, the elderly should be welcomed into their own families. Moreover, children have an obligation of human and Christian justice and love to keep closely in touch with aging parents and to do what lies in their power to care for them in their old age. "If anyone does not provide for his own relatives and especially for members of his immediate family, he has denied the faith; he is worse than an unbeliever."[59] The community should provide for those who lack families and, in doing so, attend to all their needs, not just physical ones. Here the Church has played and con-

---

[58]Cf., United States Catholic Conference, *Society and the Aged: Toward Reconciliation,* May 5, 1976.
[59]1 Tm 5:8.

tinues to play a special role. The elderly must be cherished, not merely tolerated, and the Church community, through parishes and other agencies, should seek to mediate to them the loving concern of Jesus and the Father.

56. Euthanasia or mercy killing is much discussed and increasingly advocated today, though the discussion is often confused by ambiguous use of the slogan "death with dignity." Whatever the word or term, it is a grave moral evil deliberately to kill persons who are terminally ill or deeply impaired. Such killing is incompatible with respect for human dignity and reverence for the sacredness of life.

57. Something different is involved, however, when the question is whether hopelessly ill and painfully afflicted people must be kept alive at all costs and with the use of every available medical technique.

58. Some seem to make no distinction between respecting the dying process and engaging in direct killing of the innocent. Morally there is all the difference in the world. While euthanasia or direct killing is gravely wrong, it does not follow that there is an obligation to prolong the life of a dying person by extraordinary means. At times the effort to do so is of no help to the dying and may even be contrary to the compassion due them. People have a right to refuse treatment which offers no reasonable hope of recovery and imposes excessive burdens on them and perhaps also their families. At times it may even be morally imperative to discontinue particular medical treatments in order to give the dying the personal care and attention they really need as life ebbs. Since life is a gift of God we treat it with awesome respect. Since death is part and parcel of human life, indeed the gateway to eternal life and the return to the Father, it, too, we treat with awesome respect.

The Family and Society

59. Marriage and the family are deeply affected by social patterns and cultural values. How we structure society, its approach to education and work, the roles of men and women, public policy toward health care and care of the young and old, the tone and cast of our literature, arts, and media—all these affect the family. The test of how we value the family is whether we are willing to foster, in government and business, in urban planning and farm policy, in education and health care, in the arts and sciences, in our total social and cultural environment, moral values which nourish the primary relationships of husbands, wives, and children, and make authentic family life possible.

The Nation

60. Our nation is committed in principle to the inviolable dignity of the human person, to respect for religious faith and the free exercise of religion, to social and legal structures by which citizens can participate freely in the governmental process, and to procedures by which grievances can be adjudicated and wrongs can be righted. This commitment is a constant challenge, and at times we have failed to live up to its demands. Nevertheless, it remains possible to develop here a social order "founded on truth, built on justice, and animated by love."[60]

The Individual and the Nation

61. While the ultimate and most substantive values inherent in individuals, individuality and community are inseparable elements of the moral life. So, for instance, honesty, courage, and hope, which abide only in individuals, can be fostered by freedom to learn, protection from violence, adequate income, and the availability of health care.
62. As followers of Jesus we are called to express love of neighbor in deeds which help others realize their human potential. This, too, has consequences for the structures of society. Law and public policy do not substitute for the personal acts by which we express love of neighbor; but love of neighbor impels us to work for laws, policies, and social structures which foster human goods in the lives of all persons.

Respect for the Unborn

63. It is therefore as ironic as it is tragic that, in a nation committed to human rights and dignity, the practice of legalized abortion is now widespread. Every human life is inviolable from its very beginning. While the unborn child may not be aware of itself and its rights, it is a human entity, a human being with potential, not a potential human being. Like the newborn, the unborn depend on others for life and the opportunity to share in human goods. Their dependence and vulnerability remind us of the social character of all human life: to live and thrive as a human being, each of us needs the help and support of others.[61]
64. To destroy these innocent unborn children is an unspeakable crime, a crime which subordinates weaker members of the human community to the interest of the stronger. God who calls us to Himself loves the helpless and weak; like Him we should affirm the unborn in their being, not close our eyes to their humanity so that we may

---

[60]Vatican Council II, *The Church in the Modern World*, 26.
[61]Cf., Vatican Council II, *The Church in the Modern World*, 51.

more easily destroy them. Their right to life must be recognized and fully protected by the law.

65. While many today seek abortion for frivolous and selfish reasons, there are women who see it as a tragic solution to agonizing problems. They deserve society's help in meeting and resolving these problems so that they will not feel a need to resort to the inhuman expedient of abortion. Recognition of the incomparable dignity of all human beings, including the unborn, obliges us to assume loving responsibility for all who are in need. The Church must take appropriate initiatives in providing support to women with problems during pregnancy or after, and in doing so bear witness to its belief in human dignity.[62]

Women in Society

66. As society has grown more sensitive to some new or newly recognized issues and needs (while at the same time growing tragically less sensitive to others), the movement to claim equal rights for women makes it clear that they must now assume their rightful place as partners in family, institutional, and public life. The development of these roles can and should be enriching for both women and men.

67. Even today some still consider women to be men's inferiors, almost their property. It is un-Christian and inhuman for husbands to regard their wives this way; they ought instead to "love (them) as Christ loved the Church."[63] Such un-Christian and inhuman attitudes are expressed in a truly degraded manner when they take the form of exploiting women for pleasure and financial profit through prostitution and pornography.

68. Efforts to win recognition that women have the same dignity and fundamental rights as men are praiseworthy and good. But the same cannot be said of views which would ignore or deny significant differences between the sexes, undermine marriage and motherhood, and erode family life and the bases of society itself. Liberation does not lie in espousing new modes of dehumanization, nor in enslavement to an ideology which ignores the facts of human sexuality and the requirements of human dignity.

69. There is much to be done in the Church in identifying appropriate ways of recognizing women's equality and dignity. We have every reason and precedent for doing so, since our tradition has always honored the Mother of God and recognized Mary as the one in whom, next to Jesus Himself, human nature is expressed most perfectly. In canonizing so many women over the centuries, including our own

---

[62]National Conference of Catholic Bishops, *Pastoral Plan for Pro-Life Activities*, November 20, 1975.
[63]Eph 5:25.

country's St. Frances Xavier Cabrini and St. Elizabeth Seton, the Church has proposed them to both women and men as models of what it means to live the life of Christ. Thus we fully support constructive efforts to remove demeaning attitudes and customs with respect to women, however subtle and unconscious in origin they may be.

Respect for Racial and Ethnic Groups

70. The members of every racial and ethnic group are beings of incomparable worth, yet racial antagonism and discrimination are among the most persistent and destructive evils in our nation.[64] Those victims of discrimination of whom we are most conscious are Hispanic Americans, black Americans, and native Americans. The Catholic community should be particularly sensitive to this form of injustice because it, too, has experienced prejudice and discrimination in America based on national origin and religion.

71. It is sometimes said to be pointless to lecture those who are not personally guilty of causing or directly contributing to racism and other ills of society. But the absence of personal fault for an evil does not absolve one of all responsibility. We must seek to resist and undo injustices we have not caused, lest we become bystanders who tacitly endorse evil and so share in guilt for it.

72. It is also wrong to say that those whose energy and motivation have been sapped by social injustices bear sole responsibility for bettering themselves. Instead, the struggle for a just social order requires programs to undo the consequences of past injustices.

73. Law has an important role to play in the fight against racial discrimination. Just laws alert people that some deeds are forbidden and others are required if all members of society are to share equitably in its goods. Laws may not be able to change attitudes, but they can deter those who might otherwise seek to violate the rights of others. By protecting minority groups and also those who wish to respect them and their rights, laws at least can foster actions and institutions essential to racial justice. Finally, and especially at a time when many are confused about morality, good laws can contribute to educating people to know right from wrong.

74. Thanks in great part to law and the courts, we have made progress in recent years in removing some social, political, and cultural structures which support racism. But we are far from final success. For example, the principles of legitimacy, proportionality, and restraint have sometimes been violated in law enforcement within our nation. Racial justice in such areas as housing, education, health care,

---

[64]The National Conference of Catholic Bishops and its predecessor, the National Catholic Welfare Conference, have often spoken on racial justice. Cf., for example, *The National Crisis*, NCCB, April 25, 1968.

employment, and the administration of justice must be given high priority. The Church, too, must continue efforts to make its institutional structures models of racial justice while striving to eliminate racism from the hearts of believers by reminding them of what it means to be sons and daughters of God and brothers and sisters in Christ. "There is no Greek or Jew here, circumcised or uncircumcised, foreigner, Scythian, slave, or freeman. Rather, Christ is everything in all of you."[65]

Employment

75. Chronic unemployment is a strong factor paralyzing some groups in our nation. "Minorities" are not its only victims. Women and young workers suffer disproportionately.

76. Behind the statistics of joblessness lie human tragedies. For example, the father who cannot feed his family in desperation often lapses into a pattern of life whose effects spread in an ever widening circle: crime, the use of drugs, alcoholism, mental illness, family breakdown—all increase along with unemployment.

77. Blessed with God-given gifts that include creativity and imagination, the people of this affluent nation can and must find means by which everyone who is able to work can have gainful, productive employment. If we settle for less we are allowing ourselves to be ruled by our economy instead of ruling it.[66]

78. An injustice to which we have frequently drawn attention is the systematic exploitation of agricultural workers, many of them migrants.[67] These neighbors whose work puts food on our tables are often compelled to live without decent housing, schooling, health care, and equal protection of the law. The economic risks of the industry they serve do not justify denying them the right to negotiate for their own protection and betterment. If exploitation is the cost of lower food prices, it is too high a price to pay.

Housing

79. In many American cities affluent and impoverished neighborhoods are divided mostly along racial lines. If this were a result simply of ethnic preference or the preservation of property values, we would still be concerned that the genuine "neighborhood" was being thwarted. But, in fact, the actions of government, banks, and the real estate industry at times converge to deprive some racial groups of financing

---

[65]Col 3:11.

[66]Cf., United States Catholic Conference, *The Economy: Human Dimensions.* November 20, 1975.

[67]Cf., for example, National Conference of Catholic Bishops, *Resolution on Farm Labor,* November 16, 1973.

for housing and to manipulate real estate values for the profit of insiders, with the result that our cities remain divided and hostile. All Americans should be able to live where they wish and their means allow. Furthermore, while society must provide decent housing for the poor, public housing may not be used as a device for consistently isolating some groups from the rest of the community.[68]

80. In saying this, we wish also to note the many human values preserved in ethnic neighborhoods, where people are united by a common culture, common origin, and sometimes even a common language other than English. Only when their boundaries become barriers and their values are cherished in ways that exclude others from participation do such neighborhoods become elements in a larger pattern of social strife.

81. Clearly, though, it is not just Americans of moderate means, whether in or out of ethnic neighborhoods, who should bear the burden of achieving racial justice. This is a duty of the well-to-do as well as the less affluent, of suburbanites as well as city residents: in short, of all social and economic classes. We do not have answers to all the complex issues raised by specific measures for the desegregation of schools and neighborhoods, but we believe these reflections have a significant bearing on them.

Crime and Correction

82. People have a right and need to live in peace, yet one of the urgent issues in our country today is crime. Violent urban crime receives most of the attention, but the apparently growing amount of white collar criminal fraud and corruption is also ominous, for it indicates a collapse of respect for virtues such as truthfulness and honesty which hold society together.

83. In both categories, merely emphasizing sterner law enforcement while ignoring factors which occasion criminal acts will accomplish very little. Poverty and injustice, as well as our society's spirit of acquisitiveness, contribute to crime. Whatever improvements may be needed in law enforcement and the administration of justice, society will not come to grips with the crime crisis until it seriously addresses these underlying problems.

84. Ironically, our penal system itself is sometimes a cause of increased crime. Long delay of trial and unequal application of the law are unjust and a source of increase in crimes. Often enough imprisonment only confirms inmates in criminal attitudes and practices. Sometimes prisons are also settings for gross violations of prisoners' rights. Prisoners, like the rest of us, are beings of transcendent value, and

---

[68]Cf., United States Catholic Conference, *The Right to a Decent Home*, November 20, 1975.

incarcerating them in prisons which dehumanize is a form of brutality. They have a right to protection against assault and against threats to their lives and well being. They have a right to proper food, health care, and recreation, and to opportunities to pursue other human goods such as education and the cultivation of their skills. Reform of our nation's penal system in light of these and the other human rights of prisoners is urgent and long overdue.[69]

The Nation and the Individual

85. We have spoken often of the need for just laws and wholesome public policies, for all that government can do to create a setting in which fundamental values are protected and can flourish in human lives. Among the other contributions which government should make to the creation of a more wholesome society are responsible, constitutional steps to stem the flood of pornography, violence, and immorality in the entertainment media. Yet we are aware of the limitations of government and the risk of seeming to suggest that it is all-important. Just laws and policies, taxes and programs, are necessary but they will not by themselves secure justice and peace. Such values must be built upon the foundations of good and dedicated individual human lives.

The Community of Nations

86. Our allegiance must extend beyond the family and the nation to the entire human family. In Christ we are brothers and sisters of people whose customs are unfamiliar to us, but whose Father is our Father.
87. Human interdependence is constantly increasing in today's world, so that many issues which pertain to human dignity call for the collaboration of a true community of nations.[70] Perhaps the central global issue of our day is how to create such a community out of a world of states. Pope John grasped the meaning of this challenge when he described the structural defect in the present situation: the lack of authority and institutions adequate to address the problems humanity faces.[71] Most people agree about the problems and their seriousness: hunger, environmental pollution, population growth, glaring disparities of wealth, and the persistent danger of war, to mention only a few. But agreement is lacking on ways to cooperate in dealing with them.

---

[69]Cf., United States Catholic Conference, *The Reform of Correctional Institutions in the 1970s.* November 14, 1973.
[70]Cf., Vatican Council II, *The Church in the Modern World,* 26.
[71]*Pacem in Terris,* 132-135.

88. Believing that the human family is called to live in unity, we speak of two goals for the community of nations which will also help bring it into being: the development of peoples and peace on earth. From the perspective of the United States, both are best addressed in the context of power. Our nation's enormous military and economic power make it essential that we understand how power should be used in the pursuit of these goals.

The Development of Peoples

89. All power is from God[72] and is an expression of His being. God uses His power on our behalf: by creating us and sustaining us in existence, by bestowing His gifts upon us, by enabling us to grow in likeness to Him. As His creatures and children, we are to use the power He grants us for the good of others.

90. Power may never be used to attack the dignity of persons, to subjugate them, to prevent them from seeking and realizing the goods to which their humanity gives them a claim. Beyond this, the powerful have a duty to work positively for the empowerment of the weak and powerless: to help others gain control over their own lives, so that as free and responsible persons they can participate in a self-determining manner in the goods proper to human beings.

91. The powerful must therefore work for the liberation of the oppressed and powerless. Though liberation in the fullest sense is what "Christ Himself announced and gave to man by His sacrifice," it is not possible to foster such liberation in oneself and others without also "promoting in justice and peace the true, authentic advancement" of humankind.[73]

92. Our nation's power, wealth, and position of leadership in the world impose special obligations upon us. Americans have always responded generously to foreign crises involving immediate human suffering: to floods and droughts, earthquakes and famines, and the ravages of war. This is to our credit. But the obligations of which we now speak extend further. We must work creatively for a just international order based on recognition of interdependence. We must live by the principle that all nations and peoples are entitled to an equitable share of the world's goods as well as respect for their right of self-determination.

93. The values which comprise the international common good are threatened by existing patterns of international political and economic relations. Our lives, policies, and patterns of consumption and production should be examined in light of their impact on other nations and peoples. Pope Paul has urged such examination: When so many

---

[72]Cf., Jn 19:11; Rom 13:1.
[73]Pope Paul VI, *Evangelii Nuntiandi,* 38, 31.

people are hungry, so many families are destitute, so many enchained by ignorance, so many schools, hospitals, and homes worthy of the name have yet to be built, all public or private squandering of wealth, all expenditure prompted by national or personal ostentation, and the exhausting arms race become intolerable scandals.[74]

94. The discussion of international justice and of institutions for its realization has become more specific as a result of the call at the United Nations for a New International Economic Order. Its significance lies in its effort to change the language of the debate from that of aid and charity to that of obligation and justice. The traditional question about foreign aid has been how much we of the industrial nations would choose to give others within the framework of the existing international order. By contrast, a discussion cast in terms of justice would examine the rules by which the system works—such things as trade treaties, commodity prices, corporate practices, and monetary agreements—with a view to making them more just. New rules would clarify obligations among the parties. Politically, they would be designed to improve the bargaining position of the developing nations in relation to the industrialized countries.

95. Such discussion of rules for relationships and the distribution of power on the international level may be new to us as Americans but the themes are familiar to our experience. The American tradition emphasizes that rules of fairness are central to a just political system. The developing countries argue that it is precisely rules of fairness in economic relations which do not now exist. Similarly, quest for a new and more equitable form of bargaining power in relation to us echoes the drive for bargaining power by American workers over the last century.

Peace

96. We are also obliged as Americans and especially as Christians to reflect profoundly upon war and, more importantly, upon peace and the means of building it.[75]

97. The Church has traditionally recognized that, under stringent conditions, engaging in war can be a form of legitimate defense.[76] But modern warfare, in both its technology and in its execution, is so savage that one must ask whether war as it is actually waged today can be morally justified.

98. At the very least all nations have a duty to work to curb the savagery of war and seek the peaceful settlement of disputes. The

---

[74]*Populorum Progressio*, 53.
[75]Cf., National Conference of Catholic Bishops, *Human Life in Our Day, II.* November 15, 1968.
[76]Cf., Vatican Council II. *The Church in the Modern World*, 79.

right of legitimate defense is not a moral justification for unleashing every form of destruction. For example, acts of war deliberately directed against innocent noncombatants are gravely wrong, and no one may participate in such an act.[77] In weighing the morality of warfare today, one must also take into consideration not only its immediate impact but also its potential for harm to future generations: for instance, through pollution of the soil or the atmosphere or damage to the human gene pool.

99. A citizen entering the military service is fulfilling a conscientious duty to his or her country. He or she may not casually disregard the nation's conscientious decision to go to war in self-defense. At the same time, no nation, our own included, may demand blind obedience. No members of the armed forces, above all no Christian who bear arms as "agents of security and freedom,"[78] can rightfully carry out orders or policies requiring direct force against noncombatants or the violation of some other moral norm. The right to object conscientiously to war in general and the right of selective conscientious objection to a particular war should be acknowledged by government and protected by law.[79]

100. With respect to nuclear weapons, at least those with massive destructive capability, the first imperative is to prevent their use. As possessors of a vast nuclear arsenal, we must also be aware that not only is it wrong to attack civilian populations, but it is also wrong to threaten to attack them as part of a strategy of deterrence. We urge the continued development and implementation of policies which seek to bring these weapons more securely under control, progressively reduce their presence in the world, and ultimately remove them entirely.

101. The experience of the last fifteen years shows clearly that it is not only nuclear weapons which pose grave dangers and dilemmas. We must learn from the moral and political costs, to ourselves and others, of conventional war as it was waged in Vietnam. With much of the world undergoing or approaching a deep and sometimes drastic change, there is need for restraint and for clear reflection about the purposes which can justify the use of force. The moral reasons and political purposes said to call for even conventional force of arms, besides being valid, must be clear and convincing before any commitment is made to a policy of force.

102. Today, however, the human family longs for peace which is more than the mere absence of war, peace rooted in justice and brought alive by charity. Such peace truly reflects Christ's vision of human

---

[77] Cf., *ibid.*, 80.

[78] *Ibid.*, 79.

[79] Cf., United States Catholic Conference, *Declaration on Conscientious Objection and Selective Conscientious Objection*, October 21, 1971.

life. Why is it so difficult to achieve?

103. Peace depends upon both the policies of states and the attitudes of peoples. A policy of peace can only be conceived and supported where a commitment to peace prevails. Cultivating this commitment and carrying forward this policy are intricate, delicate tasks. It is not that some among us desire war, but that those who speak of the risks of weakness are likely to dominate public debate. So the race to accumulate ever more destructive weapons continues in this and other nations.

Human Rights

104. There are considerable differences between what is required internationally and what is required domestically to preserve peace and promote justice. On another broad issue, however, the protection and promotion of human rights,[80] the values sought in our domestic political life and our foreign policy converge.

105. This nation's traditional commitment to human rights may be its most significant contribution to world politics. Today, when rights are violated on the left and the right of the international political spectrum, the pervasive presence of our nation's political power and influence in the world provides a further opportunity and obligation to promote human rights. How this should be done will vary from case to case; at the very least, however, national policy and our personal consciences are challenged when not only enemies but close allies use torture, imprisonment, and systematic repression as measures of governance.

106. The issue of human rights in foreign policy is ultimately a question of values. There is a direct, decisive bond between the values we espouse in our nation and the world we seek to build internationally. When human rights are violated anywhere without protest, they are threatened everywhere. Our own rights are less secure if we condone or contribute even by passive silence to the repression of human rights in other countries.

III. Conclusion

107. Many institutions of society have roles to play in realizing the vision we have attempted to sketch here. In a pluralistic society, religiously neutral public institutions and structures cannot be expected to embody the beliefs of any one religious group, nor indeed should they reflect an anti-religious view of life. They can and should help create the conditions in which values flourish in human lives and

---

[80]Cf., Second General Assembly of the Synod of Bishops, 1971, *Justice in the World*.

persons committed to Christian goals can pursue them without hindrance, without surrendering their rights, and with full opportunity to transmit their principles to future generations.

108. The obligation of creating these conditions rests in different ways upon different elements in society:

109. Upon Government: (a) to infringe upon the authentic rights of none;

(b) to create through the instruments of law and public policy conditions for the fullest possible flowering of the rights of all, with particular attention to family values and family needs;

(c) to seek a true community of nations with international structures able to address the real problems of today's world and work for the common good of all nations and peoples.

110. Upon Business and Industry, Labor and the Professions: (a) to define their roles not in relation to narrow self-interest but in relation to the well-being of all members of this society, especially the poor and the vulnerable;

(b) to seek for all a good life encompassing a broad spectrum of values in addition to economic ones;

(c) to show by responsible actions that the common good can be realized in our nation with intrusion by the state into ever more areas of life.

111. Upon the Media, Education, and All Who Transmit Information and Help Form Attitudes: (a) to be deeply committed to the truth;

(b) to be respectful of persons and scrupulous to avoid advocating or inculcating false and corrosive values;

(c) to be eager to foster such community-building values as justice, charity, and the understanding that all human beings have a claim upon the goods of human life.

112. Upon Churches and Religious Groups: (a) to be teachers of holiness and justice;

(b) to give witness to their teaching through policies and practices which seek to further the realization of human goods in the lives of all, those who are not their members as well as those who are;

(c) to exercise a prophetic role in society by calling individuals, groups, and institutions to be every more mindful and supportive of authentic values.

113. With all this said, however, the most important thing is still unsaid. The values proclaimed by Jesus Christ are not expressed by structures and institutions if they are not lived by men and women. Jesus is not the way, the truth, and the life for corporate abstractions like 'government,' 'business,' and 'religious groups' but for human beings.[81] Yet people live in and depend upon communities and social structures of many kinds; and so the reason for cherishing moral values in families, nations, and the community of nations, and the test of how well they are fostered there, are individual human lives lived according to God's will for us made manifest in Jesus Christ. For Christians the goal is holiness.

114. Because we have been made holy in Jesus, we are, He teaches us, also to be "made perfect . . . as your heavenly Father is perfect."[82] All of us are to be perfectly what we really are: living temples of the holy God. "All the faithful of Christ of whatever rank or status are called to the fullness of the Christian life and to the perfection of charity."[83] We are all challenged to grow in holiness according to our "own personal gifts and duties," and above all by loving service, which guides and energizes all the paths of holiness.[84] To do this requires self-discipline and self-sacrifice. But it is possible in the strength of Christ and His Spirit which we share. Recognizing its possibility is a step toward making it real. We, your bishops, pray that these reflections will help bring this possibility more alive in our lives and the lives of many, will help open our hearts and yours, our brothers and sisters in Christ, to God's immeasurable love for us all.

115. St. John of the Cross tells us that at life's nightfall "we will be examined in love."[85] A life of faith is one measured constantly throughout its course in light of the love and life of Christ in us. When we come to die, much we have cherished will seem worthless, many things deemed urgent and attractive now will appear useless or worse. What will matter then is how much we love now and how we live in response to our Father's love for us.

116. The cross of Jesus Christ shows us the deficiency of other value systems. Jesus yielded up His life for us in perfect loving union with the Father's will, and this is the meaning of His life which also gives meaning to our lives as His followers. If we can acknowledge selfishness as folly and self-sacrifice as victory, if we can love enemies, be vulnerable to injustice and, in being so, still say that we have triumphed, then we shall have learned to live in Christ Jesus.

---

[81] Jn 14:6.
[82] Mt 5:48.
[83] Vatican Council II, *Constitution on the Church*, 40.
[84] *Ibid.*, 41, cf., 39-42.
[85] *Spiritual Sentences and Maxims*, 57.

Resolution in Honor of Cardinal Krol

A Resolution Passed by the
National Conference of Catholic Bishops

November 1976

1. *Whereas* an International Eucharistic Congress is a gathering of the universal Church in a particular country for the purpose of deepening the understanding of the Holy Eucharist, enriching our love for Christ in the Eucharist, fostering devotion to the Holy Eucharist, and providing an opportunity to proclaim the Good News of the Eucharist in the human family at large; and

2. *Whereas* the Forty-first International Eucharistic Congress, held during the height of the United States' Bicentennial in the city where American independence was declared two hundred years ago, officially opened in the Cathedral of Saints Peter and Paul in the heart of Philadelphia on Sunday, August 1, 1976, and concluded with the *Statio Orbis* Mass in John F. Kennedy Stadium on Sunday, August 8, 1976; and

3. *Whereas* under the theme *Eucharist and the Hungers of the Human Family* the eight days of the Congress were devoted to presenting the relationship of the Eucharist to human hungers for: God; Food; Freedom and Justice; Love; Truth; Peace; Understanding; Jesus, the Bread of Life; and

4. *Whereas* His Holiness, Pope Paul VI, in the letter designating James Robert Cardinal Knox as Papal Legate to preside over the Forty-first Eucharistic Congress, notes that the name *Philadelphia* denoting the *City of Brotherly Love* is especially in harmony with the Eucharistic mystery which is the font and food of charity in the heart of the Church; and

5. *Whereas* in that same letter His Holiness, Pope Paul VI, singles out His Eminence, John Cardinal Krol, Archbishop of Philadelphia, for his zealous, methodical, and energetic work to prepare both the souls of the faithful and the externals of the celebration; and

6. *Whereas* His Eminence, John Cardinal Krol, served so effectively as Chairman of the National Conference of Catholic Bishops, as Chairman of the *ad hoc* Committee for the Eucharistic Congress, and as

Chairman of the Congress Board of Governors to guarantee that every event of the Congress be marked by a tone of dignity, order and impeccable taste, reflecting the sublimity of the Blessed Sacrament as well as the high esteem and love of the people of God for Jesus in the Eucharist; and

7.   *Whereas* throughout his life, and especially through the priest-hood, the episcopacy, and the cardinalate, His Eminence, John Cardinal Krol, has manifested a deep devotion to the Holy Eucharist, beautifully proclaiming by word and example the exhortation *Live What You Receive*; now, therefore, be it

8.   *Resolved by the National Conference of Catholic Bishops*, that the members of this Conference, in behalf of all the members of the Catholic Church in the United States of America, do hereby express our profound gratitude and heartiest congratulations to His Eminence, John Cardinal Krol, on the tremendous success of his tireless efforts to bring the Forty-first International Eucharistic Congress to Philadelphia during the nation's bicentennial, and to continue its enduring effect as an instrument of spiritual renewal in the Church.

Resolution on Haitian Refugees

A Resolution Prepared by the
Ad Hoc Committee on Migration and Tourism,
National Conference of Catholic Bishops

May 2, 1977

Men have a native right to use the material and
spiritual goods that 'allow . . . relatively thor-
ough and ready access to their own fulfillment'
(Gaudium et Spes) but if a state suffers from
poverty combined with great population and
cannot supply such use of goods to its inhabi-
tants, or where the state places conditions that
offend human dignity, people possess the right
to emigrate, to select a new home in foreign
lands and to seek conditions of life worthy of
man.

Paul VI, Pastoralis Migratorum

1. Many who have sought, out of direct necessity, to exercise that right described by the Holy Father and affirmed repeatedly by the magisterium of the Church, have encountered particularly grave obstacles in recent years. Among those groups of immigrants who have lately sought refuge in our country, few have met as much official opposition, hostility, and discrimination as have the refugees from Haiti.

2. Some have been deported, some are presently being held in American jails, and the majority are still denied refugee status and the right to work and move freely within this society. Virtually all live in daily fear of being arrested and forcibly repatriated.

3. We urge the officials of our government in the executive, judicial, and legislative branches to consider the matter of the Haitian refugees a priority concern that requires speedy, just, and compassionate resolution.

4. Specifically, we urge immediate cessation of all deportation proceedings against Haitian refugees, release of all Haitian refugees now imprisoned solely for reasons of immigration, and the granting of amnesty or full refugee rights to all such Haitians now in this country.

5. We urge that the United Nations convention and protocol relating to the status of refugees be scrupulously adhered to by our government and not be restrictively interpreted as applying only to persons fleeing from particular kinds of repressive societies.

6.   We urge that the appropriate committees of the House and Senate hold full and extensive hearings on the status of human rights in Haiti, given the expressed dissatisfaction of many in the Haitian community with both such hearings as have been held in the recent past and the report issued on December 31, 1976, by the Department of State on Human Rights and U.S. Policy.

7.   Finally, we recognize that several of the local churches, especially in areas where there are concentrations of Haitian immigrants and refugees, have reached out in fraternal solicitude to these recent arrivals, extending to them the hand of welcome and the opportunity to incorporate themselves into the life of the Church in the United States. We urge these churches to continue this pastoral care, and we also urge those churches which have not inaugurated such programs to do so as soon as practical.

Statement on Recombinant DNA Research

*A Statement Prepared by the Bishops'
Committee for Human Values*

May 2, 1977

1. The Bishops' Committee for Human Values has followed the discussion of recombinant DNA (deoxyribonucleic acid) research with interest. It is an issue which illustrates the endeavor of scientists and the public to ensure scientific progress in a fashion that respects human values. We recognize that this debate has not yet come to full maturity; that it is too early to determine precisely how to reconcile scientific inquiry, public health, human values, and policy in this matter. It is not too early, however, to outline its many dimensions and to urge informed public participation.

2. We have several purposes in speaking to this issue. A primary objective is educational. This is just one of several important areas in science policy about which not only scientists and specialists but the general public should be informed. The responsibility to be informed is especially critical for those in teaching and pastoral roles. Secondly, since recombinant DNA is a paradigm of other scientific issues having value and public policy dimensions, the approach in this instance will be normative of the way these other matters are handled.

3. We should like to call attention then to the moral dimensions beyond the hazards issue and offer some guidelines in moral reasoning concerning recombinant DNA research.

4. The modern era of molecular biology began more than twenty years ago with the identification of DNA as the chemical basis of heredity and the discovery of its general structure. Advances in molecular biology now permit the joining of portions of DNA molecules from different species into "DNA recombinants," which are then inserted into bacterial cells. This technique will facilitate increased knowledge of basic biological processes because it makes possible the study of individual genes and their component parts.

5. Recombinant DNA research has already increased our understanding of the organization of genes in lower organisms and of gene duplication. It is thought that there will be beneficial practical applications as well. On the other hand, the research is a cause of concern because some experiments may pose new, unanticipated risks. Biologists are altering the genes of living things without being able to predict the outcome.

6. Because this technology has the potential to modify all forms of life, it requires full exploration of the ends it serves and the means to these ends. Serious, thoughtful reflection on these matters as well as responsible collaboration between scientists and the public are morally and pragmatically imperative. This process of reflection was initiated by the scientific community on an international level and has expanded to include members of the public in local communities. The nature and extent of the debate calls for respectful, patient, responsible behavior on the part of all participants.

7. Simply stated, the dilemma is this: investigation involving recombinant DNA promises great theoretical advances. Moreover, this technique may have practical applications (e.g., in medicine and agriculture). At the same time, because the research is new (in some cases involving pathogenic substances and sometimes new organisms) it may involve unknown and potentially grave risks. It is generally agreed that there is need for caution since DNA molecules could escape from the laboratory with consequences which cannot be foreseen. Parties to the controversy adopt various stances ranging from the opinion that already too much time has been lost and work should proceed apace, to the other extreme which would ban all recombinant DNA research as inherently too risky.

8. Without detailing the history of the entire controversy, several commendable aspects of the debate should be noted. The issue came to public attention through the responsible action of scientists themselves who were concerned about the possible hazards. Furthermore, molecular biologists voluntarily imposed a moratorium on the conduct of certain types of recombinant DNA research while the situation was reviewed. The process of deliberation about the technique and its hazards was open. In other words, there has been a serious effort on the part of some scientists to consider the risk dimension of the matter.

9. Last June a yearlong discussion of safeguards resulted in the publication of guidelines by the National Institutes of Health which specify how grantees of NIH must conduct recombinant DNA research. These guidelines stipulate two types of containment: physical and biological. The physical containment requirements are designed to confine organisms containing recombinant DNA to the laboratory. The biological containment requirements stipulate the use of weakened strains of host cells, so that, should any organisms escape from physical containment, they could not survive. Agreement is lacking, however, on the adequacy of the guidelines to prevent such an occurrence. The guidelines do not apply to industrial and other private research.

10. Proponents of recombinant DNA research cite its potential benefits (e.g., the development of new methods for understanding and controlling disease) and the adequacy of the NIH guidelines to prevent any undesirable consequences which, they contend, are at this point merely hypothetical. Critics of the technique tend to focus on the potential for health hazards (e.g., novel and uncontrollable epidemics) and on the unknown and lasting effects of such intervention in the evolutionary process.

11. There are basic ethical questions about recombinant DNA research which should be raised and dispassionately addressed. Have we sufficiently investigated the potential for hazard to justify this research? To exercise a moderating influence on recombinant DNA studies, does one need to identify or only suspect substantial risk? Who should judge the acceptability of risk? Has there been sufficiently wide dissemination of balanced, accurate information about recombinant DNA for the public to contribute intelligently to policy making in this regard? Are the NIH guidelines adequate? Can they be enforced and if so, how? Is legislation a satisfactory way of managing or controlling this research? What is the responsibility of the United States on an international level in dealing with recombinant DNA? Have we sufficiently reflected on this method of intervening in the process of evolution? Is recombinant DNA only a prelude to more extensive genetic modification, i.e., to human engineering? How far do we want to advance in genetic engineering?

12. The controversy surrounding these techniques highlights the issue of freedom of scientific inquiry and the role of the public in science policy. Among the values prized by the scientific community are, understandably, scientific knowledge and the freedom to pursue it. With these as with all values, however, the potential exists for conflict with other human values. Knowledge gained in recombinant DNA research ought not be at the expense of other fundamental values. Because the well-being and health of human and other forms of life may be at stake, concerned persons should become involved in the dialogue. These remarks do not answer the question of precisely how to balance the value of scientific inquiry with responsibility of humanity at large. It seems wise, however, to inject a note of caution and prudence in the awesome task of so doing.

13. A fundamental issue in this debate concerns the public's relationship to scientific research. Contrary to the notion of value-free science, almost every scientific endeavor has transcientific dimensions—dimensions which pertain to aspects of human life other than the scientific. These dimensions involve ethical and public policy implications. In keeping with the right of self-determination, the public should know about scientific research and be able to judge for itself the acceptability of the risk which such experimentation entails for present and future generations. Furthermore, if the discussion includes an informed public, the debate is likely to consider more than the specific issue of biohazards. The focus may expand from the means of achieving greater knowledge to include the end or goal of the activity. A multi-disciplinary effort should consider the social, political, economic, and ethical implications of such research. Reflection is called for on the meaning of the direction microbiology is taking in recombinant DNA research.

14. The Church, while recognizing its limitations in scientific matters, has something to contribute to this reflection. *The Pastoral Constitution on the Church in the Modern World* observes that "recent research and discoveries in the sciences, in history, and philosophy bring up new problems which have an important bearing on life itself and demand new scrutiny by theologians." In other words, the new circumstances which challenge traditional understandings of human values must be met with creativity and imagination, reflecting a fuller and deeper understanding of the values at stake. We can undoubtedly come to still greater appreciation of our intellectual and creative capacities.

15. Yet, in this era of unprecedented scientific capabilities, the pursuit of knowledge or truth is not the sole criterion for responsible scientific inquiry, especially in light of the limitations of our human condition. A desire to control the totality of life, coupled with increased technological might, produces an inflated sense of autonomy and tends to obscure the fact that our intelligence and creativity are limited. There is more to reality than what is subject to scientific investigation and manipulation. Each scientific advance does not necessarily constitute real human progress. This realization should cause us to pause before we pursue everything which is scientifically feasible. Wisdom is also necessary if the good of humankind is really to be achieved.

16. The fundamental moral imperative is that good is to be pursued and evil to be avoided. We are strictly obliged to avoid harm, but we are not obliged to accomplish all "good." It is possible to harm future generations by negligently omitting to accomplish some things via science. On the other hand, we are not obliged to accomplish everything possible through science at whatever risk or at the price of assaulting time-honored values. Christians have always refused to vest absolute value in any human good or endeavor. We ought not now to follow slavishly the technological imperative that, "All that can be done, must be done."

17. In determining what should be done we must be wary of a strictly utilitarian mode of reasoning. We do not look only to consequences. Our actions must not only point to or produce future goods. They must also respect and reflect the range of human goods in the process. A good end or good purpose does not justify any means. There might well be a worthy scientific goal which ought not be pursued if it unjustifiably violates another human good. In other words, ethical constraints might slow down, or even preclude, some scientific advances.

18. In light of the above remarks it can be seen that the controversy surrounding recombinant DNA research should not be viewed solely from the perspective of a risk-benefit calculus. To frame the issues in terms of the increased knowledge and beneficial applications is to risk obscuring the other values at stake. There has been an urgency to recombinant DNA research which resulted in the formulation of guidelines in advance of research about the potential hazards of such research. That urgency should not be allowed to short-circuit reflection on: the purpose and implications of these forms of DNA modification; the effect of this type of genetic research on our understanding of ourselves and of our relation to nature; and the correlation between the scientific advance possible through recombinant DNA research and human progress as judged by a variety of criteria.

19. Discussion of the rights and limits of scientific inquiry in the instance of recombinant DNA well illustrates the necessity of striving always for open communication between science and the public. Such collaboration is necessary if wisdom and humility are to effect enlightened public policy.

Statement of the United States Catholic Bishops on American Indians

A Statement Issued by the
United States Catholic Conference

May 4, 1977

1. In this Statement, we wish to share our reflections on the relationship of the Catholic Church in the United States with the American Indian peoples.

2. As American Catholics, we have learned only gradually and with difficulty that the building of one community can only be authentic if it is based upon respect for the distinctive traditions, customs, institutions, and ways of life of its peoples. Indeed, we are only now beginning to understand that unity which grows through dialogue and respect for diversity is far stronger and deeper than conformity forged by dominance.

3. We recall with gratitude the great dedication and sacrifice of the many priests, religious, and lay persons, past and present, who have sought to share with the Indian people the Good News of Jesus Christ. They learned the Indian languages, and, insofar as they were able within their own cultural limits, they adapted themselves to Indian cultures. In the name of the Church, these missionaries also offered to the Indian communities their talents and knowledge of medicine and education.

4. Some who have worked with American Indians, however, recognize that efforts of the Church to promote the Gospel among Indian communities have at times been attempted in ways that actually failed to respect Indian cultures. We come to this Statement with a keen awareness of our not infrequent failures to respect the inherent rights and cultural heritage of our American Indian brothers and sisters. We offer this reflection on our attitudes and actions in the spirit of reconciliation and with a stronger commitment to be more sensitive and just in our relationships with American Indians.

Faith and Culture

5. The Church, by its very nature, must always and everywhere proclaim and give witness to God's saving love revealed by Jesus Christ in the Holy Spirit. This is the center and foundation of the Church's mission—to proclaim that in Jesus Christ, the Incarnate

Word, who died and rose from the dead, salvation is offered to all people as a gift of God's grace and mercy.[1]

6.   This Good News of salvation is not bound by time or human structures, Christ's Gospel of love and redemption, addressed to all people, transcends national boundaries, cultural differences, and divisions among peoples. It cannot be considered foreign anywhere on earth; nor can it be considered identical with any particular culture or heritage.[2] It is the common blessing of all.

7.   But persons are vitally dependent upon the institutions of family and community that have been passed down to them. These institutions—political, social, economic, and religious—shape their self-understanding and are necessary to their full development as persons. Indeed, the Second Vatican Council affirmed that persons can come to an authentic and full humanity only through those distinct cultures which form the basis and heritage of each human community.[3]

8.   The Christian faith should celebrate and strengthen the many diverse cultures which are the product of human hope and aspiration. The Gospel message must take root and grow within each culture and each community. Faith finds expression in and through the particular values, customs, and institutions of the people who hear it. It seeks to take flesh within each culture, within each nation, within each race, while remaining the prisoner of none. Pope Paul VI, in his recent statement on evangelization, stressed these themes in calling for "fidelity both to a message whose servants we are and to the people to whom we must transmit it."[4]

The Church and Justice

9.   The Church is also required by the Gospel and by its tradition to promote and defend human rights and human dignity. Pope Paul VI has underscored the fact that "between evangelization and human advancement—development and liberation—there are in fact profound links. . . . The necessity of ensuring fundamental human rights cannot be separated from this just liberation which is bound up with evangelization and which endeavors to secure structures safeguarding human freedoms." The Church, Pope Paul continued, "has the duty to proclaim the liberation of millions of human beings—the duty of assisting the birth of this liberation, of giving witness to it, of

---

[1]Pope Paul VI. *Exhortation on Evangelization in the Modern World*, 5. 14-16. 26-27: Vatican II, *Decree on the Missionary Activity of the Church*, 2-4.
[2]Pope Paul VI, 20, 28; Vatican II, *Dogmatic Constitution on the Church*, 48: *Decree on the Missionary Activity of the Church*, 8.
[3]Vatican Council II, *The Church in the Modern World*, 53.
[4]Pope Paul VI, 4.

ensuring that it is complete. This is not foreign to evangelization."[5]
10. In all its activities the Church must seek to preach and act in ways that lead to greater justice for all people. Its ministry cannot neglect the violations of human rights resulting from racism, poverty, poor housing, inadequate education and health care, widespread apathy and indifference, and a lack of freedom. These realities are fundamentally incompatible with our faith and the Church is required to oppose them. Pope Paul VI stressed the profound link between the Church's mission to preach the Gospel and action on behalf of justice: "How in fact can one proclaim the new commandment without promoting justice?"[6]

The American Experience

11. We, as American Catholics, should be especially sensitive to these aspects of the Church's mission. Over the centuries, peoples from every continent and heritage have joined in the formation of the United States. Each group to come has constructed its communities and established its institutions. Gradually, all Americans learned the lesson that to build a nation free and independent, a people must be prepared to engage in a never-ending process of change and dialogue. Each group has experienced the tensions that arise between the legitimate cultural independence that people claim for themselves and the pressing need for true and fruitful dialogue with other groups.
12. Today, we Americans are called to reflect upon past injustices and to consider again the need for both unity and diversity, to become one nation built upon respect for the distinctive traditions and values of many peoples and cultures. Both respect for cultural diversity and dialogue between cultures are indispensable if the legitimate quest for cultural identity is to lead to human development and social progress and not simply perpetuate the bitter divisions of the past. The challenge of this effort is placed before the nation by black Americans, by Spanish-speaking Americans, by the heirs of Europe's migrations and by the persevering voice of the oldest Americans, the American Indians.

American Indians

13. The American Indian peoples had developed rich and diverse cultures long before the first Europeans came to the American continent. Migrating across this great continent, the Indians dispersed

---

[5]Pope Paul VI, 31; 39; 30.
[6]Pope Paul VI, 29-36; Vatican Council II, *The Church in the Modern World*, 41.

over thousands of years, from the coasts of the Pacific Northwest to the arid mesas of the Southwest, the vast grasslands of mid-America and the mountains and woodlands of the East. Adapting themselves to changing environments as they went, they developed over two hundred distinct languages and a variety of carefully developed social, economic, and political institutions to meet their needs.

14. But the arrival of later immigrants created conflicts not yet resolved. Indian ways of life were challenged; their very existence was continually threatened by newcomers who were their superiors in the arts of war. For the Indians, the saga of nation building in America has been a story filled with sorrow and death.

15. American Indians in the United States today comprise less than one percent of our total population. In all, they belong to more than two hundred fifty distinct tribes and bands.

16. Many tribes have retained a special trust status with the United States and continue to live on reservation lands held in trust for them by the federal government. Over the long years, however, many tribes have been deprived of their communal lands, and with them have partially or entirely lost the traditional vestiges of their cultures, their languages, customs, and ways of living.

17. During recent decades, increasing numbers of American Indians, especially the young people, have migrated to cities in search of jobs, shelter, and social services which are sorely lacking on many reservations. Those who have chosen or been forced to migrate to cities in response to promises of employment and a better life have too often found only new frustrations and broken dreams. Many contend with a deep sense of uprootedness, trying to maintain ties with their families and tribes while coping with the economic hardships and social prejudices, even racism, of urban society.

18. American Indians today are struggling against great obstacles to renew the special values of their unique heritage and to revitalize the ways of their ancestors. They are striving to achieve economic development and social justice without compromising their unique cultural identity. For some American Indian peoples the struggle is to retain rights to their land and resources; for some it is to gain employment and economic security; and for others, it is to obtain political power in order to set their own goals and to make decisions affecting their own futures. These goals, to be achieved within the framework of Indian culture and traditions, test the strength of the American ideal of liberty and justice for all. America must respond, not to atone for the wrongs of the past, for that in a sense is beyond our power, but to be faithful to our national commitment and to contribute to a truly human future for all.

The Role of the Church

19. As American Catholics, we have a special responsibility to examine our attitudes and actions in light of Jesus' command to love our neighbor and to proclaim the Gospel message and its implications for society. The Church is compelled, both through its institutions and through its individual members, to promote and defend the human rights and dignity of all people.

20. Accordingly, we recognize our own responsibility to join with our American Indian sisters and brothers in their ongoing struggle to secure justice. We realize there is much that we can and must do within our Church and in society to make our support real. We must first of all increase our understanding of the present needs, aspirations, and values of the American Indian peoples. This responsibility can only be carried out effectively in dialogue with American Indians.

21. We are encouraged in our efforts by the many hopeful initiatives that Catholic communities in various parts of the country have undertaken on behalf of American Indians. From the national level, the Campaign for Human Development, the National Conference of Catholic Charities, and the Commission for Catholic Missions Among the Colored People and the Indians have provided support to many constructive local efforts.

22. For over 90 years, the Commission for Catholic Missions Among the Colored People and the Indians, together with the Bureau of Catholic Indian Missions, has had a particular responsibility to support efforts to advance the life of the Church among American Indian communities. The historical success of this work reflects the generosity of Catholics in the United States. We are particularly encouraged by the recent revitalization of these organizations and hope to see their efforts renewed and redoubled in the coming years. We should also support efforts to broaden the involvement of Indian peoples in the work of the Bureau of Catholic Indian Missions.

23. We note also the serious and sustained efforts in several dioceses to improve the Church's ministry among American Indians. In particular, the bishops of Minnesota have offered their own reflection on the Church's relationship with American Indians in their Statement, *A New Beginning*.

24. We recommend that other dioceses and Catholic organizations make similar efforts to improve their ministry with American Indians, and we pledge our own efforts to cooperate with the American Indian peoples and the local Catholic churches in these endeavors.

25. One area which deserves our special attention is that of government policy and legislation. Perhaps no other group of people in the United States is so vitally affected by government policies and programs as are American Indians. We have a responsibility to examine these systems and policies in light of the Gospel and the Church's social teachings and to urge the adoption of more just policies and legislation affecting American Indians. It seems to us that such efforts must include advocacy of: the speedy and equitable resolution of treaty and statute questions; protection of Indian land and resource rights; more adequate housing and delivery of social, educational, and health care services; and increased levels of funding and technical assistance necessary to aid American Indians in achieving political and economic self-determination and full employment.

26. We understand that such efforts will mean little if they are not accompanied by honest reflection on the entire ministry of the Church with American Indians. We must examine the Church's liturgical expressions and social and educational services within Indian communities to ask if they indeed reflect an appreciation of Indian heritage and cultural values. We would encourage national and diocesan liturgical offices to provide assistance to Indian communities to incorporate their languages and prayer forms in the liturgy and other worship services. We urge Catholic educational institutions to examine their textbooks and curriculums, and to promote programs and activities that will enable students at all levels to appreciate American Indian history, cultures, and spirituality.

27. We also urge that Church property and facilities adjacent to Indian lands or located in the midst of urban Indian neighborhoods be made more available for use by Indian communities for such activities as religious celebrations, group meetings, programs for the elderly, day-care centers, and educational programs.

28. Perhaps the most important task before us is the development of Indian leadership—clerical, religious, and lay—within the Church. This is necessary if the Church is to prosper in Indian communities. We are especially encouraged by the efforts of several dioceses to include American Indians in their permanent diaconate programs and hope that this effort is expanded. In addition, efforts should be made to ensure that American Indians have representation and a voice in all decisions made by Church agencies and organizations affecting their communities.

29. Drawing on the two themes of faith and culture, and the Church and justice, and working with all others of good will, we hope to fashion a renewed commitment to serve Indian peoples. In turn, their participation in and challenge to our Christian community will strengthen our common witness to Jesus and the Gospel message.

Religious Liberty in Eastern Europe
A Test Case for Human Rights

A Statement Issued by the
United States Catholic Conference

May 4, 1977

1. The protection of human rights continues to be a major preoccupation among those who pursue peace, and with just cause. As Christians, we have become increasingly aware that the defense and promotion of human rights is a central task of the ministry of the Church. As Pope Paul VI in his 1977 Peace message has indicated: "where human rights are truly professed and publicly recognized and defended, Peace becomes the joyful and operative atmosphere of life in society."

2. Today, human rights in many places in the world are severely restricted. While no nation is faultless in the defense and promotion of human rights, we are obliged to note two recent statements by episcopal conferences—the bishops of West Germany and of Poland—deploring the denial of the human right to religious liberty in Eastern Europe.

3. We feel all the more obliged because so many American Catholics have their ancestral roots in these countries or are themselves refugees from the oppressive regimes of Eastern Europe. The denial of religious freedom in the countries from the Baltic Sea in the north to the Black Sea in the south is a tragic episode in humanity's efforts to defend and promote human rights. Churches and individual religious believers are continually hindered by governments in the practice of their religion. In some cases, they are subjected to outright persecution, and, in others, as in the instance of Eastern Catholic churches, they have been forcibly suppressed. No religion is spared: Christians, Jews, and Moslems all suffer. The intensity and the scale of the suppression of religion is vigorous and comprehensive.

4. Attacks on the churches vary from country to country in Eastern Europe, reflecting the diversity of cultural traditions in each country, the depth and variety of religious conviction among the people, and the degree of tenacity and pragmatism of the Communist party leadership. Despite the differences in degree, a general pattern of religious oppression is clearly evident.

5. It is especially at the level of the individual believer that the infringement of the person's human right to practice his or her religion is most insidious, since in all of the Eastern European countries

211

atheism is supported by the full apparatus of the state. For example, membership in a Christian community disqualifies one from becoming a teacher, a civil servant, or an official in the goverment. In some situations, even visits to the sick and the administration of the sacraments to the dying require prior official permits. Conditions are especially severe in Lithuania where the church is subjected to constant and intense persecutions. In the Ukraine, no churches of the Ukrainian Catholic Rite and Ruthenian Rite, are permitted or open, while in Albania there exists perhaps the most systematic repression of the Church in all of Eastern Europe.

6.   Religious instruction is constantly hindered by a variety of intimidating measures taken against students and their parents by state officials. This process of violations of human rights was the subject of a recent courageous pastoral letter of the Polish bishops (September 1976). While Catholics in Poland have displayed remarkable resilience in the face of persistent and official suppression, the bishops said that the Church is now being subjected to a sophisticated program of atheization: existing building regulations are used to restrict the construction of needed churches in expanding urban centers; employment opportunities are reserved for persons who declare themselves to be nonbelievers or at least nonpracticing Catholics; and admission to some schools is made dependent upon a declaration of nonbelief. Similar practices are common throughout the Eastern European bloc.

7.   In Czechoslovakia, the regime is under the control of the most hardened Stalinists. More than half of the Catholic dioceses do not have bishops because the intransigent government refuses to acknowledge the Holy See's nominees and refuses even to dialogue on the issue. The clergy are under severe repression as are the seminaries. The very existence of the religious orders of women is especially precarious. The law forbids women from joining religious orders, and the indications are that, due to the regime's restrictions, the women's orders may be virtually extinct within twenty-five years.

8.   In summary, the lives of individual believers and the existence of the Christian community in Eastern Europe are both in serious jeopardy. Both are subject to the capricious whims of state bureaucrats, the intellectual abuse of ideologies, and the continuous harassment—with the ultimate goal of extinction—by the state apparatus.

9.   Since World War II, the political fate of Eastern Europeans has depended heavily upon relations between the United States and the Soviet Union. This relationship has been dominated by U.S. fears that provocation in Eastern Europe might precipitate a nuclear holocaust. This grim prospect has inhibited U.S. relations with the East.

10.   The resulting U.S. policy of noninterference in the affairs of Eastern European nations has prevented the United States from making any form of effective protest against Communist oppression. Advocates for the defense of human rights, including courageous dissenters in the East, have earnestly appealed to the West to apply multiple kinds of pressures against regimes in Eastern Europe, including the Soviet Union.

11. A series of recent developments—the signing of the Helsinki Accords, an increase in the volume of commercial and cultural exchanges between the United States and the Eastern European nations, and a growing sense of independence within the bloc itself—may have given the United States a potentially greater measure of influence with Communist governments in the region. The real question is whether and how we can use that influence to protect one of humanity's most precious rights: the individual's religious freedom.

12. While we do not have any illusions about the political realities of international affairs, it does appear to us that circumstances and events suggest that new opportunities are present for the United States, which, if utilized, may contribute to the defense of human rights in Eastern Europe. We therefore urge the U.S. policymakers to give respect for religious freedom a more prominent role in the conduct of our relationship with these nations. We take note of the Congress' efforts to protect human rights and encourage it to expand on these efforts.

13. Specifically, we encourage the new Administration to engage seriously in the preparations for the follow-up to the Helsinki Accords scheduled for 1977. These include the establishment of an appropriate monitoring system to measure the compliance of nations—ours as well as the Eastern Europeans—in implementing the Helsinki Accords. We also encourage U.S. trade officials, businessmen, intellectuals, performing artists, technicians, and scientists to introduce the issue of religious liberty, as well as other human rights, into their relationships with individuals and groups in Eastern Europe. And, further, advocates of corporate responsibility are encouraged to apply to Eastern Europe the same norms for evaluating the appropriateness of U.S. business presence and activities there as they do in the Third World.

14. We recall that the 1974 Roman Synod of Bishops affirmed that the promotion of human rights is required by the Gospel and is central to the Church's ministry. However, in some countries, members of the Church cannot speak up about human rights, while in others, they can do so only at great peril. We, in the United States, are not hampered in this regard. Therefore, we pledge ourselves to continue to make the public advocacy of human rights a matter of our prime concern.

15. We associate ourselves in solidarity with the persecuted Church in those regions around the world where the human right of religious freedom is severely restrained by overt acts of suppression or by subtle intimidations. We especially ally ourselves with the bishops of Eastern Europe in their suffering and their ministry to their oppressed peoples. We recognize that the best efforts of nations, private groups, and concerned individuals will not necessarily thwart those who "persecute believers and speak all kinds of slander . . ." (Mt 5:11-12). While pledging ourselves to support these efforts, we pray that those who suffer will recall Jesus' assurance that public persecution bears witness to His name and contributes to the evangelization of the world (Mk 13:9-13).

16. We also acknowledge that there is a power beyond that of policy-makers and politicians. Therefore, as we pray for the persecuted Church throughout the world, we also pray for its persecutors. In this way, we trust that God's wisdom and grace may provide what is lacking in our own efforts.

The Bicentennial Consultation
A Response to the Call to Action

A Statement Issued by the
National Conference of Catholic Bishops[1]

May 5, 1977

I

1. For two years, as part of the Catholic contribution to the bicentennial, a committee of our conference sought to involve people across the nation in a reflection on justice. At the national level it conducted seven three-day hearings at which bishops and other Church leaders listened to invited experts and concerned local persons. At the local level dioceses were encouraged to join a parish program and invite Catholics to reflect on their experience and practice of justice.

2. Many bishops, scholars, and persons active in social ministry reviewed and summarized the results of this consultation. Finally, 1,350 delegates and 1,000 observers gathered last October at a conference entitled A Call to Action to consider the results of the hearings and discussions as reflected in working papers on humankind, personhood, nationhood, ethnicity and race, the Church, neighborhood, family, and work. The convocation met for three days and produced more than one hundred eighty recommendations.

3. We invited this process of structured public discussion in the Church so that we might listen to the needs of our own people and through their voices come to know more specifically and to share more intimately "the joys and the hopes, the griefs and the anxieties" of the people of our age. Admittedly, the process of consultation was imperfect and there are some conclusions which are problematical and in some cases untenable. This has been a source of concern. Yet, this two-year process was marked by trust and respect among nearly all who took part. It gave many people a good opportunity to speak directly to Church leaders. It identified issues and a number of constructive suggestions for action. It helped dramatize how the Church and its leadership are perceived by some. We are grateful to all who shared their insights with us. We reaffirm our commitment to the principle of shared responsibility in the contemporary Church, and we assert our intention to improve consultation with our people.

---

[1]Collective statement of the American bishops reflecting an initial response to the NCCB bicentennial program and the recommendations of the Call to Action conference.

4.   The bicentennial program must be understood in light of what Vatican Council II has said about the Church. Throughout the universal Church, pastors and people have been engaged in the work of designing methods, structures, and processes for bringing the conciliar vision of the Church to fruition at the level of the parish, the diocese, the nation and, indeed, the world. The conciliar vision is contained in a unique way in the two documents on the Church: *Lumen Gentium* (The Dogmatic Constitution on the Church) and *Gaudium et Spes* (The Pastoral Constitution on the Church in the Modern World). It is in the light of the ecclesiological principles of these documents that the process, results, and future implications of the bicentennial program must be evaluated.

5.   Fundamental to the theological vision of *Lumen Gentium* is its description of the Church as the People of God.[2] The focus given to this concept by the Council has opened the way for many movements of renewal in the last decade. The image of the Church as the People of God affirms that all of us derive our dignity from the same source: the free, unmerited love of God Who has called us out of darkness into His own wonderful light to share in the life of the risen Lord Jesus Christ, thus giving us a new identity as a people uniquely His own. At this most fundamental level of the life of the Church, there are no distinctions among us. Holiness and openness to grace are the most important aspects of the life of the Church, to which everything is ordained. The hierarchical ministry in the Church is ordained entirely to the service of this plan of God, making it possible for those He has called to hear His word, become His people, and enjoy the life of the community of Jesus, the Messiah.[3] Thus the Second Vatican Council teaches that bishops, as successors of the apostles, have received from the Lord the mission of teaching authoritatively all peoples so that all may attain salvation through faith, baptism, and the observance of the commandments.[4] As pastors who are teachers, we are called both to listen and to learn from our people and also to repond to what we hear by announcing the Good News in all its implications, unfolding its riches, and applying it to contemporary circumstances.

6.   In any process of dialogue in the Church, we listen, as all Christians do, for the voice of the Spirit in the Church[5] and the world; we also exercise the charism of judgments and discernment in the Church in a special way. For bishops are "authentic teachers, that is, teachers endowed with the authority of Christ, who preach the faith to the people assigned to them, the faith which is destined to inform their

---

[2]*Lumen Gentium*, 9, 10, 11, 12.
[3]*Lumen Gentium*, 18.
[4]*Lumen Gentium*, 24.
[5]*Lumen Gentium*, 4.

thinking and direct their conduct."[6] In responding to the consultative process we have begun, therefore, we are seeking to judge and discern, to guide and direct a process which we believe can bear much fruit in the Church today. We have to be both pastors who can listen and teachers who can speak. We seek to do this sensitively, intelligently, and compassionately. We are addressing our response especially to those Christians whose faith in Christ is nurtured within the Roman Catholic Church. In this community, with its specific understanding of authority, we are called to live in truth and by love, and to be free with the liberty Christ has gained for us. One of the greatest tests of the Catholic Christian's interior freedom is to respond to God's word in the Church even when a decision may be contrary to one's own views and to abide by that decision with a profound inner peace and joy.

7. The particular process of consultation which culminated in the proposals of the Call to Action conference was helpful and important. However, it cannot be the sole factor in determining the pastoral agenda for the Church. It is our task to assess those proposals in the context of God's plan as revealed in and through Christ.

8. One of the demands of the divine plan is action to support a way of life in conformity with the justice which God has revealed and communicated to us in Christ Jesus. Both *Gaudium et Spes* and the synodal document, *Justice in the World*, affirm direct and intimate connection between the mission of the church and the ministry of justice.[7] This connection is so strong that the plan of salvation, which the Church is meant to proclaim and serve, is understood by the Bible as one of "justification," that is, as the transformation of human life by the righteousness or justice of God. This has powerful implications for the entire Church. In communion with our people, we have an obligation to address many issues of individual and social life in the light of this divine justice.[8] The bicentennial program was initiated by us to clarify and specify the implications for the Church in the United States of a social ministry at the service of the justice of God.[9]

9. Because this is the justice we preach, we also recognize that we may not simply equate earthly progress with the spread of the Kingdom of God or confuse the Church's role and competence with respect

---

[6]*Lumen Gentium*, 25.
[7]*Gaudium et Spes*, 40, 43; *Justice in the World*: Introduction, Parts I and II.
[8]*Lumen Gentium*, 25; cf., also *Christus Dominus*, 12: "Let (bishops) explain also how high a value, according to the doctrine of the Church, should be placed on the human person, on his liberty and bodily life; how highly we should value the family, its unity and stability, the procreation and education of children, human society and its laws and professions, its labor and leisure, its arts and technical inventions, its poverty and abundance. They should expound likewise the principles governing the solution of those very grave problems concerning the possession, increase and just distribution of material goods, concerning peace and war, and the fraternal coexistence of peoples."
[9]*Octagesima Adveniens*, 4.

to each. The principles of revelation do not provide specific solutions to many social problems, nor do they constitute a blueprint for organizing society. In proposing concrete policies in the social order, the Church is aware that often the more specific a proposal or program, the more room there may be for persons of sincere faith to disagree.

10. The Church is called to engage in continuing self-examination in order to make its own structures and procedures more effective instruments of and witness to this divine justice. In doing this, we must keep in mind that the Church is a unique reality into which we are graciously incorporated and a society which is essentially designed by Christ. In reflecting upon its structures, therefore, we can learn much from human organizations but we may not draw too heavily upon them. The Christian life is given to us as an undeserved gift, a grace; it does not originate in our efforts and aspirations although it requires our full cooperation. Reflection upon the roles and rights of members of the Church must take place in light of this fact.

11. In this preliminary and partial response we can speak to only some of the many recommendations, general and specific, presented to us. All are being referred for study to committees of the National Conference of Catholic Bishops and the United States Catholic Conference. How they will be addressed is described in the final section of this document. Our purpose at this time is to provide an overall assessment of what has been placed before us.

II

12. The bicentennial consultation reflected the participants' willingness to take personal responsibility for building the Christian community and sharing in its mission. Forthright in requesting episcopal action, they were equally direct in challenging one another and the community at large. The most lasting response will be in dioceses, parishes, and the lives of individuals.

13. The consultation, itself an exercise in shared responsibility, appropriately recommended "the further development of both structures and practices of consultation and shared responsibility at every level of the Church."[10] We shall seek to develop such ways of helping to discern the needs and gifts of the faithful in the light of the Gospel. We have already encouraged the formation of parish councils and diocesan pastoral councils. We wish to encourage these councils again as good forums for this dialogue to take place.

14. We support the thrust of recommendations for continued efforts to eradicate racial and ethnic discrimination, even when unconscious and unintended, in both the Church and society; to protect and foster

---

[10]Call to Action, *Church*, 1,3.

the rights of Church employees; to carry forward the practice of financial accountability; and to observe due process procedures in Church life. Catholic institutions and officials should regularly engage in formal review of their personnel policies and other practices in this light.

15. Hispanic, black, and Indian Catholics deserve continued support in their efforts to articulate their needs, as do the many other ethnic groups which demonstrate the values of cultural diversity and pluralism within the Church and society. We readily express our "desire to respond to proposals for action which come from ethnic, racial and cultural organizations," and we further strive to "facilitate and encourage efforts of such groups to formulate pastoral and social action programs to meet their needs."[11] There is much to commend in recommendations calling attention to minority needs of a cultural, liturgical, and social nature. We see the value of new forms of training for ministry, responsive to cultural diversity,[12] and of efforts to foster appropriate multicultural expressions within the Church, especially in relation to worship, pastoral planning, and education. Clearly, though, all such efforts must be consistent with the essential unity of the community of faith.

16. Since racism is "among the most persistent and destructive evils in our nation,"[13] we shall continue to address this abuse in words and actions. In view of the recommendation for a collective pastoral "on the sin of racism in both its personal and social dimension,"[14] we shall seek to develop such a document, either as a pastoral letter or in some other appropriate form.

17. Inner city neighborhoods clearly require "priority attention by the Church,"[15] yet there is also a great need for its efforts "to improve the quality of life in rural areas."[16] The dilemma with which such recommendations can confront the Church in allocating its limited resources does not permit us to abandon one area of need in favor of another; it underlines the urgent need for all the people of the Church, not only its bishops, to be sensitive and generous in responding.

18. The consultation spoke often of family concerns and the need for family ministry. Participants found much evidence of discrimination against families in society today, and some expressed the belief that even the Church gives too little attention to family life. "The whole Church, through the example of the lives of its members and through action undertaken in cooperation with other religious and civic groups, [should] combat those contemporary social, economic and cultural

---

[11]CTA, *Ethnicity and Race*, II, 2.
[12]Cf., *Ethnicity and Race*, II, 3.
[13]NCCB, *To Live in Christ Jesus*.
[14]*Ethnicity and Race*, IV, 8.
[15]*Neighborhood*, II, 7.
[16]*Neighborhood*, IV.

forces which threaten families."[17] Comprehensive pastoral planning for family ministry is required, involving Church leadership and family representatives.[18] On the national level this effort has begun and will continue through our Commission on Marriage and Family Life. Families, diocesan offices, and national Church bodies, together with other religious and civic groups, should give particular attention to the media's impact on family life and undertake programs to encourage their wholesome use by families "as part of a pastoral social justice program related to media."[19] We encourage our national communication structures to move forward vigorously in this area. Also, noting the recommendation for a "family year,"[20] we ask the appropriate NCCB/USCC structures, in collaboration with other interested bodies, to give immediate attention to this suggestion as a possible vehicle for new initiatives in this critically important field.

19. Recommendations supportive of vocations to the priesthood, the diaconate, and the religious life reflect a commendable appreciation of these forms of service to God and humanity. Beyond question, God's people who have "the right to competent pastoral care," also have "the responsibility to further vocations . . . by prayer, by participation in religious vocation programs and by active encouragement of those in seminaries and those training for the religious life."[21] Moreover, the Catholic community should offer understanding and support to bishops, priests, deacons, and religious in their work. While continuing to seek ways to improve the quality of pastoral care available to our people, we urge them also to assume their own responsibilities in this regard.

20. Some recommendations suggested the possibility of change in the Church's discipline concerning priestly celibacy and the ordination of married men as priests. We concur instead with the longstanding view of the Church, as expressed overwhelmingly by the 1971 Synod of Bishops. Priestly celibacy has great value as an eschatological sign and an instrument for pastoral service, and "the law of priestly celibacy existing in the Latin Church is to be kept in its entirety." Also, "excepting always the right of the Supreme Pontiff, the priestly ordination of married men is not permitted, even in particular cases."[22]

21. Much attention has been given the several recommendations concerning the ordination of women to the priesthood. We affirm the conclusion of the Hold See's recent *Declaration on the Question of the Admission of Women to the Ministerial Priesthood*—that the Church "does not consider herself authorized to admit women to priestly ordina-

---

[17] CTA, *Family*, I, 3.
[18] *Family*, I, 3.
[19] Cf., *Family*, II, 4.
[20] *Family*, I, 3.
[21] *Church*, I, 5.
[22] *The Ministerial Priesthood*.

tion."[23] We invite theologians to join us in a serious study of the issues to which the document addresses itself. Further study and clarification of these issues may allay some of the anguish felt by many whose love for the Church is unquestioned. There is a pressing need to "identify, formally authenticate, and expand ministries" performed by women in the Church.[24] Efforts to open up new and greater opportunities for leadership by women are imperative. We shall vigorously pursue this matter, as well as questions of justice for women in society, within our conference and other Church structures.

22. Other specific recommendations pertaining to pastoral ministry concern the aged, youth, and young adults. The needs of the elderly in our parishes and communities are urgent. In our pastoral approach to the elderly we must all recognize "the principle of dynamic growth in every age span and give consideration to the spirituality of the aging as a resource to the Church."[25] As we indicated a year ago in our statement, *Society and the Aged: Toward Reconciliation*, we intend to increase our efforts to ensure that their pastoral needs are met, that they are included in all phases of the Church's life, and that Church agencies and institutions for social service and social action give them high priority. Youth and young adults need similar attention, including opportunities for greater direct participation in the Church's life and work.[26] We welcome creative, practical proposals by agencies and individuals familiar with youth and young adult ministry. Similarly, recognizing "the unique gifts handicapped persons have to offer the Church," we shall seek ways more effectively to achieve "their integration into full participation in the Christian community."[27]

23. Other issues addressed during the consultation concern contraception, ministry to homosexuals, and the pastoral care of separated and divorced Catholics.

24. We have frequently expressed our fidelity to the Church's teaching on birth control. As pastors and teachers we, too, are concerned over "conflict and anguish" with respect to this issue.[28] In rejecting contraception as a morally legitimate means of limiting births, the Church is proclaiming and defending the value of procreation itself, "a value attacked, though in different ways, by both the ideology of contraception and by contraceptive acts."[29] For this reason, we have urged, and urge again, prayerful reflection concerning the necessity to live according to this teaching, so that the grace of God will give

---

[23]Sacred Congregation for the Doctrine of the Faith, October 15, 1976.
[24]*Church*, II, 5.
[25]CTA, *Personhood*, II, 5.
[26]Cf., *Personhood*, II, 5.
[27]*Personhood*, II, 6.
[28]*Personhood*, III, 2.
[29]*To Live in Christ Jesus*.

to all couples the power to be faithful to their mission of expressing in their lives the lifegiving love of Christ for His people. In continuing to seek effective means of "safeguarding the holiness of marriage"[30] in our times, we are determined to observe the dual reminder given us by Pope Paul: "To diminish in no way the saving teachings of Christ constitutes an eminent form of charity for souls. But this must ever be accompanied by patience and goodness, such as the Lord Himself gave example of."[31]

25. While we acknowledge the need for sensitive and compassionate ministry to homosexuals and support their basic human rights[32] we also emphasize that "homosexual activity . . . as distinguished from homosexual orientation, is morally wrong."[33] The moral obligations for such persons which arise from this fact carry a corollary obligation for all of us to respond to their need for pastoral care.

26. Recommendations concerning separated and divorced Catholics call for a clear but sensitive response in deeds as well as words.[34] In fidelity to Christ, the Church teaches firmly that sacramental marriages are indissoluble. The staggering rate and number of divorces in our country at the present time, many of them involving Catholics, reflect the tragedy of marital failure in a society which shows little appreciation for the sanctity of marriage. In light of this, the Church has a two-fold responsibility. It must proclaim more strongly, not less, the indissolubility of Christian marriage. It must also extend special pastoral care to separated and divorced Catholics, so that, even as they experience the heartache of marital failure, they may also experience Christ's loving concern and understanding mediated through their Church. This pastoral care must include a strong effort to strengthen, where needed, the personnel and expertise of those exercising ministry in our marriage tribunals. These must be properly equipped to render justice expeditiously to those who request adjudication of their marriage status by a plea of nullity.

27. Participants in the consultation spoke forcefully of their concern for many issues of justice and peace in our country and world. Recognizing that only with sacrifice will this nation be able to provide meaningful jobs, decent housing, quality education, and equal opportunity for all its people, while furthering the cause of peace, development, and human rights internationally, the recommendations express a clear commitment, which we share, to continue to work for

---

[30]*Humanae Vitae*, 30. The encyclical adds that this "implies concerted pastoral action in all the fields of human activity, economic, cultural, and social; in fact, only a simultaneous improvement in these various sectors will make it possible to render the life of parents and of children within their families not only tolerable, but easier and more joyous."

[31]*Humanae Vitae*, 29.

[32]Cf., *Personhood*, III, 4.

[33]*To Live in Christ Jesus*.

[34]Cf., *Family*, III.

these goals. In particular, we encourage our national offices to seek to develop "new models of justice education at all levels" and to encourage research and evaluation projects in this area.[35]

28. The concern for human life expressed in the consultation and the recognition of the need to restore legal protection to the unborn are praiseworthy. Comprehensive and consistent commitment to the sanctity of life in all contexts and at all stages of its development, before birth as well as after, is demanded of us as followers of Christ. Such commitment requires many practical forms of action, including restoration to the unborn of their legal right to life through an amendment to the Constitution.[36]

29. The consultation proposed a large agenda for national policy on many other issues also concerned with the sanctity of life. There were recommendations on such matters as public action to achieve full employment, income security, decent housing and health care, equal access to quality education, public and private, responsive agricultural and resource policy, sensitive immigration laws, reform of the criminal justice system, respect for human rights in foreign policy, arms control and disarmament, and many other issues. We wish in particular to state our recognition of "the dangers and evils of the arms race and an aggressive military posture" and to acknowledge our responsibility, in collaboration with others, to encourage "peace education programs" which will illuminate the moral dimensions of this urgent issue and foster responsible efforts on behalf of arms control and disarmament.[37]

30. In most cases, the recommendations on domestic and international issues are consistent with our publicly stated positions and provide a welcome impetus for continued efforts. A few, however, involve matters with which we have not dealt up to now; in some cases, the issues appear more complex than the recommendations would suggest. We strongly encourage our committees and offices to continue to study these questions and develop policy recommendations for our consideration. These efforts should go forward in recognition of the responsibility of the Church "to promote a critical reordering of national priorities and policies to give primary consideration to human rights and human needs[38] in this country and abroad.

---

[35]CTA, *Humankind*, I, 5.
[36]Cf., *Personhood*, II, 3.
[37]*Humankind*, III, 3.
[38]*Nationhood*, II.

III

31. As these remarks suggest, the different recommendations of the bicentennial consultation must be approached in several different ways. Some pertain to the teaching or discipline of the universal Church; in regard to them we recall our duty, as members of the college of bishops united with the Holy Father, to respect the principles of collegiality and universality and, in particular, our fundamental obligation of fidelity to the teaching of Christ entrusted to the Church. The conflict, between a few of the recommendations and what the Church teaches, underlines our responsibility to express this teaching more clearly and effectively. As bishops we cannot compromise Catholic teaching. Yet we have the responsibility to do whatever we can, with God's grace, to clarify the evangelical principles which lie behind these teachings, as we strive to improve our efforts to catechize on these matters. Other recommendations pertain specifically to dioceses, parishes, other structures and individuals, and the final response must come at these levels. Some matters involve existing programs of NCCB/USCC or questions now being studied by it; in such cases the recommendations will be fully considered in planning future initiatives at the national level. Still others raise new, complex questions; these too, will be examined very carefully. As part of the evaluation process, the availability of material resources to accomplish what has been suggested must necessarily be given serious and realistic consideration.

32. Among matters which are beyond the competence of our conference, as such, to influence directly, we note several themes concerning the parish which emerged from the consultation. It is worth doing this in order to indicate our support in principle.

33. In speaking of their parishes, some Catholics tend to measure the health of the Church by the presence of the sense of commitment. They express a desire to experience community in ways they find more meaningful. Requests for home Masses, parish welcoming and outreach committees, greater liturgical variety, more opportunities for cultural expression and reinforcement, and improved communication between priests and people all point to the importance of developing the community of faith in families, parishes, and informal gatherings of Christians.[39]

34. Clearly, the parish community must become closely involved with the neighborhood and its problems to witness Christian concern for a better life for all and its work for justice at the local level. Parish life should provide challenges and opportunities for the believing community to confront sin, suffering, and injustice within and beyond

---

[39] *Neighborhood*, I, 3.

the local community. This theme was articulated in repeated requests for adult education programs, especially those involving formation in Christian responsibility in the political and social realm.[40] Effective utilization of the new sacramental rites and of catechetical instruction for the young was also urged. Other recommendations, made in relation to social justice, noted the need to involve the parish in the surrounding neighborhood or rural community through prayer, service, and education. This underlines the need for supportive structures and programs at the diocesan level relating to pastoral planning for social justice, increased support for community organization, education for justice, the achievement of equal opportunity, and family life.

35. The Church in the United States is both a community of believers, pledged to fidelity to the Gospel, and a body of concerned citizens. Reflecting this dual role and the obligations arising from it, participants in the consultation expressed a keen interest in the Church's involvement in the formation of public policy and the political ethos. We, too, are intensely interested in the quality of Catholic citizenship, and, we agree that "parishes, dioceses and other groups within the Church . . . [should] continue or initiate programs of education aimed at greater understanding of: a) the way public policy is made; b) the relationship between the public policy and the Gospel of Jesus Christ, and the traditions and experiences of the Catholic people themselves, and; c) the duties of citizenship."[41]

36. We cite these two areas as representative of those where response must essentially come at the local level and where early positive action is to be encouraged. In doing so, we also note the desirability of continued consultation at various levels in the Church concerning the implementation of such recommendations.

37. As we have already said, every recommendation from the bicentennial consultation will also be studied by one or more of the committees of NCCB/USCC. Conscious of the fact that the hearings and the Detroit conference aimed at providing us the material for a five-year "Plan of Action," we direct the president of the NCCB to appoint, as soon as possible, an ad hoc committee to be chaired by a bishop, and to be composed of members of the NCCB and of members drawn from the Advisory Council. This commitment will have as its charge to develop the five-year "Plan of Action," in consultation with our NCCB and USCC committees. It will establish appropriate deadlines for its work, and once the "Plan of Action" has been accepted by the NCCB, it will have responsibility for oversight of its implementation. Finally, this committee will submit a written report on the implementation process at each of our general meetings in November for

---

[40]Cf., for example, *Church*, III, 2.
[41]*Nationhood*, I, 1.

the next five years. We believe these steps will ensure effective implementation and responsible accountability, to us and to all others, on
the part of our national structures.

38. The present preliminary and partial response is not intended as
a total response to the bicentennial consultation. Such a response
must come in carefully planned actions carried out over a period of
time. But we do not forget the fact that hundreds of people came to
us to describe situations of injustice which they had seen or worked
in. All came with hope that the Church can be a sign and source of
social justice and peace in the world today. We have been moved by
these voices. Perhaps the major result of this extensive consultation
is the hope it has given us that together we can bear witness to the
unity of the Church of Christ by the justice and peace in which we
all live.

Resolution on *Jesus of Nazareth*

A Resolution Passed by the
National Conference of Catholic Bishops

May 1977

Jesus of Nazareth, the recent television dramatization of the life of Our Lord, was a profoundly spiritual experience for millions of viewers. We commend Franco Zeffirelli, the National Broadcasting Company, the sponsors, and all associated with the program for this contribution to the religious and cultural life of the nation. We are also happy to note that the large audience attracted by *Jesus of Nazareth* demonstrates conclusively that, when treated with sensitive professionalism, religious themes are capable of winning widespread viewer acceptance in prime time television.

Statement concerning
Human Sexuality

*A Statement Prepared by the Committee on
Doctrine, National Conference of
Catholic Bishops*

November 15, 1977

1. The Committee on Doctrine exists to assist the bishops in their apostolic mandate "to profess the truth in love" (Eph 4:15). It is in this perspective that it has considered the book *Human Sexuality, New Directions in American Catholic Thought* (Paulist Press, 1977), the final report of a committee established by the Catholic Theological Society of America. We offer this assessment to the bishops, recalling that they themselves have already addressed many of these issues in *To Live in Christ Jesus* (November 1976). The Committee also acknowledges the statements of many bishops who have already spoken to the faithful of their own dioceses on this study.

2. The Committee recognizes the importance and value of theological discussion and research; without these the Church could hardly fulfill its teaching mission. But in exercising their respective tasks both the bishops and the theologians have certain obligations: they are bound by the written Word of God along with Sacred Tradition, the *sensus fidei*, the documents in which the faith of the Church has been set forth, and by pastoral and missionary concern for the world.[1] In the words of the International Theological Commission: "Although the magisterium of the Supreme Pontiff and of the bishops is specifically called 'pastoral,' the scientific character of their work does not free theologians from pastoral and missionary responsibility, especially given the publicity which modern communications media so quickly give to even scientific matters."[2] The Committee does not object to a theological study of sexuality offered as a stimulus for discussion among theologians and other qualified people. But it rejects the idea that a tentative study such as *Human Sexuality* can offer "helpful pastoral guidelines to beleaguered pastors, priests, counsellors, and teachers" as well as guidance for the faithful in forming their consciences when such a study contradicts theological tradition and the Church's clear magisterial teaching refined over the centuries and recently reaffirmed in the Vatican Declaration on Sexual Ethics

---

[1]Cf., International Theological Commission, *Theses on the Relationship Between the Ecclesiastical Magisterium and Theology* (USCC, 1977); thesis 3, p. 2.
[2]ITC, *Theses on Magisterium and Theology*; thesis 3, 4, p. 3.

and the American Bishops' Pastoral Letter.

3.   The Committee on Doctrine regrets to find in the report a rather impoverished concept of the role the written Word of God must play as a foundation for theology. While critical exegesis contributes to the Church's understanding of the sacred texts, it cannot be considered the ultimate source of their meaning. God's Word is proclaimed in the living reality of the Church which by its teaching, its liturgy, and the witness of its saints continues to reveal the riches of this Word. The Church is the locus and guardian, established by the Lord, in which His thought is authentically preserved and unfolded. This ongoing interpretation of Scripture in the daily life of the Church under the influence of the Holy Spirit is guided by the Magisterium.

4.   The sexual behavior of those called and empowered to be children of God must be based on God's plan in creating human beings male and female. This is how the Church understands Genesis 1:27-28 and Genesis 2:21-24. Because God made His human creatures male and female they are able to become "two in one flesh" and participate in His continuing creation by reproducing His image and likeness in men and women. In fidelity to this plan the Church has condemned such behavior as fornication, adultery, and masturbation as sinful. The unitive and procreative dimension of human sexual activity as it came from the hands of God can be properly realized only within the marriage covenant. God's plan for human sexuality cannot be learned from studies which stress the Bible as so culturally conditioned as to suggest that it has little of value to say on the subject to the men and women of our time. As Pope Paul VI said to the American bishops on the occasion of the Canonization of St. John Neumann: "We have no hope outside the Word of God. Apart from it there are no valid solutions to the problems of our day" (June 21, 1977).

5.   The Committee recognizes the importance and value of empirical studies (cf., Chap. 3), but it is also aware of the inadequacy of such studies by themselves to establish moral norms or alter them. Social scientific research has an important role to play in providing the raw material for theological reflection. It is one way of "consulting the faithful" about their problems and insights. However, no responsible social scientist claims that his efforts describe behavior the way it ought to be; rather it describes behavior as it in fact is. Moral values are not produced by social research and social research makes no claim that its findings are normative.

6.   We do not find in the report sufficient respect for this dialogic aspect of the relationship between research and values. Nor do we find even a sufficient critical attitude towards specific social analyses. Some research enterprises are more elaborate and more sophisticated than others. The theologian who proposes to use "input" from surveys must be careful to maintain a nuanced and critical attitude towards the relative merits of the various studies he employs.

7. The *Pastoral Constitution on the Church in the Modern World* and Pope Paul's encyclical *Humanae Vitae* expressed a careful balance between the procreative and unitive functions of human sexuality. The authors of the report neglect this balance in their effort to explore a broader concept of human sexuality. The goals of human sexuality substituted by the report (creative growth toward integration, intra-personal and interpersonal growth) are too vague to apply with any kind of precision or assurance. In effect, they remove the essential connection between sexual activity and procreation, sexual activity and marital love. Similarly, the second-level values proposed (sexual activity must be self-liberating, other-enriching, etc.) offer little guidance. By abandoning norms that make specific demands, the report reaches the conclusion that sexual activity outside of marriage can be permissible or even virtuous.

8. While the report departs from the procreative and unitive purposes of sexuality set by Vatican II, it claims to endorse the norm the Council prescribes for sexual activity, that is, that it be in accord with "the nature of the person and his acts." But the authors of the report, in the development of their study, actually ignore the second half of this norm, i.e., the requirement that what is done be in accord with the nature of the human act. As stated in the *Pastoral Constitution on the Church in the Modern World,* "When it is a question of harmonizing married love with the responsible transmission of life, it is not enough to take only the good intention and evaluation of motives into account; the objective criteria must be used, criteria drawn from the nature of the human person and human action, criteria which respect the total meaning of mutual self-giving and human procreation in the context of true love. . . ."[3] The human sexual act has both a procreative and unitive dimension, and both dimensions must be taken into account if sexual activity is to be judged by the nature of the act as well as by the nature of the human person.

9. The suggested pastoral guidelines of the report (Chap. 5) depart from the teaching of the Church in many specific areas as the authors themselves admit (cf., pp. 126, 134, 164f., 214ff.). Pastors, confessors, counsellors, and teachers cannot adopt these guidelines and remain faithful to the mission of proclaiming God's Word which has been entrusted to them.

10. The Committee also finds that *Human Sexuality* gives little attention to the supernatural aspects of marital love and fidelity in the life of the Christian. Christian marriage is meant to symbolize the love of Christ for His Church. The love and fidelity of husband and wife are to make His love and fidelity visible to the world. There is no limit to the challenge here which goes beyond simple duty or obligation. The Christian cannot be satisfied with a minimal sexual moral-

---

[3] *Pastoral Constitution on the Church in the Modern World,* #51.

ity if this challenge is to be met. But the Church believes that through the grace of God married couples can grow beyond themselves, and love beyond their merely human capacity (cf., *To Live in Christ Jesus* [USCC, 1976] p.14). The pastoral guidelines (Chap. 5) show little sensitivity to this dimension of marriage and sexuality.

11. The Committee on Doctrine appeals to the theological community in pursuance of its pastoral responsibility to continue its work in the development of a response to the problems Christians must face in the whole field of sexual ethics. We welcome the continued discussion and professional research of theologians in developing a comprehensive morality that is sensitive to the Word of God, to the mystery of Christ in His Church, to God's call to every human being to be perfect as He is perfect, and to the developing nature of the human response to that call.

12. We understand and appreciate the need for compassion in dealing with human nature, weakened as it is by sin and subject to strong cultural pressures, particularly in the area of sexual morality.

13. Since we have spoken at length of moral norms and values, it would be good to recall that whenever Christian Revelation speaks of these it adds at once the consideration of the grace that saves and makes our effort possible. The Lord, who sets us free from the works of death (cf., Rom 7:24) and raises us to the dignity of sharing God's life, will make possible the realization of human dignity on the natural and supernatural level.

14. "The Son of Man has come to search out and to save what was lost" (Lk 19:10), and though He was intransigent with evil, yet He was merciful toward individuals. In their difficulties the faithful should always find, in the words and in the heart of a priest, the echo of the voice and love of the Redeemer (cf., *Humanae Vitae*, #29).

15. However, we must also warn against the temptation to respond to this need for pastoral compassion by weakening the demands of sound morality. Rather than compassion this would turn out to be cruelty. We do this in the spirit of Pope Paul's message to the American bishops on the occasion of the Canonization of St. John Neumann: "The most profound pastoral understanding, the deepest human compassion exist only in fidelity to God's Word . . . (without this) our apostolic charity is incomplete . . . Understanding? Yes! Sensitivity? Yes! But supernatural sensitivity to Christ and to His Cross and Resurrection."

Principles and Guidelines for Fund Raising in the United States by Arch/Dioceses, Arch/Diocesan Agencies, and Religious Institutes

A Statement Promulgated by the
National Conference of Catholic Bishops

November 16, 1977

Foreword

1. These principles and guidelines reflect a shared concern on the part of the National Conference of Catholic Bishops, the Leadership Conference of Women Religious, and the Conference of Major Superiors of Men that all fund-raising efforts within the Catholic Church should reflect Christian motivation.

2. They have been developed collaboratively by the three Conferences and approved by them. Widespread consultation with the members of the three groups, as well as within the fund-raising community, was part of the process.

3. Promulgated by the National Conference of Catholic Bishops, the principles and guidelines apply to fund raising not only by dioceses and diocesan institutions but also by religious institutes. This is in line with the declaration of the apostolic letter of Pope Paul VI concerning implementation of Vatican II's *Christus Dominus* (the Decree on the Pastoral Office of Bishops in the Church), that: "The episcopal conference of any country can, after consultation with the interested religious superiors, establish norms for seeking alms which must be observed by all religious" (*Ecclesiae Sanctae, #27*).

Stewardship

4. Christian stewardship is the practical realization that everything we have is a gift from God. Stewardship expresses itself as an integral force in Christian life by motivating us to share our goods with others. We are absolute owners of nothing; rather, we are stewards of all we receive and we must use such resources responsibly in our lifelong work of building up the Kingdom of God.

5. For men and women especially committed to building up the Kingdom of God, stewardship heightens an awareness of responsibilities in matters of material concern no less than in spiritual endeavor.

6. We are particularly conscious of the sacred relationship of trust that is established when we, in God's name and for His work, ask others for financial support. Our obligation in stewardship mandates a fitting proportion between the importance of the work to be funded and the magnitude and cost of fund raising.

7. Requests for support, besides being truthful and forthright, must be made on a theologically sound basis and should always be in good taste to strive to lift the hearts and minds of men and women to a greater love of God and neighbor.

Stewardship Guidelines

8. (1) The fund-raising appeal should be directed toward motivating the faithful to participate in apostolic works in fulfillment of their responsibility to share with others.

9. (2) No organization should ask the faithful to fund its total and absolute security. Nor should an organization engage in fund-raising efforts for undefined future needs.

10. (3) The trust relationship between donor and fundraiser requires that funds collected be used for the intended purpose and not be absorbed by excessive fund-raising costs.

11. (4) Appeals for funds must be straightforward and honest, respectful, and based on sound theological principles. The donor must be informed how the donated funds will be used and assured that the funds given are used for the purpose intended and that restrictions stated by the donor will be observed.

Religious Authority

12. Effective stewardship recognizes the role of authority. All religious authority comes from God and is exercised in faith, in His name. Religious authority promotes and regularizes the building of the Kingdom of God, ever attentive to God's glory and the enhancement of humanity's condition.

13. Approbation by religious authority is required to authenticate and sanction an endeavor conducted under the aegis of God's Church. On a functional level we recognize in this authority the principle of subsidiarity which, without diminishing the responsibility of ultimate authority, makes possible a more fruitful Kingdom through the promotion of initiative and self-control.

14. All who collect funds under Catholic auspices, consequently, must have the approval of appropriate Church authority. This authorization must be clear and explicit because the Church's integrity relies upon that authority as responsible for the method and scope of fund raising, for the faithful disposition of the monies collected, and for the prevention of abuses.

Religious Authority Guidelines

15. (1) Religious institutes and diocesan agencies should observe those prescriptions of Canon Law and their own regulations which require approval of major superiors and/or the ordinary of the place to solicit funds.

16. (2) The approval of fund raising by proper authority should express the purpose for which the funds are raised and the methods to be used in raising them. Effective control of fund-raising programs should be maintained through periodic review and, where necessary, appropriate sanction.

17. (3) Religious or diocesan agencies may not proceed in the collection of funds by public subscription without the consent of the ordinaries of those places where the funds are collected (see note below).

18. (4) Major superiors of religious institutes should, as a moral duty, provide the ordinary of the place where the fund raising originates with significant information about the fund-raising programs and the apostolates they support.

Accountability

19. The very nature of religious fund raising places the fundraisers, viewed here particularly as the responsible religious organizations seeking the funds, in special relationships of accountability: to God in whose name they ask, to the Church whom they represent, to those whom they serve, and to the benefactors whose partners they are in this apostolic work. The relationship between fundraiser and benefactor goes far beyond the transfer of money. The fundraiser must recognize that giving as an expression of religion has a sacramental nature and is in itself an apostolic activity.

20. As every person is accountable to God for his or her stewardship, fundraisers are accountable to the donor for the disposition of monies received. As a first step, this accountability demands that funds be used for the causes promoted, always respecting the specified wishes of the donor. Furthermore, fundraisers should make available to donors an appropriate report of significant financial aspects and the apostolic dimensions of the endeavor to which they have contributed.

NOTE: See Apostolic Letter, *Ecclesiae Sanctae*, August 6, 1966, No. 27(2). Some canonists regard "public subscription" as an appeal for donors to contribute toward a stated purpose on the implied condition that others will contribute to the same cause. The appeal is "public" not because it may be directed to a widespread audience, as are some mail campaigns, but because of attendant circumstances, such as endorsements by Church and civil officials, with notable publicity.

Accountability Guidelines

21. (1) Accountability requires the fundraiser to provide timely reports on the extent to which promises expressed or implied in the solicitation of funds have been fulfilled.

22. (2) Fund-raising reports should be prepared in scope and design to meet the particular concerns of those to whom reports are due: namely, the governing body and membership of the fund-raising organization itself, religious authorities who approved and must monitor the fund-raising effort, donors to the particular organization and the giving public at large, and those who are beneficiaries of the funds given.

23. (3) Fund-raising reports should provide both financial information and a review of the apostolic work for which the funds were raised. The availability of these reports to benefactors on a regular basis or on reasonable request should be publicized.

24. (4) Fund-raising organizations should provide their governing bodies with an annual audit prepared in accordance with generally accepted accounting principles, and, where size warrants, by a certified public accountant.

25. (5) All financial reports of a fundraiser should be consistent with the annual audit. At minimum, a fundraiser's report, regardless of scope, should set forth the amount of money collected, the cost of conducting the fund-raising effort, and the amount and use of the funds disbursed.

26. (6) Donations should be acknowledged with promptness; reasonable requests from donors for information about their particular gift should be met.

Technique

27. Technique as a tool of stewardship can promote effectiveness and guard against the weakness of our human condition. Fundraisers should utilize the management technique of internal controls in administrative practice. Exclusive authority over all aspects of fund raising should not be vested in any single person. Separation of such financial functions of fund raising as collection, allocation, and accounting, is essential for internal control.

28. Adherence to legal requirements and respect for professional guidelines are fundamental to sound management of the fund-raising function. There are as many ways of raising funds as there are many and far-reaching apostolates to be funded. Each fund-raising method has its own specialized purpose and technique. But responsible and effective fund-raising methodology should never drown out the voice of the Spirit of God that must permeate our total efforts. The raising of funds for gospel works is indeed a vocation and a grace working hand in hand with the direct ministry for which the funds are raised.

Technique Guidelines

29. (1) Funds beyond operating expenses should not be accumulated by a fund-raising office, but should be turned over at regular intervals to the appropriate allocating office of the organization.

30. (2) Fund-raising authority and investment authority should not be vested in any single person.

31. (3) Special care should be taken to see that ethical business relationships are maintained by fundraisers with suppliers of goods and service.

32. (4) Contracts between a religious fundraiser and commercial suppliers and consultants should ensure that control over materials, designs, money, and general operations remain fully in the hands of the religious fundraiser.

33. (5) In no case should agreements be made which directly or indirectly base payment either to the commercial firm or to the religious fundraiser on a percentage basis.

34. (6) Requests for funds should not be associated with material objects which are inconsistent with the apostolic purposes of the appeal.

Implementation Guidelines

35. (1) Local ordinaries and major superiors, within their respective jurisdiction, should exercise control over fund-raising activities to achieve conformity with these guidelines. Particularly in response to formal complaints, legitimate authority should be prompt to investigate charges and remedy abuses, even to the point, when necessary, of terminating a fund-raising program.

36. (2) In virtue of their endorsement of these guidelines, the National Conference of Catholic Bishops, the Leadership Conference of Women Religious, and the Conference of Major Superiors of Men agree to assist their respective constituencies in achieving appropriate control of fund-raising activities and in obtaining effective sanction for abuses. Accordingly, each conference will, through its president:

 (a) promulgate these guidelines and other suitable norms for responsible fund raising;

 (b) help correct abuses through

  (1) cooperative efforts with the responsible authorities

(2) a meeting of the presidents of the three conferences (NCCB, LCWR, CMSM), to collaborate on further action should an abuse on the part of a member of these constituencies not be resolved by that member's responsible authority.

The Gospel of Peace and the Danger of War

*A Statement Issued by the Administrative Board
of the United States Catholic Conference*

February 15, 1978

1. In his Day of Peace Message for 1978, Pope Paul VI again called upon the community of the Church and the entire human community to reflect upon the meaning of peace in a world still marked by multiple forms of violence. Among these the spectre of technological warfare is the unique menace of the age. Listen to the Holy Father:

> We would like to be able to dispel this threatening and terrible nightmare by proclaiming at the top of our voice the absurdity of modern war and the absolute necessity of Peace—Peace not founded on the power of arms that today are endowed with an infernal destructive capacity (let us recall the tragedy of Japan), nor founded on the structural violence of some political regimes, but founded on the patient, rational, and loyal method of justice and freedom, such as the great international institutions of today are promoting and defending. We trust that the magisterial teachings of our great predecessors Pius XII and John XXIII will continue to inspire on this fundamental theme the wisdom of modern teachers and contemporary politicians (Paul VI, *No to Violence, Yes to Peace*, January 1, 1978).

2. As teachers in the Church these words of Pope Paul speak to us with a special resonance. His annual messages on the Day of Peace constitute a striking fulfillment of the mandate of Vatican Council II: "to undertake an evaluation of war with an entirely new attitude" (*Gaudium et Spes*, par. 80). Such a new attitude was clearly evident in the 1976 intervention of The Holy See at the United Nations when it said that the arms race is "to be condemned unreservedly" as a danger, an injustice, and a mistake ("A Plea for Disarmament," *Osservatore Romano*, June 1976).

The dangers of the arms race are a concern and a challenge to the whole human family. Moreover, all the members of the universal Church are called to witness to the Gospel of Peace. For the Church in the United States, however, the prophetic words of the Holy Father have a special significance. No nation has a more critical role in determining the delicate balance between the dangers of war and the possibilities of peace. It is an illusion to think the U.S. bears this responsibility alone; but is a more dangerous deception not to recognize the potential for peace that our position in the world offers to us.

3.   In 1978 two events will highlight the U.S. role and responsibility in the arms race. The first is the forthcoming VIII Special Session of the United Nations on Disarmament. The second is the continuing debate in the U.S. about a SALT II agreement with the Soviet Union designed to place new limits on nuclear weapons. It is not our purpose in this statement to engage in a detailed analysis of either of these topics, but to identify them as two instances of political debate in which the moral issues of the arms race can be articulated along with its technical dimensions.

4.   The primary moral imperative is that the arms race must be stopped and the reduction of armaments must be achieved ("A Plea for Disarmament"). In pursuit of these objectives several specific choices must be made to bring the superpower arms race under control quantitatively and qualitatively, to restrain the proliferation of nuclear weapons, and to place restrictions on the rapid growth of conventional arms sales in the world.

5.   Each of these complex issues requires separate treatment so that the relationship of moral and technical factors can be articulated and weighed. The evaluation must occur within the policy process and in the wider ambit of informed public discussion. Catholic teaching on the morality of war has traditionally been designed to speak to both of these audiences. The teaching seeks to establish a moral framework for policy debate and to provide pastoral guidance for individuals. It is incumbent upon us as bishops and other members of the Church, especially lay Catholics with particular competencies relevant to preserving peace, to fulfill this task today.

6.   The contemporary resources of Catholic teaching on war and peace are rich. The doctrine of *Pacem in Terris* (1963) and *Gaudium et Spes* (1965) supplies new and fresh religious and moral perspectives to support those who in conscience choose the way of nonviolence as a witness to the Gospel. These same documents affirm, as Catholic teaching traditionally has acknowledged, that some uses of force in defense of the common good are legitimate. Both of these moral positions are rooted in the Gospel and provide for Catholics and others a reasonable and sound means of evaluating questions of war and peace in the modern world. In an effort to contribute to the policy and public debate in the months to come, we will draw from both of these moral positions to speak to specific issues in the arms debate.

7.   Beyond this important task of moral analysis, however, the Church has another role. The Church must be a prophetic voice for peace. In the tradition of the last three popes the Church in our land must explain the meaning of peace, call people and governments to pursue peace, and stand against those forces and elements which prevent the coming of true peace. To pursue peace in the political process requires courage; at times it means taking risks for peace. The Church in a competent and careful manner must encourage reasonable risks for peace. To risk requires a degree of faith and faith in turn is based on the hope that comes from prayer. As the Church in this nation we seek to be a moral voice placing restraints on war, a prophetic voice calling for peace, and a prayerful community which has the courage to work for peace.

Statement on Small-Boat Refugees in Southeast Asia

*A Statement Issued by the Administrative Committee
of the National Conference of Catholic Bishops*

February 16, 1978

1. We urge the President and Congress to respond in a more forceful and humane manner to the anguished cries of the men, women, and children who, seeking a new life of freedom, are fleeing Southeast Asia by land and in small boats.

2. The number of these refugees, sixty percent of them children, has grown in recent months due to oppressive actions by new Communist regimes in some nations in Southeast Asia which are forcing families to undertake an almost suicidal endeavor in search of asylum.

3. As is generally the case in large-scale refugee movements in hostile circumstances, some do not reach their goal and there is a corresponding loss of life.

4. In the Southeast Asian turmoil there are firsthand reports of the terrors of the overland march from Laos and Cambodia and of the loss of life of an estimated fifty percent in the almost suicidal small-boat movement from Vietnam. For every two persons who start out, only one survives.

5. In Thailand there are approximately 100,000 refugees from Vietnam, Laos, and Cambodia. They have found a highly temporary asylum in thirteen separate refugee compounds controlled by the government of Thailand. Approximately 5,000 new refugees are entering Thailand each month, around 1,500 by small boat from Vietnam and more than 3,000 overland from Cambodia and Laos. Despite traditional kindness founded in national history and religion, the Thai government is in a most precarious position from internal and diplomatic points of view, since the country is surrounded by well-armed Communist nations.

6. There is no way of knowing how many refugees have been turned back at the borders by local Thai officials. The United States press reported some months ago that a group of twenty-nine had been returned to Cambodia and immediately executed.

7. Among the tragic aspects of this refugee movement is the reluctance of larger vessels plying the South China Sea to pick up those in distress in small boats. Past experience has taught the masters of these vessels that to do so can involve them and their shipping companies in many complications. Some countries, learning that refugees are aboard a vessel, will not permit even the crew to disembark. No landing rights are given to refugees, and the ship must keep them on board while hoping to reach a port that will grant temporary asylum. In some instances ships have sailed nearly around the world, dropping off refugees in South Africa, Kuwait, Italy, and other places.

8. It is an appalling fact that, after braving the terrors of the sea, refugees find that what awaits them is not really asylum. A proliferation of reports indicate that their boats are often driven off shore or towed back to the open sea. These refugees have no alternative but to seek haven in other countries bordering the South China Sea (the Philippines, Korea, Macao, Hong Kong, and Taiwan) or, in desperation, to set sail in their small, unseaworthy craft for Australia, over 3,000 miles away.

9. On August 11, 1977, the U.S. government authorized the admission of 7,000 boat cases and 8,000 land-based refugees. On January 25 of this year, the Attorney General authorized the admission of 7,000 additional boat refugees. These admissions are stopgap measures. Some type of established admission procedure is needed to avoid unimaginable disaster.

10. The government of France has instituted a humane procedure and is accepting approximately 1,000 refugees each month as it has done for some time. The governments of Australia, Canada, and some nations of Europe have made more limited commitments.

11. In appealing to the President and Congress to respond in a more humane and forceful manner to the tragic situation of the small-boat refugees in Southeast Asia, we are not unmindful of the responsibility of the business world and of the Church itself in this matter. The business world, particularly the shipping interests of the United States, must not abandon these men, women, and children to the perils of the sea. The ancient tradition of rendering aid to the occupants of boats and ships in distress on the high seas must be continued by American ship masters and crews, and indeed by the masters and crews of the ships of all nations.

12. As for the Church, we renew our commitment to aid the refugees of any nation, regardless of religion and political ideology. We call on the dioceses, parishes, and individual Catholics of the United States to expand their works of mercy through sponsoring and resettling those refugees who will come to our shores. We are mindful of the words of Pope Paul VI: "The pastoral care of migrants has always attracted the motherly attention and the solicitude of the Church. In fact, it has never ceased throughout the centuries to help in every way those who, like Christ in exile in Egypt with the family of Nazareth, were compelled to emigrate to lands far away from their country" (*Pastoralis Migratorum Cura*).

To Do the Work of Justice

A Statement Issued by the
*National Conference of Catholic Bishops**

May 4, 1978

1. Christian faith continually calls the Church and each of its members to decisive action to bring faith alive in the concrete circumstances of human history. Throughout the world today churches are bearing witness to Christ's saving presence by courageous efforts to speak God's Word boldly; to renew themselves; and to confront with hope and courage the critical issues of human rights, social justice, and world peace. Sharing and having shared in this renewal, we seek here to identify some of the work which remains to be done in the years ahead. This plan of action springs from our vision of our Church's ministry to the pressing needs of all the world's people. A challenge to us and our people, it is also an invitation to every bishop, priest, religious, and lay person in the Catholic Church in the United States to join in a deliberate, systematic effort to be of service to all people in their struggle for dignity, justice, and peace.

2. A year ago we issued a preliminary response to the consultation on social justice entitled "Liberty and Justice For All," which we conducted on the occasion of our national bicentennial. This consultation, in which the bishops listened to the voices of many groups and individuals, was intended to help us formulate a plan to establish goals and programs in the area of social justice over the next five years. As bishops we were called both to listen and to exercise judgment in teaching an extremely vital part of the Gospel of Jesus pertaining to the mission on behalf of social justice. Through this process of structured public dialogue, we learned much about the needs of our own people and about the problems of justice and peace which they face in their own lives and communities. Convinced that this program could bear much fruit in the Church today, we undertook a detailed evaluation of all of the recommendations through the committees of the National Conference of Catholic Bishops and the United States Catholic Conference. In addition, we directed the president of the NCCB to appoint an ad hoc committee to coordinate the evaluation process and develop a five-year pastoral plan of action based on its results. We are now prepared to set forth this plan and we invite the cooperation of the entire Catholic community in its implementation. We do so in the firm conviction that our growth as the

---

Call to Action plan approved by the Catholic bishops of the United States May 4, 1978.

community of God's people and our ministry of service to the world are inseparable dimensions of our common Christian commitment. We must, and we will, continue to grow in love and care for one another even as we enter more actively into the pursuit of justice and peace. Our participation in that pursuit, indeed, will be authentic and productive only if it truly reflects the quality of our life of fellowship with one another.

3.   The programs and activities proposed here are not our only response to the needs expressed during the bicentennial consultation. Our continuing collective commitment to the social mission of the Church and the achievement of a more just social order has long been evident in the work of our episcopal conference, its secretariats and committees. Resolutions adopted by the Call to Action conference on such issues as full employment, human rights, disarmament, housing, political responsibility, the aged, criminal justice, and world hunger echo similar positions adopted and advocated by the USCC and the NCCB in recent years. The Campaign for Human Development, the Catholic Relief Services, the USCC Migration and Refugee Services, and other social service, education, and advocacy programs carried out under the auspices of the bishops reflect our determination to meet human needs and to serve the cause of social justice.

4.   Since our meeting a year ago, we have responded to many of the concerns reflected in the Call to Action program. We have created a new Secretariat for the Laity and we have launched new initiatives pertaining to parish life and the family. We have engaged in consultation and articulated principles on teacher unionization in parochial schools, adopted standards for fund raising within the Church, and issued statements of concern on the American Indian, human rights in Eastern Europe, the Panama Canal treaties, the U.S. defense policy, and crime. Our sponsorship of the Segundo Encuentro Pastoral, a national conference designed to identify and promote the pastoral and human needs of our Hispanic people, and our continuing consultation on increasing leadership opportunities for women in the Church are illustrative of the wide range of activities in our episcopal conference designed to renew the life of the Catholic community in this nation.

5.   Many dioceses, parishes, schools, and Catholic organizations have already undertaken programs of response to the Call to Action conference. Some dioceses, for example, have sponsored consultations focusing upon its recommendations, while others have instituted significant pastoral and social programs which respond to the needs articulated. Still other dioceses and organizations have incorporated the program's results into their planning processes. These various responses are in keeping with our statement last spring inviting action at every level of Church life.

6.   During the bicentennial consultation, we found that the vision of the universal Church as an effective agent of social justice and as an advocate for human rights lives in the people of our dioceses and parishes. In expressing, from their living experience, their aspirations for the Church in our day, they reaffirmed their hopes for justice and peace. We began our bicentennial consultation as part of an attempt to implement the directive of Pope Paul VI that each Christian community, through a process of reflection and action, should apply the norms of the Gospel and the teachings of the Church to the conditions in its nation and local communities. The issues which people specified for us reflected the abiding interests of the Church today: the dignity of the person, the welfare of the family, the quality of life in cities and rural areas, the horror of modern war, and the need to abolish hunger and poverty from our land and our world.

7.   We cannot address all these issues—or indeed any of them—as a conference of bishops. The call to a ministry of justice and peace is a call to the whole Church. It is a call for the Church to do the work of justice in society and, equally important, a call for the Church to be just in its own life. In shaping a response by NCCB/USCC we have selected six major areas of emphasis. They do not exhaust the total agenda in the ministry of justice and peace, but they do reflect some of its major components. These issues are both local and national; they touch our own land and our relations with other nations. They are chosen because of their intrinsic significance and because they symbolize the larger range of issues which we challenge others in the Church and in the nation to address, even as we try, with others, to address them.

I. Education for Justice

8.   We believe that to realize the goals we have set we must expand and improve our programs of education for justice. This education must cut across generational lines, institutional structures, and various educational agencies. It requires teaching and learning the tradition of Catholic social thought, the creation of an environment for learning that reflects a commitment to justice, and an openness on the part of all Catholics to change personal attitudes and behavior. In Catholic thought, social justice is not merely a secular or humanitarian matter. Social justice is a reflection of God's respect and concern for each person and an effort to protect the essential human freedom necessary for each person to achieve his or her destiny as a child of God. Because education for justice is such a vast and all-encompassing process, we choose, within the framework of the principle of subsidiarity, to suggest here only a few of the actions we can take at the national level to encourage and complement local programs in families, schools, parishes, and dioceses.

9.   We shall establish within the USCC Office of Social Development and World Peace a center for the coordination of ongoing activities in justice education. A staff person, working closely with other national agencies concerned with education for justice, will identify areas in which further initiatives are needed, make available consultative services, facilitate the exchange of information among diocesan and regional offices of social justice, and provide materials and resources for schools, workshops, symposia, and other programs requested by diocesan offices and other appropriate agencies. Recognizing the indispensable role of catechesis in forming individuals and communities in the Church, we request that social justice be given appropriate attention and treatment in catechetical programs, using the *National Catechetical Directory* as a base, particularly Chapter VII, "Catechesis for Social Ministry."

10.   The NCCB/USCC will invite scholars and universities to undertake serious research into issues of justice and peace. In doing so we will seek funding from potential sources of research grants, besides cooperating, as circumstances may dictate, in the establishment of a structure for the selection of grantees and a method of collaboration with associations involved in Catholic higher education. We shall cosponsor with appropriate groups seminars on topics, such as shared responsibility, which are central to the full development of this plan of action.

11.   To those responsible for directing seminaries, we encourage in-service courses, workshops, and seminars for faculties and administrators to help them develop programs of justice education, and we request that these programs be strengthened. Seminarians and others preparing for ministry should continue to be instructed in the social thought of the Church and have a variety of experiences with social problems and cultural conditions in order to deepen their awareness of injustice and develop the knowledge and skills which will enable them to provide leadership in the Church's ministry of justice and peace.

12.   We request that preparation for ministry for justice continue to be included as an integral part of pastoral preparation in seminaries. Commitment to the promotion of justice should continue to be among the criteria used in evaluating candidates for ordination. We ask the NCCB Committee on Priestly Formation to assess carefully the commitment to justice ministry on the part of a seminary within the committee's regular program of seminary visitation.

13.   We also request that preparation for ministry for justice be continued, and where necessary intensified, as an integral part of diaconate training programs and that positions in ministry for justice be identified and supported as works for permanent deacons. Commitment to the promotion of justice should be among the criteria used in evaluating candidates for ordination.

14. We urge Catholic colleges and universities to develop degree programs in justice and peace education and to provide resource centers for local justice education projects. We ask all Catholic educational institutions, including elementary and secondary schools, to ensure that their students are exposed to fundamental Catholic social teaching as reflected in papal encyclicals and pronouncements, conciliary and synodal documents, and episcopal teaching. At the same time, we strongly urge dioceses to seek actively to extend career opportunities in the areas of social ministry and justice education.

15. We request each diocese to initiate an in-service justice education program for teachers, school administrators, and school boards, as well as health care personnel. We request that diocesan offices of religious education develop programs of preparation for the sacraments which will highlight their social as well as individual dimension. Finally, in dioceses where such instrumentalities do not exist, we recommend that consideration be given to the establishment of agencies to promote and coordinate justice education and social action: or, where this is not possible, that the sharing of resources and programs on a regional basis be investigated instead. In this connection, we pledge the assistance and support of the USCC Department of Social Development and World Peace.

II. Family Life

16. The Church's mission to create and sustain community runs as a theme throughout the Call to Action resolutions. The resolutions place special emphasis on the basic community of the family. Participants in the bicentennial consultation called upon their Church to support family life, foster reconciliation within and among families, enhance the family's teaching, sacramental, and social ministries. The family is a vital agent in both Church and society; it preserves tradition and develops the values of the past; it supports persons in their present responsibilities and actively prepares them to meet the challenges of the future. Effective family ministry supports these indispensable functions while embracing all the diverse living situations in which people find themselves.

17. At this time our episcopal conference is preparing to undertake a special plan of pastoral action for family ministry designed as a response to the report of the USCC Commission on Marriage and Family Life. This plan takes into account the results of the bicentennial consultation and involves a comprehensive approach to family ministry—one that sees the development and strengthening of family life as integral to the total mission of the Church in society. It seeks as well to extend the impact made by Christian families on the formation of public policy and social legislation.

18. A diocesan family life committee or advisory board, under the direction of the family life officer, will be asked to assess family needs and to evaluate present diocesan ministry and social involvement programs. Programs to be taken into account include marriage preparation, family planning, human sexuality education, marriage and family enrichment practices, family social policy, education and leadership training for couples and families.

19. The 1980 Family Year will highlight parish programs of family ministry and encourage assessment of them. This assessment and subsequent planning should give consideration to ministry to six groups: the premarried, including young adults and engaged couples; married couples, including newlyweds, middle-aged, and retired couples; parents, including the widowed, parents of the very young, expectant parents, parents of adolescents in crisis, with particular attention to the unique pastoral and social needs of single-parent families; "developing" families, including those facing the needs of beginning their families, issues pertaining to family spirituality and technological pressures upon and within families; "hurting" families, including those confronting the problems of poverty, alcoholism, drug abuse, issues of sexuality, separation, and divorce; and "leadership" families, including parish coordinating couples and couples engaged in family social action and the family apostolate, together with their children.

20. While this plan of action for total family ministry is designed to involve the Church at all levels, it places special emphasis on the parish. The year 1979 has been designated as a year of special diocesan preparation and planning, leading to a Family Year in 1980 and to a decade of family research and renewed ministry thereafter. The USCC, through its departmental agencies, will design educational programs for family social missions and family involvement in social policy formation. It will also continue preparation for the 1979 White House Conference on Families through a special coordinating committee involving other Catholic agencies, organizations, and movements.

21. This parish-level action plan will reach out to involve families in parish ministry, small support groups, and social action programs. The aim of the plan is to renew the family, the neighborhood, and the parish community, a goal vital to the Church and society.

III. The Church: People, Parishes, and Communities

22. The Church is the community of God's people sharing a common faith while engaged in responding to the needs of all. A pastoral plan of action for justice must involve efforts to deepen our life as a community and improve our ways of living and working together. This present plan recognizes certain basic pastoral principles designed to strengthen our community as we go forth to serve. These include the creative interaction of bishops, theologians, and Church leaders, and the people and their authentic representatives; specification of pastoral needs based on listening to one another in parishes and dioceses and in the nation; and careful efforts to develop consensus through open and informed discussion, prayerful deliberation, and equitable procedures for making decisions. In this section we recommend programs to bring our people into closer touch with one another and to strengthen our ability to establish pastoral objectives based upon people's real needs. Community at the local level, especially in the parish, will have our closest attention during the next five years; it is there that all of us participate most directly in the life and mission of the Church.

23. The NCCB has already established an Ad Hoc Committee on the Parish to carry out a parish renewal project. Enlisting the cooperation of every diocese, this program will be a major priority of our episcopal conference. It will consider pastoral care, liturgical life, ethnic, cultural, and doctrinal pluralism, parish councils and their roles in the mission of the Church. Its work will involve not only studies of parish life, but the preparation of aids, identification and communication of successful renewal programs, and the gathering of parish personnel to share experiences.

24. In reporting to the episcopal conference on its work, we suggest that the Ad Hoc Committee on the Parish highlight progress in the following areas: (a) steps by which parishes can become more creatively involved in the life of their communities; (b) effective models for parish programs of social service and social action; (c) steps by which the rich multicultural heritage of the Church can be strengthened at the local level; and (d) proposals for policies which will insure to every Catholic, whatever his or her income, sex, age, race, or social status, the right to share fully in the life of a vital Christian community, and through that community, to participate fully in the mission of the Church.

25. While continuing our support for the work of the NCCB/USCC Secretariat for Hispanic Affairs, we shall also seek means to encourage development of a National Hispanic Research Center. We request that our Committee for Liaison with the National Office for Black Catholics report by 1980 on further steps which may be taken, beyond those recommended elsewhere in this plan, to improve and encourage community life among black Catholics. Committees of our conference have indicated that they will be striving to improve ministry to diverse ethnic communities so as to incorporate multicultural awareness in Christian education and to insure adequate formation of candidates for ministry in the social teachings of the Church. We will request that these committees provide annual public reports on their progress.

26. Each diocese is asked to undertake an evaluation of its rural ministry, profiling the social and pastoral needs of its rural people, and assessing current resources and programs. Each diocese is encouraged to designate a person to coordinate this program and to make recommendations to diocesan agencies concerning needed reform.

27. Interested in the quality of Catholic citizenship, we shall ask our Catholic conference directors to undertake a consultation on political responsibility with the goal of devising programs and methods to promote a greater understanding of the way public policy is made and the duties of citizenship.

IV. Economic Justice

28. Catholic social teaching has consistently maintained that economic life must serve people's needs and be governed by justice. Over the past century, papal encyclicals, conciliar documents, and the statements of bishops have often called attention to the social and moral dimensions of economic life. In its teaching, the Church has noted a number of basic human rights in economic life, including the right to productive employment, the right to just wages, the right to an adequate income, the rights of workers to organize and bargain collectively, the right to own property for the many as a protection of freedom, and the right to participation in economic decisions.

29. Each of these rights carries with it responsibilities, such as the duty to work, the duty of property owners to exercise ownership for the common good, and the obligation to provide a just wage. These rights and responsibilities are still not fully guaranteed in our society. While poverty and joblessness still plague millions, workers are subject to harassment for their attempts at collective bargaining, and full employment and economic security are not yet operative goals of public policy. The Christian community must intensify its efforts on behalf of these human rights. We propose the following program to make our rich heritage of Catholic teaching come alive in the ministry of the Church and the life of every believer.

30. Our episcopal conference will continue to speak out for full employment, adequate income, the rights of workers to organize, and defense of the poor and the victims of economic injustice. In particular, we shall seek to make our voice heard more effectively in our own Catholic community and where public policy is made. Economic injustice will be a major concern in our teaching ministry and in our relations with the government. In addition, economic justice as well as economic development will continue to be a major emphasis of concern of our Campaign for Human Development. We shall continue to call for a more responsible rate of economic consumption on the part of the people of our nation in order to effect economic justice for the poor in our country and throughout the world.

31. In 1981, the USCC will convene a major consultation on economic justice. We will bring together leaders of government, business, labor, and consumers, economists, and theologians to dialogue on how the Christian community can best apply its teaching of economic justice to contemporary conditions. The consultation will focus on ways by which the Church, business, labor, and government, as well as individual citizens, can contribute to greater respect for human rights and basic justice in our national economy and in the international economic order. In all such discussions, the poor and those suffering from economic injustice will share. From these discussions may come the feasibility of forming a National Commission on Economic Justice. Such a commission might contribute to broadening and deepening our involvement in the moral and social dimensions of economic issues, make our efforts more effective, visible, and productive, and provide an ongoing forum for dialogue over Catholic principles and economic life. The scope and purpose of such an undertaking will be dependent upon the above-planned consultation.

V. Human Rights

32. The Church has seen increasingly the defense and promotion of human rights as inseparable from its gospel mandate. The tradition of Catholic social teaching is clear and emphatic in calling the community to justice. It is also consistent in linking justice to the protection of human rights and the satisfaction of human needs on the local, national, and international levels. The recent USCC publication, *Human Rights/Human Needs—An Unfinished Agenda*, provides a tool for education the community to a wide range of human rights addressed by and rooted in Catholic tradition. We call for a coordinated educational effort in the Catholic community regarding this significant topic during 1978, the thirtieth anniversary of the U.N. Universal Declaration of Human Rights.

33. The right to life, as a most fundamental human right, is and will remain the object of priority efforts on the part of the Church. We are committed to this work by our vision of human life and destiny, by the teaching of the Church, and, in a special way, by our own *Pastoral Plan for Pro-life Activities*. Therefore, in speaking of our determination to work for human rights, we deem it fitting to speak first of our intention to strive to win greater recognition and respect for this right, which had a prominent place among the Call to Action recommendations. Further consideration of human rights in this section, however, will be limited to only a few of the issues emphasized in the Call to Action recommendations.

34. Racism remains a major concern. This blight on American society is of special concern for the Church because of its deep moral implications. We hope to issue a pastoral letter dealing with this issue in 1979 and anticipate that it will treat such themes, noted in the Call to Action recommendations, as discrimination in both Church and society, pluralism, as well as the distinction between race and ethnicity, and the need to enhance and strengthen cultural pluralism. We shall attempt to address individual, cultural, and institutional racism and to initiate a process aimed at overcoming all forms of racism in the Church and in society.

35. Discrimination based on sex, because it radically undermines the personal identity of both women and men, constitutes a grave injustice in our society. At this point in history, marked, as Pope John indicated in *Pacem in Terris*, by the growing struggle of women to achieve full development, it is urgent that the Church give tangible evidence of its commitment to the rights of women, affirming their dignity as persons, and promoting their expanded participation in ecclesial and civic life. We will further purposefully study and dialogue regarding issues of concern to women and the eradication of sexist discrimination in current practices and policies.

36. Cutting across race, ethnicity, sex, and age, discrimination in American society urgently demands our attention. In addition to the pastoral letter we shall undertake the following actions: (1) A USCC statement will be issued by the fall of 1979 which will analyze the pluralism of the American experience, affirm it as a positive value in our culture with profound moral implications for social justice and peace, and include appropriate pastoral directives; (2) A set of guidelines for affirmative action will be published by mid-1979 for diocesan evaluation and implementation. Our own conference offices, in their hiring practices, are prepared to take leadership in the implementation of such guidelines; (3) An organized program of action based on the USCC Statement, *Society and the Aged: Toward Reconciliation*, will begin in mid-1980. Action will emphasize parish programs of ministry to the elderly and advocacy programs by Church agencies to assist the elderly and to protect their human rights, especially as they are affected by legislative and governmental action.

37. In order to ensure an increasingly effective response to the pressing needs of the handicapped, we will continue our work with them through the National Advisory Committee on Ministry to the Handicapped and other appropriate groups. The advisory committee, it is to be noted, came into being as a result of our direct invitation, and the conference continues to serve the committee in the role of both convenor and participant. Our pressing efforts in this regard are focusing on a mutual determination of the most effective approach to ensuring across-the-board involvement of our national conferences as well as that of other Church organizations at the regional and local levels.

38. This involves, as a necessary precondition, an in-depth needs analysis to identify more specifically the priority concerns of this important segment of the Church and of society in general. Although more specific action awaits completion of this present stage of dialogue, one important item already of our forward agenda is a pastoral letter on ministry to the handicapped.

39. Better understanding of the international dimensions of human rights is urgently needed. A consultation of diocesan representatives on this topic, sponsored by the USCC, by the spring of 1979, will assist the Church at the local level to engage its constituents in this vital work.

40. From such a consultation, specific programs for promoting human rights internationally should emerge; e.g., the celebration of a World Day of Peace and the formation of groups for disarmament, for opposition to the arms race, for promotion of international economic structural changes and for providing support to the suffering Church in the Third World and in Eastern Europe.

VI. World Hunger

41. The basic human right to eat continues to be denied to hundreds of millions of people in the United States and overseas.

42. In an effort to combat world hunger, our offices at the United States Catholic Conference will continue to monitor U.S. food policy, including constant appraisal of national policies affecting food exports, domestic food programs (e.g., food stamps, school lunch programs), and agricultural policies. We shall also continue to prepare educational materials on these matters and to present testimony before appropriate congressional committees.

43. Dioceses are urged to continue to support local efforts to provide remedial programs such as food banks and food kitchens for the needy, advocacy support for persons eligible for government assistance, and support for programs such as the Catholic Relief Services, Operation Rice Bowl, Bread for the World, and World Food Day.

44. On the domestic level, the USCC will provide dioceses and parishes with a Lenten program in 1980 designed to provide American Catholics with a prayer period for examining their personal life styles in relation to eating habits and patterns of energy consumption.

Conclusion

45. In setting forth this six-part program, we pledge ourselves for the next five years to an ongoing effort to monitor and evaluate its implementation. At the end of that five-year period there will be an evaluation and review of the plan of action which we have set forth in terms of its impact on the Church and society. Further, we call upon the Department of Social Development and World Peace, the Department of Education, and the Department of Communication of the United States Catholic Conference to assist in the implementation of this plan by calling together national, regional, and diocesan social ministry, catechetical and communications personnel to enlist their aid in publicizing and implementing this plan of action.

46. We are all learning how to live the Gospel anew today. We have truly heard a "call to action" both from our Holy Father and from our Catholic people across the land. The programs we have outlined offer a sufficient challenge to all our leadership groups to engage in generous service to the Word.

47. Ultimately, the call is directed to each Catholic in America. It is an invitation to each to make a personal commitment to seek justice and to live justly. There is no "program" for bringing this about. The action needed does not lie essentially in plans, projects, or statements. Rather, we know as Christians that the most effective response to the ills of the world is ours to make, the duty to seek justice and equality resides with each of us. Here, in the painfully slow changing of our own lives and in the agony of living out our vocations, lies the essential key to a more decent and more human world.

48. We pray and we trust that God's love, alive in the hearts of our people, will fire their imaginations and enkindle in them a desire for a more simple way of life, free from dependency on luxuries mistaken for necessities; that it will liberate them from prejudgments about others which are an obstacle to sharing the faith with them; and will enable them to view with an objective eye the deleterious effects on human beings of unjust social structures and to strive with courageous hearts to change these for the better; that it will intensify their commitment to service out of love for the One Who has first loved us. So also we pray and trust the same for ourselves.

The Plan of Pastoral Action for Family Ministry: A Vision and a Strategy

A Statement Issued by the
National Conference of Catholic Bishops

May 1978

1. Changing circumstances in today's world call for a new approach within the Church to pastoral service to families. The Catholic community is becoming increasingly aware of the crucial issues facing contemporary marriage and family life. In view of this, a plan of pastoral action is needed so that a genuine renewal might take place in the family ministry of the Church.

2. At the outset we affirm that the faithful proclamation of the Gospel in word and sacrament is fundamental to all such planning in the Church. Also, integral to this plan of action is the deep conviction that the Church's leadership considers it essential to listen perceptively, trustingly and compassionately to what people are saying about their Christian understanding of marriage, sexuality and family life. The potential for development as well as the problems confronting people in their daily lives will be perceived correctly only if this openness is central to our pastoral outlook and ministry.

Preparatory Steps

3. The actual process of listening and discernment began over two years ago. At that time a special Ad Hoc Commission was established within the United States Catholic Conference to address the issues of marriage and family life. In addition, family concerns surfaced as a central theme in the hearings that formed part of the Bishops' Bicentennial Consultation. This led in turn to certain recommendations on families in the 1976 Call To Action Conference.

4. The concerns voiced by married couples, single people and others aware of the needs of young people and families were brought to bear on the work of the USCC Commission on Marriage and Family Life. This Commission composed of bishops, diocesan family life personnel, married couples and scholars was instructed to devise a "comprehensive strategy"[1] to be carried out at all levels of the Church in

---

[1]See *Final Report on the United States Catholic Conference Ad Hoc Commission on Marriage and Family Life*, Washington, D.C., Nov. 14, 1977, p. 2.

the United States in support of marriage and family life.

5. As a prior step to convening this Commission, diocesan family life personnel in twelve regional meetings were asked to assess the present condition of the family, survey existing programs and articulate issues in family ministry.[2] The Marriage and Family Life Commission then met in late 1976 and early 1977 to analyze the results. It studied various research reports and pastoral surveys. Proposals were developed to deal with the wide range of issues and concerns expressed. To cover the whole span of family pastoral and social needs, the Commission's work culminated in a report with forty-five recommendations.

6. Certain basic themes run through these recommendations and point to the crucial areas where the Church's mission to young people, married couples and families must be developed.

7. The need for research is frequently mentioned. A number of recommendations call for deeper theological study of sexuality and the foundations of family ministry along with a spirituality of marriage and family life. Others recommend research into successful forms of family living as well as problematic areas. The formation of better curricula relating to marriage and family life is indicated as an urgent need. Clearly, interdisciplinary dialogue and scholarly exchange with social scientists are strongly recommended.

8. The development of programs for all persons engaged in family ministry—priests, deacons, religious and lay people—receives considerable attention. Note is also made of programs for professionals— physicians, lawyers and educators. Affirmative, developmental and preventive programs are proposed that should be adapted to the needs of particular groups and family styles. In such programs the concept of family should include the engaged, newly marrieds, those in the middle and later years of married life, extended families and young singles searching together for a Christian understanding of sexuality and marital commitment. Special attention should be given to military families and minority families with particular racial, cultural and ethnic heritages. Not to be overlooked are the widowed, separated and divorced Catholics and one-parent families.

9. Certain major issues are identified within the area of family ministry. Particular attention is asked to be given to sexist discrimination and the Christian clarification of men's and women's roles. The pastoral issues arising in the areas of contraception and natural family planning are also pointed to. The importance of assisting families to deal with problems related to technological change and mass media, especially television viewing, is indicated.

10. Great emphasis is placed on the need to develop family social consciousness. Proposals call for education in family social mission

---

[2] *Ibid.*, pp. 6-7.

to enable the family members to understand their social role as part of total family ministry, which also includes family-centered prayer and catechesis. The development of ministries for ethnic and racial minority families receives special attention and recommendations that call for a thorough assessment of present approaches, especially those to Hispanic, black and Native American families. In conjunction with the development of governmental policy for families, the potential of the 1981 White House Conference on Families is cited.

11. Certain key recommendations call for adequate staffing, funding and structuring of family ministries and programs. Planning and needs assessment at *all* levels of the Church with continuing consultation of families themselves are urged. Finally, the Commission assigns the highest priority to a comprehensive vision and planning process, a plan of action that would embody a "practical and pastoral"[3] response to family issues. Its intent is to be sensitive, discerning and adaptable to local conditions as well as to draw on grassroots opinion and scholarly research.

Planning Process

12. This plan of action focuses primarily on a *process* designed to involve the Church at all levels. Guided by the teaching of the Church, it is founded on four specific principles, which will help the Church itself to touch the real needs of families. Moreover, since the family is called to be an expression of God's creative and redemptive love, this process unites the spiritual with the material and psychological dimensions of human existence.

13. First, this pastoral plan seeks to raise the awareness of the Church to the sacramental nature of Christian marriage and to the realities now facing married couples and families. In addition, it aims to help families themselves become aware of their special charisms, talents and potential for self-help and ministry to others.

14. Such awareness can be encouraged in a variety of ways. First of all, it should come through participation in the liturgical and sacramental life of the Church and prayerful reflection on lived experience. At other times, dialogue, assessment of needs and shared mutual insights into family life are necessary to bring it about. Such consciousness-raising can be assisted by experts and the instruments of professional research properly and sensitively employed.

15. Secondly, the Church is seeking through this plan of action ways to enable couples and families to be caring. It is concerned with helping family members develop their potential for nurturing and healing each other, for reaching out in active concern for others. This caring

---

[3]*Ibid.*, p. 44.

involves a participation in God's creative action and the redemptive mission of Jesus.

16. As it responds to those in need, active caring takes the step beyond mere awareness and reaches out to touch individuals and groups by showing God's loving, renewing presence. The need for such a presence is obvious today. For it to happen, a positive climate is encouraged by this process, an atmosphere of warmth that will enable people to reflect on their experience more deeply, judge it in the light of Gospel values and then make the decision to act.

17. Thirdly, when we speak of a true and authentic Christian service of families, we speak of a ministry that flows from a sense of Christian mission. This call to real ministry involving the lay person in the family, not only the priest, deacon, or religious, is the genuine realization of Christian vocation and the basis of the apostolate.

18. The call from the Holy Spirit and recognition from the Church community will lead a couple or even a whole family to a deeper sense of vocation as family life ministers. Such a calling must be adequately supported and formed. In this way the Church will come to have deeply motivated, well-trained and competent leadership in this and other areas of pastoral ministry.

19. Attention should be given to another factor that will help to form family ministers who can truly serve. Notably we point to the importance of like-to-like ministry, whereby people with similar experience and inclination help others. Examples of this are married couples ministering to engaged or young people interested in marriage; parents with longer experience helping newer parents; older married couples assisting newlyweds; the widowed or persons with a particular difficulty ministering to others in similar life circumstances.

20. Fourthly, this plan of action stresses the need to establish structures that will facilitate marriage and family ministry. This is not a call to a multiplicity of new structures for their own sake; it may even require phasing out irrelevant or cumbersome structures. Yet structures that truly facilitate are important for helping the Church as a community care for and effectively serve those in need.

21. It will first of all be necessary to make sound and wise decisions about the various structures of the Church's operation on the national and regional levels. But more concretely and directly, family ministry committees or advisory commissions on the diocesan and parish levels should themselves sensitively discern the types of structures and programs needed. They should especially have a voice in forming the structures that will make family ministry effective within the everyday lives of people in the thousands of parishes and millions of families in our country.

22. In summary, this plan of action calls for a process directed to awareness that understands, caring that enables, ministry that serves and structures that truly facilitate.

National Effort for Family Ministry

23. To begin such a plan we will concentrate on developing the resources and program aids during 1978 and 1979 to enable dioceses and parishes to do their vital part. These resources will include a more detailed outline of the approaches to the planning process as applied concretely to diocesan and parish communities. They will also include specific programmatic models which allow for local application and variations.

24. We designate 1979 as a year of special diocesan preparation and planning, leading to a Family Year in 1980. We hope that this Family Year, dedicated to the celebration of family values and ministry, will usher in a decade of research into Christian marriage and family life and a time for the development of outstanding programs in family ministry.

25. To oversee this plan and related family life issues, we have established a new Commission on Marriage and Family Life. Through its membership, consisting of bishops, priests, and married lay people, which will include adequate representation from ethnic and racial minorities, we hope to communicate our concern for the value and vitality of sacramental marriage and Christian family life.

26. Already in 1978 the Department of Education of the United States Catholic Conference has been directed to serve diocesan offices in this area of ministry. It has been instructed to publish the results of its survey on marriage and family enrichment programs in order to encourage further diocesan efforts. Likewise, the emphases placed by the *National Catechetical Directory* on family-centered religious formation are to be encouraged.

27. The Department has been authorized to develop curriculum guidelines for family living and sexuality education from early childhood through young adulthood. These are to include design principles for teacher and parent preparation with suggestions for diocesan implementation. This Department will involve bilingual-bicultural personnel to assist in curriculum development and the process of implementation.

28. Several other projects also call for the attention of the Education Department. In consultation with educators and other specialists, educational guidelines are to be developed to help fathers and mothers improve their parenting skills. Resource materials and program information for families with handicapped members are to be provided. Help is to be given to diocesan offices in designing educational programs relating to family social mission and policy. New programs are to be initiated for ethnic groups to meet their special needs.

29. Because the family always exists in relationship to the wider society, careful attention must be given toward the constructive influence of public policy as it relates to family life. Implicit government policy and explicit government planning and programs can contribute to an erosion of the health and vitality of the family. Examples of this process are urban and neighborhood revitalization developments which favor the wealthy rather than the displaced poor, the creation of suburban sprawl which is determined primarily by the priorities of big business and real estate developers, and the spread of giant agribusiness at the expense of the small family farm.

30. Comprehensive decisions of a national or regional scope must take into account their impact on family life. Families, especially those whose influence is lessened by poverty or social status, must be allowed their rightful input in those decisions which affect their daily lives. This delicate, yet decisive, relationship between the society and the family demands careful study, and, where destructive influences on family are apparent, society ought to be challenged in support of the rights of families.

31. In order to influence the development of family governmental policy based on principles of Christian social justice, an effort will be made to encourage Catholic participation in the White House Conference on Families. This is especially to be effected through the Catholic Coordinating Committee for the White House Conference on Families.

Diocesan Planning for Family Ministry

32. During 1979 diocesan planning should begin. It is to be coordinated by the diocesan family life committee or advisory board working in cooperation with other diocesan agencies, such as education and Catholic Charities offices. The diocesan family life office is to take the initiative in this process through its director, who should oversee the planning process as well as other family-related programs, organizations and movements. Research and consultation with representative families of diverse backgrounds should help the diocese make the necessary allocation of funds and staff.

33. We pledge to give particularly close attention to leadership formation in family ministry. This training will include both ordained and non-ordained leaders. Unless this takes place, the total implementation of this plan will not be realized in the diocese.

34. We pledge to foster communication and coordination among various movements and organizations in this field such as Engaged Encounter, Marriage Encounter, Christian Family Movement, Families for Prayer, Teams of Our Lady, Marriage Retorno, Movimiento Familiar Cristiano and Cursillo. These and other groups are reminded to pay particular attention to the unity of the family apostolate within the diocese and the needs of the parish community.

35. To promote sound laws and better public policies pertaining to marriage and family life, we will, where possible, work with our state

Catholic conferences. State, county and city laws should be evaluated for their impact upon the quality of family life. Full use of the communication media will be encouraged in order to promote support for favorable public policy as well as to publicize this plan of pastoral action.

Parish Implementation

36. Looking beyond this initial period of diocesan planning, we designate 1980 "Family Year" during which parishes are asked to join the total diocesan effort to renew family life. It is to be a particular time for the celebration of family values and for initiating the decade of total family renewal.

37. During this year every parish should begin to undertake its own planning process with appropriate support from the diocesan family life office or bureau. Resource materials, which will help them assess their families' needs, develop a plan for family ministry, select suitable programs and activities, train parish-level leadership and begin to implement their own action plan, will be made available. The Family Year effort at the parish level will lay the foundation for parish family ministry renewal for the decade.

38. Emphasis is placed within this entire plan on flexibility so that dioceses, parishes and interrelated institutions, such as Catholic schools, social justice offices, retreat centers, Catholic Charities and health care facilities can proceed in ways that work best for them.

39. In assessing the pastoral needs of its people, the parish in particular should give attention to six areas of pastoral ministry. These areas are not rigidly divided from one another, but together form a comprehensive approach for building up Christian family life through total family ministry.

1. Ministry for Pre-Marrieds and Singles

40. To undertake the renewal of marriage and family life the Church must address the question of its ministry to young people and those who are not married. This begins in the remote preparation of young people for their vocation through quality programs in family living and sexuality education from their earliest years. The proximate preparation for marriage calls for ministry for engaged couples who should be encouraged through their engagement period to deepen their commitment to creative fidelity and sacramental marriage. A number of programmatic efforts already exist, but do not always touch the majority of the engaged, especially at the parish level. These programs should treat all significant topics related to contemporary married life. The need for the development of a sensitive ministry for single persons of all ages is likewise encouraged. This includes ministry programs and activities for middle-aged and elderly people who live alone.

2. Ministry for Married Couples

41. The need for spiritual growth and continuing development in the marriage relationship is more pronounced today than ever before. Particular attention should be given to helping couples understand communications and practical Christian approaches to questions of economics and sexuality. A special aspect of this ministry is directed to newlyweds, since many marriages end in divorce in the early years. The recent emergence of a number of programs and movements for enriching the relationship of married couples of all ages, including the middle and older years, offers parishes a variety of ways to minister. This ministry needs to touch the lives of many more couples from all economic and cultural backgrounds within the parish.

3. Ministry for Parents

42. More and better ways are needed for helping Christian parents— including widowed and other "single" parents—to carry out their responsibilities. Parenting programs are growing in numbers and depth. The need for this ministry extends from expectant parents and parents of very young children to parents of adolescents. The last mentioned often express the need for help in intergenerational communication skills and in understanding cultural change. Special help is needed for parents of children with learning disabilities. All need assistance in their role as the primary catechists of their children.

4. Ministry for "Developing" Families

43. Families with children of varying ages need different approaches designed to foster Christian family development and enrichment. Special needs are voiced by families just beginning and families with adolescent members. Supportive association, in the context of a community of faith with other families of like ideals, is a crucial element in family stability and enrichment. Family spirituality needs to be promoted through various approaches involving family sacramental preparation, home prayer formation, family nights, parish family liturgies, and other religious cultural events. Family social ministry programs require particular support in order to encourage the development of a sense of the social mission of the family toward the total human community.

5. Ministry for "Hurting" Families

44. The anguish and fragmentation of so many married couples and family members call for both a preventive and a remedial ministry for families. This includes specialized counseling, and a ministry of reconciliation that touches the psychological, economic and spiritual realities of family life. Clergy and couples engaged in family ministry should be encouraged and helped to acquire specialized skills for dealing with such complex issues as poverty, aging, alcoholism, drug abuse and homosexuality. There is a great need for ministry to separated and divorced persons as well as to children of divorced parents. The needs of families with handicapped members and those with members living in institutions should not be overlooked in this area of pastoral ministry.

6. Ministry for Leadership Couples and Families

45. The need for ministry to families and couples actively involved in family ministry can easily be overlooked. This area of ministry should include parish coordinating couples, family social action couples and leadership people in family movements. These generous, dedicated people deserve help in their efforts to grow spiritually and emotionally through their own experience of marriage and family life, and their involvement in family ministry. They need assistance in learning leadership skills as well as knowledge of how to deepen their understanding of the Christian principles influencing marriage and family life.

46. In order to plan its own family ministry program, every parish should have a family ministry committee chaired by a volunteer couple or a full- or part-time coordinator of family ministry. Responsibility for particular areas of ministry or programs (e.g., marriage preparation, natural family planning, education in human sexuality, parenthood education, marriage and family enrichment, family social education) can then be assigned to designated lay leaders with appropriate training and formation. Parishioners involved in lay apostolic movements should be encouraged to place their talents at the service of the parish.

47. Existing parish structures and institutions (e.g., parish councils, parish catechetical programs, parochial schools, etc.) are reminded of their potential for marriage and family ministry within their special areas of competence. Parish schools and parent-teacher associations can develop effective home programs and lines of communication with families. Likewise, parish religious education structures can attend to family needs through different types of family-centered approaches. These and other opportunities exist at the parish level and can be acted upon through alert pastors, parish ministry teams, principals, teachers, coordinators and parish councils.

Future Action Areas

48. That the apostolic concern expressed in this initial effort move ahead, we see a number of other areas that require a response during the coming years.

49. Candidates for the priesthood and permanent diaconate should receive better preparation for family ministry; this ministry should also be a major element in the continuing education of the clergy.

50. There is a need for theological reflection on the family's role as an agent of evangelization, as well as for practical steps to involve more family members in the full apostolate of the laity and the renewal of parish life as a whole. There must be careful coordination of evangelization, parish renewal and family life ministry.

51. Family participation in the liturgical life of the Church should be encouraged, especially through the development of forms of family prayer and sacramental celebration.

52. Research is needed concerning the factors which influence religiously "mixed" marriages. This analysis should study the impact of such marriages on the Catholic identity of spouses and children and on ecumenical cooperation.

53. The high priority need for the Church to investigate appropriate ways of ministering to minority and ethnic families should be recognized and acted upon. Specific attention should be given to the familial needs of blacks, Hispanics, Asians and American Indians. The unique sense of the extended family among Catholic racial and ethnic groups in our national experience should be examined.

54. Solid research about the impact of sociocultural and technological change on the family should be undertaken and related to the ways in which one generation passes on its beliefs and values to the next.

55. The role of women in society and the Church requires further investigation. Particular attention should be paid to the phenomenon of a family situation in which both parents work outside the home.

56. Additional efforts should be made to offer couples education and counseling in the natural methods of family planning and to inform them of the scientific advances in this field.

57. There is likewise a serious need for deeper study of theological and interdisciplinary issues related to human sexuality so as to overcome the present malaise or credibility problem among many Catholic couples and individuals.

58. While pledging to move forward in these areas, we affirm the need for cooperation with other agencies in society for continued research into and necessary action for the renewal of marriage and family life.

Vital Participation of Families

59. If this plan of pastoral action does not touch or change the lives of family members and their relationship to the total Church community, then it will have failed in its purpose. The plan's success, however, presupposes efforts on the part of families themselves, supported by others in pastoral ministry. It is crucial that this pastoral vision focus on the need for spiritual renewal and conversion within the lives of families as is indicated in the teachings of conciliar, papal and other documents of the Second Vatican Council and of the Church's magisterium in the times following the Ecumenical Council.[4]

60. Wherever possible, husband and wife should set aside time to reflect on their vocation as a couple to make their marriage an effective sign of Christ's self-giving, faithful love. They should examine their ministry to each other, the opportunities they share for spiritual growth, the responsibility as Christian parents to lead their children to Christ, their call as individuals and as a couple to a wider mission within the Church, especially to their parish, and to society with particular concern for their own neighbors. They should explore the possibility of forming a network of friends and neighbors who will mutually reinforce marriage and family ideals.

61. Likewise, families with children should try to dialogue about their role in witness, worship and service. They should look for opportunities beyond the immediate family to minister to the needs of others, especially needy neighbors, relatives and parishioners. Christian charity and justice call them to go out to serve the physical and spiritual needs of others in the local community, the country and the world. Support groups of other families can reinforce their Christian idealism and way of life.

62. Ideally, this family-centered ministry should be based on a perception of the Gospel foundations of the family's own mission. These have been initially elaborated upon in the teachings of the Second Vatican Council[5] and in the apostolic exhortation on "Evangelization

---

[4]Cf. *Lumen Gentium, Gaudium et Spes, Apostolicam Actuositatem, Humanae Vitae* (1968), *Address to Teams of Our Lady* by Pope Paul VI (1970), *Evangelii Nuntiandi* (1975) as well as *Human Life in Our Day* (1969), *To Teach as Jesus Did* (1973) and *To Live in Christ Jesus* (1975) of the United States Bishops.

[5]Cf. *Lumen Gentium* #11, 30-37; *Apostolicam Actuositatem* #11; *Gaudium et Spes* #48-50, 52.

in the Modern World."[6] In these documents the importance of the family's Christian ministry as a witnessing community, a worshipping community and a serving community is communicated.

A Word of Hope

63. This plan of action provides the framework for far-reaching pastoral renewal. Since it involves commitment to a type of ministering not only to but also *with* people through a particular participation of the family members themselves, it also presents a challenge.

64. The Fathers of Vatican II in pointing out the importance of family ministry spoke to the family as the "foundation of society."[7] They declared that: "The well-being of the individual person and of human Christian society is intimately linked with the healthy condition of that community produced by marriage and the family."[8] More recently Pope Paul VI pointed out: "Today, concern for marriage and family is one of the most pressing duties of any pastoral work . . . the family is the chief cell, not only of human society, but also of the Church."[9]

65. The pressures of social change and the ensuing moral crisis are indeed to be acknowledged. However, we see this primarily as a time to be hopeful. What could be viewed as a breakdown of marriage and family life, we hope will be a breakthrough for families and society itself. Our Christian optimism, based as it is on Christ's own victory in the face of apparent defeat, gives us reason to see a time coming when, through the renewal of the Church's ministry, a better world will come about for the entire human family.

---

[6] *Evangelii Nuntiandi* #71.
[7] *Gaudium et Spes* #52.
[8] *Ibid.*, #47.
[9] Pope Paul VI, Address to the Bishops of Austria, *L'Osservatore Romano*, Eng. ed., Sept. 29, 1977, p. 10.

Pastoral Statement of the United States Catholic Bishops on Handicapped People

A Statement Issued by the
United States Catholic Conference

November 15, 1978

1.   The same Jesus who heard the cry for recognition from the handicapped of Judea and Samaria 2,000 years ago calls us, His followers, to embrace our responsibility to our own handicapped brothers and sisters in the United States. The Catholic Church pursues its mission by furthering the spiritual, intellectual, moral, and physical development of the people it serves. As pastors of the Church in America, we are committed to working for a deeper understanding of both the pain and the potential of our neighbors who are blind, deaf, mentally retarded, emotionally impaired, who have special learning problems, or who suffer from single or multiple physical handicaps—all those whom disability may set apart. We call upon people of good will to re-examine their attitudes toward their handicapped brothers and sisters and promote their well-being, acting with the sense of justice and the compassion that the Lord so clearly desires. Further, realizing the unique gifts handicapped individuals have to offer the Church, we wish to address the need for their fuller integration into the Christian community and their fuller participation in its life.

2.   Prejudice starts with the simple perception of difference, whether that difference is physical or psychological. Down through the ages, people have tended to interpret these differences in crude moral terms. "Our" group is not just different from "theirs"; it is better in some vague but compelling way. Few of us would admit to being prejudiced against handicapped people. We bear these people no ill will and do not knowingly seek to abrogate their rights. Yet handicapped people are visibly, sometimes bluntly different from the "norm," and we react to this difference. Even if we do not look down upon handicapped people, we tend all too often to think of them as somehow apart—not fully "one of us."

3.   What the handicapped individual needs, first of all, is acceptance in this difference that can neither be denied nor overlooked. No act of charity or justice can be of lasting value to handicapped people unless it is informed by a sincere and understanding love that penetrates the wall of strangeness and affirms the common humanity underlying all distinction. Scripture teaches us that "any other commandment [is] summed in this sentence: 'You shall love your neighbor as yourself.'" In His wisdom, Jesus said, "as yourself." We must love others from the inside out, so to speak, accepting their difference from us in the same way that we accept our difference from them.

The Church's Response to the Handicapped Person

4.   Concern for handicapped people was one of the prominent notes of Jesus' earthly ministry. When asked by John's disciples, "Are you he who is come or are we to look for another?" Jesus responded with words recalling the prophecies of Isaiah. "Go and relate to John what you have heard and seen; the blind see, the lame walk, the lepers are cleansed, the deaf hear, and the poor have the Gospel preached to them." Handicapped persons became witnesses for Christ, His healing of their bodies a sign of the spiritual healing He brought to all people. "Which is less trouble to say, 'Your sins are forgiven' or 'Stand up and walk?' To help you realize that the Son has authority on earth to forgive sins"—He then said to the paralyzed man—"Stand up! Roll up your mat and go home."

5.   The Church that Jesus founded would surely have been derelict had it failed to respond to His example in its attention to handicapped people. It remains faithful to its mission when its members become more and more a people of the Beatitudes, a people blessed in their meekness, their suffering, their thirst for righteousness. We all struggle with life. As we carry on this struggle in a spirit of mutual love, we build a community of interdependent people and discover the Kingdom of God in our midst.

6.   The Church, through the response of its members to the needs of others and through its parishes, health-care institutions, and social service agencies, has always attempted to show a pastoral concern for handicapped individuals. However, in a spirit of humble candor, we must acknowledge that at times we have responded to the needs of some of our handicapped people only after circumstances or public opinion have compelled us to do so. By every means possible, therefore, the Church must continue to expand its healing ministry to these persons, helping them when necessary, working with them, and raising its voice with them and with all members of society who are their advocates. Jesus revealed by His actions that service to and with people in need is a privilege and an opportunity as well as a duty. In extending our healing hands to others, we are healed ourselves.

7.   On the most basic level, the Church responds to handicapped individuals by defending their rights. Pope John XXIII's encyclical *Pacem In Terris* stresses the innate dignity of all men and women. "In an ordered and productive community, it is a fundamental principle

that every human being is a 'person' . . . [One] has rights and duties
. . . flowing directly and spontaneously from [one's] very nature.
These rights are therefore universal, inviolable and inalienable."

8.   The word "inalienable" reminds us that the principles on which
our democracy is founded also guarantee certain rights to all Americans, regardless of their circumstances. The first of these, of course,
is the right to life. We have spoken out on this issue on many occasions. We see defense of the right to life of handicapped persons as
a matter of particular urgency, however, because the presence of
handicapping conditions is not infrequently used as a rationale for
abortion. Moreover, those severely handicapped babies who are permitted to be born are sometimes denied ordinary and usual medical
procedures.

9.   All too often, abortion and postnatal neglect are promoted by
arguing that the handicapped infant will survive only to suffer a life
of pain and deprivation. We find this reasoning appalling. Society's
frequent indifference to the plight of handicapped citizens is a problem that cries aloud for solutions based on justice and conscience,
not violence. All people have a clear duty to do what lies in their
power to improve living conditions for handicapped people, rather
than ignoring them or attempting to eliminate them as a burden not
worth dealing with.

10.   Defense of the right of life, then, implies the defense of other
rights which enable the handicapped individual to achieve the fullest
measure of personal development of which he or she is capable. These
include the right to equal opportunity in education, in employment,
in housing, as well as the right to free access to public accommodations, facilities, and services. Those who must be institutionalized
deserve decent, personalized care and human support as well as the
pastoral services of the Christian community. Institutionalization will
gradually become less necessary for some as the Christian community
increases its awareness of disabled persons and builds a stronger and
more integrated support system for them.

11.   It is not enough merely to affirm the rights of handicapped people. We must actively work to make them real in the fabric of modern
society. Recognizing that handicapped individuals have a claim to
our respect because they share in the one redemption of Christ, and
because they contribute to our society by their activity within it, the
Church must become an advocate for and with them. It must work
to increase the public's sensitivity toward the needs of handicapped
people and support their rightful demand for justice. Moreover, individuals and organizations at every level within the Church should
minister to handicaped persons by serving their personal and social
needs. Many handicapped persons can function on their own as well
as anyone in society. For others, aid would be welcome. All of us
can visit the homebound, offer transportation to those who cannot

drive, read to those who cannot read, speak out for those who have difficulty pleading their own case. In touching the lives of handicapped men, women, and children in this way, we come closest to imitating Jesus' own example, which should be always before our eyes.

The Handicapped Person and the Ecclesial Community

12. Just as the Church must do all in its power to help ensure handicapped people a secure place in the human community, so it must reach out to welcome gratefully those who seek to participate in the ecclesial community. The central meaning of Jesus' ministry is bound up with the fact that He sought the company of people who, for one reason or another, were forced to live on the fringe of society. These He made the special object of His attention, declaring that the last would be first and that the humble would be exalted in His Father's Kingdom. The Church finds its true identity when it fully integrates itself with these "marginal" people, including those who suffer from physical and psychological disabilities.

13. If handicapped people are to become equal partners in the Christian community, injustices must be eliminated and ignorance and apathy replaced by increased sensitivity and warm acceptance. The leaders and the general membership of the Church must educate themselves to appreciate fully the contribution handicapped people can make to the Church's spiritual life. Handicapped individuals bring with them a special insight into the meaning of life; for they live, more than the rest of us perhaps, in the shadow of the cross. And out of their experience they forge virtues like courage, patience, perseverance, compassion, and sensitivity that should serve as an inspiration to all Christians.

14. In the case of many handicapped people, integration into the Christian community may require nothing more than issuing an invitation and pursuing it. For some others, however, full participation can only come about if the Church exerts itself to devise innovative programs and techniques. At the very least, we must undertake forms of evangelization that speak to the particular needs of handicapped individuals, make those liturgical adaptations which promote their active participation, and provide helps and services that reflect our loving concern for those with serious problems.

15. This concern should be extended also to the families and especially the parents of handicapped people.

16. No family is ever really prepared for the birth of a handicapped child. When such a child does come into the world, families often need strong support from their faith community. That support must remain firm with the passage of years. The path to independence for handicapped individuals can be difficult. Family members need to know that others stand with them, at least in spirit, as they help their children along this path.

17. The central importance of family members in the lives of all handicapped people, regardless of age, must never be underestimated. They lovingly foster the spiritual, mental, and physical development of the handicapped person and are the primary teachers of religion and morality. Ministers working in the handicapped apostolate should treat them as a uniquely valuable resource for understanding the various needs of those they serve.

18. Full participation in the Christian community has another important aspect that must not be overlooked. When we think of handicapped people in relation to ministry, we tend automatically to think of doing something for them. We do not reflect that they can do something for us and with us. As noted above, handicapped people can, by their example, teach the nonhandicapped much about strength and Christian acceptance. Moreover, they have the same duty as all members of the community to do the Lord's work in the world, according to their God-given talents and capacity. Because handicapped individuals may not be fully aware of the contribution they can make, Church leaders should consult with them, offering suggestions on practical ways of serving.

Parish Level

19. For most Catholics the community of believers is embodied in the local parish. The parish is the door to participation for handicapped individuals, and it is the responsibility of the pastor and lay leaders to make sure that this door is always open. We noted above that the task, on occasion, may not be an easy one; involving some handicapped people in parish life may challenge the ingenuity and commitment of the entire congregation. Yet, in order to be loyal to its calling, to be truly pastoral, the parish must make sure it does not exclude any Catholic who wishes to take part in its activities.

20. If the participation of handicapped persons and their families is to be real and meaningful, the parish must prepare itself to receive them. This preparation might begin with a census aimed at identifying parishioners and those with no Church affiliation who have significant disabilities. Parish leaders could then work with individuals and their families to determine what steps, if any, are needed to facilitate their participation in parish life.

21. It may be necessary at this initial stage to place considerable emphasis upon educating the members of the parish community on the rights and needs of local handicapped people. All too often, one hears that there are too few persons with disabilities in a given parish to warrant ramped entrances, special liturgies, or education programs. Some say that these matters should be handled on the diocesan level. Although many parishes have severely limited resources, we encourage all to make the best effort their circumstances permit. No parishioner should ever be excluded on the basis of disability alone.

22. The most obvious obstacle to participation in parish activities faced by many handicapped people is the physical design of parish buildings. Structurally inaccessible buildings are at once a sign and a guarantee of their isolation from the community. Sometimes all that is required to remedy the situation is the installation of outside ramps and railings, increased lighting, minor modification of toilet facilities, and, perhaps, the removal of a few pews and kneelers. In other cases, major alterations and redesign of equipment may be called for. Each parish must examine its own situation to determine the feasibility of such alterations. Mere cost must never be the exclusive consideration, however, since the provision of free access to religious functions for all interested people is a clear pastoral duty.

23. Whenever parishes contemplate new construction, they should make provision for the needs of handicapped individuals in their plans. If both new construction and the adaptation of present buildings are out of the question, the parish should devise other ways to reach its handicapped members. In cooperation with them, parish leaders may locate substitute facilities, for example, or make a concerted effort to serve at home those who cannot come to church.

24. It is essential that all forms of the liturgy be completely accessible to handicapped people, since they are the essence of the spiritual tie that binds the Christian community together. To exclude members of the parish from these celebrations of the life of the Church, even by passive omission, is to deny the reality of that community. Accessibility involves far more than physical alterations to parish buildings. Realistic provision must be made for handicapped persons to participate fully in the Eucharist and other liturgical celebrations such as the sacraments of Reconciliation, Confirmation, and Anointing of the Sick. The experiences and needs of handicapped individuals vary, as do those of any group of people. For some with significant disabilities, special liturgies may be appropriate. Others will not require such liturgies, but will benefit if certain equipment and services are made available to them. Celebrating liturgies simultaneously in sign language enables the deaf person to enter more deeply into their spirit and meaning. Participation aids such as Mass books and hymnals in large print or Braille serve the same purpose for blind or partially sighted members.

Handicapped people can also play a more active role in the liturgy if provided with proper aids and training. Blind parishioners can serve as lectors, for example, and deaf parishioners as special ministers of the Eucharist. In this connection, we look forward to the day when more handicapped individuals are active in the full-time, professional service of the Church, and we applaud recent decisions to accept qualified candidates for ordination or the religious life in spite of their disabilities.

25. Evangelization and catechesis for handicapped individuals must be geared in content and method to their particular situation. Specialized catechists should help them interpret the meaning of their lives and should give witness to Christ's presence in the local community in ways they can understand and appreciate. We hasten to add, however, that great care should be taken to avoid further isolation of handicapped people through these programs which, as far as possible, should be integrated with the normal catechetical activities of the parish. We have provided guidelines for the instruction of handicapped persons and for their participation in the liturgical life of the Church in "Sharing the Light of Faith: National Catechetical Directory for Catholics of the United States."

26. Finally, parishes must be sensitive to the social needs of handicapped members. We have already touched on some ways in which Christians can express their concern for their handicapped brothers and sisters. These actions and others like them can help solve some of the handicapped individual's practical problems and dispel a sense of isolation. They also create an opportunity for handicapped and nonhandicapped people to join hands and break down the barriers that separate them. In such an interchange, it is often the handicapped person who gives the gift of most value.

Diocesan Level

27. Efforts to bring handicapped people into the parish community are more likely to be effective if the parishes are supported by offices operating at the diocesan level. At present, the social-service needs of handicapped individuals and their families are usually addressed by established diocesan agencies. The adequacy of this ministry should be re-evaluated in the light of present-day concerns and resources. Where it is found to be inadequate, the program should be strengthened to assure that specialized aid is provided to handicapped people. In those cases where there is no program at all, we urge that one be established.

28. The clergy, religious, and laity engaged in this program should help the parish by developing policy and translating it into practical strategies for working with handicapped individuals. They should serve as advocates for handicapped people seeking help from other agencies. Finally, they should monitor public policy and generate

multifaceted educational opportunities for those who minister to and with handicapped people.

29. Many opportunities for action at the diocesan level now exist with regard to public policy. Three pieces of federal legislation that promise significant benefits to handicapped individuals have been passed within the past few years; each calls for study and possible support.

30. We refer to the Rehabilitation Act of 1973, the rehabilitation amendments of 1974, and the Education for All Handicapped Children Act of 1975. Enforcement of the regulations implementing section 504 of the Rehabilitation Act, which forbids discrimination on the basis of handicapping conditions, is a matter of particular interest. In response to the rehabilitation amendments, the executive branch of the federal government has also taken recent action, sponsoring a White House Conference on Handicapped Individuals in 1977. This conference was attended by official state delegations, and there would be value in determining which of its recommendations are being applied in the state or states where a given diocese is located. Diocesan offices will also wish to keep abreast of general public policy and practice in their states.

31. Dioceses might make their most valuable contribution in the area of education. They should encourage and support training for all clergy, religious, seminarians, and lay ministers, focusing special attention on those actually serving handicapped individuals, whether in parishes or some other setting. Religious education personnel could profit from guidance in adapting their curricula to the needs of handicapped learners, and Catholic elementary and secondary school teachers could be provided in-service training in how best to integrate handicapped students into programs of regular education. The diocesan office might also offer institutes for diocesan administrators who direct programs with an impact on handicapped persons.

32. The coordination of educational services within the dioceses should supplement the provision of direct educational aids. It is important to establish liaisons between facilities for handicapped people operating under Catholic auspices (special, residential, and day schools; psychological services and the like) and usual Catholic school programs. Only in this way can the structural basis be laid for the integration, where feasible, of handicapped students into programs for the nonhandicapped. Moreover, in order to ensure handicapped individuals the widest possible range of educational opportunities, Catholic facilities should be encouraged to develop working realtionships both among themselves and with private and public agencies serving the same population.

National Level

33. As the most visible expression of our commitment, we the bishops now designate ministry to handicapped people as a special focus for the National Conference of Catholic Bishops and the U.S. Catholic Conference. This represents a mandate to each office and secretariat, as it develops its plans and programs, to address the concerns of handicapped individuals. Appropriate offices should also serve as resource and referral centers to both parochial and diocesan bodies in matters relating to the needs of our handicapped brothers and sisters.

Concluding Remarks

34. Handicapped people are not looking for pity. They seek to serve the community and to enjoy their full baptismal rights as members of the Church. Our interaction with them can and should be an affirmation of our faith. There can be no separate church for handicapped people. We are one flock that serves a single shepherd.

35. Our wholeness as individuals and as the People of God, we say again, lies in openness, service, and love. The bishops of the United States feel a concern for handicapped individuals that goes beyond their spiritual welfare to encompass their total well-being. This concern should find expression at all levels. Parishes should maintain their own programs of ministry with handicapped people, and dioceses should make every effort to establish offices that coordinate this ministry and serve as resource and referral centers for parish efforts. Finally, the National Conference of Catholic Bishops and the U.S. Catholic Conference will be more vigilant in promoting ministry with handicapped persons throughout the structure of the Church.

36. We look to the future with what we feel is a realistic optimism. The Church has a tradition of ministry to handicapped people, and this tradition will fuel the stronger, more broadly based efforts called for by contemporary circumstances. We also have faith that our quest for justice, increasingly enlisted on the side of handicapped individuals, will work powerfully in their behalf. No one would deny that every man, woman, and child has the right to develop his or her potential to the fullest. With God's help and our own determination, the day will come when that right is realized in the lives of all handicapped people.

Statement on the Middle East
The Pursuit of Peace with Justice

A Statement Issued by the
United States Catholic Conference

November 16, 1978

1. The challenge of achieving peace with justice in the Middle East confronts the conscience of the international community. As bishops of the Catholic Church in the United States we feel a dual responsibility to respond to the moral and religious dimensions of this challenge. On the one hand, we are bound to the Middle East by ties of history, tradition, and faith. On the other hand, we are citizens of a nation which plays a direct and continuing role in the Middle East.

2. We address this problem as pastors whose pastoral ministry involves a constant concern for protecting human life and dignity by fostering justice and peace at every level of society. We are vividly aware of the complexity of the political, legal, religious, and moral problems of the Middle East, and we acknowledge with respect and gratitude the multiple efforts of political leaders who have labored to resolve this tragic conflict. We wish in the first place to encourage them and to give voice to the silent hopes of all people everywhere who long for a common effort for peace in one of the world's most dangerous political areas.

3. We seek in this Statement to bring the problem of the Middle East before the Catholic community in the United States, so that this universal challenge to conscience may be in their thoughts and prayers. We seek also to make a constructive contribution to the public debate in a nation whose impact on the Middle East is recognized throughout the world. We realize that the specific technical questions at the heart of the Middle East conflict must be resolved in the diplomatic arena, but it is our conviction that on an issue at once so politically and emotionally significant, public opinion in a society shapes the atmosphere for political choices. In accord with this conviction we offer the following.

I. 1973-1978

4. In our 1973 Statement, *Toward Peace in the Middle East*, we specified a series of principles which should be part of an effective political solution. While acknowledging the process of continuous change that marks the life of that region, we believe the central elements of our 1973 Statement to be still valid and useful guidelines for a comprehensive approach to peace and justice in the Middle East. Therefore, we again call for a comprehensive political solution involving the following:

(a) *The rights of Israel*: to existence as a sovereign state within secure and recognized boundaries;

(b) *The rights of the Palestinian Arabs*: to participate in negotiations affecting their destiny, and to a homeland of their own;

(c) *Compensation*: just compensation should be provided for all parties concerned, of whatever national origin, deprived of home and property by the three decades of conflict;

(d) *The status of Jerusalem*: recognition of its unique religious significance which should be preserved through an international guarantee of access to the holy places and through the preservation of a religiously pluralist citizenry;

(e) *U.N. Resolution 242*: its continuing utility as a basis for a just settlement in the region.

5.   These elements set a framework for understanding the key issues of justice and peace in the Middle East. The problems posed by them persist in spite of multiple efforts to resolve them. In seeking to address these continuing dimensions of the issue, two other developments must be considered: the tragedy of Lebanon and the event of Camp David.

II. Lebanon

6.   Since the outbreak of civil war in Lebanon, where almost one-third of the population (750,000) have become refugees, its fate has been directly tied to the question of a regional settlement in the Middle East. On the one hand, it is clear that Lebanon is highly vulnerable to a multiplicity of regional and international forces which directly influence its domestic life. On the other hand, the fate and future of the Palestinians, whose refugee status evokes our sympathy, join the internal problem of Lebanon to the regional problems of the Middle East. While a regional peace is a *de facto* condition for peace in Lebanon, it is not a sufficient condition. The internal dimensions of the Lebanese problem—political, social, economic, and religious—must be addressed with a blend of political wisdom and moral courage as a first step toward peace. The value of Lebanon to the Middle East, to Christianity, and the world is a truth we cannot forget. The independence of Lebanon and its fabric of political and religious pluralism must be preserved. We call upon our government to have a special concern for all these elements.

7. The dimensions of the Lebanese problems are so great that a grave responsibility for assistance lies not only with a group of nations, but requires the interest, care, and action of the international community, especially the continuing involvement of the United Nations. The urgent needs of the nation are that the cease-fire be preserved, that the Lebanese army be rebuilt to provide for the internal security of the country, that discussions among local parties be fostered to establish a new constitution safeguarding the human rights and religious liberty of all inhabitants in Lebanon, and that the sovereignty of Lebanon be securely preserved.

8. The neutrality of Lebanon must be guaranteed and preserved in order to keep the country independent and sovereign. The Lebanese must be the principal agents of their destiny, but they may rightly expect from the United States and other key actors in the international community both diplomatic assistance and the significant economic aid which rehabilitation in Lebanon will require. We commend the efforts of the Catholic Relief Services, the Catholic Near East Welfare Association, and the Pontifical Mission for Palestine in alleviating the suffering of the victims of the conflict in Lebanon and we urge the continued support of their endeavors.

III. Camp David

9. The Camp David agreements involving Egypt, Israel, and the United States already have earned a unique status in the modern history of the Middle East. The contents of the agreements and their ultimate impact on the region are complex issues which do not yield to a simple standard of judgment. To evaluate it adequately, Camp David ought to be seen as part of a process of peacemaking in the Middle East.

10. In our view the Camp David accords have an intrinsic value which ought to be praised and supported, and they have limitations which need to be acknowledged and amended. The symbolic and substantive value of a peace treaty which now seems possible between two principal states in the Middle East conflict is an achievement of the highest importance. It not only reorients the political process away from conflict and toward peace for Egypt and Israel, it provides hope that progress is possible in the Middle East. It is of the essence of diplomatic greatness to act boldly and courageously in the face of complexity and ambiguity. Camp David is such an action and deserves our support.

11. At the same time it is necessary to recognize that if Camp David is part of a process, the diplomatic initiatives taken there must be broadened. The limitations of the Camp David accords involve both the scope and terms of the agreements. One form of limitation is evidenced by the need to bring other key actors in the Middle East into the peacemaking process. This in turn is related to the terms of the agreements: It is partially due to some dimensions of the accords that key parties are unwilling to participate in the process. Two issues which exemplify the substantive limits of the accords, and which the principles of this Statement make us particularly concerned about, are the status of Jerusalem and the fate of the Palestinians, those living in the occupied territories and in the region of the Middle East. The question of Palestinian sovereignty remains unresolved by the accords and calls for further negotiations. What has been initiated at Camp David must be extended with the same boldness and vision.

IV. Beyond Camp David

12. The Middle East problem is now set in the context of new signs of hope mixed with continuing elements of danger. Aware of the conflicted and tragic history of the recent past, we are cautious but choose to emphasize the signs of hope: Peace is possible. In transforming the possibility into a reality, we see the same basic dimensions of the problem at work which structured our 1973 statement.

13. First, the international community, especially its principal diplomatic actors, inevitably influences the future of the Middle East; all those who touch the problem have an enormous responsibility to act with wisdom and vision.

14. Second, the United Nations is a vital element in any Middle East negotiations, and its diplomatic and peacekeeping role will undoubtedly be crucial to a long-term resolution of the conflict.

15. Third, the regional parties, whose conflicting claims of justice are the essence of the political and moral problem in the Middle East, are the key to peace. In their political vision, moral courage, and will for peace lie our hopes for a peaceful future.

16. Finally, the religious communities with roots in the Middle East must reflect the best of our traditions in supporting the movement for peace with justice for all the people of the region. We have a continuing concern for the protection of the basic rights, both civil and religious, of the Christian minorities in the Middle East and we encourage the local churches there to continue their steadfast witness to the faith.

17. We call upon the inhabitants of the Holy Land to renew and intensify their efforts to build a spirit of peace, by drawing upon the rich resources of the three great religious traditions which venerate the Holy Land as a sacred place. We pray that the Prince of Peace who lived and taught and prayed in the Middle East will bless the efforts of all who hope and strive for justice and peace in the land which is still called holy.

II. The Dawn of a New Era
1979 – 1983

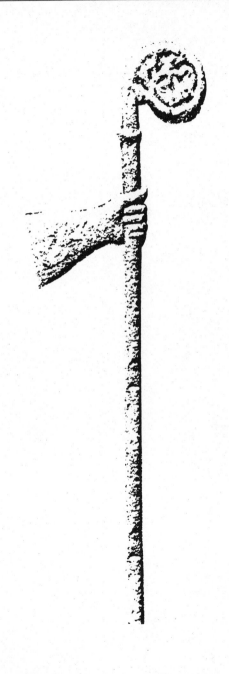

Introduction

The meeting, May 1-3, 1979, focused on an in-depth examination of the purpose and goals of the NCCB and USCC conferences with a view to possible future changes. No statements were issued.

On October 26, 1979, the Administrative Board of the USCC published a Statement entitled *Political Responsibility: Choices for the 1980s*, as the national elections approached.

Lamenting that voter participation in the United States is "now among the lowest in the world," the board identified three of the major causes: powerlessness, complexity of issues, widespread poverty, and said, "the poorer a person is, the less likely the person is to vote." The Statement calls for the amelioration of these conditions, for better government, and pleads with people to exercise their privilege of voting.

The bishops teach in this Statement that the Church's role in the political order includes education, analysis of issues for social and moral dimensions, measurement of public policy against Gospel values, speaking out with courage, skill, and concern on public issues involving human rights, social justice, and the life of the Church in society.

In not-too-veiled an answer to those persons, even some Catholics, who say: "The Church should stay out of politics," the bishops affirmed: "We believe that the Church has a proper role and responsibility in public affairs flowing from its Gospel mandate and its respect for the dignity of the human person. We hope these reflections will contribute to a renewed political vitality in our land, both in terms of citizen participation in the electoral process and the integrity and accountability of those who seek and hold public office."

On November 14, 1979, the NCCB adopted the Committee on Conciliation and Arbitration's Procedures. These *Procedures* were the outgrowth of a November 1969 mandate given to the committee by the Conference to develop procedural rules to guide the committee in dealing with cases that would reach it. Originally, the committee concentrated on due process at the local or diocesan level where the most fruitful resolution of disputes can take place.

These *Procedures*, however, are intended to help the committee to function at the Conference level. They contain no *vis obligativa* and are to be used only when a bishop member of the Conference freely chooses to use the services of the committee, and only then are they operative.

The committee preparing the *Procedures* was chaired by Most Reverend George Guilfoyle, Bishop of Camden, assisted by Bishops John F. Kinney, Daniel P. Reilly, and Sylvester W. Treinen. Their chief consultant was the Reverend Robert T. Kennedy of the Department of Canon Law, The Catholic University of America.

To date these *Procedures* have had no substantive modification.

Bishop Edward D. Head of Buffalo, chairman of the Committee on Social Development and World Peace, at the November 1979 meeting introduced to the body of bishops, *Brothers and Sisters to Us: U.S. Bishops' Pastoral on Racism in Our Day.* He recalled that the bishops, in responding to the recommendations of the Bicentennial "Call to Action" Conference in Detroit 1976, made a commitment to issue such a Pastoral Letter on racism. He noted that his committee had established a subcommittee to work on the Pastoral, chaired by Auxiliary Bishop Joseph Francis of Newark, a black bishop. After describing the wide consultation process that had been engaged in during the drafting of the Pastoral, Bishop Head then introduced Bishop Francis, who commented on the Pastoral as follows: "My brother bishops, I have only one point to make in presenting this statement to you for reflection and discussion, and that is the following: It is important that we make a strong and honest statement on racism. It must be forthright in its recognition of racism, explicit in its denunciation of racism, and challenging in its call to eradicate racism.

"Given the current atmosphere in our nation, this will certainly not be an easy task. The predominant public sentiment with respect to racial equality seems to be that great progress has been made, that most of the iniquities have been removed, and that as a society we can relax our efforts to achieve racial justice. Indeed, many believe that racial equality has now been achieved and some go so far as to suggest that too much has been done for racial minorities."

Bishop Francis then cited some startling facts. In the job market, for example, unemployment for nonwhites is twice as high as for whites; since 1973, the number of blacks and Hispanics beneath the poverty line has actually increased, while the number of whites below the poverty line has not changed; since 1974 the median income for minority families has actually decreased as a percentage of white family income. In the area of education, twenty-five years have passed since the *Brown* decision outlawing school segregation, yet more black and brown children attend racially isolated schools today than in 1954.

Bishop Francis continued: "In short, despite impressive gains made by some blacks and Hispanics, the evidence suggests that for society as a whole the gap between whites and nonwhites is now increasing, not decreasing. . . .

"Finally, if I may add just a brief personal note, let me say that I have felt the sting of racism in my own life. I have lived with discrimination in society as well as in the Church. And I have seen many of my brothers and sisters suffer the injustices of racism. I assure you—racism in our nation and in our Church is very real. Its continued existence among us requires that we address the subject with language that makes unmistakably clear our commitment to eradicate this injustice."

During the final consideration of this letter the bishops added some sixty amendments, several in response to concerns expressed by some prelates that it did not have either a sufficient theological base or enough footnotes and other references to past statements and teachings of the Church.

But even this did not satisfy Auxiliary Bishop Roger M. Mahony of Fresno, who said he was unequivocally in favor of a statement on racism but felt that the document, as amended, still was not satisfactory, protesting: "I think it [the racism statement] should be the finest document we can produce." For the Fresno prelate: "Even with the amendments, the statement still flowed from a sociological and not a theological base." Christology and theology "should be the underpinning from which the document should flow." Bishop Mahony argued for using more theology throughout than merely the Pastoral Letter's identification of racism as a sin, "a sin that divides the human family, blots out the image of God among specific members of that family, and violates the fundamental human dignity of those called to be children of the same Father."

Several bishops agreed that the document might not be perfect or could be improved, but argued that it was urgently needed at this time when racism—in forms such as the Ku Klux Klan and neo-Nazi groups—seems to be making a comeback.

Bishop Mahony proposed that a complete new draft of the proposed letter be circulated among the bishops this winter in time for consideration at their next meeting in May in Chicago.

His motion failed by voice vote—although a substantial number of bishops voiced support for this recommendation. The amended Pastoral Letter was approved 214 to 30.

The dreadful violation of human rights in Cambodia caused the bishops, assembled at their November 1979 meeting, to adopt a *Resolution on Cambodia* presented by Bishop Edward D. Head of Buffalo. Bishop Joseph McNicholas of Springfield moved the addition of "a word of thanks to the Catholics who responded so generously to the special collection for Cambodia." Several other minor amendments were accepted and the Resolution as amended was approved by voice vote.

At the same November 1979 meeting, Bishop Head moved the *Resolution on Iran*, where hostages were being held in the American embassy in Tehran. "The survival and safe return of the hostages is the first priority in this tragic dilemma," stressed the Resolution, which concluded by begging prayers "for a peaceful and successful resolution of this tragic drama." Bishop Edward O'Rourke of Peoria moved the addition of: "We as teachers of moral principles reaffirm the rights of innocent persons to immunity from terrorists' actions which threaten their well-being and lives. The end does not justify the means." His motion was seconded and approved on a voice vote.

The *Resolution on Iran* was approved by a voice vote.

At the November 1979 meeting, the NCCB president, Archbishop Quinn, reported that, in accord with approved Conference procedures, he had appointed Archbishop Rembert Weakland, O.S.B., Bishop Norbert Gaughan, and Bishop Daniel Reilly to draft a *Resolution on the Visit of Pope John Paul II* to the United States. The committee circulated a preliminary draft which was modified by amendments submitted to the drafting committee.

In their Resolution the bishops saw the papal visit as an occasion of special grace to our country, "one of the greatest events in the history of the Church in the United States." After mentioning some of the themes the Pope touched on during his visit, the Resolution states: "Responding to the Pope's message . . . we acknowledge our particular duty to give witness to the episcopal ministry of holiness and truth. . . . In union with the Holy Father we bishops wholeheartedly and with God's help rededicate ourselves to preaching the Word in season and out of season." Asking God to bless the Holy Father, the prelates hoped the papal visit would be for all "a call to the gospel message of truth, love, and service to the world."

The lengthy resolution, as amended, passed on a voice vote with no audible dissent.

On February 15, 1980, the Administrative Board of the USCC issued a *Statement on Registration and Conscription for Military Service*. This timely Statement taught that there is no objection in principle to the registration of men both in peacetime and in times of national emergency provided there are convincing reasons. The board went on record as opposed to any reinstitution of military conscription except in case of national emergency. However, the bishops' unequivocal support for "the right of selective conscientious objection" was the Statement's greatest advance and the teaching that drew the greatest notice nationally. These prelates opposed strongly the registration and conscription of women.

One of the more embarrassing diplomatic situations for the United States in the twentieth century was the 1980 seizure of American citizens as hostages by Iran in the American embassy in Tehran. The incident, fraught with international danger, perplexed the nation.

Mindful of the personal danger of the hostages, the assembled bishops on May 1, 1980, pleaded in their timely, much-amended *Resolution on Iran*: "The survival and the safe return of the hostages is the first priority in this tragic dilemma. Inflammatory words and actions should be avoided in both official policy and public debate. . . . As a nation we must combine firm resolve with rational restraint."

The Resolution recommended that diplomatic and other forms of peaceful pressure be used in support of the hostages. "Most importantly, as religious leaders, we call upon Catholics and all believers to pray without ceasing for a peaceful and successful resolution of this tragic drama." Fortunately, those prayers were heard and the hostages were released unharmed immediately after this carefully worded resolution.

In presenting the *Resolution on Cuban and Haitian Refugess* to the May 1980 meeting of the bishops, Archbishop Edward McCarthy of Miami explained that the Resolution was designed to express pastoral and human concern for the dreadfully oppressed boat people of the Caribbean. He noted that the Resolution urged government action and emphasized that the responsibility for these refugees rested on both the national and the local level. He pointed out that the Statement was intended to demonstrate the Church's concern for the black Haitians as well as the white Cubans.

The archbishop stated that it was urgent that the bishops take a public stand on such a current and pressing question, which would hopefully encourage more decisive government action and assure the government that the Church is ready and anxious to help with the resettlement of these refugees.

Bishop Rene Gracida of Pensacola-Tallahassee, chairman of the *ad hoc* Committee for Migration and Tourism, said that his committee endorsed the Statement and observed that it fitted into the pattern of past actions taken by the Conference.

The Resolution was passed on a voice vote with no audible dissent.

To commemorate the twentieth anniversary of the Vatican's founding of the Secretariat for Promoting Christian Unity in 1960, the Administrative Committee of the NCCB issued on November 9, 1980, a *Statement on Promoting Christian Unity* prepared by the NCCB's Ecumenical and Interreligious Affairs Committee, chaired by Bishop Ernest L. Unterkoefler of Charleston.

This Statement noted that a true ecumenical revolution is in progress and with Pope John Paul II hopes that the third milennium would dawn on a full refound communion of all churches. While encouraging every form of dialogue among churches, the bishops beg for prayers acknowledging that the unity we seek is not to be the product of human achievement "but a gift from God to His people."

In the May 1977 meeting, Archbishop Philip Hannan of New Orleans urged that a complete paper on the errors of communism be issued by the body of bishops. He said that there is a growing tendency among a number of people, especially youth, to consider Marxism or national socialism as a good substitute for the free enterprise system. The Statement, in his view, should deal basically with the religious content of Marxism, but should also indicate the disasters that have befallen the countries which accepted these ideologies. In order to be balanced, the Statement should also indicate excesses in our nation's present system. He felt that such a Statement would benefit Latin American bishops who are trying to contain the spread of communism, and it would also serve to support the words of the Holy Father who recently branded communism the gravest error of our time. He moved therefore "that the body of bishops direct one of its departments or establish an *ad hoc* committee to prepare a Statement on communism and present it at the next general meeting in November."

After the motion was seconded, Archbishop Bernardin asked Archbishop Hannan to withdraw the stipulation concerning the time when the paper would be presented. He noted that three committees would have to be involved, as well as the Administrative Committee. Archbishop Hannan then withdrew the provision concerning time, but warned that he would expect an accounting.

Bishop George Guilfoyle of Camden felt that a statement of this sort should address all unsound philosophies in our time, but Cardinal Carberry supported Archbishop Hannan's proposal, noting the apparent indifference of the people in Italy to the advance of communism.

Bishop Basil Losten, Eparch of Stamford, supported Archbishop Hannan's request and urged the episcopal conference to take a serious stand against communism.

After several reports in previous meetings, Bishop Joseph McNicholas of Springfield was introduced at the November 1980 meeting for the final discussion on the *Pastoral Letter on Marxist Communism*. He moved that the proposed letter with the approved amendments be accepted. He then explained some of the amendments, noting that the new preamble referred to violations of human rights by citing the USCC statement on *Religious Liberty in Eastern Europe* and by embodying a new quotation from a recent issue of *Civilta Cattolica* reflecting current thinking on the relation of the Vatican to Communist nations. Regarding specific amendments, Bishop McNicholas said *Una Sancta* had first been changed to *universal Church* and then later to "a very large portion of the human race."

Auxiliary Bishop Peter Rosazza of Hartford said that he supported the Pastoral Letter and he commended Bishop McNicholas and the committee, and especially Dr. Louis Dupre of Yale. He noted the importance of making a comparison with capitalism and he said, "If we do publish a document on Marxism, we'll be criticized elsewhere for not seeing the faults in our own system if we make no reference to capitalism." He asked if a motion could be made at another time to refer the suggested final sentence amendment he had submitted with six other bishops to the committee for return to the bishops in November 1981. The president, Archbishop Quinn, said that he could make such a motion later.

Bishop Edward Swanstrom, Auxiliary in New York, said he was glad the preamble had been changed to make reference to the human rights violations, an important move for world leaders to be reminded of the sufferings endured throughout the world.

Bishop F. Joseph Gossman of Raleigh said he was not terribly convinced about the need for such a document, and he asked whether possibly noninclusive language in the proposed text might be changed. Bishop McNicholas said he would ask at the end of debate for authorization to make such needed editorial changes.

Bishop William Weigand of Salt Lake City said that he had worked for ten years in Latin America and the present document does not address the situation there. He thought it would be good to include a paragraph on the evils of capitalism. He said Pope Paul VI had been careful to balance his statements at Medellin and in *Popularum Progressio*, and John Paul II has addressed us on our own life style and on materialism in our society. He said there is a danger of seeing the sliver in someone else's eye and not the block of wood in our own. He continued, saying that what gives the basis to the neo-Marxist thrust in Latin America are the evils of unregulated capitalism.

Archbishop William D. Borders of Baltimore said that the paper is a good study but does not follow the norms of our regular pastoral letters. He asked whether it should be issued as something other than a Pastoral Letter.

Bishop McNicholas said that it it were issued in some other form, the bishops would be saying that they could never speak in a pastoral way on a technical subject. Two problems would be that the bishops would be saying that the paper would be only academic and that it would not be considered as a teaching document of the American bishops.

Cardinal Krol spoke in favor of the motion and of the Pastoral Letter. He said he favored both its thrust and its content. He noted that he had been broadcasting for more than thirty years over Radio Free Europe and the Voice of America, and warned against getting into any discussion of the different types of communism, such as Leninism, Stalinism, Marxism, etc. Being asked why fascism and nazism went down the drain so quickly while communism has been around for more than sixty years, he said that the reason is the integrated philosophy which is materialistic, and he said the bishops must attack such an error in the interest of truth. He noted that the leaders of Italian and French communism speak sweet statements but have never repudiated the materialism and opposition to transcendence which characterize their philosophy. His Eminence's intervention seemed to satisfy the body of bishops as to which approach the letter should take.

The *Pastoral Letter on Marxist Communism* was approved by a written ballot of 236 to 17, with two invalid votes and one abstention.

The letter is widely used on college and university levels. Aimed at explaining in simple language just what Marxism is, the letter shows how this system can appeal to the poor in many parts of the world and portrays the challenge, if not threat, this is for the Church even in predominantly Christian countries.

Unlike some of the strong opposition to communism taken in the past by bishops and popes, this letter speculates that Marxism could "undergo radical changes in its attitude toward religion." Recognizing political realities as well as philosophical differences, the document points out the pressing necessity "to focus upon two problems requiring common efforts across the ideological divide: keeping the peace and empowering the poor."

No weakening of principle mars the document which courageously notes the bishops "are not blind to the horrendous violations of human rights perpetrated in the name of communism or the invasions of the territorial integrity of sovereign nations," yet the bishops in this letter warn that obsessive consumerism "makes poorer nations look upon us as the wastrels of this world . . . a sober and responsible life style would be more effective than anticommunist propaganda in dissuading the uncommitted from joining the Marxist camp."

In his presentation at the November 1980 meeting of the Statement, *Called and Gifted: The American Catholic Laity,* Bishop Albert Ottenweller of Steubenville explained that in 1976 when Archbishop Edward McCarthy of Miami was chairman of the Bishops' Committee on the Laity, the Administrative Committee authorized a Declaration affirming the Catholic laity in the Church of the United States. Under his direction, and continuing with the same members, the committee took this mandate seriously and during the last three and one-half years expended a great deal of effort on this project.

Steubenville's bishop said that "Reflection," an original name, has gone through many revisions and several consultations. "We think now is a happy time to proclaim it, because November 18, the Tuesday after our general meeting, will be the fifteenth anniversary of the *Decree on the Apostolate of the Laity.*"

The National Advisory Council to the NCCB/USCC Administrative Committee had unanimously endorsed the document. After noting that the Statement also had wide consultation with a number of lay groups and theologians, Bishop Ottenweller said that his committee stands strongly behind the document. "We think it will affirm the laity and call them to be a strong force in the Church, especially challenging them to holiness and to be about building the Kingdom of God in the world."

Bishop Ottenweller then moved that the Conference approve this Statement on the laity. A discussion followed in which the bishops proposed that several minor amendments, mostly stylistic, be considered *en bloc*; and approval was given to all these amendments.

Bishop Ottenweller then introduced several other amendments with the pertinent recommendations of the committee. In each case, the committee's recommendations were accepted; in several instances the proposer withdrew his amendment before a formal vote was taken.

The Statement, *Called and Gifted: The American Catholic Laity*, as amended, passed on a voice vote with no negatives recorded.

Auxiliary Bishop Daniel Pilarczyk of Cincinnati introduced, at the November 1980 meeting, the proposed *Catholic Higher Education and the Pastoral Mission of the Church*. He noted that it traced its origins to the Committee of Bishops and Catholic College and University Presidents. Bishop Pilarczyk observed that the bishops had not previously addressed themselves to the subject of higher education in a pastoral letter. He also said that there was a growing awareness among Catholic colleges of the need to maintain their religious identity in order to continue to exist. He added that the Pastoral Letter would acknowledge the great ecclesial efforts of Catholic colleges and universities, and could also serve as an instrument to continue and expand the ongoing dialogue between local bishops and such institutions in their dioceses. However, he warned that the letter was designed to address neither all of the problems of Catholic colleges and universities nor all existing local abuses.

Bishop Pilarczyk mentioned that a draft of the Pastoral had been sent to bishops, inviting them to share it with Catholic college and university presidents. As a result of that consultation, a second draft of the Pastoral had been prepared and sent to the bishops for *modi* (amendments). The Cincinnati auxiliary concluded by thanking Monsignor John Murphy, formerly on the staff of the National Catholic Educational Association, and Sister Alice Gallen, currently on the staff of NCEA, for their help in preparing the drafts.

Later in the meeting, Bishop Pilarczyk distributed to the bishops thirty-seven amendments received during the meeting and reviewed by the committee. Several of the amendments were withdrawn, principally because they overlapped others, but the majority of the amendments were accepted by the assembled bishops.

The Pastoral was approved on a written ballot.

Dr. Edmund D. Pellegrino, The Catholic University of America president, and eminent educator, remarked that he welcomed the Pastoral Letter as "timely," saying he was grateful for the "very positive reflections of the bishops on the way in which our Catholic institutions of learning contribute to the Church's mission to human culture and human society."[1] Noting that the bishops clearly share the Catholic institution's optimism about their future, Dr. Pellegrino praised the letter as a concrete expression of the bishops' concern and support.

---

[1] *Envoy of The Catholic University of America Alumni*, December 1980.

On July 2, 1974, the United States Supreme Court decided in effect to reinstate capital punishment by upholding the constitutionality of death penalty statutes in Florida, Texas, and Georgia. At that time the bishops went on record to oppose capital punishment, but the court's decision accelerated at a surprising rate the return of the death penalty. In all, thirty-eight states enacted death penalty legislation during the 1970s.[2]

In his November 1980 presentation of the *Statement on Capital Punishment* to the assembled bishops, Bishop Edward Head of Buffalo stressed that the Statement is both timely and important—timely because of the intense public concern over crime and violence; important because of the many people calling for a return to the death penalty as one solution for wiping out serious crime. "The Statement before you opposes the use of capital punishment," commented Buffalo's Ordinary, with the reflection that the Statement makes a prudential pastoral judgment about the application of the death penalty, a judgment "informed by Christian values of faith, love, and respect for life."

In summary, the Statement noted that the primary reasons for the reinstatement of capital punishment are deterrence, reform, and retribution; but there is no conclusive evidence the death penalty deters crime. The death penalty leaves no room for reform and taking life is not a valid act of retribution. Six "inherent difficulties" with capital punishment include the possibility of a mistake, delays in carrying out the sentence, and the "stark truth" that the application of the death penalty is "unfair and discriminatory." The poor and members of the racial and ethnic minorities are "more likely to die."

In his presentation of the Statement, Bishop Head cautioned that there is a great need for education of Catholics and all Americans on this subject. He mentioned that the Office of Social Development will be asked to produce educational materials in the form of study guides and other resources to be used in Catholic parishes.

A written ballot followed. Bishop Thomas Kelly, O.P., secretary, reported that 217 votes had been cast: 145 in favor of the Statement, 31 against, and 41 abstentions. He said that in the computation of the vote, abstentions are not counted and that the document therefore had achieved a two-thirds vote and was accepted as a Conference Statement.

Possibly the greatest single piece of publicity given to the Statement was by Bishop Ernest L. Unterkoefler of Charleston, who on April 27, 1982, testified against capital punishment to the Senate Judiciary Committee. Bishop Unterkoefler, who as a former prison chaplain accompanied six men to the electric chair, one of whom to this day the bishop is convinced was innocent, based his testimony on

---

[2]George M. Anderson, "The Death Penalty in the United States: The Present Situation," *America*, November 20, 1982.

the bishops' *Statement on Capital Punishment*.

He, too, testified that the most enduring solution to violence can be found in working to improve social conditions, alleviating poverty, inequality, and racial discrimination, "breeding grounds for hatred and a loss of self-respect." He also repeated the NCCB's call for an effective gun control law, observing that the easy availability of guns spreads violence.

The *Statement on Capital Punishment* put the American Catholic Church on record in a fuller manner on a far from settled social question. In an editorial commenting on the penalty by lethal injection, *The New York Times* protested: "Call the new technique 'humane' if you like. The sentence of death is still an expression of vengeance and it is still barbaric."[3]

On January 4, 1981, the Bishops' Committee on Social Development and World Peace, with the approval of the Administrative Board of the USCC, published *Cultural Pluralism in the United States*. This Statement is the bishops' response to a plea of the 1976 "Call to Action" conference in Detroit that more attention be given to "the ethnic riches of our blessed land and the diversity of cultures that have contributed to contemporary America."

The committee rejects totally the melting pot theory of American society and teaches that the total homogenization of people within a nation is no less disastrous than that same process among nations. Denouncing past and present discriminations, the committee continues that there is definitely a place for national parishes and that the mingling of cultures brings positive elements of enduring value to the family, the Church, and the country itself. Asserting that Americanization does not call for the abandonment of cultural differences but for their wider appreciation, the bishops begged all Americans to accept religious and cultural pluralism not as an historic oddity or a sentimental journey into the past, but as a vital, fruitful, and challenging phenomenon of our society.

The Statement called for action in support of the existence, expression, development, and mutual experience of cultural diversity in general society and especially in the Church—on diocesan, parochial, and educational levels. Minority groups were delighted with this Statement.

On March 25, 1981, for the first anniversary of the assassination of Archbishop Oscar Romero of El Salvador, in the name of the NCCB president, Archbishop John Roach released a *Statement on El Salvador*. For Archbishop Roach the continuing glorious witness of the Church in Latin America is symbolized most dramatically in the total witness given by the martyred Archbishop Romero. "After expressing deep concern for the suffering, defenseless people of El Salvador, the State-

---

[3]*The New York Times*, August 15, 1982.

ment expressed the prayerful hope of the Church in both Americas for
a political solution committed to a more just and equitable society."

The forty-five member Administrative Committee, which con-
ducts activities of the National Conference of Catholic Bishops between
annual plenary sessions of the American hierarchy, issued a *Pro-life
Statement* on March 26, 1981, renewing the call for a constitutional
amendment "in defense of the unborn human life."

While noting "remarkable pro-life gains in our society," the NCCB
Administrative Committee said it is reaffirming its position on a constitutional amendment on the basis of a 1974 congressional testimony
in which NCCB argued that an amendment is "the only way to reverse"
court decisions resulting in ready access to abortion.

The committee also noted positive increases "in the level of public
awareness of the humanity of the unborn and the inherent cruelty
of abortion; in the level of involvement of so many persons providing
competent and compassionate care for the woman who is pregnant
and in need, and in the growing number of legislative actions and
judicial decisions favoring the unborn."

But the committee was unanimous in expressing its conviction
that a constitutional amendment is the only action which will reverse
the Supreme Court's 1973 abortion decisions and which will "provide
some constitutional basis for the legal protection of the unborn child."

On April 2, 1981, the USCC Committee on Social Development
and World Peace, with the approval of the Administrative Board,
issued a Statement, *Reflections on the Energy Crisis*, in which they asked
policy makers to address energy issues "with moral insight and commitment." Humbly and honestly the committee acknowledges that
the Statement constitutes no pronouncement but rather an invitation
to further study and prudent action on the fundamental problem in
the crisis: "the need to effect a transition from primary dependence
on oil and natural gas to primary dependence on something else in
the near future."

Because "energy is one of these touchstone issues like arms control or the limits of federal power whose resolution will profoundly
affect society in the 21st century," it is important that the Church
take part in the national discussion of energy. After examining various energy sources and the issues of energy distribution and control,
the committee strives "to situate energy issues in a moral context"
by raising "human considerations which are often ignored."

Without such a moral perspective, it teaches "decision makers
will have little to rely on but the hard and rather analytical tools that
have guided energy development in the past." Among the six moral
principles offered for guiding the energy debate, possibly the outstanding two are giving special attention to the poor and the poorer
nations and having all citizens accept an appropriate share in formulating energy policy. Admitting many central energy questions are

hard to define, much less answer, the bishops ask the Catholic Christian community to be a continuous presence in the energy debate as long as issues so closely touching the welfare of all humanity go unresolved.

To date the energy crisis is far from resolved. However, this Statement did show the Church's concern for as just a solution as possible.

The Administrative Board of the USCC on April 13, 1981, in its *Resolution on El Salvador*, reiterated opposition to U.S. military aid to the government of El Salvador. These bishops, in a reaction to erroneous political insinuations about three nuns and a lay missionary murdered in December 1980, said in their statement:

> These selfless and brave women were engaged in the ministry of the Gospel: feeding, sheltering and defending the refugees who are the product of the injustice and violence in El Salvador today. No one should impugn the evangelical character of the lives of these women or question the sacrificial character of their deaths.

An August 1981 State Department briefing showed that the American Catholic bishops and the Reagan administration continued to have "very significant differences with respect to U.S. policy in Central America." Bishop Thomas C. Kelly, O.P., reported: "Nothing we heard at our investigative briefing changes our conviction that no outside military aid should go to either side of the El Salvador civil war."

At the spring 1980 meeting, Archbishop Quinn called on Bishop Edward Head of Buffalo, chairman of the Committee on Social Development and World Peace, to present the draft of the Pastoral Letter, *Health and Health Care*.

Bishop Head emphasized that approval of the draft was not being sought at the spring meeting. A vote would be taken in the meeting to determine only whether the bishops approved the general approach of the document; a final draft would be the subject of debate at the general meeting in November. In preparation for the November debate, Bishop Head invited all bishops to submit in writing their reflections on specific issues and problems to his committee.

Several bishops then recommended that other areas of concern be emphasized in the Pastoral. Archbishop William Borders of Baltimore, agreeing with the strong emphasis on social justice, suggested that the draft should develop pastoral ministry further. Bishop George Guilfoyle of Camden called for strong emphasis on moral issues; Cardinal Krol agreed. Bishop Walter Sullivan expressed his hope that certain key issues, such as national health insurance and collective bargaining in Catholic hospitals, not be deleted from the text. Auxiliary Bishop Austin Vaughan of New York recommended that some reference be made to the positive, redemptive value of suffering.

Bishop Head assured the bishops that his committee would take note of these interventions. He moved that the bishops approve the committee's overall approach to the Pastoral. The motion was seconded and passed on a voice vote without further discussion. The document required far more rewriting than had been expected.

At the November 1981 meeting, Bishop Mark Hurley, chairman of the Committee on Social Development and World Peace, in presenting the Pastoral Letter, *Health and Health Care*, noted that the Pastoral had been redrafted to incorporate the revisions suggested by the bishops; other interested individuals and groups, such as the Catholic Health Association, were given the opportunity to comment and make additional suggestions. He mentioned that in June the draft was unanimously passed, as amended, by the Committee on Social Development and World Peace and its Subcommittee on Health, and that the Pastoral has four specific purposes:

1) To reflect on the biblical and theological principles which undergird the Church's vision of health and healing; 2) To remind all Catholics of their responsibilities for their own health and for their share in the healing apostolate of the Church; 3) To express full commitment to the Catholic health care apostolate and to support and encourage professionals in the health field; 4) To offer basic principles for public policy on health.

He assured the bishops that an extensive dialogue with the Catholic Health Association and the National Conference of Catholic Charities had been conducted on this subject. The set of principles which were developed in that dialogue were incorporated into the public policy section of this draft.

Reassuring his fellow bishops regarding medical-moral issues, Bishop Hurley noted that the language referring to the *Ethical and Religious Directives for Catholic Health Facilities* had been strengthened and clarified, and he explained that on the delicate subject of collective bargaining, the text had been modified to provide a balance between the rights and responsibilities of employees.

In the section of the document dealing with public policy, the bishops noted endorsement of the concept of national health insurance. Realistically, Bishop Hurley added, it is unlikely that a national health insurance program will be enacted in the immediate future, but this concept is included in the letter because the USCC is on record since 1974 in support of national health insurance. Unwilling to retreat from that position, the committee reasserted this endorsement in their Pastoral as a principle and goal, even though they are convinced such insurance on the national level is unlikely legislation in the near future. Tens of millions of Americans are still without health insurance—a compelling reason for the bishops to continue "to work for some type of universal and comprehensive national health insurance."

Asking for additional amendments to the text, Bishop Hurley commented that the current draft placed more emphasis on the role of the sacraments, the role of the parish, and the question of science and scientific values than in earlier drafts.

The following action was taken on the new amendments. Bishop Hurley moved the approval of amendments 1-11, 13-36, and 38-43 *in globo*. After due discussion of the substantive amendments, Archbishop Roach called for a vote on *Health and Health Care* which received unanimous approval.

Of the November 16-18, 1981 meeting, NCCB President Archbishop John R. Roach could say: "The combined impact of deliberations made the meeting the most momentous in my ten years in the hierarchy."

Among the more sharply debated items at that meeting was the *Statement on Central America*, asking the end of all United States military aid to El Salvador and urging the Reagan administration to maintain economic aid to Nicaragua. Indicative of the stormy battle the Statement would meet on the floor were the fourteen modifications submitted beforehand for this rather brief document, including four more substantial recommendations by Bishop Raymond Lucker of New Ulm.

Bishop Mark Hurley, chairman of the Committee on Social Development and World Peace, made the opening presentation of the Statement which he said was initiated by Archbishop Roach and the General Secretary, Bishop Thomas Kelly, O.P., after their return from an Inter-American Bishops Meeting in Costa Rica the previous May. Bishop Hurley mentioned the subcommittee they appointed: Archbishop John L. May of St. Louis, assisted by Bishop John O'Connor of the Military Ordinariate, and Professor Dominguez of Harvard University.

After a general sketch of the Statement, Bishop Hurley introduced Archbishop May who commented, "I believe the heart of the document is the El Salvador section and the position the USCC has taken for eighteen months. We oppose military aid from all sources and call again for a political solution to the conflict. This is the position repeatedly taken by Bishop Rivera y Damas.

"Our El Salvador position has had a positive impact on the U.S. policy debate against military action and has reoriented the discussion toward a more political direction. The Statement reaffirms these two points at this crucial time in our national debate when there are new proposals for military measures."[4]

The archbishop remarked that the Statement coincides with the position of the Bishops Conference in Guatemala, published less than six months previously.

---

[4] *The New York Times*, November 20, 1981.

The archbishop continued, "Regarding Nicaragua, we have a very limited purpose in the Statement. Conscious of the complexity of the internal situation there, we are just speaking to how U.S. policy may affect Nicaragua. Our Statement affirms that it would not be wise to isolate Nicaragua economically and politically at this time. We should not push them toward the Soviets.

"In summary, I recommend that we reaffirm the strong stance we have already taken on Central America."

Bishop Theodore McCarrick of Metuchen asked why the Statement went directly from the subcommittee of the Committee on Social Development and World Peace to the Administrative Board without the full committee's having an opportunity to review it. Also, he wondered whether sufficient consultation had been had with the bishops of Guatemala and Nicaragua. Bishop Hurley answered that the full committee meets only twice a year and the Conference leadership wanted the Statement considered at the present meeting. He admitted there had been no direct contact with the Guatemalan bishops.

Archbishop James Hickey of Washington, D.C., thought the Statement was timely, well founded, and expected since the death of Archbishop Oscar Romero of El Salvador. He admitted there would be risk in issuing the Statement but greater risk in not issuing it.

Possibly the strongest protest of all was an intervention by Bishop John O'Connor, auxiliary bishop of the Military Ordinariate, a member of the subcommittee preparing the proposed document on Central America.

Stating that he was not an apologist for this or any other administration, Bishop O'Connor declared: "I must still ask that when we issue a statement recommending specific policies to our own government or to any other, we be meticulously careful that we know precisely what we are talking about . . . and I simply do not understand why it would be inappropriate to confer further with the hierarchies of the countries involved." He continued that he would defer to others if the proposed Statement concerned *only* El Salvador, but the Statement addresses Nicaragua and Guatemala as well, "not merely in protesting murder and oppression but again in addressing political, economic, and military specifics." The New York auxiliary wondered if any bishops in either of these two countries were requesting the American hierarchy to address such matters.

"Finally," Bishop O'Connor concluded, "we repeatedly call this a *Statement on Central America*. It addresses three countries, El Salvador, Nicaragua, Guatemala. It does not address Belize, Costa Rica, or Honduras, the three other countries of Central America."

After lamenting the time pressures put on the subcommittee of which he was a member, in the preparation of the document, Bishop O'Connor declared: "I simply do not believe a Statement of such importance, with implications for the Church universally and the

Holy See, can be appropriately prepared in this fashion."

Procedurally, the bishop recommended that (a) any proposed Statement on Central America be sent to the respective hierarchies of all countries addressed in the Statement; (b) after these hierarchies are given a reasonable period of time, the Statement should be remanded to the subcommittee for whatever reworking would be appropriate; (c) the completed Statement should be submitted to the Administrative Committee, via the Committee on Social Development and World Peace and published by the Administrative Committee if it concurs with the Statement.

Other bishops, fearing the dropping or the defeat of the Statement since it needed a two-thirds majority, pleaded strongly about the need for such a statement. The Statement was approved.

Among the few bishops casting "no" votes was John Cardinal Krol, archbishop of Philadelphia. Cardinal Krol said, "I am in favor of a Statement, but I have grave apprehensions about issuing a Statement without clearance with the local bishops (in Central America)."[5]

Cardinal Krol said that because the issue was multinational he would favor clearance of the Statement not only by the local church in Central America but also by the Holy See in Rome. "In a free country we can make all kinds of statements, but in most countries you make statements and somebody else is going to pay for it. In other words, it doesn't have a guaranteed positive effect," the Cardinal said, alluding to the possibility of more violence in Central America because of the U.S. bishops' forthright views.

The materials from the May 1981 meeting's discussions of the purpose and goals of the NCCB/USCC, together with individual input, were collated into a Statement by an *ad hoc* committee and presented by Auxiliary Bishop Daniel Pilarczyk of Cincinnati at the November 1981 meeting. Bishop Pilarczyk moved approval of the Statement, which had been circulated among the bishops, and asked for debate.

Archbishop Charles A. Salatka moved that the title of the Statement be changed from "Mission Statement" to "Statement of Purpose." He feared that the word "mission" might be misleading; some people might take it as referring to "the Missions."

Bishop Pilarczyk said that the committee responsible for drafting the Statement preferred to keep the title as it stands. *Mission Statement* is an acknowledged technical term; moreover, this title has been used all through the process of producing the Statement. Archbishop Salatka's motion failed by voice vote.

Archbishop Rembert Weakland, O.S.B., asked whether there were any mechanisms for revising the Statement if that should become necessary on the publication of the new *Code of Canon Law*. Bishop Pilarczyk replied that he assumed that it could be revised at will, and

---

[5] *Philadelphia Inquirer*, November 20, 1981.

that an appropriate process for revision would be set in motion should the new *Code of Canon Law* seem to require it. Bishop Pilarczyk added that the Statement is compatible with the draft of the Code that is currently available.

The *NCCB/USCC Mission Statement* was then approved on a voice vote with no audible dissent.

Also at the November 1981 meeting the NCCB approved new rules governing public statements, regarding their nature and authority.

(1) Public statements of committees of the U.S. Catholic Conference require pre-publication approval by a majority of the administrative board.

(2) "An NCCB or USCC statement or publication will have a preface signed by the general secretary that will clearly distinguish the statement's origin and authority from the approval of its text. The preface will also explicitly identify the person or persons who officially approved the statement's text and are accountable for it."

(3) "Committee statements . . . do not commit the entire membership of the conference to a position, but they do offer important guidance for assessing the subjects they treat."

At the May 1977 meeting, Bishop Bernard Law spoke of the need for planning a council-like gathering of the bishops. He saw this as necessary to get at "root principles" and form appropriate pastoral analysis. Bishop McManus supported this suggestion, and noted that at least one-third of the bishops present at the general meeting did not have the opportunity to participate in the Second Vatican Council. In view of the interest expressed, Archbishop Bernardin said that the matter would be pursued.

A planning committee headed by Bishop James W. Malone of Youngstown was formed; and a first-of-its-kind closed assembly of United States Bishops for Prayer and Reflection on Episcopal Ministry was attended by two hundred fifty-two bishops, June 13–23, 1982, on the campus of St. John's University, Collegeville, Minn. Bishop Malone explained the purpose was to invite Catholic bishops in the United States to come together in a prayerful and reflective atmosphere, and to consider various implications for pastoral ministry in the 1980s in light of the Second Vatican Council.

No statement was issued.

In March of 1983, the Administrative Board of the NCCB approved the *Statement on Social Security System*, which noted that Social Security is the largest and one of the most successful social programs in the United States. Because of recent problems that have arisen in regard to Social Security, the prelates 1) reaffirmed their support for the system; 2) hoped to highlight moral principles that would prove helpful to the public debate over Social Security; 3) hoped to offer practical guidance concerning participation in Social Security by Catholic institutions and employees of the Church.

The Board warned that the Social Security system in the United States is a program that is vital to the protection of human dignity for millions of Americans. "It makes our society more humane and is a program that merits full support of all Americans."

On October 22, 1971, John Cardinal Krol of Philadelphia told the international synod delegates in Rome that the armaments race is not the way to protect human life or foster peace.[6] On the contrary, he said, little by little it aggravates the causes of war. The fact is that "the destructive power in the arsenals of the world cannot prevent mass destruction of life. It can at best retaliate, causing a greater loss of life." The Philadelphia archbishop's address also included a defense of the rights of both total and selective conscientious objectors. Henceforth, Cardinal Krol, who was president of NCCB from 1971–1974, worked and prayed for an NCCB Statement on peace.

At their November 1980 meeting, the Catholic bishops of the United States discussed the religious and moral dimensions of the arms race, and came to a consensus that it was time to make a pastoral Statement about nuclear war. Two months later President Archbishop John Roach appointed the calm and competent Archbishop Joseph L. Bernardin chairman of an *ad hoc* committee to write such a pastoral letter. Auxiliary Bishops George Fulcher of Columbus, Thomas Gumbleton of Detroit, and Daniel Reilly of Boston, and Bishop John O'Connor of the Military Ordinariate agreed to serve on the well-balanced committee. This committee was assisted by Edward Doherty and Father Bryan Hehir from the USCC. They, in turn, were assisted by Bruce Russett, Professor of Political Science at Yale University and editor of *Journal of Conflict Resolution*, one of the leading peace research journals in the United States. The committee was also privileged to have the assistance of Immaculate Heart of Mary Sister Juliana Casey and Holy Cross Father Richard Warner, from the Leadership Conference of Women Religious and the Conference of Major Superiors of Men, respectively.

In addition to this structured committee, a roster of consultants spanning the fields of biblical studies; moral theology; foreign and defense policy; and strategic experts, as well as interested voices in local movements on war and peace, were utilized in the preparation of the Pastoral. It would be difficult to find a document more widely researched and discussed more during its formation from the very beginning.

After months of taking testimony from these and a wide variety of other experts, the bishops produced the first draft entitled, "God's Hope in a Time of Fear." Released June 11, 1982, it was marked "confidential" but was leaked to the secular as well as religious press. So extensive

---

[6]The complete text of Cardinal Krol's address can be found in *Origins*, November 4, 1971.

was the commentary and criticism that the committee had to append to its second draft: "The volume of response required a postponement of the planned November 1982 vote on the document."

The second draft went further in challenging the political order and called the three hundred-year-old political principle of absolute national sovereignty obsolete. Specifically, the committee declared: "We do not perceive any situation in which the deliberate mitigation of nuclear war, on however restricted a scale, can be morally justified." A first strike in nuclear war is "one of the worst political and moral evils which could be perpetrated. . . . Under no circumstances may nuclear weapons or other instruments of mass slaughter be used for the purpose of destroying population centers or other predominantly civilian targets."

In his half-hour introduction of the second draft, Archbishop Bernardin told the more than two hundred seventy bishops that nuclear weapons and strategy today "pose a qualitatively new moral and political challenge." He said that the committee recognizes the delicacy of the deterrence issue but believes its conclusion is fundamentally correct. He admitted the committee was not satisfied with the formulation of the present theoretical argument, "and we are keenly aware of how important it is that the bishops present in this Pastoral a moral theory which is in conformity with the totality of the Church's moral teaching. We will continue to refine our arguments in the light of the comments at this meeting and the written commentaries we receive from theologians."

To prompt discussion of the second draft, Chairman Bernardin addressed four topics:

(1) the nature of the problem posed by modern warfare;
(2) the context in which the pastoral fits;
(3) the content of the second draft;
(4) the contribution it can make to both Church and society.

Under each point a key thought will be cited on the nature of the problem. Archbishop Bernardin thinks that the Church must be a participant in the process of protecting the world and its people from the spectre of nuclear destruction, because the nuclear issue is not simply political, but also a profoundly moral and religious question. In regard to the second point, the archbishop mentioned that the American bishops hope to make a contribution to this "new moment" with a teaching document striving to keep open the dialogue in the Church and society about steps needed to reverse the arms race and reduce the danger of war, a dialogue most important in such a superpower as the United States.

In reference to the content of the Pastoral, the chairman stated that the bishops' task is to call the Catholic community to address the issues of war and peace in all their complexity, to provide practical moral guidance on the most pressing questions, but not to solve all the theoretical issues which are at the root of these questions. He cited again, in particular, the delicacy of the deterrence issue and that most bishops, in their suggestions, want a stronger prophetic challenge raised against deterrence than the second draft presents.

On the final point, "the contribution," the archbishop declared that the letter, at once a pastoral guide, a policy statement, and a word of hope in the face of nuclear fear, will be a crucial element in fashioning a Church at the service of peace.

The bishops opened their discussion of nuclear weapons on November 15, 1982, and on November 16, 1982, there was a letter from the White House to Archbishop Joseph Bernardin, chairman of the drafting committee, written "on behalf of President Reagan, Secretary Schultz, Secretary Weinberger, Director Rostow and other administration officials," and signed by William P. Clark, National Security Director. One may agree or disagree with their policies, but one must admit they constitute, by position, an imposing array.

Unfortunately, Clark's letter, written in the name of the president of the United States, was first given—the night before delivery to Archbishop Bernardin—to *The New York Times*. Frankly, the bishops were not pleased by such a procedure. In his response to the letter the archbishop noted that his committee members were "somewhat surprised to read it first in *The New York Times*. We did, of course, confer earlier with officials designated by the administration in preparation for the first draft of our proposed pastoral letter and are not unfamiliar with the points contained in Mr. Clark's letter. We recognize the value of new and continuing opportunities for discussion. The letter . . . is another link in the dialogue invited by the bishops' *ad hoc* Committee on War and Peace. . . . Certainly Mr. Clark's letter will be given careful consideration as the Committee begins modifying the second draft in accordance with guidance provided by our brother bishops."

Then five prelates were invited to offer five-minute comments on the revised draft: the late Terence Cardinal Cooke of New York, John Cardinal Krol of Philadelphia, Archbishop Raymond G. Hunthausen of Seattle, Archbishop John Quinn of San Francisco, and Archbishop Philip Hannan of New Orleans.

In December 1981, Cardinal Cooke founded the Pope John Paul II Center of Prayer and Study for Peace which endeavors to promote a worldwide prayer-for-peace network and to develop sophisticated computer programs to help leaders solve conflicts without going to war. So it was not surprising that one of the most original of his comments on the second draft was the recommendation for the establishment of a permanent international committee, preferably within the United Nations, which would have no other agenda than "to mobilize our finest resources in the cause of lasting peace." His Eminence proposed that this committee possess a global authority and have the technology to monitor and verify multilateral disarmament and the power effectively to prevent the first effort toward war by any nation. ". . . I am convinced that it can be a part of a multinational effort on the part of men and women of good will to work together toward lasting peace and toward the elimination of the very capacity to wage war . . . war is no longer an acceptable alternative."

In September 1979, Cardinal Krol testified before the Senate Foreign Relations Committee that SALT II should be ratified as a "partial and imperfect step in the direction of halting the proliferation of nuclear weapons and as part of an ongoing process." A pioneer in seeking a solution to the nuclear arms problem, Cardinal Krol asked, "Is it not time that we concentrate our efforts on peace rather than war? Is it not time we take that first step toward peace: gradual, bilateral, negotiated disarmament?"

The overriding aim of U.S. policy, His Eminence thinks, ought to be the reduction and eventual elimination of nuclear weapons. This testimony was reported and lauded nationally and internationally so the bishops were well acquainted with his stand: "gradual, bilateral, negotiable disarmament."

Cardinal Krol remarked that the second draft was nearly fifty typewritten pages longer than the first and urged that when the document is finally approved a *precis* (summary) also be issued to highlight its key points. His Eminence, with all due respect for Pope John Paul II calling deterrence "morally acceptable," suggested that the term "tolerable" be used rather than "acceptable." "Toleration," explained Cardinal Krol, "is a passive living with something that is less than satisfactory, and doing so only for a greater good."

Most Reverend Raymond Hunthausen, archbishop of Seattle, told his fellow bishops that the second draft would more clearly proclaim the Good News of Jesus Christ if they were able to state the following: "That the strategy of deterrence is a root cause of the arms race." He continued, "We acknowledge in the draft that peace is a gift from God. How then can we accept a strategy which makes nuclear weapons 'the absolute basis' for our security?" He gives a stunning answer to his own question: "That's idolatry."

Archbishop John R. Quinn of San Francisco, a former president of the NCCB, stated that the second draft is a balanced document whose strengths far outweigh its weaknesses. He thought the letter recognized the utter importance of creating a psychology of peace based on the conviction that peace is really possible. He appreciated the "new moment" described in the draft "because concern for peace and opposition to nuclear arms is no longer sporadic and selective but widespread and sustained."

Not all the experts' judgments were encouraging. Archbishop Philip Hannan of New Orleans bluntly recommended: "Withdraw the Pastoral . . . it has so many defects," and issue in its place two "vastly superior statements" on war and peace, made by Pope John Paul II on the World Day of Peace and to the United Nations.

In the afternoon small group discussions of the second draft were held, and the results given as input to the committee resulted in this survey.

Initial Reactions to the
Second Draft of the Pastoral Letter on War and Peace
Monday, November 15, 1982

Regarding the Document's

A. *sociopolitical analysis* of the signs of our times:

I basically agree	234
I have major reservations	44
I am in basic disagreement	6

B. *citations from Scripture,* and *presentation of Catholic tradition and teaching* regarding war and peace

I basically agree	202
I have major reservations	64
I am in basic disagreement	4

C. *theological principles* and *moral conclusions* regarding nuclear war and war-preparedness

I basically agree	141
I have major reservations	114
I am in basic disagreement	2

D. *practical strategies for peace*

I basically agree	191
I have major reservations	68
I am in basic disagreement	3

E. *purpose:* tone, style, length, intended audience

I basically agree	110
I have major reservations	139
I am in basic disagreement	6

Given the above, *I find myself*

basically in agreement with the Document	195
with major reservations about the Document	71
in basic disagreement with the Document	12

The Washington Post noted that the federal government last summer tried, after publication of the first draft of the letter, to soften some parts of the document which will ultimately form the basis of the U.S. Church's teachings on the subject.

On November 12, 1982, Marjorie Hyer wrote in *The Washington Post* that the nation's Roman Catholic bishops will not be "intimidated" by a White House complaint that they have misread administration policy in drafting their proposed Pastoral Letter condemning nuclear war.

"Obviously there is a difference of opinion on a number of issues. We will see who is misreading whom," Archbishop Joseph L. Bernardin responded to the letter sent in President Reagan's behalf by White House National Security Adviser William P. Clark.

Most of the bishops willing to comment on the Clark letter indicated that they too were undeterred by it. Cardinal Krol of Philadelphia, certainly one of the most knowledgeable prelates in the nuclear question, was delighted the White House reacted and admonished: "They are saying what they think and we are going to say what we think."

The second largest Protestant denomination in the country, The Council of Bishops of the United Methodist Church, then meeting in Birmingham, Ala., sent "warmest greetings" and "strong support" for the Catholic hierarchy's efforts.[7] "We thank God for your courageous witness on behalf of peace with justice." The Methodist bishops had adopted a similar but shorter and less detailed pastoral letter earlier this year.

Between the second and third drafts of the Pastoral Letter, the drafting committee met in Rome on January 18-19, 1983, with Vatican officials and representatives from the bishops' conferences of Great Britain, France, Belgium, the Netherlands, Italy, and West Germany. At the end of the meeting Cardinal Bernardin stated that the document would remain the same, but in the final version more attention would be paid to the concept of "just war" and that a distinction would be made between the differing political systems of the United States and the Soviet Union. A Vatican communiqué reported, at the conclusion of the meeting, that the Catholic bishops in the United States and Europe "reaffirmed the responsibility and the moral authority of the Church concerning problems of war and peace."[8]

The one hundred fifty-page third draft was circulated early in April 1983. *The Catholic Standard and Times* thought that this draft of the bishops' letter did indeed seem to be an improvement over earlier versions in the quality of its analysis. The addition of a two thousand seven hundred-word summary preamble was an excellent concept, because it was believed that it could be the only part of the paper most people would read. The extended text would be of interest to scholars, students, and professionals.[9]

---

[7]*The Washington Post*, November 18, 1982.
[8]*St. Anthony Messenger*, April 1983.
[9]The *précis* had been suggested by Cardinal Krol, April 14, 1983.

Not all, however, were pleased with the third draft. On April 15, 1983, in the *National Catholic Reporter*, Arthur Jones sharply criticized that "if this is the best the bishops can do given the amount of time that's gone into it, given the expectations for some bold Christian step forward on the most shameful and fearsome threat to Creation we have yet devised, then, truly, Gold help us."

Archbishop Philip Hannan continued to oppose the Pastoral Letter and in a last minute appeal said: "I would ask a delay on passage of the letter until after the general elections in 1984, or barring that, at least until the disarmament negotiations, now under way, are complete."[10]

For George F. Kennan, the teaching in the Pastoral Letter insisted that military values, even when they legitimately exist, must never be treated as absolutes and hence carried to self-defeating extremes. They must rather be seen as relative and conditional: relative to the fundamental need of civilization for survival and conditional on the observance of those elementary moral scruples beyond which horror becomes unlimited and hope impossible. According to Kennan, "There is surely no lesson that this generation of Americans needs more to learn."[11]

Seventy scientists, who contributed to the development of the first atomic bomb in 1943, signed a statement regarding the third draft. Among the signatories were five Nobel Prize winners—Hans Bethe, Owen Chamberlain, Richard Feynman, Ed McMillan, and Emilio Segre. Others who signed included Robert Marshak, Victor Weisskopf, and Frank Oppenheimer.

The statement read: "Our one hope is that both the United States and the Soviet Union will recognize the futility of trying to outbuild the other in nuclear strength and also the cataclysmic danger inherent in the effort to do so. We urge upon the leaders of both countries that this recognition be made a cornerstone of national policy and that it lead to the beginning of a mutually agreed upon reduction of nuclear armaments and, for all nations, to the ultimate goal of the total elimination of such weapons."[12]

In a February 25 interview about the final draft, Cardinal Bernardin explained for *The Chicago Catholic* that the Church has a responsibility to teach moral principles, but it also has a responsibility to show how they apply to political and social issues. The more specifically churchmen do this, the more detail they go into on recommending technical solutions, the more vulnerable they become to criticism—sometimes legitimate criticisms—for far exceeding their competence. It is important, of course, that they make clear that these

---

[10]*The Chicago Catholic*, April 29, 1983.
[11]*The New York Times*, May 1, 1983.
[12]*The New York Times*, April 24, 1983.

are their perceptions of the facts, not necessarily church teaching which is binding on everyone.

On the other hand, the demand that churchmen "stay out of politics" is often a knee-jerk reaction from people who find it embarrassing to be told of the implications of morality for social and political life. Beneficiaries of exploitation and repression would rather not be reminded that the Gospel condemns this behavior.

How specific should the Church be on social issues? There is no definitive answer. "But in general I would say: more specific—with all the risks that that entails—than many people would like, but less specific than some would hope. The challenge always is to strike a proper balance. That can be difficult indeed," Cardinal Bernardin said.

On the final day of discussion about the Pastoral Letter, there was printed in the May 3, 1983, *Sun Times* a letter signed by McGeorge Bundy, national security adviser to President John F. Kennedy; Sidney Drell, professor of physics at Stanford University; Robert S. McNamara, former secretary of defense and treasury and former president of the World Bank; Stanley Resor, former secretary of war and former ambassador to the Mutual Balanced Force Reduction talks in Vienna, Austria; Herbert Scoville, Jr., former director for science and technology, Central Intelligence Agency; Paul Warnke, chief U.S. negotiator for President Jimmy Carter at the SALT II talks; Victor Weisskopf, a Massachusetts Institute of Technology (MIT) physicist who served on the World War II Manhattan Project that developed the atomic bomb; Jerome Weisner, an electrical engineer, who was president of MIT and science adviser to President Kennedy; and Herbert York, professor of physics and former chancellor of the University of California at San Diego. The letter stated: "We congratulate the Catholic bishops of the United States for the clarity and comprehensive scope of their analysis of the problems of nuclear weapons and modern war as set forth in their proposed pastoral letter. . . ."

Before the opening of the final debate on the third draft, *The Chicago Catholic* on April 29, 1983, declared that no collective Pastoral Letter ever considered by the U.S. hierarchy has received so much attention by the bishops themselves and by a worldwide public. Catholics and others in the White House, in Congress, and throughout the world, have watched the development of the letter. Comments have been solicited, but beyond that, there has been outspoken comment from almost everywhere.

Indicative of the national atmosphere in which the Pastoral Letter was discussed, is the following quotation from an April 3 *The New York Times* editorial just a month before the letter's approval: "Well, what's it to be, Mr. President—a holy war against Soviet evil or a sober struggle to find a way to share the planet with the devil?

"But the needed consensus can be regained—by a President who believes that Americans, no less than Russians, will respond to displays of patience, determination and national unity. Such a President could indeed make this a memorable Easter. . . ."

The second draft had called for a "halt" to the testing, production, and deployment of new strategic systems; the third draft called for a "curb" on testing, production, and deployment of new nuclear weapons systems. A number of stories said the committee had made the change because of pressure from the Reagan administration.[13]

The third draft attracted considerable attention and praise from the Reagan administration which had been sharply critical of the earlier drafts. Shortly after the release of this draft, a statement from the State Department said: "We are pleased that the letter endorsed many of the far-reaching objectives which the administration seeks, notably negotiated agreements for substantial 'equitable and verifiable reduction in nuclear arsenals.'"[14]

Representative Henry Hyde (R-Ill.) circulated a letter opposing a freeze resolution in the House by saying "the Roman Catholic bishops have refused to endorse the nuclear arms freeze."[15]

In an April 8, 1983, statement Archbishop John Roach, president of the NCCB, and Cardinal Bernardin repudiated the federal administration claims that the latest draft of the bishops' war and peace Pastoral "endorses many of President Reagan's arms policies." "We would not accept any suggestion that there are relatively few and insignificant differences between U.S. policies and the policies advocated" in the U.S. bishops' proposed Pastoral Letter on war and peace.[16]

"The third draft is explicitly critical . . . of many central elements of U.S. policy," they added. Although they did not spell out which "administration spokesmen" they had in mind, the prelates' statement came in the wake of a number of efforts to make political use of the newly released third draft.[17]

They acknowledged that the administration had provided "helpful information" to the drafting committee, but commented: "In the final analysis, however, the third draft is far more the product of reflection and dialogue within the Catholic community than between the drafting committee and administration."

On the question of a nuclear freeze, neither the second nor the third drafts of the proposed Pastoral Letter advocated a freeze as such, they said. But, the archbishop added, "in both drafts the clear intent is a call to cap the arms race and reduce the weapons on both sides

---

[13]*Our Sunday Visitor*, May 1, 1983.
[14]*The New York Times*, April 10, 1983.
[15]*Our Sunday Visitor*, May 1, 1983.
[16]*Origins*, April 21, 1983, p. 738.
[17]*The Catholic Standard and Times*, April 14, 1983.

as rapidly as possible, with particular emphasis on potentially de-stabilizing systems."

In concluding, the prelates declared that they would welcome reactions to the third draft of the Pastoral Letter from administration spokesmen and all other interested parties. This exchange of views has been integral to the evolution of the document to date. "Come May 2-3, however, the decision will rest with the bishops and only them."[18]

In introducing the third draft of the peace Pastoral, Cardinal Bernardin called on everyone to accept moral responsibility for the issues of the nuclear age and assured all that the bishops wrote this letter "as American citizens" to contribute to the policy that all nations "must choose if humanity is to survive." His Eminence outlined the major changes in the third draft and comapred it with the second. An important difference was the emphasis placed on the distinction between the statement of moral principles and the application of such principles to concrete cases. The source of this change was the meeting of the drafting committee with the Holy See and representatives of several European episcopal conferences. Cardinal Bernardin explained that the section on the morality of warfare was extensively rewritten preserving the right of the state to use force as the last resort in fulfilling its duty to defend society. The separate section on "Nonviolence" allowed for an individual to opt for nonresistance. A particular concern of the third draft, according to the cardinal, had been to show the relationship of the "Just War" teaching and the "Nonviolent" position.

The treatment of "Deterrence" was recast, by stating its moral arguments in new terms. The positive task of building peace was expanded with much greater detail. Recognizing that all good is not on one side and all evil on the other, the new draft's section on U.S.-Soviet relations was expanded. It identified those aspects of Soviet behavior that have created fear and mistrust, and it acknowledged the aspects of U.S. policy that require criticism by ourselves and others. This same discussion declared that both the United States and the Soviet Union have an overriding global responsibility in preventing the use of nuclear weapons. Again, the principal source of this section's modifications was the committee's meeting in Rome, and the concerns expressed there by the European bishops.

Two changes in the third draft came from meetings with U.S. government specialists. They dealt with the U.S. targeting policy and the specific identification, by name, of the U.S. arms control proposals at the Geneva negotiations.

His Eminence repeated: "We speak not as technicians or politi-cians but as teachers of moral and religious principles. . . . As Catholic

---

[18]*Origins*, April 21, 1983, p. 738.

bishops in the United States, we face the momentous pastoral responsibility of relating moral and religious teaching to the issues facing one of the two major nuclear powers." He explained that this Pastoral Letter is designed to address both public policy and personal moral questions on war and peace.

Real debate on the over seven hundred amendments and four hundred pages of comment began May 2, 1983, at the general meeting of the bishops in Chicago. Only a few outstanding amendments can be discussed here.

One of the most crucial points debated in the meeting was the passage that recommends "support for immediate, bilateral, verifiable agreements to curb testing, production and deployment of new nuclear weapons systems." Bishop James W. Malone of Youngstown and ten other bishops proposed to change "curb" to "halt" in order to support a nuclear freeze and set the tone for the rest of the Pastoral.

Cardinal Bernardin said his committee supported the amendment, with eleven bishops speaking in favor, and two against. One who spoke against the amendment was Bishop John J. O'Connor of the drafting committee. He cited that several experts have advised that the use of "halt" could bring the opposite effect of what the bishops seek. He also mentioned that it could be seen to support a specific political party.

John Cardinal Krol of Philadelphia, highly respected by his fellow bishops in the area of the nuclear weapons problem, reminded the assembly that the goal of the documentation and speeches was "not simply the reduction but elimination" of nuclear weapons. He said "halt" is more consistent with the entire presentation. Cardinal Krol also proposed a footnote to the use of "halt" to say that having nuclear weapons would be morally acceptable as a deterrent.

Archbishop Edmund C. Szoka of Detroit proposed adoption of neither "curb" nor "halt," but use of the word "cease." He said that use of "halt" or "curb" could be seen as a victory for one side or the other on the question of disarmament. But use of "cease" would make the document "say what we want it to say,"—eliminate nuclear weapons.

Auxiliary Bishop Thomas J. Gumbleton of Detroit, a member of the drafting committee, strongly supported the use of "halt."

Refusing to substitute "cease" for "halt," the bishops approved "to *halt* the testing, production and deployment of new nuclear weapons systems." They also approved appending the suggested deterrence footnote to use the word "halt," as suggested by Cardinal Krol.

An important amendment dealing with initiating nuclear war was proposed by Archbishop John Quinn of San Francisco and approved over the committee's disapproval. It substituted "morally unjustifiable to initiate nuclear war in any form" for "an unacceptable moral risk to initiate nuclear way in any form." Moving a step further, the

Conference approved Amendment 16 by Archbishop Quinn that changed: "Precisely because of this skepticism, we judge that resort to nuclear weapons to counter a conventional attack is morally unjustifiable."

Another one of Archbishop Quinn's many amendments advanced still further the Pastoral's stand against nuclear weapons. It perfected a passage that stated: "Consequently we seek to strengthen the barrier against easy or quick resort to nuclear weapons in any form," by changing it to, "Consequently we seek to reinforce the barrier against any use of nuclear weapons." Archbishop Quinn said the change would be straightforward, and chairman Cardinal Bernardin noted the change would be in accordance with the basic thrust of the letter. This amendment, number 21, passed easily.

Many amendments were withdrawn for various reasons and those that overlapped were dropped so that after two days of arduous, dedicated work with masterful parliamentary procedure, all the remaining amendments were considered by the body of the bishops. In a vote of 238 to 9 the bishops approved *The Challenge of Peace: God's Promise and Our Response.*

The official twenty-seven hundred word summary of the letter, written by the same committee that drafted the forty-four thousand word Pastoral, was approved by the nation's bishops in a mail ballot and released on June 9, 1983. It is incorporated at the beginning of the Pastoral.

The following summaries of these prelates' opinions offer a sample of the NCCB's thought regarding the achieved Pastoral Letter. Archbishop James A. Hickey of the nation's capital explained:

> We want to be a peacemaking Church. But a peacemaking Church is also a community that raises fundamental moral questions about policies. We should be building a constituency of conscience. We should be helping to shape public opinion in a way that supports genuine efforts to curb the arms race and obtain peace. This is why our letter is a tremendous achievement. The issues cannot be left to technicians or to a few leaders. This document places the moral and ethical dimensions of nuclear arms in the center of the national debate.

Archbishop John R. Quinn of San Francisco admitted:

> This is a difficult matter, in the sense that it has many scientific and political complexities dealing with the nation's freedom and integrity. But it is something about which people are informed and for which they are eager to find a moral focus. I have found mine. I now firmly believe that any use of nuclear weapons is morally wrong. I recognize some ambiguities in terms of possessing nuclear arms, because there is the element of deterrence. But it is morally wrong to let that continue.

Bishop Raymond W. Lessard of Savannah faced the vexing problem of military personnel:

> We have an enormous military presence in my diocese. A lot of our people are in the military or used to be. I've been surprised over the last two years by their response. They're principled people and they want to have guidance. I sent the second draft of the letter to our local Army general. He had no trouble with it. So I'm not as worried as I was before that there might be difficulties.

Bishop Edward D. Head of Buffalo looked to the future:

> Of course, we haven't ended anything with this letter; we've only reached a certain point in the journey. I'd like to see us press for some organization or group at the United Nations to zero in on nuclear arms. I'd like to see us continue our open discussions, exchanging views especially with bishops' conferences in Europe. We may find that the letter is not acceptable to our brother bishops, but it will have given us an agenda.

But to the majority of the European conferences of bishops the teaching in the letter was evidently most acceptable.

About the same time, the West German bishops issued their own Pastoral that substantially agreed with the American letter and it also supported deterrence to the degree it contributes to arms reductions. The Dutch bishops issued a brief Pastoral strikingly similar to *The Challenge of Peace*. On July 28, 1983, the Irish Catholic Bishops Conference issued a joint statement saying that permanent reliance on a strategy of deterrence is insane. "The lack of proportion is most likely obtained when the use of nuclear weapons is involved."[19] In their Statement the Belgian bishops defended the installation of forty-eight cruise missiles if disarmament talks fail.

On November 8, 1983, at Lourdes, the French Bishops Conference issued a five thousand word Statement, *Winning Peace*. In many ways it parallels the U.S. Statement. The French called the threat of nuclear arms "the basis of deterrence" and stressed that this is not the same as actual use. "That [teaching] is often forgotten in attributing to the threat the same moral qualifications applied to the use" of nuclear weapons, they explained. For them: "Unilateral disarmament can even provoke the aggressiveness of neighbors by feeding the temptation to seize too easy a victim. It still serves peace to discourage the aggressor by forcing him into the beginning of prudence through an appropriate fear." These French leaders also emphasized, "the constant pressure exercised on Western democracies to neutralize them and bring them into the sphere of influence of Marxist-Leninist ideology."

Canada's bishops also congratulated the U.S. bishops for the challenge of the document, calling it "thoughtful, courageous and prophetic. . . ."

---

[19] *St. Anthony's Messenger*, October, 1983.

Archbishop Henri Legare, president of the Canadian Conference of Catholic Bishops said Canada's bishops will encourage their people to read and study "this milestone in mankind's search for peace."[20]

In mid-May the governing board of the National Council of Churches voted 260 to 2 to commend the National Conference of Catholic Bishops for *The Challenge of Peace: God's Promise and Our Response*. The Council, which has member churches totaling 40 million Protestant and Orthodox Christians, expressed "the deepest gratitude to God for the work of the Spirit moving among our Roman Catholic sisters and brothers."[21]

America's May 21 editorial explained that the bishops are under no illusions that their Pastoral Letter represents some utopian solution to the dilemmas of the nuclear age. It stated: "Instead they offer their Pastoral as one contribution, the carefully wrought reflections of a group of religious leaders, to a debate and a process that concerns all the citizens of the planet and that should enlist the intelligence and commitment of all."

The same editorial noted that while the strategy of deterrence has achieved a kind of peace over the last four decades, the cost to the world's economies has been prohibitive and, as the stockpiles increase and possession of nuclear weapons proliferates, the probability of the actual use of nuclear weapons mounts. In the view of the same editor, the third section on the promotion of peace in the interdependent world may prove more helpful than the specific judgments the bishops make on the various uses of nuclear weapons. "Perhaps more important is the strategy [prayer and fasting] for making peace with which they conclude their Pastoral and propose to their fellow Catholics and all men and women of good will 'the challenge of peace.'"

The London *Tablet* reported that it is certainly a great day for the bishops since, for very many American Catholics, they are heroes. "They have confronted the biggest issue of the times, withstood political and ideological pressures of the most intense kind and forthrightly specified how Catholics should approach the issues of nuclear war and work for a peace which is more than a balance of terror."[22]

Time concluded in its lead article that "The U.S. bishops' pastoral letter explicitly states that only the church's broad moral principles are absolute (for example, the immorality of indiscriminate killing of innocent civilians); it also concedes that Catholics of good will might differ over how these principles apply to the intricacies of nuclear weaponry.[23] But the bishops also contend that their 'moral judgment in specific cases, while not binding on conscience, is to be given

[20]*Catholic Trends*, July 30, 1983.
[21]*America*, May 28, 1983.
[22]May 28, 1983.
[23]May 16, 1983, p. 65.

serious attention and consideration' by America's 50 million Catholics as they develop their own thinking on the morality of nuclear arms."

In a news conference the final day of the meeting, Archbishop Thomas Kelly, O.P., of Louisville, Ky., said: "We do not know of any case where nuclear weapons may be used. There may be but we do not know of any."[24]

The National Catholic Reporter, never exactly a champion of Cardinal Krol, archbishop of Philadelphia, did publish: "Perhaps the most pleasant exception in this peace pastoral is Cardinal John Krol, a Pius XII bishop . . . . Catholics generally might do well to ponder the extent to which Krol's strength on the nuclear issue, and his stature among his own generation of bishops helps provide an equaminity of purpose that finally carried the day."[25]

The Presbyterian General Assembly voted to send a copy of the Pastoral to each of their thirteen thousand congregations. The Methodist bishops declared that they stand in solidarity with the Roman Catholic bishops. James Lehnard, associate executive secretary of the American Friends Service Committee [Quakers], solidly endorsed and supported the stand of the bishops against nuclear weapons.

At the same time, Cal Thomas, vice-president for Communications for the Moral Majority, thought the Statement naive and that it would be used merely as a Soviet propaganda tool. The Catholic War Veterans, at their national convention, voted to accept the Pastoral but backed development of the neutron bomb and did not support a nuclear freeze.

Even the controversial *National Catholic Reporter* on May 13 had to admit: "U.S. Catholics have a peace pastoral. What does this mean? First, that they have reason to be proud of their bishops. Next, that the world's poor have reason to hope."

In its October 1983 issue, *St. Anthony's Messenger* reported that obviously the Pastoral has fueled a great debate that will have important consequences for you, me, and everyone in the world. It is imperative that "all of us who want peace understand what is involved in and what will flow from the decisions to be made about weapons and armaments, and that we enter into the debate and decision-making process."

Lately there have been several stories of tension between the Vatican and the U.S. hierarchy. At the November 1983 NCCB meeting, Archbishop Roach admitted that the bishops' relationship with the Holy See is "marked by occasional misunderstandings, misperceptions and tensions."[26]

---

[24] *The New York Times*, May 4, 1983.
[25] May 13, 1983.
[26] *America*, December 17, 1983.

It has been mentioned that the peace Pastoral may have contributed to the tension. There is an indication that the American letter does have acceptance in Rome. The Vatican's Secretary of State, Cardinal Agostino Casaroli, analyzed issues of war and peace in the nuclear age in a November 18, 1983, address at the University of San Francisco, and there was no substantive difference between his analysis and the teachings of *The Challenge of Peace*. The Vatican spokesman taught that nuclear deterrence cannot be considered an end in itself. It has a "provisional nature" and while serving "to avoid the worst, it also has to serve to give time for seeking agreement and understanding."[27]

Church leaders of all denominations and scholars in diverse fields throughout the world think that the impact of this document has only begun to be felt. Furthermore, the present precarious world conditions are accelerating the need to study it. Materials have been prepared to facilitate its study at the parish and home levels. From the university down to the junior high school level, this Pastoral is being discussed in every type of academic surrounding, secular as well as religious.

---

[27] *Origins*, December 8, 1983, vol. 13: no. 26.

Political Responsibility: Choices for the 1980s

*A Statement Issued by the Administrative Board
of the United States Catholic Conference*

October 26, 1979

1. The hallmark of a democratic nation is its ability to engage the voice of its people in a broad range of public decisions. The United States, we fear, may be losing this capacity.

2. Consider the evidence. Fewer of our citizens are registering to vote. Fewer of the registrants are actually going to the polls. Our voting rolls have lost 15 million citizens in the last ten years. For our national elections, the rate of participation has been dropping for the last twenty years. Thus, the rate for the 1976 election was down sharply from the 1960 turnout and the rate for 1978 was the lowest for a national election since 1942. Our voter participation rates are now among the lowest in the world.[1]

3. Clearly, fewer and fewer Americans believe it is worth their time and concern to follow campaigns, form positions on the candidates and issues, and assert those positions at the polls. The result of this disaffection is also clear; an erosion in the very foundations of American political life. Thus, we take the eve of the national campaign year as the occasion to affirm again the importance of responsible political participation.

4. In 1976 we issued a statement calling for "a committed, informed citizenry to revitalize our political life."[2] We now reiterate that call with a greater sense of urgency and we ask all citizens to help restore our elections as the vital and popular forum they can and must be if our nation is to address democratically the crucial issues of the coming decade.

I. Public Responsibility and the Electoral Process

5. The reasons for the crisis in voter disaffection are many and complex, but we would like here to cite just three of its major causes.

---

[1] In the 1978 congressional elections, 37.9 percent of those eligible to vote actually did so. In contrast, forty-six percent voted in 1960. In the 1976 presidential elections, 54.4 percent of eligible voters turned out as compared to 63.8 percent in 1960.
[2] "Political Responsibility: Reflections on an Election Year," Feb. 12, 1976.

6.   First, large numbers of Americans evidently feel a sense of powerlessness. To a large degree, this feeling is justified by the evidence of our eyes and ears.

7.   Some leaders of the political estate have done much in recent years to weaken it and even to discredit it. We know too well their abuses of power, evasions of responsibility, and refusals to face up to tough choices. Many of our citizens have simply thrown up their hands and turned away from politics and government per se.

8.   We can share some of these feelings without also condoning the withdrawal they have caused. It makes little sense to let these difficulties force us to abandon citizenship, since this only invites the problems to deepen and threaten to become a permanent feature of our political life. If this happens, what hope can there be? The sensible response is to return to citizenship with the will and dedication to breathe new life into it.

9.   Second, as the patterns of our national life evolve, popular debate of issues becomes more complex and harder for the ordinary person to follow. Because of economic pressures and rapid social change, some of the traditional organizing principles of American politics no longer carry the force they once did—for example, the long-standing loyalties and identities of social institutions, geographic regions, and political parties. At the same time, we have yet to see a fresh and vital set of organizing principles take shape either to review or supplant the older ones.

10.   The avenues of contemporary communications hold the promise of shaping new forums for popular debate, but we have yet to see compelling evidence that the mass media will fulfill this promise. They seem as likely to abet disaffection as to help to remedy it.

11.   Finally, another cause of low participation is the persistent fact of widespread poverty in America. The poorer a person is, the less likely the person is to vote. Voting relies on a degree of hope, and there seems to be little reason for the people most in need to feel hopeful in this economy. Poverty shuts off the gates to the American mainstream and its institutions of influence and power. Thus, the poor have little concrete reason to see a stake in voting.

12.   Consequently, unless we address America's social and economic inequities in the coming campaign and election, we will continue to weaken the franchise of millions of our people, run the risk of creating an insidious form of dual citizenship, and jeopardize the great democratic experiment we proudly call America.

13.   We fear that some of the current popular reactions against the government and government programs reveal an excessive individualism and a decline in our commitment to the common good. It is important for all Americans to realize the extent to which we are all interdependent members of a national community. Increasingly, our problems are social in nature, demanding solutions that are likewise social. To fashion these solutions in a just and humane way requires the active and creative participation of all. It requires a renewed faith in the ability of the human community to cooperate in governmental structures that work for the common good. It requires, above all, a willingness to attack the root causes of the powerlessness and alienation that threaten our democracy.

14. All Christians have a call to citizenship and political life. In the words of Pope Paul VI: "The Christian has the duty to take part in the organization and life of political society."[3] Accordingly, we urge all citizens to use their franchise by registering to vote and going to the polls. Demand information from the campaigns themselves and from the media coverage of those campaigns. Make candidates declare their values, so you can compare those values with your own. Take stands on the candidates and the issues.

15. If the campaign year is to engage the values of the American people, the campaigners and voters alike must share the responsibility for making it happen. Become involved in the campaign or party of your choice. Finally, use the debates of the coming year to better understand the issues and inform your conscience.

II. The Church and the Political Order

16. It is appropriate in this context to offer our own reflections on the role of the Church in the political order. Christians believe that Jesus' commandment to love one's neighbor should extend beyond individual relationships to infuse and transform all human relations from the family to the entire human community. Jesus came to "bring good news to the poor, to proclaim liberty to captives, new sight to the blind and to set the downtrodden free" (Lk 4:18). He called us to feed the hungry, clothe the naked, care for the sick and afflicted, and to comfort the victims of injustice (Mt 25). His example and words require individual acts of charity and concern from each of us. Yet they also require understanding and action upon the broader dimensions of poverty, hunger, and injustice which necessarily involve the institutions and structures of economy, society, and politics.

17. The Church, the People of God, is itself an expression of this love and is required by the Gospel and its long tradition to promote and defend human rights and human dignity.[4] In his recent encyclical, *Redemptor Hominis*, Pope John Paul II declares that the Church "must be aware of the threats to [humanity] and of all that seems to oppose the endeavor 'to make human life ever more human' and make every

---

[3]Pope Paul VI, "A Call To Action," 1971, no. 24.
[4]1974 Synod of Bishops, "Human Rights and Reconciliation."

element of life correspond to humanity's true dignity—in a word, [the Church] must be aware of all that is opposed to that process."[5]

18. This view of the Church's ministry and mission requires it to relate positively to the political order, since social injustice and the denial of human rights can often be remedied only through governmental action. In today's world, concern for social justice and human development necessarily requires persons and organizations to participate in the political process in accordance with their own responsibilities and roles.

19. The Church's responsibility in the area of human rights includes two complementary pastoral actions: the affirmation and promotion of human rights, and the denunciation and condemnation of violations of these rights. In addition, it is the Church's role to call attention to the moral and religious dimensions of secular issues, to keep alive the values of the Gospel as a norm for social and political life, and to point out the demands of the Christian faith for a just transformation of society. Such a ministry on the part of every Christian and the Church inevitably involves political consequences and touches upon public affairs.

20. Christian social teaching demands that citizens and public officials alike give serious consideration in all matters to the common good, to the welfare of society as a whole, which must be protected and promoted if individual rights are to be encouraged and upheld.

21. In order to be credible and faithful to the Gospel and to our tradition, the Church's concern for human rights and social justice should be comprehensive and consistent. It must be formulated with competence and an awareness of the complexity of issues. It should also be developed in dialogue with other concerned persons and respectful of the rights of all.[6]

22. The Church's role in the political order includes the following:

(a) Education regarding the teachings of the Church and the responsibilities of the faithful;

(b) Analysis of issues for their social and moral dimensions;

(c) Measuring public policy against Gospel values;

(d) Participating with other concerned parties in debate over public policy; and

(e) Speaking out with courage, skill, and concern on public issues involving human rights, social justice, and the life of the Church in society.

23. Unfortunately, our efforts in this area are sometimes misunderstood. The Church's participation in public affairs is not a threat to the political process or to genuine pluralism, but an affirmation of

---

[5]Pope John Paul II, *Redemptor Hominis*, 1979, no. 14.
[6]"A Call to Action," op. cit., nos. 4, 50; Vatican Council II, "The Church in the Modern World," 1965, no. 43.

their importance. The Church recognizes the legitimate autonomy of government and the right of all, including the Church itself, to be heard in the formulation of public policy.

24. As Vatican II declared:

> By preaching the truth of the Gospel and shedding light on all areas of human activity through her teaching and the example of the faithful, she [the Church] shows respect for the political freedom and responsibility of citizens and fosters these values. She also has the right to pass moral judgments, even on matters touching the political order, whenever basic personal rights or the salvation of souls make such judgments necessary.[7]

25. A proper understanding of the role of the Church will not confuse its mission with that of government, but rather see its ministry as advocating the critical values of human rights and social justice.

26. It is the role of Christian communities to analyze the situation in their own country, to reflect upon the meaning of the Gospel, and to draw norms of judgment and plans of action from the teaching of the Church and their own experience.[8]

27. In carrying out this pastoral activity in the social arena, we are confronted with complexity. As the 1971 Synod of Bishops pointed out: "It does not belong to the Church, insofar as she is a religious and hierarchical community, to offer concrete solutions in the social, economic and political spheres for justice in the world."[9] At the same time, it is essential to recall the words of Pope John XXIII: "It must not be forgotten that the Church has the right and duty not only to safeguard the principles of ethics and religion, but also to intervene authoritatively with her children in the temporal sphere when there is a question of judging the application of these principles to concrete cases."[10]

28. The application of Gospel values to real situations is an essential work of the Christian community. Christians believe the Gospel is the measure of human realities. However, specific political proposals do not in themselves constitute the Gospel. Christians and Christian organizations must certainly participate in public debate over alternative policies and legislative proposals, yet it is critical that the nature of their participation not be misunderstood.

29. We specifically do not seek the information of a religious voting bloc; nor do we wish to instruct persons on how they should vote by endorsing candidates. We urge citizens to avoid choosing candidates simply on the personal basis of self-interest. Rather, we hope that voters will examine the positions of candidates on the full range

---

[7] "The Church in the Modern World," op. cit., no. 76.
[8] "A Call to Action," op. cit.
[9] 1971 Synod of Bishops, "Justice in the World."
[10] Pope John XXIII, *Pacem in Terris*, 1963, no. 160.

of issues as well as the person's integrity, philosophy, and performance.

30. We seek to promote a greater understanding of the important link between faith and politics and to express our belief that our nation is enriched when its citizens and social groups approach public affairs from positions grounded in moral conviction and religious belief. Our view is expressed very well by Pope Paul VI when he said:

> While recognizing the autonomy of the reality of politics, Christians who are invited to take up political activity should try to make their choices consistent with the Gospel and, in the framework of a legitimate plurality, to give both personal and collective witness to the seriousness of their faith by effective and disinterested service of [humanity]."[11]

31. The Church's responsibility in this area falls on all its members. As citizens we are all called to become informed, active, and responsible participants in the political process. The hierarchy has a responsibility as teachers and pastors to educate the faithful, support efforts to gain greater peace and justice, and provide guidance and even leadership on occasion where human rights are in jeopardy. The laity has major responsibility for the renewal of the temporal order. Drawing on their own experience and exercising their distinctive roles within the Christian community, bishops, clergy, religious, and laity should join together in common witness and effective action to bring about Pope John's vision of a well-ordered society based on truth, justice, charity, and freedom.[12]

32. As religious leaders and pastors, our intention is to reflect our concern that politics receive its rightful importance and attention and that it become an effective forum for the achievement of the common good. For, in the words of John Paul II, "[humanity's] solution in the modern world seems indeed to be far removed from the objective demands of the moral order, from the requirements of justice, and even more of social love. . . . We have before us here great drama that can leave nobody indifferent."[13]

III. Issues

33. Without reference to political candidates, parties, or platforms, we wish to offer a listing of some issues which we believe are important in the national debate during 1980. These brief summaries are not intended to indicate in any depth the details of our positions in

---

[11]"A Call to Action," op. cit., no. 46.
[12]*Pacem in Terris*, no. 35.
[13]*Redemptor Hominis*, 16.

these matters. We refer the reader to fuller discussions of our point of view in the documents listed in the summary which appears below. We wish to point out that these issues are not the concerns of Catholics alone; in every case we have joined with others to advocate these positions. They represent a broad range of topics on which the bishops of the United States have already expressed themselves and are recalled here in alphabetical order to emphasize their relevance in a period of national debate and decision.

A. Abortion

34. The right to life is a basic human right which should have the protection of law. Abortion is the deliberate destruction of an unborn human being and therefore violates this right. We reject the 1973 Supreme Court decisions on abortion which refuse appropriate legal protection to the unborn child. We support the passage of a constitutional amendment to restore the basic unconstitutional protection of the right to life for the unborn child (*Documentation on the Right to Life and Abortion*, 1974, 1976; *Pastoral Plan for Pro-Life Activities*, 1975).

B. Arms Control and Disarmament

35. The dangers of the arms race are a challenge and a concern to the whole human family. The primary moral imperative is that the arms race be stopped and the reduction of armaments achieved. With respect to nuclear weapons, at least those with a massive destructive capability, the first imperative is to prevent their use. As possessors of a vast nuclear arsenal, we must also be aware that not only is it wrong to attack civilian populations but it is also wrong to threaten to attack them as part of a strategy of deterrence. We urge the continued development and implementation of policies which seek to bring these weapons more securely under control, progressively reduce their presence in the world, and ultimately remove them entirely (*To Live in Christ Jesus*, 1976; *The Gospel of Peace and the Danger of War*, 1978).

C. Capital Punishment

36. In view of our commitment to the value and dignity of human life, we oppose capital punishment. We believe that a return to the use of the death penalty can only lead to further erosion of respect for life in our society. We do not question society's right to punish the offender, but we believe that there are better approaches to protecting our people from violent crimes than resorting to executions. In its application, the death penalty has been discriminatory toward the poor, the indigent, and racial minorities. Our society should reject the death penalty and seek methods of dealing with violent crime which are more consistent with the gospel vision of respect for life and Christ's message of healing love (*Community and Crime*, 1978).

D. The Economy

37. Our national economic life must reflect broad values of social justice and human rights. Above all, the economy must serve the human needs of our people. It is important to call attention to the fact that millions of Americans are still poor, jobless, hungry, and inadequately housed and that vast disparities of income and wealth remain within our nation. These conditions are intolerable and must be persistently challenged so that the economy will reflect a fundamental respect for the human dignity and basic needs of all.

38. We recognize that the present political atmosphere is characterized by a heavy emphasis on budget austerity, particularly with regard to federal spending. Some believe that the reduction of government spending for social programs is the most effective way of combating inflation.

39. There is no doubt that inflation is a serious national problem. It weakens the economic stability of our nation and erodes the economic security of our citizens. Moreover, its impact is most severe on the poor and those who live on fixed incomes. However, economic policies which attempt to reduce inflation by cutting back on human needs programs or by increasing unemployment are simply unacceptable.

40. Current levels of unemployment and the tremendous human costs which they represent are unnecessary and should not be tolerated. We support an effective national commitment to genuine full employment as the foundation of a just and responsible economic policy. We believe that all Americans who are willing and able to work have a right to useful and productive employment at fair wages. We also call for a decent income policy for those who cannot work and adequate assistance to those in need (*The Economy: Human Dimensions*, 1975).

E. Education

41. All persons of whatever race, condition, or age, by virtue of their dignity as human beings, have an inalienable right to education. We advocate:

(1) Sufficient public and private funding to make an adequate education available for all citizens and residents of the United States of America and to provide assistance for education in our nation's program of foreign aid.

(2) Governmental and voluntary action to reduce inequalities of educational opportunity by improving the opportunities available to economically disadvantaged persons.

(3) Orderly compliance with legal requirements for racially integrated schools.

(4). Voluntary efforts to increase racial ethnic integration in public and nonpublic schools.

(5) Equitable tax support for the education of pupils in public and nonpublic schools to implement parental freedom in the education of their children (*Sharing the Light of Faith*, 1979; *To Teach as Jesus Did*, 1972).

F. Family Life

42. The test of how we value the family is whether we are willing to foster, in government and business, in urban planning and farm policy, in education and health care, in the arts and sciences, in our total social and cultural environment, moral values which nourish the primary relationships of husbands, wives, and children and make authentic family life possible.

43. Implicit government policy and explicit government planning and programs can contribute to an erosion of the health and vitality of the family. Comprehensive decisions of a national or regional scope must take into account their impact on family life. Families, especially those whose influence is lessened by poverty or social status, must be allowed their rightful input in those decisions which affect their daily lives (*A Vision and Strategy: The Plan of Pastoral Action for Family Ministry*, 1978).

G. Food and Agricultural Policy

44. The right to eat flows directly from the right to life. We support a national policy aimed at securing the right to eat to all the world's people.

45. Internationally, U.S. food aid should effectively combat global hunger and malnutrition, be aimed primarily at the poorest countries and neediest peoples without regard to political considerations. In order to help stabilize prices and assure adequate supplies, the United States should join in a world grain reserve fair to both producers and consumers. Economic assistance should emphasize helping other nations move toward food self-sufficiency.

46. Domestically, nutrition programs should help meet the needs of hungry and malnourished Americans, especially children, the poor, the unemployed, and the elderly. It is essential that the food-stamp program be funded at adequate levels (*Food Policy and the Church: Specific Proposals*, 1975).

47. Through its income-support programs, its credit and research programs, its tax policies, its strategies for rural development, and its foreign aid, the United States should support the maintenance of an agricultural system based on small and moderate-sized family farms both at home and abroad (*The Family Farm*, 1979).

H. Health Care

48. Adequate health care is an essential element in maintaining a decent standard of living. Yet the high costs of health care and uneven access to resources make it impossible for many in our society to meet their basic health needs. Therefore, we support the enactment of a national health insurance program. While endorsing no particular legislative proposal at this time, we have identified a set of principles which should govern the development of a national health plan. For example:

(1) Access to adequate health care is a basic human right.

(2) Coverage should be universal in scope.

(3) National standards for health services should be adopted.

(4) Benefits should be comprehensive, including preventive health care.

(5) The program should give consumers a reasonable choice of providers.

(6) Cost controls should be established and used to encourage provider initiative and lower the cost of service (*USCC Statement on National Health Insurance*, 1974).

I. Housing

49. Decent housing is a basic human right. A greater commitment of will and resources is required to meet our national housing goal of a decent home for every American family. Housing policy must better meet the needs of low- and middle-income families, the elderly, rural areas, and minorities. It should also promote reinvestment in central cities and equal housing opportunity. Preservation of existing housing stock and a renewed concern for neighborhoods are required (*The Right to a Decent Home*, 1975).

J. Human Rights

50. Human dignity requires the defense and promotion of human rights in global and domestic affairs. With respect to international human rights, there is a pressing need for the United States to pursue a double task: 1) to strengthen and expand international mechanisms by which human rights can be protected and promoted; and 2) to take seriously the human rights dimensions of U.S. foreign policy.

Therefore, we support U.S. ratification of the international covenants on civil and political rights and on economic, social, and cultural rights. Further, we support a policy which gives greater weight to the protection of human rights in the conduct of U.S. affairs. The pervasive presence of American power creates a responsibility to use that power in the service of human rights. (*U.S. Foreign Policy: A Critique From Catholic Traditions*, 1976).

51. Domestically, human rights is also a subject of great importance. Discrimination based on sex, race, ethnicity, or age continues to exist in our nation. Such discrimination constitutes a grave injustice and an affront to human dignity. It must be aggressively resisted by every individual and rooted out of every social institution and structure (*To Do the Work of Justice*, 1978).

K. Mass Media

52. We are concerned that the communications media be truly responsive to the public interest and that future laws that govern the airwaves fully protect the common good. We strongly oppose government control over television-programming policy. At the same time, we deplore unilateral decision making by networks. We firmly believe that responsible licensing, use, and programming of the public airwaves cannot be accomplished simply by relying on the forces of the marketplace. We recommend exploring ways to reduce the commercial orientation of the broadcasting industry to better serve the public (*Statement on the Family Viewing Policy*, 1975).

L. Regional Conflict in the World

53. Three situations of regional conflict which are of significance for the whole international system, and where U.S. policy has a substantial, indeed a decisive, influence are South Africa, the Middle East, and Central America.

54. We address ourselves particularly to South Africa, not unmindful of the urgency of achieving majority rule in Rhodesia and the independence of Namibia. Nevertheless, South Africa is the object of substantial economic, political, and military interest on the part of the United States. Both U.S. foreign policy and its influence on corporate activity in South Africa should be directed toward change of the racial policies of that government. Even more effective leverage would be achieved if the United States, as the leader of the Western nations, could develop a coordinated policy with them regarding South Africa (*Southern Africa: Peace or War*, 1976).

55. In the Middle East, the quest for peace continues and the relevant parties bear distinct yet interdependent responsibilities. First, the international community, especially its principal diplomatic actors, inevitably influences the future of the Middle East. Second, the United Nations is a vital element in any Middle East negotiations, and its diplomatic and peacekeeping role will undoubtedly be crucial to a long-term resolution of the conflict. Third, the regional parties, whose conflicting claims of justice are the essence of the political and moral problem in the Middle East, are the key to peace.

56. Finally, the religious communities with roots in the Middle East must reflect the best of our traditions in supporting the movement for peace with justice for all the people of the region. We have a continuing concern for the protection of the basic rights, both civil and religious, of the Christian minorities in the Middle East, and we encourage the local churches there to continue their steadfast witness to the faith (*The Middle East: The Pursuit of Peace With Justice*, 1978).

57. In Central America, challenges to long-standing patterns of injustice and domination by large sectors of the population have been met by brutal repression. Fundamental social, economic, and political changes advocated by the Church at the Puebla conference call us in the United States to examine how our policies of military assistance and economic investment are related to existing patterns of injustice. U.S. policy should be directed toward fostering peaceful but fundamental change designed to benefit the poor of Central America.

58. This is not an exclusive listing of the issues that concern us. As Pope John Paul II has said, "The Church cannot remain insensible to whatever serves true human welfare any more than she can remain indifferent to whatever threatens it. . . ."[14] Thus we are also advocates for the civil and political rights of the elderly, the handicapped, immigrants, and aliens. We oppose excessive government interference in religious affairs as well as any unjust bias of government against religious institutions. We support measures to reform our criminal justice system. We are concerned about protection of the land and the environment as well as the monumental question of peace in the world.

IV. Conclusion

59. In summary, we believe that the Church has a proper role and responsibility in public affairs flowing from its gospel mandate and its respect for the dignity of the human person. We hope these reflections will contribute to a renewed political vitality in our land, both in terms of citizen participation in the electoral process and the integrity and accountability of those who seek and hold public office.

60. We pray that Christians will provide courageous leadership in promoting a spirit of responsible political involvement. May they follow

---

[14] *Ibid.*, 13.

the example of Jesus in giving special concern for the poor, and may all their actions be guided by a deep love of God and neighbor.

61. For in the world of American politics, as in all human communities, the words of Pope John Paul II apply: "What is in question here is the human person. We are not dealing with the 'abstract' [human person] but the real, 'concrete,' 'historical' person. . . . Every person coming into the world on account of the mystery of the redemption is entrusted to the solicitude of the Church. . . . The object of her care is [human persons] in their unique, unrepeatable human reality, which keeps intact the image and likeness of God himself. . . ."[15]

---

[15] *Ibid.*

Committee on Conciliation and Arbitration

*Procedures Adopted by the General Membership
of the National Conference of Catholic Bishops*

November 14, 1979

Article I. Functions of the Bishops' Committee on Conciliation and Arbitration

1. It shall be the primary function of the Bishops' Committee on Conciliation and Arbitration to facilitate the resolution of disputes which involve claims of injustice,[1] which have not been resolved on the local or regional level,[2] and which involve individual members, groups of members or structural affiliates of the National Conference of Catholic Bishops as one or more parties.

2. Such facilitation shall involve the Bishops' Committee on Conciliation and Arbitration, according to the norms set forth in the Articles which follow, in two forms of dispute-resolution: conciliation and arbitration.

---

[1] ". . . disputes involving claims of injustice. . . ." This expression is intended to limit the competence of the Committee to disputes in which a violation of a *right* is alleged, and not allow recourse to the Committee whenever a dispute arises over a matter of *prudential judgment* which is not alleged to involve injustice.

One of the serious confusions that has arisen in the area of ecclesiastical conciliation and arbitration has resulted from pulling these processes out of the "due process" context into which the NCCB plan had placed them, and viewing them instead as they are generally viewed in American civil society. "Due process" is concerned with the protection of *rights*, with the alleviation of injustice (be it deliberate or, as is more often the case, inadvertent). In American society, however, Conciliation and Arbitration are chiefly used not as instruments for the resolution of conflicts of *rights*, but for the resolution of conflicts of *interest* (chiefly in labor-management disputes). Such was not the intention of the NCCB in employing Conciliation and Arbitration (which have canonical roots in the Code of Canon Law) as instruments in a "due process" concern for *rights*. Hence, in the Church, Conciliation and Arbitration should not be available for the resolution of grievances that arise simply because the "aggrieved" party *disagrees prudentially* with the judgment, policy, or decision of an administrator or administrative body. Where administrative authority is involved, discretionary judgment has been vested in the administrator; there it must remain, and not be subject to overthrow by a panel of arbitrators. In such cases, Conciliation and Arbitration should be confined to grievances in which it is claimed that the administrative use of discretion had violated some *right* of the aggrieved party, has worked (or is threatening to work) some injustice.

[2] ". . . which have not been resolved on the local or regional level. . . ." This expression is intended to make clear the preference for local resolution of disputes whenever such resolution is possible. Inability to resolve a dispute on the local level could stem *either* from the unwillingness of one party to utilize such local structures as do exist, *or* from the failure of local efforts to resolve the dispute.

3. It shall be the secondary function of the Bishops' Committee on Conciliation and Arbitration to be available as a resource to assist, upon request, with the development and improvement of local-level structures for the resolution of disputes.

Article II. Relationship to NCCB and to Apostolic Signatura

In facilitating the resolution of disputes in accord with the norms which follow, the Bishops' Committee on Conciliation and Arbitration acts for the National Conference of Catholic Bishops. Recourse from decisions of the Bishops' Committee may be taken, in accord with the norms which follow, solely to the Apostolic Signatura.

Article III. Competence of the Committee

Any person or group of persons in conflict with a member, group of members, or structural affiliate of the National Conference of Catholic Bishops may seek the assistance of the Bishops' Committee on Conciliation and Arbitration provided the following conditions are fulfilled:

(1) The dispute involves injustice, that is, the claim that some action or inaction has violated a right recognized as such in the law of the Church or in the documents of the magisterium;[3]

(2) Good faith efforts at local resolution of the dispute have been unsuccessful.

---

[3] ". . . recognized as such in the law of the Church or in the documents of the magisterium. . . ." This phrase is intended to give some measure of specificity to the notion of "rights," a claimed violation of which is essential to the Committee's cognizance of the dispute.

While in civil society the sole source of recognized rights is the positive law of the society, such is not the case in the Church. In addition to universal and particular law, the Church also has the *magisterium* as a source of the Church's understanding of the rights of its people—human rights (flowing from the dignity of the human person and often said to be dictates of the "natural law"), ecclesial rights (flowing from baptism), and ecclesiastical rights (flowing from a particular office or responsibility in the Church). The documents of Vatican II, for example, are replete with teaching on all three categories of rights. The positive *law* of the Church does not presume to be a comprehensive compendium of all of the rights of the People of God. Nor does it propose to resolve by antecedent legislation all of the possible conflicts of rights that can arise in ecclesial society. Hence, restriction of the processes of Conciliation and Arbitration to disputes involving claimed *violations of law* would be far too limited a concern for justice within the Church.

Article IV. Access to the Committee

1. Access to the Committee shall be by written petition directed to the Chairman of the Bishops' Committee on Conciliation and Arbitration.

2. Such petition shall set forth the names of all parties to the dispute, the basic facts and issue or issues involved in the dispute according to the understanding of the petitioner, a precise statement of the right or rights alleged to have been violated or threatened with violation, and the details of fulfillment of the conditions hereinabove set forth in Article III.

3. Such a petition directed to the Chairman of the Bishops' Committee on Conciliation and Arbitration shall be construed as a petition for the assistance of the Bishops' Committee in facilitating *conciliation* of the dispute in accord with the norms set forth in the Articles which follow. Only after every reasonable effort at resolution of the dispute through the Christian informality of conciliation has failed will the Bishops' Committee consent to facilitate *arbitration* of the dispute.

4. Upon receiving such a petition, the Chairman of the Bishops' Committee shall contact, both by telephone and in writing[4] the party or parties named in the petition as respondent(s), apprise said party or parties of the contents of the petition, forward a copy or copies of the written petition, and request that a written response to the petition be sent promptly to the Chairman of the Bishops' Committee on Conciliation and Arbitration.

5. Upon receiving a written response to the petition, the Chairman of the Bishops' Committee, after consulting the other members of the Committee if in the judgment of the Chairman such consultation seems advisable, shall determine if the petition states a *prima facie* case for conciliation in accordance with these procedures. If such determination is negative, the petition shall be dismissed and notice of such dismissal, with the reasons for it, shall be sent to all parties. If such determination is affirmative, the Chairman shall inquire if the respondent(s) will accept conciliation, requesting a prompt reply to such inquiry.

---

[4] ". . . both by telephone and in writing. . . ." The suggested requirement of contact by telephone is in the interest of informality, personal concern, urgency, and certainty of direct communication with the named respondent(s). The requirement of written contact is in the interest of an accurate record of the actions of the Committee.

Article V. Selection of Conciliator

1.   Upon receiving an affirmative response to the inquiry concerning acceptance of conciliation, the Chairman shall inquire of the respondent(s) which of the members of the Committee would be acceptable as conciliator, requesting a prompt reply to such inquiry.

2.   Upon learning which of the members of the Committee would be acceptable to the respondent(s) as conciliator, the Chairman shall forward the acceptable names to the petitioner and ask for prompt indication of which of the submitted names would be acceptable to the petitioner.

3.   If no member of the Committee is mutually acceptable to petitioner and respondent(s), the Chairman of the Committee shall ask each party to submit promptly a list of five names of persons, preferably but not necessarily bishops, who would be acceptable as conciliators. The Chairman may also suggest names of possible conciliators.

4.   Upon receiving indications of mutually acceptable persons as conciliators, the Chairman of the Bishops' Committee shall select *one* of the mutually acceptable persons to act as conciliator in the dispute.

5.   If no mutually acceptable conciliator can be found after several attempts by the Chairman to elicit mutually acceptable names, the process of conciliation cannot proceed. The Chairman shall prepare a brief document indicating the inability of the Bishops' Committee to aid in the resolution of the dispute by conciliation due to the failure of the parties to agree upon a mutually acceptable conciliator.

6.   If the respondent(s) express unwillingness to enter into a process of conciliation, the Chairman shall make every reasonable effort to persuade said respondent(s) to cooperate with such a process. If all such efforts fail, the process of conciliation cannot proceed. The Chairman shall prepare a brief document indicating the inability of the Bishops' Committee to aid in the resolution of the dispute by conciliation due to the unwillingness of the respondent(s) to enter such a process.

Article VI. Process of Conciliation

1.   Within two weeks of the selection of the Conciliator by the Chairman of the Bishops' Committee, the Conciliator shall meet with each participant separately for oral discussion of the dispute.

2.   Within one week of the second of these conferences, the Conciliator shall meet with both participants together and endeavor to guide them to a peaceful resolution of their problem. The Conciliator shall schedule as many of these joint meetings as seem to be necessary in order to achieve conciliation.

3.   The Conciliator shall endeavor to assure that each participant answers the questions which the other participant believes are essential if he is to understand the actions of the other. The Conciliator should encourage a trust in candor on both sides.

4.   The first joint meeting of the participants and the Conciliator shall be restricted to these persons. Thereafter, in the discretion of the Conciliator, each participant may be accompanied by one or two advisers of the participant's own choosing. In the event one participant desires to have such advisers, and the Conciliator agrees, the Conciliator shall notify the other participant of the opportunity to be accompanied by an equal number of advisers. In the discretion of the Conciliator, and with the agreement of the participants, other members of the Bishops' Committee on Conciliation and Arbitration or other persons may join the meetings from time to time.

5.   If the problem is resolved by agreement, the Conciliator shall prepare a summary statement of the dispute and its resolution, and shall submit it for the approval and signature of the participants. If the problem is unresolved after the meetings arranged by the Conciliator have been held, and in any event if the problem is unresolved within six months, the Conciliator shall ask the participants if they are willing to continue discussion of the problem with the same or another conciliator. If the participants agree in their response, the Conciliator shall arrange the desired continuation. If one or more participants decline to engage in further discussion, the Conciliator shall file a report with the Bishops' Committee on Conciliation and Arbitration. This report shall contain the names of the participants, a summary of the dispute and the discussion taken to resolve it, and certification by the Conciliator that, despite the good faith of the participants, no resolution could be reached.

6.   The Conciliator shall have no power to force the participants to adopt a solution. He shall have power, however, to determine that any participant is not cooperating in good faith. Such facts as failure to attend three scheduled meetings, failure to respond to a substantial number of questions which the Conciliator believes appropriate, or failure to suggest any way of accommodating the interests of the other participant may be taken as evidence of a lack of good faith. In the event that for these or other good reasons the Conciliator believes that a participant is not cooperating in good faith, he shall notify the Chairman of the Bishops' Committee on Conciliation and Arbitration. The Chairman shall endeavor to persuade the participant to cooperate.

7.   Meetings shall be private and without publicity. All communications made in the process of conciliation shall be treated as confidential by all who share in them. If the dispute is resolved by agreement, and the parties agree to publicizing the solution, announcement of it shall be made, after consultation with the Ordinaries of the

participants. If there is no agreement on a solution or on publicizing it, no announcement shall be made.

8. Expenses incurred in the process of conciliation shall be borne equally by the parties, unless they agree otherwise, or unless the Conciliator determines otherwise according to the circumstances of a particular case.

Article VII. Initiation of Arbitration

1. When a dispute which is within the competence of the Bishops' Committee on Conciliation and Arbitration cannot be resolved by conciliation because of inability to select a mutually acceptable conciliator (cf. Article V, 5, *supra*), or because of unwillingness on the part of the respondent(s) to conciliate (cf. Article V, 6, *supra*), or because no resolution could be reached despite good faith participation in the conciliation process (cf. Article VI, 5, *supra*), any party to the dispute may petition the Bishops' Committee for assistance in facilitating arbitration of the dispute.

2. Such petition shall set forth the names of all parties to the dispute, the basic facts and issue or issues involved in the dispute according to the understanding of the petitioner, a precise statement of the right or rights alleged to have been violated or threatened with violation, and a statement regarding the failure of the conciliation process to have resolved the dispute.

3. Such petition shall be accompanied by the appropriate document from the Chairman of the Bishops' Committee (cf. Article V, 5 and 6, *supra*) or from the Conciliator (cf. Article VI, 5, *supra*) attesting to the failure of efforts to resolve the dispute by conciliation.

Article VIII. Exclusions from Arbitration

1. The following shall not be subject to settlement by arbitration:

(a) Criminal cases in the strict sense (not administrative sanctions and disciplinary actions). The process for arbitration shall extend to disputes about penalties imposed or declared administratively only if the arbitrators confine themselves to investigating whether or not the norms on the manner of proceeding have been justly and equitably observed, so that if they judge that the manner of proceeding is not to be approved, they shall refer the matter to the bishop;

(b) Non-criminal cases where there is a question of dissolving or annulling a marriage;

(c) Matters pertaining to benefices when there is litigation about the title itself to a benefice unless the legitimate authorities sanction arbitration;

(d) Spiritual matters whenever the award requires payment by means of temporal goods.

2.   Disputes involving temporal ecclesiastical goods or those things which, though annexed to the spiritual, can be dealt with apart from their spiritual aspect, may be settled through arbitration but the formalities of law for the alienation of ecclesiastical property must be observed if the matter is of sufficient importance.

Article IX. Selection of Arbitrators

1.   Upon receiving a petition in accord with the provisions of Article VII, *supra*, the Chairman of the Bishops' Committee on Conciliation and Arbitration shall contact, both by telephone and in writing, the party or parties named in the petition as respondent(s), apprise said party or parties of the contents of the petition, forward a copy or copies of the written petition, and inquire if said party or parties will accept arbitration, requesting a prompt reply to such inquiry.

2.   Upon receiving an affirmative response, the Chairman shall request the respondent(s) to submit a prompt written response to the petition. The Chairman also shall forward to the respondent(s) two lists of persons judged by the Bishops' Committee to be qualified as arbitrators, one list being composed of the names of bishops, and the other list being composed of priests, men and women religious and laity. The Chairman of the Bishops' Committee shall inquire of the respondent(s) which names on each list would be acceptable as arbitrators, requesting a prompt reply.

3.   Upon learning which persons from each list would be acceptable to the respondent(s) as arbitrators, the Chairman shall forward the acceptable names to the petitioner and ask for prompt indication of which of the submitted names from each list would be acceptable to the petitioner.

4.   If no mutually acceptable name is presented from the list of bishops, or two mutually acceptable names are not presented from the list of non-bishops, the Chairman of the Bishops' Committee shall ask each party promptly to submit a list of five names of bishops and five names of persons who are not bishops. The Chairman may also suggest names of possible arbitrators.

5.   Upon receiving indications of mutually acceptable persons as arbitrators, the Chairman of the Bishops' Committee shall select three of the mutually acceptable persons to act as arbitrators in the dispute. At least one of those selected must be a bishop.

6. If no mutually acceptable arbitrators can be found after several attempts by the Chairman of the Bishops' Committee to elicit mutually acceptable names, the process of arbitration cannot proceed. The Chairman shall prepare a brief document indicating the inability of the Bishops' Committee on Conciliation and Arbitration to aid in the resolution of the dispute by arbitration due to the failure of the parties to agree upon mutually acceptable arbitrators.

7. If the respondent(s) express unwillingness to enter into a process of arbitration, the Chairman shall make every reasonable effort to persuade said respondent(s) to cooperate with such a process. If all such efforts fail, the process of arbitration cannot proceed. The Chairman shall prepare a brief document indicating the inability of the Bishops' Committee on Conciliation and Arbitration to aid in the resolution of the dispute by arbitration due to the unwillingness of the respondent(s) to enter into such a process.

Article X. Arbitration Agreement

Within five days of receiving the names of three arbitrators chosen by the Chairman of the Bishops' Committee in accord with Article IX, 5, *supra*, the parties to the dispute shall submit to the Chairman in writing their acceptance of the named arbitrators, their agreement to submit to arbitration under the norms set forth in Article XI, *infra*, and their commitment to accept the decision of the arbitrators as binding.

Article XI. The Arbitration Process

Time and Place of Hearing

1. The Arbitrators shall appoint a time and place for hearings and notify the parties not less than five days before each hearing.

Representation by Counsel

2. Parties to the dispute may be represented at hearings by counsel or other authorized representative.

Attendance at Hearings

3. It shall be in the discretion of the Arbitrators to determine the propriety of the attendance of persons, other than parties, having a direct interest in the arbitration or of any other persons.

Adjournment

4. For good cause the Arbitrators shall adjourn the hearing upon request of a party, upon their own initiative, or when all the parties agree thereto.

Arbitration in the Absence of a Party

5. Arbitration may proceed in the absence of any party who, having received due notice, fails to be present without reason judged by the Arbitrators to be sufficient.

Evidence

6. The Arbitrators shall hear and resolve the controversy upon the evidence produced. Parties may offer such evidence as they desire and shall produce such additional evidence as the Arbitrators may deem necessary to an understanding and determination of the dispute. All testimony shall be given under oath. The Arbitrators shall judge the relevancy and materiality of the evidence offered, and conformity to legal rules of evidence shall not be necessary. All evidence shall be taken in the presence of all the Arbitrators and all of the parties except where any of the parties is absent in default or has waived his right to be present. The Arbitrators may require the parties to submit books, records, documents, and other evidence.

Evidence by Affidavit

7. The Arbitrators shall have the power to administer oaths and to take evidence from witnesses by deposition whenever witnesses cannot attend the hearing.

Order of Proceedings

8. A hearing shall be opened by the recording of the place, time and date of hearing, the presence of the Arbitrators and parties, the presence of counsel, if any, and of any persons admitted pursuant to Section 3 of this Article, and the receipt by the Arbitrators of initial statements setting forth the nature of the dispute and the remedies sought. The Arbitrators may, in their discretion, vary the normal procedure under which the petitioner first presents evidence, but in any case shall afford full and equal opportunity to all parties for presentation of relevant proofs. The names and addresses of all witnesses, and exhibits offered in evidence, shall be made a part of the record.

Majority Decision

9. In the course of the hearing, all decisions of the Arbitrators shall be by a majority vote. The award shall also be made by majority vote unless the concurrence of all is expressly required by the terms of a particular arbitration agreement.

Closing of Hearings

10. The Arbitrators shall inquire of all parties whether they have any further proofs to offer or witnesses to be heard. Upon receiving negative replies, the hearings shall be declared closed. The hearings may be reopened by the Arbitrators on their own motion, or on the motion of either party, for good cause shown, at any time before the award is made.

Time of Award

11. The award shall be rendered promptly by the Arbitrators and, unless otherwise agreed by the parties, not later than ten days from the date of closing the hearings, or if oral hearings have been waived, from the date of transmitting the final statements and proofs to the Arbitrators.

Form of Award

12. The award shall be in writing and shall be signed by the Arbitrators.

Record of Proceedings

13. Upon agreement of all parties, the entire proceedings shall be tape recorded; and, at the request of either party, or at the discretion of the arbitrators, a written transcript shall be prepared of all or of portions of the recorded proceedings. The total cost of the tape recording shall be shared equally among parties, and the cost of providing written transcripts shall be shared equally among all parties ordering copies of the transcripts, unless the parties agree otherwise, or unless the Arbitrators determine otherwise according to the circumstances of a particular case.

Meetings

14. Meetings shall be private and without publicity. All communications made in the process of Arbitration shall be treated as confidential by all who share in them. If the dispute is resolved, and the parties agree to publicizing the solution, announcement of it shall be made after consultation with the Ordinaries of the participants. If the dispute is not resolved by Arbitration, or if the parties do not agree on publicizing the solution, no announcement shall be made.

Interpretation and Application of Rules

15. Questions concerning the interpretation of these rules shall be referred for final decision to the Chairman of the Bishops' Committee on Conciliation and Arbitration.

Expenses

16. The expenses of witnesses shall be paid by the respective parties producing witnesses, unless the Arbitrators determine otherwise according to circumstances of a particular case. Traveling and other expenses of the Arbitrators, and the expenses of any witnesses or the cost of any proofs produced at the direct request of the Arbitrators, shall be borne equally by the parties unless they agree otherwise, or unless the Arbitrators determine otherwise according to circumstances of a particular case.

Article XII. Appeal from Decision in Arbitration

1.   Since the parties to arbitration have voluntarily committed themselves to abide by the decision of the Arbitrators (cf. Article X), no appeal on the merits may be taken from a decision in arbitration.

2.   Appeal from a decision in arbitration may be taken only where it is alleged that:

(a) The award was procured by corruption, fraud, or other undue means;

(b) There was evident partiality on the part of an Arbitrator;

(c) The Arbitrators exceeded their powers;

(d) The Arbitrators refused to postpone a hearing notwithstanding the showing of sufficient cause for such postponement, or refused to hear evidence material to the controversy, or otherwise conducted the hearing so as prejudicially to affect a substantial right of one of the parties;

(e) The decision was based on documents which are spurious;

(f) New evidence has been discovered of a character which demands a contrary decision;

(g) Principles of fundamental procedural fairness were violated.

3. Such appeal as is allowed by this Article, Section 2, shall be taken either to the full membership of the Bishops' Committee on Conciliation and Arbitration, or to the Apostolic Signatura, at the option of the appealing party.

Brothers and Sisters to Us

A Pastoral Letter Issued by the
United States Catholic Bishops

November 14, 1979

1.   Racism is an evil which endures in our society and in our Church. Despite apparent advances and even significant changes in the last two decades, the reality of racism remains. In large part it is only the external appearances which have changed.

2.   In 1958 we spoke out against the blatant forms of racism that divided people through discriminatory laws and enforced segregation. We pointed out the moral evil that denied human persons their dignity as children of God and their God-given rights.[1] A decade later in a second pastoral letter we again underscored the continuing scandal of racism and called for decisive action to eradicate it from our society.[2]

3.   We recognize and applaud the readiness of many Americans to make new strides forward in reducing and eliminating prejudice against minorities. We are convinced that the majority of Americans realize that racial discrimination is both unjust and unworthy of this nation.

4.   We do not deny that changes have been made, that laws have been passed, that policies have been implemented. We do not deny that the ugly external features of racism which marred our society have in part been eliminated. But neither can it be denied that too often what has happened has been only a covering over, not a fundamental change. Today the sense of urgency has yielded to an apparent acceptance of the status quo. The climate of crisis engendered by demonstrations, protests, and confrontation has given way to a mood of indifference; and other issues occupy our attention.

5.   In response to this mood, we wish to call attention to the persistent presence of racism and in particular to the relationship between racial and economic justice. Racism and economic oppression are distinct but interrelated forces which dehumanize our society. Movement toward authentic justice demands a simultaneous attack on both evils. Our economic structures are undergoing fundamental changes which threaten to intensify social inequalities in our nation. We are entering an era characterized by limited resources, restricted job markets and dwindling revenues. In this atmosphere, the poor and racial

---

[1] *Discrimination and Christian Conscience.* National Catholic Welfare Conference. 1958.
[2] *National Race Crisis.* National Conference of Catholic Bishops. 1968.

minorities are being asked to bear the heaviest burden of the new economic pressures.

6.   This new economic crisis reveals an unresolved racism that permeates our society's structures and resides in the hearts of many among the majority. Because it is less blatant, this subtle form of racism is in some respects even more dangerous—harder to combat and easier to ignore. Major segments of the population are being pushed to the margins of society in our nation. As economic pressures tighten, often those people who are black, Hispanic, native American, and Asian—and always poor—slip further into the unending cycle of poverty, deprivation, ignorance, disease, and crime. Racial identity is for them an iron curtain barring the way to a decent life and livelihood. The economic pressures exacerbate racism, particularly where poor white people are competing with minorities for limited job opportunities. The Church must not be unmindful of these economic pressures. We must be sensitive to the unfortunate and unnecessary racial tension that results from this kind of economic need.

7.   Mindful of its duty to be the advocate for those who hunger and thirst for justice's sake, the Church cannot remain silent about the racial injustices in society and in its own structures. Our concern over racism follows, as well, from our strong commitment to evangelization. Pope John Paul II has defined evangelization as bringing consciences, both individual and social, into conformity with the Gospel.[3] We would betray our commitment to evangelize ourselves and our society were we not to strongly voice our condemnation of attitudes and practices so contrary to the Gospel. Therefore, as the bishops of the United States, we once again address our pastoral reflections on racism to our brothers and sisters of all races.

8.   We do this, conscious of the fact that racism is only one form of discrimination that infects our society. Such discrimination belies both our civil and religious traditions. The United States of America rests on a constitutional heritage that recognizes the equality, dignity, and inalienable rights of all its citizens. Further, we are heirs of a religious teaching which proclaims that all men and women, as children of God, are brothers and sisters. Every form of discrimination against individuals and groups—whether because of race, ethnicity, religion, gender, economic status, or national or cultural origin—is a serious injustice which has severely weakened our social fabric and deprived our country of the unique contributions of many of our citizens. While cognizant of these broader concerns, we wish to draw attention here to the particular form of discrimination that is based on race.

---

[3]Pope John Paul II, Address at the Third General Assembly of The Latin American Bishops, Puebla, Mexico, January 28, 1979, p. 1.2.

The Sin of Racism

9.   Racism is a sin: a sin that divides the human family, blots out the image of God among specific members of that family, and violates the fundamental human dignity of those called to be children of the same Father. Racism is the sin that says some human beings are inherently superior and others essentially inferior because of race. It is the sin that makes racial characteristics the determining factor for the exercise of human rights. It mocks the words of Jesus: "Treat others the way you would have them treat you."[4] Indeed, racism is more than a disregard for the words of Jesus; it is a denial of the truth of the dignity of each human being revealed by the mystery of the Incarnation.

10.   In order to find the strength to overcome the evil of racism, we must look to Christ. In Christ Jesus "there does not exist among you Jew or Greek, slave or freeman, male or female. All are one in Christ Jesus."[5] As Pope John Paul II has said so clearly, "Our spirit is set in one direction, the only direction for our intellect, will and heart is— toward Christ our Redeemer, toward Christ, the Redeemer of [humanity]."[6] It is in Christ, then, that the Church finds the central cause for its commitment to justice, and to the struggle for the human rights and dignity of all persons.

11.   When we give in to our fears of the other because he or she is of a race different from ourselves, when we prejudge the motives of others precisely because they are of a different color, when we stereotype or ridicule the other because of racial characteristics and heritage, we fail to heed the command of the Prophet Amos: "Seek good and not evil, that you may live; then truly will the Lord . . . be with you as you claim! . . . Then let justice surge like water, and goodness like an unfailing stream."[7]

12.   Today in our country, men, women, and children are being denied opportunities for full participation and advancement in our society because of their race. The educational, legal, and financial systems, along with other structures and sectors of our society, impede people's progress and narrow their access because they are black, Hispanic, native American, or Asian.

13.   The structures of our society are subtly racist, for these structures reflect the values which society upholds. They are geared to the success of the majority and the failure of the minority. Members of both groups give unwitting approval by accepting things as they are. Per-

---

[4] Mt 7:12.
[5] Gal 3:28.
[6] *Redemptor Hominis*, 7. Pope John Paul II. 1979.
[7] Am 5:14,24.

haps no single individual is to blame. The sinfulness is often anonymous but nonetheless real. The sin is social in nature in that each of us, in varying degrees, is responsible. All of us in some measure are accomplices. As our recent pastoral letter on moral values states: "The absence of personal fault for an evil does not absolve one of all responsibility. We must seek to resist and undo injustices we have not caused, lest we become bystanders who tacitly endorse evil and so share in guilt for it."[8]

Racism Is a Fact

14. Because the courts have eliminated statutory racial discrimination and Congress has enacted civil rights legislation, and because some minority people have achieved some measure of success, many people believe that racism is no longer a problem in American life. The continuing existence of racism becomes apparent, however, when we look beneath the surface of our national life: as, for example, in the case of unemployment figures. In the second quarter of 1979, 4.9 percent of white Americans were unemployed; but for blacks the figure was 11.6 percent; for Hispanics, 8.3 percent; and for native Americans on reservations, as high as forty percent. The situation is even more disturbing when one realizes that thirty-five percent of black youth, 19.1 percent of Hispanic youth, and an estimated sixty percent of native American youth are unemployed.[9] Quite simply, this means that an alarming proportion of tomorrow's adults are cut off from gainful employment—an essential prerequisite of responsible adulthood. These same youths presently suffer the crippling effects of a segregated educational system which in many cases fails to enlighten the mind and free the spirit, which too often inculcates a conviction of inferiority, and which frequently graduates persons who are ill-prepared and inadequately trained. In addition, racism raises its ugly head in the violence that frequently surrounds attempts to achieve racial balance in education and housing.

15. With respect to family life, we recognize that decades of denied access to opportunities have been for minority families a crushing burden. Racial discrimination has only exacerbated the harmful relationship between poverty and family instability.

16. Racism is only too apparent in housing patterns in our major cities and suburbs. Witness the deterioration of inner cities and the segregation of many suburban areas by means of unjust practices of

---

[8]*To Live in Christ Jesus*, p. 25. National Conference of Catholic Bishops. 1976.
[9]*Employment and Earnings*, Vol. 26, No. 10, Dept. of Labor, Bureau of Labor Statistics, October, 1979. Precise data on youth employment among Native Americans are not available. The sixty percent unemployment figure is an estimate by the U.S. Dept. of Labor.

social steering and blockbusting. Witness also the high proportion of Hispanics, blacks, and Indians on welfare and the fact that the median income of nonwhite families is only sixty-three percent of the average white family income. Moreover the gap between the rich and the poor is widening, not decreasing.[10]

17. Racism is apparent when we note that the population in our prisons consists disproportionately of minorities; that violent crime is the daily companion of a life of poverty and deprivation; and that the victims of such crimes are also disproportionately nonwhite and poor. Racism is also apparent in the attitudes and behavior of some law enforcement officials and in the unequal availability of legal assistance.

18. Finally, racism is sometimes apparent in the growing sentiment that too much is being given to racial minorities by way of affirmative action programs or allocations to redress long-standing imbalances in minority representation and government-funded programs for the disadvantaged. At times, protestations claiming that all persons should be treated equally reflect the desire to maintain a *status quo* that favors one race and social group at the expense of the poor and nonwhite.

19. Racism obscures the evils of the past and denies the burdens that history has placed upon the shoulders of our black, Hispanic, native American, and Asian brothers and sisters. An honest look at the past makes plain the need for restitution wherever possible—makes evident the justice of restoration and redistribution.

A Look at the Past

20. Racism has been part of the social fabric of America since its European colonization. Whether it be the tragic past of the native Americans, the Mexicans, the Puerto Ricans, or the blacks, the story is one of slavery, peonage, economic exploitation, brutal repression, and cultural neglect. All have suffered indignity; most have been uprooted, defrauded, or dispossessed of their lands; and none have escaped one or another form of collective degradation by a powerful majority. Our history is littered with the debris of broken promises and treaties, as well as lynchings and massacres that almost destroyed the Indians, humiliated the Hispanics, and crushed the blacks.

21. But despite this tragic history, the racial minorities of our country have survived and increased. Each racial group has sunk its roots deep in the soil of our culture, thus helping to give to the United States its unique character and its diverse coloration. The contribution of each racial minority is distinctive and rich; each is a source of

---

[10]*Widening Economic Gap*, National Urban League, Research Dept., 1979. See also "Consumer Income," Current Population Report, Series P60 #118, 1979.

internal strength for our nation. The history of all gives a witness to a truth absorbed by now into the collective consciousness of Americans: their struggle has been a pledge of liberty and a challenge to future greatness.

Racism Today

22. Crude and blatant expressions of racist sentiment, though they occasionally exist, are today considered bad form. Yet racism itself persists in covert ways. Under the guise of other motives, it is manifest in the tendency to stereotype and marginalize whole segments of the population whose presence is perceived as a threat. It is manifest also in the indifference that replaces open hatred. The minority poor are seen as the dross of a postindustrial society—without skills, without motivation, without incentive. They are expendable. Many times the new face of racism is the computer print-out, the graph of profits and losses, the pink slip, the nameless statistic. Today's racism flourishes in the triumph of private concern over public responsibility, individual success over social commitment, and personal fulfillment over authentic compassion. Then too, we recognize that racism also exists in the attitudes and behavior of some who are themselves members of minority groups. Christian ideals of justice must be brought to bear in both the private and the public sector in order that covert racism be eliminated wherever it exists.

23. The new forms of racism must be brought face-to-face with the figure of Christ. It is Christ's word that is the judgment on this world; it is Christ's cross that is the measure of our response; and it is Christ's face that is the composite of all persons, but in a most significant way of today's poor, today's marginal people, today's minorities.

God's Judgment and Promise

The Voice of Scripture

24. The Christian response to the challenges of our times is to be found in the Good News of Jesus. The words that signaled the start of His public ministry must be the watchword for every Christian response to injustice, "He unrolled the scroll and found the passage where it was written: The spirit of the Lord is upon me; therefore, he has anointed me. He has sent me to bring glad tidings to the poor, to proclaim liberty to captives, recovery of sight to the blind and release to prisoners, to announce a year of favor from the Lord. Rolling up the scroll he gave it back . . . and sat down. . . . 'Today this

Scripture passage is fulfilled in your hearing.'"[11]

25. God's Word proclaims the oneness of the human family—from the first words of Genesis, to the "Come, Lord Jesus" of the Book of Revelation. God's Word in Genesis announces that all men and women are created in God's image; not just *some* races and racial types, but *all* bear the imprint of the Creator and are enlivened by the breath of His one Spirit.

26. In proclaiming the liberation of Israel, God's Word proclaims the liberation of all people from slavery. God's Word further proclaims that all people are accountable to and for each other. This is the message of that great parable of the Final Judgment: "When the Son of Man comes in his glory, escorted by all the angels of heaven . . . all the nations will be assembled before him. Then he will separate them into two groups. . . . The king will say to those on his right: 'Come. You have my Father's blessing!. . . For I was hungry and you gave me food, I was thirsty and you gave me drink. I was a stranger and you welcomed me. . . . I assure you, as often as you did it for one of my least brothers, you did it for me.'"[12]

27. God's Word proclaims that the person "who listens to God's word but does not put it into practice is like a man who looks into a mirror at the face he was born with . . . then goes off and promptly forgets what he looks like."[13] We have forgotten that we "are strangers and aliens no longer. . . . [We] are fellow citizens of the saints and members of the household of God. [We] form a building which rises on the foundation of the apostles and prophets, with Christ Jesus himself as the capstone."[14]

The Voice of the Church

28. This is the mystery of our Church, that all men and women are brothers and sisters, all one in Christ, all bear the image of the eternal God. The Church is truly universal, embracing all races, for it is "the visible sacrament of this saving unity.[15] The Church, moreover, follows the example of its founder and, "through its children, is one with [people] of every condition, but especially with the poor and the afflicted."[16]

29. This Church has a duty to proclaim the truth about the human being as disclosed in the truth about Jesus Christ. As our Holy Father Pope John Paul II has written: "On account of the mystery of the Redemption [every human being] is entrusted to the solicitude of the

---

[11] Lk 4:17-21.
[12] Mt 25:31-40.
[13] Jas 1:23-24.
[14] Eph 2:19-20.
[15] *Dogmatic Constitution on the Church*, 9.
[16] *Decree on the Church's Missionary Activity*, 12.

Church." The human being is "the primary and fundamental way for the Church."[17]

30. It is important to realize in the case of racism that we are dealing with a distortion at the very heart of human nature. The ultimate remedy against evils such as this will not come solely from human effort. What is needed is the recreation of the human being according to the image revealed in Jesus Christ. For He reveals in Himself what each human being can and must become.

31. How great, therefore, is that sin of racism which weakens the Church's witness as the universal sign of unity among all peoples! How great the scandal given by racist Catholics who would make the body of Christ, the Church, a sign of racial oppression! Yet all too often the Church in our country has been for many a "white Church," a racist institution.

32. Each of us as Catholics must acknowledge a share in the mistakes and sins of the past. Many of us have been prisoners of fear and prejudice. We have preached the Gospel while closing our eyes to the racism it condemns. We have allowed conformity to social pressures to replace compliance with social justice.

33. But past mistakes must not hinder the Church's response to the challenges of the present. Worldwide, the Church today is not just European and American; it is also African, Asian, Indian, and Oceanic. It is western, eastern, northern, and southern, black and also brown, white and also red and yellow. In our own country, one quarter of the Catholics are Spanish-speaking. A million black Catholics make Catholicism one of the largest denominations among black Americans today. Among our nation's original inhabitants, the native Americans, the Church's presence is increasingly becoming developed and expressed within the cultures of the various native American tribes.

34. It is a fact that Catholic dioceses and religious communities across the country for years have committed selected personnel and substantial funds to relieve oppression and to correct injustices and have striven to bring the Gospel to the diverse racial groups in our land. The Church has sought to aid the poor and downtrodden, who for the most part are also the victims of racial oppression. But this relationship has been and remains two-sided and reciprocal; for the initiative of racial minorities, clinging to their Catholic faith, has helped the Church to grow, adapt, and become truly Catholic and remarkably diverse. Today in our own land, the face of Catholicism is the face of all humanity—a face of many colors, a countenance of many cultural forms.

35. Yet more is needed. The prophetic voice of the Church, which is to be heard in every generation and even to the ends of the earth, must not be muted—especially not by the counterwitness of some of

---

[17]*Redemptor Hominis*, 13, 14.

its own people. Let the Church speak out, not only in the assemblies of the bishops, but in every diocese and parish in the land, in every chapel and religious house, in every school, in every social service agency, and in every institution that bears the name Catholic. As Pope John Paul II has proclaimed, the Church must be aware of the threats to humanity and of all that opposes the endeavor to make life itself more human. The Church must strive to make every element of human life correspond to the true dignity of the human person.[18] And during his recent visit to this country, Pope John Paul II discussed the direct implications of this for the Church in the United States:

> It will always remain one of the glorious achievements of this nation that, when people looked toward America, they received together with freedom also a chance for their own advancement. This tradition must be honored also today. The freedom that was gained must be ratified each day by the firm rejection of whatever wounds, weakens or dishonors human life. And so I appeal to all who love freedom and justice to give a chance to all in need, to the poor and the powerless. Break open the hopeless cycles of poverty and ignorance that are still the lot of too many of our brothers and sisters; the hopeless cycles of prejudices that linger on despite enormous progress toward effective equality in education and employment; the cycles of despair in which are imprisoned all those that lack decent food, shelter or employment. . . .[19]

36. Therefore, let the Church proclaim to all that the sin of racism defiles the image of God and degrades the sacred dignity of humankind which has been revealed by the mystery of the Incarnation. Let all know that it is a terrible sin that mocks the cross of Christ and ridicules the Incarnation. For the brother and sister of our Brother Jesus Christ are brother and sister to us.

The Voice of the World

37. We find God's will for us not only in the word of Scripture and in the teaching of his Church but also in the issues and events of secular society. "The Church . . . recognizes that worthy elements are found in today's social movements, especially an evolution toward unity, a process of wholesome socialization and of association in civic and economic realms."[20] Thus spoke the Church in the Second Vatican Council. That same Council urged the Church, especially the laity, to work in the temporal sphere on behalf of justice and the unity of humankind.[21]

---

[18] *Redemptor Hominis,* 14.
[19] Homily at Battery Park, New York. Pope John Paul II. October 1979.
[20] *Pastoral Constitution on the Church in the Modern World,* 42.
[21] *Pastoral Constitution on the Church in the Modern World,* 43.

38. With this in mind, we pay special tribute to those who have struggled and struggle today for civil rights and economic justice in our own country. Nor do we overlook the United Nations' Universal Declaration of Human Rights which still speaks to the conscience of the entire world and the several international covenants which demand the elimination of discrimination based on race. None of these, unfortunately, have been ratified by our country, whereas we in America should have been the first to do so. All have a duty to heed the voice of God speaking in these documents.

Our Response

39. Racism is not merely one sin among many; it is a radical evil that divides the human family and denies the new creation of a redeemed world. To struggle against it demands an equally radical transformation in our own minds and hearts, as well as in the structure of our society.

40. Conversion is the ever-present task of each Christian. In offering certain guidelines for this change of heart as it pertains to racism, we note that these are only first steps in what ought to be a continuing dialogue throughout the Catholic community and the nation at large. In this context we would urge that existing programs and plans, such as those dealing with family ministry, parish renewal, and evangelization, be used as vehicles for implementing the measures addressed here.

Our Personal Lives

41. To the extent that racial bias affects our personal attitudes and judgments, to the extent that we allow another's race to influence our relationship and limit our openness, to the extent that we see yet close our hearts to our brothers and sisters in need,[22]—to that extent we are called to conversion and renewal in love and justice.

42. As individuals we should try to influence the attitudes of others by expressly rejecting racial stereotypes, racial slurs, and racial jokes. We should influence the members of our families, especially our children, to be sensitive to the authentic human values and cultural contributions of each racial grouping in our country.

43. We should become more sensitive ourselves, and thereby sensitize our acquaintances, by learning more about how social structures inhibit the economic, educational, and social advancement of the poor. We should make a personal commitment to join with others in polit-

---

[22]I Jn 3:17.

ical efforts to bring about justice for the victims of such deprivation.

Our Church Community

44. The Church must be constantly attentive to the Lord's voice as He calls on His people daily not to harden their hearts.[23] We urge that on all levels the Catholic Church in the United States examine its conscience regarding attitudes and behavior toward blacks, Hispanics, native Americans, and Asians. We urge consideration of the evil of racism as it exists in the local Church and reflection upon the means of combatting it. We urge scrupulous attention at every level to ensure that minority representation goes beyond mere tokenism and involves authentic sharing in responsibility and decision making.
45. We encourage Catholics to join hands with members of other religious groups in the spirit of ecumenism to achieve the common objectives of justice and peace. During the struggle for legal recognition of racial justice, an important chapter in American history was written as religious groups, Jewish, Protestant, and Catholic, joined in support of a civil rights movement which found much of its initiative and inspiration within the black Protestant churches. This cooperation should continue to serve as a model for our times.
46. All too often in the very places where blacks, Hispanics, native Americans, and Asians are numerous, the Church's officials and representatives, both clerical and lay, are predominantly white. Efforts to achieve racial balance in government, the media, the armed services, and other crucial areas of secular life should not only be supported but surpassed in the institutions and programs of the Catholic Church.
47. Particular care should be taken to foster vocations among minority groups.[24] Training for the priesthood, the permanent diaconate, and religious life should not entail an abandonment of culture and traditions or a loss of racial identity but should seek ways in which such culture and traditions might contribute to that training. Special attention is required whenever it is necessary to correct racist attitudes or behavior among seminary staff and seminarians. Seminary education ought to include an awareness of the history and the contributions of minorities as well as an appreciation of the enrichment of the liturgical expression, especially at the local parish level, which can be found in their respective cultures.

---

[23] Ps 94:8.
[24] Concerns for vocations from minority groups and the preparation of priests to serve in a multi-cultural and multi-racial society have been previously expressed in *The Program for Priestly Formation*, which was developed and approved by the National Conference of Catholic Bishops, 1976.

48. We affirm the teaching of Vatican II on the liturgy by noting that "the liturgy is the summit toward which the activity of the Church is directed."[25] The Church must "respect and foster the spiritual . . . gifts of the various races and peoples"[26] and encourage the incorporation of these gifts into the liturgy.

49. We see the value of fostering greater diversity of racial and minority group representation in the hierarchy. Furthermore, we call for the adoption of an effective affirmative action program in every diocese and religious institution.

50. We strongly urge that special attention be directed to the plight of undocumented workers and that every effort be made to remove the fear and prejudice of which they are victims.

51. We ask in particular that Catholic institutions such as schools, universities, social service agencies, and hospitals, where members of racial minorities are often employed in large numbers, review their policies to see that they faithfully conform to the Church's teaching on justice for workers and respect for their rights. We recommend that investment portfolios be examined in order to determine whether racist institutions and policies are inadvertently being supported; and that, wherever possible, the capital of religious groups be made available for new forms of alternative investment, such as cooperatives, land trusts, and housing for the poor. We further recommend that Catholic institutions avoid the services of agencies and industries which refuse to take affirmative action to achieve equal opportunity and that the Church itself always be a model as an equal opportunity employer.

52. We recommend that leadership training programs be established on the local level in order to encourage effective leadership among racial minorities on all levels of the Church, local as well as national.

53. In particular, we recommend the active spiritual and financial support of associations and institutions organized by Catholic blacks, Hispanics, native Americans, and Asians within the Church for the promotion of ministry to and by their respective communities. There is also need for more attention to finding ways in which minorities can work together across racial and cultural lines to avoid duplication and competition among themselves. There is also a need for cooperative efforts between racial minorities and other social action groups, such as labor and the women's movement.

54. Finally, we urgently recommend the continuation and expansion of Catholic schools in the inner cities and other disadvantaged areas. No other form of Christian ministry has been more widely acclaimed or desperately sought by leaders of various racial communities. For a century and a half the Church in the United States has been distin-

---

[25]*Constitution on the Sacred Liturgy*, 10.
[26]*Constitution on the Sacred Liturgy*, 37.

guished by its efforts to educate the poor and disadvantaged, many of whom are not of the Catholic faith. That tradition continues today in—among other places—Catholic schools, where so many blacks, Hispanics, native Americans, and Asians receive a form of education and formation which constitutes a key to greater freedom and dignity. It would be tragic if today, in the face of acute need and even near despair, the Church, for centuries the teacher and the guardian of civilization, should withdraw from this work in our own society. No sacrifice can be so great, no price can be so high, no short-range goals can be so important as to warrant the lessening of our commitment to Catholic education in minority neighborhoods. More affluent parishes should be made aware of this need and of their opportunity to share resources with the poor and needy in a way that recognizes the dignity of both giver and receiver.

Society at Large

55. Individuals move on many levels in our complex society: each of us is called to speak and act in many different settings. In each case may we speak and act according to our competence and as the Gospel bids us. With this as our prayer, we refrain from giving detailed answers to complex questions on which we ourselves have no special competence. Instead, we propose several guidelines of a general nature.

56. The difficulties of these new times demand a new vision and a renewed courage to transform our society and achieve justice for all. We must fight for the dual goals of racial and economic justice with determination and creativity. Domestically, justice demands that we strive for authentic full employment, recognizing the special need for employment of those who, whether men or women, carry the principal responsibility for support of a family. Justice also demands that we strive for decent working conditions, adequate income, housing, education, and health care for all. Government at the national and local levels must be held accountable by all citizens for the essential services which all are entitled to receive. The private sector should work with various racial communities to ensure that they receive a just share of the profits they have helped to create.

57. Globally, we live in an interdependent community of nations, some rich, some poor. Some are high consumers of the world's resources; some eke out an existence on a near-starvation level. As it happens, most of the rich, consuming nations are white and Christian; most of the world's poor are of other races and religions.

58. Concerning our relationship to other nations, our Christian faith suggests several principles. First, racial difference should not interfere with our dealing justly and peacefully with all other nations. Secondly, those nations which possess more of the world's riches must,

in justice, share with those who are in serious need. Finally, the private sector should be aware of its responsibility to promote racial justice, not subordination or exploitation, to promote genuine development in poor societies, not mere consumerism and materialism.

Conclusion

59. Our words here are an initial response to one of the major concerns which emerged during the consultation on social justice entitled "A Call to Action," which was part of the U.S. Catholic participation in the national bicentennial. The dialogue must continue among the Catholics of our country. We have proposed guidelines and principles and as the bishops of the Catholic Conference in the United States, we must give the leadership to this effort by a commitment of our time, of personnel, and of significant financial resources. Others must develop the programs and plan operations. There must be no turning back along the road of justice, no sighing for bygone times of privilege, no nostalgia for simple solutions from another age. For we are children of the age to come, when the first shall be last and the last first, when blessed are they who serve Christ the Lord in all His brothers and sisters, especially those who are poor and suffer injustice.

Resolution on Cambodia

A Resolution Passed by the
United States Catholic Conference

November 1979

1. Pope John Paul II, in his homily at Yankee Stadium, said that the parable of Lazarus had a special significance for the United States. The starvation and devastation of the Cambodian people illustrate the meaning of the Holy Father's words. Their suffering lays a claim on our consciences. We have already called upon the Catholic community to contribute, through a special collection, to the heroic work of the Catholic Relief Services in meeting the needs of the Cambodian people.

2. We wish to thank our people again for their generosity and to commend the work of the Catholic Relief Services. But, we have only begun; the situation in Cambodia will require concerted international action for many months to avert the death of a nation.

3. We call upon our representatives in government to continue and intensify its diplomatic and humanitarian activity. We must say to our government and to others that politics cannot take priority over saving human lives in such circumstances. We commend the efforts of all agencies, governmental bodies and voluntary groups, which are striving to forestall starvation and death. We ask Catholics to support by word and sacrificial deeds policies and programs which are directed toward the survival of the people of Cambodia. We pray that the God of all consolation may provide strength and hope to them in this time of suffering.

Resolution on Iran

A Resolution Passed by the
United States Catholic Conference

November 1979

1. The events in Iran are a test of law for the international community and a test of policy for the United States. Overriding both of these aspects, however, is the central question: the safety and well-being of the hostages held in the American embassy in Teheran. The survival and safe return of the hostages are the first priority in this tragic dilemma. The intervention of Pope John Paul II on their behalf provides a model for action of others.

2. In support of this primary imperative, two requirements exist. First, the international community should make clear by word and deed that the violation of diplomatic immunity, a traditional imperative of international law, cannot be sanctioned, condoned or supported in any way. Second, we as teachers of moral principles reaffirm the rights of innocent persons to immunity from terrorists' actions which threaten their well-being and lives. The end does not justify the means. As a nation, we must combine firm resolve with rational restraint. Diplomatic and other forms of peaceful pressure need to be used in support of the hostages. Inflammatory words and action should be avoided in both official policy and public debate. The measures of conservation required in support of the economic decision taken by the President deserve our cooperation.

3. Most importantly, as religious leaders, we call upon Catholics and all believers to pray without ceasing for a peaceful and successful resolution of this tragic drama.

Resolution on the Papal Visit

A Resolution Passed by the
National Conference of Catholic Bishops

November 1979

1. After the pastoral visit of Pope John Paul II to our country, we the bishops of the United States offer these reflections to our people. We see this visit as an occasion of special grace to our country. It was truly one of the greatest events in the history of the Church in the United States. The warm response of so many millions of people, not only Catholics but also Christians of other communities and those of other faiths, testifies to a thirst for spiritual values and leadership and for a readiness to hear the saving message of the Lord Jesus.

2. In reflecting on this historic visit, we thank first of all God in his providence for this gift to our nation. We are grateful next to the Holy Father himself, successor to Peter and Vicar of Christ, who came among us as spiritual leader, first teacher in the Church, and friend witnessing in our day to the primacy of charity and pastoral concern inherent in his papal ministry. We are grateful also to all those who helped make this visit such a cherished moment: the public and civic officials, the media personnel whose coverage was both full and professional, and all of the dedicated people who contributed to the success of this pastoral journey.

3. For us and our people this event was a source of inspiration and a reason for hope. The Holy Father, in his person and by his words, reminded us that Christ speaks his message of truth and love today as always. His example renews our courage to make this message ours and to teach it faithfully.

4. Pope John Paul II touched on many poignant themes during those days in October: the quest of peace, the scandal of poverty, the dignity of the human person. He challenged our youth to be witnesses of hope for the future of the Church and society. To assist the poor in this and other nations, he urged us with these words: "Take of your substance, not of your abundance." He reaffirmed Catholic teaching of the sanctity of human life, including the unborn, the values of fidelity and commitment to vocations in all states of life— single and married, religious and ordained. He stressed the need for chastity and self-discipline in respect to sexuality and married love.

Responding to the Pope's message and to this occasion of grace, we acknowledge our particular duty as bishops to give witness to "the episcopal ministry of holiness and truth" (Address to the Bishops, October 5, 1979). As we pursue our ministry and listen to the needs of our people, we recognize the hard but consoling fact that, "As we proclaim the truth in love, it is not possible for us to avoid all criticism, nor is it possible to please everyone. But it is possible to work for the real benefit of everyone" (*Ibid.*). In union with the Holy Father, we bishops wholeheartedly and with God's help rededicate ourselves to preaching the Word in season and out of season.

5.   We ask God to bless the Holy Father in his ministry to the universal Church and to make of his visit among us a call to renewed fidelity to the Gospel message of truth, love and service to the world; and renewed love, devotion and fidelity to him personally as the Vicar of Christ.

Statement on Registration and Conscription for Military Service

*A Statement Issued by the Administrative Board
of the United States Catholic Conference*

February 14, 1980

1. We have followed closely the public debate on the reinstitution of registration for military service with the possible renewal of military conscription to follow. The questions of registration and conscription for military service are part of the broader political-moral issue of war and peace in the nuclear age. But registration and conscription bear so directly on the moral decision making of citizens that they require specific attention.

2. The U.S. Catholic Conference (USCC), and its predecessor, the National Catholic Welfare Conference (NCWC), have spoken to the question of peacetime military conscription five times since 1944. The present debate in Congress and the media raises both old and new questions; we offer in this Statement a body of principles and a series of positions in response to the public debate.

3. We recognize, of course, that the questions of registration and conscription arise, as Vatican II said, because "war has not been rooted out of human affairs." In the face of the sad truth of this statement, our response as teachers in the Church must be the same as that of all the popes of this century. We call in season and out of season for the international community to turn from war and to do the works of peace. The primary obligation of the nuclear age is to banish resort-to-force from the daily affairs of nations and peoples. From Pius XII to John Paul II the cry of the Church and the prayer of all believers is a reiteration of the words of Paul VI: "No more war, war never again!" This must remain our primary response to war today.

4. Only in the context of this Statement can we consider the question of what is the legitimate role of governments and the responsibilities of citizens regarding military conscription. We see registration, conscription, and participation in military service as moral questions as well as political issues. Our perspective on these issues is shaped by Catholic moral teaching on the role of the state, and the rights and responsibilities of citizens, when both citizen and state are confronted by questions of war and peace.

5. With Vatican II we recognize that: "As long as the danger of war remains and there is no competent and sufficiently powerful authority at the international level, governments cannot be denied the right to legitimate defense once every means of peaceful settlement has been exhausted." This principle acknowledges the right of the state to call citizens to acts of "legitimate defense." To this right there corresponds the duty each citizen has to contribute to the common good of society, including, as an essential element, the defense of society. Both the right of the state and the responsibility of the citizen are governed by moral principles which seek to protect the welfare of society and to preserve inviolate the conscience of the citizen.

6.   The moral right of the state to use force is severely limited both in terms of the reasons for which force is employed and the means to be used. While acknowledging the duty of the state to defend society and its correlative right to use force in certain circumstances, we also affirm the Catholic teaching that the state's decision to use force should always be morally scrutinized by citizens asked to support the decision or to participate in war. From the perspective of the citizen, the moral scrutiny of every use of force can produce a posture of responsible participation in the government's decision or conscientious objection to some *reasons* for using force, some *methods* of using force, or even some specific branches of the service, because of the missions they may be asked to perform (cf., *Human Life in Our Day*).

7.   In light of these general principles, we are led to the following specific positions:

(1) *Registration*. We acknowledge the right of the state to register citizens for the purpose of military conscription, both in peacetime and in times of national emergency. Therefore, we find no objection *in principle* to this action by the government. However, we believe it necessary to present convincing reasons for this at any particular time.

(2) *Military Conscription*. We are opposed to any reinstitution of military conscription except in the case of a national defense emergency. We support the present standby draft system which requires the chief executive to obtain a new authorization to induct a specific number of men into the armed forces if clear purposes of adequate defense demand conscription.

(3) *Conscientious Objection*. We regard this question in all its dimensions as a central element in Catholic teaching on the morality of war. First, we support the right of conscientious objection as a valid moral position, derived from the Gospel and Catholic teaching, and recognized as well in U.S. civil law. The legal protection provided conscientious objectors is a commendable part of our political system which must be preserved in any policy of conscription.

8.   Secondly, we support the right of selective conscientious objection (SCO) as a moral conclusion which can be validly derived from the classical moral teaching of just war theory. The position of SCO

has not yet found expression in our legal system, but a means should be found to give this legitimate moral position a secure legal status. The experience of the Vietnam war highlighted the moral and political significance of precisely this question. We are sure of the moral validity of SCO; we would welcome a dialogue with legislators, lawyers, ethicists, and other religious leaders about how to transpose this moral position into effective legal language.

(4) *Universal National Service.* We continue to oppose, as we have in the past, a universal or national service corps; our opposition rests upon its compulsory character when a proportionate threat to the nation or need for it is not clearly evident.

(5) *Women and Military Conscription.* One of the new questions in the public debate about registration and conscription is whether women should be registered and conscripted on the same basis as men. This is a complex question which touches several issues. It is our position that the past practice of making military service an option for women but not an obligation has served us well as a society. We do not see good reasons for changing this practice and so we oppose both the registration and the conscription of women.

(6) *Methods of Registration.* While we acknowledge the right of the state to register citizens, we are disturbed by proposals to use methods of registration which would require schools to provide information for registration. Such direct access by public authorities to records for this sensitive moral issue could raise serious issues of church and state. We express our opposition to this method of registration; we support methods which do not directly involve the private or religious sector in the registration process.

9. In light of these principles and policy considerations, there is a final point to be made directly to the community of the Church. The primary relationship of the Church to questions of war and peace is as a moral teacher. With Vatican II we affirm that: "All those who enter the military service in loyalty to their country should look upon themselves as the custodians of the security and freedom of their fellow countrymen: and when they carry out their duty properly, they are contributing to the maintenance of peace." We also affirm that the decision to enter military service and subsequent decisions in the line of military duty involve moral questions of great importance. Hence, the issues of registration and conscription raise questions of the kind and quality of moral education that takes place in our educational system. Specifically, it raises the question of what educational and counseling resources are available to a person facing registration or conscription. In adopting this statement of public policy on registration and conscription we call upon schools and religious

educators to include systematic formation of conscience on questions of war and peace in their curricula, and we pledge the assistance of appropriate diocesan agencies in counseling any of those who face questions of military service.

Cultural Pluralism in the United States

A Statement Issued by the
United States Catholic Conference

April 14, 1980

I. Introduction

1. "The world is charged with the grandeur of God."[1] Not the least of this grandeur is found in the wide diversity of the creation that surrounds us and of which we are so much a part. Just as nature in nearly all its forms is marked by variety, so humankind as well expresses the hand of the Creator in a many-splendored spectacle of distinct and disparate signs. In the single human family there appear, by a divine largesse, multiple expressions of language, talent, culture, and native land. Like Jacob fashioning a coat of many colors for his favorite son, Joseph, so has God put His approval on humankind by His wide and manifold gifts.

2. In spite of all this, the human family remains forever one; in the vast galaxy of tribes and peoples there is an enduring humankind. "God, who has fatherly concern for everyone, has willed that all men should constitute one family and treat one another in a spirit of brotherhood. For having been created in the image of God, who 'from one person has created the whole human race and made them live all over the face of the earth' (Acts 17:26), all are called to the same goal, namely, God himself."[2] This unity in origin and destiny must give direction to all the acts of persons and nations; "everyone must consider his every neighbor without exception as another self, taking into account first of all his life and the means necessary to living with dignity."[3]

3. Many times in the sacred writings, the inspired authors touch upon the varied distinctions that separate us one from another—we read of the table of nations that make up "the sons of Noah" and the confusion of speech at the Tower of Babel.[4] The story of Pentecost, however, in a most striking manner illustrates the reality by which the mystery of many tongues expounds a simple faith expressed in words understandable to each—"each of us heard them speaking in his own tongue about the marvels God has accomplished."[5] Diversity

---

[1] *God's Grandeur*, Gerard Manley Hopkins.
[2] *Gaudium et Spes*, 24 (The Documents of Vatican II; Abbott and Gallagher, 1966).
[3] *Ibid.*, 27.
[4] Genesis, Chaps. 10, 11 (The New American Bible, USCC. 1972).
[5] Acts 2:11 (The New American Bible, USCC. 1972).

here, far from being a threat, sees each contributing to that universal blessing which is God's message to His people.

4.   The Lord Himself chose the stranger—the Samaritan—as the sign of our neighbor and enjoined us in the great commandment "you shall love your neighbor as yourself."[6] St. Paul, writing to the Christians in Rome, reminded them: "Just as each one of us has one body with many members . . . so too we, though many, are one body in Christ. . . . We have gifts that differ according to the favor bestowed on each of us."[7]

5.   Since that first Pentecost more than nineteen centuries ago, Catholic missionaries have proclaimed the wonderful works of God to the peoples on all the continents, even to people in places that are most remote and not easily accessible. The Church embraces peoples of varying races, languages, and cultures. The Church is indeed catholic and universal, in name and in fact.

6.   It is a historic fact that there is no government and there is no organization that has as continuous and enduring an existence in form and structure as the Catholic Church. Faithful to the teaching of Jesus Christ, the Church insists that, as the people of God, we are members of the body of Christ, of the one human family, bound in a unity which transcends the diversities of origin, culture, education, or personality.

7.   Against this background, men and women in the world, while conscious of the individuality that gives each one character, must turn with familial affection toward those who in the wondrous gallery of geography and history see themselves and are seen in different ways. The easy human decision that reckons unity as uniformity and oneness as the enemy of pluralism, must be denied. For our part, we, the Committee on Social Development and World Peace, with the approval of the administrative board of the U.S. Catholic Conference, respond in these pages to the plea of the recent Call to Action meeting in Detroit, which asked us to give attention to the ethnic riches of our blessed land and the diversity of cultures that have contributed to contemporary America.

8.   In another place the bishops have spoken of the race question and of its history and its contemporary expression; here we speak more specifically of the various national and cultural experiences which have become part of the flesh and fiber of America.

9.   We should note that the Gospel, as Pope John Paul II reminds us, "is not identified with cultures and transcends them all. But the kingdom which the Gospel announces is lived by men profoundly linked with culture; the building of the kingdom cannot be dispensed from borrowing elements of human cultures (cf., *Evangelii Nuntiandi*, #20).

---

[6]Mt 22:39 (The New American Bible, USCC. 1972).
[7]Rom 12:4-6 (The New American Bible, USCC. 1972).

And even evangelization must help these cultures to cause to arise from their own living tradition original expressions of Christian life, celebration, and thought (cf., *Catechesi Tradendae*, #53). The Holy Spirit asks us to believe in fact that the leaven of the Gospel, in its authenticity, has the strength to raise up Christians in the various cultures, with all the riches of their patrimony, purified and transfigured."[8]

II. History of Immigrations and Cultures

10. In our country we must be especially conscious of the variety of persons that can call this place their homeland. With a short national history extending over two hundred years, we know, of course, that the discovery and exploration of the New World stretches back over nearly five centuries. In its earliest colonizations the Atlantic shore was settled largely by people of Anglo-Saxon heritage, but both France and Spain contributed mightily to the settlement of the South and West. As the nation took shape and grew, the settlers "created conflicts not yet resolved. Indian ways of life were challenged; their very existence was threatened by newcomers who were their superiors in the arts of war. For the Indians, the saga of nation building in America has been a story filled with sorrow and death."[9] Vast numbers of immigrants, meanwhile, settled the cities, new and old, and made their homes in the wide and fertile plains. Unique among the many groups who formed America were the blacks who were brought against their will from Africa, and who experienced here the harsh realities of slavery and oppression which did violence to their cultures, preventing their expression and, in some measure, their very survival.
11. By the second decade of this century mass immigrations were halted, but by that time millions of new arrivals, representing a mosaic of nations, had begun to give shape to the "making of America."[10] The country, however, is still expanding, with new patterns emerging. A long-established Hispanic population has become a part of the new America that largely developed in the Southwest and continues to spread into new environments. Meanwhile, the earlier population, long the only residents of the area, now find people of new and different cultures moving in with them. This phenomenon can be seen in enlarging urban centers and in developing lands, such as Alaska. This ebb and flow must be of particular concern to the Church. The long story of change, so often told, drifts in and out of our

---

[8]To the Bishops of Zaire, May 3, 1980, N.C., par. 4.
[9]U.S. Catholic Bishops, *American Indians* (1977), par. 14.
[10]There is a rich tradition of papal documents on the subject of immigration: Leo XIII (1893) *Quam aerumnosa*; Pius XII (1952) *Exsul familia*; Paul VI (1969) *Pastoralis migratorum cura.*

national consciousness, but the large picture and its implications for our citizens rarely receives the full study that can draw from it the rich lessons it affords to our contemporary society.

12. For many years, we were taken up with a concept that described the nation as "the melting pot." The clear meaning behind this metaphor argued in favor of the mingling of peoples and cultures which, in the long or short run, would give us a nearly homogeneous America. One day, it seemed to say, we would all be of a single pattern; one culture and heritage would prevail; there would be "an American way" from "sea to shining sea." Attractive as this might appear at first glance, any measure of reflection would indicate that this would not, and indeed should not, be the future for America. The total homogenization of peoples *within* a nation is no less disastrous, as history shows, than that same process *among* nations.

13. The American experience has influenced the growth and development of the Catholic Church in America, as indeed it has touched all other institutions. Unlike the Church in older lands, most often nations of one culture or two, our country, and consequently our Church, grew and flourished with the mingling of varied Catholic peoples. The religious traditions of many lands took firm root in the immigrant scene and made a true Pentecost of the growing Church. We should not omit from our attention those earliest settlers whose coming preceded the massive immigrations of the nineteenth century. Notable among these for us was the early colonizing of Maryland with its distinctly Catholic features. Whether it was before the founding of the republic or after its establishment, Catholic arrivals in the new country, with different expressions of a single faith, maintained their religious unity as a part of the universal Church.

14. What has developed for us has been a new and durable understanding of the place of cultural diversity in a land of many peoples. We have witnessed the integration of the many without that perilous assimilation in which all identity is lost. To be sure, this places burdens of sensitivity not only on the whole population, but on each ethnic group as well. Moreover, it is a continuing process that demands constant vigilance, not just on the part of lawmakers and public policy designers, but also on the total citizenry. All institutions must reflect this commitment in order to live up to the American ideal—business, industry and agriculture, education and government, labor, the arts, sciences, and the media. In a special way, because of their moral authority, the churches must be leaders in upholding human dignity lest society itself lose the benefit of their example and influence.

15. In recent years we have heard the expression, "new ethnicity." This does not suggest that the consciousness of tradition is a new-found element in our country—but it strongly asserts that there is a new way of being conscious of one's own cultural origin, a way which includes being aware also of the different heritage of others. An understanding of our own ethnic heritage should enhance our appreciation not only of our own behavior but also the behavior of others. No group now lives in isolation, and to understand any one group requires an understanding of its relation to others. All ethnic groups are part of the mainstream of American life, and any attempt to discourage or reject their presence, subtly or overtly, is an unacceptable return to "nativism" and "ethno-centrism."

16. Let us recall without rancor the sad history of immigrant days, even in this century, when religion, language, origin, customs, color, culture, and poverty were bases for discrimination and even ridicule. The Irish, the Germans, the Italians, the Poles and other Eastern Europeans, the Swedes, the Jews, and those from Arab lands were all victims of a long litany of popular derision which was the lot of the "stranger" in our land. The American Indians, blacks, Asians, and Hispanics continued to be subject to harsh oppression. It is comforting to want to feel that those days have passed, but in truth they have in some measure merely taken on new guise. For some Americans, of course, there is only the smallest consciousness of prejudice based on ethnic differences, and they seldom experience incidents of discrimination. For too many, however, discrimination has taken on more subtle and less visible forms and continues to erode the good society that should be the common patrimony of all. The Catholic ethnic in a special way has been singled out in some circles, as if this identification handicapped such a one for reasons both of religion and national origin. No one can be confident that we have a healthy society as long as this situation endures.

17. Let us acknowledge here that one form of discrimination is inter-ethnic, which is to say that ill feeling and prejudice often mark the relations of one group with another. The differences that created this are not new and are not easily dispelled. Because one has been the victim of discrimination oneself is no guarantee that one will not practice it against a neighbor. The rivalry among ethnic groups for economic opportunity, for neighborhood space, and for political power has contributed to separation and misunderstanding. But there were other elements that rested directly on language, folkways, and cultural patterns. While this bitterness becomes dissipated with time and social change, a residue of tension still remains. Various boundaries of ethnic association still must be recognized as barriers.

18. A further point should be made concerning many Americans especially those of early origin here, whose ethnic differentiation has disappeared, and who do not associate themselves with any ethnic group. These citizens also deserve our honor and respect.

19. Within the Church herself in the United States, cultural diversities have long existed and are still among us. The "national" parish, as it is called, served an admirable function in the immigrant years—it made familiar the spiritual exercise of people in a strange land. These parishes bore witness to the concreteness of Catholic diversity. They kept alive the many languages in which Christians have prayed for centuries. They added cultural strength to city neighborhoods and rural communities. They were often the center for many social and economic services. They also represented a remarkable aesthetic achievement, a patrimony of historic value today. Nor is their work finished; as immigration continues, they are and must be, in certain special circumstances, resources for new Americans, offering their strength and solace to a new generation. The many great ministries rendered by these parishes have not received the praise, gratitude, and support they have deserved, neither from historians of the past nor from scholars of the present day.

20. A source of strain within the Church was centered on the matter of Church leadership itself. The longtime rivalries among groups of Catholics of different ethnic traditions were often seen in terms of an ecclesiastical power struggle in the appointment of members of the hierarchy. We must remember that the nineteenth-century migrations of the Germans and Irish were followed by large Eastern European (Slavs and others) and Italian arrivals later in that century and in this one. So today this issue remains, although in milder form, as many ethnic groups feel the need of better representation in the Church leadership. Much has been done to achieve this end, but with the renewed interest in ethnic origins and expression, this issue may persist and even grow.

21. We ignore at our own risk, particularly in these days of ecumenical dialogue with the Eastern Orthodox, discrimination against ecclesiastical minorities where these exist within our Church. The Catholic Church in the United States includes several Eastern Catholic groups, popularly referred to as Eastern Rites, which are in reality "Eastern Catholic Churches." These Churches, along with the Western Church, are "of equal dignity" and "fully enjoy the right, and are in duty bound, to govern themselves."[11] The differences which the Catholic Eastern Churches reflect are differences of theological insight, spirituality, liturgical practice, and Church discipline. Despite the rapidly increasing numbers of such fellow Catholics in our country, discrimination against them in the valid expressions of their traditional customs, practices, and discipline seems to persist. In this context we must emphasize the principle of "unity in diversity," so precious in the history of our faith.

22. These few reflections allow us to see some of the many factors that have influenced the social development of the people of the United States, as it touches upon their ethnic origins. We have not emphasized the rich traditions that this outpouring of the ancient lands brought to the New World; it would simply be impossible to

---

[11]*Orientalium Ecclesiuum*, 1964. Par. 3, 5 (Documents of Vatican II).

catalogue them. But let us remind ourselves that the mingling of cultures, which sometimes created tensions, also brought positive elements of enduring value to the family, the Church, and the country itself. This treasure continues to flourish among us, developing in a variety of ways from generation to generation. Any move to suppress or even to neglect this resource would make our total nation poorer. If those responsible for its growth and development would fail to support it, it would be regrettable; if others, through discrimination or prejudice, would throttle its potential, it would be inexcusable. The multicolored marble that is America has veins of many hues and patterns; in their joining and confluence they contribute their own element of beauty to the Church and the land we love.

III. Principles of Action

23. The duty of the Church is to scrutinize the signs of the times,[12] and to draw from the light of the Gospel and the experience of the ages those meaningful guides that direct God's people in their pilgrimage. In this, the Church does not seek to provide the particular response to the changing anxieties of every moment, but rather to make ever more clear the Christian ideals which, like a torch raised in the night, illumine the ways of human choice. The fathers of Vatican Council II, mindful of their responsibility to humanity in its broadest aspects, wrote meaningfully of the place of culture in human life:

> The word 'culture' in its general sense indicates all those factors by which man refines and unfolds his manifold spiritual and bodily qualities. It means his effort to bring the world itself under his control by his knowledge and his labor. It includes the fact that by improving customs and institutions he renders social life more human both within the family and in the civic community. Finally, it is a feature of culture that throughout the course of time man expresses, communicates, and conserves in his works great spiritual experiences and desires, so that these may be of advantage to the progress of many, even of the whole human family.[13]

24. The fathers speak also in an anthropological and theological sense:

> Various conditions of community living, as well as various patterns for organizing the goods of life, arise from diverse ways of using things, of laboring, of expressing oneself, of practicing religion, of forming customs, of establishing laws and juridical institutions, of advancing the arts and sciences, and of promoting beauty. Thus the customs handed down to it form for each human community its proper patrimony. Thus, too, is fashioned the specific historical

---

[12] *Gaudium et Spes*, 4 (Documents of Vatican II).
[13] *Ibid.*, 53.

environment which enfolds the men of every nation and age and from which they draw the values which permit them to promote human and civic culture.[14]

25. Pope Paul VI referred all of this to the Church, especially in its work of evangelization:

> Nevertheless this universal Church is in practice incarnate in the individual Churches made up of such or such an actual part of humankind, speaking such and such a language, heirs of a cultural patrimony, of a vision of the world, of an historical past, of a particular human substratum. Receptivity to the wealth of the individual Church corresponds to a special sensitivity in the modern person.

> Let us be very careful not to conceive of the universal Church as the sum, or, if one can say so, the more or less anomalous federation of essentially different individual Churches. In the mind of the Lord the Church is universal by vocation and mission, but when she puts down her roots in a variety of cultural, social and human terrains, she takes on different external expressions and appearances in each part of the world.[15]

26. Pope John Paul II, speaking in Chicago in 1979, saluted Americans for "the common history and union which you built from the richness of your different cultural and ethnic heritages—those heritages that you now rightly want to know and to preserve."

27. He further reminded us, ". . . we are all bound together, as the people of God, the body of Christ, in a unity that transcends the diversity of our origin, culture, education and personality—in a unity that does not exclude a rich diversity. . . ."[16] Constantly emphasizing the unity which binds all humans, the Church has insisted on respecting the cultures, languages, and rites of the various peoples. She has never accepted the theory of assimilation of cultures and peoples, nor the rather extreme type of ethnicity or nationalism which is incompatible with the essential unity of all humans—of the one human family.

28. In theory and in practice the Church has insisted on the freedom of all peoples to remain faithful to their cultural heritage, their particular language, and their traditions. At the same time, recognizing the reality that culture is ever subject to development, that it is not something static but dynamic, the Church has favored the normal process of integration of cultures—sometimes described as acculturation—as distinguished from assimilation and from the extreme of exaggerated nationalism.

29. We can, then, look with confidence to the Church when, faithful to her true mission, she describes for us those safeguards that are

---

[14]*Ibid.*, 53.
[15]*Evangelii Nuntiandi*, 62. USCC, 1976.
[16]*Pilgrim of Peace*, USCC, pp. 125-126.

intended to preserve culture, to set its limits, and to make possible its authentic development.

> . . . the Church recalls to the mind of all that culture must be made to bear on the integral perfection of the human person, and on the good of the community and the whole of society. Therefore the human spirit must be cultivated in such a way that there results a growth in its ability to wonder, to understand, to contemplate, to make personal judgments, and to develop a religious, moral, and social sense.
>
> Because it flows immediately from man's spiritual and social nature, culture has constant need of a just freedom if it is to develop. It also needs the legitimate possibility of exercising its independence according to its own principles. Rightly, therefore, it demands respect and enjoys a certain inviolability, at least as long as the rights of the individual and of the community, whether particular or universal, are preserved within the context of the common good.[17]

30. The sovereign nature of culture and its survival was carefully enunciated in the papal address to UNESCO on June 2, 1980:

> By all the means at your disposal watch over the fundamental sovereignty which every nation possesses by virtue of its own culture. Protect it as you would your very eyes for the future of the great human family. Protect it. Never permit it to become the prey of a political or economic interest. Never permit it to become the victim of totalitarianism, imperialisms or hegemonies. . . .[18]

31. Recently Pope John Paul II, in his extended visit to Brazil, explained how the Church "values and promotes . . . every authentic form of culture and seeks to maintain communication and dialogue with culture." "Culture," the Pontiff said, "ought to cultivate man and each man and woman within the compass of an integral and full humanism. . . . Culture has the essential aim of promoting the being of man and of providing him with the tools necessary to the development of his individual and social being."[19]

IV. Call to Action

32. From all of this we can see emerging a guide for the Christian. The believer, who is also a product of history, culture, and environment, is in contact with unfamiliar cultures, ethnic differences, and the many disparate customs and qualities of his or her neighbor. These are neither threatening nor offensive, for they express in their own context the legitimate aspirations of the human soul and its basic

---

[17]*Gaudium et Spes*, 59 (Documents of Vatican II).
[18]*Origins* 10, 4, p. 62.
[19]N.C. News, July 1, 1980, par. 1.

dignity. For all of these differences we should seek acceptance and understanding, since they represent deep stirrings of the human heart and beat to the pulse of the common heart of all.

33. We, therefore, summon our Catholic people, and all others as well, to welcome wholeheartedly the new expressions of ethnic diversity, not as a sign of division, but one of recognition of the richness of the American heritage. This means the encouragement of scholars to new studies in this area, the patronage of the ethnic arts, the appreciation of proper liturgical expressions, the recognition of pluralism as a fact of American life, and the educational effort to make the new generation aware of its total heritage.

34. We call upon neighborhoods—a traditional American expression of ethnicity—to acknowledge their wide and diverse ethnic loyalties, excluding undesirable isolation or rivalries. The open character of neighborhood development, very often what we call its "League of Nations" quality, is itself a source of strong cultural vitality. Our neighborhoods are not enclaves of shame or disparagement but authentic expressions of the history of our people as a nation.

35. We urge all Americans to accept the fact of religious and cultural pluralism, not as an historic oddity or a sentimental journey into the past, but as a vital, fruitful, and challenging phenomenon of our society. Americanization does not call for the abandonment of cultural differences but for their wider appreciation. We solicit the help of all thoughtful citizens of this republic in an effort to blot out of public and private life the stains of ethnic prejudice and discrimination. This element becomes all the more despicable when linked, as it too often has been, to anti-Catholic "nativism."

36. We ask that the public and private sectors give consideration to those ethnic groups who have too long been unrepresented in large and important areas of American life. With special urgency we call public attention to the continued immigration of the large Hispanic population, one of the oldest ethnic American groups, which is just now beginning to receive appropriate recognition.

V. Church Agenda

37. Within the Church herself we have a task set before us that cannot be taken lightly.

38. Parishes must not fear to be centers of cultural as well as spiritual inspiration, relating the customs and folkways of people to contemporary gospel teaching. This may often require special language provisions in catechesis and worship. Insensitivity on the pastoral level can alienate even the most devout.

39. Church organizations, whether local or national, should encourage participation in the wide range of opportunities offered by the ethnic diversity of the People of God in our country.

40. Church schools and Catholic education on every level must strive to make Catholics more conscious of the broad range of cultural experience available in our multiple Church traditions. This should not be limited to history, but related also to contemporary ethnic expression.

41. In the life of the Christian family an opportunity of singular importance is provided for the inculcation of values in the developing minds of the young. Here parents can eradicate stereotyping and develop appreciation of the principle of human diversity, which will be enriched by the growing experience of the youthful mind.

42. Liturgical life, so fruitful a vehicle for understanding, should reflect the Catholic traditions of the whole human family, helping to promote the community of all. The feast of Pentecost itself might appropriately suggest both liturgy and celebration acknowledging and rejoicing in the variety of ethnic riches.

43. Seminaries must take special care to include the history of the ethnic communities and their cultures in the training of young men for the ministries, as already directed by the Conference of Bishops.[20] Moreover, the seminary environment itself must be such as to include broad ethnic appreciation. In this connection, the several religious orders, which have so effectively supported ethnic identity in the seminaries, should be lauded for their fidelity and foresight. Eastern Catholic Churches—their origins and Church practices—can also be made familiar in the Western Church, even where certain disciplines and theological insights of these "sister Churches" may appear unusual.

44. Leadership positions in Church life should be open to those of all ethnic backgrounds who are canonically eligible and qualified. The Spirit blows when and where He wills.

45. We remind social service agencies, public and private, and human service systems generally, of their obligations to respect the diverse traditions of their clientele and be responsive to their special needs. All aspects of public policy should be attentive to these concerns. We call attention, in particular, to juvenile justice and criminal justice systems to bring understanding to their responsibilities under the law.

46. Aware of the powerful effect of the mass media, we encourage a wider public expression of Church life in all its forms, with a special emphasis on pluralism within the Church as it manifests itself in the arts, literature, and devotional practice. We must censure the practice of stereotyping ethnic groups in a negative and often offensive manner. Even when this is done for humor and entertainment, it betrays a lack of sensitivity which society should not accept.

47. A thoughtful development of the relationship of theology and cultural pluralism, already discussed at meetings of the Catholic Theological Society of America, should be further promoted. We com-

---

[20]*Program of Priestly Formation*, 1976, 542-557 and *passim*.

mend and encourage new studies in this area which cannot fail to give depth and meaning to public dialogue and understanding.

48. The Great Seal of the United States expresses an American ideal that should inspire us in its motto: *"E Pluribus Unum"*—out of many, one. This motto, recognizing national unity out of widest diversity, reflects the reality that our nation is a nation of immigrants. The original inhabitants of America, a small but important percentage of our present population, are the only nonimmigrant peoples among us. We respect, then, the best of our history as a nation when we honor the motto of our Great Seal, and we respect also the highest traditions of our faith when we seek one human family under God.

49. It is evident that in these few pages we have only touched upon a multifaceted question which should be subject to additional research and reflective study by American scholars. The many authors and commentators now writing in this field must be supported in their endeavors and urged on to new ones. For our part, we call the attention of our people to this growing national concern and enlist their interest.

VI. Conclusion

50. We refer once again to the words of Vatican Council II for the perspective in which we should plan and proceed:

> The social order and its development must unceasingly work to the benefit of the human person if the disposition of affairs is to be subordinate to the personal realm and not contrariwise, as the Lord indicated when He said that the Sabbath was made for man, and not man for the Sabbath.

> This social order requires constant improvement. It must be founded on truth, built on justice, and animated by love; in freedom it should grow every day toward a more humane balance. An improvement in attitudes and widespread changes in society will have to take place if these objectives are to be gained.

> God's Spirit, who with a marvelous providence directs the unfolding of time and renews the face of the earth, is not absent from this development. The ferment of the gospel, too, has aroused and continues to arouse in man's heart the irresistible requirements of his dignity.

> Coming down to practical and particularly urgent consequences, this Council lays stress on reverence for man; everyone must consider his every neighbor without exception as another self, taking into account first of all his life and the means necessary to living it with dignity, so as not to imitate the rich man who had no concern for the poor man Lazarus.[21]

---

[21]*Gaudium et Spes*, 26, 27 (Documents of Vatican II).

51. In this spirit the Church in the United States has sought to find her way since her earliest days on this continent. The Church record during the days of mass immigration was a glorious chapter. Despite the fact that Catholics were in a minority and personnel and fiscal resources were minimal, the Church attended to the spiritual and religious needs of her immigrant flock and often to socioeconomic needs as well. The effort, though heroic, was not everywhere perfect—not in every situation adequate to the demands of the new peoples. Yet there is no institution among us whose records can compare in size and extent to this effort. The national or language churches, as we have mentioned, are monuments to the Church's dedication to the unity and diversity of Americans.

52. Presently we note that this work continues—extended to refugees and displaced persons after World War II, and since that time with Cambodians, Vietnamese, Chinese, Koreans, Cubans, Haitians, and so many others. We therefore summon our people to follow their own most noble traditions now and in the time ahead as our work continues under the full inspiration of the ideals of God and country.

53. Our thoughts turn, in closing, to the familiar words of the Master speaking to us from the pages of the Gospels concerning our neighbor.[22] Indeed, has not the phrase, "the Good Samaritan," passed into all the languages of the world! For the Christian there is no stranger, no one so different in origin or ways that such a one can be set outside of the true human family. We accept men and women for *what* they are, created and redeemed by God; we accept them *as* they are, the product of history and culture. In them and through them, God's grace works among us.

54. And so with resolute heart, and under the guidance of the Spirit, let us turn our face to the work of examination and action that lies before us "asking his blessing and his help, but knowing that here on earth God's work must truly be our own."[23]

---

[22]Mt 19:19 (The New American Bible, USCC. 1972).
[23]*Presidential Inaugural Address*, January 1961.

Resolution on the Iranian Crisis

A Resolution Passed by the
United States Catholic Conference

May 1980

1. Our pastoral concern for our country, which includes the obligation to speak about the moral implications of public issues, prompts us to address the Iranian crisis. We wish first to express our prayerful concern for the hostages and their families. We have urged and will continue to urge prayer in our churches for their welfare and safe return.

2. To the families of those killed in the rescue mission we offer our sympathy; but even more we voice our respect for the courage and selflessness of those who died for their fellow citizens. Their heroism will serve always as an inspiration for the sacrifices we all might be asked to make to resolve this national crisis. It is our prayer that their deaths will not be in vain but will remind us of the tragedy that war is.

3. We recognize that we are faced with a situation of escalating danger. The essence of the danger is that the use of military force in Iran has the potential of spreading throughout the Persian Gulf, raising in turn the spectre of superpower confrontation.

While we recognize the grievances of the Iranian people in the light of our shared history, we nonetheless condemn, on religious, moral and legal grounds, the taking and holding of hostages.

4. We understand and share the frustration of the American people over the repeated thwarting of our President's patient and restrained negotiations to free the hostages from imprisonment. The teaching of the Church on peace, however, affirms that resort to military force is not justifiable when other courses of action are available. It is our conviction that resorting to military force, in the present circumstances, would not meet the moral criteria of prudence and justice.

Resolution on Cuban and Haitian Refugees

A Resolution Passed by the
United States Catholic Conference

May 1980

1. Once again the United States faces an urgent challenge to its capacity for humanitarian response to the situation of people in need—the plight of the "boat people" from Cuba and Haiti.

2. Only a year ago, Americans were appalled by the policies of other countries which drove Southeast Asian boat people from their shores or granted them only marginal landing rights. Now we confront a parallel situation in our own hemisphere.

3. We request President Carter immediately to grant asylum and permanent residence to the boat people of both Cuba and Haiti who are seeking asylum and safety on our southern shores.

4. We assure the administration, as we have in the past, that the Church will do its utmost to provide resettlement opportunities, including employment and housing, for these people. The dimensions of this human tragedy are so great that it will require a national effort, so that the full burden of caring for the Cubans and Haitians will not fall on one section of our country.

5. The measure of the Church's concern, like the measure of its effectiveness, is the living example of over 175,000 Southeast Asians and over 500,000 Cubans whom the Church has helped to resettle already.

6. There is need for an immediate response to provide for our Haitian and Cuban brothers and sisters who are daily risking their lives in their search for security and freedom.

Statement on Tubal Ligation

*A Statement Issued by the National Conference
of Catholic Bishops*

July 3, 1980

Since we note among Catholic health care facilities a certain confusion in the understanding and application of authentic Catholic teaching with regard to the morality of tubal ligation as a means of contraceptive sterilization (cf. nos. 18, 20, *Ethical and Religious Directives for Catholic Health Facilities*) the National Conference of Catholic Bishops makes the following clarification:

(1) The traditional teaching of the Church as reaffirmed by the Sacred Congregation for the Doctrine of the Faith on March 13, 1975 clearly declares the objective immorality of contraceptive (direct) sterilization even if done for medical reasons.

(2) The principle of totality does not apply to contraceptive sterilization and cannot be used to justify it.

(3) Formal cooperation in the grave evil of contraceptive sterilization, either by approving or tolerating it for medical reasons, is forbidden and totally alien to the mission entrusted by the Church to Catholic health care facilities.

(4) The reason for justifying material cooperation as described in the NCCB Commentary on the SCDF response refers not to medical reasons given for the sterilization but to grave reasons extrinsic to the case. Catholic health care facilities in the United States complying with the *Ethical and Religious Directives* are protected by the First Amendment from pressures intended to require material cooperation in contraceptive sterilization. In the unlikely and extraordinary situation in which the principle of material cooperation seems to be justified, consultation with the Bishop or his delegate is required.

(5) The local Ordinary has responsibility for assuring that the moral teachings of the Church be taught and followed in health care facilities which are to be recognized as Catholic. In this important matter there should be increased and continuing collaboration between the Bishop, health care facilities and their sponsoring communities. Local conditions will suggest the practical structures necessary to insure this collaboration.

(6) The NCCB profoundly thanks the many physicians, administrators and personnel of Catholic health care facilities who faithfully maintain the teaching and practice of the Church with regard to Catholic moral principles.

Pastoral Letter on Marxist Communism

A Pastoral Letter Issued by the
National Conference of Catholic Bishops

November 12, 1980

Preamble

1. Our Holy Father, John Paul II, has stressed incessantly the responsibility which bishops have to be teachers in the Church. To fulfill this mandate, our teaching must be rooted in the Word of God, shaped by the tradition of the Church, and responsive to the questions, issues, and currents of thought which move the spirit, the intellects, and hearts of men and women of our day.

2. In this Pastoral Letter we have chosen to address a topic of the highest import for the Church in our time, the relationship of Christian faith and Marxism. We are conscious of the complexity of this topic, of the different forms the issue takes in the diverse cultures of the world, and of the fact that several other bishops' conferences and the Holy Father himself have addressed this issue. Even though the question does not appear to have the urgency or interest in the United States that it has in other parts of the world, Marxism nevertheless challenges us intellectually, morally, and politically. Above all, it challenges the content and the practice of our faith.

3. We are not blind to the horrendous violations of human rights perpetrated in the name of communism or the invasions of the territorial integrity of sovereign nations. Previous documents of the USCC such as the one concerning religious liberty in Eastern Europe (May 4, 1977) have addressed some of these crimes.[1]

---

[1] "Today, human rights in many places in the world are severely restricted. While no nation is faultless in the defense and promotion of human rights, we are obliged to note two recent statements by episcopal conferences—the bishops of West Germany and of Poland—deploring the denial of the human right to religious liberty in Eastern Europe. . . .

It is especially at the level of the individual believer that the infringement of the person's human right to practice his or her religion is most insidious, since in all of the East European countries atheism is supported by the full apparatus of the state. For example, membership in a Christian community disqualifies one from becoming a teacher, a civil servant or an official in the government. In some situations, even visits to the sick and the administration of the sacraments to the dying require prior official permits. Conditions are especially severe in Lithuania where the Church is subjected to constant and intense persecutions" (USCC Statement on *Religious Liberty in Eastern Europe*; Washington, 1977).

4.   But the present document deals with the theory and practice of Marxism/Leninism as they generally affect the Christian view of life and the respect for human rights in our time. It deliberately avoids discussing political, economic, and military actions taken by Marxist regimes in various parts of the globe, however important we consider these actions to be.

5.   Through this Pastoral Letter the U.S. bishops wish to take a stand on a question that preoccupies a sizable portion of the American intellectual community and that daily confronts millions of people all over the world. Such a document is, by its very nature, forced to consider the issues in their full complexity and cannot be satisfied with blanket endorsements or condemnations. In adopting this method we follow the example set by the Holy See in recent encyclicals as well as by Catholic hierarchies in other countries in pastoral letters on Marxist communism.[2] In fulfillment of our teaching ministry to guide and strengthen the faith of the People of God, we present this letter, not as a polemical or political tract, but as a Christian reflection on the Marxist world view. We hope to have shed light rather than heat on questions which touch the thought and practice of Christian faith, and we urge you to study this document in the spirit in which it was written.

Introduction

6.   In its Pastoral Constitution on the Church in the Modern World, *Gaudium et Spes*, Vatican II admonishes the Christians of our time: "It is the task of the whole people of God, particularly of its pastors and theologians, to listen to and distinguish the many voices of our times and to interpret them in the light of the divine Word" (*Gaudium et Spes*, #44). One of the most powerful voices is undoubtedly that of Marxist communism. Radically secular in origin and belligerently antireligious in its development, it once drew its followers exclusively from dechristianized circles in our society. Recently, however, Communist leaders in Italy, Spain, France, and some parts of Latin America have begun to invite religious believers to join their movement

---

[2]A recent editorial in the influential Catholic monthly *Civilta Catolica* (October 18, 1980) interprets the position of the Church as follows: "The church condemns the atheism, historical and dialectic materialism, the class struggle, the reduction of man to 'homo economicus' (an economic being), the purely earthly quest for 'heaven on earth'. . . . But it does not condemn values like the aspiration to justice and the overcoming of social and economic situations which allow the exploitation of men by men; the aspiration to create a more just and fraternal society; the consideration in which work is held and, even more, the preeminence given to the poorest classes of society; the commitment to fight for the betterment of social conditions of humanity; the importance which economic and social structures have in creating and maintaining great human masses in conditions of inferiority and underdevelopment."

while fully maintaining their religious convictions. Many, including priests and religious, have given credence to the promise of ideological freedom in the socialist society of the future. With this conciliatory policy, Western Communist leaders resume earlier attempts to persuade believers of the compatibility of their party policy with Christian faith.[3]

7.   At the same time, Communist governments in Eastern Europe, particularly in Poland and Hungary, in order to avoid paralyzing conflicts, have entered into dialogue with the Church. A certain *modus vivendi* with the secular authorities has emerged that allows the Church to exercise its pastoral functions in return for restraining from all political intervention. The Holy See itself has for some years been pursuing political agreements with various Eastern European governments—the so-called Ostpolitik—in order to secure for Christians at least a modicum of religious freedom.

8.   The new situation confronts millions of Christians with momentous decisions. Recent papal teaching, from *Pacem in Terris* to *Redemptor Hominis*, has reexamined again and again the constantly shifting attitude of Marxist parties toward the Church. National episcopates in countries where the matter requires immediate attention have already issued pastoral letters to guide the faithful in an increasingly difficult choice. We in the United States have not felt the practical urgency of the new encounter. Marxism in our country presents mainly an intellectual movement most visible in scholarly publications. The existing Communist parties seem to exercise but little attraction on North American Christians. Even so, we must not remain indifferent to what has become a vital and daily concern to a very large portion of the human race.

9.   We therefore wish to convey our pastoral reflections on this and to re-examine both the sources and the recent developments of the Marxist movement in the light of the Christian tradition. It is, of course, impossible to take account of all the variants in Marxist theory

---

[3]In his historical address of October 26, 1937, the secretary of the French Communist party, Maurice Thorez, had reminded Catholics that Leo XIII had denounced economic injustice "in almost the same terms as Marx's *Communist Manifesto* had used half a century earlier," while his successor, Pius XI, on the fortieth anniversary of that encyclical, had criticized "economic liberalism" as strongly as any communist ever had. Why, then, should Christians not join Marxists in their struggle for a better world, if they were given assurances of full freedom of conscience as well as the right to grant their children a religious education? At that time (1937) the prevailing policies in the Soviet Union cast some doubts upon the sincerity of promises of religious tolerance made by a party that remained unconditionally loyal to Stalin's regime. The climate of freedom in which the Eurocommunist leaders repeat their invitations today gives their promises a far greater credibility. In 1976 George Marchais, Thorez's successor, pointed out that the religious situation in France would be intrinsically different from that of Eastern European countries where the Church, he claimed, had been traditionally connected with the old order. "We will never declare war on religion," he promised.

and practice, significant as they may be. But, as Pope Paul VI reminded us, it would be "illusory and dangerous" to forget "the intimate link which binds [these variants] together" (*Octogesima Adveniens*, #34). What is needed, above all, is the kind of cautious discernment that allows us to recognize what unites and what separates the two principal world views of our age. Can a Christian in any way cooperate with the Marxist movement without jeopardizing the integrity of his or her faith?

10. A first distinction, indispensable for correctly evaluating the Marxist movement in its origins as well as in its later development, is the one between theory and practice. John XXIII alluded to its significance when he wrote in *Pacem in Terris*:

> Neither can false philosophical teachings regarding the nature, origin and destiny of the universe and of man be identified with historical movements that have economic, social, cultural or political ends, not even when these movements have originated from those teachings and have drawn and still draw therefrom (#159).

11. Clearly Marxism is less a logically coherent theory than a system of action of which theory forms an essential but subordinate part.[4] The political and revolutionary activity of the working class toward social-economic emancipation determines both practical value and theoretical truth. The theoretical principles of the movement are based upon an historical practice. Rather than a philosophy, then, Marxism is, by its own account, a social movement that, inevitably though freely, emerges from the economic conditions of industrial capitalism, and that, in the course of its development, creates the theoretical structures necessary to legitimate and support its practical activity. Such at least was Marx's concept of the social struggle.

12. Meanwhile, however, Leninist Marxism, especially in countries where it has gained control over the state, has developed a set of principles that, far from following actual practice, rather dictates it in all areas of social and cultural life, according to the interpretation of a single authoritative body—the Communist party. Yet since those principles have been abstracted from Marx's and Engles's writings, these writings, despite their different perspective, remain the principal basis for a discussion of the compatibility of the Christian and the Marxist world views.

---

[4] Paul VI likewise distinguishes 1) the active practice of class struggle; 2) the exercise of political and economic power under the direction of a single party; 3) a socialist ideology based on historical materialism; 4) a rigorous scientific method of examining social and political reality (*Octogesima Adveniens*, #33-34).

I. Two World Views

13. That the world view underlying the Marxist movement differs profoundly from the Christian conception of life requires no argument. The question is, rather, whether the difference is so fundamental as to exclude any meaningful dialogue. To decide this we must compare the two views on such crucial issues as the nature of man, of his alienation in the present, and his redemption in the future.

A. Marxist and Christian Humanism

14. Marxism, as well as Christianity, claims to be rooted in a respect for the dignity of the human person. Yet, clearly, the two conceptions of humanism are radically different. In the Christian vision the person is *sacred*. The relation to God constitutes an integral part of the person's very being. To be a person, to the Christian, is to be a living image of God, to be intrinsically dependent on a transcendent reality, to manifest a divine presence in the world. In short, to the Christian, the person is a living relation to God. This divine character of the person constitutes both the content and the principal effect of God's revelation in Christ. Such a transcendent dimension is obviously absent from a Marxist view of human nature. Strangely enough, some well-meaning Christians today tend to question Marx's overt and unambiguous atheism. Marx, they say, rejected only "idols," that is, spurious symbols of transcendence; the religious dimension itself was never at stake in his polemics with traditional faiths. Such a presentation misleadingly oversimplifies the case.

15. It is true enough that the belligerent atheism which prevails in most Communist countries cannot claim Marx's authority. Indoctrination or practice directly aimed at the suppression of religious beliefs conflicts with the general trend of his theory. Marx taught that the revolutionary ought to direct his activity at the social situation which religion merely *expresses* and attempts to justify. To attack religion itself rather than the conditions which produce it, is both ineffective and wrong according to Marx. Religion mythologizes human alienation: it does not *constitute* it. The emancipation of the person takes more than abolishing religion.

16. What should be attacked are the social-economic conditions that drive people to religion. Indeed, the presence of the religious illusion is a living protest against an inhuman life. In an essay of his early period Marx uses the famous expression that religion is the opium of the people. Yet he adds immediately: "The abolition of religion as the illusory happiness of men is a demand for real happiness. The call to abandon their illusions about their condition is *the call to abandon* *a condition which requires illusions."*[5]

17. Marxists have pointed out that this is not an outright rejection of religion. As an expression of human misery and an implicit protest against it, religion criticizes the structure of society. It raises the right questions, even though it offers the wrong answers.[6] Even this benign interpretation of Marx's position fails to provide a legitimate basis for the continuance of religion in the future society. Indeed, it does not even justify its present existence. For in Marx's view, the religious way of questioning weakens the oppressed's resistance to their present condition by directing their hope toward a future, otherworldly happiness.

18. So, even as an expression of social protest, religion can only slow down the advent of the Communist society. The first step toward a solution, therefore, would consist in abandoning the wrong manner of posing the problem. Yet the abandonment of religion is merely a precondition and not, as Marx's atheist friends believe, the solution itself. Communism is much more than atheism, even though atheism is a preliminary requirement for it. "Communism begins from the outset with atheism; but atheism is at first far from being *communism;* indeed, that atheism is still mostly an abstraction."[7]

19. It is small comfort to religion that Marx considers it an authentic cry of distress if he does not take seriously the content of this cry. For Marx religion is a symptom of social disease, not an articulate symbol. Whatever truth the symptom contains will disappear with the disease. Marx's distaste for speculative atheism is due, not to a more open attitude toward religion, but to his conviction that such an atheism misinterprets the origin of the believer's illusion. Atheism attempts to cure the symptoms without eradicating the disease, namely, man's social-economic condition. Theism will never be compatible with a free society, according to Marx, yet neither is atheism sufficient to produce such a society. To unmask the religious "deception," we must be clear about the question: What causes man to deceive himself religiously? No atheist philosophers ever seriously attempted to answer that question. If they had, "the critique of heaven would have been transformed into a critique of earth."[8]

---

[5]"Introduction to a Critique of Hegel's Philosophy of Right" (1884). The same metaphor had been used by other writers before him, not always in a pejorative sense. Rousseau speaks of religion as a sedative that should be used with moderation in *Julie, ou la nouvelle Héloise* (Bk VI, #8), while Hölderlin writes of the religion of the philistine: "His so-called religion has no more effect on him than an opiate." In an anonymous pamphlet written by Marx's friend Bruno Bauer with possible collaboration by Marx himself, the same metaphor appears.

[6]French party secretary George Marchias comments: "Religion here is not merely the expression of the distress of the poor; it also protests against that distress" *Communistes et Chrétiéns* (Paris: 1976) p. 31. Also: *Roger Garaudy: From Anathema to Dialogue,* trans. Luke O'Neill (New York: Herder, 1966) pp. 89-90.

[7]Marx-Engels: *Collected Works* (New York: International Publishers, 1974) 3, p. 297.

[8]*Ibid.,* p. 176.

20. A full reappropriation of what man has alienated from himself cannot be achieved by a mere annulment of God, but only by an annulment of the social structures that produce the need for God. To be effective, atheism must be supported by Communist reform. "Atheism being the supersession [overcoming] of God is the advent of theoretical humanism, and communism as the supersession of private property is the vindication of real human life as man's possession and thus the advent of practical humanism."[9] Soon after he wrote these words, Marx found the definitive expression for his critique of religion. Henceforth, he would refer to religion as an *ideology*, that is, "an ideal expression of the ruling material relations," that has no meaning or development of its own, but merely reflects the material conditions of production.

21. Every ideology is characterized: 1) by a dependence upon the more elementary forms of consciousness that direct economic production and its social structures; 2) by an illusory consciousness of independence that distinguishes it from a true, scientific consciousness (such as Marx's own social critique claims to be). It is this illusory character that makes religion intrinsically false. A critique of religion, then, should consist above all in a critique of the illusory consciousness in general—not in a critique of particular dogmas or beliefs. As Marx later noted in the text in which he exposed this theory: "Religion is first and foremost consciousness of transcendence."[10]

22. Both in rationalist atheism and in religion, theoretical constructions have become detached from their real social basis. In Marx's view, speculative atheism, no less than religion, overlooks the *practical* origin of ideas, of the idea of God as well as of its own critique of it, and mistakes for independent, logical conclusions what, in fact, primarily reflects social conditions.[11]

23. But has Marx's outright rejection of speculative atheism not opened at least the possibility of a religious perspective? Before raising any hopes on this basis, we should consider that the same argument which disposes of speculative atheism also disposes of religion. Any mode of consciousness which fails to recognize that it is rooted in, and determined by, a particular social form of production, lacks the very basis of truth according to Marx. But in his religious attitude the believer claims to go beyond this social basis altogether. To Marx the person is both a "natural" and a social being that in the process of

---

[9] *Philosophical and Economic Manuscripts* (1844); in *Collected Works*, 3, p. 341.
[10] Marx-Engels: *Werke* (Berlin: Dietz Verlag, 1926) 3, p. 54.
[11] Of those "scientific" interpretations that fail to view religion in its social-economic setting, Marx wrote in a later edition of *Capital* I: "Any history of religion that makes abstraction of this material basis is itself not critical. It is, indeed, much easier to discover through analysis the earthly core of the misty formations of religion than to do the opposite, namely, to develop on the basis of the vital, real relations of life, their cloudy forms" Marx-Engels, *Werke*, 23, p. 392.

creating itself through its own productive activity brooks no interference from any transcendent source. Even the question, "How did man and nature originate?", is meaningless for him, since it assumes as nonexistent the very act from which all intelligible existence derives. The range of intelligibility does not extend beyond the human practice. Through its unpredictable and ever greater achievements, the human race constantly makes and remakes itself.

24. The theory developed by Marx's followers deviates considerably from this absolute primacy of concrete social and political action. They elevate materialism and atheism to the status of independent speculative principles. Thus for Engels and Plekhanov (an early Russian Marxist), religion is "bad science" that must be refuted rather than be left to wither away of its own accord (as Marx had held). With Lenin this theoretical struggle against religion adopted a virulent practical character. What Marx had considered a spontaneous side effect of unsatisfactory social conditions, Lenin regarded as a poison, deliberately administered for sinister social purposes by the bourgeois class. Thus Leninist communism took the harshly polemical attitude toward religion expressed in base, antireligious propaganda and in the innumerable harassments that have reduced the Church in most of Eastern Europe to a church of silence with no other voice but that of suffering.[12] Even in its early, more tolerant form, the Marxist attitude toward religion modeled itself after Prometheus, the mythical hero who attacked the gods and whose defiant words in Aeschylus' tragedy Marx placed as epitaph above his doctoral dissertation: "In one word, I hate all the gods. . . ."

25. The Christian vision has incorporated the relation to the transcendent which Marx so clearly rejected into its very concept of the person. Its humanism is vertically open: as a relation to God as well as to himself, man shapes his own destiny in dependence upon the God to whom he owes his origin as well as his entire creative activity.

B. Alienation and Sinfulness

26. As fundamental as his concept of self-creation is Marx's critique of a social-economic condition that in his view has estranged the person from an authentically human existence. According to Marx, bourgeois society has detached objects from the person's creative freedom. Giving preference to *having* over *being* has sacrificed genuine socialization to effective methods of exchanging products. Already in his early writings (Paris, 1844) Marx had defined "alienation" as a social condition derived from a particular mode of production that separates the workers from the fruit of their work and, consequently, also from their own vital activity expressed in this production. Under

---

[12]Cf., Pope Paul VI: *Ecclesiam Suam*, #61.

those circumstances industrial labor debases the person instead of humanizing him, as work should do. Rather than expanding the person's cultural and social horizon, it remands him to the kind of primitive struggle for survival that excludes any genuine relation to others. In his early days, Marx saw this alienation institutionalized and perpetuated in the unconditional right to possess and acquire private property. Later he stressed other aspects of what he considered capitalism's single-minded concern with maximizing the exchange of commodities. Thus he denounced a division of labor controlled by productivity regardless of its ill effects upon the producer. In *Capital*, Marx refers to a civilization in which commodities have become ends instead of means by the religious term "fetishism."

27. Through the enormous interest generated by the rediscovery of Marx's early writings, his concept of alienation has entered the mainstream of social thought. Nearly every contemporary critique of our culture has incorporated it in some way or other. The popularity of the term is due to the fact that it expresses, though with increasing vagueness, a serious flaw in the very orientation of our culture. Even our Holy Father, Pope John Paul II, in his first encyclical, *Redemptor Hominis*, partly appropriates Marx's critique when he writes:

> The man of today seems ever to be under threat from what he produces, that is to say from the result of the work of his hands and, even more so, of the work of his intellect and the tendencies of his will. All too soon, and often in an unforeseeable way, what this manifold activity of man yields is not only subjected to "alienation," in the sense that it is simply taken away from the person who produces it, but rather it turns against man himself, at least in part, through the indirect consequences of its effects returning on himself. It is or can be directed against him. This seems to make up the main chapter of the drama of present-day human existence in its broadest and universal dimension (#15).

28. It is impossible to deny the inhumanity of a system that aims exclusively at producing as much exchange value as possible, without any regard for the ultimate effect its products may have upon the workers, the consumers, and the natural environment.

29. But a radical social critique must also confront the question: What induces people to adopt attitudes that result in such destructive social-economic systems of production? The existential sadness hidden in this question does not vanish with the optimistic predictions of a better future. Those who adopt such attitudes and created such structures were persons endowed with the same inclinations as we are and future generations will be. No structural revolution can entirely cure a disease that is man himself. It is to this deeper distortion, this disposition to the inhuman and even the antihuman, that Revelation addresses itself. The Christian faith, as most religions, has always interpreted the fundamental estrangement of the person from his or her humanity as an alienation from God.

30. Its vivid awareness of a deeper, more substantial evil must not be interpreted as a lack of concern for the immediate, social-economic problems that beset the lives of millions of our contemporaries. For almost a century, papal encyclicals have dealt more with questions of social justice than with any other topic. Again and again the supreme pontiffs have warned against the uninhibited pursuit of economic gain. Already Leo XIII, in his momentous encyclical *Rerum Novarum* (1891), asserted that work should not be regarded as a mere commodity, since it is the only source from which men draw their livelihood (#34). Moreover, unregulated competition, the Pope adds, threatens the person's dignity and elementary well-being. Even private property, though a natural right, must not be used without consideration for the welfare of others. Forty years later Pius XI repeated those principles with even more emphasis in *Quadragesimo Anno* (1931). Pope John XXIII in *Mater et Magistra* adapted them to the new, intensively socialized world of our own day, insisting upon the priority of the common good not only in a particular region or nation but in the world community as a whole. In a *unified* world, aid to less economically developed regions is not merely desirable—it is a social duty. In *Populorum Progressio* Pope Paul VI made an exceptionally strong appeal to the social conscience of our contemporaries, stating that "the common good at times demands the expropriation of an estate if it happens that some estates impede the common prosperity either on account of their vast size or because of their small or negligible cultivation, or cause extreme poverty to the population or bring serious harm to the country" (#24).

31. These documents unambiguously show how deeply the Church has been concerned with the social problems of our time. In no way do they detract from Marx's merit in having clearly, though not always correctly, formulated the problems resulting from the discrepancy between economic development and social structures in an advanced industrial society. One need not agree with Marx's interpretation of capitalism, and even less with the methods he advocates for accelerating social change, in order to recognize the major significance of his words and of the movement he created in drawing worldwide attention to the urgency of the social question.

32. On the other hand, any interpretation that restricts the human predicament to a single, well-circumscribed problem, soluble through structural changes alone, is bound to be dangerously one-sided. Even to expect the solution of all human suffering or all social justice from revolution or social reform is to prepare oneself for bitter disillusionment. Moreover, such a view is likely to disregard entire areas that are essential to an integral human development. In its very concrete concern for the "wretched of the earth," the Church has always refused to reduce its message to the single task, however crucial, of creating social justice and harmony. In any human "alienation," including the social one, the Church insists on searching out and addressing the even more fundamental estrangement of the person from the source of all good. She considers all negative experiences of the human condition expressions of our separation from God—our sinfulness.

33. By no coincidence was the earliest meaning of the term alienation religious: it referred to the person's estrangement from the sphere of Absolute Being. This awareness of a more general existential condition of alienation should not dispense the faithful from committing themselves to remedying with all possible means social-economic as well as all other forms of human suffering. Many Christians of the last centuries may well deserve the Marxist charge of a lack of serious social commitment. Yet their indolence is not supported by the principles of their faith. To acquaint oneself with the *authentic* Christian attitude, one should look at the heroic devotion to others displayed by the saints, not, or not exclusively, at the ever-present mediocrity of the ordinary. St. Frances Cabrini, St. Elizabeth Seton, St. Vincent de Paul, St. Peter Claver, St. John Bosco, as well as some heroic women and men in our own day, are social reformers as well as spiritual leaders. But they, and all who take Christ's precept of charity seriously, refuse to reduce the entire message of the Gospel to a call to social reform.

34. It is out of a more realistic awareness of a total condition that requires redemption, not out of a lack of social concern, that the Church rejects a revolutionary interpretation of salvation. Social revolution or reform is not sufficient to redeem the entire person. Our contemporaries have generally not been much disposed to consider their condition as affected by radical evil, and even less to interpret this evil in terms of sin. However pessimistic their outlook on the present state of affairs may be, most people's view of human nature appears amazingly optimistic. Throughout all the disasters of the modern age they have clung to a naive belief in technical and scientific progress, and even in an overall improvement of the human condition.

35. The teachings of the Church transcend such passing moods of the time. The Gospel, as Pope Paul VI wrote, does not yield to any illusions about the natural goodness of the person nor to any despairing resignation to the incurable corruption of human nature (*Ecclesiam Suam*, #61). Through the ages the Church has insisted that we live in an imperfect state from which only God's grace can redeem us. To those who witnessed the collapse of the ancient world with the demise of the Roman Empire, the Christian message sounded incredibly optimistic. To those living in recent centuries when history came to be equated with progress, the warning of fundamental sinfulness appeared gloomy. Today, in the aftermath of unprecedented wars in which millions were slaughtered, and at a time when the impact of the technology that continued to nurture the belief in progress has become dubious in many of its achievements and prospects, a more sober state of mind, once again, invites us to question the uncritical optimism of the recent past.

36. In that light we are no more disposed to believe that social-economic reform than that technical inventiveness can cure all the ills of the human condition. We repeat, the more realistic view of human nature expressed in the Christian message conveys no mandate to inertia. The Beatitudes of the Sermon on the Mount, the model of Christ's own poverty and love of the poor, as well as the countless women and men who in each of the twenty centuries of Christianity have dedicated their lives to the assistance of the destitute, the care of the sick, and education of the children without allowing themselves as much as the joy of a personal home—these are eloquent witnesses enough of Christ and his Church's real and practical concern for the downtrodden.

37. Even now dedicated Christians are daily risking their lives in some areas of the globe for the sake of gaining some elementary social justice for their brothers and sisters. But they did so and they do so in a constant awareness of that deeper need for salvation of which the Gospel speaks. Without this transcendent perspective, social experiments all too easily turn into power structures that, unconcerned about the individual, generate more human misery than they relieve.

C. Marxist Eschatology and Christian Hope

38. But Marxism is more than a critique of the present: it offers, to the poor and the humble of this world, a confident prospect of hope. Underneath the appearances of a closed economic theory, Marxism hides a vision of an ever-expanding future in which gradually all human faculties will be allowed to develop their limitless potential.[13] Liberated from the present social-economic oppression, we will uninhibitedly develop our humanity. This ideal of human emancipation beyond anything we can conceive today has incited thousands of Marxists to sacrifice their lives for the anticipated well-being of later generations. Some have seen in this powerful vision of an ideal future an unavowed religious Messianism, others a secularized eschatology.[14]

---

[13]In the preparatory notes for what was to become *Capital*, Marx wrote: "When the limited bourgeois form is stripped away, what is wealth other than the universality of individual needs, capacities, pleasures, productive forces, etc., created through universal exchange? The full development of human mastery over forces of nature, those of so-called nature as well as of humanity's own nature? The absolute working out of his native potentiality with no presupposition other than the previous historic development, which makes this totality of development, i.e., the development of all human powers as such the end in itself, not as measured on a *predetermined* yardstick" *Grundrisse* (New York: Vintage, 1973) p. 488.

[14]Pope Pius XI referred to it as "a false Messianic idea" (*Divini Redemptoris*, #8).

39. It is undoubtedly this "spiritual" character that accounts for much of Marxism's uncommon appeal and that distinguishes it from all other political movements of our time. From the beginning Marx's theory has been a powerful catalyst of mankind's utopian aspirations. The religious idea of the poor, who through their suffering would in the end bring redemption to all the people, forcefully combined with the dialectic of history, undoubtedly played a significant role in the Bolshevik revolution. Today even Marxist thinkers have come to recognize the religious sources of their vision of the future and some have attributed a unique social significance to what they consider to be the utopian nature of religion. Only the bold eschatological visions of Judaism and Christianity are, in their opinion, sufficiently detached from the bonds of the present to give form and shape to the aspirations of their own revolutionary ideals.[15]

40. Yet precisely as a spiritual phenomenon, Marxism, for all its clear affinities, stands at the opposite side of Christianity. The Marxist ideal of a surpassing future intrinsically differs from an object of Christian hope—that goes beyond our future achievements as well as our present ones. Marxist transcendence is a form of *self*-transcending: it remains within the scope of human attainment. Christian transcendence consists in being assumed into an order totally beyond the reach of human endeavor. To the Marxist the ideal future contains more than man can conceive today, but not more than he will achieve tomorrow. To the Christian the promised future descends as a gift from God's mercy.

41. Atheistic socialism has been described as a heresy of Christianity. Today it has become its most insidious transformation. Its own earthly spirituality has seduced many a Christian to reinterpret the Kingdom of God into a worldly realm of social harmony. In fact, contemporary Marxism appears as the final stage of a secularizing movement that, begun more than two centuries ago, has gradually substituted the search for the absolute with the search for adequate social structures. Its secularized vision attempts to *comprehend* in its totality what the Christian view left open to transcendence.[16]

42. The seriousness of those differences should not allow the Christian community to neglect the lessons it can learn from its most redoubtable adversary. In his responsibility for shaping the future of humankind, the Marxist constantly reminds Christians that our transcendent perspective by no means dispenses us of a wholehearted commitment to the building of the City of Man. All too often Christians are faulted with a certain indifference toward earthly projects,

---

[15]Cf., for example, Ernst Bloch: *Das Prinzip Hoffnung* (Frankfurt: Suhrkamp Verlag, 1959) and Roger Garaudy: *From Anathema to Dialogue* (New York: Herder and Herder, 1966).

[16]Cf., Friedrich Gogarten: *Verhängnis und Hoffnung der Neuzeit* (1958) 1966; Hannah Arendt: *On Revolution*, p. 159-60; also Eric Weil: "Die Säkularisierung der Politik," in *Marxismusstudien* IV, pp. 144-162.

as if one could not fully count on us for radical social reform. The charge may be unfair, but the danger is real enough. Our hope in another life must not be allowed to seduce believers into neglecting our task in the present one.

II. Ends and Means

43. While the basic views of Christianity and Marxism on the concept of the person, the nature of the present, and the expectation of the future fundamentally disagree, they nevertheless retain a sufficient common basis for fruitful comparison. Regarding the means, however, which the Marxist movement has traditionally advocated for attaining its goals, its opposition to Christian practice appears irreconcilable. Communists have always considered a polarization between social classes necessary for achieving a more equitable social system. They consider revolution, even violent revolution, an indispensable instrument of social progress.[17] Such a polarization of class opposition is unacceptable to the Christian. Indeed, as Leo XIII pointed out (*Rerum Novarum*, #15), the Christian cannot even accept the assumption that one class is the natural enemy of any other class. To be sure, human beings tend to attribute what they consider evil or undesirable to another race, nation, class, or any group other than their own. But experience should inform them that such a view, though conveniently relieving their own moral responsibility, is seldom justified. Christians have a right and a duty to fight injustice. We may even have the duty to do so by strong means when all others fail, but we have no right to regard any person or group as a permanent enemy. Indeed, any movement that claims to achieve social harmony by means of unmitigated class struggle should naturally arouse our suspicions.

44. In refusing to accept class war as the only possible means for achieving social justice, the Christian does not deny the all too real existence of those actual class antagonisms that result from both a blatantly unequal distribution of material possessions and a tenacious, often violent defense by the possessing classes of their privileged position. As the Roman pontiffs have repeatedly emphasized in their recent encyclicals, and as accepted Catholic morality has always taught, whenever a person or a group is deprived of its basic necessities, expropriation is justified.[18] In such an extreme case the poor have not chosen social warfare: it is imposed upon them by the injus-

---

[17]Recently some Communist parties in Western Europe have claimed to abandon all nondemocratic means for obtaining and maintaining political power. This entirely new position still awaits the confirmation of an actual victory and a subsequent defeat at the ballot box.

[18]Cf., John Paul II: Address to Rural and Peasant People (Oaxaca), ORIGINS (VIII, #34) 8 February 1979; Paul VI: *Populorum Progressio*, #24.

tices of the possessors. Yet even then there is no sufficient ground to consider all those who belong to the ruling class as their irreconcilable enemies.

45. The recent guidelines of Pope John Paul II in Mexico and Brazil have clearly defined the rights but also the limits imposed upon the efforts of the oppressed to redress their wrongs; nor do these limits prevent Christians from *effectively* participating in the struggle for social justice. No one who has followed the recent social movement in Latin America can claim in good faith that the Church merely serves as an instrument for support of the established social-economic system.

46. The real difference between Marxists and Christians in the social struggle lies in the absence or presence of unconditional moral restrictions. Marx's social-economic concept of history admits no moral norms extrinsic to social practice. The point is not that Marxist theory rejects currently existing moral systems in favor of a different one. It simply declares any definition of good and evil by absolutes, that is, nonhistorical criteria, "ideological" reflections of a particular social state which the ruling class, in its attempt to preserve them, presents as absolute. "There is no recognition of any right of the individual in his relation to the collectivity; no natural right is accorded to human personality, which is a mere cogwheel in the communist system" (Pius XI: *Divini Redemptoris*, #10). Individual deeds must be judged exclusively by their conformity to what Marxists declare to be the inescapable course of history. The only "moral" attitude consists in actively cooperating to facilitate and accelerate the development of the social-economic laws of history. Immoral is what slows down this development, that is, concretely, what delays the working class from carrying out its historical mission of abolishing a classless society. No moral absolutes exist. No deeds are intrinsically evil—whether violent expropriation, incarceration, or even, when revolutionary action requires it, execution; all must be judged by their relation to ultimate social-economic "progress." Clearly such a theory of historical necessity undermines the very foundations of morality.[19] As history has shown abundantly, the practical consequences are equally disquieting.

47. We do not doubt the moral courage of many Marxist men and women. But the issue is not whether individual Marxists are more moral or less moral than others. The real issue is whether the theory itself allows a scale of values according to which certain acts are prescribed and others forbidden under all circumstances. Marxism has not developed the kind of moral absolutes that are essential to a Christian world view. Choices in matters of life and death cannot be left to any individual's interpretation of "the direction of history," even less to the wisdom of a political party. The memory of the

---

[19]Cf., the sharp analysis of Leszek Kolakowski, at that time a leading Marxist theoretician, in *Toward A Marxist Humanism* (New York: Grove Press, 1969) p. 122.

millions of persons deported, imprisoned, "liquidated" for political reasons, the continuing, constant violation of basic human rights, the conquest and submission of sovereign nations that characterize Soviet history prove that our concerns are not unfounded; nor has the contempt for human rights been restricted to the past nor to a single regime. These acts, it is often said, were temporary deviations in no way representative of Communist practice. But even if all political crimes could be dismissed as past errors (which they cannot), nothing in the system itself prevents them from occurring again. That the violent policy of the past has proven to be less effective than the more moderate one of the present, is not a sufficient ground for allaying our apprehensions.

48. The absolute priority of effective social action over theory may well, in the end, be Marxism's most questionable principle, for it denies the very possibility of a normative order beyond the one created in and through man's productive activity. Revolutionary praxis recognizes no pre-existing standards and admits no ulterior judgment. No natural bond restricts man's appropriating activity; no inherent structure calls for a specific mode of behavior; no natural law derives from the very *nature* of the person and of the world any rules of right action. Society and the natural world are no more than conditions of human activity: they have lost all normative character. The transforming process is the only absolute. Instead of answering the fundamental questions of ends and means, reason is reduced to a purely instrumental, technical role. Rather than *directing* activity, it merely functions as an instrument of that activity. It fails to question whether the goals of that activity are themselves rationally justified, because it lacks the norms for ultimate questions.

III. Practical Conclusions

49. At the end of this letter we return to the practical issues that confront Christians in their relation to Marxism: the possibility of cooperation, the extent of resistance. Religious beliefs are clearly incompatible with Marx's theory *as he developed* it. The self-sufficient dialectic between the person and nature, vertically closed, yet horizontally expanding without limits, excludes what is the very basis of the religious awareness, namely that dimension of experience by which we know ourselves to be passive and absolutely dependent. We possess no evidence that modern forms of Marxism have seriously modified their position on this crucial issue. Even George Marchais, the secretary-general of the French Communist party, repeated in the very address in which he invited Catholics to join him:

No tactical reason will ever induce us to water down what distinguishes our theory from others or to seek the impossible and illusory philosophical agreement. Communist theory is based upon scientific materialism.

50. Yet this inherent atheism should not discourage the educated Christian from seriously studying a theory which so overtly conflicts with his faith. As we have pointed out, much in Communist theory stems from our own religious heritage. Conversely, the impact of Marxism on faith *contains* a lesson which the Christian would do well to heed. For the secularism that Marxists so openly profess has imperceptibly affected our whole culture to the point where it influences its entire manner of thinking and valuing. Living in such a cultural climate, religious believers cannot but profit from openly confronting a secularism that has surreptitiously infiltrated our own lives.

51. Both Pope Paul in his encyclical, *Ecclesiam Suam* (#104), and Vatican II in *Gaudium et Spes* (#19, 20), declared atheism to be the most serious problem of our time. It affects believers as well as unbelievers and has become a general characteristic of modern culture. It is not sufficient, then, for the Christian to denounce atheism as the fundamental error which it undoubtedly is. We must also attempt to understand how it was able to convince so many of our contemporaries. In attempting to do so, Christians will have to confront their own often deep-seated secularism.

52. Must the opposition between Marxist theory and Christian doctrine always remain antagonistic? It is impossible to give a definitive answer to this question, because its essentially practical orientation forces Marxism to adapt its doctrine constantly to historical developments. Until now Marxist theory has positively excluded any kind of transcendence. But is it possible that in the future a change in praxis may result in an open humanism and a genuine respect for the other dimension of man's existence? Such a change would undoubtedly transform Marx's entire theory. Yet the possibility, unlikely as it appears today, cannot be ruled out. Theory in Marxism is never primary, and hence a change in practice would eventually force theory to follow.

53. Both Pope John XXIII and Pope Paul VI entertained the possibility that the Communist movement might undergo radical changes in its attitude toward religion, even though the doctrine has been defined in uncompromisingly atheist terms (*Pacem in Terris*, #54; *Ecclesiam Suam*, #109). Some political parties in Western Europe already claim to have accomplished a shift towards religious neutrality. In his October 1977 reply to Bishop Luigi Bettazzi's inquiry about the anticipated Communist policy toward the Church, Enrico Berlinguer, secretary of the Italian Communist party, stated:

> We use Marxism critically for teaching. We do not read it like an immutable text. Now from its large legacy of ideals and cultural orientation, you ask, have we fashioned a party that will impose a specific ideology and atheism in political life and in the State? My answer is "no".... We want to construct a lay and democratic State that is neither theist, atheist or antitheist.[20]

54. Thus far those professions of democratic openness have had no occasion to be tested. It is too early to decide whether Western Communist parties have decisively broken with the antireligious heritage of Marxism/Leninism or whether they are merely making a temporary concession to the political realities in which they operate. Yet we cannot but wonder whether Communist parties can abstract from their unique world view without losing their distinctive character altogether. At this time we follow the development of Eurocommunism with open-minded interest, hoping that at least it may constitute a lesser threat to the Church than the old-style communism. Meanwhile Leninist communism continues to dominate Eastern Europe and to display its traditional, unmitigated hostility toward any religion that refuses to submit itself entirely to the high authority of the government.

55. Still, the ideological outlook of the Communist movement is not the only factor that determines cooperation on the part of Christians. In some areas of universally human concern, collaboration with Communist governments or Communist parties has become a practical necessity. Due to the socialization which Pope John XXIII recognized as one of the distinctive characteristics of our time, modern life requires the cooperation of all men and women of good will. Citizens of a world united by unrestricted technology and instant communication, yet devoid of an effective international authority, have no choice but to seek common approaches and concerted action in attacking global problems.

56. Pope John XXIII devoted the entire pastoral section of his encyclical *Pacem in Terris* to this issue:

> Today the universal common good poses problems of worldwide dimensions, which cannot be adequately tackled or solved except by the efforts of public authorities endowed with a width of powers, structures and means of the same proportions; that is, of public authorities which are in a position to operate in an effective manner on a worldwide basis. The moral order itself, therefore, demands that such a form of public authority be established (*Pacem in Terris,* #137).

57. The Church recognizes the depth and dimensions of the ideological differences that divide the human race, but the urgent practical need for cooperative efforts in the human interest overrules these

---

[20]*Rinascita* (October 14, 1977) Comments in *L'Osservatore Romano* (October 17, 1977).

differences. Hence Catholic teaching seeks to avoid exacerbating the ideological opposition and to focus upon two problems requiring common efforts across the ideological divide: keeping the peace and empowering the poor. Conscious of the great delicacy and complexity of keeping the peace in the age of nuclear deterrence and prolifera- tion, the supreme pontiffs of the past four decades have, again and again, turned their attention to the question of war and peace. John XXIII insistently appealed:

> Justice, then, right reason and humanity urgently demand that the arms race should cease; that the stockpiles which exist in various countries should be reduced equally and simultaneously by the par- ties concerned; that nuclear weapons should be banned; and that a general agreement should eventually be reached about progressive disarmament and an effective method of control (*Pacem in Terris*, #112).

58. The efforts to control the proliferation of arms, however, ought to be a work of true cooperation, aimed at effective control of the nuclear arms race in all its dimensions. Moreover, the Christian's obligation to work for world peace does not require that he cease to recognize the right to autonomy of nations or national groups that have been illegitimately deprived of their freedom.

59. In *Populorum Progressio* Paul VI focused on the question of the global poor. In his words, the new name for peace is development. The ideological divide and the great danger of nuclear war has been principally an "East-West" question. The line between social wealth and poverty, in contrast, runs between North and South. Neither East nor West has responded adequately to the needs of the poor in the Southern hemisphere. Yet solidarity with the poor has become a duty for the richer nations of an interdependent world:

> Their obligations stem from a brotherhood that is at once human and supernatural, and take on a three-fold aspect: the duty of human solidarity—the aid that the rich nations must give to developing countries; the duty of social justice—the rectification of inequitable trade relations between powerful nations and weak nations; the duty of universal charity—the effort to bring about a world that is more human towards all men, where all will be able to give and receive without one group making progress at the expense of the other. The question is urgent, for on it depends the future of the civilization of the world (*Populorum Progressio*, #44).

60. It is in these two perspectives—maintenance of world peace and eradication of global poverty—that North American Catholics are most immediately confronted with the task of cooperation with Marxist regimes.

61. In engaging in practical and humanitarian dialogue, two points require their serious attention. First, in judging social and political situations in other parts of the world, they should avoid identifying the essential principles of the Christian doctrine of society with our own social-economic structures, and even more, with the theories of economic liberalism. In defending those structures or theories as the only acceptable ones to the Christian, they impose them in cases where they have, at best, a limited application and could, at worst, lead to grave social injustice. Indeed, Catholics should remain aware of the very severe judgment which the Roman pontiffs and various European hierarchies have passed on unrestricted economic liberalism.

62. In *Quadragesimo Anno* Pope Pius XI referred to the liberal theory of uncontrolled competition as a "poisoned spring" from which have originated all the errors of individualism. The French hierarchy, commenting upon the same pope's letter on communism, stated:

> By condemning the actions of communist parties, the Church does not support the capitalist regime. It is most necessary that it be realized that in the very essence of capitalism—that is to say, in the absolute value that it gives to property without reference to the common good or to the dignity of labor—there is a materialism rejected by Christian teaching.[21]

63. The second point is of a more practical nature. In past contacts with the poor of this world, North Americans, especially American Catholics, have traditionally displayed a generous attitude in sharing some of their wealth with others. Yet this exercise of traditional charity, in evidence even to our day, has often not been matched by a sensitivity to the deeper requirements of justice which touch the very political and economic structures through which the United States relates to the developing world.

64. In addition, our obsessive consumerism that leads us to use up a far greater share of the earth's resources than any other country in history, makes poorer nations look upon us as the wastrels of this world. It is not merely envy but rightful indignation about our spending habits that accounts for the little friendship we generally receive from the poorer nations. Such habits are particularly objectionable in the followers of Him who had no stone on which to rest His head. They greatly weaken our credibility in dealing with the poverty of the world. By indulging in such habits the most powerful nation in history, and perhaps the most generous of its age, fails to provide the example and moral leadership that others, especially those living in oppression and misery, rightfully expect from it.

65. Whatever else may distinguish us from those who are forced to live in a political system based upon the principles of dialectical materialism, it certainly is not the absence of materialist attitudes. Yet a

---

[21] Anne Freemantle, ed., *The Social Teaching of the Church* (New York: Menton-Omega Books, 1963) p. 105.

sober and responsible life style would be more effective than anti-communist propaganda in dissuading the uncommitted from joining the Marxist camp. When Pius XI claimed that there would be neither socialism nor communism if the rulers of the nations had not scorned the teachings of the Church, he undoubtedly implied that sober-mindedness and control of our natural greed of material possessions are an essential condition of social justice (*Divini Redemptoris*, #38). In his first encyclical, when surveying the state of the Church and the need for reform, Pope Paul VI wrote as one of his primary concerns:

> We consider that the inner freedom which is derived from the spirit of evangelical poverty makes us more sensitive to, and more capable of understanding, the human aspects of economic questions, by applying to wealth and to the progress it can effect the just and often severe standard of judgment that they require, by giving to indigence our most solicitous and generous attention, and finally, by expressing the wish that economic goods be not the source of conflicts of selfishness and of pride among men, but that they be used in justice and equity for the common good and accordingly, distributed with greater foresight (*Ecclesiam Suam*, #57).

Catholic Higher Education and the Pastoral Mission of the Church

A Statement Issued by the
National Conference of Catholic Bishops

November 13, 1980

Part One: The Ministry of Catholic Higher Education

1. As we enter the twentieth decade of Catholic higher education in the United States, we wish to express in a formal fashion our profound gratitude and esteem for those in this ministry. They serve the entire American people in every field of learning. They also serve the Church in three indispensable ways. Catholic colleges and universities strive to bring faith and reason into an intellectually disciplined and constructive encounter. In addition, they are called to be communities of faith and worship that provide the young men and women of our country and Church with opportunities to mature in mind, body, heart, and soul. Without that maturity, they cannot function effectively as the future leaders of American business, government, culture, and religion. Finally, our schools are serving increasingly the educational needs of adults as they seek to advance their learning at various stages of their lives.

2. During his recent visit in the United States, our Holy Father, Pope John Paul II, emphasized the importance of these functions of Catholic colleges and universities. Speaking to representatives of these institutions at The Catholic University of America, he stated that Catholic colleges and universities

> must train young men and women of outstanding knowledge, who, having made a personal synthesis between faith and culture, will be both capable and willing to assume tasks in the service of the community and of society in general, and to bear witness to their faith before the world.[1]

3. Catholic colleges and universities of the United States have been a significant part of the Catholic community and of American higher education since Georgetown University was founded in 1789 by the first Bishop of Baltimore, John Carroll. Their growth since then has been extraordinary. They constitute the largest group of Catholic

---

[1] Pope John Paul II, "Excellence, Truth and Freedom in Catholic Universities," *Origins: NC Documentary Service*, Vol. 9, No. 19 (October 25, 1979): 307.

institutions of higher education in the world, a striking testimonial to the generosity and commitment of the clergy, religious, and laity in our country. They have produced great numbers of American leaders both in public life and in the Church.

4. From the schools at Antioch and Alexandria, the monastic and cathedral schools, to the medieval universities of Paris and Bologna, the Church has fostered schools dedicated to the integration of the Christian faith and culture. This same concern led to the creation of such institutions in the New World as the University of Santo Domingo in 1533 and the many others which followed it.

5. The Second Vatican Council clarified the reason for the Church's commitment to higher education when it said that people who devote themselves to the various disciplines of philosophy, history, science, and the arts can help elevate the human family to a better understanding of truth, goodness, and beauty, and to the formation of judgments which embody universal values.[2]

6. The world is good because it reflects its Creator. Human culture is good to the extent that it reflects the plan and purpose of the Creator, but it bears the wounds of sin. The Church wishes to make the Gospel of Jesus Christ present to the world and to every sector of humanity at every stage of history. The Catholic college or university seeks to do this by educating men and women to play responsible roles in the contemporary world in the framework of that most important historical fact: the sending of the Son by the Father to reconcile, to vivify, to spread the Good News, to call all the world to a restoration in Christ Jesus.[3]

7. The Catholic Church is, of course, not the only religious body in the United States to recognize the enormous importance of colleges and universities that seek to broaden human knowledge and understanding as part of their commitment to a particular religious faith. We note the ongoing contribution of Jewish and Protestant colleges and universities. At the recent National Congress of Church-Related Colleges and Universities, delegates of twenty-three churches and their affiliated colleges came to a deeper understanding of their need for each other. They discovered that they have many of the same problems and challenges, and can assist one another in facing them.

8. During the decade of the 80s, all church-related colleges and universities will meet new challenges and new pressures. The burdens of inflation and of excessive governmental regulation will probably

---

[2]Second Vatican Council, *Gaudium et Spes* (Constitution on *"The Church in the Modern World"*), par. 57.
[3]Pope John Paul II, "Sapientia Christiana," *Origins: NC Documentary Service*, Vol. 9, No. 3 (June 7, 1979): 37.

increase.[4] Moreover, the number of men and women of traditional college age will decline at a rate of almost half-a-million a year,[5] placing great economic stresses on all colleges and universities. Finally, there will be the continuing need for a clear definition by each institution of its religious identity and mission. All who are dedicated to the vitality of church-related higher education must work to surmount these challenges.

9. The future of church-related education is essential to the preservation of pluralism in higher education. The historic vitality of American Catholic colleges and universities has been indispensable to that pluralism.

10. A distinctive contribution to that pluralism has been the significant role played by women. To have so many women as presidents, major administrators, and faculty of Catholic colleges has been unique in the annals of American higher education.

Part Two: A Pastoral Message to Catholic Colleges and Universities

11. Our statement is intended as a pastoral message addressed first of all to those engaged in the ministry of Catholic higher education and then to the Church at large. It speaks about the pastoral dimension of the life of the Catholic college and university.

12. This dimension is only one aspect of Catholic higher education. The Church attaches great importance to higher learning, both for its own sake and for the life of the Church. This was acknowledged in "The Catholic University in the Modern World," issued by the Second Congress of Delegates of the Catholic Universities of the World, convened in November of 1972 by the Sacred Congregation of Catholic Education.[6] The document, "Relations of American Catholic Colleges and Universities with the Church," issued in 1976 by the Association

---

[4]Indeed, during the past decade some colleges and universities, founded by Catholics, lay or clerical or religious, which have long presumed and styled themselves to be Catholic, have found themselves required to refrain from such designation as a condition for government aid to the institution. We regret the presence of such pressures and look to their removal in a timely fashion.

[5]U.S. Bureau of the Census, Current Population Reports, Series P-25, No. 704, 1977, pp. 38-60 and No. 721, 1978, pp. 9-11, as cited in Exhibit 3. *Policy Analysis Service Reports*, Vol. 4, No. 2 (Washington DC: American Council on Education, December 1978).

[6]"The Catholic University in the Modern World," *College Newsletter* of the National Catholic Educational Association, Washington, DC, Vol. XXXV, No. 3 (March 1973). Cf., also, the letter to Presidents of Catholic Universities from Cardinal Garrone, then Prefect of the S. Congregation for Catholic Education, and dated April 25, 1973, appearing in the same issue of *College Newsletter*, pp. 11-12.

of Catholic Colleges and Universities,[7] describes how Catholic colleges and universities function in the American context. This pastoral message need not restate all that in detail but it does reaffirm the intellectual importance of Catholic colleges and universities in the modern world.

Identity and Mission

13. One of our expectations is that Catholic colleges and universities continue to manifest, with unmistakable clarity, their Catholic identity and mission. The Holy Father has said that their character must be safeguarded,[8] and that the term "Catholic" should never be "a mere label, either added or dropped according to the pressures of varying factors."[9]

14. The Catholic identity of these institutions should be evident to faculty, students, and the general public. Policies, practices, programs, and general spirit should communicate to everyone that the institution is a community of scholars dedicated to the ideals and values of Catholic higher education.

15. Trustees and administrators have an extremely important role to discharge in maintaining fidelity to the nature of the institution and the kind of education the students experience. We look in a special way, however, to faculties for the leadership to accomplish this.

16. The many faculty members who come from other religious traditions can make a special contribution to the breadth of your students' experience. However, those faculty members who completely share the Catholic vision and heritage of faith carry the greatest responsibility to maintain the Catholic character of these institutions. The recruitment and retention of committed and competent Catholic faculty are essential.

17. Many Catholic colleges and universities are making serious efforts to renew their Catholic identity and mission within the guidelines provided by the Second Vatican Council, and thus remain true to their heritage while they adapt to modern circumstances. Academic freedom and institutional independence in pursuit of the mission of the institution are essential components of educational quality and integrity; commitment to the Gospel and the teachings and heritage of the Catholic Church provide the inspiration and enrichment that make a college fully Catholic.

---

[7]"Relations of American Catholic Colleges and Universities with the Church," *Occasional Papers on Catholic Higher Education*, Vol. II, No. 1 (Washington, DC: Association of Catholic Colleges and Universities, April 1976).
[8]Pope John Paul II, "Catholic Universities for an Apostolate of Culture . . ." Address to members of the Council of the International Federation of Catholic Universities, and Rectors of the Catholic Universities of Europe, Rome, February 24, 1979, *L'Osservatore Romano*, English edition (March 5, 1979): 6.
[9]Pope John Paul II, "Excellence, Truth and Freedom in Catholic Universities," *loc. cit.*

Liberal Arts

18. The Catholic identity of a college or university is effectively manifested only in a context of academic excellence. Policies, standards, curricula, governance, and administration should accord, therefore, with the norms of quality accepted in the wider academic community. **19.** A necessary, though not sufficient, element in the identity of undergraduate programs in Catholic institutions is the provision of a liberal education of high quality. But that education must go beyond secular humanism which also emphasizes the liberal arts. Catholic institutions of higher learning can uniquely fuse the traditional study of arts and sciences with the light of faith in the synthesis we call Christian and Catholic humanism. That synthesis provides an integral view of human existence—one that gives true meaning, purpose, and value to the study of all the disciplines. Indeed the Christian and Catholic view of human nature is a sound guide through the moral dilemmas that are so frequent in contemporary society and technology.

We are concerned that the erosion in the teaching of the liberal arts in American higher education today might compromise their important part in teaching the ideals of Christian humanism. That is why we urge Catholic colleges and universities to preserve and strengthen the teaching of the liberal arts in undergraduate and pre-professional education. Particularly in professional and graduate programs, the faculty and students should address human and religious issues that are intrinsic to a humane education. An institution's Catholic identity is largely expressed in a curriculum that shows how the values of the Judeo-Christian view of life illuminate all fields of study and practice.

Theology

20. Theological education is a major concern of the bishops since we are responsible before God and before His people for

> A heritage of faith that the Church has the duty of preserving in its untouchable purity, and of presenting . . . to the people of our time in a way that is as understandable and persuasive as possible.[10]

For its part,

> One of the principal tasks of a Catholic university, and one which it alone is able to accomplish adequately, will be to make theology relevant to all human knowledge and reciprocally all human knowledge relevant to theology.[11]

---

[10]Pope Paul VI, *Evangelii Nuntiandi (On Evangelization in the Modern World)*, Apostolic Exhortation (December 8, 1975): par. 3.
[11]"The Catholic University in the Modern World," *op. cit.* pp. 2-3.

21. The early American Catholic colleges were founded, in part, to protect the faith of students. The mission of Catholic institutions has broadened considerably since that time. They are full partners in the higher education community of the nation, offering wide diversity of academic programs and degrees. With all this diversity, however, theological education has maintained a role that is central to their mission. We are grateful for this continued emphasis and take note of the improvement of education in theology and religious studies in Catholic colleges since the Second Vatican Council. Recent progress in exegesis and patristic research has enriched biblical, liturgical, and historic theology, and has contributed to progress in systematic, pastoral, and moral theology. We also appreciate the efforts to pursue the ecumenical and interreligious directives of the Council by providing students with the opportunity to learn of other religious traditions.

22. Theology is not the same as faith or spirituality or holiness. These, too, are important values of Catholic education, but here we want to emphasize that the distinguishing mark of every Catholic college or university is that, in an appropriate academic fashion, it offers its students an introduction to the Catholic theological heritage. This is a moral obligation owed to Catholic students. In fulfilling this obligation, a theological faculty should take "prudent account of the maturity and previous preparation of the students,"[12] and should be cautious about private speculation of a kind that might undermine the students' foundations of faith in God's revealed truth. It is advisable, however, that students be encouraged to cope with their personal problems of faith and to consider the religious dimensions of the major issues in our contemporary culture and society. Theology should enable students to think and to act within a vision of life that includes religious values. A truly liberating and elevating education is incomplete without the study of theology or religion.

23. For this reason, scholars in theology and other religious studies

> . . . make an indispensable contribution to the integrity of the university, which in order to embrace the fullness of human experience, must take its religious dimension into account.[13]

24. Although the majority of Catholic institutions are undergraduate colleges, some are universities with graduate and professional programs of theology. Graduate teachers and students, enriched by sacred Scripture, the traditions of the Church, and the Church's magisterium, can utilize the professional tools of their discipline to explore Catholic teaching in depth and to discern its applicability to the problems of our times. Because many of the graduates of these programs in theology will be engaged in the ministry of teaching religion, the

---

[12]*Ibid.,* p. 9. Cf., also, Pope Paul VI, *Evangelii Nuntiandi, op. cit.,* par. 78.
[13]*Ibid.,* p. 6.

faculty will have special reason to show respect for the authentic teaching of the Church.

Christian Formation of Teachers

25. The Christian formation of teachers has always been basic to the educational mission of the Church. Until a few years ago, Catholic schools were staffed almost exclusively by men and women, priests and religious, who had not only received training in a formal Christian formation program, but who also had available ongoing opportunities for growth and development in their spiritual and professional lives.

26. Today lay persons have become the overwhelming majority in virtually every Catholic school. They come to Catholic schools with a variety of teacher preparation backgrounds, motivations, and perspectives. Usually, this formation is achieved at secular universities where the prospective teacher is exposed to either a theological pluralism, or receives no special training at all in this field. This is in stark contrast to those who previously were formed in a specifically Catholic environment and emerged certain and secure in their understanding of Catholic tradition and practice.

27. Therefore, teacher preparation programs adequate for public schools are inadequate for teachers in Catholic schools. They omit the necessary spiritual and ministerial formation which must be an integral part of the professional preparation of the Catholic school teacher. This need is urgent and can best be met by the Catholic colleges and universities who alone possess the unique resources and desire to be of service to the Catholic community.

28. Catholic institutions of higher education which have teacher preparation programs are urged to provide Christian formation programs for educators who are evangelizers by call and covenant and mission. Only those teachers who have been formed theologically and spiritually can respond adequately to the call of professional ministry in Christian education according to the vision of Jesus Christ and His Church.

Theologians and Bishops

29. We bishops, for our part, look to biblical scholars and theologians for assistance in understanding and explicating the gospel message within the framework of the Church's theological traditions, and for helping the Church's judgment to mature on current questions.[14] In the words of the Second Vatican Council,

---

[14]Second Vatican Council, *Dei Verbum* (Constitution *On Divine Revelation*) (November 18, 1965), par. 12.

Furthermore, while adhering to the methods and requirements proper to theology, theologians are invited to seek continually for more suitable ways of communicating doctrine to the men and women of their times. For the deposit of faith or revealed truths are one thing; the manner in which they are formulated without violence to their meaning and significance is another.[15]

30. The Holy Father, when speaking at The Catholic University of America, said:

I want to say a special word of gratitude, encouragement, and guidance for the theologians. The Church needs her theologians, particularly in this time and age so profoundly marked by deep changes in all areas of life and society. The bishops of the Church, to whom the Lord has entrusted the keeping of the unity of the faith and the preaching of the message—individual bishops for their dioceses; and bishops collegially, with the successor of Peter for the universal Church—we all need your work, your dedication and the fruits of your reflection. We desire to listen to you and we are eager to receive the valued assistance of your responsible scholarship.[16]

31. Tension sometimes occurs as we seek to satisfy the respective claims of faith and reason, and to distinguish the doctrinal and pastoral responsibilities of bishops from the particular tasks of theologians. The Pope alluded to this tension when he said

The theologian's contribution will be enriching to the Church only if it takes into account the proper function of the bishops and the rights of the faithful. It devolves upon the bishops of the Church to safeguard the Christian authenticity and unity of faith and moral teaching . . .[17]

32. Bishops and the theological community share a mutual but not identical responsibility to the Church. Like theology, the ecclesiastical magisterium is subject to the Word of God, which it serves.[18] As Pope John Paul II has reminded us,

In putting themselves at the service of the truth, the magisterium and the theologians are joined together by common ties, namely by the word of God, by the *sensus fidei*, which has been alive in the Church in the past and is alive today, by the documents of tradition in which the faith of the people in general is set forth, and finally by pastoral and missionary considerations.[19]

33. Conscious of our different roles in the Church, and also of our mutual responsibilities, we seek a fruitful cooperation with theolo-

---

[15]Second Vatican Council, *Gaudium et Spes* (Constitution on *The Church in the Modern World*), *op. cit.*, par. 9.
[16]Pope John Paul II, "Excellence, Truth and Freedom in Catholic Universities," *loc. cit.*
[17]*Ibid.*, p. 308.
[18]Second Vatican Council, *Dei Verbum* (Constitution *On Divine Revelation*), par. 10.
[19]Pope John Paul II, "Papal Address to International Theological Commission," *Origins: NC Documentary Service*, Vol. 9, No. 24 (November 29, 1979): 394-395.

gians. Together we must work to build up the body of Christ and to bring the truth and power of the Gospel to our society and culture with due respect for the legitimate autonomy of culture and of the sciences.[20]

34. We encourage the universities to develop ways which will bring bishops and theologians together with other members of the Church and the academy to examine theological issues with wisdom and learning, with faith, and with mutual charity and esteem. We shall all need to recall and to work for that "delicate balance . . . between the autonomy of a Catholic university and the responsibilities of the hierarchy."[21] There need be no conflict between the two.

Philosophy

35. Another major concern of ours is the study of philosophy. We do not see philosophy as merely one more subject area in the field of liberal arts, nor as an academic luxury for those of speculative bent, but rather as an essential component of any education worthy of the name. It is philosophy which familiarizes the student with the laws and patterns of human thought. It brings the student to face, in a disciplined academic fashion, the great questions about God, the world, and humanity. It brings with itself an ever-increasing sense of the proportion and relationship that exist between the various aspects of reality and learning. Without solid philosophical grounding, both teachers and students in all fields of study cannot avoid the risk of superficiality and fragmentation.

Ethics

36. Catholic colleges and universities have the obligation to study and teach the moral and ethical dimensions of every discipline. They must guarantee that the moral considerations of the Catholic tradition are related to all programs of study and that the ethical implications of new findings are probed in what Pope John Paul II called a "proportionate development."[22] This is especially urgent in professional and technical studies because in a technologically oriented society it is often the professional who in fact makes many decisions involving human values.

---

[20]Second Vatican Council, *Gaudium et Spes* (Constitution on *The Church in the Modern World*), par. 59.

[21]"The Catholic University in the Modern World," *op. cit.*, p. 9.

[22]Pope John Paul II, *Redemptor Hominis (The Redeemer of Man)* (March 4, 1979), par. 15.

Justice

37. Education for justice is a significant element in the general call to gospel holiness. We issued a call to justice on the occasion of our nation's bicentennial in 1976 and we repeat now that "we must expand and improve our programs of education for justice."[23]

38. Those who enjoy the benefits of Catholic higher education have the obligation to provide our society with leadership in matters of justice and human rights.

39. Knowledge of economics and politics will not in itself bring about justice, unless it is activated by human and religious ideals. However, religious ideals without the necessary secular expertise will not provide the kind of leadership needed to influence our complex society.

40. Many Catholic colleges and universities integrate social justice teaching with field education and experience. Students and faculty are encouraged to become personally aware of problems of injustice and their responsibility to be involved in the social process. These are responses we should expect from institutions which take the Gospel seriously.

41. For the college or university to be an authentic teacher of social justice, it must conduct its own affairs in a just way.[24] "Modern man listens more willingly to witnesses than to teachers, and if he does listen to teachers, it is because they are witnesses."[25] It is important that Catholic institutions of higher education continually review their policies and personnel practices in order to ensure that social justice is a reality on campus. Fidelity to the social teachings of the Church in this basic witness means there is no contradiction between practice and theory.

Minority Concerns

42. Another aspect of justice is the treatment of minority concerns. For much of its history, the Catholic Church in the United States bore the title of the "Church of the Immigrants," and these same immigrants frequently found opportunities for higher education in the Catholic colleges and universities. As new minority groups seek educational opportunities, Catholic institutions should strive to respond to their legitimate needs, providing student aid and an education which respects their culture while offering the benefits of the Chris-

---

[23]The National Conference of Catholic Bishops, *To Do The Work of Justice* (Washington, DC: United States Catholic Conference, 1978), p. 5.

[24]Carnegie Council on Policy Studies in Higher Education, *Fair Practices in Higher Education* (Washington, DC: Jossey-Bass Publishers, 1979).

[25]Pope Paul VI, "Address to the Members of the Concilium de Laicis," October 2, 1974, as cited in the Apostolic Exhortation "On Evangelization in the Modern World," *op. cit.*, 41.

tian heritage. We have in mind blacks, Native Americans, Orientals, and other minorities, but, especially, Hispanic-Americans, whose own Catholic culture is so rich and whose numbers are so great. We encourage our colleges and universities to institute precollege programs for disadvantaged persons. We ask that attention be given to the need for the presence of minority persons on boards of trustees and faculties of these institutions.

The International Viewpoint

43. Because the unity of all people under God our Father is a fundamental principle of Catholic theology, an international point of view should be evident on the Catholic campus. Modern means of transportation and communication make possible a closer union of the peoples of the world by diminishing the distances that separate us. The way is thus being prepared for the familial closeness, the mutuality of service, and the union of hearts which lie at the core of the Gospel and to which the human family is called. The present climate of competition, hostility, and violence must be replaced by a constructive sharing of the earth's goods in a secure and peaceful environment. This suggests that international studies have an important place in the curriculum. It is also important and beneficial for students from other nations to be present on Catholic campuses. Their presence provides an opportunity for close associations which make possible an increased appreciation of others' culture and point of view.

Campus Ministry

44. This pastoral document envisions a Catholic university or college as an enterprise wholly committed to evangelical ministry. To relegate this ministry to the institution's periphery in an isolated department or office of "campus ministry" is to fault the university's or college's essential Catholic identity.

45. Trustees, administrators, faculties, parents, and, above all, students need to see their whole college or university experience as a unique opportunity for the discovery of God's abiding presence and influence in the lives of people and in the signs of the times. At most and at best an office of campus ministry can be a catalyst to spark and to energize the total institution's involvement in a gospel-oriented evangelism. This office is badly degraded if it is regarded only as something like a bookstore or student union, some sort of a convenience for those students who want a little religion on the side of their higher education.

46. A university or college which has an ongoing, dynamic program to clarify its Catholic identity will expect the office of campus ministry to have a voice in a policy-making level and to insist in season and out of season on the preservation and enrichment of the institution's religious traditions.

47. Because campus ministry includes elements of parish ministry, e.g., counseling, preparation for the sacraments, preaching, liturgical worship, and cooperation with diocesan activities, we are obliged to grant appropriate jurisdiction and authority to duly approved campus ministers at institutions of higher education in our dioceses. We see this duty not as one needlessly to restrict the highly commendable pastoral practices in campus ministry but rather as one to give our official support, and, as far as possible, our assistance to a ministry for which we have a share of responsibility. For this reason, we believe it to be of utmost importance that those who are selected for this important ministry, whether they be clergy, religious, or lay, be prepared for this kind of apostolate theologically and philosophically. They should present the authentic teaching of the Church in a pastoral manner in the context of the academic communities in which they serve.

48. We would like university and college students to feel that they are not mere visitors in our diocese but are temporary residents for whose spiritual welfare we pray and work. There is merit, therefore, in a growing trend for bishops personally to visit university and college campuses for the celebration of liturgies and, on occasion, for close up dialogue with students. Pope John Paul II has set a good example for our face to face conversations with students.

49. Though much progress lately has been made in improving the quality and extent of campus ministry on Catholic campuses, there still is vast room for upgrading this important element of Catholic higher education. To a large extent, we fear, campus ministry still suffers badly from inadequate budgets and from too limited a staff. A very encouraging development, however, is team ministry in which laity, religious, and priests combine their talents and experience for efficacious ministry.

50. In this ministry the gospel adage is controlling: "I know mine, and mine know me." To do the work of the Lord Jesus Himself on a Catholic university or college campus is to have close personal contact with students who are ready to share their intimate hopes and anxieties with a person who truly can say, "I know you, and you know me." Obviously, this ministry should not and cannot be limited to persons formally designated as campus ministers even though they rightfully are expected to take the lead.

51. We bishops, as best we can, wish to pledge our active cooperation with this kind of ministry on the campuses in our dioceses.

A Community of Faith

52. Pope John Paul II has repeatedly called for the Catholic campus to be a community of faith. In Mexico and in Poland, in Rome and in Washington, he has again and again returned to the same theme.[26] No more fitting ideal can be sought than to build a community which encourages intellectual growth and which calls to and supports a personal religious commitment.[27]

53. Growth in Christ is never an easy task. Indeed, in our times, it is exceedingly difficult to live a fully Christian life. We honor those persons—especially young people—who reject the patterns of behavior which surround them and, as "children of light,"[28] attempt to respond with fidelity to the grace of their Baptism. It is that very grace which calls us to support one another as a company of believers.

54. All Catholic activity must of necessity be pointed to an objective that is ultimately religious: how to know God better and serve Him more faithfully. The goals of a Catholic college are specified by its very nature as a place of learning. But learning itself does not constitute the perfect and fulfilled life. It needs to be integrated with our search for the Lord and in our living with our neighbor a life of faith in Him and fidelity to His way. Our concern, then, is that students and faculty find on our campuses the community of faith which can encourage and support them in reaching for that goal. Unless a Catholic institution of higher learning fosters such a faith community, it contradicts its own mission.

55. Residential students can more easily experience a campus-based community. For commuter students the formation of community is more difficult. We encourage dedicated persons to develop new ways to draw more students and faculty into communities of friends who help one another live strongly religious lives.

Adult Learners

56. Our concern for the welfare of the younger college students does not exclude the growing number of older students. These men and women seek education for new careers, to complete an interrupted education, or for the pleasure of learning. They constitute a growing proportion of the student body on our campuses. Their needs for an integrated Catholic education are similar to those of the younger students, but they must be addressed in different ways.

---

[26]"To be what it ought to be, a Catholic college or university must set up, among its faculty and students, a real community which bears witness to a living and operative Christianity, a community where sincere commitment to scientific research and study goes together with a deep commitment to authentic Christian living." Pope John Paul II, "Excellence, Truth and Freedom in Catholic Universities," *loc. cit.*

[27]"The Catholic University in the Modern World," *op. cit.*, p. 3.

[28]Eph 5:8.

57. We appreciate the many programs developed by Catholic institutions to provide theological renewal and training for ministry to Catholic adults in the years since the Second Vatican Council. These programs illustrate a distinct form of service to the Church community, which we hope will grow as we learn how to use the many resources of our institutions more effectively.

The Campus and Ecumenism

58. The Second Vatican Council called for strong ecumenical initiatives. The Catholic colleges have been responding not only with courses designed to acquaint Catholic students with other religious traditions, but with faculty members drawn from those traditions who have added a rich new dimension to departments of theology and religious studies. The Catholic college or university can be a fertile environment for further ecumenical activity, and we encourage cooperative work with the local (and national) Church to that end. Catholic faculty trained in biblical and theological sciences can offer leadership in the explorations and study in which we join with others outside the Catholic community.

Research

59. The Church has always encouraged the advancement of human knowledge, because the more we know of truth the closer we come to God in Whom truth ultimately resides. Catholic scholars, as Pope John Paul II urged, should examine all the fundamental questions in human culture with the highest degree of intellectual rigor. These scholars also have a special obligation to undertake research closely related to human and spiritual needs.[29] It is for this reason that the bishops of America in their 1976 bicentennial conference, *A Call to Action*, urged scholars to undertake research in areas of pastoral concern, especially in issues of justice and peace.[30] In these efforts the Church would be materially assisted if cooperative efforts could be organized to mobilize the combined research capabilities of the Catholic universities of this country. We shall work with the universities to find the resources necessary for research of high quality and utility.

---

[29]Cf., Pope John Paul II, "Excellence, Truth and Freedom in Catholic Universities," *loc. cit.*
[30]The National Conference of Catholic Bishops, *To Do the Work of Justice, loc. cit.*

Part Three: Support for Catholic Higher Education

60. We have addressed in particular those who work and study in Catholic colleges and universities; now we want to urge upon all in the Church a firm support for this important ministry.

Religious Congregations

61. The entire Church owes much to those generations of sisters, brothers, and priests who provided higher education to their students, financed by their own labors, and often by their own funds.
62. Today the numbers of clergy and religious are smaller at many Catholic colleges and universities. This is due, in part, to the decline in religious vocations, and, in part, to entry into other fields of ministry. It is important that the mission of Catholic higher education remain a high priority among religious communities. The nurturing of tomorrow's leadership through service in Catholic colleges and universities is an effective way of building the Christian community and of preparing the next generation of leaders for our society.

Parents

We join with Pope John Paul II to offer gratitude and appreciation

> . . . to the parents . . . who, sometimes at the price of great personal and financial sacrifice, look toward the Catholic universities and colleges for the training that unites faith and science; cultures and the Gospel values.[31]

63. Combinations of federal, state, and institutional student aid programs make it possible, although not without sacrifice, for parents to encourage and support the attendance of their sons and daughters at Catholic institutions. These programs narrow the tuition gap between the independent college and the state institution which is heavily subsidized by all taxpayers. Consequently, some exercise of choice is possible for many students. In helping a son or daughter select a college, parents should give a priority, where possible, to the Catholic institution. Adult Catholic leaders need adult Catholic education. The religious learning of the child will not suffice for the religious needs and demands of the adult.

---

[31]Pope John Paul II, "Excellence, Truth and Freedom in Catholic Universities," *op. cit.*, p. 307.

The American Church at Large

64. We appeal, finally, to the entire American Church for support of Catholic higher education. Catholic foundations, as well as Catholic individuals and families, should see generous and long-term support of Catholic institutions as one of the top priorities in our Church. The stability of institutions of higher learning in America in our time is based on a firm underpinning of endowment funds. The Catholic colleges and universities have relied through their history on the "living endowment" of religious and clergy, as well as on the generous assistance of lay persons. The day has now come when we American Catholics of the present must reciprocate the gifts we have received from the past. To all Catholics who believe with us that Catholic higher education is important for the life of the Church, we appeal for financial support, so that the benefits we have enjoyed will be preserved for the next generation of Catholic Americans.

65. We conclude by noting once again the historic interest of the Catholic Church in higher education. We thank the clergy and religious and laity in ever-increasing numbers, who staff the colleges and universities of our country. We commend all who are undertaking the renewal of Catholic higher education as part of that renewal to which the Holy Spirit through the Vatican Council has called the whole Church.[32]

---

[32]Since this message has addressed exclusively Catholic higher education, we were unable to speak of the excellent intellectual and pastoral leadership of many Catholics engaged as teachers, administrators, and campus ministers in the colleges and universities which are not Catholic. We hope for a future opportunity to speak of their invaluable contribution to the intellectual life of our country.

Called and Gifted: The American Catholic Laity

A Statement Issued by the
National Conference of Catholic Bishops

November 13, 1980

Introduction

1. Among the most enduring contributions of the Second Vatican Council is its description of the Church as the People of God.

> This was to be the new People of God. For, those who believe in Christ, who are reborn not from a perishable but from an imperishable seed through the Word of the living God (1 Pt 1:23), not from the flesh but from water and the Holy Spirit (Jn 3:5-6), are finally established as 'a chosen race, a royal priesthood, a holy nation, a purchased people . . . You who in times past were not a people, but are now the people of God (1 Pt 2:9-10)' (*Lumen Gentium*, #9).

2. This image, drawing on a rich biblical and historical tradition, gives marvelous expression to the role of the Church as the sign of the Kingdom of God. It was this Kingdom which Jesus came to announce and to inaugurate by his life, death, and resurrection. "After John's arrest, Jesus appeared in Galilee proclaiming the good news of God. 'This is the time of fulfillment. The reign of God is at hand. Reform your lives and believe in the gospel'" (Mk 1:14-16).

3. Jesus established the Church to bear witness to God's Kingdom especially by the way His followers would live as the People of God. "This is my commandment: love one another as I have loved you" (Jn 15-12).

4. The image of the People of God has many dimensions; its meaning is best grasped through a variety of experiences. Each sheds light on the whole and enables us to appreciate and live it more deeply.

5. At the present time the light shed on the meaning of the People of God by the laity is especially noteworthy and exciting. In an exercise of our charism of "bringng forth from the treasury of Revelation new things and old" (*Lumen Gentium*, #25), we bishops praise the Lord for what is happening among the laity and proclaim as well as we can what we have been experiencing and learning from them.

6. While focusing on the laity, we wish to address the whole Church. We affirm the vision of the Second Vatican Council and the importance it gives to the laity. We look forward to what is still to come under the guidance of the Holy Spirit, making the Church more and

417

more the perfect image of Christ. We also acknowledge that these continuing developments may require new concepts, new terminology, new attitudes, and new practices. In prayerful dialogue with all our sisters and brothers we are prepared to make those changes which will aid in building the Kingdom.

The Call to Adulthood

7. As the *Decree on the Apostolate of the Laity* of Vatican II says:

> Indeed, everyone should painstakingly ready himself or herself personally for the apostolate, especially as an adult. For the advance of age brings with it better self-knowledge, thus enabling each person to evaluate more accurately the talents with which God has enriched each soul and to exercise more effectively those charismatic gifts which the Holy Spirit has bestowed on all for the good of others (#30).

8. One of the chief characteristics of lay men and women today is their growing sense of being adult members of the Church. Adulthood implies knowledge, experience and awareness, freedom and responsibility, and mutuality in relationships. It is true, however, that the experience of lay persons "as Church members" has not always reflected this understanding of adulthood. Now, thanks to the impetus of the Second Vatican Council, lay women and men feel themselves called to exercise the same mature interdependence and practical self-direction which characterize them in other areas of life.

9. We note the response of many lay persons to different opportunities for faith development. There is the "coming to faith in Jesus" and a strengthening of commitment to Him and His mission which we commonly call evangelization. There is also the adult catechesis movement which allows persons to grow and deepen their faith, and there are those who in faith are seeking greater understanding through theological reflection. These and other adult lay persons have taken responsibility in their parish or diocese by serving in leadership positions on committees and boards.

10. Adult Christian living is also noticeable, though not always as publicized, in the daily struggle to live out Christian values in family, neighborhood, school, government, and work. This is a hopeful sign because the laity are uniquely present in and to the world and so bear a privileged position to build the Kingdom of God there. "You are the light of the world. . . . Your light must shine before all so that they may see goodness in your acts and give praise to your heavenly Father" (Mt 5:14-16).

11. The adult character of the People of God flows from Baptism and Confirmation which are the foundation of the Christian life and min-

istry. They signify initiation into a community of believers who, according to their state of life, respond to God's call to holiness and accept responsibility for the ministry of the Church.

The Call to Holiness

Thus it is evident to everyone that all the faithful of Christ of whatever rank or status are called to the fullness of the Christian life and to the perfection of charity. By this holiness a more human way of life is promoted even in this earthly society (*Lumen Gentium*, #40).

12. The Second Vatican Council clearly proclaimed the universal call to holiness. Not only are lay people included in God's call to holiness, but theirs is a unique call requiring a unique response which itself is a gift of the Holy Spirit. It is characteristic that lay men and women hear the call to holiness in the very web of their existence (*Lumen Gentium*, #31), in and through the events of the world, the pluralism of modern living, the complex decisions and conflicting values they must struggle with, the richness and fragility of sexual relationships, the delicate balance between activity and stillness, presence and privacy, love and loss.

13. The response of lay people to this call promises to contribute still more to the spiritual heritage of the Church. Already the laity's hunger for God's word is everywhere evident. Increasingly, lay men and women are seeking spiritual formation and direction in deep ways of prayer. This has helped to spur several renewal movements.

14. These developments present a challenge to the parish because, for the most part, the spiritual needs of lay people must be met in the parish. The parish must be a home where they can come together with their leaders for mutual spiritual enrichment, much as in the early Church: "They devoted themselves to the apostles' instruction and the communal life, to the breaking of bread and the prayers" (Acts 2:42).

15. We call special attention to the effect this should have on liturgy. The quality of worship depends in great measure on the spiritual life of all present. As lay women and men cultivate their own proper response to God's call to holiness, this should come to expression in the communal worship of the Church.

16. Simultaneously, as lay persons assume their roles in liturgical celebration according to the gifts of the Spirit bestowed on them for that purpose, the ordained celebrant will be more clearly seen as the one who presides over the community, bringing together the diverse talents of the community as a gift to the Father.

17. Whatever else the growing spiritual life of the community entails, it certainly means a more intense sharing among the whole People of God of the gifts of the Spirit. And this we wish to reinforce.

The Call to Ministry

From the reception of these charisms or gifts, including those which are less dramatic, there arise for each believer the right and duty to use them in the Church and the world for the good of humankind and for the upbuilding of the Church (*Decree on the Apostolate of the Laity, #3*).

18. Baptism and Confirmation empower all believers to share in some form of ministry. Although the specific form of participation in ministry varies according to the gifts of the Holy Spirit, all who share in this work are united with one another. "Just as each of us has one body with many members, and not all the members have the same function, so too we, though many, are one body in Christ and individually members of one another. We have gifts that differ according to the favor bestowed on each of us" (Rom 12:4-6).

19. This unity in the ministry should be especially evident in the relationships between laity and clergy, as lay men and women respond to the call of the Spirit in their lives. The clergy help to call forth, identify, coordinate, and affirm the diverse gifts bestowed by the Spirit. We applaud this solidarity between laity and clergy as their most effective ministry and witness to the world.

Christian Service: Ministry in the World

The laity, by their vocation, seek the Kingdom of God by engaging in temporal affairs, and by ordering them according to the plan of God (*Lumen Gentium, #31*).

20. Christian service in the world is represented in a pre-eminent way by the laity. It is sometimes called the "ministry of the laity" and balances the concept of ministry found in the ecclesial ministerial services. Because of lay persons, Christian service or ministry broadly understood includes civic and public activity, response to the imperatives of peace and justice, and resolution of social, political, and economic conflicts, especially as they influence the poor, oppressed, and minorities.

21. The whole Church faces unprecedented situations in the contemporary world, and lay people are at the cutting edge of these new challenges. It is they who engage directly in the task of relating Christian values and practices to complex questions such as those of business ethics, political choice, economic security, quality of life, cultural development, and family planning.

22. Really new situations, especially in the realm of social justice, call for creative responses. We know that the Spirit moves among all the

People of God, prompting them according to their particular gifts and offices to discern anew the signs of the times and to interpret them boldly in light of the Gospel. Lay women and men are in a unique position to offer this service.

23. Just as by divine institution bishops, priests, and deacons have been given through ordination authority to exercise leadership as servants of God's people, so through Baptism and Confirmation lay men and women have been given rights and responsibilities to participate in the mission of the Church. In those areas of life in which they are uniquely present and within which they have special competency because of their particular talents, education, and experience, they are an extension of the Church's redeeming presence in the world. Recognition of lay rights and responsibilities should not create a divisiveness between clergy and laity but should express the full range of the influence of the People of God. We see this and affirm it.

Ministry in the Church

As sharers in the role of Christ the Priest, the Prophet, and the King, the laity have an active part to play in the life and activity of the Church (*Decree on the Apostolate of the Laity*, #10).

24. Since the Second Vatican Council, new opportunities have developed for lay men and women to serve in the Church. We acknowledge gratefully the continuing and increasing contributions of volunteers and part-time workers who serve on parish and diocesan councils, boards of education, and financial, liturgical, and ecumenical committees, as well as those who exercise roles such as special minister of the Eucharist, catechist, and pastoral assistant. We are grateful too, for the large numbers of lay people who have volunteered and are serving in the missions.

25. Growing numbers of lay women and men are also preparing themselves professionally to work in the Church. In this regard religious sisters and brothers have shown the way with their initiative and creativity.

26. Ecclesial ministers, i.e., lay persons who have prepared for professional ministry in the Church, represent a new development. We welcome this as a gift to the Church. There are also persons who serve the Church by the witness of their lives and their self-sacrificing service and empowerment of the poor in works such as administration, housing, job development, and education. All these lay ministers are undertaking roles which are not yet clearly spelled out and which are already demanding sacrifices and risks of them and their families. As lay persons increasingly engage in ecclesial ministry, we recognize and accept the responsibility of working out practical dif-

ficulties such as the availability of positions, the number of qualified applicants, procedures for hiring, just wages, and benefits.

27. Special mention must be made of women who in the past have not always been allowed to take their proper role in the Church's ministry. We see the need for an increased role for women in the ministries of the Church to the extent possible. We recognize the tensions and misunderstandings which arise on this question, but we wish to face these as part of a sincere attempt to become true communities of faith.

28. The combination of all these responses to the challenges of our time proclaims the interrelated oneness of ministry as a gift of the Spirit, and we rejoice in this.

The Call to Community

For from the wedlock of Christians there comes the family, in which new citizens of human society are born. By the grace of the Holy Spirit received in baptism these are made children of God, thus perpetuating the People of God through the centuries. The family is, so to speak, the domestic Church (*Lumen Gentium*, #11).

29. Most lay persons have a primary identification with family. This influences the expectations of and contributions to the Church as the People of God. The family, as a way of life, is often taken as a model for the Church. In most families life is interdependent. Ideally, strengths and weaknesses are blended so that a growthful atmosphere is maintained.

30. And yet we must frankly admit that failure occurs, that in many families the ideal is not reached. For example, divorce and neglect are realities. The parish has a vital contribution to make to all families struggling to be faith communities, for the parish can serve as a model and resource for families.

31. Because lay women and men do experience intimacy, support, acceptance, and availability in family life, they seek the same in their Christian communities. This is leading to a review of parish size, organization, priorities, and identity. It has already led to intentional communities, basic Christian communities, and some revitalized parish communities.

32. It is likely that this family characteristic of the laity will continue to influence and shape the community life of Christians. If it does, this should enable the clergy to give the kind of overall leadership which their office requires. Such trends are welcome in the Church.

Conclusion

33. The Church is to be a sign of God's Kingdom in the world. The authenticity of that sign depends on all the people: laity, religious, deacons, priests, and bishops. Unless we truly live as the People of God, we will not be much of a sign to ourselves or the world.

34. We are convinced that the laity are making an indispensable contribution to the experience of the People of God and that the full import of their contribution is still in a beginning form in the post-Vatican II Church. We have spoken in order to listen. It is not our intention rigidly to define or control, to sketch misleading dreams, or bestow false praise. We bishops wish simply to take our place and exercise our role among the People of God. We now await the next word.

Statement on Promoting Christian Unity

*A Statement Issued by the
Administrative Committee of the
National Conference of Catholic Bishops*

November 15, 1980

1. In our day, the Catholic Church has many serious concerns which arise from reflection on the Gospel. Among the concerns of the Church, Pope John Paul II has stressed the priority of ecumenism. Very clearly he has pointed out that this is, "A priority imposed on our actions, in the first place, because it corresponds to the very location of the Church. The ecumenical effort is not engaged in for reasons of opportuneness and is not dictated by contingent situations or circumstances, but is based on God's will" (Address to the Roman Curia, June 30, 1980).

2. As this new decade begins, it is the responsibility of the whole Church to keep before itself this priority. Since the establishment of the Secretariat for Promoting Christian Unity twenty years ago, this year much has been accomplished to sustain the trend for the restoration of Christian unity. Indeed, there is evidence that a true ecumenical revolution is in progress. This ecumenical revolution is bringing about the healing of divisions inherited from the past. Also, it is bringing Christian churches into deeper, more open, and more complete relationships with one another.

3. The Roman Catholic Church has been particularly blessed by the partnership, dialogue, and common witness with Christian communions. Many times, other churches have offered us this opportunity through their sincere collaboration, and for this we are profoundly grateful. This trend is a gift of God. It has been so sustained and has become so widespread that it seems to mark the dawn of a new era for Christian people. This era will stand in marked contrast to the division and discord among Christians that arose during preceding centuries.

4. The Holy Father has summarized what appears to be a major redirection of the course of Christian history saying, "The second millenium witnessed our progressive separation. The opposite movement has begun everywhere. It is necessary and I beseech 'Father of Lights' from whom every perfect gift comes down [cf., Jas 1:17] to grant that the dawn of the third millennium shall rise on our full refound communion" (Address to the Secretariat for Promoting Christian Unity, Feb. 8, 1980).

5.   In the next twenty years, for so great a goal to come about, many tasks must be accomplished. Foremost among these is the continuation of theological dialogue, conducted with clarity, openness, humility, and charity—the continuing joint study of the principal doctrinal differences which in the past were at the root of the divisions which still separate Christians today. If, as Pope John Paul II has said, "the dawn of the century that is approaching must find us united in full communion," we must conclude with him that "the theological dialogue will have to overcome the disagreements that still exist" (Address to the Curia, June 30, 1980).

6.   The task of the theological dialogue makes serious demands on our Catholic theologians and scholars of other churches. Together, they have carried it forward with a scholarly and religious commitment that has our sincere appreciation and continued support. The various dialogues underway are so many efforts leading to the same goal. We contemplate them proceeding through successive stages, each building on the foundations laid for it in an earlier stage. Some of these dialogues are soon to reach a certain maturity which will enable the Catholic Church "to make an official pronouncement and draw the consequences for the stage that will follow" (Address to the SPCU, Feb. 8, 1980).

7.   For the dialogues to achieve their ultimate purpose they must be accompanied at the same time by a clear realization among the Catholic people of the necessity of our ecumenical commitment. No one has stated this more forcefully than the Holy Father: "It is certain that in the present historical situation of Christianity and the world the only possibility we see of fulfilling the church's universal mission . . . is that of seeking sincerely, perseveringly, humbly and also courageously the ways of drawing closer and of union . . . To all who, for whatever motive, would wish to dissuade the church from seeking the universal unity of Christians the question must once again be put: Have we the right not to do it? (*Redemptor Hominis*, n. 6, March 22, 1979).

8.   So ecumenism is not only a theological task; it engages every dimension of the Church's life.

> "The task of promoting unity," as the Holy Father has said, "is essentially a *pastoral* task. It is pastoral in that the bishops are the principal ministers of unity within the local churches and therefore 'have a special responsibility for promoting the ecumenical movement' (Ecumenical Directory II, 65). It is pastoral also in that all who are entrusted with this work must see it as primarily ordered to the building up of the Body of Christ and the salvation of the world. As long as Christians are divided, so long will the work of preaching the Gospel be hampered; divisions among Christians impair the credibility of the Gospel, the credibility of Christ himself. . . . This service of unity is a service of Christ, of the Gospel, and of all humanity. It is, then, a truly pastoral service. A high *priority* attaches to this truly pastoral work" (Address to Representatives of National Ecumenical Commissions, Nov. 24, 1980).

In stating our commitment to the priority of this task we commend
it as well to all the Catholic people and ask their continued dedication
to it.

9.   In a special way we commend it to their prayers. While not stint-
ing in the efforts required of us, we know that the unity which we
seek is not to be the product of human achievement but a gift from
God to His people. "Only God allows us to advance in fulfillment of
Christ's supreme desire *ut unum sint*" (Address to the Curia, June 30,
1980).

Statement on Capital Punishment

A Statement Issued by the
United States Catholic Bishops

November 1980

1. In 1974, out of a commitment to the value and dignity of human life, the U.S. Catholic Conference, by a substantial majority, voted to declare its opposition to capital punishment. As a former president of the National Conference of Catholic Bishops pointed out in 1977, the issue of capital punishment involves both "profound legal and political questions" as well as "important moral and religious issues."[1] And so we find that this issue continues to provoke public controversy and to raise moral questions that trouble many. This is particularly true in the aftermath of widely publicized executions in Utah and Florida and as a result of public realization that there are now over five hundred persons awaiting execution in various prisons in our country.

2. The resumption of capital punishment after a long moratorium, which began in 1967, is the result of a series of decisions by the United States Supreme Court. In the first of these decisions, *Furman v. Georgia* (1972), the Court held that the death penalty as then administered did constitute cruel and unusual punishment and so was contrary to the Eighth Amendment to the Constitution. Subsequently in 1976 the Court upheld death sentences imposed under state statutes which had been revised by state legislatures in the hope of meeting the Court's requirement that the death penalty not be imposed arbitrarily. These cases and the ensuing revision of state and federal statutes gave rise to extended public debate over the necessity and advisability of retaining the death penalty. We should note that much of this debate was carried on in a time of intense public concern over crime and violence. For instance, in 1976 alone, over 18,000 people were murdered in the United States. Criticism of the inadequacies of the criminal justice system has been widespread, even while spectacular crimes have spread fear and alarm, particularly in urban areas. All these factors make it particularly necessary that Christians form their views on this difficult matter in a prayerful and reflective way and that they show a respect and concern for the rights of all.

---

[1] *Statement on Capital Punishment*, Archbishop Joseph L. Bernardin, President, National Conference of Catholic Bishops, January 26, 1977. Cf. *Community and Crime*, Statement of the Committee on Social Development and World Peace, United States Catholic Conference, February 15, 1978, p. 8.

3. We should acknowledge that in the public debate over capital punishment we are dealing with values of the highest importance: respect for the sanctity of human life, the protection of human life, the preservation of order in society, and the achievement of justice through law. In confronting the problem of serious and violent crime in our society, we want to protect the lives and the sense of security both of those members of society who may become the victims of crime and of those in the police and in the law enforcement system who run greater risks. In doing this, however, we must bear in mind that crime is both a manifestation of the great mysteries of evil and human freedom and an aspect of the very complex reality that is contemporary society. We should not expect simple or easy solutions to what is a profound evil, and even less should we rely on capital punishment to provide such a solution. Rather, we must look to the claims of justice as these are understood in the current debate and to the example and teaching of Jesus, whom we acknowledge as the Justice of God.

I. Purposes of Punishment

4. Allowing for the fact that Catholic teaching has accepted the principle that the state has the right to take the life of a person guilty of an extremely serious crime, and that the state may take appropriate measures to protect itself and its citizens from grave harm, nevertheless, the question for judgment and decision today is whether capital punishment is justifiable under present circumstances. Punishment, since it involves the deliberate infliction of evil on another, is always in need of justification. This has normally taken the form of indicating some good which is to be obtained through punishment or an evil which is to be warded off. The three justifications traditionally advanced for punishment in general are retribution, deterrence, and reform.

5. Reform or rehabilitation of the criminal cannot serve as a justification for capital punishment, which necessarily deprives the criminal of the opportunity to develop a new way of life that conforms to the norms of society and that contributes to the common good. It may be granted that the imminence of capital punishment may induce repentence in the criminal, but we should certainly not think that this threat is somehow necessary for God's grace to touch and to transform human hearts.

6. The deterrence of actual or potential criminals from future deeds of violence by the threat of death is also advanced as a justifying objective of punishment. While it is certain that capital punishment prevents the individual from committing further crimes, it is far from certain that it actually prevents others from doing so. Empirical studies in this area have not given conclusive evidence that would justify the imposition of the death penalty on a few individuals as a means of preventing others from committing crimes. There are strong reasons to doubt that many crimes of violence are undertaken in a spirit of rational calculation which would be influenced by a remote threat of death. The small number of death sentences in relation to the number of murders also makes it seem highly unlikely that the threat will be carried out and so undercuts the effectiveness of the deterrent.

7.   The protection of society and its members from violence, to which the deterrent effect of punishment is supposed to contribute, is a value of central and abiding importance; and we urge the need for prudent firmness in ensuring the safety of innocent citizens. It is important to remember that the preservation of order in times of civil disturbance does not depend on the institution of capital punishment, the imposition of which rightly requires a lengthy and complex process in our legal system. Moreover, both in its nature as legal penalty and in its practical consequences, capital punishment is different from the taking of life in legitimate self-defense or in defense of society.

8.   The third justifying purpose for punishment is retribution or the restoration of the order of justice which has been violated by the action of the criminal. We grant that the need for retribution does indeed justify punishment. For the practice of punishment both presupposes a previous transgression against the law and involves the involuntary deprivation of certain goods. But we maintain that this need does not require nor does it justify taking the life of the criminal, even in cases of murder. We must not remain unmindful of the example of Jesus, who urges upon us a teaching of forbearance in the face of evil (Mt 5:38-42) and forgiveness of injuries (Mt 18:21-35). It is morally unsatisfactory and socially destructive for criminals to go unpunished, but the forms and limits of punishment must be determined by moral objectives which go beyond the mere inflicting of injury on the guilty. Thus we would regard it as barbarous and inhumane for a criminal who had tortured or maimed a victim to be tortured or maimed in return. Such a punishment might satisfy certain vindictive desires that we or the victim might feel, but the satisfaction of such desires is not and cannot be an objective of a humane and Christian approach to punishment. We believe that the forms of punishment must be determined with a view to the protection of society and its members and to the reformation of the criminal and his reintegration into society (which may not be possible in certain cases). This position accords with the general norm for punishment proposed by St. Thomas Aquinas when he wrote: "In this life, however, penalties are not sought for their own sake, because this is not the era of retribution; rather, they are meant to be corrective by being conducive either to the reform of the sinner or the good of society,

which becomes more peaceful through the punishment of sinners."[2]

9.   We believe that in the conditions of contemporary American society, the legitimate purposes of punishment do not justify the imposition of the death penalty. Furthermore, we believe that there are serious considerations which should prompt Christians and all Americans to support the abolition of capital punishment. Some of these reasons have to do with evils that are present in the practice of capital punishment itself, while others involve important values that would be promoted by abolition of this practice.

II. Christian Values in the Abolition of Capital Punishment

10.   We maintain that abolition of the death penalty would promote values that are important to us as citizens and as Christians. First, abolition sends a message that we can break the cycle of violence, that we need not take life for life, that we can envisage more humane and more hopeful and effective responses to the growth of violent crime. It is a manifestation of our freedom as moral persons striving for a just society. It is also a challenge to us as a people to find ways of dealing with criminals that manifest intelligence and compassion rather than power and vengeance. We should feel such confidence in our civic order that we use no more force against those who violate it than is actually required.

11.   Second, abolition of capital punishment is also a manifestation of our belief in the unique worth and dignity of each person from the moment of conception, a creature made in the image and likeness of God. It is particularly important in the context of our times that this belief be affirmed with regard to those who have failed or whose lives have been distorted by suffering or hatred, even in the case of those who by their actions have failed to respect the dignity and rights of others. It is the recognition of the dignity of all human beings that has impelled the Church to minister to the needs of the outcast and the rejected and that should make us unwilling to treat the lives of even those who have taken human life as expendable or as a means to some further end.

12.   Third, abolition of the death penalty is further testimony to our conviction, a conviction which we share with the Judaic and Islamic traditions, that God is indeed the Lord of life. It is a testimony which removes a certain ambiguity which might otherwise affect the witness that we wish to give to the sanctity of human life in all its stages. We do not wish to equate the situation of criminals convicted of capital

---

[2]Thomas Aquinas, *Summa Theologiae*, II-II, 68, 1; tr. Marcus Lefebvre, O.P. (London: Blackfriars, 1975).

offenses with the condition of the innocent unborn or of the defenseless aged or infirm, but we do believe that the defense of life is
strengthened by eliminating exercise of a judicial authorization to take
human life.

13. Fourth, we believe that abolition of the death penalty is most
consonant with the example of Jesus, who both taught and practiced
the forgiveness of injustice and who came "to give his life as a ransom
for many" (Mk 10:45). In this regard we may point to the reluctance
which those early Christians who accepted capital punishment as a
legitimate practice in civil society felt about the participation of Christians in such an institution[3] and to the unwillingness of the Church
to accept into the ranks of its ministers those who had been involved
in the infliction of capital punishment.[4] There is and has been a certain
sense that even in those cases where serious justifications can be
offered for the necessity of taking life, those who are identified in a
special way with Christ should refrain from taking life. We believe
that this should be taken as an indication of the deeper desires of the
Church as it responds to the story of God's redemptive and forgiving
love as manifest in the life of his Son.

III. Difficulties Inherent in
Capital Punishment

14. With respect to the difficulties inherent in capital punishment,
we note first that infliction of the death penalty extinguishes possibilities for reform and rehabilitation for the person executed as well
as the opportunity for the criminal to make some creative compensation for the evil he or she has done. It also cuts off the possibility
for a new beginning and of moral growth in a human life which has
been seriously deformed.

15. Second, the imposition of capital punishment involves the possibility of mistake. In this respect, it is not different from other legal
processes; and it must be granted our legal system shows considerable care for the rights of defendants in capital cases. But the possibility of mistake cannot be eliminated from the system. Because death
terminates the possibilities of conversion and growth and support
that we can share with each other, we regard a mistaken infliction of
the death penalty with a special horror, even while we retain our
trust in God's loving mercy.

16. Third, the legal imposition of capital punishment in our society
involves long and unavoidable delays. This is in large part a consequence of the safeguards and the opportunities for appeal which the

---

[3]Tertullian, *De Idolatria*, c. 17.
[4]Code of Canon Law, Canon 984.

law provides for defendants; but it also creates a long period of anxiety and uncertainty both about the possibility of life and about the necessity of reorienting one's life. Delay also diminishes the effectiveness of capital punishment as a deterrent, for it makes the death penalty uncertain and remote. Death Row can be the scene of conversion and spiritual growth, but it also produces aimlessness, fear, and despair.

17. Fourth, we believe that the actual carrying out of the death penalty brings with it great and avoidable anguish for the criminal, for his family and loved ones, and for those who are called on to perform or to witness the execution. Great writers such as Shakespeare and Dostoyevsky in the past and Camus and Orwell in our time have given us vivid pictures of the terrors of execution not merely for the victim but also for bystanders.[5]

18. Fifth, in the present situation of dispute over the justifiability of the death penalty and at a time when executions have been rare, executions attract enormous publicity, much of it unhealthy, and stir considerable acrimony in public discussion. On the other hand, if a substantial proportion of the more than five hundred persons now under sentence of death are executed, a great public outcry can safely be predicted. In neither case is the American public likely to develop a sense that the work of justice is being done with fairness and rationality.

19. Sixth, there is a widespread belief that many convicted criminals are sentenced to death in an unfair and discriminatory manner. This belief can be affirmed with certain qualifications. There is a certain presumption that if specific evidence of bias or discrimination in sentencing can be provided for particular cases, then higher courts will not uphold sentences of death in these cases. But we must also reckon with a legal system which, while it does provide counsel for indigent defendants, permits those who are well off to obtain the resources and the talent to present their case in as convincing a light as possible. The legal system and the criminal justice system both work in a society which bears in its psychological, social, and economic patterns the marks of racism. These marks remain long after the demolition of segregation as a legal institution. The end result of all this is a situation in which those condemned to die are nearly always poor and are disproportionately black.[6] Thus forty-seven percent of the inmates on Death Row are black, whereas only eleven percent of the American population is black. Abolition of the death penalty will not eliminate racism and its effects, an evil which we are called on to combat in many different ways. But it is a reasonable judgment that racist attitudes and the social consequences of racism have some influ-

---

[5]William Shakespeare, *Measure for Measure*, Act II, Scene 1; Fyodor Dostoyevsky, *The Idiot*; George Orwell, "A Hanging"; Albert Camus, "Reflections on the Guillotine."
[6]Cf. Charles Black, Jr., *Capital Punishment* (New York: Norton, 1974), pp. 84-91.

ence in determining who is sentenced to die in our society. This we do not regard as acceptable.

IV. Conclusions

20. We do not propose the abolition of capital punishment as a simple solution to the problems of crime and violence. As we observed earlier, we do not believe that any simple and comprehensive solution is possible. We affirm that there is a special need to offer sympathy and support for the victims of violent crime and their families. Our society should not flinch from contemplating the suffering that violent crime brings to so many when it destroys lives, shatters families, and crushes the hopes of the innocent. Recognition of this suffering should not lead to demands for vengeance but to a firm resolution that help be given to the victims of crime and that justice be done fairly and swiftly. The care and the support that we give to the victims of crime should be both compassionate and practical. The public response to crime should include the relief of financial distress caused by crime and the provision of medical and psychological treatment to the extent that these are required and helpful. It is the special responsibility of the Church to provide a community of faith and trust in which God's grace can heal the personal and spiritual wounds caused by crime and in which we can all grow by sharing one another's burdens and sorrows.

21. We insist that important changes are necessary in the correctional system in order to make it truly conducive to the reform and rehabilitation of convicted criminals and their reintegration into society.[7] We also grant that special precautions should be taken to ensure the safety of those who guard convicts who are too dangerous to return to society. We call on governments to cooperate in vigorous measures against terrorists who threaten the safety of the general public and who take the lives of the innocent. We acknowledge that there is a pressing need to deal with those social conditions of poverty and injustice which often provide the breeding grounds for serious crime. We urge particularly the importance of restricting the easy availability of guns and other weapons of violence. We oppose the glamorizing of violence in entertainment, and we deplore the effect of this on children. We affirm the need for education to promote respect for the human dignity of all people. All of these things should form part of a comprehensive community response to the very real and pressing problems presented by the prevalence of crime and violence in many parts of our society.

---

[7]Cf. *The Reform of Correctional Institutions in the 1970s,* Statement of the United States Catholic Conference, November 1973.

22. We recognize that many citizens may believe that capital punishment should be maintained as an integral part of our society's response to the evils of crime, nor is this position incompatible with Catholic tradition. We acknowledge the depth and the sincerity of their concern. We urge them to review the considerations we have offered which show both the evils associated with capital punishment and the harmony of the abolition of capital punishment with the values of the Gospel. We urge them to bear in mind that public decisions in this area affect the lives, the hopes and the fears of men and women who share both the misery and the gandeur of human life with us and who, like us, are among those sinners whom the Son of Man came to save.

23. We urge our brothers and sisters in Christ to remember the teaching of Jesus, who called us to be reconciled with those who have injured us (Mt 5:43-45) and to pray for forgiveness for our sins "as we forgive those who have sinned against us" (Mt 6:12). We call on you to contemplate the crucified Christ, who set us the supreme example of forgiveness and of the triumph of compassionate love.

Resolution on the Hostages in Iran

A Resolution Passed by the
National Conference of Catholic Bishops

November 1980

The status of the hostages in Iran remains at a critical stage. It is not our intention, at this time, to comment on the terms for their release set by the Iranian authorities or on the manner in which the United States government should respond. Instead, we pledge to continue our prayers for the speedy release of the hostages and for a settlement of the differences between the United States and Iran which respects the legitimate interests of both countries. We express our sentiments of sympathy to the families of the hostages and also our admiration for their patience and courage throughout these trying months. As we approach the feasts of Thanksgiving and Christmas so dear to families, we pray that God will continue to give them strength and hope. With all people of good will we look forward to the day when we can offer thanks to God for the hostages' safe return home.

Resolution on El Salvador

*A Resolution Passed by the Administrative Board
of the United States Catholic Conference*

March 1981

1. A year ago, March 24, 1980, Archbishop Oscar Arnulfo Romero was assassinated while offering the Eucharist. He died, as he lived, in the service of the poor. His life and his death have been a vivifying witness for the Church in El Salvador, in the United States and especially for his brother bishops.

2. A month before he was murdered, Archbishop Romero had written to President Carter asking that no military assistance be provided to the Government of El Salvador. Responding to this prophetic action, the bishops of the United States have consistently opposed all military assistance by the United States to El Salvador.

3. In the year since Archbishop Romero's assassination, the war in El Salvador has claimed the lives of over 10,000 people. Every human life is equally sacred, but not all are equally vulnerable. The poor have borne the burden of injustice for decades in El Salvador; they now are most exposed to the violence of the war.

4. A symbol of the vulnerability of the poor was the brutal murder, in December 1980, of the four American missionaries who worked daily among the poor. These selfless and brave women were engaged in the ministry of the Gospel; feeding, sheltering and defending the refugees who are the product of the injustice and violence in El Salvador today. No one should impugn the evangelical character of the lives of these women or question the sacrificial nature of their deaths. Indeed this Administrative Board has just reaffirmed its urgent call to the U.S. Government to press for prompt and thorough completion of the investigation surrounding their deaths. Their ministry and their murders should focus our attention on the basic problem in El Salvador: the quest for justice and human rights by the majority of the population, which has too long been denied both.

5. In two recent testimonies before the Congress, the U.S. Catholic Conference (USCC) has sought to keep this essential dimension of the conflict in El Salvador before the eyes of the American public and especially those who shape U.S. policy. As members of the Administrative Board of the USCC, we wish to endorse the recommendations of these testimonies. We are conscious that the situation in El Salvador is both complex and changing. We speak on the basis of the best knowledge we have available to us at this time. We do not speak lightly or hastily. Our desire is to further the public debate on an issue of great moral and political importance to the people of the United States and El Salvador.

6. We speak as bishops and pastors of the Catholic Church, which has been called by the Second Vatican Council to stand as the sign and safeguard of the dignity of the person. We speak to the policy question of El Salvador because public policies affect people. We continue to have serious doubts about and substantial differences with U.S. policy toward El Salvador.

7. Specifically, we wish to reiterate our opposition to military aid and intervention by the major outside powers. We oppose intervention in any form by the Soviet Union and its allies; we likewise oppose U.S. military aid or intervention in the war. We urge, instead, that greater attention be given by the U.S. Government to a political resolution of the conflict in El Salvador by encouraging a dialogue among all parties. We support economic assistance to the people of El Salvador, but we also realize that its full effectiveness requires a basic political resolution of the conflict.

8. In conclusion, we speak again to the Church in El Salvador, to its bishops, priests, sisters and laity and the missionaries who serve there. We thank them for their evangelical witness, we pledge our continued support and we pray for a just and peaceful resolution of the war in El Salvador.

Reflections on the Energy Crisis

*A Statement Issued by the Committee on Social
Development and World Peace, United States
Catholic Conference*

April 2, 1981

I. Introduction

1.   The fading of the petroleum age disquiets the entire world. Cheap oil and natural gas not only powered the dramatic transformation of Western society in the twentieth century, they underlie much of the material progress developing countries have made. Now it is only a matter of time until oil and gas production peaks and starts to drop.[1] In the years ahead, the nations of the earth, both rich and poor, must learn to conserve what supplies they can obtain. They must also find some way of switching over to dependence on alternative sources of energy without sinking into economic chaos.

2.   The United States cannot ignore this imperative. Almost half the energy we use comes from oil and forty percent of this oil is imported.[2] The abrupt price surges of recent years, besides affecting consumers directly, have contributed heavily to inflation and unemployment. Middle-class families find their budgets increasingly tight, while the poor are faced with the terrible prospect of choosing between fuel and decent clothing, fuel and health care, even fuel and food. Clearly, energy costs will prove to be a growing burden to millions of our people.

3.   Moreover, the American economy is frighteningly vulnerable to outright disruption. The embargo of 1973-74 and the more recent war between Iran and Iraq demonstrate that the nation lacks reliable access to foreign petroleum. If the flow of oil from Africa and the Persian

---

[1]Dr. V. Paul Kenney, professor of physics at the University of Notre Dame, served as technical consultant to the USCC subcommittee on energy. He comments, "Estimation of oil and gas reserves is more art than science, but it seems likely that we passed our domestic peak about 1970 and that world production will pass its peak between 1990 and 1995." A well-respected study concludes, "Even if imports of oil were maintained at the 1976 level of about 40 percent, and oil and gas consumption grew at an annual rate of 2 percent, conventional domestic oil and natural gas resources would not last much beyond the year 2000." Sam H. Schurr, project director, *Energy in America's Future: The Choices Before Us,* a study by the staff of resources for the future. Johns Hopkins University Press (Baltimore, 1979), p. 26.

[2]The sources of energy used in the United States in 1979 were as follows: oil, 47.5 percent; natural gas, 25.4 percent; coal, 19.6 percent; hydroelectric, four percent; nuclear, 3.5 percent. Power Systems Sector, General Electric Co., United States Energy Data Book, General Electric Co., (Fairfield, Conn., 1980), p. 7. The percentage of our oil that is imported has fallen from a high of 46.6 in 1977 (see footnote 6).

Gulf were suddenly cut off, the production of goods would shrink, jobs would disappear, and the delivery of necessary services would be hampered.[3] Under such circumstances, those who have less would presumably suffer more. In a competition for scarce energy and for reduced goods and services, only the wealthy could win.

4. Because of its economic and political power, the United States bears a responsibility to the international community as well as to its own citizens. There are few greater gifts we can offer the people of other lands than openhearted cooperation in the effort to develop a global policy to bring about future energy security. This duty takes a special moral urgency from the fact that America is the leading energy consumer. A half-century of plentiful oil has made us careless; we waste what other countries need.

5. Our power can be as much a force for evil as for good. Should we fail to help the world toward security, we increase the chance that we will lead it to destruction. In the absence of well-developed alternative systems, what happens when the oil and gas run out? Even before the wells dry up, what happens as global supplies dwindle and prices soar? Even before supply problems became acute, what happens if there is another, longer embargo or if turmoil engulfs the OPEC nations? Early in 1980, the president of the United States asserted America's readiness to defend its vital energy interests with force. The black seed of the final holocaust may lie beneath the sands of the Middle East.

II. The Moral Dimensions of Energy Policy[4]

6. The threat of war, the danger that scarcity poses for the poor— such considerations are reason enough for the Church to take part in the national discussion of energy. Further, energy is one of those touchstone issues like arms control or the limits of federal power whose resolution will profoundly affect society in the twenty-first century. Unless some new perspectives are brought to bear, decision makers will have little to rely on but the hard and rather narrow analytical tools that have guided energy development in the past. In his first encyclical, *Redemptor Hominis*, Pope John Paul II said: "The development of technology and the development of contemporary

---

[3]"The denial of [foreign] oil supplies—to us or to others—would threaten our security and provoke an economic crisis greater than that of the Great Depression 50 years ago, with a fundamental change in the way we live." President Jimmy Carter, State of the Union Address, Jan. 23, 1980.

[4]Rev. John T. Pawlikowski, OSM, professor of social ethics at the Catholic Theological Union in Chicago, served as theological consultant to the USCC subcommittee on energy.

civilization, which is marked by the ascendancy of technology, demand a proportional development of morals and ethics. For the present this last development seems unfortunately to be always left behind" (#15).

7.   The present Statement offers no solutions to the swirling controversies that surround the formation of energy policy. It constitutes an invitation, not a pronouncement—an invitation to further study, to conscientious judgment, to prudent action at all levels. At the same time, it seeks to situate energy issues in a moral context, to arouse sensitivity to human considerations that are often ignored. Catholic social teaching suggests certain clear principles that should be borne in mind as Americans, remembering their brothers and sisters in other nations, strive to adjust to a world where oil and natural gas are no longer readily available.

Moral Principles

8.   (1) *Upholding the right to life.* It is clear that no overall energy strategy is free from risk to human life. Claims that there is a completely safe option are illusory; the choice is not between black and white but among shades of gray. Furthermore, a given policy can threaten life in various ways. For example, developing energy source A may consign miners or local residents to death, while failing to develop it may indirectly kill others if supply falls short of essential demand.

9.   The Church recognizes these sad facts. It is deeply committed to the defense of human life, however, and this commitment is uppermost in its approach to energy. Energy planners and those in authority must do all in their power to safeguard human life. They must especially avoid exposing people to danger without giving them the opportunity to accept or reject that danger. As the bishops gathered at the Second Vatican Council said:

> At the same time, however, there is a growing awareness of the exalted dignity proper to the human person, since he stands above all things and his rights and duties are universal and inviolable. Therefore, there must be available to all people everything necessary for leading a life truly human, [including] the right . . . to [required] information, [and] to activity in accord with the upright norm of one's own conscience. . . . Hence, the social order and its development must unceasingly work to the benefit of the human person if the disposition of affairs is to be subordinate to the personal realm and not contrariwise (*Gaudium et Spes,* #26).

10.   (2) *Accepting an appropriate share of responsibility for the welfare of creation.* Judeo-Christian tradition views human beings not in isolation but as part of a larger whole—as creatures in the midst of creation. This tradition counsels respect for the natural world, emphasizing that we have duties as well as rights in its use. Since we derive all

our energy from nature, the relationship of humanity and environment has the broadest implications for energy policy.

11. In the religious community, this relationship is often described as "responsible stewardship"; we are stewards to whose care the Master has entrusted His creation. The technological strides we have made since World War II require a sharpening of that concept. The human race has the capacity to alter nature, even to destroy it, and the scope of our responsibility grows with the scope of our power. We are no longer called upon simply to tend the garden God has given us. It is now in our hands to determine whether our descendants will inherit an earth capable of sustaining them.

12. This awesome responsibility has led some analysts to advance the notion that humanity is an intruder in nature; they advocate extreme measures, including methods of population control that are destructive of liberty. There is no question that in our present state of knowledge we cannot obtain adequate energy supplies without imposing some costs on the environment. But surely our response should not be to alienate ourselves from nature, to spurn the gifts God has given us. Pope John Paul gave the context in which we should approach the task of designing an ecologically sound energy program when he declared that "exploitation of the earth . . . and the uncontrolled development of technology outside the framework of a long-range authentically humanistic plan often bring with them a threat to our natural environment . . . and remove us from nature. Yet it was the Creator's will that humanity should communicate with nature as an intelligent and noble master and guardian, and not as a heedless exploiter and destroyer" (*Redemptor Hominis*, #15).

13. (3) *Accepting limitation in a Christian spirit.* When a certain young man questioned Jesus on what he should do to be saved, Jesus advised him to sell what he had, take up his cross and follow. The young man "went away sad, for his possessions were many" (Mt 19:16-22). If preservation of the common good, both domestic and global, requires that we as individuals make sacrifices related to energy use, we should do so cheerfully. Americans have become used to the idea that rapid economic expansion is an unqualified, even inevitable good. Future resource restrictions may force us to rethink our expectations; they may even lead to substantial changes in our way of life. Insofar as these adjustments affect excess possessions, we should welcome them. They are a blessing.

14. Adopting this attitude will free us to face the energy situation with hope. God did not put us here to build up His Kingdom only to strike the requisite tools from our hands. The problems that close us in can be solved if we will seek the right solutions. This means rising above a preoccupation with material gain.

15. (4) *Striving for a more just society.* The energy debate is not about abstractions and statistics. It is about war and famine and suffering;

its content is the struggle against cold, against dark, against isolation. The energy policies we choose must reflect a search after justice for all, not only on the level of individual rights but also with regard to the structures of society.

16. Catholic social teaching has touched on these themes time and again. *Gaudium et Spes* declares, "Meanwhile that conviction grows . . . that it devolves on humanity to establish a political, social and economic order which will increasingly serve people and help individuals as well as groups to affirm and develop the dignity proper to them" (#9). Pope John XXIII, in sounding a similar note, emphasized that every human being is spirit and body, multifaceted, born to pursue a varied perfection. His words in *Mater et Magistra* remind us that economic considerations impinge on the development of energy policy in more ways than one. The desire for economic justice must dominate.

> 'National wealth'—as our predecessor of happy memory, Pius XII, rightfully observed—'inasmuch as it is produced by the common efforts of the citizenry, has no other purpose than to secure without interruption those material conditions in which individuals are enabled to lead a full and perfect life. . . . For the system whereby both the common prosperity is achieved and individuals exercise their right to use material goods, conforms fully to norms laid down by God the Creator.' From this it follows that the economic prosperity of any people is to be assessed not so much from the sum total of goods and wealth possessed as from the distribution of goods according to norms of justice, so that everyone in the community can develop and perfect themselves. For this, after all, is the end toward which all economic activity of a community is by nature ordered (#74).

17. Finally, Pope John Paul teaches in *Dives in Misericordia* that the spirit of justice must be perfected by the spirit of mercy.

> Certainly, the Second Vatican Council also leads us in this direction when it speaks repeatedly of the need to make the world more human and says that the realization of this task is precisely the mission of the church in the modern world. Society can become ever more human only if we introduce into the many-sided setting of interpersonal and social relationships, not merely justice, but also that 'merciful love' which constitutes the messianic message of the Gospel (#14).

18. Public discussion of energy policy has been sharply polarized. Too often advocates of a particular point of view refuse to even consider the arguments of those they oppose. It is difficult to see how these attitudes, the antithesis of fraternal charity, can help create a more just social order. The Church would be false to its Founder if it did not take up the cause of the oppressed. But it must also insist that justice is not to be meted out to some and denied to others. Just as utility companies should not raise rates above the level needed to ensure a fair return for honest and efficient service, for example, consumers should not demand that rates be held below the same level.

19. (5) *Giving special attention to the needs of the poor and members of minority groups.* The first Letter of John asks, "If someone who has the riches of this world sees his brother in need and closes his heart to him, how does the love of God abide in him?" (1 Jn 3:17). As noted above, poor people, especially those with fixed incomes, will feel the sting of rising energy prices more keenly than their affluent neighbors. Moreover, racist attitudes may affect both price and access to supply. In circumstances where energy is essential to the maintenance of life, health, or human dignity, there is but one course to follow. Private agencies and federal, state, and local authorities must take whatever steps are necessary to ensure an adequate supply to people whom poverty or discrimination place at a disadvantage. No energy policy is acceptable that fails to deal adequately with basic needs.

20. No one will quarrel with the proposition that Christians cannot stand idly by while people freeze in their homes for lack of fuel. The Church goes further in its advocacy for the poor, however. In "A Call to Action," Pope Paul VI outlines the attitude we should adopt toward those who suffer deprivation. He also shows why the poor should be singled out for special attention in dealing with the energy crisis.

> In teaching us charity, the Gospel instructs us in the preferential respect due to the poor and the special situation they have in society: The more fortunate should renounce some of their rights so as to place their goods more generously at the service of others. If beyond legal rules there is really no deeper feeling of respect for and service to others, then even equality before the law can serve as an alibi for flagrant discrimination, continued exploitation and actual contempt (#23).

21. Our concern for the poor must extend beyond America's borders. Domestic policy, far from imposing burdens on the economies of other nations, should be consistent with the goal of promoting sound development throughout the world.

22. (6) *Participating in the decision-making process.* Fairness requires that groups and individuals representing a broad spectrum of opinion have an opportunity to take part in formulating energy policy. Even local energy decisions often involve danger to life and health, and national ones can have major economic effects and can help determine the patterns of power in society. The stakes are too high both practically and morally for the ordinary citizen to ignore the processes through which such decisions are reached.

23. Given the inequalities that pervade American society, fairness may also require active assistance to those whose voice is rarely heard in policy discussions. Pope Paul's words in "Justice in the World" describe the situation well:

> Unless combated and overcome by social and political action, the influence of the new industrial and technological order favors the concentration of wealth, power and decision making in the hands of a small public or private controlling group. Economic justice and lack of social participation keep a person from attaining basic human and civil rights (#9).

24. The principle of subsidiarity, as outlined in *Quadragesimo Anno* and reaffirmed in *Mater et Magistra*, is relevant to any discussion of citizen participation. In general terms, the principle holds that social functions that can be performed by an individual should not be transferred to a group, and that functions that can be performed by a smaller "collectivity" (the local community, for example) should not be transferred to a larger "collectivity" (state or, at the next stage, federal government). Pope Pius XI gave the reason: "Inasmuch as every social activity should, by its very nature, prove a help to members of the body social, it should never destroy or absorb them" (quoted in *Mater et Magistra*, #53). In order for energy decisions to be broadly based, they must be taken in accessible forums.

Commitment

25. These principles are offered as a framework for moral reflection and action regarding energy policy. They are lenses through which such policy can be examined, benchmarks by which it can be judged. However, the principles have their limitations. Because they are general, different people will reach different conclusions when applying them, say, to nuclear power or coal use. The element of informed individual judgment remains critical. In the same way, the principles cannot move anyone to take Christian morality seriously in grappling with energy. That is a matter of faith, a matter of religious commitment.

26. Our redemption makes us capable of seeking just, generous, and loving solutions to the problems we face. But we are too sinful, too given to selfishness, to pursue this difficult search without a conviction that all humanity is one in Christ. Pope John urged his readers in *Pacem in Terris*, "in the light of their Christian faith and led by love, to ensure that the various institutions—whether economic, social, cultural or political in purpose—will be such as . . . to facilitate or render less arduous humanity's self-perfection in both the natural order and the supernatural" (#146). Jesus, in St. John's account, spoke more simply:

> As the Father has loved me, so I have loved you. Live on in my love. You will live in my love if you keep my commandments, even as I have kept my Father's commandments and live in his love. All

this I tell you that my joy may be yours and your joy may be complete. This is my commandment: Love one another as I have loved you (Jn 15:9-12).

III. Making the Transition: Sources of Energy

27. As annoying as they may be, gas lines and temporary crimps in the supply pipeline are not the "energy crisis." Even our reliance on oil imports is only one element in the crisis. The fundamental problem, simply put, is the need to effect a transition from primary dependence on oil and natural gas to primary dependence on something else in the fairly near future.

28. From the moral perspective just presented, it makes a great deal of difference how this transition is handled and where it leads. Will the development of alternative sources of energy contribute to a just society in which access to the necessities of life is universal? Will it reduce the risk of self-destruction through war that competition for energy supplies now poses? Will it help balance the need for economic development with the need for environmental integrity? Can it be a creative force in shaping a more hopeful future than the world seems to face today? In the remaining years of this century, the human community will answer these questions for better or worse.

Conventional Oil and Natural Gas

29. This nation will not wean itself overnight from oil and natural gas. Great disruptions would result if it tried. America moves on petroleum; with minor exceptions, our entire transportation system is bound to it. Moreover, large-scale technologies cannot now use any substitute energy source except coal or nuclear fission, and conversion takes time and money.

30. Not only will the United States continue to burn conventional oil and gas, it will continue to trade on the world oil market. Ideally, this trade is good. If governed by fair cooperative arrangements between oil producers and importers, it serves as a reminder of the interdependence of nations and benefits all. As noted above, though, many considerations make a sharp decrease in our use of foreign oil desirable. Such a step can even be seen as an act of justice toward importing countries struggling to develop their economies.[5]

---

[5]"National policies of conservation, fuel substitution and domestic supply enhancement which reduce oil imports have effects beyond the borders of the country which acts. They tend to lower energy prices, lessen stresses on the international financial system, and improve the prospects for political and economic stability. In doing so, they make both the country that reduces imports and all other oil importers better off." Schurr, pp. 418-19.

31. American imports have dropped significantly since 1977,[6] and there seems to be room for further improvement. Even though domestic oil production has apparently peaked, industry can contribute by searching for new strikes and employing new techniques for forcing more crude from old wells. Such efforts have clear value.

32. Given the certainty that our resources are finite, however, oil production should not be overemphasized. Why pursue a policy that guarantees the early exhaustion of domestic supplies, especially when oil has certain uses (in the production of pharmaceuticals, for instance) that would be very difficult to replace? Without ignoring the need to produce for today's demand, it is prudent to begin identifying an alternative or mix of alternatives immediately. As long as oil remains our primary fuel, we are on a collision course with nature.

Conservation

33. What to do in this dilemma? One response comes quickly to mind. Pope John Paul, in an address to the Pontifical Commission on Justice and Peace in 1978, said that "Christians will want to be in the vanguard in favoring ways of life that decisively break with a frenzy of consumerism, exhausting and joyless." Sadly, few Americans take such exhortations to heart and fewer still think of energy when they think of consumerism. Yet all people of good will do have a positive duty to conserve energy and to use energy efficiently under the conditions prevailing in the nation and the world. Those who have adopted simple styles of life deserve praise for their courage and commitment.

34. The duty to conserve will vary from individual to individual, depending on each one's health, economic status, and other circumstances. For example, older people who set their thermostats too low run the risk of illness or death from a gradual decline in body temperature (accidental hypothermia). Those who live outside metropolitan areas do not have the option of switching to mass transit systems to get to work. Poor people are not in a position to weatherize their homes out of their own pockets. Conservation is a matter of judgment, informed by a lively conscience.

35. The recent downturn in gasoline sales and slowed growth in demand for electricity show that conservation has gained a certain momentum.[7] It is up to ordinary men and women to make sure that this movement remains strong. Most of us can take some of the small

---

[6]The United States imported 8.8 million barrels of oil a day in 1977 and 8.2 million barrels a day in 1979. Energy Data Book, p. 46. Preliminary estimates for 1980 put imports at less than 7 million barrels per day.

[7]For electrical demand, see Energy Data Book, p. 15. The drop in gasoline sales, a recent phenomenon, has been widely reported. The current recession may well be responsible for part of this cutback, but the extent of its influence is unknown.

but important steps to save energy that citizens' groups, government agencies, and others are constantly proposing. A striking statistic highlights the urgency of the need: More than ten percent of the oil the entire world produces each day vanishes into the tanks of American cars.[8]

36. Relatively minor adjustments in the way we live can have only a limited impact of course. There are opportunities for conservation throughout the economy. For example, much can be done in the industrial sector by "co-generating" electricity with process heat, recycling discarded materials, phasing in more energy-efficient equipment and procedures, and so on. State and federal governments can offer incentives for such innovations where sound economics does not dictate them. Government can also stimulate other wide-ranging improvements in America's use of energy. It can establish stringent performance standards for automobiles, buildings, and other products; institute weatherization programs (thereby creating job opportunities as well); and, in general, guide the country in an orderly and sensible conservation effort.

37. Some shy away from conserving energy because it connotes sacrifice or because they suspect industry of exploiting the market for private gain. Such a response makes little practical sense. A barrel of oil that is not burned today is available for tomorrow; every act of conservation brightens our chances of making a smooth transition to reliance on alternative sources of energy. Conversely, a rejection of small sacrifices today could enforce large sacrifices tomorrow. It is not yet clear whether Americans will have to accept fundamental changes like abandoning inefficient suburban housing and shopping centers accessible only by car for efficient central-city apartments and stores served by mass transit. But such changes are certainly more likely to be necessary if we bury our heads in the sand.

Coal

38. Conservation only saves oil; it cannot replace it. Leaving aside the transportation sector, the leading alternative to oil is coal. About seventy-five percent of the coal we now consume goes to make electricity, with most of the rest consigned to industry.[9] It is tempting to increase coal production. America has abundant reserves of the mineral,[10] and the technology surrounding its use is well developed. Coal

---

[8]The Washington Post, Sept. 25, 1979, p. A10.

[9]Committee on Nuclear and Alternative Energy Systems, National Academy of Sciences, Energy in Transition, 1985-2010, W.H. Freeman (San Francisco, 1980), p. 158.

[10]"The United States has more mineable coal reserves than any other country, a supply that will last hundreds of years. Current annual excess production capacity in the industry stands at nearly 200 million tons." President's Commission on Coal, "Rec-

could become the key transitional fuel, bridging the gap between petroleum and renewable energy sources.

39. However, the advantages of accelerated coal production must be evaluated in the light of some very serious disadvantages. As the Appalachian bishops' pastoral statement "This Land Is Home to Me" points out, the history of coal is a tale of sweat, of suffering, of bloody conflict, of disease, of early death. Even today, miners lose their lives in accidents and black lung remains a crippling curse. New mining also threatens local residents. In Appalachia, it can lead to increased blasting, flooding, and road damage. In the West, it can disrupt communities, turning them into overnight "boom towns." The economic and social health of some small towns and cities has already been shattered; these places are blazing a sad trail that many others may follow.

40. Environmental considerations loom large. First, strip mining has heavily damaged land and poisoned water supplies in the past; and recently enacted federal law has not yet effectively halted this devastation. Second, burning coal releases huge amounts of sulphur and nitrogen oxides and other pollutants into the atmosphere. The oxides can combine with water to create "acid rain," which is suspected of wiping out fish populations in lakes and damaging some crops.[11] More important, air pollution poses a danger to human health, killing thousands of people every year.[12]

41. The use of coal (and other fossil fuels as well) has been associated in recent scientific investigation with a darker, more shadowy threat than mining accidents or pollution. Combustion releases carbon dioxide and a buildup of this gas over time could affect temperatures worldwide in ways that are difficult to predict. Such a phenomenon could cause significant climatic changes, jeopardize food supplies by altering growing conditions in agricultural areas, perhaps even trigger catastrophic flooding by melting parts of the polar ice caps. No one is sure how great an increase in carbon dioxide levels would be necessary to produce such consequences or if they would happen at all.

---

ommendations and Summary Findings" (Washington, D.C., Government Printing Office, 1980), p. 7. The U.S. Senate Committee on Energy and Natural Resources offers a more precise estimate: "Recoverable coal reserves amount to at least 150 billion tons, which is equal to at least two centuries of consumption at current levels." "Energy: An Uncertain Future" (Washington, D.C., Government Printing Office, 1978), p. 35.

[11] Carroll L. Wilson (project director), *Coal: Bridge to the Future*, report of the world coal study (Cambridge, Mass., Ballinger Publishing Co., 1980), p. 144.

[12] There is considerable uncertainty concerning the number of deaths that air pollution may be said to cause. One study comments, "Although we have given two estimates of deaths attributable to air pollution—9,000 and 140,000—we emphasize that reliable quantitative estimates of the overall health impact of air pollution do not exist." Hans H. Landsberg, et al., *Energy: The Next Twenty Years* (Cambridge, Mass., Ballinger Publishing Co., 1979), p. 365. Dr. Kenney adds, "Air-pollution epidemiology studies suggest that sulfate and particulate emissions from coal-fired plants may cause some 50,000 to 100,000 premature deaths yearly across the entire U.S. population."

But it would be the height of folly to tamper in ignorance with the ecology of the entire planet.[13]

42. Unlike the question of conservation, the question of increased coal use does not present the Christian with a clear moral choice. As with many other issues related to energy, there are many gaps and uncertainties in the facts about coal. How great a risk does atmospheric carbon dioxide imply? What elements in air pollution are most toxic? How dangerous will contaminated rain be at higher levels of acidity? Moreover, the facts change over time. Until now, neither voluntary compliance nor federal requirements for pollution abatement have been notably successful.[14] Coal's supporters note, however, that future power plants will be designed to conform to rigorous emission standards and that promising new techniques to remove sulphur during combustion are being developed. The basis for moral judgment will shift as our knowledge improves.

43. The present state of affairs certainly calls for caution in accepting a more prominent role for coal in America's future. The Church cannot ignore the benefits coal offers; it is an energy "cushion" that the average person might one day be very glad to have. But neither can the Church ignore the attendant dangers to human health and the environment. If a commitment to coal is made, it should be balanced by a simultaneous commitment to improved mine safety and strict ecological and community-protection standards. To act otherwise is to seek a just end through unjust means.

Nuclear Fission

44. Besides coal, the only developed and expandable alternative to oil for large-scale electrical generation is nuclear fission. It is based on a domestic resource, uranium, and could provide power for a very long time if the breeder reactor were perfected on a commercial scale. America already has a functioning nuclear industry, with some seventy plants in operation and another ninety under construction or cleared for construction.[15] Since atomic energy produces about twelve percent of our electricity nationwide,[16] the question is not whether to use it. Rather, we must decide whether to continue using it and, if so, whether to use more of it.

---

[13]This discussion of the carbon dioxide problem is drawn from a symposium before the Senate Committee on Government Affairs, July 30, 1979. The word "uncertainty" dominated the discussion. While the majority opinion is that increased levels of carbon dioxide will cause a warming of the atmosphere, for example, some scientists think it may produce a cooling. See also Wilson, pp. 147-50.

[14]General Accounting Office, "Improvements Needed in Controlling Major Air Pollution Sources" (Washington, D.C., General Accounting Office, 1978).

[15]General Accounting Office, "Questions on the Future of Nuclear Power: Implications and Trade-Offs" (Washington, D.C., General Accounting Office, 1979), pp. 1, 8.

[16]Energy Data Book, p. 77.

45. Nuclear power has been aptly described as standing at the center of an incomplete system.[17] The byproducts of fission are hazardous radioactive wastes. These high-level wastes must be totally isolated from the environment for a very long time, and scientists disagree on whether that is possible in all cases.[18] There are also unresolved safety questions in the operation of nuclear plants, as the 1979 accident at Three Mile Island forcefully demonstrated.[19] The effects of low-level radiation on uranium miners and others is the subject of intense and confusing debate. Finally, the spread of nuclear technology here and abroad raises the specter of nuclear arms proliferation.[20]

46. As everyone knows, atomic energy is fiercely controversial. Many uncertainties surround this complex technology and both pro- and anti-nuclear advocates seem prone to exaggerated claims, creating an atmosphere in which rational public discussion is difficult. Under these circumstances, it is hardly surprising that individuals disagree in good faith on the course national policy should follow. Some favor shutting down existing nuclear plants; others press for a moratorium on licensing or construction; still others want to build new reactors while working to solve the problems implicit in the fission fuel cycle.

47. This controversy, which has been conducted largely in moral terms, will persist. It should be dominated by a concern for human life, both now and in the future, and by a desire to mold a just society where everyone has access to the necessities. According to one viewpoint, these principles support the continued development of nuclear energy. Failure to pursue the technology could eventually put the United States at a disadvantage vis-à-vis other nations in supplying power to its people. Abandoning the nuclear option altogether creates more immediate risks. Those who would close plants or forbid new ones

---

[17]Robert Stobaugh and Daniel Yergin, *Energy Future* (New York, Random House, 1979), p. 117.

[18]Many estimates have been given as to the length of time nuclear wastes must be isolated from the environment. According to a panel discussion sponsored by the Forum of the National Academy of Sciences in Washington, D.C., Nov. 19, 1979, the most critical period is the first 1,000 years. A transcript of the discussion, titled "Nuclear Waste: What to Do With It?" is available from the National Academy of Sciences. See also Schurr, pp. 499-500.

[19]Bishop Joseph Daley of Harrisburg issued a formal statement in the wake of the Three Mile Island accident calling for a moratorium on the licensing of new nuclear plants until the government can "guarantee" their safety.

[20]The question of the connection between the U.S. nuclear power industry and nuclear arms proliferation is problematical. Dr. Kenney comments: "It is certainly technically feasible to apply sufficient overall security measures to ensure the integrity of our domestic reactor fuel cycle. . . . Reactor fuel supplied to nations overseas is the real focus of our proliferation problem. Recent attempts by the United States to dissuade the lesser-developed nations from further reliance on nuclear power have been rebuffed. Moreover, regardless of what nuclear stance this nation assumes, it is already clear that nuclear fuel and technology will be supplied to those who ask for it by other industrialized countries in both Western and Eastern Europe." For a more detailed discussion that draws similar conclusions but emphasizes the need for a nonproliferation policy, see Landsberg, pp. 442-46 and 454-65.

must concretely demonstrate how conservation and alternative energy sources can provide for essential services.[21]

48. Without discounting such arguments, we should be aware that nuclear power's share in electrical generation remains fairly small. Our commitment to atomic energy could still be reversed through careful planning. This possibility deserves careful consideration. While nuclear energy is not evil in itself, it can do great evil. The consequences of a core meltdown or an accident involving "hot" wastes could be catastrophic, far outweighing any good society derives from the electricity fission could supply. It may be unwise to cooperate in the spread of nuclear technology through the world, despite the fact that many nations seek this technology. Finally, the effect that hundreds of nuclear plants and their stored wastes may have on our descendants must be taken into account. If the defenders of nuclear power are to prevail, they must be able to demonstrate its safety beyond reasonable doubt.

49. Because of the risks involved, people's right to participate democratically in decisions that affect them deserves special emphasis where atomic energy is concerned. The average person has the opportunity to vote for government officials, to speak up at public hearings and the like. However, some states have turned to a more direct and potentially more inclusive instrument for registering citizen opinion on nuclear power: the referendum. Industry advocates presumably have a financial advantage in putting their position before the public, but this advantage can be nullified through spending limitations. If fair referenda were held on such questions as the operation of nuclear· plants or the disposal of wastes, the outline of a national consensus might emerge. At the very least, responsible leaders of various persuasions would have the chance to educate people on the choices they faced, helping dispel the mythology and reduce the tensions that cloud the nuclear issue.[22]

Geothermal Energy

50. Geothermal generating plants have been suggested as another substitute for facilities that burn fossil fuels, since in theory geothermal energy reserves are very extensive. But the contribution steam

---

[21]"Questions on the Future of Nuclear Power," p. 26: "The trends we have projected indicate that if actions are taken to limit or halt the growth of nuclear power, they must be accompanied by actions to severely limit electricity requirements or programs to expand coal supply or other non-nuclear fuels. Otherwise, serious shortfalls of electricity supply are likely to occur in the 1980s."

[22]Granted that nuclear power represents a special case because it has been so highly politicized, such referenda might logically be held on all major energy projects where social costs and benefits must be weighed: for example, the construction of large dams, the opening of new coal fields, and the installation of windmill systems and large solar arrays.

and water from the earth can make to our energy supply is limited by the fact that they can be tapped only in certain locations. They also entail heavy economic and environmental costs. Research into the possibility of drawing on geopressurized zones and on hot dry rock and magma formations may expand the potential of geothermal in the next few decades.[23]

Synthetic Oil and Gas

51. Electricity, of course, is only one form of energy and it is not suited to all tasks. Our immediate fuel crisis is largely a liquid-fuel crisis centered on transporation. As a result, the federal government is giving considerable attention to synthetic oil and gas derived from coal, oil shale, biomass, and other hydrocarbons. The United States has massive stores of raw materials, from which synthetics can be made.[24] Furthermore, the corporations that trade in conventional oil and gas can both produce and market synthetic fuels, using techniques related to those they presently employ.

52. The major emphasis today is on products synthesized from coal and oil shale. Unfortunately, most of the human and environmental problems associated with accelerated coal combustion apply in varying degrees to the liquefaction and gasification processes under consideration.[25] Manufacturing these substances also requires great quantities of water. In semiarid Western states, public officials would face some very hard choices between water for coal conversion and water for agriculture and home use.

53. Clearly, the moral concerns mentioned in connection with burning coal are relevant here as well. A serious disruption of our transportation system in the future could have a disastrous effect on millions of people and threaten the stability of the entire economy. However, the legitimate need to find a replacement liquid fuel should not make us less vigilant in protecting human life and environment. We will pay a price for fossil-derived synthetics, perhaps a heavy one. It would be irresponsible not to weigh the risks very seriously and not to examine any promising alternative technology before embarking on a massive "synfuels" program.

54. Proceeding with care should not cause excessive delay. At present, the United States has no commercial synthetic-fuel plants. Although

---

[23]This discussion of geothermal energy is based on General Accounting Office, "Geothermal Energy: Obstacles and Uncertainties Impede Its Widespread Use" (Washington, D.C., General Accounting Office, 1980).

[24]For coal reserves, see footnote 10; for oil shale, see Schurr, p. 231; for biomass, see Schurr, pp. 260-61.

[25]There is still considerable uncertainty about the exact environmental impacts of synfuel production, but they would be substantial. For shale oil, see National Academy of Sciences, pp. 138-39. For coal liquids, see National Academy of Sciences, p. 181. For coal gas, see National Academy of Sciences, p. 143.

the practicality of several liquefaction and gasification technologies has been demonstrated on a relatively small scale, further research will be required to develop the most desirable methods and to make sure that large-scale production is feasible.[26] While these economic and technical questions are being settled, we should also study the social and environmental implications of synthetic-fuel production, both for America and other nations. We will probably discover that we can have a synthetics industry. We must then decide whether we should have one.

Solar Power

55. Given the severe difficulties they present, one cannot help viewing most energy sources with a touch of apprehension. By contrast, the general reaction to solar power is hope. (The term "solar power" includes energy from the sun; from wind, wave, and falling water; and from biomass.) The sun is an inexhaustible fount of energy for a variety of purposes, with the probable exception of tasks requiring high heat—firing utility and industrial boilers, for example. Its effects on people and the environment are relatively benign.[27] Since some small solar applications are appropriate for use in poor as well as developed countries, we can render the whole human family a service by perfecting the relevant technology. Most important, solar power can help open the way to permanent energy security, pointing beyond the end of fossil fuels.

56. Hope centers on something yet to be realized. Hydroelectric generation is an established energy source and working solar units of various kinds are scattered throughout the country. But the rewards of solar power lie mainly in the future, partly for technical reasons and partly as a result of social, economic, and institutional barriers. Moreover, since most solar technologies are still in an early stage of development, it is extremely difficult to predict their potential—or for that matter the unforeseen problems they may present. This accounts for much of the controversy surrounding energy from the sun. The value of pursuing the solar option is not in serious dispute. But analysts disagree vehemently on when various solar devices will come into general use and how strong a contribution they will make, individually and collectively, to our energy supply.[28]

---

[26]See Schurr, pp. 55-58.

[27]The most obvious exception to this rule is the hydroelectric facility. When a dam bursts, people die and the local environment certainly suffers. Some solar systems— the solar power satellite is the most frequently cited example—may pose very serious risks to humanity and nature.

[28]As is well known, the Carter administration set a goal of obtaining twenty percent of our energy from solar sources by the year 2000. The National Academy of Sciences study mentioned above, which has been widely attacked as being anti-solar, holds that this goal can only be reached if the government provides "vigorous incentives"

57. The matter of timing is critical in a discussion of the transition period from primary dependence on oil and natural gas to alternative sources—roughly the next twenty or thirty years. Again, few would deny that the sun may provide a significant share of our power in the long run. Will it prove practical in the short run? The way different people answer this question helps determine their attitude not only toward solar but also toward the energy sources solar is intended to replace or supplement.

58. How quickly scientists and engineers can develop solar systems is a technical issue that does not invite moral reflection. However, two related considerations deserve stress. First, energy is a tool for fulfilling essential human needs. No energy policy is just which fails to meet these needs; that is the fundamental requirement. Those who question the near-term effectiveness of some solar devices, therefore, raise a legitimate concern. Second, solar energy, because it is renewable and generally benign, possesses key advantages over the rest of the field. It follows that energy planners, while making sure that essential needs are served, should favor the development of selected solar technologies, offering generous public incentives and attempting to remove the obstacles that impede rapid advance.

59. Active and passive systems for space and water heating, the leading direct solar applications, are the likeliest vehicle for ushering in a solar age.[29] In the present state of the art, solar heating remains beyond the reach of the poor, and even affluent people will exercise care in purchasing equipment whose performance is relatively untried. However, the benefits of these systems will increase as the price of fossil fuels rises and they can provide valuable buffer against interruptions in oil supply.

---

to promote solar technologies (pp. 346-49); in the absence of such incentives, the authors argue, solar will meet only five percent of our energy needs in 2000. Stobaugh and Yergin, who are more optimistic on solar energy's prospects, say, "We believe that given reasonable incentives, solar could provide between a fifth and a quarter of the nation's energy requirements by the turn of the century" (p. 183). Denis Hayes, a leading solar advocate and head of the Solar Energy Research Institute, takes the whole world into account in his projection: "By the year 2000, such renewable energy sources could provide 40 percent of the global energy budget; by 2025, humanity could obtain 75 percent of its energy from solar resources" (*Rays of Hope*, New York, W.W. Norton, 1977), p. 155.

[29]See Schurr, p. 482: "Solar space and water heating may offer a near-term opportunity to shift from depletable to renewable energy sources. This technology may help to fill energy requirements and also supply a prototype for a series of long-term shifts as the energy sector changes over time. On institutional as well as technical grounds, therefore, the solar space and water heating enterprise has far-reaching implications that give it an important role among energy initiatives." This view of solar heating has wide support. Michael D. Yokell, formerly of the Solar Energy Research Institute, concludes in a recent article in *Public Interest Economics*: "Is the role for solar energy then limited to hot water and space heating in newly constructed buildings plus a few special applications? In the short run, the candid answer must be yes." Vol. 5, No. 1 (Spring 1980), pp. 1, 8.

60. On the basis of continuing research, the prospects seem good for using solar radiation to produce other forms of energy besides heat. Photovoltaics, the direct conversion of sunlight into electricity with silicon cells, may be extremely important to a society so thoroughly electrified as ours is.[30] Mention has already been made of biomass (nonfossilized organic materials ranging from garbage to crop residues to trees to manure) as a feedstock for synthetic liquids and gases. If one or more of the conversion techniques under study proves successful on a commercial scale, the outlook for solving our transportation fuel problems could brighten considerably.[31]

61. Support for biomass conversion must be qualified, however. The creation of large "energy farms" featuring fast-growing plants destined for the factory could cause serious erosion and water pollution problems. Planning should include steps to minimize these effects. The well-established trend toward fermenting alcohol from grain for gasohol also bears watching. While it is true that the grain presently used for this purpose is surplus, the alcohol-fuels industry could become a powerful competitor in the world food market. Research into ways of deriving ethanol from materials without food value should be encouraged.

Perspectives

62. Although it is necessary for analytical purposes to separate one energy source from another, they are intertwined as closely as threads in a tapestry. Because oil and natural gas are such versatile fuels, replacing them requires broad adjustments across the entire energy spectrum. Moreover, changing the role one source plays in supplying America's energy has an impact on the role alternative sources play. Increasing the use of coal for electrical generation, for example, might well have any or all of the following consequences: decreasing the need for nuclear power; retarding the development of photovoltaics; retarding research on new ways to tap geothermal energy; and impeding (through production and transportation bottlenecks) the rapid establishment of a synthetic-fuels industry. When one adds to this the further complications associated with human health, the environment, and world peace, the impossibility of isolating one aspect of the energy situation becomes clear. Wise decisions can only come from maintaining perspective on the whole.

---

[30]See National Academy of Sciences, p. 40: "Unlike solar thermal conversion (photovoltaics) is a field in which fundamental research could yield dramatic returns, and recent technical progress has been very rapid."

[31]In a speech at the Bio-Energy '80 World Congress in Atlanta April 24, 1980, Thomas E. Stelson, assistant secretary for conservation and solar energy at the U.S. Department of Energy, estimated that biomass could produce from eight to thirteen quads (using widely shared projections of demand, about seven percent to ten percent of total energy use) by the year 2000.

63. Humility also has a particular value in the debate over energy sources. The hallmarks of the field seem to be uncertainty and change. Experts work with educated guesses as to demand, supply, and the timing of both. Furthermore, we cannot see very clearly over the rim of the century. While a technology like nuclear fusion will have no immediate impact, it is the subject of intense research and development and holds considerable promise in the longer run. Breakthroughs in fusion or in such areas as hydrogen research or energy-storage capacity may shift the range of choices. While these considerations must not be allowed to paralyze energy planning, they should serve to keep it undogmatic.

64. The most valuable perspective of all, of course, comes from giving moral and ethical standards the attention they deserve. How shall we choose the energy sources we rely on, and how shall we handle them once chosen? The Church must answer, "as creatures and as fellow creatures." The love of God and the love of humanity must guide us if we are not to injure ourselves in the search for energy security.

IV. Making the Transition: Energy Distribution and Control

65. The national debate is not exclusively a discussion of where our energy will come from. It also takes in the structures that control the flow of energy through American society and the uses to which energy is ultimately put. The Church's interest in these topics is quite straightforward. To the extent that energy is necessary for human life and health, and for life with dignity, access to it is a matter of justice. Institutions and energy policies that fail to take human need sufficiently into account violate rights which the Church must defend. In doing so, it both espouses the common good and reaffirms its special sense of identity with the poor.

The Distribution of Energy

66. Late in 1980, the Congress of the United States appropriated about $2 billion to help low-income people pay their fuel bills. Some question the adequacy of this funding. Others see the need for government aid as an indictment of the economic system that produced the need in the first place. Whatever its precise implications, the legislation makes a two-pronged statement about our society. It acknowledges the fact that the days of cheap and plentiful power are over. It also acknowledges society's responsibility to respond by making sure that the poor are not denied necessities. Just as food stamps are an attempt to deal with inequitable food distribution, this assistance is an attempt to deal with inequitable energy distribution.

67. If anything, the problem is likely to get worse. Our oil-supply system is so vulnerable to disruption that we must expect a series of spot shortages and/or price increases in the future.[32] The price of oil, in turn, will draw the price of other fuels upward, magnifying the effects of rising construction costs, high interest rates, and general inflation. These conditions, devastating to the poor, will progressively squeeze other groups of Americans as well.

68. There are basically two ways to allocate energy among all its possible users and uses. The first is reliance on the marketplace, tempered, perhaps, by the social conscience of individual companies. The value of such an approach is that it generally reflects the cost of energy to each individual and the economy as a whole and encourages conservation. Its primary disadvantage is that some people and some activities lose out in the competition for energy supplies. When money is the only consideration, affluent citizens can maintain even their most frivolous amusements while their less wealthy neighbors go without fuel for heating and cooking.

69. The second approach to energy allocation is through government fiat. Public officials, either alone or in cooperation with the private sector, choose the activities and classes of citizens that are to receive help in obtaining energy and decide what form this aid is to take. This method allows for comprehensive planning that protects the interests of all members of society. However, it involves a degree of government intervention in private decision making that many people find offensive.

70. The United States has chosen to combine elements of both these approaches in dealing with the energy situation. For instance, the federal government has decontrolled oil prices and is in the process of decontrolling natural gas prices. At the same time, it is giving the poor some help and trying to spread part of the benefits of decontrol by means of the "windfall-profits tax."

71. Christians will differ on how to justly distribute energy supplies, but principle will lead them to agree on certain goals. Even as they offer a neighborly hand to distressed individuals in their own communities, they will back public energy assistance for all low-income people offered in a spirit of respect for the recipient's dignity. They will not be content, indeed, unless such aid completely offsets price increases attributable directly or indirectly to decontrol. It is mani-

---

[32]John F. O'Leary, former deputy secretary of energy, called supply interruptions "almost inevitable in the 1980s" in an editorial in The Washington Post (Jan. 22, 1980, p. A19). He also asked, "Will we see a repetition of the downslide of real prices in the years to come? The answer almost certainly is no, because the major factor contributing to falling prices—chronic and sustained surpluses—has disappeared. In fact, it is fair to predict that from this time forward, at least during the 1980s, we shall see constant upward pressure on price."

festly unfair that the poor should have to spend an ever greater percentage of their meager income on necessary power as a result of measures aimed at cutting excess consumption.

72. Government assistance should take other forms besides simple payments. Money used for fuel is immediately helpful, but it does nothing to improve one's long-range situation. Substantial funding should also be invested in weatherizing the homes of low-income people and, where feasible, in installing solar heating equipment. Further, government should work with utility companies to bring about the adoption of rate structures that protect the interests of the poor.[33]

73. Steps must be taken to ensure that in times of shortage the essential functions of society do not falter for lack of fuel. Authorities on all levels should perfect contingency plans for supplying energy to farms, to health facilities, to basic transportation systems, and to other elements in the social fabric that are most important for sustaining life and health. In the absence of such plans, the disruption that a major crisis would cause could explode into chaos.

74. Concern for the poor and for essential services takes priority in designing strategies for energy distribution because they involve necessities. Beyond that the standard must be equity. To take a concrete example, there is nearly unanimous agreement that the United States should move to free itself from excessive dependence on imported oil. The common good this move would serve is the good of the whole human race, given the threat of nuclear war. Obviously, however, cutbacks in oil could have significant implications for energy distribution, both in terms of access and price. The burden of such a policy must be fairly shared.

The Control of Energy

75. The energy industry is dominated by very large companies, ranging from the oil "majors" to the utilities that supply electricity. Moreover, many of the strongest corporations have substantial interests in more than one energy source.[34] This concentration of economic power has become increasingly controversial.

---

[33]"Life-line rates" and "time-of-day rates" have been prominently mentioned in this connection. Time-of-day rates would encourage people to reduce their use of energy during certain hours in order to eliminate the need for costly "peak-load" facilities. Life-line rates would establish a basic charge for a certain minimum amount of power for necessary uses, and impose higher charges for energy consumed above that minimum. Life-line rates, though good in concept, would have to be carefully structured to avoid discriminating against some of the very people they are intended to protect. For example, a childless middle-class couple where both husband and wife worked might use very little energy at home and thus qualify for the basic charge, while a poor woman with young children might require more power for heating, cooking, and so on, and fail to qualify.

[34]Robert M. Wolcott, "Monolith in the Making," *Public Interest Economics,* Vol. 5, No. 1 (Spring 1980), pp. 2, 7.

76. Public discussion of the role of the great oil companies illustrates the point best. Undeniably, our rapid economic development has been based in large part on the availability of cheap energy. The argument can be made that industry concentration was necessary to achieve this end, that it would have been impossible to obtain the requisite supply of oil and natural gas from domestic and foreign wells, transport it, refine it, distribute it, and sell it at low prices unless vast resources were invested in a few corporations. If this premise is granted, the companies plausibly claim some credit for America's well-being.

77. On the other hand, many stress the harm these firms have done. Concentration in the oil industry, critics say, has led to profiteering and monopolistic pricing policies, to the exploitation of people and of nature's gifts, and to the creation of a power structure that undermines democratic ideals. In this view, our material progress has been won at the expense of other nations, which have been denied fair access to humanity's common heritage, the riches of the earth.[35]

78. This debate, as it applies to the oil companies or to other components of the energy industry, involves enormous complexities that cannot be analyzed here. It is worth noting, however, that since the publication of *Rerum Novarum* in 1891, the Catholic Church has warned against the dangers of unbridled capitalism.[36] Concentrated economic power is as much a threat to individual liberty as concentrated political power where necessities are concerned. In theory, any corporations that controlled the food supply or the clothing supply or the energy supply could, in the absence of regulation, do what they pleased with the consumer. Their decisions could mean life or death for those unable to pay the price.

79. In fact, no corporation has such power in America today, and many are run by good people who reject unethical practices. There have been serious abuses, however. In recent years people have suffered great hardships because the firms that supplied their heating fuel cut them off for failing to pay their bills.[37] While it is true that a business cannot continue to operate—cannot supply fuel to anyone— if customers default, cold-weather cutoffs are not a legitimate remedy. Companies should subordinate their economic rights to the higher right to life. Likewise, while the Church fully recognizes the right to collective bargaining, workers should avoid strikes that force suspen-

---

[35]For a skeptical though not hostile history of the oil industry, see Anthony Sampson, *The Seven Sisters* (New York, Viking Press, 1975).
[36]Pope John XXIII quotes Pope Pius XI on this point and adds his own observations in *Mater et Magistra*, 35-40. See also Pope Paul VI, *Populorum Progressio*. #26.
[37]The Community Services Administration has published a booklet telling people what to do when the heat fails as a result of a cutoff or for some other reason. Among the suggestions: Wrap yourself in newspapers to avoid freezing. See Greg E. Welsh, "No More Heat? A Self-Help Booklet!" (Washington, D.C., Community Services Administration, 1979).

sions of service in winter.

80. The development of certain solar technologies offers a limited but real opportunity for counteracting the undesirable effects of concentration. Clearly the need for large, centralized, impersonal production and distribution facilities will not fade away. But if solar heating systems proliferate and other small-scale devices prove reliable and affordable, substantial decentralization could occur.[38] Movement in this direction would permit some people—even the poor, if installation funds were available—to insulate themselves against complete reliance on outside sources of power. The homeowner with an array of solar cells on the roof of a passive solar house, the farmer with a windmill and equipment for distilling fuel alcohol from crop residues or waste, the tenant with a safe wood stove would have a species of control over their lives that most Americans now lack.

81. Decentralization through solar power could also have an important side benefit. While analysts disagree on the relationship between energy policy and employment,[39] the installation of small-scale solar devices in homes and businesses is by nature a labor-intensive activity. It should lead to the creation of new jobs, especially when combined with efforts to properly weatherize the buildings where solar power is used.

82. Prudent efforts to achieve some decentralization clearly deserve encouragement. At the same time, there are more direct ways to guard against potential and actual abuses of power. One, of course, is government regulation. Another was briefly mentioned in the discussion of nuclear power: citizen participation in the decision-making process. Whether they are expressing their views on the risks associated with some energy source or helping ensure that corporate actions respect human needs, people have every right to intervene when energy policy is designed and implemented.

83. What form might such interventions take? With respect to energy companies themselves, they could range from orderly protests to testimony at public hearings to consumer representation on corporate boards. They could also include advocacy in the political arena aimed at influencing the content of legislation or regulation. The possibilities are as varied as the institutions that control energy in this country.

---

[38]"However, where fuel transport costs are very high, or scale economies are weak or non-existent, decentralization may be more desirable. For example, if the direct rays of the sun are the fuel, the possible economic advantage of collecting and using that energy domestically for home heating, as opposed to collecting it for later distribution in a centralized electrical network, becomes a calculation of great interest for energy planning" Schurr, pp. 324-25. "Indeed, because arrays of PV (i.e., photovoltaic) cells may show little or no scale economies, small- and medium-scale installations could well be a more intelligent use of this technology" Schurr, p. 331.

[39]See Paul Keegan, "Employment Is the Name of the Game as Solar Advocates Press Their Case," *National Journal* (Dec. 15, 1979), pp. 2100-03.

84. Generally speaking, the smaller the entity responsible for a particular decision—individual rather than group, state rather than federal government, local distributor rather than multinational corporation—the better chance an informed citizenry has of affecting it. Some policies must be made on the highest levels; only Washington, for example, can commit the nation to greatly increased coal production. Nevertheless, those holding authority in the public and private sectors should be constantly looking for ways to center energy decision making as near the grass roots as possible. While adopting this course might lessen efficiency, it should produce results more satisfactory to the people and utlimately to the institutions that serve them.

The Problem of Systemic Evil

85 Most socioeconomic systems are established for worthy purposes. However, in a world made imperfect by sin, problems inevitably arise in their application. Obeying some law of institutional inertia, these systems tend to perpetuate themselves and the evil they do is tolerated for the sake of the good. Partly for this reason, the status quo never lacks defenders and reformers never lack zeal.

86. Certainly the control and distribution of energy in America today occasion as much structural sin as any major feature of our national life. Some corporations neglect or deny their social responsibilities, government sometimes acts without due regard for the common good, and pressure groups relentlessly pursue their narrow goals in defiance of others' legitimate concerns.

87. People who seek justice must do their best to sort out the evil from the good and act on their perceptions. Obviously, this will not end controversy; it may at times have the opposite effect. But by approaching the debate in a certain spirit—again, as creatures and as fellow creatures—we elevate it. We also increase the likelihood that it will lead one day to a broad consensus, since sound conclusions flow from sound premises.

V. Conclusion

88. The word "energy" appears only a handful of times in papal or conciliar documents and even these scant references have little application to the current discussion in the United States. That is hardly surprising. Pope Paul VI, commenting on social justice in "A Call to Action," said, "There is of course a wide diversity among the situations in which Christians . . . find themselves according to regions, sociopolitical systems and cultures." Therefore, "it is up to these Christian communities . . . to discern the options and commitments which are called for in order to bring about the social, political and economic changes seen in many cases to be urgently needed" (#4).

89. The Catholic Christian community in America, as part of the large religious community and in association with all people of good will, faces a most challenging task in dealing with energy. Some matters are fairly clear: the primacy of serving human needs, the necessity of avoiding occasions of war, the duty of conserving energy wisely, the desirability of responsibly developing renewable energy sources, to name a few. However, many of the central questions in the energy field are hard to define, much less to answer. The Catholic Christian community should be a continuous presence in the energy debate as long as issues so closely touching the welfare of humanity go unresolved.

90. It should be present through Catholic parishes, which can act to save energy in their own buildings, assist the poor, educate adults and children, and provide means for people to organize for advocacy.

91. It should be present through Catholic primary and high schools, which can emphasize the link between science and morality.

92. It should be present through Catholic colleges and universities, where theologians and ethicists can join with scientists, engineers, and others to design practical ways to bring moral considerations to bear on energy policy and practice.[40]

93. It should be present through Catholic seminaries and novitiates, which can prepare priests and religious to approach matters of social justice with informed sensitivity.

94. It should be present through religious and secular Catholic organizations, which can sponsor energy-related projects, aid the work of appropriate American and international bodies, and highlight the moral dimensions of energy policy in many other ways.

95. It should be present through participation in interfaith groups and compatible secular coalitions, which can broaden support for laudable goals.

96. Finally, the Catholic community should be present through Catholic people of every calling who are willing to address energy issues with moral insight and commitment.

97. A sound viewpoint on energy rises above the perspective of the producer who cares nothing for the consumer or the consumer who ignores the producer's rights. It is a viewpoint that recognizes the transition to alternative sources of energy as a movement in history, a link between episodes in the development of civilization. In this

---

[40]In a speech to scholars and students in Cologne, West Germany, Nov. 15, 1980, Pope John Paul said, "Today it is the church that is the portal for reason and science that trust in capacity for truth, which legitimizes them as human capacities; for the freedom of science, through which it has dignity as a human, personal good; for progress in service to mankind, which needs it for the safety of its life and dignity."

movement lies creative potential for promoting human solidarity, for shaping what in Jesus' eyes would be a better world. Only through steadfast loyalty to a dream of justice can we bring that world to birth—as creatures and as fellow creatures.

Statement on Central America

A Statement Issued by the
United States Catholic Conference

November 19, 1981

1. Central America has become a focal point of concern and attention in the United States. In every country of Central America the Catholic Church plays a significant role. In word and deed, in the actions of bishops, priests, religious, and lay people, the Church daily influences the flow of events precisely because it is so intimately identified with the people of those countries in their pilgrimage of faith and their pursuit of justice. In the 1979 Puebla meeting, the Latin American bishops provided a description of the fundamental force they see lying just below the surface of the sometimes confusing ebb and flow of events in their continent:

> From the depths of the countries which make up Latin America a cry is rising to heaven, growing louder and more alarming all the time. It is the cry of a suffering people who demand justice, freedom and respect for the basic rights of human beings and peoples (Puebla Document, No. 87).

2. In responding to this cry, the Church in Central America has taken its direction from the Second Vatican Council, from Paul VI's "The Progress of Peoples" (1967), from the Medellin (1968) and Puebla (1979) conferences of the Latin American bishops, and from Pope John Paul II's addresses at Puebla and in Brazil. These sources have shaped a pastoral witness in which the Church has affirmed its own need for conversion, and has tried to respond to cries of the poor by seeking to identify with its people in their struggle for true justice. The decisions have produced a new and challenging style of ministry. In turn many have paid a heavy price: a number of priests and missionaries killed in El Salvador, including Archbishop Romero and the four U.S. women missionaries; an additional number killed in Guatemala, including Father Stanley Rother, murdered on July 28, 1981. To these and other missionaries who have given their lives, we pay tribute.

3. The killing of these missionaries from the United States vividly reminds us of our relationship to the drama of Central America, but this is not our only bond. Those who go from the United States to serve in Central America, as well as local leadership of the Church in these countries, have often described the multiple ways in which the United States daily influences the destiny of people in these neighboring nations. The bonds between the United States and Central America are complex and diverse; they are political, cultural, economic, and religious. They are shaped by over two centuries of history and they differ in each country. This Statement cannot possibly examine these relationships in a detailed manner, but as bishops in the United States we feel a special tie to our brother bishops and to the Church in Central America. The witness of the Church there calls forth our own witness, one which seeks to address decisions taken in the United States whose consequences directly affect our sisters and brothers in the faith.

4.   There are many voices, both governmental and nongovernmental, which seek to shape our vision of Central America today. Even a cursory knowledge of the region impresses an observer with the complexity of events within each country. But some have argued that the dominant reality which must concern us is the place of Central America in the United States-Soviet global competition.

5.   In preparing this Statement, we have reviewed again the major arguments in the U.S. public debate on Central America. We have compared and evaluated them in the light of the information we have from the Church in Central America. Church leaders there speak primarily and most frequently about the internal reality of their countries: about the daily struggle of existence of the majority of their people, about the need for just social structures internally, and the right to self-determination, even as small nations, in their relationships with other countries.

6.   There is no question here of the ecclesiastical leadership in Central America being naive or confused about the threat which Soviet dominated forces could play in their societies. The Catholic Church in Latin America, as elsewhere, has hardly been complacent about communism. The Latin American Church has repeatedly stated in the last decade that external subversion is not the primary threat or principal cause of conflict in these countries. The dominant challenge is the internal conditions of poverty and the denial of basic human rights which characterize many of these societies. These conditions, if unattended, become an invitation for intervention.

7.   These conditions must be assessed country by country, but our general purpose here is to say again that the U.S. approach to Central America should be based upon an understanding of these internal realities and the way in which our policies and practices affect them. We do, of course, join our brother bishops in Central America, opposing as well any military assistance that Cuba or the Soviet Union may provide directly or indirectly to the contending forces in that region.

8.   Any conception of the problems in Central America which is cast principally in terms of global security issues, military responses, arms transfers, and preservation of a situation which fails to promote meaningful participation of the majority of the population in their

societies is, in our view, profoundly mistaken. It is to provide a different emphasis that we offer the following reflections.

9. *El Salvador*: In congressional testimony and previous statements of the U.S. Catholic Conference (USCC), we have addressed the problem of El Salvador on a regular basis since February 1980 when the late Archbishop Romero called for a change in U.S. policy. Our position has been and continues to be shaped by three themes.

10. First, following Archbishop Romero and now Bishop Rivera y Damas, we are convinced that outside military assistance from any source to any party is not a useful contribution but simply intensifies the cycle of violence in El Salvador. For this reason we have opposed and continue to oppose military aid from all sources, while supporting monitored economic assistance by the United States. We support political measures to prevent the flow of arms from other nations to El Salvador, even as we continue to oppose U.S. military assistance to the government of El Salvador.

11. Second, we endorse and support Bishop Rivera y Damas's call for a broad-based political solution in El Salvador. At this time we wish to call attention to the crucial and creative role the United States can and should play in supporting a political rather than a military solution to the tragic conflict in El Salvador. If the United States is to play the significant role open to it, it must make efforts to persuade the major protagonists to halt the armed conflict and engage in constructive dialogue; it must assist them in healing the wounds with economic, educational, and nutritional aid. If valid elections are to be the final product of a political solution, they will come about only after appropriate preconditions are fulfilled.

12. Third, we wish to reaffirm the position of the administrative board of the USCC regarding Salvadoran exiles now in the United States. Many have been and are being deported and others face the threat of deportation. We believe that as long as the present state of violence and turmoil exists in El Salvador, the citizens of that country, regardless of political philosophy, should not be forced to return home. Hence, we urge that a moratorium be placed on all deportations to El Salvador, at least until such time as the government in power can guarantee the safety of its citizens. We are also mindful of the suffering of large numbers of Salvadoran refugees and displaced persons in other countries; we pledge our material assistance and ask other nations also to respond to their needs.

13. *Nicaragua*: The agony of war which presently ravages El Salvador is now a memory for Nicaraguans. But they presently face major political and social questions about the future direction of their society. Two central questions confronting Nicaragua are its internal direction and its external relations.

14. Internally, Nicaragua is experiencing great difficulty in pursuing political and economic reconstruction from the devastation of war.

Although stripped of essential resources, the government and people have tried to guarantee basic necessities for the population. While acknowledging these facts, we also share the concerns expressed recently by our brother bishops in Nicaragua about increasing restrictions on human rights. It is crucially important that the religious character of the society be faithfully preserved, and that the rights of free association, speech, press, and freedom of education be protected, even as the social and economic needs of the people continue to be met.

15. The immediate question facing us as bishops in the United States is the policy of our government toward Nicaragua. We believe that a policy designed to isolate Nicaragua and prevent its access to resources crucially needed for reconstruction is neither justified by our history with Nicaragua nor useful for the Nicaraguan people. Hence we continue to support, as we have in the past, economic assistance on a bilateral and multilateral basis for Nicaragua. Such assistance should be monitored, for Nicaragua as for other countries, in terms of human rights criteria. In our view a mature, cooperative, diplomatic relationship between the United States and Nicaragua could be a force for human rights and stability in Central America.

16. *Guatemala*: We deplore the escalating violence in Guatemala as described in the statement of the Guatemalan bishops on June 13, 1980: "The acts of violence among us have taken on unimaginable forms: there are murders, kidnappings, torture, and even vicious desecrations of the victims' bodies."

17. The death toll from politically motivated murders is estimated by the U.S. Department of State to be seventy-five to one hundred per month. In a statement issued only two weeks prior to Father Rother's murder, the bishops of Guatemala asserted that they saw in the assassination of priests and religious a pattern of violence designed to silence the voice of the Church.

18. The bishops spoke again to the violence in their land on August 6, 1981:

> The Catholic Church . . . is today perhaps as never before in its history the victim of unjust attacks and of violent aggression. . . .
> In addition to the assassination or disappearance of 12 priests . . .
> and the violent deaths of numerous catechists and members of our Christian communities, it is known by everyone that in recent days there has been unleashed a publicity campaign which tends to discredit the church (Communique of the Episcopal Conference of Guatemala, August 6, 1981).

19. Numerous reports, governmental and nongovernmental, have documented the deteriorating human rights situation in Guatemala. Pope John Paul II, in a 1980 letter to the bishops of Guatemala, described the situation in the following way:

I well know the anxieties you have communicated to me on more than one occasion, even publicly, in the last few months, for the many, far too many acts of violence that have racked your country, and your repeated calls for an end to what you have rightly called "the road to self-destruction" that violates all human rights—first among them the sacred right to life—and that does not help to solve the social problems of the nation.

20. It is not our contention that the government of Guatemala is responsible for all that occurs, but we do find significant the recent human rights report of the State Department: "The government has not taken effective steps to halt abuses or carry out serious investigations" (U.S. Department of State: "Country Reports on Human Rights Practices," 1981, p. 441).

21. At this moment in Guatemalan history, U.S. diplomacy should be directed toward enhancing the protection of human rights and assisting the meeting of basic human needs, especially the need for food and for capital investment for food production. Such a policy will require a creative political vision; such vision is not manifested by the provision of military hardware in a situation already ridden with violence. We believe military assistance should not be provided from any source or in any form.

22. We offer these reflections as bishops and citizens. As bishops we are called to teach the full dimensions of the gospel message, including, as Paul VI said in 1975, questions involving justice, liberation, development, and world peace (*On Evangelization*, #31). As citizens of the most powerful nation in the Western hemisphere, we take seriously Pope John Paul II's injunction to us at Yankee Stadium, "to seek out the structural reasons which foster or cause the different forms of poverty in the world and in your own country, so you can apply the proper remedies."

23. Both of these directives impel our present Statement on Central America. We offer it in the hope that our continuing prayer for the Church and the people of that region may be complemented by our public support in this country of their human rights and needs. We renew our special bonds with the Church in Central America and we reaffirm our fraternal support to our brother bishops who serve that Church.

24. Our intention, in prayer and action, is to respond to the Lord's command heard in the prophet Isaiah: "This, rather, is the fasting I wish: releasing those bound unjustly, untying the thongs of the yoke; setting free the oppressed, breaking every yoke; sharing your bread with the hungry, sheltering the oppressed and homeless; clothing the naked when you see them and not turning your back on your own" (Is 58:6-9).

Health and Health Care

A Statement Issued by the
National Conference of Catholic Bishops

November 19, 1981

I. Introduction

1. Health and health care are subjects that profoundly touch the lives of us all. One's ability to live a fully human life and to reflect the unique dignity that belongs to each person is greatly affected by health. Not only for individuals, but likewise for society at large, health issues take on important significance because of the intimate role they play in personal and social development. Complex in their ramifications and universal in their relevance, these issues are of concern to us all—rich and poor, young and old.

2. For the Church, health and the healing apostolate take on special significance because of the Church's long tradition of involvement in this area and because the Church considers health care to be a basic human right which flows from the sanctity of human life. Recognizing the significance of health issues and the legitimate interest of all people in this subject, we address this Pastoral Letter to all Catholics in the United States.

3. Although we cannot adequately discuss in this Statement all of the technical, ethical, and religious issues that the topic calls to mind, we do wish to fulfill four specific purposes. First, we will reflect on the biblical and theological principles which undergird the Church's vision of health and healing. Second, we wish to call all Catholics to a fuller acceptance of their responsibility for their own health and for their share in the healing apostolate of the Church. Third, we want to express our full commitment to the Catholic health care apostolate and our encouragement and support of professionals in the health field. Finally, we will offer some basic principles for public policy as a means of encouraging full and responsible participation by all Catholics in the shaping of national health policies. We would like, therefore, to provide a sound framework for an ongoing discussion of health and healing in the American Catholic community. Through this Pastoral Statement we hope to contribute to a renewal of the Church's broad commitment to this most important subject.

II. The Message of the Gospel and Tradition

A. *The Example of Jesus*

4. In the earthly ministry of Jesus, the acts of healing stand out as dramatic high points. His teaching and preaching were not done in isolation but were accompanied by frequent manifestations of his healing power. Jesus used this power in a very personal and concrete way. He touched others and thereby brought them health and wholeness. He cured the leper (see Mt 8:1-4), gave sight to the blind (see Mt 9:27-31), and enabled the lame to walk (see Lk 5:17-26). On these and numerous other occasions, Jesus dramatized the importance of healing in his mission. He relieved suffering and "cured all who were afflicted" (Mt 8:16). He demonstrated that illness could be an occasion to prove God's love for his people and not a sign of punishment. The life that Jesus came to give was not in fact to end with death. He asserted emphatically: "I am the resurrection and the life: whoever believes in me, though he should die, will come to life" (Jn 11:25-26).
5. Health in the biblical perspective means wholeness—not only physical, but also spiritual and psychological wholeness; not only individual, but also social and institutional wholeness. Jesus was the Divine Healer who came to restore this health. He healed people's physical and psychological ills; he healed them to the depth of their being. Through his life and ministry he proclaimed the Kingdom of God on earth and reached out to touch and to heal our wounded humanity. He came to the world to make us fully human, to help us to realize our human dignity as creatures made in the image of God. He came to bring the fullness of life.

B. *The Church's Tradition*

6. The healing ministry of Christ is historically embodied in the Church. From the earliest traditions of the Church to the present day, the mission of evangelization to which Jesus sent his followers has included healing as a major part. "Into whatever city you go, after they welcome you . . . cure the sick there. Say to them, 'The reign of God is at hand'" (Lk 10:8-9). In the familiar story of the Last Judgment, Jesus held out to all who comfort the sick the promise of the Father's blessing. "Come. You have my Father's blessing! . . . For I was . . . ill and you comforted me. . . I assure you, as often as you did it for one of my least brothers [and sisters], you did it for me" (Mt 25:34-40).
7. Members of the Church follow the example of Jesus, therefore, when they carry out the work of healing—not only by providing care

for the physically ill, but also by working to restore health and wholeness in all facets of the human person and the human community.

8. The sacraments are an especially important part of this healing mission. The *Roman Ritual: Rite of Anointing and the Pastoral Care of the Sick* has particular significance as a sign and a prayer for the return to health.[1] This new rite is intended to help Christians understand human sickness in the context of the whole mystery of salvation. This liturgy of anointing illustrates the connection between the care of the sick and the example and teaching of Jesus. The following words from the introduction to the *Rite of Anointing and the Pastoral Care of the Sick* explain how the prayers of the priest and the anointing with oil relate to the suffering and resurrection of Jesus:

> The man who is seriously ill needs the special help of God's grace in this time of anxiety, lest he be broken in spirit and subject to temptations and the weakening of faith.
>
> Christ, therefore, strengthens the faithful who are afflicted by illness with the sacrament of anointing, providing them with the strongest means of support.
>
> The celebration of this sacrament consists especially in the laying on of hands by the presbyters of the church, their offering the prayer of faith, and the anointing of the sick with oil made holy by God's blessing. This rite signifies the grace of the sacrament and confers it.
>
> This sacrament provides the sick person with the grace of the Holy Spirit by which the whole person is brought to health, trust in God is encouraged and strength is given. . . . A return to physical health may even follow the reception of this sacrament if it will be beneficial to the sick person's salvation."[2]

9. Down through the centuries, the Church has carried on the work of healing through diverse forms and structures. The Church community from its earliest days has provided hospitable places of care and comfort for those in need of healing. Those who are ill, orphaned, widowed, poor, homeless, handicapped, or otherwise in need have found the gentle healing touch of the Lord in Church-sponsored programs and institutions. These examples of healing ministry form a rich heritage which we must confidently and gratefully renew and adapt to the needs of today.

C. Mercy and Justice

10. Because all human beings are created according to God's image, they possess a basic human dignity which calls for the utmost reverence. On the individual level this means a special responsibility to

---

[1] Decree of the Sacred Congregation for Divine Worship promulgating the *Roman Ritual: Rite of Anointing and the Pastoral Care of the Sick*, Dec. 7, 1972.
[2] *Ibid.*, Introduction, #5-6.

care for one's own health and that of others. On the societal level this calls for responsibility by society to provide adequate health care which is a basic human right. Health care is so important for full human dignity and so necessary for the proper development of life that it is a fundamental right of every human being. Thus Pope John XXIII, in his encyclical *Pacem in Terris*, listed medical care among those basic human rights which flow from the sanctity and dignity of human life.[3]

11. An essential element of our religious tradition regarding human rights is the understanding that the works of mercy and the works of justice are inseparable. This insight, especially as expressed in the Second Vatican Council and in recent papal and episcopal statements, offers special guidance and inspiration to all who participate in the work of healing.

12. The works of mercy call Christians to engage themselves in direct efforts to alleviate the misery of the afflicted. The works of justice require that Christians involve themselves in sustained struggle to correct any unjust social, political, and economic structures and institutions which are the causes of suffering. As Pope John Paul II has said, "The church cannot remain insensitive to whatever serves [humanity's] true welfare, any more than she can remain indifferent to whatever threatens it."[4]

13. Because we believe in the dignity of the person, we must embrace every chance to help and to liberate, to heal the wounded world as Jesus taught us. Our hands must be the strong but gentle hands of Christ, reaching out in mercy and justice, touching individual persons, but also touching the social conditions that hinder the wholeness which is God's desire for humanity.

III. Responsibility for Health

14. We have emphasized that health in the Christian perspective means wholeness—not only physical and emotional, but also spiritual and social. Health has to do with more than strictly medical concerns. The restoration of health and maintenance of good health are not solely the responsibility of doctors, nurses, and other medical professionals. We all bear a responsibility in this regard, both as individuals and as members of large social and religious institutions.

---

[3] *Pacem in Terris*, art. 11.
[4] *Redemptor Hominis*, art. 13.

A. Personal Responsibility

15. As individuals we show respect for our own life and dignity when we adopt life styles that enhance our health and well-being. We should seek to reject personal habits that can threaten our health, such as smoking, excessive consumption of food and drink, abusive use of alcohol and drugs, and neglect of proper exercise.

16. In the face of powerful social, cultural, and economic pressures from a consumer society, we are called to exercise moderation in the use of material goods. Out of gratitude and reverence for the unique sanctity that is ours, we must choose life and health, not death and sickness.

17. Reforms in personal habits are very important, but they are only a first step. People's health problems are not simply self-inflicted, but are often caused by forces over which they have no control. Workers disabled by unhealthy conditions in their work places are not to blame for their ill health, nor are the poor to blame for their lack of proper nutrition. Christians have the duty to address threats such as these which are rooted in the structures of society. They can do so by working with private and voluntary groups of various kinds and by cooperating with the appropriate efforts of government in such areas as occupational safety, regulation of food and drug advertising, housing code enforcement, pollution control, and health care for the poor.

B. Family

18. The family constitutes another extremely important level of responsibility in terms of health care, particularly in the area of prevention. The family unit has a great capacity to promote the health of its members, for it is the primary setting for health education and for instilling those habits that lead to the preservation of sound physical and mental health.

19. Many families face a special challenge and opportunity in caring for ill parents, children, or siblings. For example, a member of the family may be very frail or senile, retarded or physically handicapped, or afflicted with chronic or terminal illness. So far as circumstances permit, we encourage families to care for them at home, so they might benefit from the comfort that only personal love in a home setting can give. Unquestionably, the fulfillment of family responsibility to needy members calls for sacrifice; but if rendered in the gospel spirit, it is the sort of meaningful sacrifice that has its own reward in happiness, peace, and personal growth. We urge public policies to provide incentives to encourage and enable families to care for their sick members.

20. When a family member is in need of care that cannot be provided in the home, institutional care is sometimes the only alternative. Families faced with this decision should be supported and encouraged to continue their care and involvement with the patient in the long-term care facility. Many of these facilities are providing the kind of personalized, quality care that is called for in these situations.

21. Besides meeting their responsibilities toward their own members, families should reach out to other families in distress due to illness, disability, or death. This distress is often first apparent to neighbors and friends, who in times of trouble may be the best outside source of personal concern and assistance. In simple but important ways, neighbors and friends can be the presence of Christ to those who suffer. Such support can strengthen their hope in the Resurrection.

C. Parish

22. The Catholic parish, as a visible and integral part of the local community, has a significant role to play in the health apostolate as well. It should encourage parishioners in need of health care to patronize a Catholic hospital and to support its apostolate in the local community. In addition to caring for and praying for its own members who may be ill, the parish community has a responsibility to reach out. Parishioners should be encouraged to visit the homebound, the sick, the dying, and the bereaved in their homes or in local health facilities. Provided that they are sensitive and reasonably well trained, the members of a parish can penetrate the isolation and loneliness in which too many people in poor health find themselves. In this regard we are encouraged by innovations such as the National Conference of Catholic Charities parish outreach program through which local Catholic charities agencies reach out and assist parishes to minister to the social and health needs of families and individuals.

23. Many families face problems arising from illness which severely test their Christian faith. This can be true, for example, in the case of parents of a newborn with serious birth defects. It is particularly important in such instances that support be given to the family by the Christian community. Where possible, Catholic health facilities can provide training to improve and strengthen these support systems.

24. Another important role for the parish community to play is in the area of health education and preventive health measures. Parishioners can work together in utilizing local resources such as hospitals, health departments, or home health agencies in sponsoring health education programs and preventive services such as health fairs, immunization projects, and blood pressure and hypertension clinics.

25. Advocacy of the rights of others is also a responsibility in the area of health that can be carried out by the parish. Parishioners can join together to speak out on behalf of community health needs, especially those of the poor. Likewise, they can participate in health care planning; monitor important health legislation at the federal, state, and local levels; and advocate legislative action that deals justly with health problems. They can also investigate health hazards such as unsafe working conditions in local industry, unhealthy living conditions in local housing, and other issues needing community action.

D. Diocese

26. At the diocesan level, we intend to demonstrate our commitment to health care by strengthening and adapting those diocesan structures that are involved in the care and maintenance of health. Through our diocesan coordinators of health affairs, for example, we will continue the fruitful dialogue and collaboration that has existed with Catholic health care facilities, with Catholic health care professionals, and with community and state officials within our dioceses.

27. Diocesan offices and programs that deal with social, economic, and environmental issues are also important in the overall health apostolate. Factors relating to economic status and living conditions have a profound impact on the health of individuals and sometimes of whole communities. For example, inadequate housing, unemployment, lack of education, and a polluted environment are frequently causes of ill health. As Church leaders, we will continue to seek social and institutional changes that deal with these underlying problems.

IV. Formal Health Apostolate

A. A Word of Appreciation

28. We pledge ourselves to the preservation and further development of the rich heritage that is embodied in the Church's formal health apostolate. Led by religious congregations of women, the Church was a pioneer in the development of health care services in America. Thanks to the thousands of women and men who heroically and competently built this legacy, the Catholic hospital has become for generations of American Catholics and for many other citizens a familiar symbol of the healing apostolate of the Church. We urge the continuation of Catholic leadership and presence in health care. Our Catholic religious have provided and still provide outstanding service to the Church and the community at large by their work in this field. We encourage them to continue in this most important apostolate. However, the changing demographics and the decline in the number of religious have had their effect on the role of religious in the health apostolate. We urge the increased participation of the Catholic laity in the corporate structure, organization, and administration of Catholic-sponsored hospitals and health agencies.

29. Today our country is served by a variety of Catholic health care facilities: more than six hundred twenty short-term hospitals, some two hundred sixty long-term care facilities, four schools of medicine, one hundred seventy nursing schools, and numerous institutions providing research and education in the health care field. In 1915 the Catholic Hospital Association began a history of organized collaboration among the Church's health care institutions. This history has now entered a new and promising phase in the renaming of that organization as the Catholic Health Association of the United States. Recognizing the long Catholic tradition of the right to associate, we support Catholic organizations of health professionals and urge their continued inspiration and support to members involved in the service of healing.

30. In the name of the Church and of all those who have been helped by these institutions, we thank our health professionals—lay and religious—for the continuing witness they give to Christian principles in the modern world. Gratitude is due as well to all those engaged in public or voluntary health care facilities or in private practice who likewise, outside of formal Church sponsorship, follow the Lord's example in caring for the sick. As bishops of the Catholic Church in the United States, we fully endorse these apostolic efforts, both personal and institutional. We commit ourselves to do our part in maintaining and developing a Catholic institutional presence within the health care field in our country.

31. We are particularly thankful for the presence of the Catholic health care facilities in America. They are places where millions of men and women in the United States have experienced the healing touch of Jesus Christ in times of mental and physical suffering. We commend especially the religious of the Church whose resourceful leadership has been at the heart of the Catholic health apostolate since its inception. We praise all those persons whose sacrifices made possible the development of Catholic health facilities in the United States long before public law provided tax dollars to help fund health care. We also thank all those who have generously accepted the important responsibility of serving on boards of trustees of Catholic health care facilities as well as the numerous volunteers who have generously given of their time and energies.

32. We recognize the valuable programs that exist in Catholic educational institutions that include nursing and medical schools as well as basic and special programs for other health professions. As Catholic institutions, they should be centers where sound gospel and human values are inculcated by word and example as well as by formal programs of instruction and education that are consistent with the teaching of the magisterium. Christian educators should work diligently to communicate to the professionals of tomorrow a balanced appreciation of the gift of health, a critical stance toward social and cultural threats to health, an understanding of the ethical and moral dilemmas flowing from health care issues, and a compassionate concern to employ their human talents in promoting adequate health care as a basic right of all people.

B. *Catholic Identity*

33. In today's complex world, the sponsors, trustees, administrators, and other professionals in Catholic health care facilities have to struggle with a variety of new challenges calling for both prudence and boldness. These facilities are confronted with a vast array of issues, ranging from economic and technological to social and moral concerns. As an example of one of these concerns, we point to the trend toward increased concentrations of hospital ownership by the for-profit corporations. While public health policy, regulations, reimbursement methodologies, and health-systems planning have tended to unify health care, they challenge Catholic health facilities to search for ways to maintain and deepen their identity and exercise a penetrating influence in the health field.

34. Many of these problems are common to secular institutions as well, and we support the efforts of Catholic facilities to work cooperatively with others in dealing with mutual concerns. At the same time, some issues arise for Catholic health care facilities precisely because of their commitment to Christian and Catholic values. We hope that these institutions will consciously and creatively work to strengthen their Catholic identity and to reflect the values that are unique to our tradition.

35. "What is a Catholic health care facility?" "What should we do that distinguishes us?" These are questions posed by the Catholic Health Association in a recent document titled *Evaluative Criteria for Catholic Health Care Facilities*. The association's concerted efforts to draw attention to these questions and to assist its members in evaluating their own facilities in the light of Catholic values is commendable.

36. Following on this same theme, we wish to draw attention to several areas in which Catholic health care facilities can demonstrate their fidelity to the Catholic tradition.

1. Personalized Patient Care

37. The advance of medical science and technology has made healing a complex task. Catholic facilities have a special witness opportunity in this regard. They share with others the need to continually improve the technical quality of their health care. The use of highly sophisticated medical equipment is an essential element of the health apostolate in our modern world, and we are thankful for the advances brought about by such technology.

38. At the same time, we recall the words of Pope John Paul II in his recent address to health professionals. He said, "Care . . . cannot be reduced to the strictly technico-professional aspect, but must address all the elements of human being."[5] We recall as well that Jesus' own healing ministry was based on personal contact with those who were suffering. He dealt with others gently, humanely, and completely. Following his example, our health care facilities should make every effort to personalize the patient care they offer. They should strive to treat the whole person in a way that fully respects human dignity and that recognizes the multifaceted causes of illness, not limited to the physical and medical causes.

39. In this connection it is heartening to see the progress made in establishing and expanding departments of pastoral care and chaplaincy programs in Catholic and other religious facilities and in upgrading the education of pastoral care personnel in health care facilities so that they meet appropriate standards of certification. We urge increased collaboration between medical staff and the pastoral care staff. These pastoral care departments and programs, appropriately ecumenical in operation and staffed by trained men and women, give needed emphasis to the spiritual dimensions of health. Without health of the spirit, high technology focused strictly on the body offers limited hope for healing the whole person.

2. Medical-Moral Issues

40. The question of Catholic identity also involves certain medical-moral issues that confront Catholic health care facilities. It is clear that the debate of health issues in America includes a certain conflict over basic moral values. Pressures on Catholic institutions to permit practices that violate Catholic teaching are strong and pervasive. Experience bears this out in the matter of abortion. Some have noted the same pressures in the area of contraceptive sterilization. In resisting these pressures, we urge that serious consideration be given to the following words of Pope John Paul II:

> The truth is that technological development, characteristic of our time, is suffering from a fundamental ambivalence: While on the one hand it enables men and women to take in hand their own destiny, it exposes them on the other hand to the temptation of going beyond the limits of a reasonable dominion over nature, jeopardizing the very survival and integrity of the human person.

> Just consider, to remain in the sphere of biology and medicine, the implicit danger to the human's right to life represented by the very discoveries in the field of artificial insemination, the control of births and fertility, hibernation (cryobiology, ed.) and "retarded death," genetic engineering, psychic drugs, organ transplants, etc. Certainly

[5]Pope John Paul II, Address to Third National Conference of ARSI, June 19, 1979.

scientific knowledge has its own laws by which it must abide. It must also recognize, however, especially in medicine, an impassable limit in respect for the person and in protection of the right to live in a way worthy of the human being.

If a new method of investigation, for example, harms or threatens to harm this right, it is not to be considered lawful simply because it increases our knowledge. Science, in fact, is not the highest value to which all others must be subordinated. Higher up in the scale of values is precisely the individual's personal right to physical and spiritual life, to psychic and functional integrity. The person, in fact, is the measure and criterion of good or evil in all human manifestations. Scientific progress therefore cannot claim to lie in a kind of neutral ground. The ethical norm, based on respect for the dignity of the person, must illuminate and discipline both the research phase and the phase of the application of the results reached in it.[6]

41. A deep harmony unites the truths of science and the truths of faith. The Church has recognized the great benefits of science and technology to the human race, especially in the field of medicine and health care. However, applied science must be united with conscience. We call on all scientists, in close collaboration with theologians, to address these issues clearly and decisively so that the ethic of life will govern these fundamental decisions in scientific research.
42. Catholics should be among the first to support scientists in their fidelity to goals that enhance and promote life. Catholics, and especially Catholic scientists, must bear a special witness, standing firm to defend the basic dignity of the human person. It is our role to promote Christian values, to keep them present in public debate, and to join hands with others who seek to promote such values.
43. We specifically wish to call attention to the *Ethical and Religious Directives for Catholic Health Facilities* issued by the bishops several years ago at the request of those working in the Catholic health field. These directives are revised when necessary and particular pronouncements on some specific topics are issued; for example, the *Statement on Tubal Ligation*.[7] These directives serve as firm standards to be followed in the protection of Catholic values and in the continuing affirmation of Catholic identity. We call for faithful commitment to them.

3. Prophetic Role

44. We believe and hope that American society will move toward the establishment of a national policy that guarantees adequate health care for all while maintaining a pluralistic approach. As this develops, the role of Catholic institutions in the health field will change. They

---

[6]Pope John Paul II, Address to Italian Physicians and Surgeons, Oct. 27, 1980, *Origins*, Nov. 13, 1980, vol. 19, pp. 351-52.
[7]National Conference of Catholic Bishops' *Statement on Tubal Ligation*, July 3, 1980.

will take an even greater responsibility in fulfilling the prophetic role of promoting basic Christian values, championing the cause of the poor and neglected in society, and finding new ways to blend personal care and technological skills in health care service.

45. Service to the poor is one particularly important way of fulfilling this prophetic role. Here again we commend to all the emphatic words of Pope John Paul II:

> Social thinking and social practice inspired by the Gospel must always be marked by a special sensitivity towards those who are most in distress, those who are extremely poor, those suffering from all the physical, mental and moral ills that afflict humanity including hunger, neglect, unemployment and despair. . . .

> But neither will you recoil before the reforms—even profound ones—of attitudes and structures that may prove necessary in order to recreate over and over again the conditions needed by the disadvantaged if they are to have a fresh chance in the hard struggle of life. The poor of the United States and of the world are your brothers and sisters in Christ. You must never be content to leave them just the crumbs from the feast. You must take of your substance, and not just of your abundance in order to help them. And you must treat them like guests at your family table.[8]

46. All those in the health apostolate who heed this call and follow the example of Jesus will continue to serve the poor, the frail elderly, the powerless, and the alienated. Sometimes this will be at great sacrifice, and it will demand both courage and imagination. For example, when locating or relocating facilities, leaders in the health apostolate can offer special insights for health care improvement in drastically underserved inner-city and rural areas, especially among Hispanics, blacks, Native Americans, and other minorities.

47. Many of those whom the Catholic institution seeks to serve are reluctant or unable to seek help. They may be intimidated by the formality of a hospital, or live in an isolated area, or speak no English. Some may cling to an exaggerated ideal of self-reliance. Catholic health care institutions should take the initiative in reaching out to these needy people. They should not hesitate, moreover, to initiate social action programs on behalf of their patients or potential patients and their families. Such programs will sometimes involve advocacy in the cause of justice for the underprivileged. This will include working for changes in reimbursement methodologies that penalize and threaten the existence of hospitals that seek to serve the poor.

48. A second important way of fulfilling the Church's prophetic role in the health care field is the development of alternative models of health care. For example, community clinics, "satellite" clinics, and other new models of health care delivery that meet the needs of the

---

[8]Pope John Paul II, Homily at Yankee Stadium, Oct. 2, 1979.

indigent, the underserved, and the poor should be supported and developed. Hospices, which offer humane, personal care for the terminally ill, are also a welcome development in recent years. These services exemplify the all-important integration of the spiritual, physical, psychological, and social dimensions of health care.

49. We likewise encourage further innovation in personal health education programs and in preventive health care services. For example, programs of health screening for the elderly which are conducted in local parishes or in congregate housing have proven to be both effective and desirable. Home health care for the frail elderly and disabled and new developments in long-term care facilities are also welcome signs of innovation. We trust that Catholic health care facilities will continue to be leaders in the promotion of these and other alternatives in the years ahead.

4. Rights and Responsibilities of Employers and Employees

50. By its very nature a Catholic health care facility aims to take on the character of a Christian community. All who work there are participants in the Catholic health apostolate. Catholic institutions are encouraged to provide education and training programs to instruct and inform their employees in the Catholic philosophy of care of the sick. They should also foster the work of volunteers and include them in such training programs. This is especially necessary in view of the religious pluralism of employees of hospitals and health agencies. Together they can strive to make the hospital setting one that reflects the atmosphere of a Christian service community. This kind of community building within the hospital is one clear way of demonstrating the Catholic hospital's unique identity.

51. An important and indispensable responsibility of employers is the duty to deal justly with all employees. This involves not only just wages, fringe benefits, and the like, but also the effective honoring of the desire of employees "to be treated as free and responsible men and women, able to participate in the decisions which affect their life and their future."[9] This calls for the full recognition of the rights of employees to organize and bargain collectively with the institution through whatever association or organization they freely choose or through whatever other means seem appropriate without unjust pressures from their employers or from already existing labor organizations. The effort to attend fully to the teachings of the Church will, in the long run, strengthen the apostolate by safeguarding its credibility and will deepen the commitment to the principles of social justice as required by the Gospel. In this regard we call attention to Pope John Paul II's recent encyclical, *Laborem Exercens*:

---

[9]Pope John Paul II, Address at Monterey, Mexico, Jan. 31, 1979.

All these rights, together with the need for the workers themselves to secure them, give rise to yet another right: the right of association, that is, to form associations for the purpose of defending the vital interests of those employed in the various professions. These associations are called labor or trade unions. . . . It is clear that even if it is because of their work needs that people unite to secure their rights, their union remains a constructive factor of social order and solidarity, and it is impossible to ignore it.[10]

52. Justice also demands that employees realize the special responsibility that they have to their employer and the responsibilities they have as workers who care for the sick in a Christian facility. This is particularly significant in light of the importance of Catholic identity as delineated above. One of the characteristics that should be evident in a Christian-Catholic health care facility is a strong sense of community and deep commitment to human dignity and basic human rights. We hope that workers in these facilities will give special attention to developing a sense of community that will promote the delivery of personalized patient care. Out of respect for these rights, workers must take no action that endangers the life of the patients in the health care facility where they may be employed. On this matter we again refer to *Laborem Exercens*:

One method used by unions in pursuing the just rights of their members is the strike or work stoppage, as a kind of ultimatum to the competent bodies, especially the employers. This method is recognized by Catholic social teaching as legitimate in the proper conditions and within just limits.

In this connection workers should be assured the right to strike, without being subjected to personal penal sanctions for taking part in a strike. While admitting that it is a legitimate means, we must at the same time emphasize that a strike remains, in a sense, an extreme means. It must not be abused. . . .

Furthermore, it must never be forgotten that, when essential community services are in question, they must in every case be ensured, if necessary by means of appropriate legislation. Abuse of the strike weapon can lead to the paralysis of the whole of socioeconomic life, and this is contrary to the requirements of the common good of society, which also corresponds to the properly understood nature of work itself.[11]

V. Public Policy

53. It is appropriate in this context to call attention to the significant impact that public policy has on health care in our society. The government, working for the common good, has an essential role to play in assuring that the right of all people to adequate health care is

---

[10]*Laborem Exercens*, art. 20.
[11]*Ibid*.

protected. The function of government reaches beyond the limited resources of individuals and private groups. Private agencies and institutions alone are unable to develop a comprehensive national health policy, or to ensure that all Americans have adequate health insurance, or to command the vast resources necessary to implement an effective national health policy. These functions are in large part the responsibility of government. However, in accord with the traditional Catholic principle of subsidiarity, we believe voluntary institutions must continue to play an essential role in our society.

54. Christian people have a responsibility to actively participate in the shaping and executing of public policy that relates to health care. On this issue, as on all issues of basic human rights, the Church has an important role to play in bringing gospel values to the social and political order. In our statement on political responsibility issued earlier, we outline this role in more detail:

> The Church's responsibility in the area of human rights includes two complementary pastoral actions: the affirmation and promotion of human rights and the denunciation and condemnation of violations of these rights. In addition, it is the Church's role to call attention to the moral and religious dimensions of secular issues, to keep alive the values of the Gospel as a norm for social and political life, and to point out the demands of the Christian faith for a just transformation of society. Such a ministry on the part of every Christian and the Church inevitably involves political consequences and touches upon public affairs.[12]

55. We urge Catholics to fulfill their political responsibility in the area of health care policy by educating themselves on the issues and by making their views known. Acting both individually and collectively through parishes, Catholic organizations and other appropriate networks, they can make a valuable contribution toward the development of a just and humane national health policy.

Principles for Public Policy

56. In the interest of providing a sound framework for discussion and policy development, we affirm the following principles which we believe should be reflected in a national health policy. These principles are consistent with and flow from a recent constructive dialogue between the Catholic Health Association, the National Conference of Catholic Charities, and the United States Catholic Conference.

57. (1) Every person has a basic right to adequate health care. This right flows from the sanctity of human life and the dignity that belongs to all human persons, who are made in the image of God. It implies

---

[12]United States Catholic Conference Administrative Board's Statement on *Political Responsibility: Choices for the 1980's*, Oct. 26, 1979, p. 4.

that access to that health care which is necessary and suitable for the proper development and maintenance of life must be provided for all people, regardless of economic, social, or legal status. Special attention should be given to meeting the basic health needs of the poor. With increasingly limited resources in the economy, it is the basic rights of the poor that are frequently threatened first. The Church should work with the government to avoid this danger.

58. (2) Pluralism is an essential characteristic of the health care delivery system of the United States. Any comprehensive health system that is developed, therefore, should use the cooperative resources of both the public and private sectors, the voluntary, religious, and nonprofit sectors. In any national health system, provision should be made for the protection of conscience in the delivery of care. This applies not only to individual and institutional providers, but also to consumers.

59. (3) The benefits provided in a national health care policy should be sufficient to maintain and promote good health as well as to treat disease and disability. Emphasis should be placed on the promotion of health, the prevention of disease, and the protection against environmental and other hazards to physical and mental health. If health is viewed in an integrated and comprehensive manner, the social and economic context of illness and health care must become an important focus of concern and action. Toward this end, public policy should provide incentives for preventive care, early intervention and alternative delivery systems. All of these actions should be carried out in the context of our fundamental commitment to the sanctity and dignity of human life.

60. (4) Consumers should be allowed a reasonable choice of providers whether they be individual providers, groups, clinics, or institutions. Likewise, to enhance personal and family responsibility in health care, public policy should ensure broad consumer participation in the planning and decision making that affects health maintenance and health care delivery both in the community and in institutions.

61. (5) Health care planning is an essential element in the development of an efficient and coordinated health care system. Public policy should ensure that uniform standards are part of the health care delivery system. This is the joint responsibility of the private and public sectors. They should work cooperatively to ensure the provision of standards that will help to achieve equity in the range and quality of services and in the training of providers.

62. (6) Methods of containing and controlling costs are an essential element of national health policy. Incentives should be developed at every level of administering health care efficiently, effectively, and economically.

63. Following on these principles and on our belief in health care as a basic human right, we call for the development of a national health insurance program. It is the responsibility of the federal government to establish a comprehensive health care system that will ensure a basic level of health care for all Americans. The federal government should also ensure adequate funding for this basic level of care through a national health insurance program. Such a program should reflect sound human values and should, in our view, be based on the principles that we have set forth in this Statement.[13]

VI. Conclusion

64. As pastors and teachers, we feel it is opportune to issue these reflections on health and the Catholic community. If they clarify some matters and describe the scope of the Church's interest in this vital subject, part of our purpose will have been served. The rest can only be accomplished by those who share our values and our belief in the innate dignity of the human person. We hope this Statement will lead to a continuing dialogue on health and health care, a dialogue that takes its starting point from some of the issues we have raised.

65. Christians know that pain permeates the human condition. But they also know that God did not abandon us to helpless acquiescence in suffering. He promised to take upon Himself the work of human restoration and to "make all things new" again (Rv 21:5). This He did at the center of time through Jesus; this He continues to do through the healing work of His followers. In the end, since the limitations of the human condition impose a degree of suffering and ultimately death for all of us, those involved in the healing mission of Christ render a unique service by bringing a faith dimension to these crucial moments. Animated by and united in the spirit of Christ, we extend our hands to all who are sick and to all who have dedicated their lives to the work of healing. May the faith and goodness of all Christians be the light by which they heal, the light in which they live and work.

---

[13]John Paul II addresses this matter in *Laborem Exercens*, art. 19: "The expenses involved in health care, especially in the case of accidents at work, demand that medical assistance should be easily available for workers and that as far as possible it should be cheap or even free of charge."

NCCB/USCC
Mission Statement

*A Statement Adopted by the Catholic Bishops
of the United States*

November 1981

1. The National Conference of Catholic Bishops and the United States Catholic Conference are a permanent institute[1] composed of the Catholic bishops of the United States of America in and through which the bishops exercise in a communal or collegial manner the pastoral mission entrusted to them by the Lord Jesus of santification, teaching, and leadership,[2] especially by devising forms and methods of apostolate suitably adapted to the circumstances of the times.[3] Such exercise is intended to offer appropriate assistance to each bishop in fulfilling his particular ministry in the local Church, to effect a commonality of ministry addressed to the people of the United States of America, and to foster and express communion with the Church in other nations within the Church universal, under the leadership of its chief pastor, the Pope.

2. The National Conference of Catholic Bishops deals principally with matters connected with the internal life of the Church.

3. The United States Catholic Conference deals principally with affairs involving the general public, including social concerns, education, and communications, on the national level and in support of efforts at the regional and diocesan levels.

---

[1]Cf. Canon 322, 1980 *Schema Codicis Iuris Canonici*
[2]Cf. *Lumen Gentium* 21
[3]Cf. *Christus Dominus* 38.1

Statement on Social Security

A Statement Approved by the
Administrative Board of the
United States Catholic Conference

March 1983

1. Social Security is the largest and one of the most successful social programs in the United States. It provides an effective and dignified way for Americans to honor their responsibility to provide basic income security and medical insurance for the elderly, the disabled and the dependent.

2. Our support for Social Security is not new. As early as 1919 in the "Program of Social Reconstruction,"[1] Catholic bishops called for the State to provide comprehensive social insurance to provide protection against old age, disability, and illness. The Church through all the intervening years has been a strong supporter of the Social Security System because it provides precisely this kind of protection.

3. In recent years, however, Social Security has experienced a number of problems that have generated widespread concern. Certain current financial difficulties in the program have stimulated a broad public debate about how to ensure the ongoing soundness of Social Security. At the same time, we have witnessed within the Church a small but growing number of organizations, institutions, and individuals who are considering withdrawing from or not participating in the Social Security System.

4. In view of these circumstances, we wish to address the subject of Social Security with three specific objectives in mind:

 (a) to reaffirm our support for the Social Security System;

 (b) to highlight several of the moral principles from our Catholic social tradition which can help to shape the public policy debate over Social Security;

 (c) to indicate some practical implications concerning participation in Social Security by Catholic institutions and employees of the Church.

---

[1] Administrative Committee of the National Catholic War Council, "Program of Social Reconstruction" (1919) in Hugh J. Nolan, ed., *Pastoral Letters of the American Hierarchy, 1792-1970* (Huntington, Indiana: Our Sunday Visitor, Inc., 1971), p. 207.

---

1. Support for the Social Security System

5. Our general support for the Social Security System stems from Catholic social teaching concerning basic human rights and the common good. Every person is made in the image and likeness of God and is therefore endowed with a special human dignity. This dignity is protected by a set of basic human rights which are universal and inherent in the very nature of the human person. Pope John XXIII listed some of these rights in his encyclical letter, *Pacem in Terris*:

> Every person has the right to life, to bodily integrity, and to the means which are suitable for the proper development of life. . . . Therefore, a human being has the right to security in case of sickness, inability to work, widowhood, old age, unemployment. . . .[2]

6. The concept of the common good is also an essential element of our social teaching and one that has important implications for the issue of Social Security. The human person is essentially a social being, and human rights are rights that are held in community. Therefore all persons are required to work together for the sake of the common good, for the general welfare of the entire human family. All persons are called to establish social institutions and structures which protect basic human rights and reflect the dignity of the human person.

7. In the case of social insurance for the aged, the widowed, and the disabled, we are dealing with a right that is essential for the effective human development of a large segment of our citizen population. It is evident that in contemporary society this right cannot be adequately protected without the active participation of government. As stated in *Pacem in Terris*:

> It is necessary that governments make efforts to see that insurance systems are made available to the citizens, so that, in case of misfortune or increased family responsibilities, no person will be without the necessary means to maintain a decent standard of living.[3]

8. We believe that a humane social policy must include a comprehensive social insurance program that is organized through the public sector. In the United States the Social Security System provides this basic social insurance protection. It is very important, therefore, that all Americans support the system, have confidence in it, and work constructively to make it a fair and sound program. Such action will, in our view, serve the common good and help to protect human dignity.

---

[2]John XXIII, *Pacem in Terris* (1963), 11.
[3]*Ibid.*, 64.

2. The Public Policy Debate

9.   We firmly believe that our nation's lawmakers should make the necessary adjustments in the Social Security System to ensure its continued stability and soundness. The policy choices involved in this task, however, are not solely economic and political choices. They also include significant moral content. We believe our tradition of Catholic social teaching offers a number of moral principles that can provide insight and direction for this public policy debate.

10. As efforts are undertaken to amend the Social Security System and assure its financial soundness, we urge the nation's decision makers to pay special attention to the principles of distributive justice and concern for the poor. Without suggesting specific technical solutions to the financial problems that face Social Security, we do wish to call attention to several aspects of the policy debate.

(a) With respect to changes in benefits, we believe that any adjustments which are made should not penalize low-income individuals and families. Those whose resources are already very limited should not be forced to suffer a decrease in benefits.

(b) With respect to the tax structure of Social Security, we believe that any changes which are to be made should be weighted in favor of the poor. Following the general principle that taxes should be assessed according to the ability to pay, we urge policy makers to amend the Social Security tax structure in ways that do not increase the share of taxes paid by lower income families and individuals. Those who are more affluent should be required to bear a greater share of the total Social Security tax burden.

(c) We believe that the principles of equity and concern for the common good also suggest the advisability of bringing employees of nonprofit institutions under the Social Security program.

(d) We also wish to call attention to the fact that the present structure of Social Security contains a number of serious inequities with respect to the benefits received by some women. We urge that prompt action be taken to remedy these inequities.

3. Participation of Catholic Institutions and Employees

11. The principles delineated above have important implications for Catholic institutions and employees of the Church. Just as the principles of social justice lead us to support Social Security for the nation as a whole, we are compelled to strive for that same justice within the Church's own institutions. In the words of the 1971 Synod, "While the Church is bound to give witness to justice, she recognizes that anyone who ventures to speak to people about justice must first be just in their eyes."[4]

12. In addition to the moral principles we have cited above, there are significant practical advantages to Social Security that should encourage participation. It is generally agreed that the protection provided by Social Security cannot be duplicated at a comparable cost. Social Security provides comprehensive insurance coverage: disability, survivors, retirement, and health benefits. It provides protection for one's dependents; it is indexed to protect against inflation; and its coverage is portable.

13. In view of these moral and practical reasons, we strongly urge all Catholics to support and participate in the Social Security System. We encourage Catholic employers and employees to examine fully the moral and practical advantage of Social Security. Catholic institutions are urged to assist their employees by providing the necessary resources to promote a better understanding of these issues. Likewise, we hope that the educational structures and institutions of the Church will make a specific effort to teach students about the moral principles involved in this matter. Finally, in the interest of the common good we urge all of the clergy and religious to participate in Social Security.

14. In summary, we believe that the Social Security System in the United States is a program that is vital to the protection of human dignity for millions of Americans. It makes our society more humane and is a program that merits the full support of all Americans.

---

[4]Synod of Bishops, *Justice in the World* (1971), 40.

Statement on Namibia

*A Statement Approved by the
Administrative Board of the
United States Catholic Conference*

March 1983

1. In December 1981, the President of the Southern African Catholic Bishops Conference (SACBC), Archbishop Denis E. Hurley of Durban, visited the United States as part of a five-nation mission to place the views of the SACBC before the key states in the Namibian negotiations. In May 1982 the SACBC published its position in a lengthy policy document which attracted much attention in South Africa, the United Kingdom and the United States.

2. In its *Report on Namibia*, the SACBC made the following statements:

> In broad outline it is clear enough to us that there is a universal consensus, with South Africa the only dissenting voice, that South Africa has no right to be in Namibia.
>
> It also seems clear to us that the majority of Namibians have one overriding desire and that is the implementation of U.N. Security Council Resolution 435, resulting in a cease-fire, the withdrawal of South African Security Forces and the holding of elections under United Nations auspices.
>
> We conclude this report with an appeal for understanding, for a creative, humane and constructive Christian effort on the part of South Africa to conclude a just and peaceful settlement, and for sustained and fervent prayer that, with the help of God, this will be achieved.

3. In issuing its *Report on Namibia*, the SACBC continues its witness to the social dimensions of the gospel message in Southern Africa. Archbishop Hurley's visit to the United States was a demonstration of the importance the SACBC attaches to the U.S. role in the Namibia negotiations. Aware of this fact, the USCC Administrative Board issues this statement in support of our brother bishops in the SACBC and in solidarity with the other Christian churches, particularly the Lutheran church in Namibia and here in the United States, which have worked so courageously for a just resolution of the Namibian conflict.

4. The U.S. role in Namibia can and should be that of a constructive contribution to peace. We are aware of the course of negotiations over the past four years, and we recognize the way in which U.S. policy can set a tone and a direction for the diplomatic process concerning Namibia. We endorse the efforts of the five-nation "Western Contact Group" in their discussions with South Africa and the South-West

African People's Organization (SWAPO). But we now face a diplomatic stalemate and the possible breakdown of the negotiating effort.
There is a need for both renewed effort on the part of all parties and
new initiatives by the Contact Group in its search for a peaceful
solution to the conflict.

5.   The SACBC *Report on Namibia* calls for the realization of three
objectives: the withdrawal of South Africa from Namibia, a cease-fire
within Namibia and the holding of elections. We endorse these three
goals and urge the U.S. Government to pursue them aggressively.
In addition we oppose attaching other issues to the negotiations in
such a way that these three objectives endorsed by the SACBC are
endangered.

6.   The Namibian people should not be expected, much less forced,
to await the resolution of the many outstanding issues in Southern
Africa before their right to self-determination and civil peace is assured.
The United States entered the Namibian negotiations to provide a
just and peaceful resolution of the conflict. We urge our government
to be faithful to this original intention: to foster a peaceful settlement
not to frustrate it. The suffering in Namibia has continued long enough.
We join our efforts and our prayers to those of the bishops in the
SACBC for a rapid, just and peaceful settlement.

The Challenge of Peace: God's Promise and Our Response

A Pastoral Letter Issued by the
National Conference of Catholic Bishops

May 3, 1983

Introduction

1. "The whole human race faces a moment of supreme crisis in its advance toward maturity." Thus the Second Vatican Council opened its treatment of modern warfare.[1] Since the Council, the dynamic of the nuclear arms race has intensified. Apprehension about nuclear war is almost tangible and visible today. As Pope John Paul II said in his message to the United Nations concerning disarmament: "Currently, the fear and preoccupation of so many groups in various parts of the world reveal that people are more frightened about what would happen if irresponsible parties unleash some nuclear war."[2]

2. As bishops and pastors ministering in one of the major nuclear nations, we have encountered this terror in the minds and hearts of our people—indeed, we share it. We write this letter because we agree that the world is at a moment of crisis, the effects of which are evident in people's lives. It is not our intent to play on fears, however, but to speak words of hope and encouragement in time of fear. Faith does not insulate us from the challenges of life; rather, it intensifies our desire to help solve them precisely in light of the Good News which has come to us in the person of Jesus, the Lord of history. From the resources of our faith we wish to provide hope and strength to all who seek a world free of the nuclear threat. Hope sustains one's capacity to live with danger without being overwhelmed by it; hope

---

[1] Vatican II, the *Pastoral Constitution on the Church in the Modern World* (hereafter cited: *Pastoral Constitution*), #77. Papal and conciliar texts will be referred to by title with paragraph number. Several collections of these texts exist although no single collection is comprehensive; see the following: *Peace and Disarmament: Documents of the World Council of Churches and the Roman Catholic Church* (Geneva and Rome: 1982) (hereafter cited: *Documents*, with page number); J. Gremillion, *The Gospel of Peace and Justice: Catholic Social Teaching Since Pope John* (Maryknoll, N.Y.: 1976); D. J. O'Brien and T. A. Shannon, eds., *Renewing the Earth: Catholic Documents on Peace, Justice, and Liberation* (New York: 1977); A. Flannery, O.P., ed., *Vatican Council II: The Conciliar and Post Conciliar Documents* (Collegeville, Minn.: 1975); W. Abbot, ed., *The Documents of Vatican II* (New York: 1966). Both the Flannery and Abbot translations of the *Pastoral Constitution* are used in this letter.

[2] John Paul II, "Message to the Second Special Session of the United Nations General Assembly Devoted to Disarmament" (June 1982) (hereafter cited: "Message U.N. Special Session 1982"), #7.

is the will to struggle against obstacles even when they appear insuperable. Ultimately our hope rests in the God who gave us life, sustains the world by his power, and has called us to revere the lives of every person and all peoples.

3.   The crisis of which we speak arises from this fact: nuclear war threatens the existence of our planet; this is a more menacing threat than any the world has known. It is neither tolerable nor necessary that human beings live under this threat. But removing it will require a major effort of intelligence, courage, and faith. As Pope John Paul II said at Hiroshima: "From now on it is only through a conscious choice and through a deliberate policy that humanity can survive."[3]

4.   As Americans, citizens of the nation which was first to produce atomic weapons, which has been the only one to use them, and which today is one of the handful of nations capable of decisively influencing the course of the nuclear age, we have grave human, moral, and political responsibilities to see that a "conscious choice" is made to save humanity. This letter is therefore both an invitation and a challenge to Catholics in the United States to join with others in shaping the conscious choices and deliberate policies required in this "moment of supreme crisis."

I. Peace in the Modern World: Religious Perspectives and Principles

5.   The global threat of nuclear war is a central concern of the universal Church, as the words and deeds of recent popes and the Second Vatican Council vividly demonstrate. In this pastoral letter we speak as bishops of the universal Church, heirs of the religious and moral teaching on modern warfare of the last four decades. We also speak as bishops of the Church in the United States, who have both the obligation and the opportunity to share and interpret the moral and religious wisdom of the Catholic tradition by applying it to the problems of war and peace today.

6.   The nuclear threat transcends religious, cultural, and national boundaries. To confront its danger requires all the resources reason and faith can muster. This letter is a contribution to a wider common effort, meant to call Catholics and all members of our political community to dialogue and specific decisions about this awesome question.

7.   The Catholic tradition on war and peace is a long and complex one, reaching from the Sermon on the Mount to the statements of Pope John Paul II. Its development cannot be sketched in a straight

---

[3]John Paul II, "Address to Scientists and Scholars," #4, *Origins* 10 (1981):621.

line and it seldom gives a simple answer to complex questions. It speaks through many voices and has produced multiple forms of religious witness. As we locate ourselves in this tradition, seeking to draw from it and to develop it, the document which provides profound inspiration and guidance for us is the *Pastoral Constitution on the Church in the Modern World* of Vatican II, for it is based on doctrinal principles and addresses the relationship of the Church to the world with respect to the most urgent issues of our day.[4]

8.   A rule of interpretation crucial for the *Pastoral Constitution* is equally important for this pastoral letter although the authority inherent in these two documents is quite distinct. Both documents use principles of Catholic moral teaching and apply them to specific contemporary issues. The bishops at Vatican II opened the *Pastoral Constitution* with the following guideline on how to relate principles to concrete issues:

> In the first part, the Church develops her teaching on man, on the world which is the enveloping context of man's existence, and on man's relations to his fellow men. In Part II, the Church gives closer consideration to various aspects of modern life and human society; special consideration is given to those questions and problems which, in this general area, seem to have a greater urgency in our day. As a result, in Part II the subject matter which is viewed in the light of doctrinal principles is made up of diverse elements. Some elements have a permanent value; others, only a transitory one. Consequently, the constitution must be interpreted according to the general norms of theological interpretion. Interpreters must bear in mind—especially in Part II—the changeable circumstances which the subject matter, by its very nature, involves.[5]

9.   In this pastoral letter, too, we address many concrete questions concerning the arms race, contemporary warfare, weapons systems, and negotiating strategies. We do not intend that our treatment of each of these issues carry the same moral authority as our statement of universal moral principles and formal Church teaching. Indeed, we stress here at the beginning that not every statement in this letter has the same moral authority. At times we reassert universally binding moral principles (e.g., noncombatant immunity and proportionality). At still other times we reaffirm statements of recent popes and the teaching of Vatican II. Again, at other times we apply moral principles to specific cases.

10.   When making applications of these principles we realize—and we wish readers to recognize—that prudential judgments are involved

---

[4]The *Pastoral Constitution* is made up of two parts; yet it constitutes an organic unity. By way of explanation: the constitution is called "pastoral" because, while resting on doctrinal principles, it seeks to express the relation of the Church to the world and modern mankind. The result is that, on the one hand, a pastoral slant is present in the first part and, on the other hand, a doctrinal slant is present in the second part. *Pastoral Constitution*, note 1 above.

[5]*Ibid.*

based on specific circumstances which can change or which can be interpreted differently by people of good will (e.g., the treatment of "no first use"). However, the moral judgments that we make in specific cases, while not binding in conscience, are to be given serious attention and consideration by Catholics as they determine whether their moral judgments are consistent with the Gospel.

11. We shall do our best to indicate, stylistically and substantively, whenever we make such applications. We believe such specific judgments are an important part of this letter, but they should be interpreted in light of another passage from the *Pastoral Constitution*:

> Often enough the Christian view of things will itself suggest some specific solution in certain circumstances. Yet it happens rather frequently, and legitimately so, that with equal sincerity some of the faithful will disagree with others on a given matter. Even against the intention of their proponents, however, solutions proposed on one side or another may be easily confused by many people with the Gospel message. Hence it is necessary for people to remember that no one is allowed in the aforementioned situations to appropriate the Church's authority for his opinion. They should always try to enlighten one another through honest discussion, preserving mutual charity and caring above all for the common good.[6]

12. This passage acknowledges that, on some complex social questions, the Church expects a certain diversity of views even though all hold the same universal moral principles. The experience of preparing this pastoral letter has shown us the range of strongly held opinion in the Catholic community on questions of war and peace. Obviously, as bishops we believe that such differences should be expressed within the framework of Catholic moral teaching. We urge mutual respect among different groups in the Church as they analyze this letter and the issues it addresses. Not only conviction and commitment are needed in the Church, but also civility and charity.

13. The *Pastoral Constitution* calls us to bring the light of the Gospel to bear upon "the signs of the times." Three signs of the times have particularly influenced the writing of this letter. The first, to quote Pope John Paul II at the United Nations, is that "the world wants peace, the world needs peace."[7] The second is the judgment of Vatican II about the arms race: "The arms race is one of the greatest curses on the human race and the harm it inflicts upon the poor is more than can be endured."[8] The third is the way in which the unique dangers and dynamics of the nuclear arms race present qualitatively new problems which must be addressed by fresh applications of traditional moral principles. In light of these three characteristics, we wish to examine Catholic teaching on peace and war.

---

[6]*Ibid.*, #43.
[7]John Paul II, "Message U.N. Special Session 1982," #2.
[8]*Pastoral Constitution*, #81.

14. The Catholic social tradition, as exemplified in the *Pastoral Constitution* and recent papal teachings, is a mix of biblical, theological, and philosophical elements which are brought to bear upon the concrete problems of the day. The biblical vision of the world, created and sustained by God, scarred by sin, redeemed in Christ and destined for the Kingdom, is at the heart of our religious heritage. This vision requires elaboration, explanation, and application in each age; the important task of theology is to penetrate ever more adequately the nature of the biblical vision of peace and relate it to a world not yet at peace. Consequently, the teaching about peace examines both how to construct a more peaceful world and how to assess the phenomenon of war.

15. At the center of the Church's teaching on peace and at the center of all Catholic social teaching are the transcendence of God and the dignity of the human person. The human person is the clearest reflection of God's presence in the world; all of the Church's work in pursuit of both justice and peace is designed to protect and promote the dignity of every person. For each person not only reflects God, but is the expression of God's creative work and the meaning of Christ's redemptive ministry. Christians approach the problem of war and peace with fear and reverence. God is the Lord of life, and so each human life is sacred; modern warfare threatens the obliteration of human life on a previously unimaginable scale. The sense of awe and "fear of the Lord" which former generations felt in approaching these issues weighs upon us with new urgency. In the words of the *Pastoral Constitution*:

> Men of this generation should realize that they will have to render an account of their warlike behavior; the destiny of generations to come depends largely on the decisions they make today.[9]

16. Catholic teaching on peace and war has had two purposes: to help Catholics form their consciences and to contribute to the public policy debate about the morality of war. These two purposes have led Catholic teaching to address two distinct but overlapping audiences. The first is the Catholic faithful, formed by the premises of the Gospel and the principles of Catholic moral teaching. The second is the wider civil community, a more pluralistic audience, in which our brothers and sisters with whom we share the name Christian, Jews, Moslems, other religious communities, and all people of good will also make up our polity. Since Catholic teaching has traditionally sought to address both audiences, we intend to speak to both in this letter, recognizing that Catholics are also members of the wider political community.

---

[9]*Ibid.*, #80.

17. The conviction, rooted in Catholic ecclesiology, that both the community of the faithful and the civil community should be addressed on peace and war has produced two complementary but distinct styles of teaching. The religious community shares a specific perspective of faith and can be called to live out its implications. The wider civil community, although it does not share the same vision of faith, is equally bound by certain key moral principles. For all men and women find in the depth of their consciences a law written on the human heart by God.[10] From this law reason draws moral norms. These norms do not exhaust the Gospel vision, but they speak to critical questions affecting the welfare of the human community, the role of states in international relations, and the limits of acceptable action by individuals and nations on issues of war and peace.

18. Examples of these two styles can be found in recent Catholic teaching. At times the emphasis is upon the problems and requirements for a just public policy (e.g., Pope John Paul II at the U.N. Special Session 1982); at other times the emphasis is on the specific role Christians should play (e.g., Pope John Paul II at Coventry, England, 1982). The same difference of emphasis and orientation can be found in Pope John XXIII's *Peace on Earth* and Vatican II's *Pastoral Constitution*.

19. As bishops we believe that the nature of Catholic moral teaching, the principles of Catholic ecclesiology, and the demands of our pastoral ministry require that this letter speak both to Catholics in a specific way and to the wider political community regarding public policy. Neither audience and neither mode of address can be neglected when the issue has the cosmic dimensions of the nuclear arms race.

20. We propose, therefore, to discuss both the religious vision of peace among peoples and nations and the problems associated with realizing this vision in a world of sovereign states, devoid of any central authority and divided by ideology, geography, and competing claims. We believe the religious vision has an objective basis and is capable of progressive realization. Christ is our peace, for He has "made us both one, and has broken down the dividing wall of hostility . . . that He might create in Himself one new man in place of the two, so making peace, and might reconcile us both to God" (Eph 2:14-16). We also know that this peace will be achieved fully only in the Kingdom of God. The realization of the Kingdom, therefore, is a continuing work, progressively accomplished, precariously maintained, and needing constant effort to preserve the peace achieved and expand its scope in personal and political life.

21. Building peace within and among nations is the work of many individuals and institutions; it is the fruit of ideas and decisions taken

---

[10]*Ibid.*, #16.

in the political, cultural, economic, social, military, and legal sectors of life. We believe that the Church, as a community of faith and social institution, has a proper, necessary, and distinctive part to play in the pursuit of peace.

22. The distinctive contribution of the Church flows from her religious nature and ministry. The Church is called to be, in a unique way, the instrument of the Kingdom of God in history. Since peace is one of the signs of that Kingdom present in the world, the Church fulfills part of her essential mission by making the peace of the Kingdom more visible in our time.

23. Because peace, like the Kingdom of God itself, is both a divine gift and a human work, the Church should continually pray for the gift and share in the work. We are called to be a Church at the service of peace, precisely because peace is one manifestation of God's word and work in our midst. Recognition of the Church's responsibility to join with others in the work of peace is a major force behind the call today to develop a theology of peace. Much of the history of Catholic theology on war and peace has focused on limiting the resort to force in human affairs; this task is still necessary, and is reflected later in this Pastoral Letter, but it is not a sufficient response to Vatican II's challenge "to undertake a completely fresh reappraisal of war."[11]

24. A fresh reappraisal which includes a developed theology of peace will require contributions from several sectors of the Church's life: biblical studies, systematic and moral theology, ecclesiology, and the experience and insights of members of the Church who have struggled in various ways to make and keep the peace in this often violent age. This Pastoral Letter is more an invitation to continue the new appraisal of war and peace than a final synthesis of the results of such an appraisal. We have some sense of the characteristics of a theology of peace, but not a systematic statement of their relationships.

25. A theology of peace should ground the task of peacemaking solidly in the biblical vision of the Kingdom of God, then place it centrally in the ministry of the Church. It should specify the obstacles in the way of peace, as these are understood theologically and in the social and political sciences. It should both identify the specific contributions a community of faith can make to the work of peace and relate these to the wider work of peace pursued by other groups and institutions in society. Finally, a theology of peace must include a message of hope. The vision of hope must be available to all, but one source of its content should be found in a Church at the service of peace.

26. We offer now a first step toward a message of peace and hope. It consists of a sketch of the biblical conception of peace; a theological understanding of how peace can be pursued in a world marked by

---

[11] *Ibid.*, #80.

sin; a moral assessment of key issues facing us in the pursuit of peace today; and an assessment of the political and personal tasks required of all people of good will in this most crucial period of history.

A. Peace and the Kingdom

27. For us as believers, the sacred scriptures provide the foundation for confronting war and peace today. Any use of scripture in this area is conditioned by three factors. *First*, the term "peace" has been understood in different ways at various times and in various contexts. For example, peace can refer to an individual's sense of well-being or security, or it can mean the cessation of armed hostility, producing an atmosphere in which nations can relate to each other and settle conflicts without resorting to the use of arms. For men and women of faith, peace will imply a right relationship with God, which entails forgiveness, reconciliation, and union. Finally, the scriptures point to eschatological peace, a final, full realization of God's salvation when all creation will be made whole. Among these various meanings, the last two predominate in the Scriptures and provide direction to the first two.

28. *Second*, the scriptures as we have them today were written over a long period of time and reflect many varied historical situations, all different from our own. Our understanding of them is both complicated and enhanced by these differences, but not in any way obscured or diminished by them. *Third*, since the Scriptures speak primarily of God's intervention in history, they contain no specific treatise on war and peace. Peace and war must always be seen in light of God's intervention in human affairs and our response to that intervention. Both are elements within the ongoing revelation of God's will for creation.

29. Acknowledging this complexity, we still recognize in the scriptures a unique source of revelation, a word of God which is addressed to us as surely as it has been to all preceding generations. We call upon the spirit of God who speaks in that word and in our hearts to aid us in our listening. The sacred texts have much to say to us about the ways in which God calls us to live in union with and in fidelity to the divine will. They provide us with direction for our lives and hold out to us an object of hope, a final promise, which guides and directs our actions here and now.

1. Old Testament

30. War and peace are significant and highly complex elements within the multilayered accounts of the creation and development of God's people in the Old Testament.

a. War

31. Violence and war are very much present in the history of the People of God, particularly from the Exodus period to the monarchy. God is often seen as the one who leads the Hebrews in battle, protects them from their enemies, makes them victorious over other armies (see, for example, Dt 1:30; 20:4; Jos 2:24; Jgs 3:28). The metaphor of warrior carried multifaceted connotations for a people who knew themselves to be smaller and weaker than the nations which surrounded them. It also enabled them to express their conviction about God's involvement in their lives and his desire for their growth and development. This metaphor provided the people with a sense of security; they had a God who would protect them even in the face of overwhelming obstacles. It was also a call to faith and to trust; the mighty God was to be obeyed and followed. No one can deny the presence of such images in the Old Testament nor their powerful influence upon the articulation of this people's understanding of the involvement of God in their history. The warrior God was highly significant during long periods of Israel's understanding of its faith. But this image was not the only image, and it was gradually transformed, particularly after the experience of the exile, when God was no longer identified with military victory and might. Other images and other understandings of God's activity became predominant in expressing the faith of God's people.

b. Peace

32. Several points must be taken into account in considering the image of peace in the Old Testament. First, all notions of peace must be understood in light of Israel's relation to God. Peace is always seen as a gift from God and as fruit of God's saving activity. Secondly, the individual's personal peace is not greatly stressed. The well-being and freedom from fear which result from God's love are viewed primarily as they pertain to the community and its unity and harmony. Furthermore, this unity and harmony extend to all of creation; true peace implied a restoration of the right order not just among peoples, but within all of creation. Third, while the images of war and the warrior God become less dominant as a more profound and complex understanding of God is presented in the texts, the images of peace and the demands upon the people for covenantal fidelity to true peace grow more urgent and more developed.

c. Peace and Fidelity to the Covenant

33. If Israel obeyed God's laws, God would dwell among them. "I will walk among you and will be your God and you shall be my people" (Lv 26:12). God would strengthen the people against those who opposed them and would give peace in the land. The description of life in these circumstances witnesses to unity among peoples and creation, to freedom from fear and to security (Lv 26:3-16). The right relationship between the people and God was grounded in and expressed by a covenantal union. The covenant bound the people to God in fidelity and obedience; God was also committed in the covenant to be present with the people, to save them, to lead them to freedom. Peace is a special characteristic of this covenant; when the prophet Ezekiel looked to the establishment of the new, truer covenant, he declared that God would establish an everlasting covenant of peace with the people (Ez 37:26).

34. Living in covenantal fidelity with God had ramifications in the lives of the people. It was part of fidelity to care for the needy and helpless; a society living with fidelity was one marked by justice and integrity. Furthermore, covenantal fidelity demanded that Israel put its trust in God alone and look only to him for its security. When Israel tended to forget the obligations of the covenant, prophets arose to remind the people and call them to return to God. True peace is an image which they stressed.

35. Ezekiel, who promised a covenant of peace, condemned in no uncertain terms the false prophets who said there was peace in the land while idolatry and injustice continued (Ez 13:16). Jeremiah followed in this tradition and berated those who "healed the wounds of the people lightly" and proclaimed peace while injustice and infidelity prevailed (Jer 6:14; 8:10-12). Jeremiah and Isaiah both condemned the leaders when, against true security, they depended upon their own strength or alliances with other nations rather than trusting in God (Is 7:1-9; 30:1-4; Jer 37:10). The lament of Isaiah 48:18 makes clear the connection between justice, fidelity to God's law, and peace; he cries out: "O that you had hearkened to my commandments! Then your peace would have been like a river, and your righteousness like the waves of the sea."

d. Hope for Eschatological Peace

36. Experience made it clear to the people of God that the covenant of peace and the fullness of salvation had not been realized in their midst. War and enmity were still present, injustices thrived, sin still manifested itself. These same experiences also convinced the people of God's fidelity to a covenant which they often neglected. Because of this fidelity, God's promise of a final salvation involving all peoples and all creation and of an ultimate reign of peace became an integral part of the hope of the Old Testament. In the midst of their failures and sin, God's people strove for greater fidelity to him and closer relationship with him; they did so because, believing in the future they had been promised, they directed their lives and energies toward an eschatological vision for which they longed. Peace is an integral component of that vision.

37. The final age, the Messianic time, is described as one in which the "Spirit is poured on us from on high." In this age, creation will be made whole, "justice will dwell in the wilderness," the effect of righteousness will be peace, and the people will "abide in a peaceful habitation and in secure dwellings and in quiet resting places" (Is 32:15-20). There will be no need for instruments of war (Is 2:4; Mi 4:3),[12] God will speak directly to the people and "righteousness and peace will embrace each other" (Ps 85:10-11). A messiah will appear, a servant of God upon whom God has placed his spirit and who will faithfully bring forth justice to the nations: "He will not cry or lift up his voice, or make it heard in the street; a bruised reed he will not break and a dimly burning wick he will not quench; he will faithfully bring forth justice" (Is 42:2-3).

38. The Old Testament provides us with the history of a people who portrayed their God as one who intervened in their lives, who protected them and led them to freedom, often as a mighty leader in battle. They also appear as a people who longed constantly for peace. Such peace was always seen as a result of God's gift which came about in fidelity to the covenantal union. Furthermore, in the midst of their unfulfilled longing, God's people clung tenaciously to hope in the promise of an eschatological time when, in the fullness of salvation, peace and justice would embrace and all creation would be secure from harm. The people looked for a messiah, one whose coming would signal the beginning of that time. In their waiting, they heard the prophets call them to love according to the covenantal vision, to repent, and to be ready for God's reign.

2. New Testament

39. As Christians we believe that Jesus is the messiah or Christ so long awaited. God's servant (Mt 12:18-21), prophet and more than prophet (Jn 4:19-26), the one in whom the fullness of God was pleased to dwell, through whom all things in heaven and on earth were reconciled to God, Jesus made peace by the blood of the cross (Col 1:19-20). While the characteristics of the *shalom* of the Old Testament (gift from God, inclusive of all creation, grounded in salvation and covenantal fidelity, inextricably bound up with justice) are present in the New Testament traditions, all discussion of war and peace in the New Testament must be seen within the context of the unique revelation of God that is Jesus Christ and of the reign of God which Jesus proclaimed and inaugurated.

---

[12]The exact opposite of this vision is presented in Joel 3:10 where the foreign nations are told that their weapons will do them no good in the face of God's coming wrath.

a. War

40. There is no notion of a warrior God who will lead the people in an historical victory over its enemies in the New Testament. The only war spoken of is found in apocalyptic images of the final moments, especially as they are depicted in the Book of Revelation. Here war stands as image of the eschatological struggle between God and Satan. It is a war in which the Lamb is victorious (Rv 17:14).

41. Military images appear in terms of the preparedness which one must have for the coming trials (Lk 14:31; 22:35-38). Swords appear in the New Testament as an image of division (Mt 12:34; Heb 4:12); they are present at the arrest of Jesus, and he rejects their use (Lk 22:51 and parallel texts); weapons are transformed in Ephesians, when the Christians are urged to put on the whole armor of God which includes the breastplate of righteousness, the helmet of salvation, the sword of the Spirit, "having shod your feet in the equipment of the Gospel of peace" (Eph 6:10-17; cf., I Thes 5:8-9). Soldiers, too, are present in the New Testament. They are at the crucifixion of Jesus, of course, but they are also recipients of the baptism of John, and one centurion receives the healing of his servant (Mt 8:5-13 and parallel texts; cf., Jn 4:46-53).

42. Jesus challenged everyone to recognize in him the presence of the reign of God and to give themselves over to that reign. Such a radical change of allegiance was difficult for many to accept and families found themselves divided, as if by a sword. Hence, the Gospels tell us that Jesus said he came not to bring peace but rather the sword (Mt 10:34). The peace which Jesus did not bring was the false peace which the prophets had warned against. The sword which he did bring was that of the division caused by the word of God which, like a two-edged sword, "pierces to the division of soul and spirit, of joints and marrow, and discerns the thoughts and intentions of the heart" (Heb 4:12).

43. All are invited into the reign of God. Faith in Jesus and trust in God's mercy are the criteria. Living in accord with the demands of the Kingdom rather than those of one's specific profession is decisive.[13]

---

[13] An omission in the New Testament is significant in this context. Scholars have made us aware of the presence of revolutionary groups in Israel during the time of Jesus. Barabbas, for example, was "among the rebels in prison who had committed murder in the insurrection" (Mk 15:7). Although Jesus had come to proclaim and to bring about the true reign of God which often stood in opposition to the existing order, he makes no reference to nor does he join in any attempts such as those of the Zealots to overthrow authority by violent means. See M. Smith, "Zealots and Sicarii, Their Origins and Relations," *Harvard Theological Review* 64 (1971):1-19.

b. Jesus and Reign of God

44. Jesus proclaimed the reign of God in his words and made it present in his actions. His words begin with a call to conversion and a proclamation of the arrival of the Kingdom. "The time is fulfilled, and the Kingdom of God is at hand; repent, and believe in the Gospel" (Mk 1:15, Mt 4:17). The call to conversion was at the same time an invitation to enter God's reign. Jesus went beyond the prophets' cries for conversion when he declared that, in him, the reign of God had begun and was in fact among the people (Lk 17:20-21; 12:32).

45. His words, especially as they are preserved for us in the Sermon on the Mount, describe a new reality in which God's power is manifested and the longing of the people is fulfilled. In God's reign the poor are given the Kingdom, the mourners are comforted, the meek inherit the earth, those hungry for righteousness are satisfied, the merciful know mercy, the pure see God, the persecuted know the Kingdom, and peacemakers are called the children of God (Mt 5:3-10).

46. Jesus' words also depict for us the conduct of one who lives under God's reign. His words call for a new way of life which fulfills and goes beyond the law. One of the most striking characteristics of this new way is forgiveness. All who hear Jesus are repeatedly called to forgive one another, and to do so not just once, but many, many times (Mt 6:14-15; Lk 6:37; Mt 18:21-22; Mk 11:25; Lk 11:4; 17:3-4). The forgiveness of God, which is the beginning of salvation, is manifested in communal forgiveness and mercy.

47. Jesus also described God's reign as one in which love is an active, life-giving, inclusive force. He called for a love which went beyond family ties and bonds of friendship to reach even those who were enemies (Mt 5:44-48; Lk 6:27-28). Such a love does not seek revenge but rather is merciful in the face of threat and opposition (Mt 5:39-42; Lk 6:29-31). Disciples are to love one another as Jesus has loved them (Jn 15:12).

48. The words of Jesus would remain an impossible, abstract ideal were it not for two things: the actions of Jesus and his gift of the spirit. In his actions, Jesus showed the way of living in God's reign; he manifested the forgiveness which he called for when he accepted all who came to him, forgave their sins, healed them, released them from the demons who possessed them. In doing these things, he made the tender mercy of God present in a world which knew violence, oppression, and injustice. Jesus pointed out the injustices of his time and opposed those who laid burdens upon the people or defiled true worship. He acted aggressively and dramatically at times, as when he cleansed the temple of those who had made God's house into a "den of robbers" (Mt 21:12-17 and parallel texts; Jn 3:13-25).

49. Most characteristic of Jesus' actions are those in which he showed his love. As he had commanded others, his love led him even to the giving of his own life to effect redemption. Jesus' message and his actions were dangerous ones in his time, and they led to his death—a cruel and viciously inflicted death, a criminal's death (Gal 3:13). In all of his suffering, as in all of his life and ministry, Jesus refused to defend himself with force or with violence. He endured violence and cruelty so that God's love might be fully manifest and the world might be reconciled to the One from whom it had become estranged. Even at his death, Jesus cried out for forgiveness for those who were his executioners: "Father, forgive them . . . " (Lk 23:34).

50. The resurrection of Jesus is the sign to the world that God indeed does reign, does give life in death, and that the love of God is stronger even than death (Rom 8:36-39).

51. Only in light of this, the fullest demonstration of the power of God's reign, can Jesus' gift of peace—a peace which the world cannot give (Jn 14:27)—be understood. Jesus gives that peace to his disciples, to those who had witnessed the helplessness of the crucifixion and the power of the resurrection (Jn 20:19, 20, 26). The peace which he gives to them as he greets them as their risen Lord is the fullness of salvation. It is the reconciliation of the world and God (Rom 5:1-2; Col 1:20); the restoration of the unity and harmony of all creation which the Old Testament spoke of with such longing. Because the walls of hostility between God and humankind were broken down in the life and death of the true, perfect servant, union and well-being between God and the world were finally fully possible (Eph 2:13-22; Gal 3:28).

c. Jesus and the Community of Believers

52. As his first gift to his followers, the risen Jesus gave his gift of peace. This gift permeated the meetings between the risen Jesus and his followers (Jn 20:19-29). So intense was that gift and so abiding was its power that the remembrance of that gift and the daily living of it became the hallmark of the community of faith. Simultaneously, Jesus gave his spirit to those who followed him. These two personal and communal gifts are inseparable. In the spirit of Jesus the community of believers was enabled to recognize and to proclaim the savior of the world.

53. Gifted with Jesus' own spirit, they could recognize what God had done and know in their own lives the power of the One who creates from nothing. The early Christian communities knew that this power and the reconciliation and peace which marked it were not yet fully operative in their world. They struggled with external persecution and with interior sin, as do all people. But their experience of the spirit of God and their memory of the Christ who was with them nevertheless enabled them to look forward with unshakable confidence to the time when the fullness of God's reign would make itself known in the world. At the same time, they knew that they were called to be ministers of reconciliation (2 Cor 5:19-20), people who would make the peace which God had established visible through the love and the unity within their own communities.

54. Jesus Christ, then, is our peace, and in his death-resurrection he gives God's peace to our world. In him God has indeed reconciled the world, made it one, and has manifested definitively that his will is this reconciliation, this unity between God and all peoples, and among the peoples themselves. The way to union has been opened, the covenant of peace established. The risen Lord's gift of peace is inextricably bound to the call to follow Jesus and to continue the proclamation of God's reign. Matthew's Gospel (Mt 28:16-20; cf., Lk 24:44-53) tells us that Jesus' last words to his disciples were a sending forth and a promise: "I shall be with you all days." In the continuing presence of Jesus, disciples of all ages find the courage to follow him. To follow Jesus Christ implies continual conversion in one's own life as one seeks to act in ways which are consonant with the justice, forgiveness, and love of God's reign. Discipleship reaches out to the ends of the earth and calls for reconciliation among all peoples so that God's purpose, "a plan for the fullness of time, to unite all things in him" (Eph 1:10), will be fulfilled.

3. Conclusion

55. Even a brief examination of war and peace in the Scriptures makes it clear that they do not provide us with detailed answers to the specifics of the questions which we face today. They do not speak specifically of nuclear war or nuclear weapons, for these were beyond the imagination of the communities in which the Scriptures were formed. The sacred texts do, however, provide us with urgent direction when we look at today's concrete realities. The fullness of eschatological peace remains before us in hope and yet the gift of peace is already ours in the reconciliation effected in Jesus Christ. These two profoundly religious meanings of peace inform and influence all other meanings for Christians. Because we have been gifted with God's peace in the risen Christ, we are called to our own peace and to the making of peace in our world. As disciples and as children of God, it is our task to seek for ways in which to make the forgiveness, justice and mercy, and love of God visible in a world where violence and enmity are too often the norm. When we listen to God's word, we hear again and always the call to repentance and to belief: to repentance because although we are redeemed we continue to need redemption; to belief, because although the reign of God is near, it is still seeking its fullness.

B. *Kingdom and History*

56. The Christian understanding of history is hopeful and confident but also sober and realistic. "Christian optimism based on the glorious cross of Christ and the outpouring of the Holy Spirit is no excuse for self-deception. For Christians, peace on earth is always a challenge because of the presence of sin in man's heart."[14] Peace must be built on the basis of justice in a world where the personal and social consequences of sin are evident.

57. Christian hope about history is rooted in our belief in God as creator and sustainer of our existence and our conviction that the Kingdom of God will come in spite of sin, human weakness, and failure. It is precisely because sin is part of history that the realization of the peace of the Kingdom is never permanent or total. This is the continuing refrain from the patristic period to Pope John Paul II:

> For it was sin and hatred that were an obstacle to peace with God and with others: He destroyed them by the offering of life on the cross; He reconciled in one body those who were hostile (cf., Eph 2:16; Rom 12:5) . . . Although Christians put all their best energies into preventing war or stopping it, they do not deceive themselves about their ability to cause peace to triumph, nor about the effect of their efforts to this end. They therefore concern themselves with all human initiatives in favor of peace and very often take part in them. But they regard them with realism and humility. One could almost say that they relativize them in two senses: they relate them both to the self-deception of humanity and to God's saving plan.[15]

58. Christians are called to live the tension between the vision of the reign of God and its concrete realization in history. The tension is often described in terms of "already but not yet": i.e., we already live in the grace of the Kingdom, but it is not yet the completed Kingdom. Hence, we are a pilgrim people in a world marked by conflict and injustice. Christ's grace is at work in the world; his command of love and his call to reconciliation are not purely future ideals but call us to obedience today.

59. With Pope Paul VI and Pope John Paul II we are convinced that "peace is possible."[16] At the same time, experience convinces us that "in this world a totally and permanently peaceful human society is unfortunately a utopia, and that ideologies that hold up that prospect as easily attainable are based on hopes that cannot be realized, whatever the reason behind them."[17]

---

[14]John Paul II, "World Day of Peace Message 1982," #12, *Origins* 11 (1982): 477.
[15]*Ibid.*, #11-12, pp. 477-78.
[16]John Paul II, "Message U.N. Special Session 1982," #13; Pope Paul VI, "World Day of Peace Message 1973."
[17]John Paul II, "World Day of Peace Message 1982," #12, cited, p. 478.

60. This recognition—that peace is possible but never assured and that its possibility must be continually protected and preserved in the face of obstacles and attacks upon it—accounts in large measure for the complexity of Catholic teaching on warfare. In the Kingdom of God, peace and justice will be fully realized. Justice is always the foundation of peace. In history, efforts to pursue both peace and justice are at times in tension, and the struggle for justice may threaten certain forms of peace.

61. It is within this tension of kingdom and history that Catholic teaching has addressed the problem of war. Wars mark the fabric of human history, distort the life of nations today, and, in the form of nuclear weapons, threaten the destruction of the world as we know it and the civilization which has been patiently constructed over centuries. The causes of war are multiple and not easily identified. Christians will find in any violent situation the consequences of sin: not only sinful patterns of domination, oppression or aggression, but the conflict of values and interests which illustrate the limitations of a sinful world. The threat of nuclear war which affects the world today reflects such sinful patterns and conflicts.

62. In the "already but not yet" of Christian existence, members of the Church choose different paths to move toward the realization of the kingdom in history. As we examine both the positions open to individuals for forming their consciences on war and peace and the Catholic teaching on the obligation of the state to defend society, we draw extensively on the *Pastoral Constitution* for two reasons.

63. First, we find its treatment of the nature of peace and the avoidance of war compelling, for it represents the prayerful thinking of bishops of the entire world and calls vigorously for fresh new attitudes, while faithfully reflecting traditional Church teaching. Secondly, the council fathers were familiar with more than the horrors of World Wars I and II. They saw conflicts continuing "to produce their devastating effect day by day somewhere in the world," the increasing ferocity of warfare made possible by modern scientific weapons, guerrilla warfare "drawn out by new methods of deceit and subversion," and terrorism regarded as a new way to wage war.[18] The same phenomena mark our day.

64. For similar reasons we draw heavily upon the popes of the nuclear age, from Pope Pius XII through Pope John Paul II. The teaching of popes and councils must be incarnated by each local church in a manner understandable to its culture. This allows each local church to bring its unique insights and experience to bear on the issues shaping our world. From 1966 to the present, American bishops, individually and collectively, have issued numerous statements on the issues of peace and war, ranging from the Vietnam war to con-

---

[18]*Pastoral Constitution,* #79.

scientious objection and the use of nuclear weapons. These statements reflect not only the concerns of the hierarchy but also the voices of our people who have increasingly expressed to us their alarm over the threat of war. In this letter we wish to continue and develop the teaching on peace and war which we have previously made, and which reflects both the teaching of the universal Church and the insights and experience of the Catholic community of the United States.

65. It is significant that explicit treatment of war and peace is reserved for the final chapter of the *Pastoral Constitution*. Only after exploring the nature and destiny of the human person does the Council take up the nature of peace, which it sees not as an end in itself, but as an *indispensable condition* for the task "of constructing for all men everywhere a world more genuinely human."[19] An understanding of this task is crucial to understanding the Church's view of the moral choices open to us as Christians.

C. The Moral Choices for the Kingdom

66. In one of its most frequently quoted passages, the *Pastoral Constitution* declares that it is necessary "to undertake a completely fresh reappraisal of war."[20] The Council's teaching situates this call for a "fresh reappraisal" within the context of a broad analysis of the dignity of the human person and the state of the world today. If we lose sight of this broader discussion we cannot grasp the Council's wisdom. For the issue of war and peace confronts everyone with a basic question: what contributes to, and what impedes, the construction of a more genuinely human world? If we are to evaluate war with an entirely new attitude, we must be serious about approaching the human person with an entirely new attitude. The obligation for all of humanity to work toward universal respect for human rights and human dignity is a fundamental imperative of the social, economic, and political order.

67. It is clear, then, that to evaluate war with a new attitude, we must go far beyond an examination of weapons systems or military strategies. We must probe the meaning of the moral choices which are ours as Christians. In accord with the vision of Vatican II, we need to be sensitive to both the danger of war and the conditions of true freedom within which moral choices can be made.[21] Peace is the setting in which moral choice can be most effectively exercised. How can we move toward that peace which is indispensable for true human freedom? How do we define such peace?

---

[19] *Ibid.*, #77.
[20] *Ibid.*, #80.
[21] *Ibid.*, #17.

1. The Nature of Peace

68. The Catholic tradition has always understood the meaning of peace in positive terms. Peace is both a gift of God and a human work. It must be constructed on the basis of central human values: truth, justice, freedom, and love. The *Pastoral Constitution* states the traditional conception of peace:

> Peace is not merely the absence of war. Nor can it be reduced solely to the maintenance of a balance of power between enemies. Nor is it brought about by dictatorship. Instead, it is rightly and appropriately called "an enterprise of justice" (Is 32:17). Peace results from that harmony built into human society by its divine founder and actualized by men as they thirst after ever greater justice.[22]

69. Pope John Paul II has enhanced this positive conception of peace by relating it with new philosophical depth to the Church's teaching on human dignity and human rights. The relationship was articulated in his 1979 Address to the General Assembly of the United Nations and also in his "World Day of Peace Message 1982":

> Unconditional and effective respect for each one's unprescriptable and inalienable rights is the necessary condition in order that peace may reign in a society. Vis-à-vis these basic rights all others are in a way derivatory and secondary. In a society in which these rights are not protected, the very idea of universality is dead, as soon as a small group of individuals set up for their own exclusive advantage a principle of discrimination whereby the rights and even the lives of others are made dependent on the whim of the stronger.[23]

70. As we have already noted, however, the protection of human rights and the preservation of peace are tasks to be accomplished in a world marked by sin and conflict of various kinds. The Church's teaching on war and peace establishes a strong presumption against war which is binding on all; it then examines when this presumption may be overriden, precisely in the name of preserving the kind of peace which protects human dignity and human rights.

2. The Presumption against War and the Principle of Legitimate Self-Defense

71. Under the rubric, "curbing the savagery of war," the Council contemplates the "melancholy state of humanity." It looks at this world as it is, not simply as we would want it to be. The view is stark: ferocious new means of warfare threatening savagery surpass-

---

[22]*Ibid.*, #78.
[23]John Paul II, "World Day of Peace Message 1982," #9, cited. The *Pastoral Constitution* stresses that peace is not only the fruit of justice, but also love, which commits us to engage in "the studied practice of brotherhood" (#78).

ing that of the past, deceit, subversion, terrorism, genocide. This last crime, in particular, is vehemently condemned as horrendous, but all activities which deliberately conflict with the all-embracing principles of universal natural law, which is permanently binding, are criminal, as are all orders commanding such action. Supreme commendation is due the courage of those who openly and fearlessly resist those who issue such commands. All individuals, especially government officials and experts, are bound to honor and improve upon agreements which are "aimed at making military activity and its consequences less inhuman" and which "better and more workably lead to restraining the frightfulness of war."[24]

72. This remains a realistic appraisal of the world today. Later in this section the Council calls for us "to strain every muscle as we work for the time when all war can be completely outlawed by international consent." We are told, however, that this goal requires the establishment of some universally recognized public authority with effective power "to safeguard, on the behalf of all, security, regard for justice, and respect for rights."[25] *But what of the present?* The council is exceedingly clear, as are the popes:

> Certainly, war has not been rooted out of human affairs. As long as the danger of war remains and there is no competent and sufficiently powerful authority at the international level, governments cannot be denied the right to legitimate defense once every means of peaceful settlement has been exhausted. Therefore, government authorities and others who share public responsibility have the duty to protect the welfare of the people entrusted to their care and to conduct such grave matters soberly.
>
> But it is one thing to undertake military action for the just defense of the people, and something else again to seek the subjugation of other nations. Nor does the possession of war potential make every military or political use of it lawful. Neither does the mere fact that war has unhappily begun mean that all is fair between the warring parties.[26]

73. The Christian has no choice but to defend peace, properly understood, against aggression. This is an inalienable obligation. It is the *how* of defending peace which offers moral options. We stress this principle again because we observe so much misunderstanding about both those who resist bearing arms and those who bear them. Great numbers from both traditions provide examples of exceptional courage, examples the world continues to need. Of the millions of men and women who have served with integrity in the armed forces, many have laid down their lives. Many others serve today throughout the world in the difficult and demanding task of helping to preserve that "peace of a sort" of which the Council speaks. We see many deeply

---

[24] *Pastoral Constitution*, #79.
[25] *Ibid.*, #82.
[26] *Ibid.*, #79.

sincere individuals who, far from being indifferent or apathetic to world evils, believe strongly in conscience that they are best defending true peace by refusing to bear arms. In some cases they are motivated by their understanding of the Gospel and the life and death of Jesus as forbidding all violence. In others, their motivation is simply to give personal example of Christian forbearance as a positive, constructive approach toward loving reconciliation with enemies. In still other cases, they propose or engage in "active nonviolence" as programmed resistance to thwart aggression, or to render ineffective any oppression attempted by force of arms. No government, and certainly no Christian, may simply assume that such individuals are mere pawns of conspiratorial forces or guilty of cowardice.

74. Catholic teaching sees these two distinct moral responses as having a complementary relationship, in the sense that both seek to serve the common good. They differ in their perception of how the common good is to be defended most effectively, but both responses testify to the Christian conviction that peace must be pursued and rights defended within moral restraints and in the context of defining other basic human values.

75. In all of this discussion of distinct choices, of course, we are referring to options open to individuals. The Council and the popes have stated clearly that governments threatened by armed, unjust aggression must defend their people. This includes defense by armed force, if necessary, as a last resort. We shall discuss below the conditions and limits imposed on such defense. Even when speaking of individuals, however, the Council is careful to preserve the fundamental *right* of defense. Some choose not to vindicate their rights by armed force and adopt other methods of defense, but they do not lose the right of defense nor may they renounce their obligations to others. They are praised by the Council, as long as the rights and duties of others or of the community itself are not injured.

76. Pope Pius XII is especially strong in his conviction about the responsibility of the Christian to resist unjust aggression:

> *A people threatened with an unjust aggression, or already its victim, may not remain passively indifferent, if it would think and act as befits a Christian.* All the more does the solidarity of the family of nations forbid others to behave as mere spectators, in any attitude of apathetic neutrality. Who will ever measure the harm already caused in the past by such indifference to war of aggression, which is quite alien to the Christian instinct? How much more keenly has it brought any advantage in recompense? On the contrary, it has only reassured and encouraged the authors and fomentors of aggression, while it obliges the several peoples, left to themselves, to increase their armaments indefinitely . . . Among (the) goods (of humanity) some are of such importance for society, that it is perfectly lawful to defend them against unjust aggression. *Their defense is even an obligation for*

the nations as a whole, who have a duty not to abandon a nation that is attacked.[27]

77. None of the above is to suggest, however, that armed force is the only defense against unjust aggression, regardless of circumstances. Well does the Council require that grave matters concerning the protection of peoples be conducted *soberly*. The Council fathers were well aware that in today's world, the "horror and perversity of war are immensely magnified by the multiplication of scientific weapons. For acts of war involving these weapons can inflict massive and indiscriminate destruction far exceeding the bounds of legitimate defense."[28] Hence, we are warned: "Men of our time must realize that they will have to give a somber reckoning for their deeds of war. For the course of the future will depend largely on the decisions they make today."[29] There must be serious and continuing study and efforts to develop programmed methods for both individuals and nations to defend against unjust aggression without using violence.

78. We believe work to develop nonviolent means of fending off aggression and resolving conflict best reflects the call of Jesus both to love and to justice. Indeed, each increase in the potential destructiveness of weapons and therefore of war serves to underline the rightness of the way that Jesus mandated to his followers. But, on the other hand, the fact of aggression, oppression, and injustice in our world also serves to legitimate the resort to weapons and armed force in defense of justice. We must recognize the reality of the paradox we face as Christians living in the context of the world as it presently exists; we must continue to articulate our belief that love is possible and the only real hope for all human relations, and yet accept that force, even deadly force, is sometimes justified and that nations must provide for their defense. It is the mandate of Christians, in the face of this paradox, to strive to resolve it through an even greater commitment to Christ and his message. As Pope John Paul II said:

> Christians are aware that plans based on aggression, domination and the manipulation of others lurk in human hearts, and sometimes even secretly nourish human intentions, in spite of certain declarations or manifestations of a pacifist nature. For Christians know that in this world a totally and permanently peaceful human society is unfortunately a utopia, and that ideologies that hold up that prospect as easily attainable are based on hopes that cannot be realized,

---

[27]Pius XII, "Christmas Message," 1948; The same theme is reiterated in Pius XII's "Message" of October 3, 1953: "The community of nations must reckon with unprincipled criminals who, in order to realize their ambitious plans, are not afraid to unleash total war. This is the reason why other countries, if they wish to preserve their very existence and their most precious possessions, and unless they are prepared to accord free action to international criminals, have no alternative but to get ready for the day when they must defend themselves. *This right to be prepared for self-defense cannot be denied, even in these days, to any state.*"

[28]*Pastoral Constitution*, #80.

[29]*Ibid.*

whatever the reason behind them. It is a question of a mistaken view of the human condition, a lack of application in considering the question as a whole; or it may be a case of evasion in order to calm fear, or in still other cases a matter of calculated self-interest. Christians are convinced, if only because they have learned from personal experience, that these deceptive hopes lead straight to the false peace of totalitarian regimes. But this realistic view in no way prevents Christians from working for peace; instead, it stirs up their ardor, for they also know that Christ's victory over deception, hate, and death gives those in love with peace a more decisive motive for action than what the most generous theories about man have to offer; Christ's victory likewise gives a hope more surely based than any hope held out by the most audacious dreams.

This is why Christians, even as they strive to resist and prevent every form of warfare, have no hesitation in recalling that, in the name of an elementary requirement of justice, peoples have a right and even a duty to protect their existence and freedom by proportionate means against an unjust aggressor.[30]

79. In light of the framework of Catholic teaching on the nature of peace, the avoidance of war, and the state's right of legitimate defense, we can now spell out certain moral principles within the Catholic tradition which provide guidance for public policy and individual choice.

3. The Just-War Criteria

80. The moral theory of the "just-war" or "limited-war" doctrine begins with the presumption which binds all Christians: we should do no harm to our neighbors; how we treat our enemy is the key test of whether we love our neighbor; and the possibility of taking even one human life is a prospect we should consider in fear and trembling. How is it possible to move from these presumptions to the idea of a justifiable use of lethal force?

81. Historically and theologically the clearest answer to the question is found in St. Augustine. Augustine was impressed by the fact and the consequences of sin in history—the "not yet" dimension of the kingdom. In his view war was both the result of sin and a tragic remedy for sin in the life of political societies. War arose from disordered ambitions, but it could also be used, in some cases at least, to restrain evil and protect the innocent. The classic case which illustrated his view was the use of lethal force to prevent aggression against innocent victims. Faced with the fact of attack on the innocent, the presumption that we do no harm, even to our enemy, yielded to the command of love understood as the need to restrain an enemy who would injure the innocent.

82. The just-war argument has taken several forms in the history of

---

[30]John Paul II, "World Day of Peace Message 1982," #12, cited, p. 478.

Catholic theology, but this Augustinian insight is its central premise.[31]
In the twentieth century, papal teaching has used the logic of Augustine and Aquinas[32] to articulate a right of self-defense for states in a decentralized international order and to state the criteria for exercising that right. The essential position was stated by Vatican II: "As long as the danger of war persists and there is no international authority with the necessary competence and power, governments cannot be denied the right of lawful self-defense, once all peace efforts have failed."[33] We have already indicated the centrality of this principle for understanding Catholic teaching about the state and its duties.

83. Just-war teaching has evolved, however, as an effort to prevent war; only if war cannot be rationally avoided, does the teaching then seek to restrict and reduce its horrors. It does this by establishing a set of rigorous conditions which must be met if the decision to go to war is to be morally permissible. Such a decision, especially today, requires extraordinarily strong reasons for overriding the presumption *in favor of peace* and *against* war. This is one significant reason why valid just-war teaching makes provision for conscientious dissent. It is presumed that all sane people prefer peace, never *want* to initiate war, and accept even the most justifiable defensive war only as a sad necessity. Only the most powerful reasons may be permitted to override such objection. In the words of Pope Pius XII:

> The Christian will for peace . . . is very careful to avoid recourse to the force of arms in the defense of rights which, however legitimate, do not offset the risk of kindling a blaze with all its spiritual and material consequences.[34]

84. The determination of *when* conditions exist which allow the resort to force in spite of the strong presumption against it is made in light of *jus ad bellum* criteria. The determination of *how* even a justified resort to force must be conducted is made in light of the *jus in bello* criteria. We shall briefly explore the meaning of both.[35]

---

[31]Augustine called it a Manichaean heresy to assert that war is intrinsically evil and contrary to Christian charity, and stated: "War and conquest are a sad necessity in the eyes of men of principle, yet it would be still more unfortunate if wrongdoers should dominate just men" (*The City of God*, Book IV, C. 15).

Representative surveys of the history and theology of the just-war tradition include: F. H. Russell, *The Just War in the Middle Ages* (New York: 1975); P. Ramsey, *War and the Christian Conscience* (Durham, N.C.: 1961); P. Ramsey, *The Just War: Force and Political Responsibility* (New York: 1968), James T. Johnson, *Ideology, Reason and the Limitation of War* (Princeton: 1975), *Just War Tradition and the Restraint of War: A Moral and Historical Inquiry* (Princeton: 1981); L. B. Walters, *Five Classic Just-War Theories* (Ph.D. Dissertation, Yale University, 1971); W. O'Brien, *War and/or Survival* (New York: 1969), *The Conduct of Just and Limited War* (New York: 1981); J. C. Murray, "Remarks on the Moral Problem of War," *Theological Studies* 20 (1959):40-61.

[32]Aquinas treats the question of war in the *Summa Theologica*, II-IIae, q. 40; also cf., II-IIae, q. 64.

[33]*Pastoral Constitution*, #79.

[34]Pius XII, "Christmas Message," 1948.

[35]For an analysis of the content and relationship of these principles cf.: R. Potter, "The

Jus ad Bellum

85. Why and when recourse to war is permissible.

86. (a) *Just Cause:*
War is permissible only to confront "a real and certain danger," i.e., to protect innocent life, to preserve conditions necessary for decent human existence, and to secure basic human rights. As both Pope Pius XII and Pope John XXIII made clear, if war of retribution was ever justifiable, the risks of modern war negate such a claim today.

87. (b) *Competent Authority:*
In the Catholic tradition the right to use force has always been joined to the common good; war must be declared by those with responsibility for public order, not by private groups or individuals.
88. The requirement that a decision to go to war must be made by competent authority is particularly important in a democratic society. It needs detailed treatment here since it involves a broad spectrum of related issues. Some of the bitterest divisions of society in our own nation's history, for example, have been provoked over the question of whether or not a president of the United States has acted constitutionally and legally in involving our country in a *de facto* war, even if—indeed, especially if—war was never formally declared. Equally perplexing problems of conscience can be raised for individuals expected or legally required to go to war even though our duly elected representatives in Congress have, in fact, voted for war.
89. The criterion of competent authority is of further importance in a day when revolutionary war has become commonplace. Historically, the just-war tradition has been open to a "just revolution" position, recognizing that an oppressive government may lose its claim to legitimacy. Insufficient analytical attention has been given to the moral issues of revolutionary warfare. The mere possession of sufficient weaponry, for example, does not legitimize the initiation of war by "insurgents" against an established government, any more than the government's systematic oppression of its people can be carried out under the doctrine of "national security."
90. While the legitimacy of revolution in some circumstances cannot be denied, just-war teachings must be applied as rigorously to revolutionary-counterrevolutionary conflicts as to others. The issue of who constitutes competent authority and how such authority is exercised is essential.

Moral Logic of War," *McCormick Quarterly* 23 (1970):203-33; J. Childress, "Just War Criteria," in T. Shannon, ed., *War or Peace: The Search for New Answers* (New York: 1980).

91. When we consider in this letter the issues of conscientious objection (C.O.) and selective conscientious objection (S.C.O.), the issue of competent authority will arise again.

92. (*c*) *Comparative Justice:*
Questions concerning the *means* of waging war today, particularly in view of the destructive potential of weapons, have tended to override questions concerning the comparative justice of the positions of respective adversaries or enemies. In essence: which side is sufficiently "right" in a dispute, and are the values at stake critical enough to override the presumption against war? The question in its most basic form is this: do the rights and values involved justify killing? For whatever the means used, war, by definition, involves violence, destruction, suffering, and death.

93. The category of comparative justice is designed to emphasize the presumption against war which stands at the beginning of just-war teaching. In a world of sovereign states recognizing neither a common moral authority nor a central political authority, comparative justice stresses that no state should act on the basis that it has "absolute justice" on its side. Every party to a conflict should acknowledge the limits of its "just cause" and the consequent requirement to use *only* limited means in pursuit of its objectives. Far from legitimizing a crusade mentality, comparative justice is designed to relativize absolute claims and to restrain the use of force even in a "justified" conflict.[36]

94. Given techniques of propaganda and the ease with which nations and individuals either assume or delude themselves into believing that God or right is clearly on their side, the test of comparative justice may be extremely difficult to apply. Clearly, however, this is not the case in every instance of war. Blatant aggression from without and subversion from within are often enough readily identifiable by all reasonably fair-minded people.

95. (*d*) *Right Intention:*
Right intention is related to just cause—war can be legitimately intended only for the reasons set forth above as a just cause. During the conflict, right intention means pursuit of peace and reconciliation, including avoiding unnecessarily destructive acts or imposing unreasonable conditions (e.g., unconditional surrender).

---

[36]James T. Johnson, *Ideology, Reason and the Limitation of War*, cited; W. O'Brien, *The Conduct of Just and Limited War*, cited, pp. 13-30; W. Vanderpol, *La doctrine scolastique du droit de guerre*, p. 387ff; J. C. Murray, "Theology and Modern Warfare," in W. J. Nagel, ed., *Morality and Modern Warfare*, p. 80ff.

96. (e) *Last Resort:*

For resort to war to be justified, all peaceful alternatives must have been exhausted. There are formidable problems in this requirement. No international organization currently in existence has exercised sufficient internationally recognized authority to be able either to mediate effectively in most cases or to prevent conflict by the intervention of United Nations or other peacekeeping forces. Furthermore, there is a tendency for nations or peoples which perceive conflict between or among other nations as advantageous to themselves to attempt to prevent a peaceful settlement rather than advance it.

97. We regret the apparent unwillingness of some to see in the United Nations organization the potential for world order which exists and to encourage its development. Pope Paul VI called the United Nations the last hope for peace. The loss of this hope cannot be allowed to happen. Pope John Paul II is again instructive on this point:

> I wish above all to repeat my confidence in you, the leaders and members of the International Organizations, and in you, the international officials! In the course of the last ten years, your organizations have too often been the object of attempts at manipulation on the part of nations wishing to exploit such bodies. However it remains true that the present multiplicity of violent clashes, divisions, and blocks on which bilateral relations founder, offer the great International Organizations the opportunity to engage upon the qualitative change in their activities, even to reform on certain points their own structures in order to take into account new realities and to enjoy effective power.[37]

98. (f) *Probability of Success:*

This is a difficult criterion to apply, but its purpose is to prevent irrational resort to force or hopeless resistance when the outcome of either will clearly be disproportionate or futile. The determination includes a recognition that at times defense of key values, even against great odds, may be a "proportionate" witness.

99. (g) *Proportionality:*

In terms of the *jus ad bellum* criteria, proportionality means that the damage to be inflicted and the costs incurred by war must be proportionate to the good expected by taking up arms. Nor should judgments concerning proportionality be limited to the temporal order without regard to a spiritual dimension in terms of "damage," "cost," and "the good expected." In today's interdependent world even a local conflict can affect people everywhere; this is particularly the case when the nuclear powers are involved. Hence a nation cannot justly go to war today without considering the effect of its action on others and on the international community.

---

[37]John Paul II, "World Day of Peace Message 1983," #11, cited.

100. This principle of proportionality applies throughout the conduct of the war as well as to the decision to begin warfare. During the Vietnam war our bishops' conference ultimately concluded that the conflict had reached such a level of devastation to the adversary and damage to our own society that continuing it could not be justified.[38]

Jus in Bello

101. Even when the stringent conditions which justify resort to war are met, the conduct of war (i.e., strategy, tactics, and individual actions) remains subject to continuous scrutiny in light of two principles which have special significance today precisely because of the destructive capability of modern technological warfare. These principles are proportionality and discrimination. In discussing them here, we shall apply them to the question of *jus ad bellum* as well as *jus in bello*; for today it becomes increasingly difficult to make a decision to use any kind of armed force, however limited initially in intention and in the destructive power of the weapons employed, without facing at least the possibility of escalation to broader, or even total, war and to the use of weapons of horrendous destructive potential. This is especially the case when adversaries are "superpowers," as the Council clearly envisioned:

> Indeed, if the kind of weapons now stocked in the arsenals of the great powers were to be employed to the fullest, the result would be the almost complete reciprocal slaughter of one side by the other, not to speak of the widespread devastation that would follow in the world and the deadly after-effects resulting from the use of such weapons.[39]

102. It should not be thought, of course, that massive slaughter and destruction would result only from the extensive use of nuclear weapons. We recall with horror the carpet and incendiary bombings of World War II, the deaths of hundreds of thousands in various regions of the world through "conventional" arms, the unspeakable use of gas and other forms of chemical warfare, the destruction of homes and of crops, the utter suffering war has wrought during the centuries before and the decades since the use of the "atom bomb." Nevertheless, every honest person must recognize that, especially given the proliferation of modern scientific weapons, we now face possibilities which are appalling to contemplate. Today, as never before, we must ask not merely what *will* happen, but what *may* happen, especially if major powers embark on war. Pope John Paul II has repeatedly pleaded that world leaders confront this reality:

---

[38]National Conference of Catholic Bishops, *Resolution on Southeast Asia* (Washington, D.C.: 1971).
[39]*Pastoral Constitution*, #80.

[I]n view of the difference between classical warfare and nuclear or bacteriological war—a difference so to speak of nature—and in view of the scandal of the arms race seen against the background of the needs of the Third World, this right [of defense], which is very real in principle, only underlines the urgency of world society to equip itself with effective means of negotiation. In this way the nuclear terror that haunts our time can encourage us to enrich our common heritage with a very simple discovery that is within our reach, namely, that war is the most barbarous and least effective way of resolving conflicts.[40]

103. The Pontifical Academy of Sciences reaffirmed the Holy Father's theme in its November 1981 "Statement on the Consequences of Nuclear War." Then, in a meeting convoked by the Pontifical Academy, representatives of national academies of science from throughout the world issued a "Declaration on the Prevention of Nuclear War" which specified the meaning of Pope John Paul II's statement that modern warfare differs by nature from previous forms of war. The scientists said:

Throughout its history humanity has been confronted with war, but since 1945 the nature of warfare has changed so profoundly that the future of the human race, of generations yet unborn, is imperiled. . . . For the first time it is possible to cause damage on such a catastrophic scale as to wipe out a large part of civilization and to endanger its very survival. The large-scale use of such weapons could trigger major and irreversible ecological and genetic changes whose limits cannot be predicted.[41]

And earlier, with such thoughts plainly in mind, the Council had made its own "the condemnation of total war already pronounced by recent popes."[42] This condemnation is demanded by the principles of proportionality and discrimination. Response to aggression must not exceed the nature of the aggression. To destroy civilization as we know it by waging a "total war" as today it *could* be waged would be a monstrously disproportionate response to aggression on the part of any nation.

104. Moreover, the lives of innocent persons may never be taken directly, regardless of the purpose alleged for doing so. To wage truly "total" war is by definition to take huge numbers of innocent lives. Just response to aggression must be discriminate; it must be directed against unjust aggressors, not against innocent people caught up in a war not of their making. The Council therefore issued its memorable declaration:

Any act of war aimed indiscriminately at the destruction of entire cities or of extensive areas along with their population is a crime

---

[40]John Paul II, "World Day of Peace Message 1982," #12, cited.
[41]"Declaration on Prevention of Nuclear War" (Sept. 24, 1982).
[42]*Pastoral Constitution*, #80.

against God and man himself. It merits unequivocal and unhesitating condemnation.[43]

105. When confronting choices among specific military options, the question asked by proportionality is: once we take into account not only the military advantages that will be achieved by using this means but also all the harms reasonably expected to follow from using it, can its use still be justified? We know, of course, that no end can justify means evil in themselves, such as the executing of hostages or the targeting of noncombatants. Nonetheless, even if the means adopted is not evil in itself, it is necessary to take into account the probable harms that will result from using it and the justice of accepting those harms. It is of utmost importance, in assessing harms and the justice of accepting them, to think about the poor and the helpless, for they are usually the ones who have the least to gain and the most to lose when war's violence touches their lives.

106. In terms of the arms race, if the *real* end in view is legitimate defense against unjust aggression, and the means to this end are not evil in themselves, we must still examine the question of proportionality concerning attendant evils. Do the exorbitant costs, the general climate of insecurity generated, the possibility of accidental detonation of highly destructive weapons, the danger of error and miscalculation that could provoke retaliation and war—do such evils or others attendant upon and indirectly deriving from the arms race make the arms race itself a disproportionate response to aggression? Pope John Paul II is very clear in his insistence that the exercise of the right and duty of a people to protect their existence and freedom is contingent on the use of proportionate means.[44]

107. Finally, another set of questions concerns the interpretation of the principle of discrimination. The principle prohibits directly intended attacks on noncombatants and nonmilitary targets. It raises a series of questions about the term "intentional," the category of "noncombatant," and the meaning of "military."

108. These questions merit the debate occurring with increasing frequency today. We encourage such debate, for concise and definitive answers still appear to be wanting. Mobilization of forces in modern war includes not only the military, but to a significant degree the political, economic, and social sectors. It is not always easy to determine who is directly involved in a "war effort" or to what degree. Plainly, though, not even by the broadest definition can one rationally consider combatants entire classes of human beings such as schoolchildren, hospital patients, the elderly, the ill, the average industrial worker producing goods not directly related to military purposes,

---

[43]*Ibid.*
[44]John Paul II, "World Day of Peace Message 1982," #12, cited.

farmers, and many others. They may never be directly attacked.

109. Direct attacks on military targets involve similar complexities. Which targets are "military" ones and which are not? To what degree, for instance, does the use (by either revolutionaries or regular military forces) of a village or housing in a civilian populated area invite attack? What of a munitions factory in the heart of a city? Who is directly responsible for the deaths of noncombatants should the attack be carried out? To revert to the question raised earlier, how many deaths of noncombatants are "tolerable" as a result of indirect attacks—attacks directed against combat forces and military targets, which nevertheless kill noncombatants at the same time?

110. These two principles, in all their complexity, must be applied to the range of weapons—conventional, nuclear, biological, and chemical—with which nations are armed today.

4. The Value of Nonviolence

111. Moved by the example of Jesus' life and by his teaching, some Christians have from the earliest days of the Church committed themselves to a nonviolent lifestyle.[45] Some understood the Gospel of Jesus to prohibit all killing. Some affirmed the use of prayer and other spiritual methods as means of responding to enmity and hostility.

112. In the middle of the second century, St. Justin proclaimed to his pagan readers that Isaiah's prophecy about turning swords into ploughshares and spears into sickles had been fulfilled as a consequence of Christ's coming:

> And we who delighted in war, in the slaughter of one another, and in every other kind of iniquity have in every part of the world converted our weapons into implements of peace—our swords into ploughshares, our spears into farmers' tools—and we cultivate piety, justice, brotherly charity, faith, and hope, which we derive from the Father through the crucified Savior . . .[46]

113. Writing in the third century, St. Cyprian of Carthage struck a similar note when he indicated that the Christians of his day did not fight against their enemies. He himself regarded their conduct as proper:

---

[45]Representative authors in the tradition of Christian pacifism and nonviolence include: R. Bainton, *Christian Attitudes Toward War and Peace* (Abington: 1960), chaps. 4, 5, 10; J. Yoder, *The Politics of Jesus* (Grand Rapids: 1972), *Nevertheless: Varieties of Religious Pacifism* (Scottsdale: 1971); T. Merton, *Faith and Violence: Christian Teaching and Christian Practice* (Notre Dame: 1968); G. Zahn, *War, Conscience and Dissent* (New York: 1967); E. Egan, "The Beatitudes: Works of Mercy and Pacifism," in T. Shannon, ed., *War or Peace: The Search for New Answers* (New York: 1980), pp. 169-187; J. Fahey, "The Catholic Church and the Arms Race," *Worldview* 22 (1979):38-41; J. Douglass, *The Nonviolent Cross: A Theology of Revolution and Peace* (New York: 1966).

[46]Justin, *Dialogue with Trypho*, ch. 110; cf., also, *The First Apology*, chaps. 14, 39.

They do not even fight against those who are attacking since it is not granted to the innocent to kill even the aggressor, but promptly to deliver up their souls and blood that, since so much malice and cruelty are rampant in the world, they may more quickly withdraw from the malicious and the cruel.[47]

114. Some of the early Christian opposition to military service was a response to the idolatrous practices which prevailed in the Roman army. Another powerful motive was the fact that army service involved preparation for fighting and killing. We see this in the case of St. Martin of Tours during the fourth century, who renounced his soldierly profession with the explanation: "Hitherto I have served you as a soldier. Allow me now to become a soldier of God . . . I am a soldier of Christ. It is not lawful for me to fight."[48]

115. In the centuries between the fourth century and our own day, the theme of Christian nonviolence and Christian pacifism has echoed and re-echoed, sometimes more strongly, sometimes more faintly. One of the great nonviolent figures in those centuries was St. Francis of Assisi. Besides making personal efforts on behalf of reconciliation and peace, Francis stipulated that laypersons who became members of his Third Order were not "to take up lethal weapons, or bear them about, against anybody."

116. The vision of Christian nonviolence is not passive about injustice and the defense of the rights of others; it rather affirms and exemplifies what it means to resist injustice through nonviolent methods.

117. In the twentieth century, prescinding from the non-Christian witness of a Mahatma Ghandi and its worldwide impact, the nonviolent witness of such figures as Dorothy Day and Martin Luther King has had a profound impact upon the life of the Church in the United States. The witness of numerous Christians who had preceded them over the centuries was affirmed in a remarkable way at the Second Vatican Council.

118. Two of the passages which were included in the final version of the *Pastoral Constitution* gave particular encouragement for Catholics in all walks of life to assess their attitudes toward war and military service in the light of Christian pacifism. In paragraph 79 the Council fathers called upon governments to enact laws protecting the rights of those who adopted the position of conscientious objection to all war: "Moreover, it seems right that laws make humane provisions for the case of those who for reasons of conscience refuse to bear arms, provided, however, that they accept some other form of service to the human community."[49] This was the first time a call for legal protection of conscientious objection had appeared in a docu-

---

[47]Cyprian, *Collected Letters*; Letters to Cornelius.
[48]Sulpicius Severus, *The Life of Martin*, 4.3.
[49]*Pastoral Constitution*, #79.

ment of such prominence. In addition to its own profound meaning this statement took on even more significance in the light of the praise that the Council fathers had given in the preceding section "to those who renounce the use of violence and the vindication of their rights."[50] In *Human Life in Our Day* (1968) we called for legislative provision to recognize selective conscientious objectors as well.[51]

119. As Catholic bishops it is incumbent upon us to stress to our own community and to the wider society the significance of this support for a pacifist option for individuals in the teaching of Vatican II and the reaffirmation that the popes have given to nonviolent witness since the time of the Council.

120. In the development of a theology of peace and the growth of the Christian pacifist position among Catholics, these words of the *Pastoral Constitution* have special significance: "All these factors force us to undertake a completely fresh reappraisal of war."[52] The Council fathers had reference to "the development of armaments by modern science (which) has immeasurably magnified the horrors and wickedness of war."[53] While the just-war teaching has clearly been in possession for the past 1,500 years of Catholic thought, the "new moment" in which we find ourselves sees the just-war teaching and nonviolence as distinct but interdependent methods of evaluating warfare. They diverge on some specific conclusions, but they share a common presumption against the use of force as a means of settling disputes.

121. Both find their roots in the Christian theological tradition; each contributes to the full moral vision we need in pursuit of a human peace. We believe the two perspectives support and complement one another, each preserving the other from distortion. Finally, in an age of technological warfare, analysis from the viewpoint of nonviolence and analysis from the viewpoint of the just-war teaching often converge and agree in their opposition to methods of warfare which are in fact indistinguishable from total warfare.

II. War and Peace in the Modern World: Problems and Principles

122. Both the just-war teaching and nonviolence are confronted with a unique challenge by nuclear warfare. This must be the starting point of any further moral reflection: nuclear weapons particularly and nuclear warfare as it is planned today, raise new moral questions. No previously conceived moral position escapes the fundamental confron-

---

[50] *Ibid.,* #78.
[51] United States Catholic Conference, *Human Life in Our Day* (Washington, D.C.: 1968), p. 44.
[52] *Pastoral Constitution,* #80.
[53] *Ibid.*

tation posed by contemporary nuclear strategy. Many have noted the similarity of the statements made by eminent scientists and Vatican II's observation that we are forced today "to undertake a completely fresh reappraisal of war." The task before us is not simply to repeat what we have said before; it is first to consider anew whether and how our religious-moral tradition can assess, direct, contain, and, we hope, help to eliminate the threat posed to the human family by the nuclear arsenals of the world. Pope John Paul II captured the essence of the problem during his pilgrimage to Hiroshima:

> In the past it was possible to destroy a village, a town, a region, even a country. Now it is the whole planet that has come under threat.[54]

123. The Holy Father's observation illustrates why the moral problem is also a religious question of the most profound significance. In the nuclear arsenals of the United States or the Soviet Union alone, there exists a capacity to do something no other age could imagine: we can threaten the entire planet.[55] For people of faith this means we read the Book of Genesis with a new awareness; the moral issue at stake in nuclear war involves the meaning of sin in its most graphic dimensions. Every sinful act is a confrontation of the creature and the creator. Today the destructive potential of the nuclear powers threatens the human person, the civilization we have slowly constructed, and even the created order itself.

124. We live today, therefore, in the midst of a cosmic drama; we possess a power which should never be used, but which might be used if we do not reverse our direction. We live with nuclear weapons knowing we cannot afford to make one serious mistake. This fact dramatizes the precariousness of our position, politically, morally, and spiritually.

125. A prominent "sign of the times" today is a sharply increased awareness of the danger of the nuclear arms race. Such awareness has produced a public discussion about nuclear policy here and in other countries which is unprecedented in its scope and depth. What has been accepted for years with almost no question is now being subjected to the sharpest criticism. What previously had been defined as a safe and stable system of deterrence is today viewed with political and moral skepticism. Many forces are at work in this new evaluation, and we believe one of the crucial elements is the Gospel vision of peace which guides our work in this Pastoral Letter. The nuclear age has been the theater of our existence for almost four decades; today it is being evaluated with a new perspective. For many the leaven of the Gospel and the light of the Holy Spirit create the decisive dimension of this new perspective.

---

[54]John Paul II, "Address to Scientists and Scholars," #4, cited, p. 621.
[55]Cf., "Declaration on Prevention of Nuclear War."

A. *The New Moment*

126. At the center of the new evaluation of the nuclear arms race is a recognition of two elements: the destructive potential of nuclear weapons, and the stringent choices which the nuclear age poses for both politics and morals.

127. The fateful passage into the nuclear age as a military reality began with the bombing of Nagasaki and Hiroshima, events described by Pope Paul VI as a "butchery of untold magnitude."[56] Since then, in spite of efforts at control and plans for disarmament (e.g., the Baruch Plan of 1946), the nuclear arsenals have escalated, particularly in the two superpowers. The qualitative superiority of these two states, however, should not overshadow the fact that four other countries possess nuclear capacity and a score of states are only steps away from becoming "nuclear nations."

128. This nuclear escalation has been opposed sporadically and selectively but never effectively. The race has continued in spite of carefully expressed doubts by analysts and other citizens and in the face of forcefully expressed opposition by public rallies. Today the opposition to the arms race is no longer selective or sporadic, it is widespread and sustained. The danger and destructiveness of nuclear weapons are understood and resisted with new urgency and intensity. There is in the public debate today an endorsement of the position submitted by the Holy See at the United Nations in 1976: the arms race is to be condemned as a danger, an act of aggression against the poor, and a folly which does not provide the security it promises.[57]

129. Papal teaching has consistently addressed the folly and danger of the arms race; but the new perception of it which is now held by the general public is due in large measure to the work of scientists and physicians who have described for citizens the concrete human consequences of a nuclear war.[58]

130. In a striking demonstration of his personal and pastoral concern for preventing nuclear war, Pope John Paul II commissioned a study by the Pontifical Academy of Sciences which reinforced the findings of other scientific bodies. The Holy Father had the study transmitted by personal representative to the leaders of the United States, the Soviet Union, the United Kingdom, and France, and to the president of the General Assembly of the United Nations. One of its conclusions is especially pertinent to the public debate in the United States:

> Recent talk about winning or even surviving a nuclear war must reflect a failure to appreciate a medical reality: Any nuclear war

---

[56]Paul VI, "World Day of Peace Message 1976," in *Documents*, p. 198.
[57]"Statement of the Holy See to the United Nations" (1976), in *The Church and the Arms Race*; Pax Christi-USA (New York: 1976), pp. 23-24.
[58]R. Adams and S. Cullen, *The Final Epidemic: Physicians and Scientists on Nuclear War* (Chicago: 1981).

would inevitably cause death, disease and suffering of pandemonic proportions and without the possibility of effective medical intervention. That reality leads to the same conclusion physicians have reached for life-threatening epidemics throughout history. Prevention is essential for control.[59]

131. This medical conclusion has a moral corollary. Traditionally, the Church's moral teaching sought first to prevent war and then to limit its consequences if it occurred. Today the possibilities for placing political and moral limits on nuclear war are so minimal that the moral task, like the medical, is prevention: as a people, we must refuse to legitimate the idea of nuclear war. Such a refusal will require not only new ideas and new vision, but what the Gospel calls conversion of the heart.

132. To say "no" to nuclear war is both a necessary and a complex task. We are moral teachers in a tradition which has always been prepared to relate moral principles to concrete problems. Particularly in this letter we could not be content with simply restating general moral principles or repeating well-known requirements about the ethics of war. We have had to examine, with the assistance of a broad spectrum of advisors of varying persuasions, the nature of existing and proposed weapons systems, the doctrines which govern their use, and the consequences of using them. We have consulted people who engage their lives in protest against the existing nuclear strategy of the United States, and we have consulted others who have held or do hold responsibility for this strategy. It has been a sobering and perplexing experience. In light of the evidence which witnesses presented and in light of our study, reflection, and consultation, we must reject nuclear war. But we feel obliged to relate our judgment to the specific elements which comprise the nuclear problem.

133. Though certain that the dangerous and delicate nuclear relationship the superpowers now maintain should not exist, we understand how it came to exist. In a world of sovereign states, devoid of central authority and possessing the knowledge to produce nuclear weapons, many choices were made, some clearly objectionable, others well-intended with mixed results, which brought the world to its present dangerous situation.

134. We see with increasing clarity the political folly of a system which threatens mutual suicide, the psychological damage this does to ordinary people, especially the young, the economic distortion of priorities—billions readily spent for destructive instruments while pitched battles are waged daily in our legislatures over much smaller amounts for the homeless, the hungry, and the helpless here and abroad. But it is much less clear how we translate a "no" to nuclear war into the personal and public choices which can move us in a new

---

[59]Pontifical Academy of Sciences, "Statement on the Consequences of the Use of Nuclear Weapons," in *Documents*, p. 241.

direction, toward a national policy and an international system which more adequately reflect the values and vision of the Kingdom of God.

135. These tensions in our assessment of the politics and strategy of the nuclear age reflect the conflicting elements of the nuclear dilemma and the balance of terror which it has produced. We have said earlier in this letter that the fact of war reflects the existence of sin in the world. The nuclear threat and the danger it poses to human life and civilization exemplify in a qualitatively new way the perennial struggle of the political community to contain the use of force, particularly among states.

136. Precisely because of the destructive nature of nuclear weapons, strategies have been developed which previous generations would have found unintelligible. Today military preparations are undertaken on a vast and sophisticated scale, but the declared purpose is not to use the weapons produced. Threats are made which would be suicidal to implement. The key to security is no longer only military secrets, for in some instances security may best be served by informing one's adversary publicly what weapons one has and what plans exist for their use. The presumption of the nation-state system, that sovereignty implies an ability to protect a nation's territory and population, is precisely the presumption denied by the nuclear capacities of both superpowers. In a sense each is at the mercy of the other's perception of what strategy is "rational," what kind of damage is "unacceptable," how "convincing" one side's threat is to the other.

137. The political paradox of deterrence has also strained our moral conception. May a nation threaten what it may never do? May it possess what it may never use? Who is involved in the threat each superpower makes: government officials? or military personnel? or the citizenry in whose defense the threat is made?

138. In brief, the danger of the situation is clear; but how to prevent the use of nuclear weapons, how to assess deterrence, and how to delineate moral responsibility in the nuclear age are less clearly seen or stated. Reflecting the complexity of the nuclear problem, our arguments in this Pastoral must be detailed and nuanced; but our "no" to nuclear war must, in the end, be definitive and decisive.

B. Religious Leadership and the Public Debate

139. Because prevention of nuclear war appears, from several perspectives, to be not only the surest but only way to limit its destructive potential, we see our role as moral teachers precisely in terms of helping to form public opinion with a clear determination to resist resort to nuclear war as an instrument of national policy. If "prevention is the only cure," then there are diverse tasks to be performed in preventing what should never occur. As bishops we see a specific task defined for us in Pope John Paul II's "World Day of Peace Message 1982":

> Peace cannot be built by the power of rulers alone. Peace can be firmly constructed only if it corresponds to the resolute determination of all people of good will. Rulers must be supported and enlightened by a public opinion that encourages them or, where necessary, expresses disapproval.[60]

140. The Pope's appeal to form public opinion is not an abstract task. Especially in a democracy, public opinion can passively acquiesce in policies and strategies or it can, through a series of measures, indicate the limits beyond which a government should not proceed. The "new moment" which exists in the public debate about nuclear weapons provides a creative opportunity and a moral imperative to examine the relationship between public opinion and public policy. We believe it is necessary, for the sake of prevention, to build a barrier against the concept of nuclear war as a viable strategy for defense. There should be a clear public resistance to the rhetoric of "winnable" nuclear wars, or unrealistic expectations of "surviving" nuclear exchanges, and strategies of "protracted nuclear war." We oppose such rhetoric.
141. We seek to encourage a public attitude which sets stringent limits on the kind of actions our own government and other governments will take on nuclear policy. We believe religious leaders have a task in concert with public officials, analysts, private organizations, and the media to set the limits beyond which our military policy should not move in word or action. Charting a moral course in a complex public policy debate involves several steps. We will address four questions, offering our reflections on them as an invitation to a public moral dialogue:
  (1) the use of nuclear weapons;
  (2) the policy of deterrence in principle and in practice;
  (3) specific steps to reduce the danger of war;
  (4) long-term measures of policy and diplomacy.

C. The Use of Nuclear Weapons

142. Establishing moral guidelines in the nuclear debate means addressing first the question of the use of nuclear weapons. That question has several dimensions.
143. It is clear that those in the Church who interpret the Gospel teaching as forbidding all use of violence would oppose any use of nuclear weapons under any conditions. In a sense the existence of these weapons simply confirms and reinforces one of the initial insights of the nonviolent position, namely, that Christians should not use

---

[60]John Paul II, "World Day of Peace Message 1982," #6, cited, p. 476.

lethal force since the hope of using it selectively and restrictively is so often an illusion. Nuclear weapons seem to prove this point in a way heretofore unknown.

144. For the tradition which acknowledges some legitimate use of force, some important elements of contemporary nuclear strategies move beyond the limits of moral justification. A justifiable use of force must be both discriminatory and proportionate. Certain aspects of both U.S. and Soviet strategies fail both tests as we shall discuss below. The technical literature and the personal testimony of public officials who have been closely associated with U.S. nuclear strategy have both convinced us of the overwhelming probability that major nuclear exchange would have no limits.[61]

145. On the more complicated issue of "limited" nuclear war, we are aware of the extensive literature and discussion which this topic has generated.[62] As a general statement, it seems to us that public officials would be unable to refute the following conclusion of the study made by the Pontifical Academy of Sciences:

> Even a nuclear attack directed only at military facilities would be devastating to the country as a whole. This is because military facilities are widespread rather than concentrated at only a few points. Thus, many nuclear weapons would be exploded.
>
> Furthermore, the spread of radiation due to the natural winds and atmospheric mixing would kill vast numbers of people and contaminate large areas. The medical facilities of any nation would be inad-

---

[61]The following quotations are from public officials who have served at the highest policy levels in recent administrations of our government: "It is time to recognize that no one has ever succeeded in advancing any persuasive reason to believe that any use of nuclear weapons, even on the smallest scale, could reliably be expected to remain limited." M. Bundy, G. F. Kennan, R. S. McNamara, and G. Smith, "Nuclear Weapons and the Atlantic Alliance," *Foreign Affairs* 60 (1982):757.

"From my experience in combat there is no way that [nuclear escalation] . . . can be controlled because of the lack of information, the pressure of time and the deadly results that are taking place on both sides of the battle line." Gen. A. S. Collins, Jr. (former deputy commander in chief of U.S. Army in Europe), "Theatre Nuclear Warfare: The Battlefield," in J. F. Reichart and S. R. Sturn, eds., *American Defense Policy*, 5th ed., (Baltimore: 1982), pp. 359-60.

"None of this potential flexibility changes my view that a full-scale thermonuclear exchange would be an unprecedented disaster for the Soviet Union as well as for the United States. Nor is it at all clear that an initial use of nuclear weapons—however selectively they might be targeted—could be kept from escalating to a full-scale thermonuclear exchange, especially if command-and-control centers were brought under attack. The odds are high, whether weapons were used against tactical or strategic targets, that control would be lost on both sides and the exchange would become unconstrained." Harold Brown, *Department of Defense Annual Report FY 1979* (Washington, D.C.: 1978).

Cf., also: *The Effects of Nuclear War* (Washington, D.C.: 1979, U.S. Government Printing Office).

[62]For example, cf.,: H. A. Kissinger, *Nuclear Weapons and Foreign Policy* (New York: 1957), *The Necessity for Choice* (New York: 1960); R. Osgood and R. Tucker, *Force, Order and Justice* (Baltimore: 1967); R. Aron, *The Great Debate: Theories of Nuclear Strategy* (New York: 1965); D. Ball, *Can Nuclear War Be Controlled?* Adelphi Paper #161 (London: 1981); M. Howard, "On Fighting a Nuclear War," *International Security* 5 (1981):3-17.

equate to care for the survivors. An objective examination of the medical situation that would follow a nuclear war leads to but one conclusion: prevention is our only recourse.[63]

Moral Principles and Policy Choices

146. In light of these perspectives we address three questions more explicitly: (1) counter population warfare; (2) initiation of nuclear war; and (3) limited nuclear war.

1. Counter Population Warfare

147. Under no circumstances may nuclear weapons or other instruments of mass slaughter be used for the purpose of destroying population centers or other predominantly civilian targets. Popes have repeatedly condemned "total war," which implies such use. For example, as early as 1954 Pope Pius XII condemned nuclear warfare "when it entirely escapes the control of man," and results in "the pure and simple annihilation of all human life within the radius of action."[64] The condemnation was repeated by the Second Vatican Council:

> Any act of war aimed indiscriminately at the destruction of entire cities or of extensive areas along with their population is a crime against God and man himself. It merits unequivocal and unhesitating condemnation.[65]

148. Retaliatory action, whether nuclear or conventional, which would indiscriminately take many wholly innocent lives, lives of people who are in no way responsible for reckless actions of their government, must also be condemned. This condemnation, in our judgment, applies even to the retaliatory use of weapons striking enemy cities after our own have already been struck. No Christian can rightfully carry out orders or policies deliberately aimed at killing noncombatants.[66]

149. We make this judgment at the beginning of our treatment of nuclear strategy precisely because the defense of the principle of noncombatant immunity is so important for an ethic of war and because the nuclear age has posed such extreme problems for the principle. Later in this letter we shall discuss specific aspects of U.S. policy in light of this principle and in light of recent U.S. policy statements stressing the determination not to target directly or strike directly

---

[63]"Statement on the Consequences of the Use of Nuclear Weapons," cited, p. 243.
[64]Pius XII, "Address to the VIII Congress of the World Medical Association," in *Documents*, p. 131.
[65]*Pastoral Constitution*, #80.
[66]*Ibid.*

against civilian populations. Our concern about protecting the moral value of noncombatant immunity, however, requires that we make a clear reassertion of the principle our first word on this matter.

2. The Initiation of Nuclear War

150. We do not perceive any situation in which the deliberate initiation of nuclear warfare, on however restricted a scale, can be morally justified. Non-nuclear attacks by another state must be resisted by other than nuclear means. Therefore, a serious moral obligation exists to develop non-nuclear defensive strategies as rapidly as possible.

151. A serious debate is underway on this issue.[67] It is cast in political terms, but it has a significant moral dimension. Some have argued that at the very beginning of a war nuclear weapons might be used, only against military targets, perhaps in limited numbers. Indeed it has long been American and NATO policy that nuclear weapons, especially so-called tactical nuclear weapons, would likely be used if NATO forces in Europe seemed in danger of losing a conflict that until then had been restricted to conventional weapons. Large numbers of tactical nuclear weapons are now deployed in Europe by the NATO forces and about as many by the Soviet Union. Some are substantially smaller than the bomb used on Hiroshima, some are larger. Such weapons, if employed in great numbers, would totally devastate the densely populated countries of Western and Central Europe.

152. Whether under conditions of war in Europe, parts of Asia, or the Middle East, or the exchange of strategic weapons directly between the United States and the Soviet Union, the difficulties of limiting the use of nuclear weapons are immense. A number of expert witnesses advise us that commanders operating under conditions of battle probably would not be able to exercise strict control; the number of weapons used would rapidly increase, the targets would be expanded beyond the military, and the level of civilian casualties would rise enormously.[68] No one can be certain that this escalation would not occur, even in the face of political efforts to keep such an exchange "limited." The chances of keeping use limited seem remote, and the consequences of escalation to mass destruction would be appalling. Former public officials have testified that it is improbable that any nuclear war could actually be kept limited. Their testimony and the consequences involved in this problem lead us to conclude that the

---

[67]M. Bundy, et al., "Nuclear Weapons," cited; K. Kaiser, G. Leber, A. Mertes, F. J. Schulze, "Nuclear Weapons and the Preservation of Peace," *Foreign Affairs* 60 (1982):1157-70; cf., other responses to Bundy article in the same issue of *Foreign Affairs*.

[68]Testimony given to the National Conference of Catholic Bishops' Committee during preparation of this Pastoral Letter. The testimony is reflected in the quotes found in note 61.

danger of escalation is so great that it would be morally unjustifiable to initiate nuclear war in any form. The danger is rooted not only in the technology of our weapons systems but in the weakness and sinfulness of human communities. We find the moral responsibility of beginning nuclear war not justified by rational political objectives.

153. This judgment affirms that the willingness to initiate nuclear war entails a distinct, weighty moral responsibility; it involves transgressing a fragile barrier—political, psychological, and moral—which has been constructed since 1945. We express repeatedly in this letter our extreme skepticism about the prospects for controlling a nuclear exchange, however limited the first use might be. Precisely because of this skepticism, we judge resort to nuclear weapons to counter a conventional attack to be morally unjustifiable.[69] Consequently, we seek to reinforce the barrier against any use of nuclear weapons. Our support of a "no first use" policy must be seen in this light.

154. At the same time we recognize the responsibility the United States has had and continues to have in assisting allied nations in their defense against either a conventional or a nuclear attack. Especially in the European theater, the deterrence of a *nuclear* attack may require nuclear weapons for a time, even though their possession and deployment must be subject to rigid restrictions.

155. The need to defend against a conventional attack in Europe imposes the political and moral burden of developing adequate, alternative modes of defense to present reliance on nuclear weapons. Even with the best coordinated effort—hardly likely in view of contemporary political division on this question—development of an alternative defense position will still take time.

156. In the interim, deterrence against a conventional attack relies upon two factors: the not inconsiderable conventional forces at the disposal of NATO and the recognition by a potential attacker that the outbreak of large-scale conventional war could escalate to the nuclear level through accident or miscalculation by either side. We are aware that NATO's refusal to adopt a "no first use" pledge is to some extent linked to the deterrent effect of this inherent ambiguity. Nonetheless, in light of the probable effects of initiating nuclear war, we urge NATO to move rapidly toward the adoption of a "no first use" policy, but doing so in tandem with development of an adequate alternative defense posture.

---

[69]Our conclusions and judgments in this area although based on careful study and reflection of the application of moral principles do not have, of course, the same force as the principles themselves and therefore allow for different opinions, as the Summary makes clear.

3. Limited Nuclear War

157. It would be possible to agree with our first two conclusions and still not be sure about retaliatory use of nuclear weapons in what is called a "limited exchange." The issue at stake is the *real* as opposed to the *theoretical* possibility of a "limited nuclear exchange."

158. We recognize that the policy debate on this question is inconclusive and that all participants are left with hypothetical projections about probable reactions in a nuclear exchange. While not trying to adjudicate the technical debate, we are aware of it and wish to raise a series of questions which challenge the actual meaning of "limited" in this discussion.

(a) Would leaders have sufficient information to know what is happening in a nuclear exchange?

(b) Would they be able under the conditions of stress, time pressures, and fragmentary information to make the extraordinarily precise decision needed to keep the exchange limited if this were technically possible?

(c) Would military commanders be able, in the midst of the destruction and confusion of a nuclear exchange, to maintain a policy of "discriminate targeting"? Can this be done in modern warfare, waged across great distances by aircraft and missiles?

(d) Given the accidents we know about in peacetime conditions, what assurances are there that computer errors could be avoided in the midst of a nuclear exchange?

(e) Would not the casualties, even in a war defined as limited by strategists, still run in the millions?

(f) How "limited" would be the long-term effects of radiation, famine, social fragmentation, and economic dislocation?

159. Unless these questions can be answered satisfactorily, we will continue to be highly skeptical about the real meaning of "limited." One of the criteria of the just-war tradition is a reasonable hope of success in bringing about justice and peace. We must ask whether such a reasonable hope can exist once nuclear weapons have been exchanged. The burden of proof remains on those who assert that meaningful limitation is possible.

160. A nuclear response to either conventional or nuclear attack can cause destruction which goes far beyond "legitimate defense." Such use of nuclear weapons would not be justified.

161. In the face of this frightening and highly speculative debate on a matter involving millions of human lives, we believe the most effective contribution or moral judgment is to introduce perspectives by which we can assess the empirical debate. Moral perspective should be sensitive not only to the quantitative dimensions of a question but to its psychological, human, and religious characteristics as well. The issue of limited war is not simply the size of weapons contemplated or the strategies projected. The debate should include the psychological and political significance of crossing the boundary from the conventional to the nuclear arena in any form. To cross this divide is to enter a world where we have no experience of control, much testimony against its possibility, and therefore no moral justification for submitting the human community to this risk.[70] We therefore express our view that the first imperative is to prevent any use of nuclear weapons and our hope that leaders will resist the notion that nuclear conflict can be limited, contained, or won in any traditional sense.

D. Deterrence in Principle and Practice

162. The moral challenge posed by nuclear weapons is not exhausted by an analysis of their possible uses. Much of the political and moral debate of the nuclear age has concerned the strategy of deterrence. Deterrence is at the heart of the U.S.-Soviet relationship, currently the most dangerous dimension of the nuclear arms race.

1. The Concept and Development of Deterrence Policy

163. The concept of deterrence existed in military strategy long before the nuclear age, but it has taken on a new meaning and significance since 1945. Essentially, deterrence means "dissuasion of a potential adversary from initiating an attack or conflict, often by the threat of unacceptable retaliatory damage."[71] In the nuclear age, deterrence has become the centerpiece of both U.S. and Soviet policy. Both superpowers have for many years now been able to promise a retaliatory response which can inflict "unacceptable damage." A situation of stable deterrence depends on the ability of each side to deploy its retaliatory forces in ways that are not vulnerable to an attack (i.e., protected against a "first strike"); preserving stability requires a willingness by both sides to refrain from deploying weapons which appear to have a first strike capability.

164. This general definition of deterrence does not explain either the elements of a deterrence strategy or the evolution of deterrence policy since 1945. A detailed description of either of these subjects would

---

[70]Undoubtedly aware of the long and detailed technical debate on limited war, Pope John Paul II highlighted the unacceptable moral risk of crossing the threshold to nuclear war in his "Angelus Message" of December 13, 1981: "I have, in fact, the deep conviction that, in the light of a nuclear war's effects, which can be scientifically foreseen as certain, the only choice that is morally and humanly valid is represented by the reduction of nuclear armaments, while waiting for their future complete elimination, carried out simultaneously by all the parties, by means of explicit agreements and with the commitment of accepting effective controls." In *Documents*, p. 240.

[71]W. H. Kincade and J. D. Porro, *Negotiating Security: An Arms Control Reader* (Washington, D.C.: 1979).

require an extensive essay, using materials which can be found in abundance in the technical literature on the subject of deterrence.[72] Particularly significant is the relationship between "declaratory policy" (the public explanation of our strategic intentions and capabilities) and "action policy" (the actual planning and targeting policies to be followed in a nuclear attack).

165. The evolution of deterrence strategy has passed through several stages of declaratory policy. Using the U.S. case as an example, there is a significant difference between "massive retaliation" and "flexible response," and between "mutual assured destruction" and "countervailing strategy." It is also possible to distinguish between "counterforce" and "countervalue" targeting policies, and to contrast a posture of "minimum deterrence" with "extended deterrence." These terms are well known in the technical debate on nuclear policy; they are less well known and sometimes loosely used in the wider public debate. It is important to recognize that there has been substantial continuity in U.S. action policy in spite of real changes in declaratory policy.[73]

166. The recognition of these different elements in the deterrent and the evolution of policy means that moral assessment of deterrence requires a series of distinct judgments. They include: an analysis of the *factual character* of the deterrent (e.g., what is involved in targeting doctrine); analysis of the *historical development* of the policy (e.g., whether changes have occurred which are significant for moral analysis of the policy): the relationship of deterrence policy and other aspects of *U.S.-Soviet affairs*; and determination of the key *moral questions* involved in deterrence policy.

2. The Moral Assessment of Deterrence

167. The distinctively new dimensions of nuclear deterrence were recognized by policymakers and strategists only after much reflection. Similarly, the moral challenge posed by nuclear deterrence was grasped only after careful deliberation. The moral and political paradox posed by deterrence was concisely stated by Vatican II:

> Undoubtedly, armaments are not amassed merely for use in wartime. Since the defensive strength of any nation is thought to depend on its capacity for immediate retaliation, the stockpiling of arms which grows from year to year serves, in a way hitherto unthought

---

[72]Several surveys are available, for example, cf.: J. H. Kahin, *Security in the Nuclear Age: Developing U.S. Strategic Policy* (Washington, D.C.: 1975); M. Mandelbaum, *The Nuclear Question: The United States and Nuclear Weapons 1946-1976* (Cambridge, England: 1979); B. Brodie, "Development of Nuclear Strategy," *International Security* 2 (1978):65-83.

[73]The relationship of these two levels of policy is the burden of an article by D. Ball, "U.S. Strategic Forces: How Would They Be Used?" *International Security* 7 (1982/83):31-60.

of, as a deterrent to potential attackers. Many people look upon this as the most effective way known at the present time for maintaining some sort of peace among nations. Whatever one may think of this form of deterrent, people are convinced that the arms race, which quite a few countries have entered, is no infallible way of maintaining real peace and that the resulting so-called balance of power is no sure genuine path to achieving it. Rather than eliminate the causes of war, the arms race serves only to aggravate the position. As long as extravagant sums of money are poured into the development of new weapons, it is impossible to devote adequate aid in tackling the misery which prevails at the present day in the world. Instead of eradicating international conflict once and for all, the contagion is spreading to other parts of the world. New approaches, based on reformed attitudes, will have to be chosen in order to remove this stumbling block, to free the earth from its pressing anxieties, and give back to the world a genuine peace.[74]

168. Without making a specific moral judgment on deterrence, the Council clearly designated the elements of the arms race: the tension between "peace of a sort" preserved by deterrence and "genuine peace" required for a stable international life; the contradiction between what is spent for destructive capacity and what is needed for constructive development.

169. In the post-conciliar assessment of war and peace, and specifically of deterrence, different parties to the political-moral debate within the Church and in civil society have focused on one aspect or another of the problem. For some, the fact that nuclear weapons have not been used since 1945 means that deterrence has worked, and this fact satisfies the demands of both the political and the moral order. Others contest this assessment by highlighting the risk of failure involved in continued reliance on deterrence and pointing out how politically and morally catastrophic even a single failure would be. Still others note that the absence of nuclear war is not necessarily proof that the policy of deterrence has prevented it. Indeed, some would find in the policy of deterrence the driving force in the superpower arms race. Still other observers, many of them Catholic moralists, have stressed that deterrence may not morally include the intention of deliberately attacking civilian populations or noncombatants.

170. The statements of the NCCB/USCC over the past several years have both reflected and contributed to the wider moral debate on deterrence. In the NCCB pastoral letter, *To Live In Christ Jesus* (1976), we focused on the moral limits of declaratory policy while calling for stronger measures of arms control.[75] In 1979 John Cardinal Krol, speaking for the USCC in support of SALT II ratification, brought into focus the other element of the deterrence problem: the actual use of nuclear weapons may have been prevented (a moral good), but

---

[74]*Pastoral Constitution*, #81.
[75]United States Catholic Conference, *To Live in Christ Jesus* (Washington, D.C.: 1976), p. 34.

the risk of failure and the physical harm and moral evil resulting from possible nuclear war remained. "This explains," Cardinal Krol stated, "the Catholic dissatisfaction with nuclear deterrence and the urgency of the Catholic demand that the nuclear arms race be reversed. It is of the utmost importance that negotiations proceed to meaningful and continuing reductions in nuclear stockpiles, and eventually to the phasing out altogether of nuclear deterrence and the threat of mutual-assured destruction."[76]

171. These two texts, along with the conciliar statement, have influenced much of Catholic opinion expressed recently on the nuclear question.

172. In June 1982, Pope John Paul II provided new impetus and insight to the moral analysis with his statement to the United Nations Second Special Session on Disarmament. The Pope first situated the problem of deterrence within the context of world politics. No power, he observes, will admit to wishing to start a war, but each distrusts others and considers it necessary to mount a strong defense against attack. He then discusses the notion of deterrence:

> Many even think that such preparations constitute the way—even the only way—to safeguard peace in some fashion or at least to impede to the utmost in an efficacious way the outbreak of wars, especially major conflicts which might lead to the ultimate holocaust of humanity and the destruction of the civilization that man has constructed so laboriously over the centuries.
>
> In this approach one can see the "philosophy of peace" which was proclaimed in the ancient Roman principle: *Si vis pacem, para bellum.* Put in modern terms, this "philosophy" has the label of "deterrence" and one can find it in various guises of the search for a "balance of forces" which sometimes has been called, and not without reason, the "balance of terror."[77]

173. Having offered this analysis of the general concept of deterrence, the Holy Father introduces his considerations on disarmament, especially, but not only, nuclear disarmament. Pope John Paul II makes this statement about the morality of deterrence:

> In current conditions "deterrence" based on balance, certainly not as an end in itself but as a step on the way toward a progressive disarmament, may still be judged morally acceptable. Nonetheless, in order to ensure peace, it is indispensable not to be satisfied with this minimum which is always susceptible to the real danger of explosion.[78]

174. In Pope John Paul II's assessment we perceive two dimensions of the contemporary dilemma of deterrence. One dimension is the danger of nuclear war, with its human and moral costs. The posses-

---

[76]John Cardinal Krol, "Testimony on Salt II," *Origins* (1979):197.
[77]John Paul II, "Message U.N. Special Session 1982," #3.
[78]*Ibid.*, #8.

sion of nuclear weapons, the continuing quantitative growth of the arms race, and the danger of nuclear proliferation all point to the grave danger of basing "peace of a sort" on deterrence. The other dimension is the independence and freedom of nations and entire peoples, including the need to protect smaller nations from threats to their independence and integrity. Deterrence reflects the radical distrust which marks international politics, a condition identified as a major problem by Pope John XIII in *Peace on Earth* and reaffirmed by Pope Paul VI and Pope John Paul II. Thus a balance of forces, preventing either side from achieving superiority, can be seen as a means of safeguarding both dimensions.

175. The moral duty today is to prevent nuclear war from ever occurring *and* to protect and preserve those key values of justice, freedom, and independence which are necessary for personal dignity and national integrity. In reference to these issues, Pope John Paul II judges that deterrence may still be judged morally acceptable, "certainly not as an end in itself but as a step on the way toward a progressive disarmament."

176. On more than one occasion the Holy Father has demonstrated his awareness of the fragility and complexity of the deterrence relationship among nations. Speaking to UNESCO in June 1980, he said:

> Up to the present, we are told that nuclear arms are a force of dissuasion which have prevented the eruption of a major war. And that is probably true. Still, we must ask if it will always be this way.[79]

In a more recent and more specific assessment, Pope John Paul II told an international meeting of scientists on August 23, 1982:

> You can more easily ascertain that the logic of nuclear deterrence cannot be considered a final goal or an appropriate and secure means for safeguarding international peace.[80]

177. Relating Pope John Paul's general statements to the specific policies of the U.S. deterrent requires both judgments of fact and an application of moral principles. In preparing this letter we have tried, through a number of sources, to determine as precisely as possible the factual character of U.S. deterrence strategy. Two questions have particularly concerned us: 1) the targeting doctrine and strategic plans for the use of the deterrent, particularly their impact on civilian casualties; and 2) the relationship of deterrence strategy and nuclear warfighting capability to the likelihood that war will in fact be prevented.

---

[79]John Paul II, "Address to UNESCO, 1980," #21.
[80]John Paul II, "Letter to International Seminar on the World Implications of a Nuclear Conflict," August 23, 1982, text in *NC News Documentary*, August 24, 1982.

Moral Principles and Policy Choices

178. Targeting doctrine raises significant moral questions because it is a significant determinant of what would occur if nuclear weapons were ever to be used. Although we acknowledge the need for deterrent, not all forms of deterrence are morally acceptable. There are moral limits to deterrence policy as well as to policy regarding use. Specifically, it is not morally acceptable to intend to kill the innocent as part of a strategy of deterring nuclear war. The question of whether U.S. policy involves an intention to strike civilian centers (directly targeting civilian populations) has been one of our factual concerns.

179. This complex question has always produced a variety of responses, official and unofficial in character. The NCCB Committee has received a series of statements of clarification of policy from U.S. government officials.[81] Essentially these statements declare that it is not U.S. strategic policy to target the Soviet civilian population as such or to use nuclear weapons deliberately for the purpose of destroying population centers. These statements respond, in principle at least, to one moral criterion for assessing deterrence policy: the immunity of noncombatants from direct attack either by conventional or nuclear weapons.

180. These statements do not address or resolve another very troublesome moral problem, namely, that an attack on military targets or militarily significant industrial targets could involve "indirect" (i.e., unintended) but massive civilian casualties. We are advised, for example, that the United States strategic nuclear targeting plan (SIOP— Single Integrated Operational Plan) has identified sixty "military" targets within the city of Moscow alone, and that 40,000 "military" targets for nuclear weapons have been identified in the whole of the Soviet Union.[82] It is important to recognize that Soviet policy is subject to the same moral judgment; attacks on several "industrial targets"

---

[81]Particularly helpful was the letter of January 15, 1983, of Mr. William Clark, national security adviser, to Cardinal Bernardin. Mr. Clark stated: "For moral, political, and military reasons, the United States does not target the Soviet civilian population as such. There is no deliberately opaque meaning conveyed in the last two words. We do not threaten the existence of Soviet civilization by threatening Soviet cities. Rather, we hold at risk the war-making capability of the Soviet Union—its armed forces, and the industrial capacity to sustain war. It would be irresponsible for us to issue policy statements which might suggest to the Soviets that it would be to their advantage to establish privileged sanctuaries within heavily populated areas, thus inducing them to locate much of their war-fighting capability within those urban sanctuaries." A reaffirmation of the administration's policy is also found in Secretary Weinberger's *Annual Report to the Congress* (Caspar Weinberger, *Annual Report to the Congress*, February 1, 1983, p. 55): "The Reagan Administration's policy is that under no circumstances may such weapons be used deliberately for the purpose of destroying populations." Also, the letter of Mr. Weinberger to Bishop O'Connor of February 9, 1983, has a similar statement.

[82]S. Zuckerman, *Nuclear Illusion and Reality* (New York: 1982); D. Ball, cited, p. 36; T. Powers, "Choosing a Strategy for World War III," *The Atlantic Monthly*, November 1982, pp. 82-110.

or politically significant targets in the United States could produce massive civilian casualties. The number of civilians who would necessarily be killed by such strikes is horrendous.[83] This problem is unavoidable because of the way modern military facilities and production centers are so thoroughly interspersed with civilian living and working areas. It is aggravated if one side deliberately positions military targets in the midst of a civilian population. In our consultations, administration officials readily admitted that, while they hoped any nuclear exchange could be kept limited, they were prepared to retaliate in a massive way if necessary. They also agreed that once any substantial numbers of weapons were used, the civilian casualty levels would quickly become truly catastrophic, and that even with attacks limited to "military" targets, the number of deaths in a substantial exchange would be almost indistinguishable from what might occur if civilian centers had been deliberately and directly struck. These possibilities pose a different moral question and are to be judged by a different moral criterion: the principle of proportionality.

181. While any judgment of proportionality is always open to differing evaluations, there are actions which can be decisively judged to be disproportionate. A narrow adherence exclusively to the principle of noncombatant immunity as a criterion for policy is an inadequate moral posture for it ignores some evil and unacceptable consequences. Hence, we cannot be satisfied that the assertion of an intention not to strike civilians directly, or even the most honest effort to implement that intention, by itself constitutes a "moral policy" for the use of nuclear weapons.

182. The location of industrial or militarily significant economic targets within heavily populated areas or in those areas affected by radioactive fallout could well involve such massive civilian casualties that, in our judgment, such a strike would be deemed morally disproportionate, even though not intentionally indiscriminate.

183. The problem is not simply one of producing highly accurate weapons that might minimize civilian casualties in any single explosion, but one of increasing the likelihood of escalation at a level where many, even "discriminating," weapons would cumulatively kill very large numbers of civilians. Those civilian deaths would occur both immediately and from the long-term effects of social and economic devastation.

184. A second issue of concern to us is the relationship of deterrence doctrine to war-fighting strategies. We are aware of the argument that war-fighting capabilities enhance the credibility of the deterrent, particularly the strategy of extended deterrence. But the development of such capabilities raises other strategic and moral questions. The

---

[83]Cf., the comments in Pontifical Academy of Sciences "Statement on the Consequences of the Use of Nuclear Weapons," cited.

relationship of war-fighting capabilities and targeting doctrine exemplifies the difficult choices in this area of policy. Targeting civilian populations would violate the principle of discrimination—one of the central moral principles of a Christian ethic of war. But "counterforce targeting," while preferable from the perspective of protecting civilians, is often joined with a declaratory policy which conveys the notion that nuclear war is subject to precise rational and moral limits. We have already expressed our severe doubts about such a concept. Furthermore, a purely counterforce strategy may seem to threaten the viability of other nations' retaliatory forces, making deterrence unstable in a crisis and war more likely.

185. While we welcome any effort to protect civilian populations, we do not want to legitimize or encourage moves which extend deterrence beyond the specific objective of preventing the use of nuclear weapons or other actions which could lead directly to a nuclear exchange.

186. These considerations of concrete elements of nuclear deterrence policy, made in light of John Paul II's evaluation, but applying it through our own prudential judgments, lead us to a strictly conditioned moral acceptance of nuclear deterrence. We cannot consider it adequate as a long-term basis for peace.

187. This strictly conditioned judgment yields *criteria* for morally assessing the elements of deterrence strategy. Clearly, these criteria demonstrate that we cannot approve of every weapons system, strategic doctrine, or policy initiative advanced in the name of strengthening deterrence. On the contrary, these criteria require continual public scrutiny of what our government proposes to do with the deterrent.

188. *On the basis of these criteria we wish now to make some specific evaluations:*

(1) If nuclear deterrence exists only to prevent the *use* of nuclear weapons by others, then proposals to go beyond this to planning for prolonged periods of repeated nuclear strikes and counter-strikes, or "prevailing" in nuclear war, are not acceptable. They encourage notions that nuclear war can be engaged in with tolerable human and moral consequences. Rather, we must continually say "no" to the idea of nuclear war.

(2) If nuclear deterrence is our goal, "sufficiency" to deter is an adequate strategy; the quest for nuclear superiority must be rejected.

(3) Nuclear deterrence should be used as a step on the way toward progressive disarmanent. Each proposed addition to our strategic system or change in strategic doctrine must be assessed precisely in light of whether it will render steps toward "progressive disarmament" more or less likely.

189. Moreover, these criteria provide us with the means to make some judgments and recommendations about the present direction of U.S. strategic policy. Progress toward a world freed of dependence on nuclear deterrence must be carefully carried out. But it must not be delayed. There is an urgent moral and political responsibility to use the "peace of a sort" we have as a framework to move toward authentic peace through nuclear arms control, reductions, and disarmament. Of primary importance in this process is the need to prevent the development and deployment of destabilizing weapons systems on either side; a second requirement is to ensure that the more sophisticated command and control systems do not become mere hair triggers for automatic launch on warning; a third is the need to prevent the proliferation of nuclear weapons in the international system.

190. In light of these general judgments *we oppose* some specific proposals in respect to our present deterrence posture:

(1) The addition of weapons which are likely to be vulnerable to attack, yet also possess a "prompt hard-target kill" capability that threatens to make the other side's retaliatory forces vulnerable. Such weapons may seem to be useful primarily in a first strike;[84] we resist such weapons for this reason and we oppose Soviet deployment of such weapons which generate fear of a first strike against U.S. forces.

(2) The willingness to foster strategic planning which seeks a nuclear war-fighting capability that goes beyond the limited function of deterrence outlined in this letter.

(3) Proposals which have the effect of lowering the nuclear threshold and blurring the difference between nuclear and conventional weapons.

191. In support of the concept of "sufficiency" as an adequate deterrent, and in light of the present size and composition of both the U.S. and Soviet strategic arsenals, *we recommend*:

(1) Support for immediate, bilateral, verifiable agreements to halt the testing, production, and deployment of new nuclear weapons systems.[85]

(2) Support for negotiated bilateral deep cuts in the arsenals of both superpowers, particularly those weapons systems which have destabilizing characteristics; U.S. proposals like those for START (Strategic Arms Reduction Talks) and INF (Intermediate-range Nuclear Forces) negotiations in Geneva are said to be designed to achieve

---

[84]Several experts in strategic theory would place both the MX missile and Pershing II missiles in this category.

[85]In each of the successive drafts of this letter we have tried to state a central moral imperative: that the arms race should be stopped and disarmament begun. The implementation of this imperative is open to a wide variety of approaches. Hence we have chosen our own language in this paragraph, not wanting either to be identified with one specific political initiative or to have our words used against specific political measures.

deep cuts;[86] our hope is that they will be pursued in a manner which will realize these goals.

(3) Support for early and successful conclusion of negotiations of a comprehensive test ban treaty.

(4) Removal by all parties of short-range nuclear weapons which multiply dangers disproportionate to their deterrent value.

(5) Removal by all parties of nuclear weapons from areas where they are likely to be overrun in the early stages of war, thus forcing rapid and uncontrollable decisions on their use.

(6) Strengthening of command and control over nuclear weapons to prevent inadvertent and unauthorized use.

192. These judgments are meant to exemplify how a lack of unequivocal condemnation of deterrence is meant only to be an attempt to acknowledge the role attributed to deterrence, but not to support its extension beyond the limited purpose discussed above. Some have urged us to condemn all aspects of nuclear deterrence. This urging has been based on a variety of reasons, but has emphasized particularly the high and terrible risks that either deliberate use or accidental detonation of nuclear weapons could quickly escalate to something utterly disproportionate to any acceptable moral purpose. That determination requires highly technical judgments about hypothetical events. Although reasons exist which move some to condemn reliance on nuclear weapons for deterrence, we have not reached this conclusion for the reasons outlined in this letter.

193. Nevertheless, there must be no misunderstanding of our profound skepticism about the moral acceptability of any use of nuclear weapons. It is obvious that the use of any weapons which violate the principle of discrimination merits unequivocal condemnation. We are told that some weapons are designed for purely "counterforce" use against military forces and targets. The moral issue, however, is not resolved by the design of weapons or the planned intention for use; there are also consequences which must be assessed. It would be a perverted political policy or moral casuistry which tried to justify using a weapon which "indirectly" or "unintentionally" killed a million innocent people because they happened to live near a "militarily significant target."

194. Even the "indirect effects" of initiating nuclear war are sufficient to make it an unjustifiable moral risk in any form. It is not sufficient, for example, to contend that "our" side has plans for "limited" or "discriminate" use. Modern warfare is not readily contained by good intentions or technological designs. The psychological climate of the world is such that mention of the term "nuclear" generates uneasi-

---

[86]Cf., President Reagan's "Speech to the National Press Club" (November 18, 1981) and "Address at Eureka College" (May 9, 1982), Department of State, *Current Policy* #346 and #387.

ness. Many contend that the use of one tactical nuclear weapon could produce panic, with completely unpredictable consequences. It is precisely this mix of political, psychological, and technological uncertainty which has moved us in this letter to reinforce with moral prohibitions and prescriptions the prevailing political barrier against resort to nuclear weapons. Our support for enhanced command and control facilities, for major reductions in strategic and tactical nuclear forces, and for a "no first use" policy (as set forth in this letter) is meant to be seen as a complement to our desire to draw a moral line against nuclear war.

195. Any claim by any government that it is pursuing a morally acceptable policy of deterrence must be scrutinized with the greatest care. We are prepared and eager to participate in our country in the ongoing public debate on moral grounds.

196. The need to rethink the deterrence policy of our nation, to make the revisions necessary to reduce the possibility of nuclear war, and to move toward a more stable system of national and international security will demand a substantial intellectual, political, and moral effort. It also will require, we believe, the willingness to open ourselves to the providential care, power, and Word of God, which call us to recognize our common humanity and the bonds of mutual responsibility which exist in the international community in spite of political differences and nuclear arsenals.

197. Indeed, we do acknowledge that there are many strong voices within our own episcopal ranks and within the wider Catholic community in the United States which challenge the strategy of deterrence as an adequate response to the arms race today. They highlight the historical evidence that deterrence has not, in fact, set in motion substantial processes of disarmament.

198. Moreover, these voices rightly raise the concern that even the conditional acceptance of nuclear deterrence as laid out in a letter such as this might be inappropriately used by some to reinforce the policy of arms buildup. In its stead, they call us to raise a prophetic challenge to the community of faith—a challenge which goes beyond nuclear deterrence, toward more resolute steps to actual bilateral disarmament and peacemaking. We recognize the intellectual ground on which the argument is built and the religious sensibility which gives it its strong force.

199. The dangers of the nuclear age and the enormous difficulties we face in moving toward a more adequate system of global security, stability, and justice require steps beyond our present conceptions of security and defense policy. In the following section we propose a series of steps aimed at a more adequate policy for preserving peace in a nuclear world.

III. The Promotion of Peace:
Proposals and Policies

200. In a world which is not yet the fulfillment of God's Kingdom, a world where both personal actions and social forces manifest the continuing influence of sin and disorder among us, consistent attention must be paid to preventing and limiting the violence of war. But this task, addressed extensively in the previous section of this letter, does not exhaust Catholic teaching on war and peace. A complementary theme, reflected in the Scriptures and the theology of the Church and significantly developed by papal teaching in this century, is the building of peace as the way to prevent war. This traditional theme was vividly reasserted by Pope John Paul in his homily at Coventry Cathedral:

> Peace is not just the absence of war. It involves mutual respect and confidence between peoples and nations. It involves collaboration and binding agreements. Like a cathedral, peace must be constructed patiently and with unshakable faith.[87]

201. This positive conception of peacemaking profoundly influences many people in our time. At the beginning of this letter we affirmed the need for a more fully developed theology of peace. The basis of such a theology is found in the papal teaching of this century. In this section of our Pastoral we wish to illustrate how the positive vision of peace contained in Catholic teaching provides direction for policy and personal choices.

A. *Specific Steps to Reduce the Danger of War*

202. The dangers of modern war are specific and visible; our teaching must be equally specific about the needs of peace. Effective arms control leading to mutual disarmament, ratification of pending treaties,[88] development of nonviolent alternatives, are but some of the recommendations we would place before the Catholic community and all men and women of good will. These should be part of a foreign policy which recognizes and respects the claims of citizens of every nation to the same inalienable rights we treasure, and seeks to ensure an international security based on the awareness that the creator has provided this world and all its resources for the sustenance and benefit of the entire human family. The truth that the globe is inhabited by a single family in which all have the same basic needs and all have

---

[87]John Paul II, "Homily at Bagington Airport," Coventry, #2, *Origins* 12 (1982):55.
[88]The two treaties are the Threshold Test Ban Treaty signed July 3, 1974, and the Treaty on Nuclear Explosions for Peaceful Purposes (P.N.E.) signed May 28, 1976.

a right to the goods of the earth is a fundamental principle of Catholic teaching which we believe to be of increasing importance today. In an interdependent world all need to affirm their common nature and destiny; such a perspective should inform our policy vision and negotiating posture in pursuit of peace today.

1. Accelerated Work for Arms Control, Reduction, and Disarmament

203. Despite serious efforts, starting with the Baruch plans and continuing through SALT I and SALT II, the results have been far too limited and partial to be commensurate with the risks of nuclear war. Yet efforts for negotiated control and reduction of arms must continue. In his 1982 address to the United Nations, Pope John Paul II left no doubt about the importance of these efforts:

> Today once again before you all I reaffirm my confidence in the power of true negotiations to arrive at just and equitable solutions.[89]

204. In this same spirit, we urge negotiations to halt the testing, production, and deployment of new nuclear weapons systems. Not only should steps be taken to end development and deployment, but the numbers of existing weapons must be reduced in a manner which lessens the danger of war.

205. Arms control and disarmament must be a process of verifiable agreements especially between two superpowers. While we do not advocate a policy of unilateral disarmament, we believe the urgent need for control of the arms race requires a willingness for each side to take some first steps. The United States has already taken a number of important independent initiatives to reduce some of the gravest dangers and to encourage a constructive Soviet response; additional initiatives are encouraged. By independent initiatives we mean carefully chosen limited steps which the United States could take for a defined period of time, seeking to elicit a comparable step from the Soviet Union. If an appropriate response is not forthcoming, the United States would no longer be bound by steps taken. Our country has previously taken calculated risks in favor of freedom and of human values; these have included independent steps taken to reduce some of the gravest dangers of nuclear war.[90] Certain risks are required today to help free the world from bondage to nuclear deterrence and the risk of nuclear war. Both sides, for example, have an interest in avoiding deployment of destabilizing weapons systems.

---

[89]John Paul II, "Message to U.N. Special Session 1982," #8.
[90]Mr. Weinberger's letter to Bishop O'Connor specifies actions taken on command and control facilities designed to reduce the chance of unauthorized firing of nuclear weapons.

206. There is some history of successful independent initiatives which have beneficially influenced the arms race without a formal public agreement. In 1963 President Kennedy announced that the United States would unilaterally forgo further nuclear testing; the next month Soviet Premier Nikita Khrushchev proposed a limited test ban which eventually became the basis of the U.S.-Soviet partial test ban treaty. Subsequently, both superpowers removed about 10,000 troops from Central Europe and each announced a cut in production of nuclear material for weapons.

207. (a) Negotiation on arms control agreements in isolation, without persistent and parallel efforts to reduce the political tensions which motivate the buildup of armaments, will not suffice. The United States should therefore have a continuing policy of maximum political engagement with governments of potential adversaries, providing for repeated, systematic discussion and negotiation of areas of friction. This policy should be carried out by a system of periodic, carefully prepared meetings at several levels of government, including summit meetings at regular intervals. Such channels of discussion are too important to be regarded by either of the major powers as a concession or an event made dependent on daily shifts in international developments.

208. (b) The Nuclear Non-Proliferation Treaty of 1968 (NPT) acknowledged that the spread of nuclear weapons to hitherto nonnuclear states (horizontal proliferation) could hardly be prevented in the long run in the absence of serious efforts by the nuclear states to control and reduce their own nuclear arsenals (vertical proliferation). Article VI of the NPT pledged the superpowers to serious efforts to control and to reduce their own nuclear arsenals; unfortunately, this promise has not been kept. Moreover, the multinational controls envisaged in the treaty seem to have been gradually relaxed by the states exporting fissionable materials for the production of energy. If these tendencies are not constrained, the treaty may eventually lose its symbolic and practical effectiveness. For this reason the United States should, in concert with other nuclear exporting states, seriously re-examine its policies and programs and make clear its determination to uphold the spirit as well as the letter of the treaty.

2. Continued Insistence on Efforts to Minimize the Risk of Any War

209. While it is right and proper that priority be given to reducing and ultimately eliminating the likelihood of nuclear war, this does not of itself remove the threat of other forms of warfare. Indeed, negotiated reduction in nuclear weapons available to the superpowers could conceivably increase the danger of non-nuclear wars.

210. (a) Because of this we strongly support negotiations aimed at reducing and limiting conventional forces and at building confidence between possible adversaries, especially in regions of potential military confrontations. We urge that prohibitions outlawing the production and use of chemical and biological weapons be reaffirmed and observed. Arms control negotiations must take account of the possibility that conventional conflict could trigger the nuclear confrontation the world must avoid.

211. (b) Unfortunately, as is the case with nuclear proliferation, we are witnessing a relaxation of restraints in the international commerce in conventional arms. Sales of increasingly sophisticated military aircraft, missiles, tanks, antitank weapons, antipersonnel bombs, and other systems by the major supplying countries (especially the Soviet Union, the United States, France, and Great Britain) have reached unprecedented levels.

212. Pope John Paul II took specific note of the problem in his U.N. address:

> The production and sale of conventional weapons throughout the world is a truly alarming and evidently growing phenomenon . . . . Moreover the traffic in these weapons seems to be developing at an increasing rate and seems to be directed most of all toward developing countries.[91]

213. It is a tragic fact that U.S. arms sales policies in the last decade have contributed significantly to the trend the Holy Father deplores. We call for a reversal of this course. The United States should renew earlier efforts to develop multilateral controls on arms exports, and should in this case also be willing to take carefully chosen independent initiatives to restrain the arms trade. Such steps would be particularly appropriate where the receiving government faces charges of gross and systematic human rights violations.[92]

214. (c) Nations must accept a limited view of those interests justifying military force. True self-defense may include the protection of weaker states, but does not include seizing the possessions of others, or the domination of other states or peoples. We should remember the caution of Pope John Paul II: "In alleging the threat of a potential enemy, is it really not rather the intention to keep for itself a means of threat, in order to get the upper hand with the aid of one's own arsenal of destruction?"[93] Central to a moral theory of force is the principle that it must be a last resort taken only when *all* other means of redress have been exhausted. Equally important in the age of mod-

---

[91] *Ibid.* Cf., United States Catholic Conference, *At Issue #2: Arms Export Policies—Ethical Choices* (Washington, D.C.: 1978) for suggestions about controlling the conventional arms trade.

[92] The International Security Act of 1976 provides for such human rights review.

[93] John Paul II, "Address to the United Nations General Assembly," *Origins* 9 (1979):268.

ern warfare is the recognition that the justifiable reasons for using force have been restricted to instances of self-defense or defense of others under attack.

3. The Relationship of Nuclear and Conventional Defenses

215. The strong position we have taken against the use of nuclear weapons, and particularly the stand against the initiation of nuclear war in any form, calls for further clarification of our view of the requirements for conventional defense.

216. Nuclear threats have often come to take the place of efforts to deter or defend against non-nuclear attack with weapons that are themselves non-nuclear, particularly in the NATO-Warsaw Pact confrontation. Many analysts conclude that, in the absence of nuclear deterrent threats, more troops and conventional (non-nuclear) weapons would be required to protect our allies. Rejection of some forms of nuclear deterrence could therefore conceivably require a willingness to pay higher costs to develop conventional forces. Leaders and peoples of other nations might also have to accept higher costs for their own defense, particularly in Western Europe, if the threat to use nuclear weapons first were withdrawn. We cannot judge the strength of these arguments in particular cases. It may well be that some strengthening of conventional defense would be a proportionate price to pay, if this will reduce the possibility of a nuclear war. We acknowledge this reluctantly, aware as we are of the vast amount of scarce resources expended annually on instruments of defense in a world filled with other urgent, unmet human needs.

217. It is not for us to settle the technical debate about policy and budgets. From the perspective of a developing theology of peace, however, we feel obliged to contribute a moral dimension to the discussion. We hope that a significant reduction in numbers of conventional arms and weaponry would go hand in hand with diminishing reliance on nuclear deterrence. The history of recent wars (even so-called "minor" or "limited" wars) has shown that conventional war can also become indiscriminate in conduct and disproportionate to any valid purpose. We do not want in any way to give encouragement to a notion of "making the world safe for conventional war," which introduces its own horrors.

218. Hence, we believe that any program directed at reducing reliance on nuclear weapons is not likely to succeed unless it includes measures to reduce tensions, and to work for the balanced reduction of conventional forces. We believe that important possibilities exist which, if energetically pursued, would ensure against building up conventional forces as a concomitant of reductions in nuclear weapons. Examples are to be found in the ongoing negotiations for mutual balanced force reductions, the prospects for which are certainly not dim and would be enhanced by agreements on strategic weapons, and in the confidence-building measures still envisaged under the Helsinki agreement and review conference.

219. We must reemphasize with all our being, nonetheless, that it is not only nuclear war that must be prevented, but war itself. Therefore, with Pope John Paul II we declare:

> Today, the scale and the horror of modern warfare—whether nuclear or not—makes it totally unacceptable as a means of settling differences between nations. War should belong to the tragic past, to history; it should find no place on humanity's agenda for the future.[94]

Reason and experience tell us that a continuing upward spiral, even in conventional arms, coupled with an unbridled increase in armed forces, instead of securing true peace will almost certainly be provocative of war.

4. Civil Defense

220. Attention must be given to existing programs for civil defense against nuclear attack, including blast and fall-out shelters and relocation plans. It is unclear in the public mind whether these are intended to offer significant protection against at least some forms of nuclear attack or are being put into place to enhance the credibility of the strategic deterrent forces by demonstrating an ability to survive attack. This confusion has led to public skepticism and even ridicule of the program and casts doubt on the credibility of the government. An independent commission of scientists, engineers, and weapons experts is needed to examine if these or any other plans offer a realistic prospect of survival for the nation's population or its cherished values, which a nuclear war would presumably be fought to preserve.

5. Efforts to Develop Nonviolent Means of Conflict Resolution

221. We affirm a nation's right to defend itself, its citizens, and its values. Security is the right of all, but that right, like everything else, must be subject to divine law and the limits defined by that law. We must find means of defending peoples that do not depend upon the threat of annihilation. Immoral means can never be justified by the end sought; no objective, however worthy of good in itself, can justify sinful acts or policies. Though our primary concern through this statement is war and the nuclear threat, these principles apply as well to all forms of violence, including insurgency, counterinsurgency, "destabilization," and the like.

---

[94]John Paul II, "Homily at Bagington Airport," Coventry, 2; cited, p. 55.

222. (a) The Second Vatican Council praised "those who renounce the use of violence in the vindication of their rights and who resort to methods of defense which are otherwise available to weaker parties, provided that this can be done without injury to the rights and duties of others or of the community itself."[95] To make such renunciation effective and still defend what must be defended, the arts of diplomacy, negotiation, and compromise must be developed and fully exercised. Nonviolent means of resistance to evil deserve much more study and consideration than they have thus far received. There have been significant instances in which people have successfully resisted oppression without recourse to arms.[96] Nonviolence is not the way of the weak, the cowardly, or the impatient. Such movements have seldom gained headlines, even though they have left their mark on history. The heroic Danes who would not turn Jews over to the Nazis and the Norwegians who would not teach Nazi propaganda in schools serve as inspiring examples in the history of nonviolence.

223. Nonviolent resistance, like war, can take many forms depending upon the demands of a given situation. There is, for instance, organized popular defense instituted by government as part of its contingency planning. Citizens would be trained in the techniques of peaceable noncompliance and noncooperation as a means of hindering an invading force or nondemocratic government from imposing its will. Effective nonviolent resistance requires the united will of a people and may demand as much patience and sacrifice from those who practice it as is now demanded by war and preparation for war. It may not always succeed. Nevertheless, before the possibility is dismissed as impractical or unrealistic, we urge that it be measured against the almost certain effects of a major war.

224. (b) Nonviolent resistance offers a common ground of agreement for those individuals who choose the option of Christian pacifism even to the point of accepting the need to die rather than to kill, and those who choose the option of lethal force allowed by the theology of just war. Nonviolent resistance makes clear that both are able to be committed to the same objective: defense of their country.

225. (c) Popular defense would go beyond conflict resolution and compromise to a basic synthesis of beliefs and values. In its practice, the objective is not only to avoid causing harm or injury to another creature, but, more positively, to seek the good of the other. Blunting the aggression of an adversary or oppressor would not be enough. The goal is winning the other over, making the adversary a friend.

---

[95] *Pastoral Constitution*, #78.
[96] G. Sharp, *The Politics of Nonviolent Action* (Boston: 1973); R. Fisher and W. Ury, *Getting to Yes: Negotiating Agreement Without Giving In* (Boston: 1981).

226. It is useful to point out that these principles are thoroughly compatible with—and to some extent derived from—Christian teachings and must be part of any Christian theology of peace. Spiritual writers have helped trace the theory of nonviolence to its roots in scripture and tradition and have illustrated its practice and success in their studies of the church fathers and the age of martyrs. Christ's own teachings and example provide a model way of life incorporating the truth, and a refusal to return evil for evil.

227. Nonviolent popular defense does not ensure that lives would not be lost. Nevertheless, once we recognize that the almost certain consequences of existing policies and strategies of war carry with them a very real threat to the future existence of humankind itself, practical reason as well as spiritual faith demand that it be given serious consideration as an alternative course of action.

228. (d) Once again we declare that the only true defense for the world's population is the rejection of nuclear war and the conventional wars which could escalate into nuclear war. With Pope John Paul II, we call upon educational and research institutes to take a lead in conducting peace studies: "Scientific studies on war, its nature, causes, means, objectives, and risks have much to teach us on the conditions for peace . . ."[97] To achieve this end, we urge that funds equivalent to a designated percentage (even one-tenth of one percent) of current budgetary allotments for military purposes be set aside to support such peace research.

229. In 1981, the Commission on Proposals for the National Academy of Peace and Conflict Resolution recommended the establishment of the U.S. Academy of Peace, a recommendation nearly as old as this country's constitution. The commission found that "peace is a legitimate field of learning that encompasses rigorous, interdisciplinary research, education, and training directed toward peacemaking expertise."[98] We endorse the commission's recommendation and urge all citizens to support training in conflict resolution, nonviolent resistance, and programs devoted to service to peace and education for peace. Such an academy would not only provide a center for peace studies and activities, but also be a tangible evidence of our nation's sincerity in its often professed commitment to international peace and the abolition of war. We urge universities, particularly Catholic universities, in our country to develop programs for rigorous, interdisciplinary research, education, and training directed toward peacemaking expertise.

---

[97] John Paul II, "World Day of Peace Message 1982," #7, cited, p. 476.
[98] *To Establish the United States Academy of Peace: Report of the Commission on Proposals for the National Academy of Peace and Conflict Resolution* (Washington, D.C.: 1981), pp. 119-20.

230. We, too, must be prepared to do our part to achieve these ends. We encourage churches and educational institutions, from primary schools to colleges and institutes of higher learning, to undertake similar programs at their own initiative. Every effort must be made to understand and evaluate the arms race, to encourage truly transnational perspectives on disarmament, and to explore new forms of international cooperation and exchange. No greater challenge or higher priority can be imagined than the development and perfection of a theology of peace suited to a civilization poised on the brink of self-destruction. It is our prayerful hope that this document will prove to be a starting point and inspiration for that endeavor.

6. The Role of Conscience

231. A dominant characteristic of the Second Vatican Council's evaluation of modern warfare was the stress it placed on the requirement for proper formation of conscience. Moral principles are effective restraints on power only when policies reflect them and individuals practice them. The relationship of the authority of the state and the conscience of the individual on matters of war and peace takes a new urgency in the face of the destructive nature of modern war.

232. (a) In this connection we reiterate the position we took in 1980. Catholic teaching does not question the right in principle of a government to require military service of its citizens provided the government shows it is necessary. A citizen may not casually disregard his country's conscientious decision to call its citizens to acts of "legitimate defense." Moreover, the role of Christian citizens in the armed forces is a service to the common good and an exercise of the virtue of patriotism, so long as they fulfill this role within defined moral norms.[99]

233. (b) At the same time, no state may demand blind obedience. Our 1980 statement urged the government to present convincing reasons for draft registration, and opposed reinstitution of conscription itself except in the case of a national defense emergency. Moreover, it reiterated our support for conscientious objection in general and for selective conscientious objection to participation in a particular war, either because of the ends being pursued or the means being used. We called selective conscientious objection a moral conclusion which can be validly derived from the classical teaching of just-war principles. We continue to insist upon respect for and legislative protection of the rights of both classes of conscientious objectors. We also approve requiring alternative service to the community—not related to military needs—by such persons.

---

[99]United States Catholic Conference, *Statement on Registration and Conscription for Military Service* (Washington, D.C.: 1980). Cf., also, *Human Life in Our Day,* cited, pp. 42-45.

B. Shaping a Peaceful World

234. Preventing nuclear war is a moral imperative; but the avoidance of war, nuclear or conventional, is not a sufficient conception of international relations today. Nor does it exhaust the content of Catholic teaching. Both the political needs and the moral challenge of our time require a positive conception of peace, based on a vision of a just world order. Pope Paul VI summarized classical Catholic teaching in his encyclical, *The Development of Peoples*: "Peace cannot be limited to a mere absence of war, the result of an ever-precarious balance of forces. No, peace is something built up day after day, in the pursuit of an order intended by God, which implies a more perfect form of justice among men and women."[100]

1. World Order in Catholic Teaching

235. This positive conception of peace sees it as the fruit of order; order, in turn, is shaped by the values of justice, truth, freedom, and love. The basis of this teaching is found in sacred Scripture, St. Augustine and St. Thomas. It has found contemporary expression and development in papal teaching of this century. The popes of the nuclear age, from Pius XII through John Paul II, have affirmed pursuit of international order as the way to banish the scourge of war from human affairs.[101]

236. The fundamental premise of world order in Catholic teaching is a theological truth: the unity of the human family—rooted in common creation, destined for the kingdom, and united by moral bonds of rights and duties. This basic truth about the unity of the human family pervades the entire teaching on war and peace: for the pacifist position it is one of the reasons why life cannot be taken, while for the just-war position, even in a justified conflict bonds of responsibility remain in spite of the conflict.

237. Catholic teaching recognizes that in modern history, at least since the Peace of Westphalia (1648), the international community has been governed by nation-states. Catholic moral theology, as expressed for example in chapters 2 and 3 of *Peace on Earth*, accords a real but relative moral value to sovereign states. The value is real because of the functions states fulfill as sources of order and authority in the political community; it is relative because boundaries of the sovereign state do not dissolve the deeper relationships of responsibility existing in the human community. Just as within nations the moral fabric of society is described in Catholic teaching in terms of

---

[100]Paul VI, *The Development of Peoples* (1967), #76.
[101]Cf., V. Yzermans, ed., *Major Addresses of Pius XII*, 2 vols. (St. Paul: 1961) and J. Gremillion, *The Gospel of Peace and Justice*, cited.

reciprocal rights and duties—between individuals, and then between the individual and the state—so in the international community *Peace on Earth* defines the rights and duties which exist among states.[102]

238. In the past twenty years Catholic teaching has become increasingly specific about the content of these international rights and duties. In 1963, *Peace on Earth* sketched the political and legal order among states. In 1966, *The Development of Peoples* elaborated on order of economic rights and duties. In 1979, Pope John Paul II articulated the human rights basis of international relations in his "Address to the United Nations General Assembly."

239. These documents and others which build upon them, outlined a moral order of international relations, i.e., how the international community *should* be organized. At the same time this teaching has been sensitive to the actual pattern of relations prevailing among states. While not ignoring present geopolitical realities, one of the primary functions of Catholic teaching on world order has been to point the way toward a more integrated international system.

240. In analyzing this path toward world order, the category increasingly used in Catholic moral teaching (and, more recently, in the social sciences also) is the interdependence of the world today. The theological principle of unity has always affirmed a human interdependence; but today this bond is complemented by the growing political and economic interdependence of the world, manifested in a whole range of international issues.[103]

241. An important element missing from world order today is a properly constituted political authority with the capacity to shape our material interdependence in the direction of moral interdependence. Pope John XXIII stated the case in the following way:

> Today the universal common good poses problems of world-wide dimensions, which cannot be adequately tackled or solved except by the efforts of public authority endowed with a wideness of powers, structure and means of the same proportions: that is, of public authority which is in a position to operate in an effective manner on a world-wide basis. The moral order itself, therefore, demands that such a form of public authority be established.[104]

242. Just as the nation-state was a step in the evolution of government at a time when expanding trade and new weapons technologies made the feudal system inadequate to manage conflicts and provide security, so we are now entering an era of new, global interdependencies requiring global systems of governance to manage the result-

---

[102]Cf., John XXIII, *Peace on Earth* (1963), esp. #80-145.
[103]A sampling of the policy problems and possibilities posed by interdependence can be found in: R. O. Keohane and J. S. Nye, Jr., *Power and Interdependence* (Boston: 1977); S. Hoffmann, *Primacy or World Order* (New York: 1978); The Overseas Development Council, *The U.S. and World Development* 1979; 1980; 1982 (Washington, D.C.).
[104]John XXIII, *Peace on Earth* (1963), #137.

ing conflicts and ensure our common security. Major global problems such as worldwide inflation, trade and payments deficits, competition over scarce resources, hunger, widespread unemployment, global environmental dangers, the growing power of transnational corporations, and the threat of international financial collapse, as well as the danger of world war resulting from these growing tensions cannot be remedied by a single nation-state approach. They shall require the concerted effort of the whole world community. As we shall indicate below, the United Nations should be particularly considered in this effort.

243. In the nuclear age, it is in the regulation of interstate conflicts and ultimately the replacement of military by negotiated solutions that the supreme importance and necessity of a moral as well as a political concept of the international common good can be grasped. The absence of adequate structures for addressing these issues places even greater responsibility on the policies of individual states. By a mix of political vision and moral wisdom, states are called to interpret the national interest in light of the larger global interest.

244. We are living in a global age with problems and conflicts on a global scale. Either we shall learn to resolve these problems together, or we shall destroy one another. Mutual security and survival require a new vision of the world as one interdependent planet. We have rights and duties not only within our diverse national communities but within the larger world community.

2. The Superpowers in a Disordered World

245. No relationship more dramatically demonstrates the fragile nature of order in international affairs today than that of the United States and the Soviet Union. These two sovereign states have avoided open war, nuclear or conventional, but they are divided by philosophy, ideology, and competing ambitions. Their competition is global in scope and involves everything from comparing nuclear arsenals to printed propaganda. Both have been criticized in international meetings because of their policies in the nuclear arms race.[105]

246. In our 1980 Pastoral Letter on Marxism, we sought to portray the significant differences between Christian teaching and Marxism; at the same time we addressed the need for states with different political systems to live together in an interdependent world:

> The Church recognizes the depth and dimensions of the ideological differences that divide the human race, but the urgent practical need for cooperative efforts in the human interest overrules these differences. Hence Catholic teaching seeks to avoid exacerbating the ideological opposition and to focus upon the problems requiring com-

---

[105]This has particularly been the case in the two U.N. Special Sessions on Disarmament, 1979, 1982.

mon efforts across the ideological divide: keeping the peace and empowering the poor.[106]

247. We believe this passage reflects the teaching of *Peace on Earth*, the continuing call for dialogue of Pope Paul VI and the 1979 address of Pope John Paul II at the United Nations. We continue to stress this theme even while we recognize the difficulty of realizing its objectives.

248. The difficulties are particularly severe on the issue of the arms race. For most Americans, the danger of war is commonly defined primarily in terms of the threat of Soviet military expansionism and the consequent need to deter or defend against a Soviet military threat. Many assume that the existence of this threat is permanent and that nothing can be done about it except to build and maintain overwhelming or at least countervailing military power.[107]

249. The fact of a Soviet threat, as well as the existence of a Soviet imperial drive for hegemony, at least in regions of major strategic interest, cannot be denied. The history of the Cold War has produced varying interpretations of which side caused which conflict, but whatever the details of history illustrate, the plain fact is that the memories of Soviet policies in Eastern Europe and recent events in Afghanistan and Poland have left their mark in the American political debate. Many peoples are forcibly kept under Communist domination despite their manifest wishes to be free. Soviet power is very great. Whether the Soviet Union's pursuit of military might is motivated primarily by defensive or aggressive aims might be debated, but the effect is nevertheless to leave profoundly insecure those who must live in the shadow of that might.

---

[106]United States Catholic Conference, *Marxist Communism* (Washington, D.C.: 1980), p. 19.

[107]The debate on U.S.-Soviet relations is extensive; recent examples of it are found in: A. Ulam, "U.S.-Soviet Relations: Unhappy Coexistence," *America and the World, 1978*; *Foreign Affairs* 57 (1979):556-71; W. G. Hyland, "U.S.-Soviet Relations: The Long Road Back," *America and the World, 1981*; *Foreign Affairs* 60 (1982):525-50; R. Legvold, "Containment Without Confrontation," *Foreign Policy* 40 (1980):74-98; S. Hoffmann, "Muscle and Brains," *Foreign Policy* 37 (1979-80):3-27; P. Hassner, "Moscow and The Western Alliance," *Problems of Communism* 30 (1981):37-54; S. Bialer, "The Harsh Decade: Soviet Policies in the 1980s," *Foreign Affairs* 59 (1981):999-1020; G. Kennan, *The Nuclear Delusion: Soviet-American Relations in the Atomic Age* (New York: 1980); N. Podhoretz, *The Present Danger* (New York: 1980); P. Nitze, "Strategy in the 1980s," *Foreign Affairs* 59 (1980):82-101; R. Strode and C. Gray, "The Imperial Dimension of Soviet Military Power," *Problems of Communism* 30 (1981):1-15; International Institute for Strategic Studies, *Prospects of Soviet Power in the 1980s*, Parts I and II, Adelphi Papers #151 and 152 (London: 1979); S. S. Kaplan, ed., *Diplomacy of Power: Soviet Armed Forces as a Political Instrument* (Washington, D.C.: 1981); R. Barnet, *The Giants: Russia and America* (New York: 1977); M. McGwire, *Soviet Military Requirements*, The Brookings Institution (Washington, D.C.: 1982); R. Tucker, "The Purposes of American Power," *Foreign Affairs* 59 (1980/81):241-74; A. Geyer, *The Idea of Disarmament: Rethinking the Unthinkable* (Washington, D.C.: 1982). For a review of Soviet adherence to treaties, cf.: "The SALT Syndrome Charges and Facts: Analysis of an "Anti-SALT Documentary," report prepared by U.S. government agencies (State, Defense, CIA, ACDA, and NSC), reprinted in *The Defense Monitor* 10, #8A, Center for Defense Information.

250. Americans need have no illusions about the Soviet system of repression and the lack of respect in that system for human rights, or about Soviet covert operations and pro-revolutionary activities. To be sure, our own system is not without flaws. Our government has sometimes supported repressive governments in the name of preserving freedom, has carried out repugnant covert operations of its own, and remains imperfect in its domestic record of ensuring equal rights for all. At the same time, there is a difference. NATO is an alliance of democratic countries which have freely chosen their association; the Warsaw Pact is not.

251. To pretend that as a nation we have lived up to all our own ideals would be patently dishonest. To pretend that all evils in the world have been or are now being perpetrated by dictatorial regimes would be both dishonest and absurd. But having said this, and admitting our own faults, it is imperative that we confront reality. The facts simply do not support the invidious comparisons made at times, even in our own society, between our way of life, in which most basic human rights are at least recognized even if they are not always adequately supported, and those totalitarian and tyrannical regimes in which such rights are either denied or systematically suppressed. Insofar as this is true, however, it makes the promotion of human rights in our foreign policy, as well as our domestic policy, all the more important. It is the acid test of our commitment to our democratic values. In this light, any attempts to justify, for reasons of state, support for regimes that continue to violate human rights is all the more morally reprehensible in its hypocrisy.

252. A glory of the United States is the range of political freedoms its system permits us. We, as bishops, as Catholics, as citizens, exercise those freedoms in writing this letter, with its share of criticisms of our government. We have true freedom of religion, freedom of speech, and access to a free press. We could not exercise the same freedoms in contemporary Eastern Europe or in the Soviet Union. Free people must always pay a proportionate price and run some risks—responsibly—to preserve their freedom.

253. It is one thing to recognize that the people of the world do not want war. It is quite another thing to attribute the same good motives to regimes or political systems that have consistently demonstrated precisely the opposite in their behavior. There are political philosophies with understandings of morality so radically different from ours, that even negotiations proceed from different premises, although identical terminology may be used by both sides. This is no reason for not negotiating. It is a very good reason for not negotiating blindly or naively.

254. In this regard, Pope John Paul II offers some sober reminders concerning dialogue and peace:

[O]ne must mention the tactical and deliberate lie, which misuses language, which has recourse to the most sophisticated techniques of propaganda, which deceives and distorts dialogue and incites to aggression . . . while certain parties are fostered by ideologies which, in spite of their declarations, are opposed to the dignity of the human person, ideologies which see in struggle the motive force of history, that see in force the source of rights, that see in the discernment of the enemy the ABC of politics, dialogue is fixed and sterile. Or, if it still exists, it is a superficial and falsified reality. It becomes very difficult, not to say impossible, therefore. There follows almost a complete lack of communication between countries and blocs. Even the international institutions are paralyzed. And the setback to dialogue then runs the risk of serving the arms race. However, even in what can be considered as an impasse to the extent that individuals support such ideologies, the attempt to have a lucid dialogue seems still necessary in order to unblock the situation and to work for the possible establishment of peace on particular points. This is to be done by counting upon common sense, on the possibilities of danger for everyone and on the just aspirations to which the peoples themselves largely adhere.[108]

255. The cold realism of this text, combined with the conviction that political dialogue and negotiations must be pursued, in spite of obstacles, provides solid guidance for U.S.-Soviet relations. Acknowledging all the differences between the two philosophies and political systems, the irreducible truth is that objective mutual interests do exist between the superpowers. Proof of this concrete if limited convergence of interest can be found in some vitally important agreements on nuclear weapons which have already been negotiated in the areas of nuclear testing and nuclear explosions in space as well as the SALT I agreements.

256. The fact that the Soviet Union now possesses a huge arsenal of strategic weapons as threatening to us as ours may appear to them does not exclude the possibility of success in such negotiations. The conviction of many European observers that a *modus vivendi* (often summarized as "detente") is a practical possibility in political, economic, and scientific areas should not be lightly dismissed in our country.

257. Sensible and successful diplomacy, however, will demand that we avoid the trap of a form of anti-Sovietism which fails to grasp the central danger of a superpower rivalry in which both the U.S. and the U.S.S.R. are the players, and fails to recognize the common interest both states have in never using nuclear weapons. Some of those dangers and common interests would exist in any world where two great powers, even relatively benign ones, competed for power, influence, and security. The diplomatic requirement for addressing the U.S.-Soviet relationship is not romantic idealism about Soviet intentions and capabilities but solid realism which recognizes that everyone will lose in a nuclear exchange.

---

[108]John Paul II, "World Day of Peace Message 1983," #7, cited.

258. As bishops we are concerned with issues which go beyond diplomatic requirements. It is of some value to keep raising in the realm of the political debate truths which ground our involvement in the affairs of nations and peoples. Diplomatic dialogue usually sees the other as a potential or real adversary. Soviet behavior in some cases merits the adjective reprehensible, but the Soviet people and their leaders are human beings created in the image and likeness of God. To believe we are condemned in the future only to what has been the past of U.S.-Soviet relations is to underestimate both our human potential for creative diplomacy and God's action in our midst which can open the way to changes we could barely imagine. We do not intend to foster illusory ideas that the road ahead in superpower relations will be devoid of tension or that peace will be easily achieved. But we do warn against that "hardness of heart" which can close us or others to the changes needed to make the future different from the past.

3. Interdependence: From Fact to Policy

259. While the nuclear arms race focuses attention on the U.S.-Soviet relationship, it is neither politically wise nor morally justifiable to ignore the broader international context in which that relationship exists. Public attention, riveted on the big powers, often misses the plight of scores of countries and millions of people simply trying to survive. The interdependence of the world means a set of interrelated human questions. Important as keeping the peace in the nuclear age is, it does not solve or dissolve the other major problems of the day. Among these problems the pre-eminent issue is the continuing chasm in living standards between the industrialized world (East and West) and the developing world. To quote Pope John Paul II:

> So widespread is the phenomenon that it brings into question the financial, monetary, production, and commercial mechanisms that, resting on various political pressures, support the world economy. These are proving incapable either of remedying the unjust social situations inherited from the past or of dealing with the urgent challenges and ethical demands of the present.[109]

260. The East-West competition, central as it is to world order and important as it is in the foreign policy debate, does not address this moral question which rivals the nuclear issue in its human significance. While the problem of the developing nations would itself require a Pastoral Letter, Catholic teaching has maintained an analysis of the problem which should be identified here. The analysis acknowledges internal causes of poverty, but also concentrates on the way the larger

---

[109]John Paul II, "The Redeemer of Man," #16, *Origins* 8 (1980):635.

international economic structures affect the poor nations. These particularly involve trade, monetary, investment, and aid policies.

261. Neither of the superpowers is conspicuous in these areas for initiatives designed to address "the absolute poverty" in which millions live today.[110]

262. From our perspective and experience as bishops, we believe there is a much greater potential for response to these questions in the minds and hearts of Americans than has been reflected in U.S. policy. As pastors who often appeal to our congregations for funds destined for international programs, we find good will and great generosity the prevailing characteristics. The spirit of generosity which shaped the Marshall Plan is still alive in the American public.

263. We must discover how to translate this personal sense of generosity and compassion into support for policies which would respond to papal teaching in international economic issues. It is precisely the need to expand our conception of international charity and relief to an understanding of the need for social justice in terms of trade, aid, and monetary issues which was reflected in Pope John Paul II's call to American Catholics in Yankee Stadium:

> Within the framework of your national institutions and in cooperation with all your compatriots, you will also want to seek out the structural reasons which foster or cause the different forms of poverty in the world and in your own country, so that you can apply the proper remedies. You will not allow yourselves to be intimidated or discouraged by oversimplified explanations which are more ideological than scientific—explanations which try to account for a complex evil by some single cause. But neither will you recoil before the reforms—even profound ones—of attitudes and structures that may prove necessary in order to recreate over and over again the conditions needed by the disadvantaged if they are to have a fresh chance in the hard struggle of life. The poor of the United States and of the world are your brothers and sisters in Christ.[111]

264. The Pope's words highlight an intellectual, moral, and political challenge for the United States. Intellectually, there is a need to rethink the meaning of national interest in an interdependent world. Morally, there is a need to build upon the spirit of generosity present in the U.S. public, directing it toward a more systematic response to the major issues affecting the poor of the world. Politically, there is a need for U.S. policies which promote the profound structural reforms called for by recent papal teaching.

265. Precisely in the name of international order papal teaching has, by word and deed, sought to promote multilateral forms of cooperation toward the developing world. The U.S. capacity for leadership

---

[110]The phrase and its description are found in R. S. McNamara, *Report to the Board of Governors of the World Bank* 1978; cf., also, 1979; 1980 (Washington, D.C.).
[111]John Paul II, "Homily at Yankee Stadium," #4, *Origins* 9 (1979):311.

in multilateral institutions is very great. We urge much more vigorous and creative response to the needs of the developing countries by the United States in these institutions.

266. The significant role the United States could play is evident in the daily agenda facing these institutions. Proposals addressing the relationship of the industrialized and developing countries on a broad spectrum of issues, all in need of "profound reforms," are regularly discussed in the United Nations and other international organizations. Without U.S. participation, significant reform and substantial change in the direction of addressing the needs of the poor will not occur. Meeting these needs is an essential element for a peaceful world.

267. Papal teaching of the last four decades has not only supported international institutions in principle, it has supported the United Nations specifically. Pope Paul VI said to the U.N. General Assembly:

> The edifice which you have constructed must never fail; it must be perfected and made equal to the needs which world history will present. You mark a stage in the development of mankind for which retreat must never be admitted, but from which it is necessary that advance be made.[112]

268. It is entirely necessary to examine the United Nations carefully, to recognize its limitations and propose changes where needed. Nevertheless, in light of the continuing endorsement found in papal teaching, we urge that the United States adopt a stronger supportive leadership role with respect to the United Nations. The growing interdependence of the nations and peoples of the world, coupled with the extragovernmental presence of multinational corporations, requires new structures of cooperation. As one of the founders of and major financial contributors to the United Nations, the United States can, and should, assume a more positive and creative role in its life today.

269. It is in the context of the United Nations that the impact of the arms race on the prospects for economic development is highlighted. The numerous U.N. studies on the relationship of development and disarmament support the judgment of Vatican II cited earlier in this letter: "The arms race is one of the greatest curses on the human race and the harm it inflicts upon the poor is more than can be endured."[113]

270. We are aware that the precise relationship between disarmament and development is neither easily demonstrated nor easily reoriented. But the fact of a massive distortion of resources in the face of crying human need creates a moral question. In an interdependent world, the security of one nation is related to the security of all. When we consider how and what we pay for defense today, we need a broader

---

[112]Paul VI, "Address to the General Assembly of the United Nations" (1965), #2.
[113]*Pastoral Constitution,* #81.

view than the equation of arms with security.[114] The threats to the security and stability of an interdependent world are not all contained in missiles and bombers.

271. If the arms race in all its dimensions is not reversed, resources will not be available for the human needs so evident in many parts of the globe and in our own country as well. But we also know that making resources available is a first step; policies of wise use would also have to follow. Part of the process of thinking about the economics of disarmament includes the possibilities of conversion of defense industries to other purposes. Many say the possibilities are great if the political will is present. We say the political will to reorient resources to human needs and redirect industrial, scientific, and technological capacity to meet those needs is part of the challenge of the nuclear age. Those whose livelihood is dependent upon industries which can be reoriented should rightfully expect assistance in making the transition to new forms of employment. The economic dimension of the arms race is broader than we can assess here, but these issues we have raised are among the primary questions before the nation.[115]

272. An interdependent world requires an understanding that key policy questions today involve mutuality of interest. If the monetary and trading systems are not governed by sensitivity to mutual needs, they can be destroyed. If the protection of human rights and the promotion of human needs are left as orphans in the diplomatic arena, the stability we seek in increased armaments will eventually be threatened by rights denied and needs unmet in vast sectors of the globe. If future planning about conservation of and access to resources is relegated to a pure struggle of power, we shall simply guarantee conflict in the future.

273. The moral challenge of interdependence concerns shaping the relationships and rules of practice which will support our common need for security, welfare, and safety. The challenge tests our idea of human community, our policy analysis, and our political will. The need to prevent nuclear war is absolutely crucial, but even if this is achieved, there is much more to be done.

---

[114]Cf., Hoffman, cited; Independent Commission on Disarmament and Security Issues, *Common Security* (New York: 1982).

[115]For an analysis of the policy problems of reallocating resources, cf.: Bruce M. Russett, *The Prisoners of Insecurity* (San Francisco: 1983). Cf.: *Common Security*, cited; Russett, cited; *U.N. Report on Disarmament and Development* (New York: 1982); United Nations, *The Relationship Between Disarmament and Development: A Summary*, Fact Sheet #21 (New York: 1982).

IV. The Pastoral Challenge and Response

A. *The Church: A Community of Conscience, Prayer, and Penance*

274. Pope John Paul II, in his first encyclical, recalled with gratitude the teaching of Pius XII on the Church. He then went on to say:

> Membership in that body has for its source a particular call, united with the saving action of grace. Therefore, if we wish to keep in mind this community of the People of God, which is so vast and so extremely differentiated, we must see first and foremost Christ saying in a way to each member of the community: "Follow Me." It is the community of the disciples, each of whom in a different way— at times very consciously and consistently, at other times not very consciously and very consistently—is following Christ. This shows also the deeply "personal" aspect and dimension of this society.[116]

275. In the following pages we should like to spell out some of the implications of being a community of Jesus' disciples in a time when our nation is so heavily armed with nuclear weapons and is engaged in a continuing development of new weapons together with strategies for their use.

276. It is clear today, perhaps more than in previous generations, that convinced Christians are a minority in nearly every country of the world—including nominally Christian and Catholic nations. In our own country we are coming to a fuller awareness that a response to the call of Jesus is both personal and demanding. As believers we can identify rather easily with the early Church as a company of witnesses engaged in a difficult mission. To be disciples of Jesus requires that we continually go beyond where we now are. To obey the call of Jesus means separating ourselves from all attachments and affiliations that could prevent us from hearing and following our authentic vocation. To set out on the road to discipleship is to dispose oneself for a share in the cross (cf., Jn 16:20). To be a Christian, according to the New Testament, is not simply to believe with one's mind, but also to become a doer of the word, a wayfarer with and a witness to Jesus. This means, of course, that we never expect complete success within history and that we must regard as normal even the path of persecution and the possibility of martyrdom.

---

[116]John Paul II, "The Redeemer of Man," #21, cited, p. 641. Much of the following reflects the content of A. Dulles, *A Church to Believe in: Discipleship and the Dynamics of Freedom* (New York: 1982), chap. 1.

277. We readily recognize that we live in a world that is becoming increasingly estranged from Christian values. In order to remain a Christian, one must take a resolute stand against many commonly accepted axioms of the world. To become true disciples, we must undergo a demanding course of induction into the adult Christian community. We must continually equip ourselves to profess the full faith of the Church in an increasingly secularized society. We must develop a sense of solidarity, cemented by relationships with mature and exemplary Christians who represent Christ and his way of life. **278.** All of these comments about the meaning of being a disciple or a follower of Jesus today are especially relevant to the quest for genuine peace in our time.

B. Elements of a Pastoral Response

279. We recommend and endorse for the faithful some practical programs to meet the challenge to their faith in this area of grave concern.

1. Educational Programs and Formation of Conscience

280. Since war, especially the threat of nuclear war, is one of the central problems of our day, how we seek to solve it could determine the mode, and even the possibility, of life on earth. God made human beings stewards of the earth; we cannot escape this responsibility. Therefore, we urge every diocese and parish to implement balanced and objective educational programs to help people at all age levels to understand better the issues of war and peace. Development and implementation of such programs must receive a high priority during the next several years. They must teach the full impact of our Christian faith. To accomplish this, this Pastoral Letter in its entirety, including its complexity, should be used as a guide and a framework for such programs, as they lead people to make moral decisions about the problems of war and peace, keeping in mind that the applications of principles in this Pastoral Letter do not carry the same moral authority as our statements of universal moral principles and formal Church teaching. **281.** In developing educational programs, we must keep in mind that questions of war and peace have a profoundly moral dimension which responsible Christians cannot ignore. They are questions of life and death. True, they also have a political dimension because they are embedded in public policy. But the fact that they are also political is no excuse for denying the Church's obligation to provide its members with the help they need in forming their consciences. We must learn together how to make correct and responsible moral judgments. We reject, therefore, criticism of the Church's concern with these issues on the ground that it "should not become involved in politics." We are called to move from discussion to witness and action.

282. At the same time, we recognize that the Church's teaching authority does not carry the same force when it deals with technical solutions involving particular means as it does when it speaks of principles or ends. People may agree in abhorring an injustice, for instance, yet sincerely disagree as to what practical approach will achieve justice. Religious groups are as entitled as others to their opinion in such cases, but they should not claim that their opinions are the only ones that people of good will may hold.

283. The Church's educational programs must explain clearly those principles or teachings about which there is little question. Those teachings, which seek to make explicit the Gospel call to peace and the tradition of the Church, should then be applied to concrete situations. They must indicate what the possible legitimate options are and what the consequences of those options may be. While this approach should be self-evident, it needs to be emphasized. Some people who have entered the public debate on nuclear warfare, at all points on the spectrum of opinion, appear not to understand or accept some of the clear teachings of the Church as contained in papal or conciliar documents. For example, some would place almost no limits on the use of nuclear weapons if they are needed for "self-defense." Some on the other side of the debate insist on conclusions which may be legitimate options but cannot be made obligatory on the basis of actual Church teaching.

2. True Peace Calls for "Reverence for Life"

284. All of the values we are promoting in this letter rest ultimately in the disarmament of the human heart and the conversion of the human spirit to God who alone can give authentic peace. Indeed, to have peace in our world, we must first have peace within ourselves. As Pope John Paul II reminded us in his 1982 World Day of Peace message, world peace will always elude us until peace becomes a reality for each of us personally. "It springs from the dynamism of free wills guided by reason towards the common good that is to be attained in truth, justice and love."[117] Interior peace becomes possible only when we have a conversion of spirit. We cannot have peace with hate in our hearts.

285. No society can live in peace with itself, or with the world, without a full awareness of the worth and dignity of every human person, and of the sacredness of all human life (Jas 4:1-2). When we accept violence in any form as commonplace, our sensitivities become dulled. When we accept violence, war itself can be taken for granted. Violence has many faces: oppression of the poor, deprivation of basic human rights, economic exploitation, sexual exploitation and pornography,

---

[117]John Paul II, "World Day of Peace Message 1982," #4, cited, p. 475.

neglect or abuse of the aged and the helpless, and innumerable other acts of inhumanity. Abortion in particular blunts a sense of the sacredness of human life. In a society where the innocent unborn are killed wantonly, how can we expect people to feel righteous revulsion at the act or threat of killing noncombatants in war?

286. We are well aware of the differences involved in the taking of human life in warfare and the taking of human life through abortion. As we have discussed throughout this document, even justifiable defense against aggression may result in the indirect or unintended loss of innocent human lives. This is tragic, but may conceivably be proportionate to the values defended. Nothing, however, can justify direct attack on innocent human life, in or out of warfare. Abortion is precisely such an attack.

287. We know that millions of men and women of good will, of all religious persuasions, join us in our commitment to try to reduce the horrors of war, and particularly to assure that nuclear weapons will never again be used, by any nation, anywhere, for any reason. Millions join us in our "no" to nuclear war, in the certainty that nuclear war would inevitably result in the killing of millions of innocent human beings, directly or indirectly. Yet many part ways with us in our efforts to reduce the horror of abortion and our "no" to war on innocent human life in the womb, killed not indirectly, but directly.

288. We must ask how long a nation willing to extend a constitutional guarantee to the "right" to kill defenseless human beings by abortion is likely to refrain from adopting strategic warfare policies deliberately designed to kill millions of defenseless human beings, if adopting them should come to seem "expedient." Since 1973, approximately 15 million abortions have been performed in the United States, symptoms of a kind of disease of the human spirit. And we now find ourselves seriously discussing the pros and cons of such questions as infanticide, euthanasia, and the involvement of physicians in carrying out the death penalty. Those who would celebrate such a national disaster can only have blinded themselves to its reality.

289. Pope Paul VI was resolutely clear: *If you wish peace, defend life.*[118] We plead with all who would work to end the scourge of war to begin by defending life at its most defenseless, the life of the unborn.

3. Prayer

290. A conversion of our hearts and minds will make it possible for us to enter into a closer communion with our Lord. We nourish that communion by personal and communal prayer, for it is in prayer that we encounter Jesus, who is our peace, and learn from him the way to peace.

---

[118]Paul VI, "World Day of Peace Message 1977."

291. In prayer we are renewed in faith and confirmed in our hope in God's promise.

292. The Lord's promise is that he is in our midst when we gather in prayer. Strengthened by this conviction, we beseech the risen Christ to fill the world with his peace. We call upon Mary, the first disciple and the Queen of Peace, to intercede for us and for the people of our time that we may walk in the way of peace. In this context, we encourage devotion to Our Lady of Peace.

293. As believers, we understand peace as a gift of God. This belief prompts us to pray constantly, personally and communally, particularly through the reading of Scripture and devotion to the rosary, especially in the family. Through these means and others, we seek the wisdom to begin the search for peace and the courage to sustain us as instruments of Christ's peace in the world.

294. The practice of contemplative prayer is especially valuable for advancing harmony and peace in the world. For this prayer rises, by divine grace, where there is total disarmament of the heart and unfolds in an experience of love which is the moving force of peace. Contemplation fosters a vision of the human family as united and interdependent in the mystery of God's love for all people. This silent, interior prayer bridges temporarily the "already" and "not yet," this world and God's Kingdom of peace.

295. The Mass in particular is a unique means of seeking God's help to create the conditions essential for true peace in ourselves and in the world. In the Eucharist we encounter the risen Lord, who gave us his peace. He shares with us the grace of the redemption, which helps us to preserve and nourish this precious gift. Nowhere is the Church's urgent plea for peace more evident in the liturgy than in the Communion Rite. After beginning this rite of the Mass with the Lord's Prayer, praying for reconciliation now and in the Kingdom to come, the community asks God to "grant us peace in our day," not just at some time in the distant future. Even before we are exhorted "to offer each other the sign of peace," the priest continues the Church's prayer for peace, recalling the Lord Jesus Christ's own legacy of peace:

> Lord Jesus Christ, you said to your apostles: I leave you peace, my peace I give you. Look not on our sins, but on the faith of your Church, and grant us the peace and unity of your kingdom.

Therefore, we encourage every Catholic to make the sign of peace at Mass an authentic sign of our reconciliation with God and with one another. This sign of peace is also a visible expression of our commitment to work for peace as a Christian community. We approach the table of the Lord only after having dedicated ourselves as a Christian community to peace and reconciliation. As an added sign of commitment, we suggest that there always be a petition for peace in the general intercessions at every eucharistic celebration.

296. We implore other Christians and everyone of good will to join us in this continuing prayer for peace, as we beseech God for peace within ourselves, in our families and community, in our nation, and in the world.

4. Penance

297. Prayer by itself is incomplete without penance. Penance directs us toward our goal of putting on the attitudes of Jesus himself. Because we are all capable of violence, we are never totally conformed to Christ and are always in need of conversion. The twentieth century alone provides adequate evidence of our violence as individuals and as a nation. Thus, there is continual need for acts of penance and conversion. The worship of the Church, particularly through the sacrament of reconciliation and communal penance services, offers us multiple ways to make reparation for the violence in our own lives and in our world.

298. As a tangible sign of our need and desire to do penance we, for the cause of peace, commit ourselves to fast and abstinence on each Friday of the year. We call upon our people voluntarily to do penance on Friday by eating less food and by abstaining from meat. This return to a traditional practice of penance, once well observed in the U.S. Church, should be accompanied by works of charity and service toward our neighbors. Every Friday should be a day significantly devoted to prayer, penance, and almsgiving for peace.

299. It is to such forms of penance and conversion that the Scriptures summon us. In the words of the prophet Isaiah:

> Is not the sort of fast that pleases me, to break unjust fetters and undo the thongs of the yoke, to let the oppressed go free and break every yoke, to share your bread with the hungry, and shelter the homeless poor, to clothe the person you see to be naked and not turn from your own kin? Then will your light shine like the dawn and your wound be quickly healed over. If you do away with the yoke, the clenched fist, the wicked word, if you give your bread to the hungry and relief to the oppressed, your light will rise in the darkness, and your shadows become like noon (Is 58:6-8; 10).

300. The present nuclear arms race has distracted us from the words of the prophets, has turned us from peacemaking, and has focused our attention on a nuclear buildup leading to annihilation. We are called to turn back from this evil of total destruction and turn instead in prayer and penance toward God, toward our neighbor, and toward the building of a peaceful world:

> I set before you life or death, a blessing or a curse. Choose life then, so that you and your descendants may live in the love of Yahweh your God, obeying His voice, clinging to Him; for in this your life

consists, and on this depends your long stay in the land which
Yahweh swore to your fathers Abraham, Isaac, and Jacob, He would
give them (Dt 30:19–20).

C. Challenge and Hope

301. The arms race presents questions of conscience we may not
evade. As American Catholics, we are called to express our loyalty
to the deepest values we cherish: peace, justice, and security for the
entire human family. National goals and policies must be measured
against that standard.

302. We speak here in a specific way to the Catholic community.
After the passage of nearly four decades and a concomitant growth
in our understanding of the ever-growing horror of nuclear war, we
must shape the climate of opinion which will make it possible for our
country to express profound sorrow over the atomic bombing in 1945.
Without that sorrow, there is no possibility of finding a way to repu-
diate future use of nuclear weapons or of conventional weapons in
such military actions as would not fulfill just-war criteria.

303.   To Priests, Deacons, Religious, and Pastoral Ministers:

We recognize the unique role in the Church which belongs to
priests and deacons by reason of the sacrament of holy orders and
their unique responsibility in the community of believers. We also
recognize the valued and indispensable role of men and women religious. To all of them and to all other pastoral ministers we stress that
the cultivation of the Gospel vision of peace as a way of life for
believers and as a leaven in society should be a major objective. As
bishops, we are aware each day of our dependence upon your efforts.
We are aware, too, that this letter and the new obligations it could
present to the faithful may create difficulties for you in dealing with
those you serve. We have confidence in your capacity and ability to
convert these difficulties into an opportunity to give a fuller witness
to our Lord and his message. This letter will be known by the faithful
only as well as you know it, preach and teach it, and use it creatively.

304.   To Educators:

We have outlined in this letter Catholic teaching on war and
peace, but this framework will become a living message only through
your work in the Catholic community. To teach the ways of peace is
not "to weaken the nation's will" but to be concerned for the nation's
soul. We address theologians in a particular way, because we know
that we have only begun the journey toward a theology of peace;
without your specific contributions this desperately needed dimension of our faith will not be realized. Through your help we may

provide new vision and wisdom for church and state.

305. We are confident that all the models of Catholic education which have served the Church and our country so well in so many ways will creatively rise to the challenge of peace.

306. *To Parents:*

Your role, in our eyes, is unsurpassed by any other; the foundation of society is the family. We are conscious of the continuing sacrifices you make in the efforts to nurture the full human and spiritual growth of your children. Children hear the Gospel message first from your lips. Parents who consciously discuss issues of justice in the home and who strive to help children solve conflicts through nonviolent methods enable their children to grow up as peacemakers. We pledge our continuing pastoral support in the common objective we share of building a peaceful world for the future of children everywhere.

307. *To Youth:*

Pope John Paul II singles you out in every country where he visits as the hope of the future; we agree with him. We call you to choose your future work and professions carefully. How you spend the rest of your lives will determine, in large part, whether there will any longer be a world as we know it. We ask you to study carefully the teachings of the Church and the demands of the Gospel about war and peace. We encourage you to seek careful guidance as you reach conscientious decisions about your civic responsibilities in this age of nuclear military forces.

308. We speak to you, however, as people of faith. We share with you our deepest conviction that in the midst of the dangers and complexities of our time God is with us, working through us and sustaining us all in our efforts of building a world of peace with justice for each person.

309. *To Men and Women in Military Service:*

Millions of you are Catholics serving in the armed forces. We recognize that you carry special responsibilities for the issues we have considered in this letter. Our perspective on your profession is that of Vatican II: "All those who enter the military service in loyalty to their country should look upon themselves as the custodians of the security and freedom of their fellow countrymen; and where they carry out their duty properly, they are contributing to the maintenance of peace."[119]

310. It is surely not our intention in writing this letter to create problems for Catholics in the armed forces. Every profession, however,

---

[119]*Pastoral Constitution,* #79.

has its specific moral questions and it is clear that the teaching on war and peace developed in this letter poses a special challenge and opportunity to those in the military profession. Our pastoral contact with Catholics in military service, either through our direct experience or through our priests, impresses us with the demanding moral standards we already see observed and the commitment to Catholic faith we find. We are convinced that the challenges of this letter will be faced conscientiously. The purpose of defense policy is to defend the peace; military professionals should understand their vocation this way. We believe they do, and we support this view.

311. We remind all in authority and in the chain of command that their training and field manuals have long prohibited, and still do prohibit, certain actions in the conduct of war, especially those actions which inflict harm on innocent civilians. The question is not whether certain measures are unlawful or forbidden in warfare, but which measures: to refuse to take such actions is not an act of cowardice or treason but one of courage and patriotism.

312. We address particularly those involved in the exercise of authority over others. We are aware of your responsibilities and impressed by the standard of personal and professional duty you uphold. We feel, therefore, that we can urge you to do everything you can to assure that every peaceful alternative is exhausted before war is even remotely considered. In developing battle plans and weapons systems, we urge you to try to ensure that these are designed to reduce violence, destruction, suffering, and death to a minimum, keeping in mind especially noncombatants and other innocent persons.

313. Those who train individuals for military duties must remember that the citizen does not lose his or her basic human rights by entrance into military service. No one, for whatever reason, can justly treat a military person with less dignity and respect than that demanded for and deserved by every human person. One of the most difficult problems of war involves defending a free society without destroying the values that give it meaning and validity. Dehumanization of a nation's military personnel by dulling their sensibilities and generating hatred toward adversaries in an effort to increase their fighting effectiveness robs them of basic human rights and freedoms, degrading them as persons.

314. Attention must be given to the effects on military personnel themselves of the use of even legitimate means of conducting war. While attacking legitimate targets and wounding or killing opposed combat forces may be morally justified, what happens to military persons required to carry out these actions? Are they treated merely as instruments of war, insensitive as the weapons they use? With what moral or emotional experiences do they return from war and attempt to resume normal civilian lives? How does their experience affect society? How are they treated by society?

315. It is not only basic human rights of adversaries that must be respected, but those of our own forces as well. We reemphasize, therefore, the obligation of responsible authorities to ensure appropriate training and education of combat forces and to provide appropriate support for those who have experienced combat. It is unconscionable to deprive those veterans of combat whose lives have been severely disrupted or traumatized by their combat experiences of proper psychological and other appropriate treatment and support.

316. Finally, we are grateful for the sacrifice so many in military service must make today and for the service offered in the past by veterans. We urge that those sacrifices be mitigated so far as possible by the provision of appropriate living and working conditions and adequate financial recompense. Military persons and their families must be provided continuing opportunity for full spiritual growth, the exercise of their religious faith, and a dignified mode of life.

317. We especially commend and encourage our priests in military service. In addition to the message already addressed to all priests and religious, we stress the special obligations and opportunities you face in direct pastoral service to the men and women of the armed forces. To complement a teaching document of this scope, we shall need the sensitive and wise pastoral guidance only you can provide. We promise our support in facing this challenge.

318. To Men and Women in Defense Industries:

You also face specific questions, because the defense industry is directly involved in the development and production of the weapons of mass destruction which have concerned us in this letter. We do not presume or pretend that clear answers exist to many of the personal, professional, and financial choices facing you in your varying responsibilities. In this letter we have ruled out certain uses of nuclear weapons, while also expressing conditional moral acceptance for deterrence. All Catholics, at every level of defense industries, can and should use the moral principles of this letter to form their consciences. We realize that different judgments of conscience will face different people, and we recognize the possibility of diverse concrete judgments being made in this complex area. We seek as moral teachers and pastors to be available to all who confront these questions of personal and vocational choice. Those who in conscience decide that they should no longer be associated with defense activities should find support in the Catholic community. Those who remain in these industries or earn a profit from the weapons industry should find in the Church guidance and support for the ongoing evaluation of their work.

319. To Men and Women of Science:

At Hiroshima Pope John Paul said: "Criticism of science and technology is sometimes so severe that it comes close to condemning science itself. On the contrary, science and technology are a wonderful product of a God-given human creativity, since they have provided us with wonderful possibilities and we all gratefully benefit from them. But we know that this potential is not a neutral one: it can be used either for man's progress or for his degradation."[120] We appreciate the efforts of scientists, some of whom first unlocked the secret of atomic power and others of whom have developed it in diverse ways, to turn the enormous power of science to the cause of peace.

320. Modern history is not lacking scientists who have looked back with deep remorse on the development of weapons to which they contributed, sometimes with the highest motivation, even believing that they were creating weapons that would render all other weapons obsolete and convince the world of the unthinkableness of war. Such efforts have ever proved illusory. Surely, equivalent dedication of scientific minds to reverse current trends, and to pursue concepts as bold and adventuresome in favor of peace as those which in the past have magnified the risks of war, could result in dramatic benefits for all of humanity. We particularly note in this regard the extensive efforts of public education undertaken by physicians and scientists on the medical consequences of nuclear war.

321. We do not, however, wish to limit our remarks to the physical sciences alone. Nor do we limit our remarks to physical scientists. In his address at the United Nations University in Hiroshima, Pope John Paul II warned about misuse of "the social sciences and the human behavioral sciences when they are utilized to manipulate people, to crush their mind, souls, dignity and freedom. . . ."[121] The positive role of social science in overcoming the dangers of the nuclear age is evident in this letter. We have been dependent upon the research and analysis of social scientists in our effort to apply the moral principles of the Catholic tradition to the concrete problems of our day. We encourage social scientists to continue this work of relating moral wisdom and political reality. We are in continuing need of your insights.

322. To Men and Women of the Media:

We have directly felt our dependence upon you in writing this letter; all the problems we have confronted have been analyzed daily in the media. As we have grappled with these issues, we have experienced some of the responsibility you bear for interpreting them. On the quality of your efforts depends in great measure the opportunity

---

[120]John Paul II, "Address to Scientists and Scholars," #3, cited, p. 621.
[121]*Ibid.*

the general public will have for understanding this letter.

323. *To Public Officials:*
Vatican II spoke forcefully of "the difficult yet noble art of politics."[122] No public issue is more difficult than avoiding war; no public task more noble than building a secure peace. Public officials in a democracy must both lead and listen; they are ultimately dependent upon a popular consensus to sustain policy. We urge you to lead with courage and to listen to the public debate with sensitivity.

324. Leadership in a nuclear world means examining with great care and objectivity every potential initiative toward world peace, regardless of how unpromising it might at first appear. One specific initiative which might be taken now would be the establishment of a task force including the public sector, industry, labor, economists, and scientists with the mandate to consider the problems and challenges posed by nuclear disarmament to our economic well-being and industrial output. Listening includes being particularly attentive to the consciences of those who sincerely believe that they may not morally support warfare in general, a given war, or the exercise of a particular role within the armed forces. Public officials might well serve all of our fellow citizens by proposing and supporting legislation designed to give maximum protection to this precious freedom, true freedom of conscience.

325. In response to public officials who both lead and listen, we urge citizens to respect the vocation of public service. It is a role easily maligned but not easily fulfilled. Neither justice nor peace can be achieved with stability in the absence of courageous and creative public servants.

326. *To Catholics as Citizens:*
All papal teaching on peace has stressed the crucial role of public opinion. Pope John Paul II specified the tasks before us: "There is no justification for not raising the question of the responsibility of each nation and each individual in the face of possible wars and of the nuclear threat."[123] In a democracy, the responsibility of the nation and that of its citizens coincide. Nuclear weapons pose especially acute questions of conscience for American Catholics. As citizens we wish to affirm our loyalty to our country and its ideals, yet we are also citizens of the world who must be faithful to the universal principles proclaimed by the Church. While some other countries also possess nuclear weapons, we may not forget that the United States was the first to build and to use them. Like the Soviet Union, this country now possesses so many weapons as to imperil the contin-

---

[122] *Pastoral Constitution*, #75.
[123] John Paul II, "Address at Hiroshima," #2, *Origins* 10 (1981):620.

uation of civilization. Americans share responsibility for the current situation, and cannot evade responsibility for trying to resolve it.

327. The virtue of patriotism means that as citizens we respect and honor our country, but our very love and loyalty make us examine carefully and regularly its role in world affairs, asking that it live up to its full potential as an agent of peace with justice for all people.

> Citizens must cultivate a generous and loyal spirit of patriotism, but without being narrow-minded. This means that they will always direct their attention to the good of the whole human family, united by the different ties which bind together races, people, and nations.[124]

328. In a pluralistic democracy like the United States, the Church has a unique opportunity, precisely because of the strong constitutional protection of both religious freedom and freedom of speech and the press, to help call attention to the moral dimensions of public issues. In a previous Pastoral Letter, *Human Life In Our Day*, we said: "In our democratic system, the fundamental right of political dissent cannot be denied, nor is rational debate on public policy decisions of government in the light of moral and political principles to be discouraged. It is the duty of the governed to analyze responsibly the concrete issues of public policy."[125] In fulfilling this role, the Church helps to create a community of conscience in the wider civil community. It does this in the first instance by teaching clearly within the Church the moral principles which bind and shape the Catholic conscience. The Church also fulfills a teaching role, however, in striving to share the moral wisdom of the Catholic tradition with the larger society.

329. In the wider public discussion, we look forward in a special way to cooperating with all other Christians with whom we share common traditions. We also treasure cooperative efforts with Jewish and Islamic communities, which possess a long and abiding concern for peace as a religious and human value. Finally, we reaffirm our desire to participate in a common public effort with all men and women of good will who seek to reverse the arms race and secure the peace of the world.

Conclusion

330. As we close this lengthy letter, we try to answer two key questions as directly as we can.

331. Why do we address these matters fraught with such complexity, controversy, and passion? We speak as pastors, not politicians. We

---

[124]*Pastoral Constitution*, #75.
[125]*Human Life in Our Day*, cited, p. 41.

are teachers, not technicians. We cannot avoid our responsibility to lift up the moral dimensions of the choices before our world and nation. The nuclear age is an era of moral as well as physical danger. We are the first generation since Genesis with the power to virtually destroy God's creation. We cannot remain silent in the face of such danger. Why do we address these issues? We are simply trying to live up to the call of Jesus to be peacemakers in our own time and situation.

332. What are we saying? Fundamentally, we are saying that the decisions about nuclear weapons are among the most pressing moral questions of our age. While these decisions have obvious military and political aspects, they involve fundamental moral choices. In simple terms, we are saying that good ends (defending one's country, protecting freedom, etc.) cannot justify immoral means (the use of weapons which kill indiscriminately and threaten whole societies). We fear that our world and nation are headed in the wrong direction. More weapons with greater destructive potential are produced every day. More and more nations are seeking to become nuclear powers. In our quest for more and more security, we fear we are actually becoming less and less secure.

333. In the words of our Holy Father, we need a "moral about-face." The whole world must summon the moral courage and technical means to say "no" to nuclear conflict; "no" to weapons of mass destruction; "no" to an arms race which robs the poor and the vulnerable; and "no" to the moral danger of a nuclear age which places before humankind indefensible choices of constant terror or surrender. Peacemaking is not an optional commitment. It is a requirement of our faith. We are called to be peacemakers, not by some movement of the moment, but by our Lord Jesus. The content and context of our peacemaking is set, not by some political agenda or ideological program, but by the teaching of his Church.

334. Thus far in this Pastoral Letter we have made suggestions we hope will be helpful in the present world crisis. Looking ahead to the long and productive future of humanity for which we all hope, we feel that a more all-inclusive and final solution is needed. We speak here of the truly effective international authority for which Pope John XXIII ardently longed in Peace on Earth,[126] and of which Pope Paul VI spoke to the United Nations on his visit there in 1965.[127] The hope for such a structure is not unrealistic, because the point has been reached where public opinion sees clearly that, with the massive weaponry of the present, war is no longer viable. There is a substitute for war. There is negotiation under the supervision of a global body realistically fashioned to do its job. It must be given the equipment

---

[126]John XXIII, Peace on Earth (1963), #137.
[127]Paul VI, "Address to the General Assembly of the United Nations," (1965), #2.

to keep constant surveillance on the entire earth. Present technology makes this possible. It must have the authority, freely conferred upon it by all the nations, to investigate what seem to be preparations for war by any one of them. It must be empowered by all the nations to enforce its commands on every nation. It must be so constituted as to pose no threat to any nation's sovereignty. Obviously the creation of such a sophisticated instrumentality is a gigantic task, but is it hoping for too much to believe that the genius of humanity, aided by the grace and guidance of God, is able to accomplish it? To create it may take decades of unrelenting daily toll by the world's best minds and most devoted hearts, but it shall never come into existence unless we make a beginning now.

335. As we come to the end of our Pastoral Letter we boldly propose the beginning of this work. The evil of the proliferation of nuclear arms becomes more evident every day to all people. No one is exempt from their danger. If ridding the world of the weapons of war could be done easily, the whole human race would gladly do it tomorrow. Shall we shrink from the task because it is hard?

336. We turn to our own government and we beg it to propose to the United Nations that it begin this work immediately; that it create an international task force for peace; that this task force, with membership open to every nation, meet daily through the years ahead with one sole agenda: the creation of a world that will one day be safe from war. Freed from the bondage of war that holds it captive in its threat, the world will at last be able to address its problems and to make genuine human progress, so that every day there may be more freedom, more food, and more opportunity for every human being who walks the face of the earth.

337. Let us have the courage to believe in the bright future and in a God who wills it for us—not a perfect world, but a better one. The perfect world, we Christians believe, is beyond the horizon, in an endless eternity where God will be all in all. But a better world is here for human hands and hearts and minds to make.

338. For the community of faith the risen Christ is the beginning and end of all things. For all things were created through him and all things will return to the Father through him.

339. It is our belief in the risen Christ which sustains us in confronting the awesome challenge of the nuclear arms race. Present in the beginning as the word of the Father, present in history as the word incarnate, and with us today in his word, sacraments, and spirit, He is the reason for our hope and faith. Respecting our freedom, He does not solve our problems but sustains us as we take responsibility for His work of creation and try to shape it in the ways of the Kingdom. We believe His grace will never fail us. We offer this letter to the Church and to all who can draw strength and wisdom from it in the conviction that we must not fail Him. We must subordinate the

power of the nuclear age to human control and direct it to human benefit. As we do this we are conscious of God's continuing work among us, which will one day issue forth in the beautiful final Kingdom prophesied by the seer of the Book of Revelation:

> Then I saw a new heaven and a new earth; for the first heaven and the first earth had passed away and the sea was no more. And I saw the holy city, new Jerusalem, coming down out of heaven from God, prepared as a bride adorned for her husband; and I heard a great voice from the throne saying, "Behold, the dwelling of God is with men. He will dwell with them, and they shall be his people, and God himself will be with them, he will wipe away every tear from their eyes, and death shall be no more, neither shall there be mourning nor crying nor pain any more, for the former things have passed away." And he who sat upon the throne said, "Behold, I make all things new" (Rv 21:1-5).

Statement on U.S. Policy in Central America

A Statement Issued by the
President of the United States Catholic Conference

July 22, 1983

1. The critical importance of U.S.-Nicaragua relations as a policy problem and a legislative issue for the Congress is daily evident. The U.S. Catholic Conference (USCC) has advocated a diplomatic course of action for the United States as a means of addressing the war in El Salvador and a method of reversing the presently dangerous course of U.S.-Nicaraguan relations.

2. In testimony given on March 7, 1983 to a joint session of the House Subcommittee on Western Hemispheric Affairs and the Subcommittee on Human Rights and International Organizations, Archbishop James A. Hickey, speaking for the USCC, said:

> U.S. policy over the past two years has not been helpful to the moderate elements in Nicaraguan life. Rather it has served as a continuous provocation which has given a pretext for ever-increasing governmental attempts to control important elements of Nicaraguan life. The bishops of the United States called in November 1981 for a U.S. policy that would engage Nicaragua diplomatically not isolate it. My recent experience in Nicaragua has convinced me that what we said in 1981 is even more applicable today.

3. In contrast to this recommendation of positive diplomatic engagement, U.S. policy toward Nicaragua presently has the effect of deepening the internal crises in the country and escalating the dangers of war in the region. A string of U.S. actions reaching from unrelentingly hostile policy rhetoric, through U.S. actions to prevent Nicaragua from obtaining credit and loans in international financial institutions to the funding of covert activities on the Nicaraguan border have all run counter to the policy proposals made by Archbishop Hickey in March.

4. The House of Representatives will soon vote on HR2760 aimed at prohibiting further funding of covert activities. In his testimony of last March Archbishop Hickey said:

> Let me state personally that as an American bishop I find any use of U.S. tax dollars for the purpose of covert destabilization of another government to be unwise, unjustified and destructive of the very values a democratic nation should support in the world.

5. The purpose of my statement is to reaffirm this judgment as a guide for U.S. policy. Even more strongly I wish to oppose any form of U.S. military intervention in Central America. I repeat the earlier calls of our bishops' conference for a diplomatic, nonmilitary solution, a policy requiring discussions between the U.S. and Nicaragua, Honduras and Nicaragua, and support by the United States of the diplomatic efforts of other Latin American republics to resolve peacefully the crisis in Central America.

Archbishop John R. Roach
President
United States Catholic Conference

Appendix

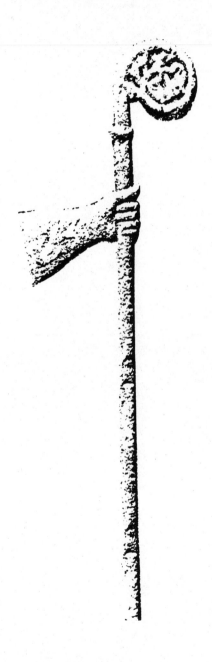

Chronological Table of Important Events in the History of the Church in the United States from 1975 to 1983

1975: The Latin Liturgy Association was founded.

1976: The "Call to Action" congress was held in Detroit during the Bicentennial of the American Revolution. The forty-first International Eucharistic Congress was held in Philadelphia.

1977: The first black bishop to hold a residential see in the United States was appointed: Joseph L. Howze of Biloxi.

1978: The Fellowship of Catholic Scholars was founded. Father Bruce Ritter was honored by the American Institute of Public Service for his work with sex-exploited young people.

1979: Catholic Relief Services gave assistance to 14 million people while spending a record $291 million in 86 countries. Pope John Paul II visited the United States in October.

1980: Pope John Paul II appointed Cardinal William Baum of Washington, D.C., prefect of the Congregation of Catholic Education. At the age of 53 the cardinal became the youngest and only American prefect in the Roman Curia. The new Apostolic Delegate, Archbishop Pio Laghi, was appointed to the United States. In the three years since its founding in 1976, Operation Rice Bowl raised $12 million to aid the poor. The statue of Mother Joseph Pariseau of the Sisters of Providence was dedicated May 1 in National Statuary Hall in the U.S. Capitol. Mother Joseph, thus honored by the State of Washington, established 29 institutions (schools, orphanages, and hospitals) during the 46 years she spent in the Northwest. She died in 1902. Pope John Paul II presided at the June 22 ceremonies for the beatification of Kateri Tekakwitha, "Lily of the Mohawks" (1656-1680). The Knights of Columbus contributed more than $26 million to charitable causes and over 8 million hours in service to their communities. On June 30 the U.S. Supreme Court ruled 5 to 4 in support of the constitutionality of federal legislation restricting the funding of abortion under the Medicaid program. Msgr. Luigi Ligutti, 85, former executive secretary of the National Catholic Rural Life Conference, was honored by the Iowa Centennial Memorial Foundation for his work on behalf of people in rural areas. The activities of Catholic Relief Services in 1979 had a total program value of more than $340 million, according to the agency's annual report. A Synod of Bishops met in Rome to discuss the "role of the family"; the topic was suggested by Cardinal John Krol of Philadelphia. Catholic diocesan newspapers increased their circulation to 70,000 subscribers for a total circulation of 4.69 million during this year.

1981: 252,900 black and 256,000 Hispanic students represented one-sixth of total enrollment in Catholic schools. Two Catholics were named to President Reagan's Cabinet: Alexander Haig, Secretary of State, and Raymond Donovan, Secretary of Labor. A record total of Catholics served in Congress: 17 in the Senate; 118 in the House of Representatives. President Reagan appointed William A. Wilson, a convert to Catholicism, as his personal representative to the Vatican. Entertainer Danny Thomas was given the Father Flanagan Award for Service to Youth by Boys Town. Archbishop Raymond G. Hunthausen of Seattle called for U.S. unilateral disarmament and suggested Christians refuse to pay up to 50 percent of their federal income tax as nonviolent resistance "to nuclear murder." Mother Teresa of Calcutta opened four shelters in the United States and received Marquette University's Pere Marquette Discovery Award. The Plowshares Eight, including Father Daniel Berrigan, received prison sentences for the break-in at the missile assembly plant in Norristown, Pa. Msgr. Paul A. Lenz, director of the Bureau of Catholic Indian Missions, reported a revitalization of the Church in the American Indian community. The NCCB paid tribute on the occasion of his death to Roy Wilkins, leader of the National Association for the Advancement of Colored People for 46 years. Protestant, Jewish, and Catholic business leaders organized to aid Catholic schools in Philadelphia and raised $77 million. By November 12, more than thirty bishops had commented on nuclear arms. The United States Supreme Court ruled that the University of Missouri at Kansas City could not deny student religious groups the use of campus facilities for worship.

1982: The National Organization of Catholic Evangelical Directors was established at a meeting of 43 persons representing various dioceses, religious communities, and national organizations. The Department of Health and Human Services announced that it had prepared new rules requiring federally subsidized family planning clinics to separate abortion activity completely from all family planning services. John Cody, Cardinal Archbishop of Chicago, died. Archbishop Joseph L. Bernardin of Chicago announced the end of an independent investigation into the financial dealings of his predecessor, Cardinal Cody, declaring that it produced no evidence of wrongdoing. Findings of a survey conducted by Americans United for Separation of Church and State indicated that a record number of 141 Catholics (17 in the Senate, 124 in the House) would be in the 98th Congress. President Reagan became the first Chief Executive to meet with pro-life marchers. Cardinal John F. Dearden became the first United States bishop to receive the Laetare Medal of the University of Notre Dame. Auxiliary Bishop Joseph Francis of Newark, N.J., announced that 133 United States bishops were on record in support of a bilateral U.S.–U.S.S.R. freeze on nuclear weapons. The National Conference on the Charismatic Renewal in the Catholic Church held at the University of Notre Dame was attended by more than 13,000 people from ten nations. The Knights of Columbus gave more than $41.7 million to charitable causes. On September 8, Msgr. Emerson J. Moore was ordained the first black bishop in the history of the Archdiocese of New York.

1983: President Reagan, in the State of the Union address, reiterated his support for a constitutional amendment on school prayer and for tuition tax credits for parents with children in private and parochial schools. He repeated these stances January 31 at the National Religious Broadcasters' convention, when he also condemned abortion. Archbishop Joseph L. Bernardin of Chicago was created a cardinal. Cardinal Joseph L. Bernardin was named to the 1982 South Carolinian of the Year Award for "dedicated service to mankind and superior accomplishments." Archbishop John R. Quinn of San Francisco was named to help guide developments in religious life in America. Humberto Medeiros, Cardinal Archbishop of Boston, died; Terence Cooke, Cardinal Archbishop of New York, died.

Growth of the Church in the United States

1975–1979[1]

Categories	1975	1979
Population	48,881,872	49,812,178
Archdioceses	32	32
Dioceses	135	138
Priests	58,847	58,621
Seminarians	17,247	13,266
Parishes	18,531	18,794

1980-1982[2]

Categories	1980	1982
Population	50,449,842	52,088,744
Archdioceses	33	33
Dioceses	138	143
Priests	58,398	57,870
Seminarians	12,468	12,054
Parishes	18,829	18,839

[1]These statistics are taken from the 1976 and 1980 editions of *The Official Catholic Directory* published by P.J. Kenedy and Sons, New York, N.Y.

The most alarming fact of this set of statistics is the decrease of 3,981 seminarians in such a brief period, very close to a drop of 1,000 students for the priesthood per year.

[2]These statistics are taken from the 1981 and 1983 editions of *The Official Catholic Directory*.

The greatest decline in the listed years is in the number of priests.

Organization and Purpose of NCCB/USCC

The National Conference of Catholic Bishops (NCCB) and the United States Catholic Conference (USCC) are the organizations of the American Catholic hierarchy. Through these distinct but closely related organizations—one a canonical entity, the other a civil corporation—the bishops fulfill their responsibilities of leadership and service to Church and nation.

The membership of NCCB consists in approximately 375 Catholic bishops of the United States. NCCB enables the bishops to exchange ideas and information, deliberate on the Church's broad concerns, and respond as a body. The conference functions through a general assembly, an administrative committee of 48 members, several executive-level committees, and some 40 standing and ad hoc committees. NCCB committees deal with pastoral matters important to the Church as a whole.

The United States Catholic Conference is the public policy agency of the Catholic bishops of America. Unlike NCCB, whose members are bishops exclusively, USCC's policy-making structures include priests, religious, and lay people. USCC shares several structures with NCCB. Its Administrative Board is the same body as NCCB's Administrative Committee, and the same executive-level committees serve both conferences. The General Secretariat in Washington, D.C., handles both NCCB and USCC business. Indeed, while most staff are assigned to one conference or the other, a significant number work for NCCB/USCC. The USCC provides an organizational structure and the resources needed to ensure coordination, cooperation, and assistance in the public, educational, and social concerns of the Church at the national or interdiocesan level.

Index

Abortion, 18-19, 23, 81-91, 134, 184-85, 223, 269, 323, 569
"Absolute poverty," 563
Abstinence from meat, 571
"Acceptable," 304
Acceptance of handicapped persons, 42
Access to buildings, 271
Access to health care, 483
Accidents, hand gun violence, 66
Accountability: fund raising guidelines, 234-35; *Teach Them*, 151; television industry, 56-58
Acid raid, 448
"Action policy," 537
"Active nonviolence," 513
Ad Hoc Commission on Marriage and Family Life (USCC), 40, 255
Ad Hoc Committee for Hispanic Affairs (NCCB), 28
Ad Hoc Committee for Pro-Life Activities, 18
Ad Hoc Committee on Migration and Tourism (NCCB), 32, 287
Ad Hoc Committee on Moral Values (NCCB), 28
Ad Hoc Committee on the Parish (NCCB), 249
Ad Hoc Committee on War and Peace, 338
Adolescence. see Youth.
Adoption of children, 85
Adult education, 401, 413-14
Advertising, television industry, 59, 65
Aeschylus, 387
Affidavits (arbitration procedure), 338
Affiliated stations (TV networks), 58, 64-65
Affirmative action, 386
Afghanistan, 559
Age discrimination, 141
Aged, 1, 22, 23, 50, 108, 138-45, 182-83, 252, 481
Aggression, 513, 514-15, 518, 521, 553, 569
Agriculture, 21, 47-48, 51, 70
Air pollution, 448
Alcohol fuels, 455
Alienation, 386-90 *passim*
Aliens in the United States, 31
"Already but not yet," 508, 509, 515, 570

Alternative models of health care, 480
Alternative sources of energy, 445
America (Jesuit magazine), 314
"American Catholic Church" (phrase), 41
American Friends Service Committee (Quakers), 315
American Indians, 2, 31, 108, 205-10, 366, 375
Americanization, 373
Annulment of marriage, 335
Anointing of the Sick (sacrament), 471
Anti-Catholicism, 373
"Anti-Colonialist Gospel," 12
Anti-Semitism, 121
Anti-Sovietism, 561
Apartheid, 16, 74-75
Apocalypse, 504
Apostolate: *Called and Gifted*, 412; Catholic higher education, 412; family apostolate, 260; fund raising guidelines, 233; handicapped persons, 270; health care, 296, 475-82
Apostolic Signatura, 331, 341
Appeals from decision of arbitration, 340
Arabs, 11
Arbitration procedures, 283, 330, 335-41
Archdioceses, *Principles and Guidelines for Fund Raising*, 232-37
Armed Forces. see United States: Armed Forces.
Arms control, 75, 547, 548
Arms race, 136, 301, 304, 310, 323, 398, 496, 521, 522, 526, 537-38, 546, 547, 552, 555, 559, 564, 572
Arms reductions, 548
Association of Catholic Colleges, 403-4
Asylum, small-boat refugees, 242
Atheism, 211, 384, 386, 392, 396
Atomic weapons. see Nuclear weapons.
Audits, fund raising guidelines, 235
Augustine, Saint, Bishop of Hippo, 78, 515-16
Australia, 242
Authority, 4, 233-34, 495-96, 517, 557
Automobiles, 447

Awareness: crisis in housing, 114;
   family ministry, 257

"Balance of terror," 529, 539
Banks, crisis in housing, 106
Baptism (sacrament), 26, 418-19,
   421
Basic Christian communities, 422
Bauer, Bruno, 385
Baum, William (Abp.), 21, 22
Beatitudes, 288, 391
Behavioral sciences, 576
Benefices, 336
Berlinguer, Enrico, 396
Bernardin, Joseph (Cardinal), 1, 2,
   4, 9, 11, 19, 20, 23, 35, 38, 39-40,
   42, 43, 300-312 *passim*
Bettazzi, Luigi (Bp.), 396
Bible. NT 267, 503-7
Bible. NT Acts, 122, 171, 364, 419
Bible. NT Colossians, 174, 187
Bible. NT I Corinthians, 78
Bible. NT Ephesians, 34, 80, 179,
   185, 348, 413, 498, 504, 507
Bible. NT Galatians, 173, 344
Bible. NT Hebrews, 172
Bible. NT James, 348
Bible. NT John, 67, 78, 79, 80, 145,
   170, 171, 174, 176, 417, 444-45,
   470, 506
Bible. NT I John, 443
Bible. NT Luke, 93, 130, 137, 177,
   231, 347, 470, 506, 507
Bible. NT Mark, 214, 417, 431, 504,
   505
Bible. NT Matthew, 78, 130, 137,
   174, 195, 214, 344, 348, 365, 418,
   429, 434, 441, 470, 504, 505, 507
Bible. NT Philippians, 177
Bible. NT Revelation, 485, 581
Bible. NT Romans, 78, 123, 124,
   170, 172, 173, 231, 365, 420
Bible. NT Timothy, 182
Bible. OT 122-23, 500-3
Bible. OT Amos, 344
Bible. OT Deuteronomy, 138,
   571-72
Bible. OT Ezekiel, 502
Bible. OT Genesis, 229, 364
Bible. OT Hosea, 178
Bible. OT Isaiah, 119, 468, 502, 503,
   511, 571
Bible. OT Jeremiah, 502
Bible. OT Leviticus, 169, 501-2
Bible. OT Psalms, 101, 174, 352, 503

Bible: Study and teaching, 125, 229,
   231, 296, 347, 406, 497, 500
Bicentennial of the United States,
   10, 22, 215-26, 245, 255
Biological warfare, 550
Biomass energy production, 452,
   453, 455
Birth control. see Contraception.
Bishops: responsibilities, 3, 322
Bishops' Committee on Conciliation
   and Arbitration, 330-41
Bishops of Appalachia, 448
Bishops of Canada, 31, 313
Bishops of Central America, 299
Bishops of El Salvador, 298
Bishops of Europe, 313
Bishops of France, 313, 399
Bishops of Germany [Federal
   Republic], 211, 313, 380
Bishops of Guatemala, 297, 298,
   467-68
Bishops of Ireland, 313
Bishops of Italy, 3
Bishops of Latin America, 288, 464
Bishops of Minnesota, 31
Bishops of Netherlands, 313
Bishops of Nicaragua, 298, 467
Bishops of Poland, 211, 380
Bishops of South Africa, 491
Bishops' Program for Social
   Reconstruction (1919), 98
Blacks, 152, 284, 349, 432
Blanchette, Romeo (Bp.), 41
Blessed Virgin Mary. see Mary,
   Blessed Virgin Mary.
Blind persons, 272
Block grants, 49
"Boat people," 38, 287, 378
Bombing (aerial bombardment), 520
Borders, William D. (Abp.), 19,
   289, 295
Brazil, 55
Bread for the World (program), 253
Bread of Life (religious education
   program), 253
Breeder reactors, 449
Broadcasting industry, 16, 33, 54-
   65, 289, 327
Brothers and Sisters to Us, 1-2, 284-
   85, 342-55
Brown, Edmund G., Jr., 21, 126
Brown, Harold, 531
Bundy, McGeorge, 308
Bureau of Catholic and Indian
   Missions, 209

Business and businessmen, 15, 194, 458-61

California, 21, 126
Call to Action (Apostolic letter, May 1971), 53, 130, 319, 322, 443, 461
Call to Action Conference (meeting, Detroit), 28, 32, 215-16, 244, 247, 251, 255, 284, 365, 414
Called and Gifted: The American Catholic Laity, 290, 417-23
Cambodia, 241-42, 285, 356
Camp David Agreements, 278-79
Campaign for Human Development, 244, 250
Campaign politics, 130
Campus ministry, 411-12
Camus, Albert, 432
Canada, 242
Canal Zone (Panama Canal), 12, 27
Canon law: conciliation/arbitration procedures, 283-84, 330; fund raising guidelines, 234
Capital punishment, 292, 293
Capitalism, 288, 289, 389, 399, 459
Carberry, John J. (Cardinal), 9, 26-27, 29, 36, 288
Carbon dioxide, 448
Carpet bombing, 520
Carter, Jimmy (President), 24, 157-58, 213, 378, 436, 453
Casaroli, Agostino (Cardinal), 315-16
Casey, Juliana, 301
Catechesi Tradendae, 366
Catechetics, 36, 148-56, 246, 273
"Catholic" (term), 404
Catholic Church: Bicentennial response, 216; Brothers and Sisters to Us, 352; Challenge of Peace, 494-500, 509-10, 566-68; cultural pluralism, 365, 371; educational mission, 401-2; Marxist Communism, 389-90; political responsibility, 283; promoting Christian unity, 424-26; society and the aged, 142-45; Statement on American Indians, 209-10
"Catholic Church in the United States" (phrase), 41
Catholic Coordinating Committee for the White House Conference on Families, 260

Catholic Health Association, 296, 476, 477, 483
Catholic Higher Education and the Pastoral Mission of the Church, 291, 401
Catholic Hospital Association, 476
Catholic-Jewish relations, 1, 21, 120-25
Catholic Near Eastern Welfare Association, 278
Catholic Relief Services, 29, 43, 253, 278, 356
Catholic Schools, 13, 22, 25, 50, 84, 121, 274, 353-54
Catholic Schools in a Declining Church (report), 25
Catholic Standard and Times (Philadelphia), 306
Catholic Theological Society of America, 34, 228, 374
Catholic University of America, The, 291
Catholic war veterans, 315
Celibacy, 220
Central America, 295, 297, 298, 328, 464-68, 582-83
Challenge of Peace: God's Promise and Our Response, 2, 3, 302, 309-16, 493-581
Chaplains, 478, 575
Charity, 42, 390, 563
Chemical warfare, 550
Chicago Catholic, 308
Chicago, Ill., 17
Child care, 159-63
Children: family ministry, 265; handicapped persons, 270-71; Let the Little Children Come to Me, 26, 159-63; nutrition programs, 14, 72; pro-life plan, 85; television viewing, 55; To Live in Christ Jesus, 180-82
Christ. see Jesus Christ.
Christian Education of Youth (December 31, 1929), 156
Christian unity, 1, 287, 424-26
Christianity, 387, 391-95
Christians in Action (1948), 4
Christus Dominus (October 28, 1965), 217, 232
Church and State questions, 321, 362, 381-82, 403, 467
Church buildings, handicapped access, 271

Church in the Modern World. see
  *Pastoral Constitution on the
  Church in the Modern World.*
Cities: *Brothers and Sisters to Us,*
  346, 353; *Challenge of Peace,* 521-
  22, 523, 532, 541; crisis in
  housing, 105-6; *Resolution on
  New York City,* 128
Citizenship (political concept), 250,
  317-19
Civil defense, 552
Civilta Catolica, 381
Clark, William P., 303, 306, 541
Class warfare, 393
Cleveland, Ohio, 66
Climate, energy crisis, 448-49
Coal as fuel, 447-49
Code Seal of Approval (motion
  pictures), 60
Cogenerating electricity, 447
Collective guilt, 122
Colleges and universities, 246, 247,
  271, 401-16
Collins, A. S., Jr., 531
Colonialism, 12, 26
Commercial broadcasting industry,
  15
Commission for Catholic Missions
  among the Colored People and
  the Indians, 209
Commission on Marriage and
  Family Life (USCC), 247, 255,
  256, 259
Commitment: Church and the
  political order, 133; energy
  crisis, 444; Plan for family
  ministry, 41; *Promoting Christian
  Unity,* 425, 426; *Teach Them,* 148-
  56
Committee for Ecumenical and
  Interreligious Affairs, 21
Committee for Migration and
  Tourism, 32, 287
Committee of Bishops and Catholic
  College and University
  Presidents, 291
Committee on Conciliation and
  Arbitration (NCCB), 283, 330-41
Committee on Doctrine (NCCB),
  34, 229, 231
Committee on Priestly Formation
  (NCCB), 246
Committee on Social Development
  and World Peace, 19, 31, 284,
  293-99 *passim,* 365

Committee on the Laity (NCCB),
  290
"Committee Statements," 300
Common good, 372, 389, 397, 441,
  482, 488, 490, 513
Communications, regulation of
  communications, 14-15, 56-57
Communism, 211-14, 241-42, 380-
  400, 465, 559
Community: Bicentennial
  consultation, 221, 225; *Called and
  Gifted,* 422; Catholic health care
  facilities, 482; Catholic higher
  education, 412; *Challenge of
  Peace,* 498, 514, 558, 566;
  Community and crime, 324;
  community of believers, 506;
  community building, 117;
  community of nations, 189-90;
  Society and the aged, 143-44;
  support of Catholic schools, 154;
  To Do the Work of Justice, 243-44,
  248-49; young adults, 221
Comparative justice, 518
Compassion: concerning human
  sexuality, 231
Competent authority for war, 517
Competition, 457
Comprehensive Test Ban Treaty,
  545
Concentration in industry, 51, 458-
  61, 477
Conciliation procedures, 283, 330-35
Conciliators, 333-35
Conduct of life, 351
Conference of Major Superiors of
  Men, 35, 232-37, 301
Confirmation (Sacrament), 418-19,
  421
Conflict of rights, 330
Conflict resolution, 552-55, 557
Congregation of the Blessed
  Sacrament, 18
Congress of Delegates of the
  Catholic Universities of the
  World, 403
Connare, William G. (Bp.), 11
Connolly, Thomas A. (Abp.), 31
Conscience: *Challenge of Peace,* 496,
  498, 555; delivery of health care,
  484; *To Live in Christ Jesus,*
  175-76
Conscientious objection to all war,
  525-26

Conscientious objection to military service, 286, 301, 361, 512-13, 516, 518, 555

Conscription for military service, 286, 360-63

Conservation of resources, 51, 438-63

Constitution on the Church in the Modern World. see Pastoral Constitution on the Church in the Modern World.

Constitution on the Sacred Liturgy, 77, 79

Consultation, 3-4, 10-11, 31, 217, 218-26, 232, 332, 333, 443

Consumers: consumerism, 290, 399, 446; domestic food policy, 47-48; television viewing, 58

Contemplative prayer, 570

Contraception, 221, 478

Contracts, fund raising guidelines, 236

Control of handguns, 67

Controversy: Bicentennial consultation, 224; bishops and theologians, 408; Brothers and Sisters to Us, 349-50; capital punishment, 427-28; Central America, 465; Challenge of Peace, 309-11, 315, 517, 529-30, 533-36, 568, 578-80; energy crisis, 294, 442, 453, 456-57; handgun control, 68; Marxist Communism, 387, 396; nuclear power, 450; recombinant DNA, 200-4; Social Security system, 489

Conventional military forces, 534

Conversion of life, 173, 351, 505, 569-70

Cooke, Terence J. (Cardinal), 18, 19, 43, 303

"Cooling off" period, handgun purchases, 67

Cooperation: Challenge of Peace, 563-64; conciliation procedures, 333; energy crisis, 439; Marxist Communism, 383, 397-98; religious education, 151; television self-regulation, 56-58

Correctional institutions, 188-89, 433

Counsel (legal representation), 337

Counter population warfare, 532

"Counterforce policy," 543

Counterrevolution, 517

Courts, capital punishment, 432

"Covenant," 502

Covert military activities, 582-83

"Covert racism," 347

Credit, crisis in housing, 111-12

Crime: El Salvador, 436; excluded from arbitration, 335; handgun violence, 16, 66; Society and the aged, 142; Statement on Capital Punishment, 427-34; To Live in Christ Jesus, 188-89

Crowley, Joseph R. (Bp.), 33

Cruise missiles, 313

Cuba, 378, 465

Cuban refugees, 287

Cultural Pluralism in the United States, 293, 364-76

Culture: Catholic higher education, 402; Marxist Communism, 388; Statement on American Indians, 205

"Curb," 311

Cyprian, Saint, Bishop, 524

Czechoslovakia, 212

Daley, Joseph (Bp.), 450

Day, Dorothy, 524

De facto war, 517

Deacons, 220, 246, 264, 572

Dearden, John F. (Cardinal), 24

Death penalty. see Capital punishment.

"Death with Dignity," 81

Decentralization of industry, 460

Declaration on Christian Education, 160, 162

Declaration on Conscientious Objection. . .(October 21, 1971), 192

Declaration on Religious Freedom, 175, 176

Declaration on Sexual Ethics, 29, 34

Declaration on the Question of the Admission of Women to the Ministerial Priesthood, 200

"Declaratory policy," 537, 538, 543

Decree on Ecumenism, 78

Decree on the Apostolate of the Laity, 290, 418, 420, 421

Decree on the Church's Missionary Activity, 348

Decree on the Ministry and Life of Priests, 79, 80

Decree on the Missionary Activity of the Church, 206
Defense, right of. see Self-defense, right of.
Defense industries, 575
Democracy, 530, 560, 578
Democratic Party of the U.S., 158
Denmark, 553
Department of Education (USCC), 26, 36, 155-56, 254, 259
Department of Social Development and World Peace (USCC), 12, 47-53, 247, 254
Destabilization of governments, 582-83
Destabilizing weapons systems, 544
Detachment (spiritual detachment), 566
Detente, 561
Deterrence of crime, 428-29
Deterrence of war, 303, 304, 310, 314, 316, 526, 529, 534, 536-40, 541-46, 575
"Developing" families, 248, 262
Development of nations, 44, 70, 355, 399, 445, 564
Development of Peoples. see *Populorum Progressio*.
Dialogue: Bicentennial consultation, 215-16; *Called and Gifted*, 418; Catholic-Jewish relations, 22, 120, 124; *Challenge of Peace*, 309, 560-61; election dialogue, 157; family ministry, 256; Marxist and Christian humanism, 384-87, 395, 398-99; political responsibility, 146-47; pro-life plan, 82-83; Promoting Christian unity, 424-26; school aid questions, 25; television industry, 57-58
Dignity of human being, 143, 165, 319-20, 430, 437, 472, 488, 510, 574
DiLorenzo, Francis, 28
Dingman, Maurice J. (Bp.), 24, 35
Dioceses: Bicentennial consultation, 225; Call to Action programs, 244; *Called and Gifted*, 421; Catholic-Jewish dialogue, 121, 124-25; crisis in housing, 116; family ministries, 259, 260; fund raising guidelines, 35, 232-37; handicapped persons, 273-74; health care, 475; *Let the Little*

Children Come to Me, 162; Plan for family ministry, 41; pro-life plan, 82-83, 88; Society and the aged, 144; *Statement on the American Indian*, 209; *Teach Them*, 155; *To Do the Work of Justice*, 247, 248, 250
Diplomacy, 561, 562, 582
Diplomatic immunities and protections, 286-87, 357
Disabled, 41-42, 269
Disarmament, 37-38, 239, 304, 313, 323, 527, 539, 540, 543, 548, 564, 577
Discipleship, 566-67
"Discriminating weapons," 542
Discrimination: Bicentennial consultation, 218-19; *Brothers and Sisters to Us*, 284-85, 343; capital punishment, 323-24, 432; Choices for the 1980s, 327; crisis in housing, 106-7; handicapped persons, 274; *Religious Liberty in Eastern Europe*, 211-14; sexism, 252, 256; Society and the aged, 140, 141, 142; *To Live in Christ Jesus*, 186-87; women in society, 185-86
Discrimination and Christian Conscience (1958), 342
Disinvestment, 106
Displaced persons. see Refugees.
Distribution of energy, 456-61
Diversity, 219, 293, 364-76
Dives in Misericordia, 442
Divini Redemptoris, 391, 394, 400
Divorce, 222, 263
DNA research, 33, 200-4
Doctrine, 495
Documentation on the Right to Life and Abortion (1974), 134
Dogmatic Constitution on the Church, 78, 176, 206, 216, 217, 238, 239, 348, 364, 370, 372, 375, 381, 396, 408, 420
Doherty, Edward, 301
Domestic food policy, 47-53
Dominguez, Jorge I., 297
Donnellan, Thomas A. (Abp.), 24, 35
Donohoe, Hugh A. (Bp.), 20, 35
Donor's rights, fund raising guidelines, 233-37
Dostoevsky, Fedor, 432
Dougherty, John J. (Bp.), 33

Draft. see Conscription for military service.
Drell, Sidney, 308
"Due process," 330
Dupre, Louis, 288

"E Pluribus Unum" (motto), 330
Eastern Europe, 30, 211-14, 380, 382, 560
Eastern Orthodox Churches, 369
Eastern Rite Catholic Churches, 369, 374
East-West questions, 398, 562
Ecclesiae Sanctae (1966), 232, 234
Ecclesial community, 270
Ecclesial ministerial services, 420, 421
Ecclesiam Suam, 390, 396, 400
Ecclesiastical goods, 336
Ecclesiology, 498
Ecological problems, 449
Economic assistance, 437, 467
Economics: Brothers and Sisters to Us, 342-43; Catholic higher education, 410; crisis in housing, 99-110 passim; food policy, 12-13; human dimensions, 20, 92-98, 134, 187, 324; Marxist Communism, 383, 389, 398-99; Panama Canal, 12; recession, 1; Reflections on the Energy Crisis, 438-63; Social Security system, 487-89; Statement on Central America, 298; To Do the Work of Justice, 250-51
Ecumenical Council. see Vatican Council II.
Ecumenism, 82-83, 287, 414
Education: adult education, 29; Bicentennial consultation, 224, 225; Catholic higher education, 401-16; Catholic schools, 25; Challenge of Peace, 555, 567-68, 576; child nutrition programs, 49; Choices for the 1980s, 324-25; cultural pluralism, 374; economic justice, 20-21; education for justice, 243, 245-47, 410; energy crisis, 462; family education, 160; family ministry, 259; handicapped persons, 274; health care, 476-77; Humanae Vitae, 222; Let the Little Children Come to Me, 26;

natural family planning, 21; nutrition education, 50; pro-life plan, 83-84; Reflections on an election year, 134; Society and the aged, 144; Statement on Capital Punishment, 292; Teach Them, 148
Education for All Handicapped Children Act of 1975, 274
Egypt, 278-79
Elderly. see Aged.
Elizabeth Seton, Saint, 148, 156
El Salvador, 293, 295, 297, 298, 436-37, 464, 466, 582
Emission standards, 449
Emmanuel (publication), 18
Empirical studies, 229, 428-29
Employment: Brothers and Sisters to Us, 284, 345, 353; Choices for the 1980s, 324; crisis in housing, 108; domestic food policy, 48; energy crisis, 460; Human dimensions of the economy, 92, 94-95, 96; To Live in Christ Jesus, 187; U.S.-Panama relations, 165
Encuentro Pastoral, 244
Endowment of higher education, 416
Ends and means, 522
Energy crisis, 438-63
"Energy farms," 455
Energy stamps, 456
Engels, Friedrich, 387
Entertainment industry, 54-65
Equality, 1-2, 142, 185-86, 284, 344, 352, 353
Eschatology, 391-93, 500, 502-3
Essential services, 458
Estrangement. see Alienation.
Ethical and Religious Directives for Catholic Health Facilities, 19, 296, 379, 479
Ethics, 409
Ethnic groups, 107, 124, 186-87, 219, 293, 367-73
"Ethnocentrism," 368
Eucharist and the Hungers of the Human Heart, 2, 17-18, 77-80
Eucharistic Congresses, 2, 17-18, 29, 30, 77, 196
Eurocommunism, 397
Europe, 380, 382, 534, 551, 559, 561
Euthanasia, 81, 84, 139-40, 144, 365, 371

Evaluative Criteria for Catholic Health Care Facilities, 477

Evangelii Nuntiandi, 190, 405, 406, 468

Evangelization, 4, 31, 205-6, 266, 273, 343, 371

Evidence, arbitration procedures, 338

Exhortation on Evangelization in the Modern World, 31

"Existential conditions," 390

Expenses, arbitration procedures, 340

Exports and imports, 14

Extreme Unction. see Anointing of the Sick.

Faith, 407, 408, 412

Families: *Brothers and Sisters to Us*, 345, 354; *Called and Gifted*, 422; Choices for the 1980s, 325; cultural pluralism, 374; domestic food policy, 49; early childhood development, 26; *Economy: Human Dimensions*, 95; Family farm, 326; handgun violence, 66-67; health care, 473-74; *Let the Little Children Come to Me*, 159-63; migration and families, 168; Plan of Pastoral action for family ministry, 40, 41; Society and the aged, 138, 143; Statement on handicapped persons, 270-71; television viewing, 14, 54-65; *To Do the Work of Justice*, 247-48; *To Live in Christ Jesus*, 178-80, 183

Family-centered ministry, 265

Family ministry, 219-20, 255-66

"Family Year" (proposed), 220, 248, 259, 261

Farms and farming, 13, 21, 48-53, 70-71, 108, 126

Fasting, 502

FBI Crime Reports, 66

Fidelity, 502

Financial reports, fund raising guidelines, 235

Finkelstein, Lydia, 5

Firearms deaths, 66

"First strike," 536, 544

Fission fuel cycle, 450

Flanagan, Bernard J. (Bp.), 43

Florida, 292, 427

Food Day (April 17, 1975), 12

Food for Peace Program, 13

Food policy and supply: Choices for the 1980s, 325; feeding the hungry, 47-53; *Food Policy and the Church*, 13-14, 69-73, 135; *Food Policy and the Church: Specific Proposals*, 325; Food Stamp program, 13, 47, 71, 141-42, 145, 456; Reflections on an election year, 135; Society and the aged, 141-42; *Statement on Central America*, 468; *To Do the Work of Justice*, 253

Ford, Gerald R. (President), 24, 157-58

Foreign Affairs (quarterly journal), 531, 533

Foreign aid, 70, 325

Forgiveness of sin, 429-30

France, 242, 289

Franchise. see Voting.

Francis, Joseph A. (Bp.), 41, 284

Francis of Assisi, Saint, 524

Freedom: *Brothers and Sisters to Us*, 350; *Challenge of Peace*, 515, 560, 578, 580; Choices for the 1980s, 321; cultural pluralism, 372; Eastern Europe, 30, 211-14; El Salvador, 466; free speech, 61; handgun violence, 67; hunger for freedom, 79; Marxist Communism, 382; Nicaragua, 467; recombinant DNA, 202; registration and conscription, 362; *Statement on American Indians*, 206-7; UN and South Africa, 74

Freeze on nuclear weapons development, 309

Friendship, 413

Fuel shortages, 438, 456-57

Fulcher, George (Bp.), 301

Fund raising, 35, 232-37

Furman *vs*. Georgia (1972), 427

Future (the future), 9, 391-93, 441

Gallagher, Raymond (Bp.), 23

Gallen, Alice, 291

Gandhi, Mahatma, 524

Gas (natural gas), 438, 439, 445, 452

Gasification of synfuel, 452, 453

Gaudium et Spes. see *Dogmatic Constitution on the Church*.

Gaughan, Norbert (Bp.), 286

General Catechetical Directory (1972), 36, 160, 161

Genetic engineering, 33, 200-4
Georgia, 292
Geothermal energy, 451
Gerety, Peter (Abp.), 23, 24
Germans in the U.S., 369
Germany (Federal Republic), 211
God: *Challenge of Peace*, 497, 499,
  500, 501, 503, 570; *Eucharist and
  the Hungers of the Human Family*,
  78; Marxist Communism, 386;
  presence of God, 258
God the Father, 171
"God's Hope in a Time of Fear,"
  301
God's people, 248
"Good Samaritan" (phrase), 376
*Gospel of Peace and the Danger of
  War*, 37, 238-40, 323
Gospel values, 132
Gossman, F. Joseph (Bp.), 289
Government: health care, 483;
  housing activity; 110-13; *To Live
  in Christ Jesus*, 194
Grace, 172-73
Gracida, Rene (Bp.), 36
Grain reserve, 70
Greeley, Andrew M., 25
Green, Francis (Bp.), 22
Grievance procedures, 330
Guaranteed adequate income, 13
Guatemala, 297, 298, 467
Guidance counseling, 162
Guidelines for Catholic-Jewish Relations
  (1967), 120
Guidelines for fund raising, 35
Guilfoyle, George (Bp.), 24, 283,
  288, 295
Guilt, collective guilt, 122
Gumbleton, Thomas J. (Bp.), 301,
  311
Guns, handgun violence, 16, 66-68

Haiti, 378
Haitian refugees, 32, 198-99, 287,
  378
"Halt," 311
Handguns, 16, 66-68
Handicapped, 1, 41-42, 109, 252,
  267-75
Hannan, Philip (Abp.), 19, 22, 23,
  24, 287, 303, 304-5, 307
Head, Edward D. (Bp.), 43, 284,
  285, 292, 296, 313
Healing, 470

Health and health care, 295, 296,
  469-85
Health care, 19, 84, 141, 295-96,
  326, 449, 469-85
Health insurance, 326, 484-85
Hearings, arbitration procedures,
  339
Heating fuels, 459
Hehir, Bryan, 43, 301
"Hellish cycle of poverty," 152
Helsinki agreements, 30, 213, 552
Hickey, James A. (Abp.), 298, 312,
  582
"Hidden Elderly," 143
Higher education. see Colleges and
  universities.
Hispanic persons in the U.S., 244,
  249-50, 366
History and historiography, 374,
  383, 394, 499, 508-10, 556
Hölderlin, Friedrich, 385
Holiness. see Sanctification.
Holy Places (Middle East), 42
Holy Spirit, 171, 258, 417-18, 421
Home health care, 473, 481
Home-School contacts, 153
Homogeneity of population, 367
Homosexuals and homosexuality,
  29, 222
Honduras, 583
Hope (virtue), 583
Hopkins, Gerard Manley, S.J., 364
Horizontal proliferation of nuclear
  weapons, 549
Hospices, 481
Hospitals, 144, 379, 474, 475, 477
Hostages crisis in Iran, 357, 377,
  435
Housing: *Brothers and Sisters to Us*,
  345; crisis in housing, 19-20;
  Reflections on an election year,
  135; *Right to a Decent Home*, 99-
  119; Society and the aged, 141,
  142, 144, 145; *To Live in Christ
  Jesus*, 187-88
Human dimensions of economy,
  92-98
Human Life Amendment, 88
Human Life Foundation, 21, 127
Human Life in Our Day, 361, 525,
  578
Human person [individual]:
  Brothers and Sisters to Us, 350;
  capital punishment, 430; health
  care, 573; Marxist Communism,

386, 391; *To Live in Christ Jesus*, 178, 184, 189

Human rights: *Challenge of Peace*, 550, 565, 575; Choices for the 1980s, 320, 326-27; Church and the political order, 131; conciliation and arbitration, 330; Haitian refugees, 199; health care, 483; Marxist Communism, 289, 380, 395; pro-life plans, 82-83; Reflections on an election year, 135-36; *Religious Liberty in Eastern Europe*, 211-14; Society and the aged, 139-42; South Africa, 16-17; *To Do the Work of Justice*, 251-53; *To Live in Christ Jesus*, 193

Human rights/human needs—An unfinished agenda, 251

Human Sexuality, 34, 228

Humanae Vitae, 222, 230, 231

Humanism, 384, 405

Humanity. see Man (mankind).

Hungary, 382

Hunger, 1, 13, 14, 29, 47-48, 69, 78-79, 253

Hunger for the Spirit, 79

Hunthausen, Raymond G. (Abp.), 303, 304

Hurley, Denis E. (Abp.), 491

Hurley, Mark J. (Bp.), 18-19, 41, 43, 296, 297, 298

"Hurting families," 263

Hyde, Henry, 309

Hydroelectric facilities, 453

Hyer, Marjorie, 306

Identity of Catholic Institutions, 404, 411-12, 477

Ideology, 289, 290, 313, 383, 386, 394, 397-98, 514-15, 559, 561

"Idolatry," 304

Immigration/Emigration, 27, 38, 167-69, 198-99, 241-42, 366, 376, 378

Imports/Exports, 445, 446, 458, 549

Income: Armed Forces, 575; *Brothers and Sisters to Us*, 346; crisis in housing, 99-100, 103, 111; domestic food policy, 13, 48; *Economy: Human Dimensions*, 95, 96; energy crisis, 443, 457; housing for elderly, 24; Social Security system, 488; Society and the aged, 140, 141, 144-45

Indians. see American Indians.

Indifference, 342, 347, 392

Indirect casualties in warfare, 541

Individualism, 318, 399

Industrial relations, 21, 126, 481, 490

Inferiority/Superiority, 344

Inflation, 95-96, 103-4, 128

Initiation of nuclear war, 533-34

Innocent lives in warfare, 521

Institutional health care, 473-74

Insulation and weatherization, 447, 458

Insurance, 295, 296, 326, 484-85, 488, 490

Intention in war, 518

Intentional communities, 422

Inter-American Bishops Meeting in Costa Rica (May 1981), 297

Interdependence, 16-17, 422, 557-58, 562-65

Interest rates, 23-24, 105, 112

Interior peace, 568

Intermediate-range nuclear forces, 544

International Court of Justice, 74

International Eucharistic Congress (Philadelphia, 1976), 17, 31, 77

International Fund for Agricultural Development, 70

International organizations, 519, 579

International relations, 1, 16-17, 42, 47, 70, 75-76, 92, 164, 192-93, 213, 238-40, 241-42, 276-79, 299, 327-28, 354, 356, 357, 360, 377, 411, 435, 439, 459, 493-581

International Theological Commission, 228

International trade, Panama Canal, 45

Interreligious Coalition for Housing, 114

Iran, 285-86, 287, 357, 377, 435

Irish in the U.S., 369

Iron Curtain Countries. see Eastern Europe.

Islam, 430

Israel (ancient Israel), 501-2

Israel, 11, 22, 124, 277, 278-79

Italians in the U.S., 369

Italy, 288, 289

Japan, 527

Jerusalem, 268

Jesus Christ, 2, 33, 78, 80, 122, 148, 344, 417-18, 431, 470, 478, 503-7, 570, 580

Jesus of Nazareth (television dramatization), 227

Jewish-Catholic relations, 1, 120-25

"Jewishness" of Catholic heritage, 122-23

Jews in U.S., 11, 21, 124

Jobs. see Employment.

John Neumann, Saint, 35, 148, 229, 231

John XXIII, Pope, 44, 94, 101, 132, 139, 164, 165, 189, 252, 268-69, 321, 322, 383, 389, 396, 397, 398, 442, 444, 472, 488, 498, 540, 557, 579

John of the Cross, Saint, 195

John Paul II, Pope, 2, 286, 289, 304, 305, 319, 322, 328, 343, 344, 348, 350, 356, 357, 358-59, 365, 372, 388, 394, 401-15 *passim*, 424, 425, 426, 439-40, 441, 446, 462, 468, 472, 478, 480, 481-82, 485, 493, 494, 496, 508, 514-15, 519, 520-21, 522, 526, 527, 536, 539, 540, 543, 547, 548, 550, 552, 554, 557, 559, 560, 562, 563, 566, 568, 573, 576, 577

John the Baptist, Saint, 268

Jones, Arthur, 307

Journal of Conflict Resolution, 301

Judaism, 120-25, 392, 430

Judeo-Christian values, 405

Judgment, 446, 495

Jus ad bellum, 516, 517-20

Jus in bello, 520-23

Just cause for war, 517

"Just war," 306, 310, 515-16, 517, 525, 555

Justice: *Brothers and Sisters to Us*, 284-85, 342-55; Catholic higher education, 410; *Challenge of Peace*, 509, 513-14, 518, 568; conciliation and arbitration, 330; domestic food policy, 52; education for justice, 151, 222-23; *Gospel of Peace and the Danger of War*, 37; health care, 471-72, 480; Human dimensions of economy, 20, 92-98; hunger for justice, 79; Marxist Communism, 393; *Panama-U.S. Relations*, 44, 165; Social Security system, 490; *Statement on*

American Indians, 206, 207; *To Do the Work of Justice*, 243-54; *To Live in Christ Jesus*, 190-91

Justice in the World (1971 Synod), 117, 217, 444

Justin Martyr, Saint, 523

Kelly, Thomas, O.P. (Bp.), 292, 295, 297, 315

Kennan, George F., 307

Kennedy, John Fitzgerald (President), 140

Kennedy, Robert T., 284

Kenney, V. Paul, 438, 450

Khrushchev, Nikita, 549

King, Martin Luther, 524

Kingdom of God, 232, 392, 418, 423, 498, 499, 500, 504, 505, 508-25 *passim*, 529, 547, 570

Kinney, John F. (Bp.), 283

Kissinger, Henry, 44-46

Knowledge, 202, 536

Kolakowski, Leszek, 394

Kosnick, Anthony, 29

Krol, John (Cardinal), 9, 18-19, 21-22, 25, 27, 28, 29, 30, 36, 38, 39, 196-97, 289, 299, 301, 303, 304, 306, 311, 315, 538, 539

Ku Klux Klan, 285

Labor. see Work.

Labor relations. see Industrial relations.

Laborem Exercens, 481-82, 485

Laity: *Called and Gifted*, 289, 417-23; Catholic higher education, 407, 416; *Choices for the 1980s*, 322; The Church and the political order, 133

Land use, 51, 109-10

Landlords, 114

Landsberg, Hans H., 448

Language and Liturgy, 369

Language problems, 142

Laos, 241-42

Last resort (war as last resort), 519

Latin America, 168, 288, 289

Law, Bernard (Bp.), 300

Law: *Brothers and Sisters to Us*, 342, 345; Catholic schools, 155; *Challenge of Peace*, 577; conscientious objection, 362; *Pastoral Plan for Pro-life Activities*, 81, 86-91; *Statement on Capital*

Punishment, 292, 427-34; *To Live in Christ Jesus*, 186
Law enforcement, 66-68
Lay persons. see Laity.
Laying on of hands, 471
Leadership: *Called and Gifted*, 418; *Challenge of Peace*, 529-30; family ministry, 260; leadership couples, 263; leadership families, 263; *Statement on American Indians*, 210
Leadership Conference of Women Religious, 35, 232-37, 301
"League of Nations" neighborhoods, 373
Leased housing programs, 112
Lebanon, 43, 277-78
Legare, Henri (Abp.), 313-14
Legislation. see Law.
Legitimacy of government, 517
Legitimate self-defense, 511, 536
Lenin, V. I., 383, 387
Leo XIII, Pope, 382, 389, 393
Lessard, Raymond W. (Bp.), 312-13
Let the Little Children Come to Me, 2, 26, 159-63
Liberal arts, 405
Liberalism (economic school), 382, 399
Liberation. see Freedom.
Liberty. see Freedom.
"Liberty and Justice for All" (1977), 243
Life: Bicentennial consultation, 223; capital punishment, 251, 429, 430; *Challenge of Peace*, 497, 556, 568, 571; energy crisis, 440; handicapped persons, 269; Human Life Foundation, 127; pro-life activities, 81-91, 294; recombinant DNA, 200-4; sanctity of human life, 157; Society and the aged, 139-40; *To Do the Work of Justice*, 251; *To Live in Christ Jesus*, 184
Lifestyle, 289, 290, 400, 446
Like-to-Like ministry, 258
"Limited nuclear wars," 531
"Limited wars," 515-16, 551
Liquefaction of synfuels, 452, 453
Lithuania, 212, 380
Liturgy: *Brothers and Sisters to Us*, 353; *Called and Gifted*, 419; *Eucharist and the Hungers of the*

Human Family, 77; handicapped persons, 270-72
"Living endowment" of religious and clergy, 416
"Living room dialogues," 120
Loans: New York City fiscal crisis, 128; Section 202 programs, 23, 24
Lobbying, 89, 144
Local church, 509
Local resolution of disputes, 331
Lohmuller, Martin N. (Bp.), 30
Long-term health care facilities, 476
Losten, Basil (Eparch), 288
Love: Church and the political order, 130-31; handicapped people, 267-68; Marxist Communism, 393; on *Human Sexuality*, 34-35; Reflections on an election year, 137; *To Live in Christ Jesus*, 170-71
Lumen Gentium. see *Dogmatic Constitution on the Church*.
Lutheran Church, 491
Lyons, Thomas W. (Bp.), 40, 41

Magisterium, 157-58: Bicentennial consultation, 226-28; bishops and theologians, 408; *Challenge of Peace*, 302, 307, 495; economic justice, 93-94, 250; *National Catechetical Directory*, 36; on *Human Sexuality*, 228; *Pastoral Letter on Marxist Communism*, 289; *To Live in Christ Jesus*, 176-77
Maguire, John J. (Abp.), 39
Maher, Leo (Bp.), 30
Mahony, Robert M. (Bp.), 285
Malnutrition, 48, 69
Malone, James W. (Bp.), 300
Man (mankind), 364, 387
Management techniques, fund raising, 235-36
Mandates of United Nations, 74
Manhood (maleness), 140
Manning, Timothy (Cardinal), 28
Manual of Accounting (NCCB), 35
Marchais, George, 382, 385, 395-96
"Marginal people," 270
Market economy, 457
Marriage, 29, 34, 220, 221-22, 230, 335
Marshall Plan, 563
Martin of Tours, Saint, 524

Marxism, 287-88, 380-400
Mary, Blessed Virgin Mary, 185, 570
Maryland, 367
Mass (Holy Sacrifice), 570
Mass media. see Media.
Mater et Magistra (encyclical), 94, 389, 443, 444
Materialism, 289, 383, 396, 399-400
Maturity, 418
McCarrick, Theodore (Bp.), 298
McCarthy, Edward (Abp.), 287, 290
McCourt, Kathleen, 25
McCready, William C., 25
McDowell, John (Bp.), 28
McFarland, Norman F. (Bp.), 35
McGrath, Marcos (Abp.), 12, 27, 45
McManus, William (Bp.), 26, 36, 300
McNamara, Robert S., 308
McNicholas, Joseph (Bp.), 19, 20, 24, 30, 31, 32, 36, 285, 288, 289
Media (mass media), 3, 136, 327, 374, 576-77
Medicare, 141, 145
Medicine, 139-40, 141, 269, 469-85, 527-28, 532
"Melting pot," 367
Mental health care, 141
Mercy, 471-72
Mercy killing. see Euthanasia.
Messiah, 503
Methodists, 306, 315
Metropolitan areas, crisis in housing, 112
Mexico, 27, 168
Middle East, 11, 22, 42, 276-79, 327-28
Middle East: The Pursuit of Peace with Justice, 328
Migration, 108, 167-69, 244
Military assistance, 295, 466
Military service, 2, 192, 286, 360-63, 504, 512-13, 524, 573
Military targets, 523
Milk programs in the schools, 13, 50, 71
Mining, 448
Ministry: broken marriages, 222; *Called and Gifted*, 420-22; campus ministry, 411-12; Catholic higher education, 401-16; cultural pluralism, 369; educational ministry, 148-49; episcopal ministry, 300; healing ministry,

470; "housing ministry," 116; social ministry, 246; *Statement on Handicapped Persons*, 268; *To Do the Work of Justice*, 249-50; see also Family ministry.
Minorities: Bicentennial consultation, 219; *Brothers and Sisters to Us*, 284, 344, 345, 346, 349, 353; Catholic higher education, 410; family ministries, 257, 264; *Statement on American Indians*, 208
Mission Statement, 299
"Missions" (term), 299
Missions and missionaries, 205, 421, 464
Monopoly, domestic food policy, 51
"Moral about-face," 579
Moral Majority, 315
Morality: arms race, 301; *Brothers and Sisters to Us*, 285; *Challenge of Peace*, 302, 307, 308, 310, 312, 313, 314, 495-96, 498, 510, 526, 528, 529, 530-31, 533, 535, 537-40, 541-46, 550, 556-58, 567, 575, 579; Choices for the 1980s, 320, 325; Church and the political order, 131-32, 158; Directives for Catholic health facilities, 19; energy crisis, 294, 439, 444, 452, 462; *Gospel of Peace and the Danger of War*, 239; health care, 296; homosexuality, 222; housing crisis, 20, 114-16; Human dimensions of economy, 377; Iranian hostages crisis, 377; Marxist Communism, 393-94; medical-moral issues, 478-79; moral values in U.S., 10; Panama Canal, 12, 26, 164; pro-life plan, 84-85; recombinant DNA, 33, 200; registration and conscription, 360-63; Social Security system, 300; *Statement on Human Sexuality*, 34-35, 228-31; television industry, 59-60; terrorism, 285-86; *To Live in Christ Jesus*, 28, 170-95; Tubal ligation, 379; UN and South Africa, 76
Mortgages, 111-12
Mothers/Motherhood, 50, 85
Motion picture industry, 59-62
Mugavero, Francis (Bp.), 21, 28
Multifamily housing units, 103

Municipal governments, 113, 128
Murder, 429
Murphy, John, 291
MX missiles, 544

Namibia, 13, 74, 491-92
National Advisory Committee on
    Ministry to the Handicapped,
    252
National Advisory Council to
    NCCB/USCC, 290
National Association of
    Broadcasters, 15, 64
National Broadcasting Company,
    227
National Catechetical Directory, 10,
    36, 246, 259
National Catholic Educational
    Association, 151, 291
National Catholic Reporter, 307, 315
National Catholic Rural Life
    Conference, 13, 20, 115
National Catholic Welfare
    Conference, 360
National Commission on Economic
    Justice, 251
National Conference of Catholic
    Bishops, 3, 9, 11, 21, 38-39, 40,
    82, 196-97, 232-37, 275, 305, 486
National Conference of Catholic
    Charities, 115, 296, 474, 483
National Congress of Church-
    Related Colleges and
    Universities, 402
National Council of Churches, 314
National Crisis (April 25, 1968), 186
National Firearms Policy, 67-68
National health insurance, 295, 296,
    326, 484-85
National Health Insurance (1974), 326
National Health Policy, 483
National Housing and Human
    Development Alliance, 116
National Housing Goal, 102-3
National Opinion Research Center,
    25, 151-52
National Parishes, 368-69
"National priorities," 223
National Race Crisis (1968), 342
National Safety Council, 66
National School Lunch Program,
    13, 49
Nationalism, 55-56, 529
Native Americans. see American
    Indians.

"Nativism," 368, 373
Natural family planning, 21, 127
Natural law, 230, 331, 395, 512
Natural resources, 44, 51
Nazism, 285
NCCB/USCC Mission Statement, 486
Negroes. see Blacks.
Neighborhoods, 105-6, 118, 188,
    210, 219, 354, 373
Networks (TV networks), 14, 54-65
Neumann, John. see John
    Neumann, Saint.
New Jersey, 4
"New moment," 302, 304, 525, 527-
    29, 530
New York City, 128
New York Times, 293, 303, 308
Newman, John Henry (Cardinal),
    128
News media, 3
Nicaragua, 297, 298, 466-67, 582-83
"No first use policy," 534, 546
No to Violence, Yes to Peace (January
    1, 1978), 238
Nolan, Hugh J., 2, 3-5
Noncombatants, 522, 523, 532, 541
Noncompliance, 553
Noncooperation, 553
"Non-inclusive language," 289
Nonresistance, 310
Nonviolence, 310, 513, 523-25, 530-
    31, 552-55
North Atlantic Treaty Organization
    (NATO), 533, 534, 551, 560
Norway, 553
Nostra Aetate (1965), 21, 120-25
Nuclear energy, 451
Nuclear fission, 449-51
Nuclear Non-Proliferation Treaty of
    1968 (NPT), 549
Nuclear proliferation, 549, 550
Nuclear weapons, 4, 29, 192, 239,
    302, 304, 309, 311, 312, 493-581
Nursing homes, 141
Nutrition, 13, 48, 69, 141-42

Oaths, 338
Obscenity, 56
Obstetrics/Gynecology, 85, 269, 379
O'Connor, John (Bp.), 298, 301, 311
Octogesima Adveniens, 383
Office of Social Development, 292
Office of Social Development and
    World Peace (USCC), 246
Oil supplies, 438, 439, 445, 452

Old people. see Aged.
"Old-Old," 140
O'Leary, John F., 457
On Poverty and Race Relations
(November 1966), 107
On the Pastoral Care of Migrants
(Motu proprio), 167, 168
One-parent families. see Single-
parent families.
Openness, 397, 425
Operation Faith Sharing, 30
Operation Rice Bowl, 29, 253
Operation Sign (volunteer
program), 30
Oppression, 346, 372, 395, 553, 559
O'Rourke, Edward, 285-86
Orthodox Churches, 369
Orwell, George, 432
Ostpolitik, 382
Ottenweller, Albert (Bp.), 290
Outreach programs in health care,
474
Ownership of land, 51

Pacem in Terris. see *Peace on Earth*.
Pacifism, 523-25, 553, 556
Paenitemini (February 17, 1966), 173
Palestine, 11, 277, 279
Panama, 11-12, 26, 44-46, 164-66
Parents: as educators, 22, 26, 62;
    Catholic higher education, 415;
    Challenge of Peace, 573; family
    ministry, 262; *Let the Little
    Children Come to Me*, 159-63;
    Society and the aged, 138, 143
Parishes, 29, 35, 40, 82-83, 88-89,
    106, 114, 115-16, 118, 143, 149,
    162, 224-25, 232-37, 244, 249,
    261, 262, 263-64, 265, 271-73,
    368-69, 412, 421, 422, 462, 474-75
Partial test ban treaty, 549
Participation in decision-making,
    443, 451, 481, 484
Participation in public affairs, 22-23,
    129-30, 319
Participation in the Liturgy, 271,
    420
Participation in war, 361
Pastoral care, 84-86, 100-1
*Pastoral Constitution on the Church in
    the Modern World*, 21, 81, 101,
    102, 127, 132, 177, 184, 203, 230,
    321, 350, 417, 422, 440, 442, 495,
    496, 497, 509, 511, 514, 521-22,
    524, 525, 532, 537, 553

*Pastoral Letter on Marxist
    Communism*, 1, 287-88, 380-400,
    558
"Pastoral letters" (term), 3, 289
*Pastoral Letters of the U.S. Catholic
    Bishops*, 1-2, 3-5
Pastoral Plan for Pro-Life Activities,
    18, 19, 134, 185, 323
*Pastoral Statement on Handicapped
    Persons*, 267-75
Pastoral theology, 35, 40, 228, 230,
    425, 478
Pastoralis Migratorum, 198
Pastoralis Migratorum Cura (Paul VI),
    242
Pastors, 154
Patients in health care facilities,
    477-78
Patriarchs of the Old Testament,
    124
Patriotism, 578
Paul, Saint, Apostle, 122-24
Paul VI, Pope, 1, 17, 20, 31, 35, 37,
    52, 53, 76, 101, 109-10, 117, 133,
    152, 156, 167, 206, 211, 222, 229,
    231, 232, 238, 242, 266, 289, 319,
    322, 360, 371, 382, 389, 390, 396,
    400, 405, 406, 410, 444, 461, 468,
    508, 519, 527, 556, 559, 564, 569,
    579
Pawlikowski, John T., O.S.M., 439
"Peace," (term), 500, 510, 547
Peace Academy (proposed), 554
Peace and war: *Brothers and Sisters
    to Us*, 352; *Challenge of Peace*, 2,
    304-16, 490-581; El Salvador,
    466; *Gospel of Peace and the
    Danger of War*, 40, 238-40;
    Iranian hostage crisis, 286-87;
    Marxist Communism, 398;
    Middle East, 276-77; Namibia,
    491; "Peace is justice," 1;
    registration and conscription,
    360; *To Live in Christ Jesus*, 191-
    93; UN and South Africa, 75
"Peace of a sort," 538, 540
Peace on Earth (encyclical), 132, 139,
    164, 239, 252, 268-69, 383, 396,
    397, 398, 444, 472, 488, 540, 556-
    57, 559, 579
Pediatrics, 269
Pellegrino, Edmund D., 291
Penance (sacrament), 86, 571
Pennsylvania, 4
Pentecost, 364-65

"People of God," 216, 417, 420-21, 507
Pershing II missiles, 544
"Personalized learning," 153
Person[hood], 268-69
Peter, Saint, Apostle, 80
Petroleum. see Oil supply.
Philadelphia, Pa., 17, 18, 29, 30, 77, 196
Philosophy: Catholic higher education, 409; *Pastoral Letter on Marxist Communism*, 288, 289, 396
Photovoltaics, 455
Pilarczyk, Daniel (Bp.), 291, 299, 300
Pius XI, Pope, 156, 382, 389, 391, 394, 399, 400, 444
Pius XII, Pope, 442, 513-14, 516, 532
"Plan of Action" (Call to Action Conference), 225-26
Plan of Pastoral Action for Family Ministry, 40, 255-66, 325
Planning process: *Challenge of Peace*, 544, 574; energy crisis, 440, 455, 457; family ministry, 257-58
"Plea for Disarmament" (*Osservatore Romano* June 1976), 238
Plekhanov, G. V., 387
Pluralism, 107, 205, 207, 277-78, 293, 346, 364-76, 484, 497
Poland, 211, 212, 382, 559
Polarization, 393, 442
Political authority, 557
Political Responsibility (May 6, 1976), 23, 146-47
Political Responsibility: Choices for the 1980s, 283, 483
Politics: Cambodia, 356; *Challenge of Peace*, 308, 558, 560, 562, 565, 567-68, 577; Choices for the 1980s, 317-29; energy crisis, 395; Marxist Communism, 395; Pro-Life plan, 87-91
Pollution of the environment, 448
Pontifical Academy of Sciences, 521, 527, 531-32
Pontifical Mission for Palestine, 278
Poor, the Poor: *Brothers and Sisters to Us*, 350, 353-54; capital punishment, 432; Central America, 468; *Challenge of Peace*, 562-63; Choices for the 1980s,

317-29; crisis in housing, 99-100, 101, 104-5, 106, 107, 108; *Economy: Human Dimensions*, 97; El Salvador, 436; energy crisis, 443, 456; family ministry, 260; food policy, 71; health care, 480; Marxist Communism, 391, 393-94, 398, 399; political responsibility, 283; *Teach Them*, 152; *To Do the Work of Justice*, 250-51
Pope John Paul II Center for Prayer & Study for Peace, 303
Popes/Papacy, 286, 288, 358-59
Popular defense, 553
Populorum Progressio, 109-10, 389, 398, 556, 557
Pornography, 28
Poverty. see Poor, the Poor.
Powerlessness, feelings of powerlessness, 22, 368
Prayer, 419, 569-71
Premarrieds, 261-62
Presbyterian General Assembly, 315
Preschool children, 159-63
Presence of God, 258
Preventive health care, 484
Preventive ministry ("hurting families"), 263
Priests and priesthood, 220, 246, 264, 419, 420, 572, 575
Priests' Eucharistic League, 18
Principles and Guidelines for Fund Raising, 35, 232-37
Prisons, 346, 433
Probability of success in war, 519
Procreative dimension of sexuality, 34, 230
Program for Priestly Formation (1976), 352
Program of Priestly Formation (1976), 374
Pro-Life activities, 18, 81-91, 352
Prometheus (hero), 387
"Prompt hard-target kill," 544
Property, 388
Prophecy, 479-80
Prophets of Old Testament, 124, 502, 505, 571
Proportionality in warfare, 519-22, 542, 549
"Proportionate development in ethics," 409
Prudence, 292
Psychology, 292

Public officials, 577
Public opinion, 81-91, 432, 433, 530
Public policy: Bicentennial
   consultation, 225; *Brothers and
   Sisters to Us*, 347; *Challenge of
   Peace*, 308, 528-29, 577-78;
   Choices for the 1980s, 317-29;
   crisis in public housing, 109-10;
   Economy: Human Dimensions, 96-
   97; handicapped persons, 273-
   74; health care, 482-85; Marxist
   Communism, 397; New York
   City fiscal crisis, 128; *Pastoral
   Plan for Pro-Life Activities*, 86-91;
   political responsibility, 283;
   Social Security system, 487-90;
   Statement on American Indians,
   209-10; *Statement on Capital
   Punishment*, 427-28; U.S. Panama
   relations, 164
Public schools, 25
"Public subscription" (term), 35,
   234
Public utilities, 443
Puebla Conference, 328, 464
Punishment, 428

*Qualities and Competencies of Teaching
   Religion* (1973), 151
Quinn, John R. (Abp.), 30, 39, 42-
   43, 286, 288, 295, 303, 304, 311,
   312

Race relations, 186-87
Racial equality, 1-2, 74
Racism: *Brothers and Sisters to Us*,
   284, 342-55; capital punishment,
   432; energy crisis, 443; *To Do the
   Work of Justice*, 252
Radioactive wastes, 450, 457
"Rating game" (television), 58, 64
Rausch, James S. (Bp.), 16
Reagan, Ronald W. (President),
   295, 297, 303, 306, 541
Recombinant DNA research, 33,
   200-4
Reconciliation: *Challenge of Peace*,
   507; pro-life plan, 85-86; Society
   and the aged, 145
Red Lion (Supreme Court Decision),
   56
Redemptor Hominis, 319, 322, 344,
   388, 439, 441, 472, 566
"Redlining," 106
Referendum elections, 451

*Reform of Correctional Institutions in
   the 1970s*, 189, 433
Refugee Service (USCC), 244
Refugees, 1: Cuban refugees, 287,
   378; cultural pluralism, 376;
   Haitian refugees, 32, 198-99,
   287, 378; Middle East, 277;
   People on the move, 167-69;
   Salvadorean refugees, 466;
   Southeast Asia, 38, 241-42
Regional conflict, 327-28
Registration for military service,
   286, 360-63
Registration of handguns, 16
Rehabilitation Act of 1973, 274
Rehabilitation of criminals, 428,
   431, 433
Rehabilitation of housing, 109
Reilly, Daniel P. (Bp.), 283, 286
Reilly, David (Bp.), 301
*Relations of American Catholic Colleges
   and Universities with the Church*,
   403
"Religion is the opium of the
   people" (Marx), 384
Religious congregations, institutes,
   and orders, 233-37, 415, 475-76
Religious education, 2, 25, 26, 30,
   36, 148, 406-7
Religious liberty. see Freedom.
Religious Liberty in Eastern Europe,
   380
Religious life: *Brothers and Sisters to
   Us*, 351; Catholic higher
   education, 291, 413; Church and
   the political order, 133; cultural
   pluralism, 368-69, 370-71;
   Marxist Communism, 289, 290,
   381, 384, 395-96; *Resolution on the
   Papal Visit*, 358-59; *Teach Them*,
   149; *To Live in Christ Jesus*, 194
Remedial ministry ("hurting
   families"), 263
Reports, fund raising guidelines,
   235
Reproductive organs, 19, 379, 479
Republic of South Africa. see South
   Africa.
Rerum Novarum, 389, 393, 459
Research: Catholic higher
   education, 408, 414; Catholic-
   Jewish dialogue, 125; *Challenge
   of Peace*, 301, 554, 576, 577, 580;
   cultural pluralism, 373, 375;
   education for justice, 246;

energy crisis, 440, 452, 454-55;
family ministry, 256, 264;
handgun violence, 66; Human
Life Foundation, 127; human
sexuality, 34, 228, 229; pro-life
plan, 86; recombinant DNA, 33,
200-4; *Teach Them*, 155
Resettlement of refugees, 378
Resolution on Farm Labor (November
16, 1973), 187
*Resolution on 25th Anniversary of
U.N. Universal Declaration on
Human Rights* (1973), 135-36
"Resolutions" (term), 308
Resor, Stanley, 308
Respect for life, 83, 143
Responsibility: Bicentennial
consultation, 218; bishops and
theologians, 408; *Called and
Gifted*, 421; *Challenge of Peace*,
580; Choices for the 1980s, 317-
29; energy crisis, 440-41; health
care, 296, 472-75, 481, 483;
parents' responsibilities, 160;
personal responsibility, 3-4;
political responsibility, 146-47,
250; sin of racism, 345;
television viewing, 15, 55
Restitution to racial minorities, 346
Resurrection of Christ, 506
Retribution (war of retribution), 517
Retribution for crime, 429
Revolution, 384, 390, 392, 394, 504,
517
Right intention (in war), 518
Right to a Decent Home, 1, 99-119,
135, 188, 326
Rights: *Called and Gifted*, 421; capital
punishment, 431; *Challenge of
Peace*, 511, 550, 565, 574-75;
Church and the political order,
131; handicapped persons, 269,
271-72, 275; health care
employees, 481; human rights,
3, 30, 110; *Religious Liberty in
Eastern Europe*, 211-14; "Right to
eat," 47; Society and the aged,
139-42; *To Do the Work of Justice*,
251-53; *To Live in Christ Jesus*,
193
Rivera y Damas, Arturo (Bp.), 297,
466
Roach, John (Abp.), 24, 35, 39, 293,
297, 301, 315, 583

Romero, Oscar (Abp.), 293, 298,
464, 466
Rosazza, Peter (Bp.), 288
Rother, Stanley, 464
Rural life: crisis in housing, 107,
112; Society and the aged, 142
Ruthenian Rite, 212
Ryan, Joseph (Abp.), 22

Sacraments, 271, 471
Sacred Congregation for the
Doctrine of the Faith, 379
Sacred Congregation of Catholic
Education, 403
Saint Anthony's Messenger, 315
Saints, 390
Salatka, Charles A. (Abp.), 299
SALT agreements (strategic arms),
38, 239, 548, 561
Salvador. see El Salvador.
Sanctification, 216, 419
"Saturday Night Specials"
(handguns), 16, 67
School administration, 154
School Breakfast Program, 49-50
School enrollments, 155, 403
School lunch program, 49
Schools: *Brothers and Sisters to Us*,
284; Catholic-Jewish dialogue,
121; domestic food policy, 49-50;
registration and conscription,
362-63; school aid, 25-26; *Teach
Them*, 148-56
Schurr, Sam H., 438, 445, 454, 460
Science, 33-34, 200-4, 307, 462, 479,
526, 576
Scoville, Herbert, Jr., 308
Screening of television programs,
58
Scripture. see Bible.
Secretariat for Hispanic Affairs,
249-50
Secretariat for Jewish-Catholic
Relations, 21
Secretariat for Promoting Christian
Unity, 287, 424
Secularism, 392, 396
Selective conscientious objection,
286, 301, 361
Selective Service. see Conscription
for military service.
Self-defense, right of self-defense,
37, 191-92, 360-61, 429, 511-15,
552, 555, 568, 569

Self-determination: UN and South Africa, 76, 492; U.S.-Panama relations, 165
Self-fulfillment, 81, 174
Self-regulation of television industry, 15, 57, 64
Seminaries, 246, 352, 374
Sensitivity: *Brothers and Sisters to Us*, 351; cultural pluralism, 367, 374; developing world, 399; military service, 574; *Panama-U.S. Relations*, 46, 165; *Statement on American Indians*, 207; *Statement on Human Sexuality*, 35
Separated marriage partners, 263
Service, 420-21, 480
Seton, Elizabeth. see Elizabeth Seton, Saint.
Sexism, 256
Sexuality, 28, 29, 34, 56, 60, 228-31, 252, 264
Shakespeare, William, 432
Sharing the Light of the Faith, 37, 273, 325
Sheen, Fulton J. (Abp.), 17
Shehan, Lawrence (Cardinal), 17
Short-range nuclear weapons, 545
Short-term health care facilities, 476
Si vis pacem para bellum, 539
Siam. see Thailand.
Sick, Anointing of the sick, 471
Sign of Peace (at Mass), 570
"Signs of the times," 370, 496, 526
Sin: *Challenge of Peace*, 508, 509; energy crisis, 460; Marxist Communism, 387; racism as sin, 285, 344-45, 349; *To Live in Christ Jesus*, 172-73
Single Integrated Operation Plan, 541
Single life (unmarried persons), 261-62
Single-parent families, 162, 256
Slavs in the U.S., 369
Small-boat refugees in Southeast Asia, 241-42
"Social Justice for All (1975-1978)," 7, 280
Social justice issues, 1, 4, 92-98, 113-14, 132, 140, 215-26, 243-54, 292, 293, 320, 384-85, 388-89, 391, 393, 398-99, 410, 420, 430, 441-42, 465, 487-90, 496-97, 562
Social sciences, 576

Social Security system, 140, 144-145, 300, 487-90
Socialism, 287
Socialization, 350
Society: *Brothers and Sisters to Us*, 354; family ministry, 265; *To Live in Christ Jesus*, 183
Society and the Aged: Toward Reconciliation, 23, 138-45, 221, 252
Solar power, 453-55, 460
Solicitation of funds, 35
South Africa (Republic of South Africa), 16, 74-76, 327, 491-92
Southern Command (Panama Canal Zone), 45, 165
Southern Hemisphere needs, 398
Southwest Africa. see Namibia.
Sovereignty, 26, 27, 44, 302, 528, 529
Soviet Union. see Union of Soviet Socialist Republics.
Spain, 45
Special ministers of the Eurcharist, 273
Speculative atheism, 386
Stafford, James Francis (Bp.), 40-41
Start Talks (strategic arms), 544
State governments, 113, 427
Statement on Family Viewing Policy (1975), 136
"Statements" (term), 3, 300
Stelson, Thomas E., 455
Sterilization, 379, 478
Stewardship of goods, 117, 232, 233, 235-37, 441
Strategic weapons systems, 309
Strikes (work stoppages), 126, 482
Strip mining, 448
Structures, family ministry, 258
Students, Catholic schools, 405, 406, 412, 413
Subsidiarity, 245, 331, 444, 460, 483
Suburban life, 346
Success in war, 519
Suffering, 295, 385, 433, 464
Sullivan, John J. (Bp.), 41
Sullivan, Walter (Bp.), 295
Sun Times (Chicago), 308
"Supersession of God" (Marx), 386
Swanstrom, Edward (Bp.), 289
Synod of Bishops (1971), 117, 131, 220, 321
Synod of Bishops (1974), 47, 79, 131, 213

Synthetic oils and gas, 452
Szoka, Edmund C. (Abp.), 311

Tablet (London), 314
Tack, Juan, 44-46
Targeting policy, 310, 537, 541, 543
Tawil, Joseph (Melkite Abp.), 22
Taxation, 45, 111, 142, 325, 457
Teach Them (May 6, 1976), 2, 25,
    148-56
"Teacher Initiated Instructional
    Programs," 153
Teachers/teaching, 4, 9, 19, 131-32,
    148-56, 289, 381, 397, 402, 404,
    411, 415, 470, 495, 498, 527, 556,
    572, 579
Team ministry, 412
Technology: *Challenge of Peace*, 520,
    576; energy crisis, 440, 441, 452,
    453, 454, 456; family ministry,
    264; health care, 477-79;
    recombinant DNA, 201, 203
Teenagers. see Youth.
Television: family viewing policy,
    14, 54-56; *Reflections on an
    Election Year*, 136; *Resolution on
    Jesus of Nazareth*, 33, 227
Temporal ecclesiastical goods, 336
Tenants, 114
Termination date for fund raising
    campaigns, 35
Terrorism, 285-86, 357, 377, 435
Test Ban Treaty, 545
Texas, 292
Textbooks, 210
Thailand, 38, 241
Theology: anti-semitism, 121-22;
    Brothers and Sisters to Us, 285;
    Catholic higher education, 405-
    9; Catholic-Jewish dialogue, 121,
    123, 125; *Challenge of Peace*, 499,
    547, 551, 554, 556, 572; cultural
    pluralism, 370, 375; family
    ministry, 264; *Human Sexuality*,
    34, 228-31; medical-moral issues,
    470; *National Catechetical
    Directory*, 10; Promoting
    Christian unity, 425
"This Land Is Home to Me," 448
Thomas, Cal, 315
Thomas Aquinas, Saint, 516
Thorez, Maurice, 382
Three Mile Island, Pa., 450
Time (magazine), 314
Time zones, 62

To Do the Work of Justice, 243-54, 410
To Live in Christ Jesus, 2, 4, 28, 34,
    39, 170-95, 228, 231, 323, 345,
    538
To Teach as Jesus Did (1972), 25, 134-
    35, 148, 149, 150, 151, 155, 325
"Tolerable," 304
Torrijos, Omar, 12
"Total Christian formation," 151
Total warfare. see Unlimited
    warfare.
Totalitarian regimes, 560
Toward Peace in the Middle East, 276-
    77
Tradition, 9, 470, 494, 511
Transcendence, 384, 392, 396
Transportation, 142
Treaties, 11-12, 27, 38, 44-46, 164,
    278-79, 286, 327, 351, 512, 547-
    49, 552, 561
Treinen, Sylvester W. (Bp.), 283
Trustees of Catholic colleges and
    universities, 411
Trustees of Catholic health care
    facilities, 476
Truth, 79, 561
Tubal ligation, 379, 479

Ukraine, 212
"*Una Sancta*" (phrase), 288
"Unacceptable damage," 536
Unborn, respect for, 184-85
Understanding: Catholic-Jewish
    relations, 120-21; *Challenge of
    Peace*, 501, 509-10; Choices for
    the 1980s, 322; conciliation and
    arbitration, 335; cultural
    pluralism, 364-65; handicapped
    persons, 270; hunger for
    understanding, 79; Marxist
    Communism, 396; role of
    television, 55; *Statement
    concerning Human Sexuality*, 34,
    230; *To Do the Work of Justice*,
    253
Unemployment (pastoral, 1930), 97
Unemployment. see Employment.
Unilateral disarmament, 548
Union of Soviet Socialist Republics
    (USSR), 37, 298, 306, 307, 308,
    310, 382, 465, 528, 531, 533, 536-
    40, 541, 544, 548, 551, 558-63,
    577
United Farm Workers of America,
    126

United Methodist Church, 306
United Nations Organization, 11,
    16, 32, 37, 44, 74-76, 198, 238,
    239, 251, 277, 279, 303, 305, 313,
    351, 491, 493, 519, 527, 539, 558,
    564, 580
United States: Agriculture
    Department, 71
United States: Armed Forces, 45,
    312-13, 360-63, 528, 552, 573-75
United States: Congress, 49, 56, 59,
    70, 89-90, 100, 242, 292-93, 456
United States: Congress. Senate,
    38, 304
United States: Constitution, 68, 81,
    89, 223, 294, 323, 427, 569
United States: Department of
    Housing and Urban
    Development, 112
United States: Farmers' Home
    Administration, 112
United States: Federal
    Communications Commission,
    15, 54, 56-59, 62-65
United States: Foreign relations, 11-
    12, 26, 37, 44-46, 70, 135-36, 238,
    242, 276-79, 286-87, 306-10, 327,
    358-59, 377, 435, 436-37, 439,
    464-68, 491, 526, 531, 536-40,
    541, 544, 547, 548, 551, 558-65,
    572, 577, 582
United States: History, 346-47, 366-
    70, 406
United States: National Academy of
    Science, 453-54
United States: National Institutes of
    Health, 33, 201-2
United States: President, 242
United States: State Department,
    199, 309, 467, 468
United States: Supreme Court, 56,
    68, 81, 86-87, 294, 323, 427
United States Catholic Conference
    (USCC), 1, 3, 9, 11, 82, 224, 244,
    246, 253, 427
Unitive dimension of sexuality, 34,
    230
Unity (religious unity), 1, 78, 287,
    348, 369, 424-26, 502
"Universal Church" (phrase), 288
Universality of the Church, 371,
    425
Universities. see Colleges and
    universities.
Unlimited war, 521

Unterkoefler, Ernest L. (Bp.), 43,
    287, 292-93
Uranium, 449
Urban life. see Cities.
U.S. Bishops on the Arms Race (1971
    Synod), 136
"Ut unum sint," 426
Utah, 427
Utility companies, 458

Values. see Morality.
Vatican Council II (1962-65), 93,
    120, 123, 132, 137, 152, 168, 264,
    265, 266, 300, 331, 350, 360, 370,
    375, 401-2, 404, 406, 414, 417,
    419, 423, 437, 442, 493, 494, 495,
    499, 509, 510, 512, 524, 526, 532,
    537, 553, 555, 577
Vaughan, Austin (Bp.), 295
Vertical proliferation of nuclear
    weapons, 549
Veterans, 575
Victims of crime, 433
Vietnam, 38, 241-42, 520
"Viewer advisory," 54, 63
Viewing periods (family viewing
    periods), 54-65
Violence: Brothers and Sisters to Us,
    346; Challenge of Peace, 501, 506,
    509, 514, 552-53, 568, 571; El
    Salvador, 295, 436; Guatemala,
    467; handgun violence, 66-68;
    motion pictures, 62; Resolution
    on Capital Punishment, 429, 430;
    television viewing, 54, 56
Visas, 168
Vision and Strategy, 325
Vocation to the religious state, 220,
    352
Volunteers, 141, 421
Voting: arbitration procedures, 339;
    Choices for the 1980s, 317-29

War and peace. see Peace and War.
Warnke, Paul, 308
"Warrior" (metaphor), 501, 504
Warsaw Pact, 551, 560
Washington Post, 305
Water supply, 452
Watergate scandals, 22
Weakland, Rembert, O.S.B. (Abp.),
    286, 299
Weatherization, 447, 458
Weigand, William (Bp.), 289
Weinberger, Caspar, 541, 548

Weisner, Jerome, 308
Weisskopf, Victor, 308
Welsh, Thomas J. (Bp.), 24, 33, 37
Western Conference of Teamsters,
    126
"Western Contact Group," 491
Whealon, John F. (Abp.), 36
White House Conference on
    Families (1979), 248, 260
White House Conference on
    Handicapped Individuals (1977),
    274
Whites (Caucasians), 343, 349
Windfall-profits tax, 457
"Winnable nuclear wars," 530
Winning Peace (publication of
    French Bishops), 313
Women: *Called and Gifted*, 422;
    family ministry, 264; military
    conscription, 362; ministries,
    220-21; pro-life plan, 84-85;
    Society and the aged, 140; *To
    Live in Christ Jesus*, 185-86; WIC
    program, 50, 72

Work: *Economy: Human Dimensions*,
    93; farm labor, 126; health care,
    473; Marxist Communism, 387-
    88; *To Live in Christ Jesus*, 194
Working mothers, 159, 162
World Day of Peace, 253
World Food Conference (Rome,
    1974), 69, 70
World Food Day, 25
World War I (1914-1918), 509
World War II (1939-1945), 494, 509,
    527, 553, 572
Worship. see Liturgy.
"Wretched of the earth," (phrase),
    389

Year of the Family (1980), 248
York, Herbert T., 308
"Young-Old," 140
Youth, 22, 30, 58-59, 138, 148-56,
    262, 401-16, 573

Zealots, 504
Zeffirelli, Franco, 227

About the Editor

Reverend Hugh J. Nolan, Professor Emeritus of Immaculata College, was ordained a priest of the Archdiocese of Philadelphia in 1941 and procured his doctorate in American Church History with distinction in 1944. He established the Master's Program in American Church History at St. Paul Seminary, St. Paul, Minnesota and has taught at La Salle, Rosemont, and Cabrini colleges, Villanova University, and The Catholic University of America. He was head of the Theology Department at Immaculata College for twenty-one years and was elected a member of the Academy of American Franciscan History.

Father Nolan is the author of *Francis Patrick Kenrick, Third Bishop of Philadelphia, 1830–1851*. He edited the *Pastoral Letters of the American Hierarchy, 1792–1970* and contributed to the *New Catholic Encyclopedia, Minnesota History, America, Ave Maria*, and the *Catholic Historical Review*. He was Editor in Chief of the *Records of the American Catholic Historical Society* for twelve years and for ten years a writer of editorials for Philadelphia's diocesan newspaper, *The Catholic Standard and Times*. He wrote "Francis Patrick Kenrick, 1830–1851" and "Dennis Cardinal Dougherty, 1918–1951" for the recent *History of the Archdiocese of Philadelphia*. Father Nolan is presently pastor of St. Isaac Jogues Parish, Valley Forge, Pennsylvania.

Credits

Design: Mack Rowe Visual Communications, Ltd.

Cover Photo: Detail of a bishop's crosier from the ruins of the Cistercian Abbey, Boyle, County Roscommon, Ireland by Dan Juday

Production

Typeface: Palatino and Palatino Semi-bold

Typography: VIP Systems, Inc.; Alexandria, Va.

Printing: Banta Company; Harrisonburg, Va.